REINING IN THE IMPERIAL PRESIDENCY

REINING IN THE IMPERIAL PRESIDENCY

Lessons and Recommendations Relating
to the Presidency of George W. Bush

House Committee on the Judiciary Majority Staff Report

to Chairman John C. Conyers, Jr.

SKYHORSE PUBLISHING

Skyhorse Publishing books may be purchased in bulk at special discounts for sales promotion, corporate gifts, fund-raising, or educational purposes. Special editions can also be created to specifications. For details, contact the Special Sales Department, Skyhorse Publishing, 555 Eighth Avenue, Suite 903, New York, NY 10018 or info@skyhorsepublishing.com.

www.skyhorsepublishing.com

10 9 8 7 6 5 4 3 2 1

Library of Congress Cataloging-in-Publication Data

Conyers, John, 1929-
Reining in the imperial presidency : lessons and recommendations relating to the presidency of George W. Bush / Chairman John Conyers, Jr.
p. cm.
ISBN 978-1-60239-930-3
1. Executive power--United States--History--21st century. 2. Bush, George W. (George Walker), 1946- 3. United States--Politics and government--2001- I. Title.
JK516.C59 2009
973.931--dc22
2009018690

Printed in Canada

Reining in the Imperial Presidency: Lessons and Recommendations Relating to the Presidency of George W. Bush

Table of Contents

Section 6 – Policy Recommendations 270

Foreword

In 1973, historian Arthur Schlesinger coined the term "Imperial Presidency" to describe a presidency that had assumed more power than the Constitution allows, and had circumvented the traditional checks and balances of our constitutional system. Until recently, the Nixon Administration seemed to represent the singular embodiment of that idea. But today, as the Bush Administration comes to a close, there can be little doubt concerning the persistence of Mr. Schlesinger's notion. More than three decades later, Mr. Schlesinger himself characterized the Bush Administration as "the Imperial Presidency redux," although he more optimistically predicted that "democracy's singular virtue – its capacity for self-correction – will one day swing into action." Today, in hindsight I can attest to the prescience of Mr. Schlesinger's warnings of unchecked power, even as we vigorously pursue the much-needed democratic self-correction he anticipated.

The Bush Administration's approach to power is, at its core, little more than a restatement of Mr. Nixon's famous rationalization of presidential misdeeds: "When the president does it, that means it's not illegal." Under this view, laws that forbid torturing or degrading prisoners cannot constrain the president because, if the president ordered such acts as Commander in Chief, "that means it's not illegal." Under this view, it is not the courts that decide the reach of the law – it is the president – and neither the judiciary nor Congress can constrain him. And where statutory law or the Constitution itself appear to impose obstacles to presidential whim, creative counselors can be relied upon to reach whatever result the president desires.

This dismissive approach to our system of checks and balances was exemplified when the Vice President's Chief of Staff, David Addington, appeared before the House Judiciary Committee on June 26, 2008. As much as any individual in the Bush Administration, David Addington is considered the architect of the concept of unchecked and unreviewable presidential powers known as the "unitary executive" (in a *New Yorker* profile, a former Pentagon attorney, Richard Schiffrin, said that he left one meeting with Mr. Addington with the impression that he "doesn't believe there should be co-equal branches"). Yet when I questioned Mr. Addington about the unitary executive theory of government during our Judiciary Committee hearing, he responded, "I frankly, don't know what you mean by unitary theory of government."

Perhaps nowhere was the range and scope of this most recent version of the Imperial Presidency more apparent than within the United States Department of Justice, the cornerstone of law enforcement in our country. While each administration re-populates the upper reaches of the Department with its own appointees, the men and women who have served there – in administrations of both political parties and throughout our Nation's history – have taken to heart the Department's core values of fair, honest, and impartial justice. Thus, at the height of Watergate, in what became known as the "Saturday Night Massacre," President Nixon's Attorney General Elliot Richardson and Mr. Richardson's Deputy William Ruckelshaus famously resigned rather than carry out the President's order to fire Special Prosecutor Archibald Cox, who had subpoenaed White House tape recordings.

The contrast with the Bush Department of Justice could not be starker. In this Administration, too many Department leaders abandoned that proud tradition of independence and integrity, and made decisions based on political objectives rather than the facts and the law. Young political operatives were given control over the most sensitive operations of the Department, and federally protected, non-partisan law enforcement positions were used to provide political patronage. The Civil Rights Division was twisted to obtain partisan electoral advantage, rather than protect the most vulnerable among us from discrimination.

In keeping with its imperial aspirations, the Administration went to extraordinary lengths to hide its conduct from scrutiny and avoid accountability. Thus, the White House refused to respond to congressional subpoenas, and insisted that presidential aides – and even former aides – are immune from subpoena, even though numerous presidential aides have testified under congressional subpoena during past administrations, as every citizen is legally obligated to do. Here, too, the Administration was following the example set by Richard Nixon. When President Nixon suggested such a claim, Senator Sam Ervin responded: "That is not executive privilege. That is executive poppycock."

The Bush Administration has relied on even more extreme claims in refusing to release documents subpoenaed by Congress. In the end, the Administration has been so recalcitrant in asserting this "executive poppycock" that the Committee was forced to pursue witnesses and documents in federal court. Even after the Committee secured a historic victory rejecting the Administration's claims, the White House still refused to relent. As of this writing, the matter remains in litigation.

There have been additional transgressions against the Constitution and the country by the Bush Administration. There was the contrived and manipulated drive to a preemptive war of aggression with Iraq. In the words of the Downing Street Minutes, "the intelligence and facts were being fixed around the policy." There was the unconscionable use of detention without cause; enhanced interrogation if not outright torture; extraordinary rendition; the extralegal use of national security letters; warrantless wiretaps of American citizens; the unilateral weakening of our regulatory system; the use of signing statements to override the laws of the land; and the intimidation and silencing of critics and whistleblowers who dared tell fellow citizens what was being done in their name.

Many think these acts rise to the level of impeachable conduct. I agree. I have never wavered in my belief that this President and Vice-President are among the most impeachable officials in our Nation's history, and the more we learn the truer that becomes.

Some ardent advocates of impeachment have labeled me a traitor – or worse – for declining to begin a formal impeachment inquiry in the House Judiciary Committee. While I reject that particular criticism, I want to make clear how much I respect those who have given so much time and energy to the cause of fighting for the impeachment of President Bush and Vice-President Cheney. While we may not agree on the best path forward, I know they are acting on the basis of our shared love of this country. These citizens are not fringe radicals, and they are obviously not motivated simply by personal feelings about President Bush, however strong those feelings may be at times. They are individuals who care deeply about our Constitution and our Nation, and who have stood up to fight for the democracy they love, often at great personal cost. Our country was founded, and our democracy has long been nurtured, by people willing to take such risks, and we should honor their vigilance and courage.

However, as I have said, while President Bush and Vice President Cheney have earned the dishonorable eligibility to be impeached, I do not believe that would have been the appropriate step at this time in our history, and I would like again to briefly explain why that is the case.

Contrary to assertions by some advocates, the predecessor to this Report – the Judiciary Committee then-Minority staff's "Constitution in Crisis" – did not call for impeachment. Rather, it concluded that there was substantial evidence of impeachable misconduct and that there should be a full investigation by a select Committee armed with subpoena power. Prior to the 2006 elections, when I saw that my views on impeachment were being misstated by friends and foes alike, I set the record straight in an essay published in *The Washington Post* titled "No Rush to Impeachment:"

> The administration's stonewalling, and the lack of oversight by Congress, have left us to guess whether we are dealing with isolated wrongdoing, or mistakes, or something worse. In my view, the American people deserve answers, not guesses. I have proposed that we obtain these answers in a responsible and bipartisan manner. It was House Republicans who took power in 1995 with immediate plans to undermine President Bill Clinton by any means necessary, and they did so in the most autocratic, partisan and destructive ways imaginable. If there is any lesson from those "revolutionaries," it is that partisan vendettas ultimately provoke a public backlash and are never viewed as legitimate.

> So, rather than seeking impeachment, I have chosen to propose comprehensive oversight of these alleged abuses. The oversight I have suggested would be performed by a select committee made up equally of Democrats and Republicans and chosen by the House speaker and the minority leader.

> The committee's job would be to obtain answers – finally. At the end of the process, if – and only if – the select committee, acting on a bipartisan basis, finds evidence of potentially impeachable offenses, it would forward that information to the Judiciary Committee. This threshold of bipartisanship is appropriate, I

believe, when dealing with an issue of this magnitude.

Nonetheless, I have been accused of "violating my oath of office" by "playing politics" with impeachment, and I have been criticized for saying that I have the Constitution in one hand and a calculator in the other. I would suggest that this argument ignores the text and history of the Constitution. There is nothing mandatory about using the power to impeach when wrongful conduct is shown, and the decision whether or not to impeach was always intended to be subject to the politics at the time. We live in a democracy, after all.

Thus, in Federalist No. 65, Alexander Hamilton described impeachable offenses as "those... which proceed from the misconduct of public men... which may with peculiar propriety be denominated POLITICAL..." (Caps in original.) To address these "political" offenses, the Constitutional Convention rejected using either a judicial tribunal (that was the approach of the "Virginia Plan") or a hybrid committee of judicial and political officers (as proposed by Gouverneur Morris and Charles Pinckney), and instead vested the authority in the legislature. As the records of the Convention detail, the Founders made this choice fully aware of the political considerations that would factor into impeachment decisions.

The simple fact is, despite the efforts of impeachment advocates, the support and votes have not been there, and could not reasonably be expected to materialize. It takes 218 votes in the House and 67 votes in the Senate to impeach and remove a president from office. The resolution I offered three years ago to simply investigate whether an impeachment inquiry was warranted garnered only 38 cosponsors in the House, and the Democratic Leader of the Senate labeled it "ridiculous." Impeachment resolutions against Vice President Cheney and President Bush offered by my friend and colleague Dennis Kucinich only garnered 27 and 11 House cosponsors, respectively.

Impeachment, if done right, also takes time. When I became Chairman of the House Judiciary Committee in January of 2007, after twelve years of Republican rule, we had to start much of our oversight from scratch, and against an Administration more dedicated to secrecy and obfuscation than any in our history. Unlike the Nixon impeachment, we did not have the benefit of the bipartisan Ervin Committee or a fearless special prosecutor such as Archibald Cox or Leon Jaworski to help lay the groundwork needed to remove a president or vice president from office.

During the failed impeachment of President Bill Clinton, many of us derided House Republicans for, in the words of Senator Bob Kerrey, "sloppily" conducting the inquiry. Without calling a single fact witness, the Republicans essentially rubber-stamped the work of Independent Counsel Ken Starr and forwarded his allegations on to defeat in the Senate. Many advocates would have had me do the same to this President based on newspaper and magazine articles. But that course would have cheapened the impeachment process itself – and would not have led to success.

The final plea was: "Why not try? What do you have to lose?" Impeachments, however, both successful and unsuccessful, have precedential consequences – they set standards for future presidential behavior. The House Judiciary Committee's rejection of an article of impeachment against President Nixon for failing to file tax returns, for example, was used as precedent in acquitting President Clinton for impeachment based on personal misdeeds.

While some of the difficulty in garnering support for impeachment results from fatigue over the recent and unjustified impeachment of President Clinton, and concern about routinizing what should be an extraordinary constitutional event – whatever the reason, an impeachment vote in the House was certain to fail. What, then, would be the precedent set by a House vote *against* the impeachment of President Bush or Vice President Cheney for deceiving our nation into war, allowing torture, engaging in warrantless domestic surveillance, and retaliating against those who attempted to reveal the truth about these acts? In my view, a failed impeachment – by an almost certainly lopsided vote – would have grossly lowered the bar for presidential behavior and caused great damage to our Constitution. More immediately, a failure to impeach President Bush and Vice President Cheney would have been trumpeted by their allies as a vindication for them and for their overreaching policies.

To all of us who treasure our constitutional form of government and our standing in the world, and mourn the loss of life in a war built on deception, I know the failure to impeach is a deeply unsatisfying outcome. As one who has participated in more impeachments than any other Member of Congress, I came to the realization that this is the reality of this moment in history. Faced with that reality, I had a choice: do nothing; or redouble my efforts to peel away the secrecy of this Administration, expose its wrongdoing, and protect the liberties and freedoms of the American people.

I chose the latter course. This is what led me to bring suit in federal court to challenge the legality of the Iraq War. This is what led me to publish my own report, "What Went Wrong in Ohio," and join with Barbara Boxer and the late Stephanie Tubbs Jones in filing an election challenge on the House floor challenging the unjust result in 2004. This is what led me to personally deliver a letter to the White House regarding the manipulation of intelligence described in the Downing Street Minutes, signed by 121 Members and more than 500,000 Americans, to challenge the warrantless surveillance of innocent Americans, and to hold a series of Minority hearings in the basement of the Capitol and the Rayburn Building regarding these matters. This is what led me to call for a special counsel to investigate the culpability of the White House in the outing of Valerie Plame. And over the last two years in the Majority, this is what led the Judiciary Committee to conduct 157 days of oversight hearings.

These choices produced results. As just one example, our Committee issued the first subpoenas of the new Congress when we learned that United States Attorneys had been mysteriously dismissed. Our investigative efforts turned up thousands of pages of documents, which were made available, in real time, on the Internet to the public. We went to court and obtained the testimony of former Justice Department/White House liaison Monica Goodling. These efforts exposed substantial wrongdoing at the Department, and resulted in passage of a new law regarding the replacement of U.S. Attorneys, the resignations of numerous high-ranking Department officials, including the Attorney General, and an ongoing criminal investigation of these officials.

When the culpability for the firing of the United States Attorneys appeared to lead into the White House, the Committee subpoenaed high-ranking presidential aides and internal White House memos. When the Administration refused to comply, our Committee held the responsible officials in contempt, and the full House followed suit. And when the Justice Department refused to prosecute, the Committee filed suit in federal court and won a landmark victory.

In addition to the appointment of Patrick Fitzgerald as Special Counsel in the Valerie Plame matter and the conviction of Scooter Libby, I released a Homeland Security Inspector General Report calling into question the rendition of Maher Arar to Syria, and obtained two GAO reports confirming the harm and danger of President Bush's signing statements. At the time of this Report, we are awaiting an Office of Professional Responsibility report concerning what may have been the selective, politically biased prosecution of former Alabama Governor Don Siegelman and others, Inspector General reports concerning the propriety of the President's warrantless surveillance program, a Special U.S. Attorney investigation into the U.S. Attorney firings, and a Special U.S. Attorney investigation into the CIA tape destruction. All of this is occurring even before the onset of a new, more open Administration.

Moreover, history is already judging President George W. Bush. As of this writing, his approval rating is in the mid-20s, dismal by any standard. The November 2008 election is widely viewed as a landslide repudiation of President Bush and his policies.

But our work is not done. The lesson I took away from Watergate and the Vietnam era spying abuses was that much of the work of reining in an Imperial Presidency takes place after the change in Administrations. It was only due to the work of the Church Committee and other reviews initiated after President Nixon resigned that we were able to pass historic legislation such as the Federal Campaign Finance Act, the Foreign Intelligence Surveillance Act, the Independent Counsel Act, the Ethics in Government Act, and the Presidential Records Act. It was Pecora Commission's work after the Wall Street Crash in 1929 that helped lay the ground work for the New Deal banking and securities reforms.

Likewise, I believe now is when much of the work to remedy the excesses of the most recent Imperial Presidency begins. That is why this Report recommends that the Judiciary Committee and the Congress pursue any unresolved subpoenas and document requests left over from the last Congress; that we create a "blue-ribbon" commission or similar select committee, along the lines of the 9/11 Commission, to investigate these matters and report to Congress, the President, and the public; and that the incoming Administration finally begin an independent criminal review of activities of the outgoing Administration, such as enhanced interrogation, extraordinary rendition, and domestic warrantless surveillance. These initiatives can and should work collectively and without prejudice to one another. The fact that Congress is pursuing responsible oversight should not impact any criminal investigations, just as the work of the Ervin Committee did not limit the prerogatives of Special Counsels Cox or Jaworski. As a matter of fact, information gleaned from one review could reinforce and galvanize others. While I understand there is a powerful desire to simply move on and focus on the many large issues facing us, we simply cannot sweep these matters under the rug of history without addressing them head on. As the world's oldest democracy, I am certain we are strong enough to survive and even prosper from these proposed inquiries.

In addition to these threshold recommendations, the Report goes on to make a total of 47 policy recommendations. These range from passing laws regarding self-serving presidential pardons, helping to protect whistleblowers from retribution, and reforming our elections; as well as commencing executive and Justice Department actions to end torture and extraordinary rendition, close Guantanamo Bay, provide due process to detainees, end the use of abusive signing statements and assertions of state secrets, and end the selective declassification and manipulation of intelligence information.

Candidate Obama repeatedly and publicly spoke out against the violations of our Constitution perpetrated by the Bush Administration. It is my hope that these recommendations will help to ensure that President Obama follows through and rolls back those excesses, and restores the checks and balances that have made our nation strong. There remain numerous questions about the Bush Administration's misdeeds, many of them described in the text that follows, and the more these facts are uncovered and aired, the stronger they will make our democracy.

———————————————

The Constitution has been sorely tested over the last eight years. But like the late Mr. Schlesinger, I am confident in our capacity to self-correct. Doing so will require much hard work and diligence, and that effort only continues with the release of this Report. Our work is far from complete.

John Conyers, Jr.
January 2009

Executive Summary

This Report has been prepared at the direction of Rep. John Conyers, Jr., Chairman of the House of Representatives Committee on the Judiciary. It was drafted to itemize and document the various abuses that occurred during the Bush Administration relating to the Committee's review and jurisdiction, and to develop a comprehensive set of recommendations to prevent the recurrence of these or similar abuses in the future. This Report is being published initially on the internet, with a print version to come shortly.

The Report begins with a preface titled "Deconstructing the Imperial Presidency," which describes and critiques the key war power memos that gave rise to the concept of broad-based, unreviewable, and secret presidential powers in time of war. These legal theories, many of which took seed shortly after September 11, 2001, rely on breathtaking assertions regarding the nature and scope of the so-called "global war on terror," such as those set forth in an October 23, 2001, memorandum concluding that the president may order extensive military operations inside the United States. As the Report documents, these theories were relied on time and again in numerous other contexts by the Bush Administration over the next seven and one half years.

The next five sections of the Report describe specific abuses of the Imperial Presidency relating to Judiciary Committee inquiries. Section 1, "Politicization of the Department of Justice," describes the Committee's U.S. Attorneys investigation and concerns relating to the politicization of the Civil Rights Division in general and the Voting Rights Division in particular. Even as this report is being released, the Justice Department's Offices of the Inspector General and Professional Responsibility have released a report further documenting politicized hiring and politicized decision-making in the Division. Section 2, "Assault on Individual Liberties," broadly details Bush Administration policies relating to detention, enhanced interrogation, extraordinary rendition, ghosting and black sites, warrantless domestic surveillance, and the issuance of national security and exigent letters. Section 3, "Misuse of Executive Branch Authority," describes concerns relating to signing statements and misuse of regulatory authorities. Section 4, "Retribution against Critics," details the facts ascertained relating to the outing of former intelligence agent Valerie Plame Wilson, and other instances of improper retribution by the Bush Administration against its critics. Section 5, "Government in the Shadows," describes multifaceted efforts of the Bush Administration to avoid accountability and culpability through a variety of legal techniques, including broad and unprecedented assertions of executive privilege, withholding testimony and information without formal assertion of privilege, extraordinary assertions of state secrets, broad uses of classification authorities, and unduly narrow construction of the Freedom of Information Act, as well as manipulation of intelligence in the run-up to the Iraq War. Each of these sections includes a comprehensive set of findings detailing specific legal and factual conclusions drawn from the review.

Section 6 of the Report sets forth a comprehensive set of 47 policy recommendations designed to respond to the abuses and excesses of the Bush Imperial Presidency. The list begins with three major threshold recommendations:

- First, that the Judiciary Committee pursue its document requests and subpoenas pending at the end of the 110th Congress.

- Second, that Congress create an independent blue ribbon commission or similar body to investigate the host of previously unreviewable activities of the Bush Administration, including detention, enhanced interrogation, extraordinary rendition, ghosting and black sites, and warrantless domestic electronic surveillance.

- Third, that the new Administration conduct an independent criminal inquiry into whether any laws were broken in connection with these activities.

In this regard, the Report firmly rejects the notion that we should move on from these matters simply because a new Administration is set to take office. This is because there never has been an independent, comprehensive review of these very serious allegations with a full report to the American public. The investigations to date have either been limited in scope or authority, hidden from the public and the Congress, or stonewalled or obstructed by the outgoing Administration behind impenetrable walls of classification and privilege. The purpose of the above-described investigations is not payback, but to uphold the rule of law, allow us to learn from our national mistakes, and prevent them from recurring. Such an effort would be a welcome sign to our friends, and a warning to our foes, that this Nation can indeed serve as a beacon of liberty and freedom without weakening our ability to combat terrorism or other threats.

The Report makes clear that even after scores of hearings, investigations, and reports, Congress and the American public still do not have answers to some of the most fundamental questions concerning the Bush Imperial Presidency. These include the following:

1. **Who created the U.S. Attorney firing list, and how were specific U.S. Attorneys included or excluded from the list?**

After more than 13 House and Senate Judiciary committee hearings and depositions with over 12 witnesses, we still do not know who created the U.S. Attorney firing list and why. Witnesses testifying included then-Attorney General Alberto Gonzales, his Chief of Staff Kyle Sampson, Deputy Attorney General Paul McNulty, White House Liaison Monica Goodling, and every other senior Department of Justice official with a reported role in the matter, but none have accepted responsibility for creating the list. Then-Attorney General Gonzales, for example, claimed that he "was not involved in seeing any memos, was not involved in any discussions about what was going on," and testified that he did not place the fired U.S. Attorneys on the list, even as he later claimed not to remember any details of the firings or the reasons those U.S. Attorneys were fired. He testified at one point that he regretted not having the Deputy Attorney General "directly involved" in the process, only to later assert that the one person he had relied upon "in particular" was the Deputy Attorney General. Mr. Gonzales defended his inability to recollect the facts by claiming that he had not spoken to key fact witnesses "to preserve the integrity" of the investigation, but Ms. Goodling said that the Attorney General had rehearsed his recollection of the facts with her.

Chairman Conyers has repeatedly stated that "the bread crumbs in this investigation have always led to 1600 Pennsylvania Avenue," yet the White House has asserted a broad and unprecedented form of executive privilege and supposed immunity from subpoena to prevent Harriet Miers and Karl Rove from testifying and to justify the refusal by the White House and the Republican National Committee refusing to turn over relevant documents and e-mails. The Bush Administration has continued to stonewall even after House votes for contempt of Congress and a federal district court decision rejecting its legal position.

2.   **Were any Laws Broken as a Result of the Enhanced Interrogation Tactics Engaged in by the Bush Administration?**

Notwithstanding various internal reports by the Bush Administration and a number of investigations and hearings in the Congress (limited and constrained in many cases by Administration obstruction), there never has been a full and independent inquiry into whether there have been criminal violations of federal statutes prohibiting torture and war crimes. Consider the following exchange between Chairman Conyers and Attorney General Mukasey at a February 7, 2008, hearing concerning admitted instances of waterboarding, an interrogation method the Bush Administration belatedly acknowledged was unlawful:

Mr. Conyers: Well, are you ready to start a criminal investigation into whether this confirmed use of waterboarding by United States agents was illegal?

Mr. Mukasey: No, I am not, for this reason: Whatever was done as part of a CIA program at the time that it was done was the subject of a Department of Justice opinion through the Office of Legal Counsel and was found to be permissible under law as it existed then.

Unanswered was how the Attorney General could know the waterboarding was done in good faith reliance on the OLC opinions and within any limits or constraints set by the Justice Department without first investigating the facts.

Consider also the following exchanges between Subcommittee Chairman Nadler, former Attorney General Aschroft, and Attorney General Mukasey at hearings on July 17, 2008, and July 23, 2008, respectively, concerning waterboarding:

Mr. Nadler: Attorney General Ashcroft, in your testimony you mentioned Abu Zubaydah, who was captured in March 2002. The Inspector General report on the FBI's role in interrogation makes clear that he was interrogated beginning in march of that year. The Yoo-Bybee legal memo [approving CIA interrogation techniques] was not issued until August

2002. So was the interrogation of Abu Zubaydah before August 2002 done without DOJ legal approval?

Mr. Ashcroft: I don't know.

Mr. Nadler: Well, did you offer legal approval of interrogation methods used at that time?

Mr. Ashcroft: At what time, sir?

Mr. Nadler: Prior to August of 2002, [in] March 2002.

Mr. Ashcroft: I have no recollection of doing that at all.

Mr. Nadler: ...Do you know if waterboarding was used on Abu Zubaydah before the DOJ approved it?

Mr. Ashcroft: I do not.

Attorney General Mukasey was no more responsive:

Mr. Nadler: [I]t is now clear that one of the detainees, Abu Zubaydah, for example, was interrogated for months in the spring and summer of 2002, before the first OLC opinion and the issue we know of, the August 1, 2002, legal memo by John Yoo was issued.... have you or anyone at the Department investigated the legality of the interrogation methods used before the August 1 Yoo memo was issued?

Mr. Mukasey: I have not investigated that myself. I think part of that question involves whether the methods employed were consistent with that memo or not, and I don't know whether they were or they were not.

Mr Nadler: Do you think someone should take a look at that?

Mr. Mukasey: I think a look at that may very well be taken or have been taken. I am not specifically aware of it as I sit here.

Mr. Nadler: Can you let us know?

Mr. Mukasey: I will take a look.

The Committee has not heard back on the matter from the Attorney General.

3. **Were any Laws Broken as a Result of the Extraordinary Rendition Tactics Engaged in by the Bush Administration?**

The Committee has uncovered considerable evidence of potential criminal culpability relating to the rendition of Maher Arar. This includes:

- A Department of Homeland Security Inspector General report found that Immigration and Naturalization Service (INS) officials had determined that it was "more likely than not" that Mr. Arar would be tortured if sent to Syria, but sent him anyway, even though the "assurances upon which INS based Mr. Arar's removal were ambiguous regarding the source or authority purporting to bind the Syrian government to protect Arar."

- The Inspector General also expressed concern about the speed with which Administration officials transferred Mr. Arar and about possible interference with his access to counsel. "The method of the notification of the [Convention Against Torture protection] interview to Mr. Arar's attorneys and the notification's proximity to the time of the interview [a phone message left at a work number at 4:30 p.m. on a Sunday for an interview that started at 9:00 p.m. that same Sunday night] were questionable."

- Former Department of Homeland Security Inspector General Clark Ervin has also testified before the Committee that: "There is no question but that given everything we know, the intention here was to render him to Syria, as opposed to Canada, because of the certainty that he would be tortured in Syria and he would not be in Canada."

While these troubling facts led to apologies to Mr. Arar by the Chairs and Ranking Members of the Judiciary Committee's Subcommittee on the Constitution, Civil Rights, and Civil Liberties, and the Foreign Affairs Committee's Subcommittee on Oversight, there has never been an adequate explanation as to why these facts have not warranted a criminal investigation.

4. **Were any Laws Broken as a Result of the the so-called "Terrorist Surveillance Program" and related activities?**

There have been numerous efforts to obtain a judicial determination of the legality of the President's warrantless domestic surveillance program. Among other things, the Electronic Frontier Foundation filed a lawsuit alleging that AT&T had collaborated with the NSA to engage in illegal surveillance (which became one of a series of consolidated cases challenging the program); the American Civil Liberties Union brought a suit alleging the program was unlawful; and Rep. Maurice Hinchey (D-NY) sought a Department of Justice Office of Professional Responsibility investigation into whether Department attorneys had violated their legal or ethical responsibilities in connection with the program.

Each and every one of these efforts has been obstructed by the Bush Administration. After unsuccesfully arguing that the Electronic Frontier Foundation suit should be dismissed as a result of the state secrets doctrine, the Bush Administration insisted that retroactive legal immunity for telcommunications companies involved in the program be included in recently enacted surveillance legislation. After a federal court in Michigan found the warrantless surveillance program to be unlawful, the Administration succeeded in having the decision reversed on appeal on procedural grounds. The Department's internal investigation died in early 2006 after President Bush denied the investigators the necessary security clearances (the investigation was belatedly revived by the new Attorney General last year, but only after substantial time on the relevant statutes of limitations had elapsed).

5. **To what extent were President Bush and Vice President Cheney involved in the outing of Valerie Plame Wilson and its aftermath?**

There is considerable evidence that culpability for the outing of Valerie Plame Wilson and subsequent obstruction goes above and beyond Scooter Libby. We have learned the following as a result of the Special Counsel and congressional investigations, and the trial and conviction of the Vice President's former Chief of Staff I. Lewis Libby:

- Mr. Libby's notes from on or before June 11, 2003, reveal that the Vice President informed Mr. Libby that Ambassador Wilson's wife, Valerie Plame Wilson, worked in the Central Intelligence Agency's Counterproliferation Division.

- That same day, Cathie Martin, Assistant to the Vice President for Public Affairs, learned that Ambassador Wilson's wife worked at the CIA, and she relayed that information to Mr. Cheney and Mr. Libby during a meeting in the Vice President's office.

- A few weeks later, on or about July 6, 2003, Mr. Cheney clipped Ambassador Wilson's *New York Times* op-ed questioning the Bush Administration's Iraq-uranium claim and, in his own hand, wrote the following rhetorical note conspicously above its title: "Have they [i.e., the CIA] done this sort of thing before? Send an ambassador to answer a question... *Or did his wife send him on a junket?*"

- The next day, Ms. Martin e-mailed White House Press Secretary Ari Fleischer with talking points on the Niger trip by Mr. Cheney. He subsequently dictated a revised set of talking points that Ms. Martin circulated to the press. It has been reported that the FBI's summary of the Special Counsel's inteview with Vice President Cheney reflects that he "was at a loss to explain how the change of the talking points focusing attention on who specifically sent Wilson to Niger would

21

not lead... to exposure" of Valerie Plame Wilson's identity.

- In the early fall of 2003, Mr. Cheney wrote a note to himself on the unfairness of Mr. Libby, alone among White House staffers, having been asked to "stick his neck in the meat grinder" in connection with the White House's response to Ambassador Wilson's op-ed.

- Mr. Libby's key disclosure of Ms. Plame Wilson's identity to *New York Times* reporter Judith Miller occurred during a meeting arranged at the behest of the Vice President.

- A redacted report of the FBI's interview with Mr. Libby that the Justice Department allowed the staff of the House Oversight Committee to review reflects that Mr. Libby told the FBI that "it was 'possible' that Vice President Cheney instructed him to disseminate information about Ambassador Wilson's wife to the press."

While this and other evidence strongly suggests vice presidential and/or presidential involvement, complete understanding of this matter has been obstructed by both the President's assertion of executive privilege and threatened assertion to deny the Oversight and Government Reform Committee and the Judiciary Committee access to relevant information, and by Mr. Libby's lies to FBI interviewers and the grand jury convened to investigate the leak. As Special Counsel Fitzgerald emphasized during his closing argument, Mr. Libby's lies put a "cloud over what the Vice President did" immediately following the publication of Ambassador Wilson's op-ed.

Given that so many significant questions remain unanswered relating to these core constitutional and legal matters, many of which implicate basic premises of our national honor, it seems clear that our country cannot simply move on. As easy or convenient as it would be to turn the page, our Nation's respect for the rule of law and its role as a moral leader in the world demand that we finally and without obstruction conduct and complete these inquiries. This can and should be done without rancor or partisanship.

_____

This Report could not have been completed absent the hearings and investigatory work undertaken by other committees, and their work is relied upon and cited throughout. In particular, this Report includes the work of the Senate Judiciary Committee, the House and Senate Select Committees on Intelligence, the House and Senate Armed Services Committees, the House Oversight and Government Reform Committee, and the House Foreign Relations Committee (which held a series of hearings in conjunction with the House Judiciary Committee). The work of the many diligent Inspectors General was also vital to the Committee's work, including in particular the Department of Justice Inspector General's office.

Preface: Deconstructing the Imperial Presidency

In the Founders' view, the "blessings of liberty" were threatened by "those military establishments which must gradually poison its very fountain." ...Except for the actual command of military forces, all authorization for their maintenance and all explicit authorization for their use is placed in the control of Congress under Article I, rather than the President under Article II.

– Justice Antonin Scalia in *Hamdi v. Rumsfeld*.[1]

"Imperial Presidency" is a term used to embody a fervently held anti-democratic belief system, rooted in a constitutionally unsupportable view of the president's power vis-à-vis the Congress, the courts, and the people of the United States.

The Imperial Presidency of George W. Bush – constructed and enforced by Vice President Dick Cheney and his chief legal advisor David Addington,[2] given legal veneer in Department of Justice Office of Legal Counsel opinions by Deputy Assistant Attorney General John C. Yoo, and endorsed by White House Counsel and later Attorney General Alberto Gonzales – has been characterized by the determined effort to arrogate for the president vast uncheckable power in large spheres of government action, coupled with the equally determined willingness to do battle with the courts and Congress for the president's right to maintain these prerogatives. For the president to seek legislative authorization from Congress, rather than simply act unilaterally (on detention policy, for example), was scorned as "giv[ing] away the President's power."[3] Even the Republican-controlled Congress was viewed by David Addington with hostility for the potential threat it posed to the president's ability to act unilaterally.[4] The determined insistence that the pesident had the right to go it alone was typified by Mr. Addington's statement: "We're going to push and push and push until some larger force makes us stop."[5]

Among the most far-reaching instances of President Bush's arrogation of power are actions he took in the aftermath of the terror attacks of September 11, 2001. Here, as will be set forth in greater detail, President Bush relied on extreme – and secret – interpretations of his constitutional powers to implement aggressive and far-reaching policies relating to detention, interrogation, and electronic surveillance. Whenever these actions have been exposed and challenged in court, the courts have generally held them to be unconstitutional – or constitutional only to the extent they were authorized by Congress.

President Bush has similarly "pushed and pushed" for presidential power vis-à-vis Congress and the courts in other significant areas of activity. For example, he has stonewalled legitimate congressional requests for information, going so far as to assert that his White House advisors need not so much as show up in response to congressional subpoenas – even in instances where there are no communications with the President involved that might support an assertion of executive privilege. He has also taken the position that, simply by issuing a "signing statement" at the time he signs a bill into law, he may excuse himself from his responsibility under the Constitution to "take care that the laws be faithfully executed."[6]

A cornerstone of the legal rationale contrived to support the Imperial Presidency has been a radically expansive view of the president's constitutional authority as Commander in Chief. The Bush Administration has asserted that the Commander-in-Chief power extends far beyond the battlefield, and that any action he takes under claim of that power, in whatever arena, is presumptively considered the equivalent to ordering the movements of troops on the battlefield, and thus can neither be limited by Congress nor reviewed by the courts. According to this view, the president alone defines the scope of circumstances in which he may exercise these Commander in Chief powers, even in connection with a "war" that has no limitation in either geographical location or duration – the conflict may be world-wide, including within U.S. borders, and may extend potentially forever.

Under this view, for example, President Bush has claimed the power to label American citizens and lawfully admitted aliens as "enemy combatants," and on that basis to seize them in the United States; hold them in military custody, in solitary confinement, without access to an attorney or any meaningful opportunity to challenge the evidentiary basis for their detention; and subject them to harsh interrogation methods, including methods condemned as torture under settled international law, and try them in closed military commissions instead of in a court of law, all in flagrant disregard of Fifth Amendment due process protections. He has also claimed the power to wiretap and record the conversations of American citizens, without obeying the Fourth Amendment requirement to obtain a warrant to do so.

Moreover, under this view, the president is not even required to inform the courts or Congress of the legal basis for asserting that his decisions are unreviewable, or the classes of decisions covered, or the definition of the "battlefield" on which these decisions operate. Rather, the decisions as to such issues of human liberty as detention, interrogation methods, and surveillance can be justified by secret internal memoranda. In effect, this view gives the president license to operate under secret interpretations of his powers, even inside the United States, and even against United States citizens.

The bare text of the Constitution says nothing about the extent of the president's Commander in Chief powers; it says only that the president "shall be Commander in Chief of the Army and Navy of the United States."[7] But such an expansive view of these powers as articulated by the Bush Administration could render the rest of the Constitution null, eviscerating the separation of powers structure designed to limit Executive power, and trampling the Bill of Rights.

The ambitious reach of the Bush Administration's imperial vision, the audacity with which it was pursued, and the extent to which its pursuit was acquiesced in, is unprecedented in our Nation's history. But the imperial impulse – and the dangers it poses to democracy, the rule of law, the public welfare, and international peace – are all too familiar to students of world history. The Founders had ready examples from their own era, beginning with King George III of England.[8] Keenly mindful of these dangers when they met in Philadelphia to draft our Constitution, the Founders carefully devised a system of checks and balances among the three Branches so as to restrain the imperial tendencies of the Executive.

After laying largely dormant for the first six years of the Bush Presidency, that system of checks and balances is now seeing new vigor. In the 110th Congress, over the past two years, the House Committee on the Judiciary, along with other Committees in both Houses of Congress, has endeavored to uncover, shine a light on, and correct the imperial excesses of the Bush Presidency, including its policies and practices in areas ranging from detention, interrogation, and rendition to electronic surveillance, to signing statements, as well as the improper politicization of federal law enforcement and its overall proclivity to secrecy.

The results to date of this endeavor are described in this Report. It will be left for others to describe the damage the Imperial Presidency has done to our standing in the world of nations; this Report focuses on the damage it has done to our constitutional values, and on what must be done to restore those values to their rightful place in our government.

Already, the harshest interrogation technique known to have been employed under the direction of Bush Administration officials – waterboarding – has been confirmed by Administration officials in testimony before Congress in 2008,[9] and Vice President Cheney himself has now admitted having given his support to its use.[10] Though the legislation updating the Foreign Intelligence Surveillance Act (FISA) is in many respects problematic, it does include features designed to ensure the primacy of the Legislative and Judicial Branches in formulating and ensuring compliance with appropriate procedures and safeguards for electronic surveillance of American citizens. Congressional investigation into the improper politicization of the Justice Department appears to have been a factor leading to the resignation of a number of key Department and White House officials, apparently bringing a halt to this corrupting influence on federal law enforcement, and the role of various White House officials is still under active investigation.

Although Congress and the courts have awakened to reassert their proper constitutional roles in the functioning of the federal government – particularly in connection with the protection of individual liberties against encroachment by the Executive Branch – further action and continued vigilance are needed. To promote and assist in those efforts, this Report reviews the rise of the Imperial Presidency in the Bush Administration, describes the response in Congress and the courts during the past two years, and sets forth recommendations as to how to restore Constitutional balance and maintain it in the future.

Benjamin Franklin, as he emerged from Independence Hall on the final day of the Constitutional Convention's deliberations, was reported to have replied when asked what kind of government the people were getting: "A republic – if you can keep it."

26

This preface provides a prelude to the overall report. It does so by honing in on the initial set of expansive legal opinions stating that the president had essential, unreviewable powers in innumerable aspects of our nation's legal policy during a time of armed conflict. These views began to take root shortly after the September 11 terrorist attacks.

The September 25, 2001, War Powers Memorandum

In the immediate aftermath of the September 11, 2001, terrorist attacks, President Bush sought authorization from Congress to use military force against those responsible for the attacks. There was little question that this use of military force was appropriate and would be authorized. Simultaneously, however, there were immediate efforts – through Vice President Cheney and David Addington – to exploit the events of 9/11, and the fact that the country was rallying behind the President, to claim for the president broad powers that went far beyond any targeted response to the 9/11 attacks.

The initial White House draft for a proposed congressional resolution authorizing the President to use military force, submitted to Congress on September 12, 2001, the day after the attacks, would have authorized the President not only to use military force to attack those responsible for the 9/11 attacks but, in addition, "to deter and pre-empt any future acts of terrorism or aggression against the United States."[11] This latter purpose, of using force to deter and pre-empt aggression has been described as being of "inescapable elasticity," because nearly any military action can be asserted or rationalized as being taken with this goal in mind.[12] This request to Congress, made within a day or two of the 9/11 attacks, embodies what became the Administration's "pre-emption" rationale for the use of military force against Iraq 18 months later; indeed, as will be discussed, it may have been intended at that time to justify an attack on Iraq as a purported response to the 9/11 attacks.

According to Senator Tom Daschle, Senate Majority Leader at the time, the Bush Administration also sought authority to use war powers within the domestic United States. In the form in which the resolution came to the Senate floor, it authorized the President to "use all necessary and appropriate force against those nations, organizations, or persons he determines planned, authorized, committed, or aided the terrorist attacks that occurred on September 11, 2001." But as Senator Daschle recounted:

> Literally minutes before the Senate cast its vote, the Administration sought to add the words "in the United States and" after "appropriate force" in the agreed-upon text. **This last-minute change would have given the president broad authority to exercise expansive powers not just overseas–where we all understood he wanted authority to act–but right here in the United States, potentially against American citizens**. I could see no justification for Congress to accede to this extraordinary request for additional authority. I refused.[13]

Ultimately, neither of these two requests for additional, extraordinary authorization – to use military force for pre-emption and deterrence, and to use military force inside the United States – was included in the final version of the Act. As signed into law on September 18, 2001, the Authorization for the Use of Military Force (AUMF) authorized the President to:

> use all necessary and appropriate force against those nations,
> organizations, or persons he determines planned, authorized,
> committed, or aided the terrorist attacks that occurred on
> September 11, 2001, or harbored such organizations or persons, in
> order to prevent any future acts of international terrorism against
> the United States by such nations, organizations or persons.[14]

Congress cited the War Powers Act in authorizing the President to use military force for the specified purposes set forth in the AUMF.[15]

Despite the fact that Congress declined to endorse either of these additional authorizations in the AUMF per the Administration's request, a memorandum prepared by Deputy Assistant Attorney General John Yoo[16] in the Justice Department's Office of Legal Counsel, dated September 25, 2001, less than a week after the President signed the AUMF into law, flatly asserted that the president possessed this authority inherently.[17]

In setting forth the legal basis for the use of military force in response to the 9/11 attacks, the memorandum, titled "The President's Constitutional Authority to Conduct Military Operations Against Terrorists and Nations Supporting Them," asserted that the president possessed nearly unlimited power in any matter that touched war policy in response to the 9/11 attacks, and explicitly rejected any constitutional role for Congress in that sphere of action. Notwithstanding the clear intent of Congress in the development of the AUMF, this War Powers Memorandum asserted that the president had authority to take military action against nations having nothing to do with the 9/11 attacks (such as Iraq) under a deterrence/pre-emption rationale, as well as authority to use military power inside the United States – subject to no congressional limitations on his exercise of these powers.

To fully appreciate the intended reach of that memorandum, it is important to remember that at the time it was written, numerous voices inside of and close to the Bush Administration expressed substantial interest in attacking Iraq as part of the response to the 9/11 attacks, even though there was little evidence that Iraq had any involvement in those attacks.[18] The 9/11 Commission, for example, in its report summarized its interviews with National Security Advisor Condoleeza Rice and Secretary of State Colin Powell in which they discussed the efforts of others (primarily Deputy Secretary of Defense Wolfowitz) to pursue an attack on Iraq:

> According to Rice, the issue of what, if anything, to do about Iraq
> was really engaged at Camp David. Briefing papers on Iraq, along

with many others, were in briefing materials for the participants. Rice told us the Administration was concerned that Iraq would take advantage of the 9/11 attacks. She recalled that in the first Camp David session chaired by the President, Rumsfeld asked what the Administration should do about Iraq. Deputy Secretary Wolfowitz made the case for striking Iraq during "this round" of the war on terrorism.

* * * * * * *

Secretary Powell recalled that Wolfowitz – not Rumsfeld – argued that Iraq was ultimately the source of the terrorist problem and should therefore be attacked... **Powell said that Wolfowitz was not able to justify his belief that Iraq was behind 9/11. "Paul was always of the view that Iraq was a problem that had to be dealt with," Powell told us. "And he saw this as one way of using this event as a way to deal with the Iraq problem."[19]**

Mr. Yoo started his War Powers Memorandum with a discussion of presidential power in general, distinguishing the "legislative" powers of Congress from the "executive" powers of the president. Under this dichotomy, the president was the "exclusive" determiner as to the use of military force, and Congress had no role in these decisions: "[C]ongress's legislative powers are limited to the list enumerated in Article I, section 8, while the president's powers include inherent executive powers that are unenumerated in the Constitution. In that "the decision to deploy military force is 'executive' in nature," Mr. Yoo asserted, it is "exclusively entrusted to the president."[20]

Mr. Yoo characterized Congress's passage of the AUMF as merely "demonstrat[ing] Congress's acceptance of the president's unilateral war power in an emergency situation like that created by the September 11 incidents."[21] Any perceived limitations on executive power set forth in the AUMF (in authorizing military force only against those who attacked the United States and in rejecting the request that the military powers could be used inside the United States) were dismissed. Mr. Yoo was explicit in his view that the president's power was broader than Congress's authorization, and included the power to engage in a "pre-emptive" war (the subsequent rationale for invading Iraq) against foreign states or actors having nothing to do with 9/11, and for which military actions had not been authorized by Congress:

> [T]he Joint Resolution [*i.e.*, the AUMF] is somewhat narrower than the President's constitutional authority. The Joint Resolution's authorization to use force is limited only to those individuals, groups, or states that planned, authorized, committed, or aided the attacks, and those nations that harbored them. It does not, therefore, reach other terrorist individuals, groups, or states,

which cannot be determined to have links to the September 11 attacks. **Nonetheless, the President's broad constitutional power to use military force to defend the Nation, recognized by the Joint Resolution itself, would allow the President to take whatever actions he deems appropriate to pre-empt or respond to terrorist threats from new quarters.**[22]

Further, even though Congress specifically rejected the President's request for authorization to use military authority within the United States, Mr. Yoo asserted that the president had inherent authority to use that power "at home or overseas":

Military actions need not be limited to those individuals, groups, or states that participated in the attacks on the World Trade Center and the Pentagon: **the Constitution vests the President with the power to strike terrorist groups or organizations that cannot be demonstrably linked to the September 11 incidents, but that, nonetheless, pose a similar threat to the security of the United States and the lives of its people, whether at home or overseas.**[23]

Though inside the Justice Department and the White House, the AUMF was regarded as a legal irrelevancy, and the Congress that enacted it as an impediment to be evaded, Mr. Yoo publically praised the AUMF, and stressed its importance, with no hint that its limitations were being flouted. Consider, for example, his statements in a 2007 interview:

Q: Is there any controversial element to [the authorization obtained from Congress in the AUMF]?

Mr. Yoo: No. In fact, I don't think so. It's passed by large majorities of the House and Senate. And remember the Senate [at] this time is controlled by Democrats, and so we spent a lot of time negotiating with them about the exact language, but the finished product is a *consensus* document. The statute says use all necessary means to stop future terrorist attacks and to find those responsible for the past attacks. It's an extremely broad statute, but Congress knew what it was doing. I know that for a fact because we negotiated very closely with them about the wording.[24]

Similarly, it is not without some irony that the Justice Department would ultimately rely on the AUMF to claim, when the Administration's detention policies later came under legal challenge, that they were undertaken pursuant to congressional authorization.[25]

Consistent with the expansive view of presidential war powers, when President Bush ordered the use of military force against al Qaeda in October 2001, he did not cite the AUMF as authority for that action. His letter informing Congress of his use of force in Afghanistan stated only that he "appreciate[d] the continuing support of Congress, including its enactment of [the AUMF]." Aside from this passing reference, his letter made clear that he was relying solely on his Constitutional power as Commander in Chief.

> I have taken these actions pursuant to my constitutional authority to conduct U.S. foreign relations as Commander in Chief and Chief Executive. It is not possible to know at this time either the duration of combat operations or the scope and duration of the deployment of U.S. Armed Forces necessary to counter the terrorist threat to the United States. As I have stated previously, it is likely that the American campaign against terrorism will be lengthy. I will direct such additional measures as necessary in exercise of our right to self-defense and to protect U.S. citizens and interests.

> I am providing this report as part of my efforts to keep the Congress informed, consistent with the War Powers Resolution and Public Law 107-40. Officials of my Administration and I have been communicating regularly with the leadership and other members of Congress, and we will continue to do so. **I appreciate the continuing support of the Congress, including its enactment of Public Law 107-40, in these actions to protect the security of the United States of America and its citizens, civilian and military, here and abroad.**[26]

The assertions of unreviewable presidential power as Commander in Chief would be advanced time and again in the context of specific presidential actions. For example, in connection with the use of military commissions (November 2001):

> [U]nder 10 U.S.C § 821 and his inherent powers as Commander in Chief, the President may establish military commissions to try and punish terrorists apprehended as part of the investigation into, or in military and intelligence operations in response to, the September 11 attacks... **Indeed, if § 821 were read as restricting the use of military commissions and prohibiting practices traditionally followed, it would infringe on the President's express constitutional powers as Commander in Chief.**[27]

In connection with whether the War Crimes Act could constrain the president in the conduct of military activity (January 2002):

> The [War Crimes Act] regulates the manner in which the U.S. Armed Forces may conduct military operations against the enemy;

as such, it potentially comes into conflict with the President's Commander in Chief power under Article II of the Constitution. As we have advised others earlier in this conflict, the Commander in Chief power gives the President the plenary authority in determining how best to deploy troops in the field. **Any congressional effort to restrict presidential authority by subjecting the conduct of the U.S. Armed Forces to a broad construction of the Geneva Convention, one that is not clearly borne by its text, would represent a possible infringement on presidential discretion to direct the military.** [28]

In connection with whether the federal torture statute could constrain the president in his choice of interrogation methods (August 2002):

Even if an interrogation method arguably were to violate [18 U.S.C. § 2340A, the felony prohibition against torture], the statute would be unconstitutional if it impermissibly encroached on the President's constitutional power to conduct a military campaign. As Commander-in-Chief, the President has the constitutional authority to order interrogations of enemy combatants to gain intelligence information concerning the military plans of the enemy... **Any effort to apply Section 2340A in a manner that interferes with the President's direction of such core war matters as the detention and interrogation of enemy combatants thus would be unconstitutional.**[29]

Regarding applicability of the criminal torture statute (March 2003):

[F]ederal criminal laws of general applicability do not apply to properly-authorized interrogations of enemy combatants, undertaken by military personnel in the course of an armed conflict. **Such criminal statutes, if they were misconstrued to apply to the interrogation of enemy combatants, would conflict with the Constitution's grant of the Commander in Chief power solely to the President.**[30]

It was this expansive view of the president's supreme, inherent powers that Vice President Cheney, David Addington, and John Yoo "pushed and pushed" – all the way to the Supreme Court.

Critique of John Yoo's Flawed Theory of Presidential Supremacy

It would be difficult to overstate how profoundly flawed the Yoo/Addington/Cheney theories of presidential supremacy are vis-à-vis the power of Congress and the courts. At their core, these theories rest on a fictionalized version of American history – one in which the Revolutionary War was fought to give the president near monarchical, uncheckable powers over foreign affairs and the use of the military; the Constitution was constructed to provide carefully limited powers to Congress but unlimited powers to the president; the president, by merely claiming that a decision touched on the exercise of military power, would enjoy nearly unfettered power to deprive United States citizens of liberties protected by the Bill of Rights, with the Congress and the courts essentially powerless to stop him.

Mr. Yoo has attempted to dismiss his critics by caricaturing them, claiming that they would have Congress micro-manage a war's execution;[31] or that "the left" is seeking, as part of its "campaign against the war," to have every captured terrorist given Miranda warnings.[32] But his notions contradict every reasonable understanding of the American experience as colonies, the events leading to the Declaration of Independence and the Revolutionary War, the intent of the Framers, and the structure and plain text of the Constitution.

Out of the wealth of writings of the Framers, many in contexts having nothing to do with war powers, there are a number of opportunities for Mr. Yoo to isolate a sentence here or there to bolster his radical contentions.[33] Refuting those contentions involves a more thoughtful study of the Federalist Papers, the full writings of Alexander Hamilton and James Madison, the experiences of the colonists with King George III that animated the Framers' concerns regarding executive power, and the seminal Supreme Court opinions from the late 1700s and early 1800s, to carefully divine the fundamental principles that remain relevant more than 200 years later.

Mr. Yoo's writings have received widespread scholarly criticism based on such study. For purposes of this Report, the following can be distilled: Mr. Yoo utterly disregarded important colonial and revolutionary experience against which the Constitution was written – a stance which led him to grossly misread the legal principles that have developed in that historical context. In particular, he failed to recognize that the Constitution explicitly grants Congress broad powers for the very purpose of checking the president, including in the sphere of war and foreign affairs. His claim that the Constitution gives the president vast "inherent" powers, while Congress's powers are limited to those enumerated, simply cannot withstand scrutiny.

For example, Mr. Yoo's treatment, in the September 25, 2001, War Powers Memorandum, of Alexander Hamilton's statement on the virtues of "energy in the executive... for protection of the community against foreign attacks" to support his assertion that the president has exclusive power in the realms of war, foreign policy, and national defense provides a useful example of his flawed approach. He wrote:

> Our reading of the text [of the Constitution] is reinforced by
> analysis of the constitutional structure. First, it is clear that the
> Constitution secures all federal executive power in the President to
> ensure a unity in purpose and energy in action. "Decision, activity,

secrecy, and dispatch will generally characterize the proceedings of one man in a much more eminent degree than the proceedings of any greater number." [The Federalist No. 70 (Alexander Hamilton).] The centralization of authority in the President alone is particularly crucial in matters of national defense, war, and foreign policy, where a unitary executive can evaluate threats, consider policy choices, and mobilize national resources with a speed and energy that is superior to any other branch. As Hamilton noted, "Energy in the executive is a leading character in the definition of good government. It is essential to the protection of the community against foreign attacks." [*Id.*] This is not less true in war. "Of all the cares or concerns government, the direction of war most peculiarly demands those qualities which distinguish the exercise of power by a single hand."' [The Federalist No. 74 (Alexander Hamilton).][34]

Mr. Yoo's analysis here is flawed in a number of important respects. To begin with, he relies on Federalist No. 70, a writing that is primarily devoted to the proposition that the Executive should be a single individual rather than several individuals or a council. This is the "unity" and "energy" that Hamilton is referencing, and the concern is simply that it would be dissipated if the executive powers were to reside in more than one person. Federalist No. 70 does *not* speak to the "unity" of the president's power in military matters or foreign affairs powers to the exclusion of Congress; indeed, it does not address the allocation of war or foreign affairs powers between Congress and the president at all.

Hamilton specifically discusses the president's war powers in Federalist No. 69, the immediate preceding writing, well known to all who have dispassionately studied this issue, though not even mentioned by Mr. Yoo. In that writing, Hamilton stresses the *limitations* on the president's war power, emphasizing that the president is *not* to have monarchical-type powers in the use of the military. Here, as elsewhere in our constitutional republic, the "energy" required of the Executive is to carry out the law as duly enacted, not to autocratically make the law.

Likewise, Hamilton's reference to the direction of a war requiring a "single hand" is no more than another reference to the proposition that the Commander in Chief should be a single individual. This understanding is unambiguous from examining the context in which the reference was written. A preceding sentence in the very paragraph of Federalist No. 69 from which Mr. Yoo extracts the "single hand" sentence mentions that the state constitutions place military power with the governor – that is, a "single hand" – and not an executive council of some sort. "Even those of them [states], which have in other respects coupled the Chief Magistrate [*i.e.*, the governor] with a Council, have, for the most part concentrated the military authority in him alone." No fair reading of the passage from which this phrase is excerpted supports the notion that Hamilton was advocating that absolute authority related to war should be placed in the hand of the president to the exclusion of Congress.

In Federalist No. 69, Hamilton sought to reassure the public, which had so recently suffered under the military adventurism and abuses of the British monarchy – by including, prominently, a discussion of the military abuses that precipitated the Declaration of Independence,[35] and by stressing that the Constitution would constrain the president's incentives to exercise military authority by placing that authority in check by Congress:[36]

> The President is to be commander-in-chief of the army and navy of the United States. In this respect his authority would be nominally the same with that of the king of Great Britain, but in substance much inferior to it. It would amount to nothing more than the supreme command and direction of the miliary and naval forces, as first General and admiral of the Confederacy.

* * * * * * *

> The one [the president] would have a right to command the military and naval forces of the nation: The other [the King] in addition to this right, possesses that of declaring war, and of raising and regulating fleets and armies by his own authority. The one [the president] would have a concurrent power with a branch of the Legislature in the formation of treaties: The other is the sole possessor of the power to making treaties...[37]

To this end, the Constitution provided to Congress – not the president – nearly each and every pertinent power which bears directly on the execution of war, with the sole exception of the Commander-in-Chief power. These included the power to:

- "provide for the common Defence and general Welfare of the United States,"

- "regulate Commerce with foreign Nations, and among the several States, and with the Indian Tribes,"

- "define and punish Piracies and Felonies committed on the high Seas, and Offenses against the Law of Nations;"

- "declare War, grant Letters of Marque and Reprisal, and make Rules concerning Captures on Land and Water,"

- "raise and support Armies, but no Appropriation of Money to that Use shall be for a longer Term than two Years,"

- "provide and maintain a Navy,"

- "make Rules for the Government and Regulation of the land and naval Forces,"

- "provide for calling forth the Militia to execute the Laws of the Union, suppress Insurrections and repel Invasions,"

- "provide for organizing, arming, and disciplining the Militia, and for governing such Part of them as may be employed in the Service of the United States, reserving to the States respectively, the Appointment of the Officers, and the Authority of training the Militia according to the discipline prescribed by Congress."[38]

To the same end, the Constitution even provided that negotiating treaties and appointing ambassadors – core "executive"- type powers in the sphere of foreign affairs – would require concurrence by the Senate.[39] And inclusion of the Third Amendment in the Bill of Rights, prohibiting the quartering of soldiers in private homes, is yet another indication of the Framers' concern with the potential for the president to abuse his military authority, and of the intent to check its exercise.

Justice Scalia relied on the guidance of the Framers in dissenting in the *Hamdi* case, on the basis that the Government's unconstitutional detention of a United States citizen in military custody without access to counsel or *habeas corpus* required that the appeals court's contrary holding be not merely vacated, but reversed:

> The proposition that the Executive lacks indefinite wartime detention authority over citizens is consistent with the Founders' general mistrust of military power permanently at the Executive's disposal. In the Founders' view, the "blessings of liberty" were threatened by "those military establishments which must gradually poison its very fountain." [The Federalist No. 45, (J. Madison).] No fewer than 10 issues of the Federalist were devoted in whole or part to allaying fears of oppression from the proposed Constitution's authorization of standing armies in peacetime... Except for the actual command of military forces, all authorization for their maintenance and all explicit authorization for their use is placed in the control of Congress under Article I, rather than the President under Article II. As Hamilton explained, the President's military authority would be "much inferior" to that of the British King:

> It would amount to nothing more than the supreme command and direction of the military and naval forces, as first general and admiral of the confederacy: while that of the British king extends to the declaring of war, and to the raising and regulating of fleets

and armies; all which, by the constitution under consideration, would appertain to the legislature." [The Federalist No. 69.]

A view of the Constitution that gives the Executive authority to use military force rather than the force of law against citizens on American soil flies in the face of the mistrust that engendered these provisions.[40]

Perhaps the most fundamental expression of the Framer's intent is that the Constitution allocates to Congress the power to declare war. Mr. Yoo attempts to dismiss the Framers' decision to give Congress this most central and critical power, on which all other war powers rest, by asserting that it is meant only to give Congress the right to recognize the existence of a war, not the authority to decide that war should be waged.[41] But James Madison refuted any such notion in 1793:

> Those who are to *conduct a war* cannot in the nature of things, be proper or safe judges, [of] whether a *war ought* to be *commenced, continued,* or *concluded.* They are barred from the latter functions by a great principle in free government, analogous to that which separates the sword from the purse, or the power of execution from the power of enacting laws.[42]

In a letter to Thomas Jefferson, Madison emphasized that the Constitution "supposes, what the History of all Gov[ernmen]ts demonstrates, that the Ex[ecutive] is the branch of power most interested in war, & most prone to it. It has accordingly with studied care, vested the question of war in the Legisl[ature]."[43]

One historian has referred to Mr. Yoo's effort to minimize the significance of the Declare War Clause of the Constitution as an example of his "fictionalizing of the founding period":

> Yoo's fictionalizing of the founding period is best exemplified by his lengthy discussion of the August 17, 1787, debate at the Constitutional Convention in Philadelphia. The surviving notes of this debate are admittedly garbled, cryptic and open to interpretation. But two things come through with ringing clarity. First, the word "declare," as the Framers used it, had a loose and fluctuating meaning. **Second, most participants in the discussion agreed on the importance of limiting the President's war powers by granting important war powers to Congress. This consensus stemmed from a conviction that war is the nurse of executive aggrandizement and that the President, whose powers balloon unnaturally in wartime, has a dangerous incentive to contrive and publicize bogus pretexts for war.**[44]

The historical record could not be more abundantly clear: The Framers, concerned that the president would have incentives toward military adventurism, carefully constructed the Constitution to assure that Congress – on behalf of the people – would have the power to keep the president's war-making and related foreign affairs powers in check. In attempting to make a case for his contrary assertions, Mr. Yoo ignores the entire sweep of history of the colonial era and the events leading to the Revolutionary War and the Constitution, including, prominently, the military abuses by the King that precipitated that War.

Mr. Yoo's corollary assertion that the executive power vested in the president in Article II of the Constitution includes unspecified inherent and implied powers, while the legislative power vested in the Congress under Article I is limited to the enumerated powers, is likewise unsupportable upon examination. Mr. Yoo asserts that:

> Article II, Section 1 provides that "[t]he executive Power shall be vested in a President of the United States."... This difference in language indicates that Congress's legislative powers are limited to the list enumerated in Article I, section 8, while the President's powers include inherent executive powers that are unenumerated in the Constitution.[45]

But the notion that the Constitution's enumeration of relatively few powers to the president should be read to imply expansive *un*enumerated powers, while the Constitution's enumeration of a far greater range of powers to Congress should be considered as a general limit on congressional power to act, makes little sense – especially where so many of the powers given to Congress can readily be seen as specifically intended to check presidential power – including in matters of war and foreign affairs.

Article II does, in fact, enumerate several specific responsibilities for the president. These powers include being Commander in Chief of the Army and Navy, having the authority to require the opinion of inferior officers in the Executive Branch, granting pardons, making treaties (with advice and consent of the Senate), appointing inferior officers, and, importantly, "tak[ing] Care that the Laws be faithfully executed." If, as Mr. Yoo claims, the Constitution granted inherent and unenumerated powers to the president by virtue of its vesting the president with the "executive Power," this enumeration of specific powers would be unnecessary.

In an effort to reconcile his contradictory assertions, Mr. Yoo posits that "the enumeration in Article II marks the points at which several traditional executive powers were diluted or reallocated [to Congress]. Any other, unenumerated executive powers, however, were conveyed to the President by the Vesting Clause."[46] This is not only the obviously strained construct of a sophist, however; it is easily refuted on its own terms, by noting that there are certain enumerated executive powers that are allocated wholly to the president, without any "dilution" – such as the power to pardon, or to employ inferior officers and secure advice from them.

More broadly, this strained construct overlooks the plain text of the Constitution. The Constitution does, indeed, speak to the allocation of residual, unenumerated power – to the Legislative Branch. Article I, section 8, the "Necessary and Proper Clause," gives Congress the power:

> To make all Laws which shall be necessary and proper for carrying into Execution the foregoing Powers, and all other Powers vested by this Constitution in the Government of the United States, or in any Department or Officer thereof.[47]

While there have been situations in which an unenumerated power must reasonably be implied in order to give effect to an enumerated power, and there may be others in the future, these judgments should be approached with due caution and humility, keeping in mind the Constitution's strong structural presumption against implicit Executive power.

Finally, as to Mr. Yoo's efforts to marginalize the courts, his assertion that the Constitution does not provide a role for the courts in checking the president's war powers is likewise flawed and manifestly contradicted by seminal Supreme Court decisions from the first decades of the Republic. Finding that assertion in a law review article Mr. Yoo had published in 1996[48] prompted Constitutional historian Louis Fisher to question how a competent law student editing Mr. Yoo's piece could have let it slip through:

> Looking initially at the first two decades, the student would have discovered the decisions of the Supreme Court in *Bas v. Tingy* (1800), *Talbot v. Seeman* (1801) and *Little v. Barreme* (1804), where the Court looked exclusively to Congress for the meaning of the war power. In the latter case, the Court decided that when a collision occurs in time of war between a presidential proclamation and a congressional statute, the statute trumps the proclamation.[49]

Mr. Fisher noted that Mr. Yoo had "ignor[ed] Chief Judge Marshall's statement in *Talbot* that the 'whole power of war being, by the constitution of the United States, vested in [C]ongress, the acts of that body can alone be resorted to as our guides in this inquiry.'"[50]

Mr. Yoo also ignores *Youngstown Sheet & Tube Co. v. Sawyer*, 343 U.S. 579 (1952), in which the Court rejected the President's claim that he had inherent constitutional authority to seize U.S. steel mills to keep them operating in the face of a scheduled labor strike. Like Mr. Yoo, the President's lawyers had relied on the provisions in Article II stating that "the executive Power shall be vested in a President"; and that the president "shall be Commander in Chief of the Army and Navy of the United States." Justice Jackson's concurring opinion rejected this argument and set out the considerations that should go into deciding, consistent with the equilibrium of separation of powers granted to the federal government under the Constitution, whether the president has a given power, emphasizing that an assertion that a power is "within [the president's] domain and beyond control by Congress" are the "circumstances which leave presidential power most vulnerable to attack and in the least favorable of possible constitutional postures."[51,52]

The Need for a Judiciary Committee Staff Report

Mr. Yoo's flawed theories metastasized into every corner of the Bush Imperial Presidency – from the politicization of the Justice Department, to defiant signing statements, to unchecked regulatory authority; from the arrogantly unilateral approach to detention and interrogation of detainees, and warrantless surveillance of Americans, to misuse of National Security Letters to evade established court oversight procedures; from manipulation of pre-war intelligence, to misuse of executive privilege and secrecy, to retaliation against critics. In these and other areas, we have seen an Administration with a single-minded determination to advance its aims even at the cost of abrogating the powers of the other Branches and abridging the rights and liberties of U.S. citizens. The dangers to our democracy of this effort to marshal these extraordinary powers into the Executive are what has compelled this Committee, over the past two years, to uncover and document this effort in all its excesses, to begin the work of remedying the damage it has done, and to help prevent any similar effort in the future.

Section 1 – Politicization of the Department of Justice

I feel a special obligation, maybe a special -- an additional burden coming from the White House to reassure the career people at the department and to reassure the American people that I'm not going to politicize the Department of Justice.[53]

– Attorney General-designee Alberto Gonzales
January 6, 2005

I work for the White House, you work for the White House.[54]

– Attorney General Alberto Gonzales
April 21, 2005

One of the most significant issues explored by the 110th Congress was the politicization of basic government functions that had occurred during the Bush Administration. Concern about this issue arose as early as 2002, when former White House aide John Dilulio complained, "[t]here is no precedent in any modern White House for what is going on in this one: a complete lack of a policy apparatus. What you've got is everything, and I mean everything, being run by the political arm. It's the reign of the Mayberry Machiavellis."[55]

When Hurricane Katrina struck and the Administration's deeply inadequate response was left to an unqualified political appointee in charge of the Federal Emergency Management Agency, the gravity of the problem became tragically clear.[56] Further reports have only heightened concern about the scope and depth of the problem, such as the recent charge by the head of the non-partisan American Association for the Advancement of Science that unqualified political appointees were "burrowing in" to the civil service and taking over career jobs with responsibility for making and administering government science policy: "You'd just like to think people have more respect for the institution of government than to leave wreckage behind with these appointments," this official charged.[57] Additionally, the House Committee on Oversight and Government Reform has documented numerous other instances of government action being driven by political considerations, such as an aggressive White House campaign to deploy government resources in support of Republican political candidates and repeated examples of White House and Administration officials overruling policy recommendations of agency career professionals for apparently political reasons.[58]

It was against this backdrop that a series of disturbing reports emerged in early 2007 of federal prosecutors being forced from office in suspicious circumstances.[59] Enterprising journalists immediately began collecting and analyzing these reports and noted that, in a number of cases the prosecutors who had been forced out were highly regarded; and that, in some cases, the prosecutors were also handling highly sensitive matters, such as political corruption investigations of Administration allies.[60] The controversy took on further life when one of the removed United States Attorneys, David Iglesias of New Mexico, stated that his removal was "a political fragging, pure and simple."[61]

The Administration's claims that the removed prosecutors were poor performers also did little to quell the controversy. In very large part, these claims were contradicted by the Department's formal evaluations of the removed prosecutors which rated their performance as excellent, and in many cases home state lawyers and others officials rose to publicly defend the prosecutors' reputations.[62]

When documents surfaced showing that the removals were the result of a lengthy process in which United States Attorneys were ranked based on their loyalty to the President and in which some prosecutors were praised as "loyal Bushies," the controversy took on yet another dimension. If some United States Attorneys were forced out for taking actions harmful to the Administration's political interests, what actions had been taken by the "loyal Bushie" prosecutors who were allowed to keep their jobs?[63]

Concern that politics may have influenced prosecution decisions only mounted when two professors published a study indicating that the Bush Administration was seven times as likely to investigate Democratic officeholders than Republican officeholders.[64] The issue sharpened when a federal appeals court reversed the politically-sensitive conviction of a Wisconsin state official named Georgia Thompson and within several hours of hearing oral argument ordered Ms. Thompson freed immediately from federal prison.[65] In the context of the unfolding controversy over the U.S. Attorney removals, many questioned whether Ms. Thompson's prosecution had been influenced by political concerns (Ms. Thompson was hired in 2001 into the civil service by the state Department of Administration, and had been indicted for allegedly awarding a state contract to a travel agency whose executives had made political contributions to Democratic Governor Jim Doyle), particularly after it was revealed that the Republican United States Attorney handling the case had been on the firing list for a time but was removed soon after he filed this indictment.[66] When a Republican lawyer from Alabama executed a sworn affidavit asserting that Karl Rove himself had urged the federal prosecution of Democratic Alabama governor Don Siegelman, it was clear that the issue of politically-selective prosecutions required thorough investigation.[67]

In addition to reports regarding the suspicious circumstances surrounding the removal of federal prosecutors, there were also widespread reports concerning the politicization of the Civil Rights Division (CRT) at the Department of Justice. Historically, the CRT had been viewed as the government engine at the forefront of the struggle to ensure equal justice under the law – from spearheading the fight to end school segregation to promoting racial, ethnic, and gender diversity and prosecuting hate crimes. The Division's image for vigorous law enforcement, fairness, and impartially had been tarnished.

Over the past eight years, the Division has received substantial criticism over charges of politicization in its decision-making and personnel hiring process. Beginning in 2002, the

42

Department came under fire for misusing its authority to ensure redistricting plans that favored Republicans.[68] Notwithstanding the Department's assertion that it was committed to fully enforcing civil rights laws, attorneys both in and out of the Department argued that the Civil Rights Division has been less aggressive in bringing discrimination cases.

In particular, staff said the Department eased up on several traditional areas of civil rights enforcement,[69] such as housing, voting, employment, and disability discrimination. According to a 2006 *Boston Globe* article, "the kinds of cases the Civil Rights Division is bringing have undergone a shift. The division is bringing fewer voting rights and employment cases involving systematic discrimination against African-Americans..."[70] Richard Ugleow, a 23-year veteran of the CRT, said the Division's statutory mandate was conscientiously fulfilled in an even-handed and judicious fashion under both Republican and Democratic Administrations, until the George W. Bush Administration.[71]

As criticism mounted over the politicization of enforcement decisions within the Division, experienced civil rights attorneys were driven out of the Department. In 2005, *The Washington Post* reported that nearly 20 percent of the division's lawyers had left, in part because of a buyout program that some lawyers believe was aimed at pushing out those who did not share the Administrations' conservative view on civil rights laws.[72] Many veteran litigators complained that political appointees had cut them out of hiring and major policy decisions, including approvals of controversial GOP redistricting plans which career staff had concluded discriminated against minority voters.[73] A *Boston Globe* article suggested that the Bush Administration was quietly remaking the Justice Department's Civil Rights Division by filling the permanent ranks with lawyers who had strong conservative credentials but little experience in civil rights.[74] Documents obtained by the *Globe* reveal that only 42 percent of the lawyers hired since 2003, after the Administration changed internal policies to give political appointees more influence in the hiring process, had civil rights experience.[75] In the two years before the change, 77 percent of those who were hired had civil rights backgrounds.[76] It is against this backdrop that the Committee commenced a series of hearings to investigate whether political considerations influenced the Department's civil rights enforcement work and hiring practices.

I.   Politicization of the Prosecution Function

A.   Hiring and Firing of U.S. Attorneys and other Department Personnel

On March 1, 2007, House Judiciary Committee Chairman John Conyers, Jr. issued the first subpoenas of the newly convened 110th Congress.[77] Those subpoenas compelled the public testimony of a group of Bush Administration United States Attorneys who had been forced from office under suspicious circumstances, and ignited a controversy that eventually would engulf the Administration. By the time the initial phase of the Committee's investigation was complete, the entire leadership of the Department of Justice as well as two key political aides at the White House had resigned. Reportedly, the President had even been compelled to seek the resignation of his closest advisor and confidant, Karl Rove, telling him in church one Sunday in Summer

2007 "there's too much heat on you."[78]

The controversy began when reports surfaced around the country of United States Attorneys being forced from office under suspicious circumstances.[79] Several Members of Congress immediately expressed concern, and Chairman Conyers and along with Courts, the Internet, and Intellectual Property Subcommittee Chairman Berman quickly wrote to Attorney General Alberto Gonzales on January 17, 2007, demanding information about the matter.[80] Mr. Gonzales testified before the Senate Judiciary Committee on January 18, 2007, that "I would, never, ever make a change in a United States attorney for political reasons or if it would in any way jeopardize an ongoing serious investigation. I just would not do it."[81] This assurance did not mitigate the significant concern about the firings that had emerged, however.

In February and March 2007, both the House and Senate Judiciary Committees held hearings to explore the reasons for the firings and to address concerns that political considerations may have influenced the Administration's decisions. Principal Associate Deputy Attorney General Will Moschella testified before the House Judiciary Committee's Commercial and Administrative Law Subcommittee on this subject, providing both a private briefing and public testimony at a March 6, 2007, hearing regarding the reasons for the forced resignations.[82] He claimed that, with one exception, the U.S. Attorneys had been fired because of their poor performance. Under questioning by Chairman Conyers, Mr. Moschella asserted the White House played only a very modest role in the matter, stating "because these are political appointees," it would be "unremarkable" to "send the list to the White House and let them know our proposal and whether they agreed with it."[83]

The same day that Mr. Moschella testified, the Subcommittee also heard from six of the removed U.S. Attorneys, who appeared pursuant to subpoena. These prosecutors described the circumstances of their removal, testifying that they were given virtually no explanation of why they were being asked to resign, and they responded to the charges of poor performance that the Administration had subsequently leveled against them.[84] In addition, evidence emerged that two of the U.S. Attorneys had received what appeared to be highly inappropriate communications from Members of Congress or their staff about pending prosecution matters, and that they had disappointed those politicians by declining to provide confidential information or to take requested action. United States Attorney David Iglesias described receiving calls from Senator Pete Domenici and Representative Heather Wilson, both Republicans from New Mexico, about a public corruption matter that allegedly implicated a New Mexico Democrat, and testified that: "My sense was that they expected me to take action on these widely reported corruption matters, and I needed to do it immediately."[85] He continued to explain that after the first of these contacts, "I had a sick feeling in the pit of my stomach that something very bad had just happened. And within six weeks, I got the phone call from Mike Battle indicating that it was time for me to move on."[86] United States Attorney John McKay also described receiving a "disconcerting" call regarding his handling of election cases from the Chief of Staff to United States Representative Doc Hastings, a Republican from Washington.[87]

This testimony substantially increased concern that the firings were politically driven. Further questions were raised by testimony that day from another fired U.S. Attorney, Bud Cummins, describing a troubling conversation he had with Mike Elston, the Deputy Attorney General's Chief of Staff, in which Mr. Elston discouraged Mr. Cummins and the other U.S. Attorneys from discussing this matter. In written testimony submitted after the hearing, Mr. Cummins elaborated on these disturbing communications.[88] Others of the U.S. Attorneys also described similar contacts from Mr. Elston.[89]

To address the questions raised by this testimony, Chairman Conyers and Subcommittee Chairwoman Sánchez immediately demanded access to documents and interviews with White House and Department of Justice personnel at the center of the firings.[90] That demand was given teeth by a vote on March 21, 2007, of the Commercial and Administrative Law Subcommittee to authorize the Chairman to issue additional subpoenas in order to compel production of documents and to obtain testimony from witnesses such as Karl Rove, Harriet Miers, Monica Goodling, and others who appeared to have played key roles.[91] The need for this vote was soon apparent as the Department of Justice's voluntary efforts at producing documents were so incomplete that the Chairman was compelled to issue a document subpoena to Attorney General Gonzales on April 10, 2007.[92]

The documents obtained from the Department of Justice only raised more questions about the firings. Multiple drafts of lists of U.S. Attorneys to be fired were produced that had passed between the White House and the Department.[93] One e-mail addressed the need to find a quick replacement for Carol Lam in San Diego, describing "the real problem we have right now with Carol Lam."[94] That e-mail was sent the very day Ms. Lam informed senior Justice Department officials that she would be executing search warrants in her expanding investigation into Republican corruption.[95] The earliest document on the matter identified by the Department was an e-mail to Kyle Sampson, the Attorney General's Chief of Staff, from a member of the White House Counsel's office with the subject line "Question From Karl Rove" asking whether U.S. Attorneys would be replaced.[96]

Unfortunately, none of these documents clearly established how or by whom the particular list of fired U.S. Attorneys was assembled. Nor did a marathon appearance by the Attorney General's former Chief of Staff Kyle Sampson – who had resigned as the scandal broke – before the Senate Judiciary Committee, nor did a series of detailed staff interviews of Department of Justice personnel. Indeed, the more the Committee learned, the less clear the answers became.

In short order, the Committee's investigation established that the so-called "performance based" reasons offered by the Administration to justify these firings were not true.[97] The U.S. Attorneys were in almost all cases top performers. Respected former Deputy Attorney General and conservative Jim Comey testified before the Commercial and Administrative Law Subcommittee on May 3, 2007, that he deeply respected and valued many of these prosecutors.[98] Interviews of numerous Justice Department officials further debunked the reasons given to

Congress and the public to support these firings.[99] For example, the reasons offered to justify the firing of John McKay arose only after he was placed on the firing list. Similarly, the notion that David Iglesias was an "absentee landlord" – the reason given to the Committee by the Justice Department to justify this firing – did not appear until after Mr. Iglesias had already been fired.[100] In the case of Arkansas United States Attorney Bud Cummins, who was asked to resign to create a place for Republican political operative Tim Griffin, the Administration also provided after-the-fact justifications that were not related to the actual decision to force his resignation, such as the apparently baseless claim that he was a poor performer or the inaccurate claim that he had already announced plans to resign.[101]

While the investigation established that the Department's justifications did not appear to be accurate, it only further raised suspicion about the real reasons for these firings. Indeed, based on the Department of Justice documents and interviews obtained by the Committee, it became increasingly apparent that a number of the U.S. Attorneys were removed for purely political reasons. Bud Cummins, for example, was apparently removed at least in part simply to make way for Karl Rove's aide Tim Griffin to obtain U.S. Attorney experience to enhance his future employment and political prospects.[102] David Iglesias appears to have been removed because of concern by New Mexico Republicans about his refusal to bring particular vote fraud prosecutions where he had concluded there was no appropriate basis to prosecute, and also because he angered New Mexico Members of Congress who had hoped he would bring other prosecutions ahead of the 2006 elections.[103] In a number of other cases, serious concerns about the role of politics in the firings remain.[104] Furthermore, it was clear that, at least in part, whether or not a U.S. Attorney was placed on or removed from the firing list depended on whether he or she had political support from Administration allies[105] – in this way, as the Justice Department Inspector General would ultimately explain to the Committee, all the firings appear to have been substantially infected by improper political considerations:

> Sampson also acknowledged that he considered whether particular U.S. Attorneys identified for removal had political support... **If a U.S. Attorney must maintain the confidence of home state political officials to avoid removal, regardless of the merits of the U.S. Attorney's prosecutorial decisions, respect for the Department of Justice's independence and integrity will be severely damaged**, and every U.S. Attorney's prosecutorial decisions will be suspect.[106]

Attorney General Gonzales appeared before the House and Senate Judiciary Committees, yet could not dispel these concerns. Mr. Gonzales claimed that he did not place any of the U.S. Attorneys on the firing list.[107] He also repeatedly claimed not to remember any of the details regarding the firing process or the reasons why these U.S. Attorneys were fired. In other significant ways, the Attorney General's testimony appeared to conflict with either his prior statements or those of his subordinates, including on whether the Deputy Attorney General had played a meaningful role in the firing process – at one point the Attorney General said that the

Deputy was a key figure, but at another point he said that the Deputy was not significantly involved – and on whether he had spoken to other participants in the firing process about their potential testimony.[108] On the later point, he first denied speaking to so-called "fact witnesses" but later admitted talking over the facts of the matter with Monica Goodling, the Justice Department's Liaison to the White House.[109] Ms. Goodling testified before the full House Judiciary Committee under compulsion of a subpoena and a limited grant of immunity that was needed to overcome her invocation of the Fifth Amendment.[110] This was the first time a witness had appeared before a Congressional Committee under compulsion of subpoena and a grant of limited immunity since 2003 and the only time it occurred during the 110th Congress. At this hearing, Ms. Goodling acknowledged "crossing the line" by considering political factors in hiring career prosecutors and immigration judges, and in approving Department personnel for important "details" in Department leadership offices.[111] This testimony led to two detailed reports by the Department's Offices of the Inspector General and Professional Responsibility that found widespread and in some cases unlawful consideration of improper political considerations in Department hiring for a diverse array of positions including Honors program entry level positions, career Assistant United States Attorney jobs, summer internships, and details to top Department offices and immigration judgeships.[112]

These findings echoed concerns stated by former Deputy Attorney General James Comey, who had previously testified before a Judiciary Subcommittee about the harm that would result if the Department was found to have taken politics into account in hiring federal prosecutors:

> [T]hat concerns me a great deal. I hope that didn't happen. I hope the investigation turns out that it didn't happen. But that is a very serious thing. U.S. Attorneys are political appointees, as the chairman said. They can be terminated for any reason. And I understood that I was a political appointee. But these AUSAs, they are the ones on whom the whole system rests. And we just cannot have that kind of political test... It's very troubling. **I don't know how you would put that genie back in the bottle, if people started to believe we were hiring our AUSAs for political reasons. I don't know that there's any window you can go to get the Department's reputation back if that kind of stuff is going on.**[113]

During her House Judiciary Committee testimony, Ms. Goodling also described a very disturbing conversation with Attorney General Gonzales in which he appears to have rehearsed his version of the facts regarding the firings with Ms. Goodling while the congressional investigation of the matter was proceeding.[114] According to Ms. Goodling, she had visited Mr. Gonzales' office as the controversy unfolded seeking a transfer or change of duties, and Mr. Gonzales instead proceeded to go over his view of the relevant events, saying, "'Let me tell you what I can remember.' And he kind of -- he laid out for me his general recollection." Ms. Goodling further stated that this conversation with the Attorney General made her uncomfortable: "And I remember thinking at that point that this was something that we were all going to have to talk about, and I didn't know that it was – I just – I didn't know that it was maybe appropriate for us to talk about that at that point, and so I just didn't."[115]

Finally, Ms. Goodling confirmed Committee concerns that the Administration had made an intentional effort to obscure and minimize the role of the White House in the matter, telling Members that Deputy Attorney General McNulty had warned her away from a Senate briefing on the issue because, if she were present, Senators might be encouraged to ask questions about the actions of the White House.[116] While it thus provided important information for the Committee's investigation, Ms. Goodling's testimony did not, however, explain who had identified these U.S. Attorneys for firing or why.

Eventually, the Committee exhausted all sources of information from within the Department of Justice without being able to answer key questions about the firings. As Mr. Conyers put it in questioning the Attorney General, there was only one more place to look for answers: "The breadcrumbs in this investigation have always led to 1600 Pennsylvania Avenue."[117] Accordingly, on June 13, 2007, the Chairman issued subpoenas for White House documents and for the appearance of former White House Counsel Harriet Miers regarding these matters.[118] That same day, Senate Judiciary Committee Chairman Leahy issued an identical document subpoena to the White House as well as a subpoena for the testimony of Karl Rove's aide Sara Taylor. Chairman Conyers also subpoenaed White House documents known to be contained on the computer servers of the Republican National Committee (RNC), which had been used by White House personnel, apparently in an effort to avoid federal record keeping requirements.[119]

On July 12, 2007, the Commercial and Administrative Law Subcommittee convened to hear the testimony of Harriet Miers. Ms. Miers, however, refused to appear for the hearing, making the unprecedented claim that, as a former aide to President Bush, she was immune from congressional subpoena.[120] The White House similarly refused to produce a single subpoenaed document, claiming that every piece of paper within the White House related to the U.S. Attorney firings was covered by executive privilege, and refusing even to provide a log describing the documents that were being withheld.[121] The RNC also refused to provide most of the subpoenaed documents or a privilege log, claiming that White House orders prevented it from doing so.[122]

On July 25, 2007, the full Judiciary Committee voted 22-17 to recommend that the House of Representatives find Harriet Miers and White House Chief of Staff Josh Bolten, as custodian of White House documents, in contempt of Congress.[123] On February 14, 2008, the contempt resolution came to the House for a vote. In support of the Committee, the full House voted to cite Ms. Miers and Mr. Bolten for contempt and refer them for criminal prosecution, by an overwhelming vote of 223-32.[124] This was the first vote to cite a person for contempt of Congress in over 25 years.

The Administration refused to prosecute the contempt however, at the direction of newly-installed Attorney General Michael Mukasey, in possible violation of the federal criminal contempt statute.[125] In response, Chairman Conyers used the authority granted to him by the House to take the matter to Court. On March 10, 2008, the Committee filed a civil action in the U.S. District Court seeking a legal ruling that the Administration's theories of immunity from subpoena and executive privilege were legally unsound.[126]

On July 31, 2008, United States District Judge John Bates granted the Committee's motion for partial summary judgment and ruled, as the Committee had argued, that Harriet Miers was not immune from congressional subpoena and that she was required to appear and testify before the Committee.[127] Judge Bates explained:

> The Executive cannot identify a single judicial opinion that recognizes absolute immunity for senior presidential advisors in this or any other context. **That simple yet critical fact bears repeating: the asserted absolute immunity claim here is entirely unsupported by existing case law**. In fact, there is Supreme Court authority that is all but conclusive on this question and that powerfully suggests that such advisors do not enjoy absolute immunity. The Court therefore rejects the Executive's claim of absolute immunity for senior presidential aides.[128]

Judge Bates also ruled that the Administration had no valid excuse for refusing to produce non-privileged documents and that the Administration was obligated to provide a more detailed listing and description of any documents withheld from the Committee's subpoena on executive privilege grounds than it previously had done.[129] The matter is now pending in the United States Court of Appeals for the District of Columbia, and the Judge's order has been stayed during the appeal.[130]

On September 29, 2008, the Department's Offices of the Inspector General and Professional Responsibility released their own detailed report on the forced resignation of the U.S. Attorneys.[131] The report confirmed the Committee's initial conclusions that the so-called performance-based reasons offered by the Administration to justify these firings were in large part untrue and that a number of the firings were politically motivated, concluding that "political partisan considerations were an important factor in the removal of several of the U.S. Attorneys."[132] The Department's report further concluded that inaccurate and misleading statements were made to the Congress and the public on this matter, and that a number of laws may have been violated by both the firings and the potential false statements of Administration officials.[133] Finally, the report described a widespread refusal by White House witnesses to cooperate with the Department's investigation and the refusal of the White House to make key documents available, and concluded that because of this obstruction, Department investigators "were unable to determine the role the White House played in these removals."[134]

Because of the seriousness of their findings and the limits on their authority to compel White House cooperation, the Department watchdogs called in this report for the appointment of a federal prosecutor to continue the investigation and evaluate whether criminal charges should be brought.[135] Accepting this recommendation, Attorney General Mukasey appointed Norah M. Dannehy, the Acting United States Attorney for the District of Connecticut, to continue the investigation.[136] As of this writing, Ms. Dannehy's investigation is ongoing.

B.   Selective Prosecution

Just as the Committee's investigation has revealed that some U.S. Attorneys who apparently were not considered sufficiently loyal were forced to resign, concerns have also been raised that political pressure may have been brought to bear on some U.S. Attorneys who were permitted to keep their jobs – including the so-called "loyal Bushies," as they were described by Kyle Sampson, Chief of Staff to then-Attorney General Gonzales.[137] These concerns were reinforced and heightened by an academic study published by Professors Donald Shields and John Cragan in February 2007 and updated for presentation at an October 23, 2007, joint hearing of the Crime, Terrorism, and Homeland Security and Commercial and Administrative Law Subcommittees that found federal prosecutors during the Bush Administration have investigated Democratic officeholders far more frequently than their Republican counterparts.[138] The updated findings – based on a sample of 820 reported cases and investigations – determined that during the Bush Administration, 80% of federal public corruption investigations have involved Democratic officeholders and only 14% have involved Republican officeholders.[139] Based on these data, the study's author testified that the Administration's investigations of Democrats are "highly disproportionate," and that there was "less than one chance in 10,000" that the over-representation of Democrats was by chance, concluding that selective prosecution of Democrats must have occurred.[140]

The Committee's investigation generated bipartisan concern about politically motivated prosecutions. During the summer of 2007, the Committee received a bipartisan petition signed by 44 former state Attorneys General calling for action.[141] At the Subcommittees' joint hearing, Ronald Reagan and George H. W. Bush Attorney General Richard Thornburgh stated his concern about "apparent political prosecution" and warned that citizens "may no longer" have "confidence that the Department of Justice is conducting itself in a fair and impartial manner without actual political influence or the appearance of political influence."[142]

Against this background, Committee staff investigated numerous allegations of selective prosecution that have surfaced around the country. In the early stages of its work, the Committee focused particularly on three cases where concerns about politically-motivated prosecutions have been especially intense: the Georgia Thompson case in Milwaukee, Wisconsin; the prosecution of the Democratic former Governor of Alabama Don Siegelman; and the criminal prosecution of Allegheny County coroner Cyril Wecht in Pittsburgh, Pennsylvania. Staff has also examined several cases brought against a group of judges and a practicing attorney in Jackson, Mississippi, including Mississippi Supreme Court Justice Oliver Diaz and trial attorney Paul Minor. Each of these matters presented at best a questionable exercise of prosecutorial discretion, and they often involved charges that appear to have elevated routine political fund-raising or similarly mundane conduct into aggressive federal criminal charges. As stated above, other cases of alleged selective prosecution have also been reported from states such as Georgia, Illinois, and elsewhere. The facts and circumstances of these prosecutions, as revealed by a detailed staff investigation, are summarized in a thorough report prepared for Chairman Conyers by the Committee's majority staff that was released on April 17, 2008.[143]

Even since that report, however, additional instances of potentially politicized decision-making within the Department have continued to arise, such as charges that the Department failed to fully prosecute corruption within the politically controversial Interior Department Oil and Gas leasing program, and that politically-connected Interior Department officials pressured Main Justice officials to overrule local prosecutors and keep the Department out of civil whistleblower cases involving that same program.[144] In one such case, the local U.S. Attorney complained on the record of being overruled "at the highest levels" of the Department and the career civil chief handling the matter reportedly suggested to the whistleblower's lawyer that "the case 'had political stuff written all over it.'"[145]

The case of former Alabama Governor Don Siegelman has raised the greatest controversy and seen the greatest level of investigative activity in this area. The House Judiciary Committee obtained sworn testimony on the case, through the September 14, 2007, deposition under oath of a Republican lawyer from Alabama, Dana Jill Simpson, who testified that she heard extensive discussion of Karl Rove pressing the Justice Department into prosecuting Don Siegelman.

As noted in Section 5, the Committee has actively pursued testimony from Karl Rove, issuing a subpoena for his testimony on May 22, 2008. When Mr. Rove refused to appear in response to subpoena, the Subcommittee and then the full Committee by a 20-14 vote recommended that the full House of Representatives cite Mr. Rove for contempt of Congress.

On the Wecht case, the United States Attorney responsible for the prosecution, Mary Beth Buchanan, was interviewed on the record by Committee majority and minority staff in connection with the broader U.S. Attorney purge investigation, although the Department (and Committee minority staff) objected to questions regarding the Wecht matter and thus she was prevented from testifying.[146]

On October 23, 2007, the Crime, Terrorism, and Homeland Security Subcommittees held a joint hearing on the subject, and heard from witnesses on the Siegelman and Wecht cases, including former Attorney General Richard Thornburgh and former United States Attorney Doug Jones, as well as one of the authors of the statistical analysis discussed above.[147] As quoted above, former Attorney General Thornburgh testified about the very disturbing facts of the Wecht case and stated his view that it appeared that politics had affected the prosecution decision. Former U.S. Attorney Jones testified about facts he learned while representing Don Siegelman in Alabama.[148] Mr. Jones explained that at one point the investigation had essentially closed, but just as the 2006 gubernatorial election primary season arrived, it heated back up. When Mr. Jones asked about this, he was told that the order came down from "Washington" to give the case a top-to-bottom review, which resulted in an entire new investigation being launched under circumstances that greatly troubled Mr. Jones.[149]

The Committee also aggressively pursued access to documents needed for this investigation. On July 17, 2007, Chairman Conyers, Commercial and Administrative Law Subcommittee Chairwoman Sánchez, and Committee Members Artur Davis and Tammy Baldwin sent a letter to then-Attorney General Gonzales seeking documents regarding the Department's handling of the Siegelman, Wecht, and Thompson cases, including materials that would explain the Department's charging analysis and decision-making process.[150] Two months later, on September 4, 2007, the Department responded by refusing to produce any "predecisional" or "deliberative" documents regarding any of these cases, relying on a statement of the Department's claimed "longstanding" position made in a 2002 letter authored by Alberto Gonzales when he served as White House Counsel.[151] The Department did provide a small number of documents (less than 30 pages) regarding the Thompson case, which it considered a "closed" matter about which information could be somewhat more freely shared, and offered to make United States Attorney Biskupic available for an untranscribed briefing on that case.[152] The Department refused, however, to provide any non-public information or documents regarding the Siegelman and Wecht cases, asserting that it could not provide such information to the Committee on "open" matters.[153]

Chairman Conyers, Chair Sánchez, and Representatives Davis and Baldwin responded by further clarifying the scope of the Committee's information request and explaining that the Department's refusal to provide any information on "open" cases or any "deliberative" materials was inconsistent with past practice and Department precedent.[154] In fact, Congress repeatedly has obtained prosecution memoranda and other deliberative materials of the Department regarding both open and closed criminal matters during past congressional investigations.[155] The Administration even made available to Congress the very prosecution memoranda that were at issue in the 2002 letter authored by Mr. Gonzales on which the Department relied.[156]

Negotiations regarding the possible production of documents continued between Committee staff and the Department's Office of Legislative Affairs. Some progress was made on the Thompson case, and a provisional agreement was reached in which Committee majority and minority staff members were permitted to review some relevant documents on Department premises, including interview memoranda and internal Department correspondence, as well as a detailed pre-indictment analysis akin to the prosecution memo, as a predicate for an untranscribed briefing by Mr. Biskupic (offered without prejudice to a subsequent transcribed interview or hearing if deemed necessary). In December 2007, Mr. Biskupic provided a confidential briefing on the Thompson case and related matters to Committee majority and minority staff during which he denied having any political motives in bringing the prosecution, and claimed that he had not even known that he was under consideration to be removed from his position as a U.S. Attorney by Department leaders.

Unfortunately, the Department largely stonewalled all further requests for information and has completely denied access to non-public materials regarding the Siegelman or Wecht matters. Accordingly, on June 27, 2008, Chairman Conyers issued a subpoena for these documents. Despite extensive negotiations, that subpoena has not been fully complied with and the Siegielman and Wecht documents have been withheld.[157] On December 10, 2008, Chairman Conyers wrote to the Attorney General demanding that these documents – and others subject to outstanding Committee subpoenas and requests – be appropriately preserved during the transition to a new administration.[158]

Recent developments have only heightened concern about these cases. On March 27, 2008, the federal appeals court in Atlanta, Georgia ruled that former Alabama Governor Siegelman should be released from prison pending his appeal, having concluded that "Siegelman has satisfied the criteria set out in the statute, and has specifically met his burden of showing that his appeal raises substantial questions of law or fact" regarding the viability of his conviction.[159] And more recently, new information has surfaced describing additional acts of apparent misconduct by the Siegelman prosecution team. On November 7, 2008, Chairman Conyers wrote the Attorney General transmitting troubling documents provided by a Department whistleblower suggesting that the Siegelman jury had improperly communicated with the prosecution during trial, contacts that were never disclosed to the defense or the judge.[160] Chairman Conyers also transmitted documents suggesting that the Republican-connected U.S. Attorney, who had purportedly recused herself from the case at the insistence of the defense, had in fact communicated information and a litigation strategy recommendation to the active members of the team. Commentators have expressed extensive concern about this new information, such as law professor Carl Tobias who said that the e-mails raise "legitimate questions" about the prosecution's conduct.[161]

Developments in the Wecht case have also only reinforced the Committee's concerns. In early April, after a two-month trial during which the prosecution presented over forty witnesses (the defense rested without putting on any evidence, arguing that the prosecution had not proved its case), and following ten days of deliberations, the jury announced that it was deadlocked and the presiding judge declared a mistrial. The prosecution immediately sought a retrial, a decision that defense lawyers criticized as having been made without due deliberation and before the reasons for the hung jury had been assessed.[162]

Subsequently, a member of the jury revealed that "[t]he majority of the jury thought he was innocent," and the *Pittsburgh Post-Gazette* editorialized that the case "added up to a big zero" and that it would be a "travesty" for the prosecution to continue and would "tarnish the integrity of the U.S. Attorney's office."[163] Indeed, on learning that a retrial was planned, the jury foreman wondered if the prosecution had any additional evidence that the jury had not seen, and stated that "as the case went on, my thoughts were this was being politically driven."[164] Other jurors apparently also had become concerned during trial that politics had played a role in the prosecution.[165] Local alarm was only further heightened by news that the prosecution had dispatched FBI agents to visit members of the jury.[166] Further demonstrating the bipartisan nature of public concern about the course of this prosecution, on April 16, 2008, a group of Republican and Democratic citizens of the Western District of Pennsylvania wrote to Attorney General Mukasey and U.S. Attorney Buchanan urging that the snap decision to retry Dr. Wecht be reconsidered.[167]

On April 17, 2008, along with the release of the Committee majority staff's report on this subject, Chairman Conyers, Chair Sánchez, and Representatives Davis and Baldwin requested a full investigation of these cases by the Department's Offices of Professional Responsibility and Inspector General, and the Office of Professional Responsibility has launched such an investigation, which remains pending as of this writing.[168]

II.   Politicization of the Civil Rights Division

A.   Factual Background

The Civil Rights Division (CRT) was created as part of the Civil Rights Act of 1957 which sought to protect the voting rights of African Americans who suffered widespread and pervasive discrimination, particularly in the Deep South. In the years that followed the passage of the Act, the Division's narrow mandate was expanded to include the enforcement of civil rights statutes aimed at eliminating discrimination in employment, housing, schools, lending institutions, public accommodations, and federally assisted programs. The Division's mandate was also extended beyond race discrimination to include discrimination based on national origin, immigration status, religion, sex, disability, and family status.[169]

During the Bush Administration, a series of news reports and complaints surfaced concerning the selective enforcement of civil rights statutes by the Justice Department. From 2002 to 2007, the CRT was embroiled in controversy surrounding the politicization of the policy decisions affecting its hiring practices, the preclearance of discriminatory redistricting plans, and the limited number of discrimination cases brought throughout the Division, particularly in the areas of voting, housing, and employment. Within that five year period, there were consistent allegations that the Division had strayed from its core mission of enforcing federal civil rights statutes aimed at eliminating discrimination and ensuring equal treatment and equal justice under law.[170]

In a 2007 report submitted to the United Nations Committee on the Elimination of Racial Discrimination, the American Civil Liberties Union (ACLU) concluded that racial and ethnic discrimination and inequality remain ongoing and pervasive in the United States, and that the U.S. Government has not done enough to address these important problems. The report cited the Civil Rights Division's enforcement work since 2001 as an example of the government's failure to take proactive steps to end racial discrimination in the United States.[171] The ACLU argued that "the Justice Department's Civil Rights Division has abandoned much of the traditional civil rights enforcement work it once pursued. For instance, the Voting Section encouraged states to limit, rather than expand, the franchise."[172]

In 2007, Bob Kengle, former Deputy Chief of the Voting Section of the Civil Rights Division and a Justice Department veteran, said that he left the Division because he reached his "personal breaking point." He explained, "in short, I lost faith in the institution as it had become. This was not the result of just one individual, such as Brad Schlozman, although he certainly did his share and then some. Rather, it was the result of an institutional sabotage after which I concluded that as a supervisor I no longer could protect line attorneys from political appointees, keep the litigation I supervised focused on the law and the facts, ensure that attorneys place civil rights enforcement ahead of partisanship, or pursue cases based solely on merit."[173]

Notwithstanding declining caseloads and intense criticism regarding the adequacy of the Department's enforcement work, the Bush Administration maintained that the Civil Rights Division continued robust and vigorous enforcement of civil rights laws. A close examination of the Division's docket, however, revealed a dramatic shift in the kinds of cases the Civil Rights Division litigated. The division brought very few voting rights and employment cases involving systematic discrimination against African-Americans and other minorities, but instead focused on cases alleging reverse discrimination against whites and religious discrimination against Christians. According to Department statistics, prosecutions for the kinds of racial and gender discrimination crimes traditionally handled by the division declined 40 percent over the past five years. Dozens of CRT attorneys found themselves handling appeals of deportation orders and other immigration matters instead of civil rights cases.[174] Shortly after it became public that political appointees within the Division approved a Georgia law requiring photo identification to vote over the strong objections of career professionals, the Voting Section leadership instituted a new rule requiring that staff members who review Section 5 voting submissions limit their written analysis to the facts surrounding the matter, and expressly prohibited the career staff from making recommendations as to whether or not the Department should impose an objection to the voting change.[175]

Much of the controversy surrounding the Voting Section centered around its enforcement of the Voting Rights Act of 1965.[176] This statute contains two sections that are key to the Department's ability to combat racial and language based discrimination in the election process: Section 5 and Section 2. Section 5 requires jurisdictions with a history of discrimination in voting to preclear, or get federal approval of, any new voting practices or procedures and to show that they do not have a discriminatory purpose or effect. Preclearance may be granted by the Attorney General or the Federal District Court for the District of Columbia. All voting changes submitted to the Department of Justice are reviewed and evaluated by the Voting Section, and if the Section finds that the submitting authority has failed to meet its burden of proving the absence of a discriminatory purpose or effect, the Justice Department can interpose an objection to prevent the implementation of the voting change. Section 2 is another critical enforcement tool the Department uses to eliminate discrimination in voting. Section 2 is a national prohibition on practices and procedures that deny individuals an equal opportunity to participate effectively in the political process on the basis of race or membership in a language minority group.[177] Section 2 is enforced through litigation brought by the Justice Department's Voting Section or private litigants.

B. Committee Actions

With this background, Chairman Conyers and Constitution Subcommittee Chairman Jerrold Nadler held a series of hearings focusing on enforcement, voting rights, fair housing, and employment discrimination. Because the greatest evidence of politicization occurred in voting, the Committee focused most of its oversight efforts on the enforcement work of the Voting Section, holding a total of seven hearings relating to the subject in the 110th Congress.

On March 7, 2007, Chairman Conyers held a full Committee hearing on "Protecting the Right to Vote: Election Deception and Irregularities in Recent Federal Elections." In his opening statement Chairman Conyers explained that, "there is no more important issue that comes before this Committee, this Congress or this Nation than protecting the right to vote. Our democracy is premised on the notion of one person, one vote. It is the keystone right of our nation, and without it, all of the other rights and privileges of our people would quickly become meaningless."

During his testimony, Ralph Neas, president of People for the American Way, explained that voter suppression techniques were used throughout the 2006 mid-term federal election to deceive voters into changing their votes, to vote on the wrong day, or to go to the wrong polling place. Some schemes attempted to convince citizens that voting will be difficult or even dangerous, or simply annoy them so much that they would stay home from the polls in disgust at the whole process.[178] For example, thousands of Latino voters in Orange County, California, received letters warning them in Spanish that, "if you are an immigrant, voting in a federal election is a crime that can result in incarceration."[179] In Maryland, "democratic sample ballot" fliers were disseminated in predominately African-American neighborhoods which deceptively identified Democratic candidates as Republicans.[180] Virginia voters received robo calls from a so-called "Virginia Elections Commission" informing them – falsely – that they were ineligible to vote. Virginia voters were also told that they couldn't vote if they had family members who had been convicted of a crime.[181] Commenting on the Department's voting enforcement record, then-Senator Obama argued that a private right of action provision was needed in the Deceptive Practices and Voter Intimidation Prevention Act "to allow individuals to go to court to stop deceptive practices while they are happening. That is important, given how uninterested the current Justice Department has proved to be in cracking down on election-season dirty tricks."[182]

On March 22, 2007, Chairman Nadler and Chairman Conyers held a hearing to evaluate the enforcement work of the Civil Rights Division. Witnesses included Wan Kim, former Assistant Attorney General for the Civil Rights Division (2005-2007), Joe Rich, former Voting Section Chief for the Civil Rights Division (1999-2005), and Leadership Conference on Civil Rights (LCCR) President Wade Henderson. This hearing, "Changing Tides: Exploring the Current State of Civil Rights Enforcement within the DOJ," coincided with the release of a report by the Citizens' Commission on Civil Rights, "The Erosion of Rights."[183]

The Commission's report provided detailed accounts of new policies implemented within the Civil Rights Division during the Bush Administration that led to a rapid decline in civil rights enforcement despite staff recommendations and complaints of discrimination. It focused on four distinct areas of the Division: Voting Section, Employment Section, Criminal Section, and personnel decisions. Of the sections highlighted, the Voting Section was by far the most controversial because of highly questionable legal and policy positions by the Department in key voting rights matters that appeared to undertaken to benefit Republicans.[184] Many current and former lawyers in the section argued that senior officials exerted political influence in many of the sensitive voting-rights cases the unit handled from 2001 to 2005 including two in Georgia,[185] one in Mississippi[186] and a Texas[187] redistricting plan orchestrated by Congressman Tom DeLay in 2003.[188] "Erosion of Rights" contends that fair and vigorous enforcement of Section 5 was compromised because of partisan political concerns. The report concluded that these actions damaged the Section 5 process, undermined the credibility of the Justice Department and the Civil Rights Division, and resulted in discriminatory voting changes being precleared.[189] In explaining the level of politicization that had seeped not only into voting rights enforcement, but also into personnel matters, Mr. Rich testified that he "was ordered to change standard performance evaluations of attorneys under his supervision to include critical comments of those who had made recommendations that were counter to the political will of the front office and to improve evaluations of those who were politically favored."[190]

Further still, some in the civil rights community have argued that the Bush Administration has undertaken a series of actions through regulations, litigation, and budgetary policy that illustrate a pattern of hostility toward core civil rights values and signal a diminished commitment to eradicating discrimination in this country.[191] In his testimony, Wade Henderson, the Executive Director of the LCCR, said, "over the last six years, we have seen politics trump substance and alter the prosecution of our nation's civil rights laws in many parts of the Division. We have seen career civil rights division employees – section chiefs, deputy chiefs, and line lawyers – forced out of their jobs in order to drive political agendas. We have seen whole categories of cases not being brought, and the bar made unreachably high for bringing suit in other cases. We have seen some outright overruling of career prosecutors for political reasons,[192] and also many cases being 'slow walked,' to death."[193]

On October 30, 2007, the Subcommittee held a hearing focusing exclusively on issues in the Voting Section. One of the key witnesses was John Tanner, then head of the Voting Section. Among other things, Mr. Tanner was questioned concerning his previous controversial comments defending the Department's decision to overrule staff in favor of preclearing the Georgia voter ID law. Mr. Tanner had explained that "primarily elderly persons" are the ones adversely affected by such laws, but "minorities don't become elderly the way white people do: They die first." So, anything that "disproportionately impacts the elderly, has the opposite impact on minorities," he added.[194] After questioning Mr. Tanner about the factual basis of his comments, Congressman Artur Davis said, "[w]ell, this is the problem. Once again, you engaged in an analysis without knowing the numbers... You are charged with enforcing the voting rights laws in this country. And if you are not fully informed about things that you're talking about and pontificating about, if you're basing your conclusions on stereotypes and generalizations, that raises a question in the minds of some of us whether or not you are the person in the best position to make these choices."[195]

Toby Moore, former Geographer and Social Science Analyst of the Voting Section of the CRT assigned to the controversial Georgia photo voter identification matter, testified that "the eagerness to conform analysis to decisions already made that characterized the Section's efforts in Ohio in 2004 and in 2003 enforcement generally led to a Georgia voter ID investigation in the summer of 2005 in which a determined effort was made to suppress evidence of retrogression, manufacture evidence in support of voter ID laws generally, and to punish those of us who disagreed. To me, it represents the nadir of Voting Section enforcement, worse even than the Section's action in the Mississippi redistricting case."[196]

In describing the impact of the Voting Section's actions in the Georgia case, Laughlin McDonald, ACLU Voting Rights Project Director, testified that "the revelations of partisan bias in the Civil Rights Division Voting Section's decision making create a lack of confidence and trust in the section." He explained that political bias undermines the Section's effectiveness and calls into question the Section's decisions about what to investigate and what kind of cases to bring. He also pointed out that "the section's recent action is a clear signal that partisanship can trump racial fairness, and thus increases the likelihood that minorities will be manipulated to advance partisan goals."[197]

Julie Fernandes, former Counsel to the Assistant Attorney General for Civil Rights, testified:

> [S]ince 2001, the Civil Rights Division has brought two cases
> alleging voting discrimination against African Americans. One, in
> Crockett County, Tennessee, was authorized under the previous
> Administration, with the complaint finally filed in April 2001. The
> other was in 2006 in Euclid, Ohio. **No cases involving voting
> discrimination against African Americans have been brought
> in the Deep South throughout the entire Administration**. Not
> one. The only case brought alleging racial discrimination in the
> Deep South was a case to protect White voters in Mississippi. Of
> course, White voters are protected by the Voting Rights Act. But it
> strains the imagination to believe that the only example of racial
> discrimination in voting in the Deep South for the past 6 years was
> a case involving White voters.[198]

Several other enforcement actions that appeared to be influenced by political considerations were addressed during the hearing. In a letter dated April 15, 2005, Hans von Spakovsky, then-Counsel to the Assistant Attorney General for the Civil Rights Division, informed the Arizona Secretary of State that, under the Help America Vote Act (HAVA), voters without identification can be denied provisional ballots.[199] This position taken by Mr. von Spakovsky reversed existing Department of Justice positions on HAVA provisional ballot requirements and ultimately was rescinded. Furthermore, the April 15, 2005, letter appeared to be issued in a manner inconsistent with Justice Department and Election Assistance Commission (EAC) protocol.[200] Another example of apparently unwarranted and restrictive voting rights intervention by the Department raised at the hearing was the agency's unsolicited October 29, 2004, letter to an Ohio federal judge, advising that challenges to voters' eligibility in Ohio are legally permissible,[201] despite the fact that such challenges to Ohio voters would appear to constitute caging, a discriminatory voter suppression tactic that is prohibited by Section 2 of the Voting Rights Act[202] and a Republican National Party Consent Decree.[203]

On February 26, 2008, the Subcommittee held a hearing to further examine the enforcement actions and priorities of the Department of Justice. At this hearing, Hilary O. Shelton, Director, Washington Bureau of the National Association for the Advancement of Colored People (NAACP), testified that "the number of voter suppression cases brought by the current Department of Justice does not reflect the number of complaints of people across the Nation who feel their rights have been violated." Mr. Shelton also said that "the NAACP, as well as representatives from almost every other civil and voting rights organization, all report an increase in the number of Americans – primarily racial and ethnic minority Americans – who say that they have been denied their Constitutional right to register and vote."[204]

Lorriane C. Minnite, Ph.D., Assistant Professor of Political Science, testified that voter fraud is rare,[205] and questioned the efficacy and fairness of the Department vote fraud investigations. She also questioned the purpose of the Department of Justice's Ballot Access and Voting Integrity Initiative, pointing out that the program has turned up very little individual voter fraud. Ms. Minnite found that, three years after the Department of Justice Ballot Access and Voting Integrity Initiative was launched in 2002, government records show that only 24 people were convicted of or pled guilty to illegal voting between 2002 and 2005, an average of eight people a year.[206] This includes 19 people who were ineligible to vote, five because they were still under state supervision for felony convictions, 14 who were not U.S. citizens, and five people who voted twice in the same election.[207]

Policy modifications and changes to the Federal Prosecution of Election Offenses Manual, published in May 2007, and which provides guidelines regarding voter fraud prosecutions, was also a topic during the hearing. In a letter admitted into the hearing record, J. Gerald Hebert, Executive Director and Director of Litigation of the Campaign Legal Center discussed the changes to the manual.[208] Mr. Hebert, a 20 year veteran of the CRT Voting Section, argued that the changes to the manual "appear to open the door for partisan abuse of election law enforcement by political appointees at DOJ." He explained that the manual removed the precautionary measures instituted to prevent partisan abuse of election law enforcement by political appointees in the timing of investigations or indictments, the pursuit of isolated instances of individual voter fraud (as compared to mass cases of voter suppression), and the types of pre-election investigations to be avoided by prosecutors.

On May 14, 2008, the Commercial and Administrative Law and Crime, Terrorism, and

Homeland Security Subcommittees held a joint hearing to examine two matters that raised serious questions about the Department's approach to allegations of voter suppression. The hearing showed how the Department's aggressive effort to prosecute questionable cases of so-called voter fraud stands in marked contrast to its far more passive approach to allegations that voting rights have been suppressed. At the outset of the hearing, the Administration's disengagement with these issues was clearly shown when it refused to send a witness to present the Department's view of the matters despite Chairman Conyers' request that they do so.[209]

The first matter explored at the hearing was the effort by Republican political operatives to jam telephones for ride-to-the polls services offered by the New Hampshire Democratic Party and the Manchester Fire Fighters Association on Election Day 2002. A federal judge found that this scheme was an "insidious" effort "to suppress as many votes for Democratic candidates as possible by sabotaging efforts to get citizens with transportation problems rides to polling places – citizens who the conspirators thought would largely vote for Democratic candidates."[210]

The hearing explored evidence that the Justice Department's investigation of this matter was limited to low-level party operatives, that leads pointing to the involvement of senior White House officials were not fully investigated, and that Administration officials obstructed and the delayed the progress of the prosecution effort to benefit Republican Party interests. For example, witness Paul Twomey who represented the New Hampshire Democratic Party in a civil suit related to the matter testified that "the slow pace of this case has been occasioned by delays caused by individuals at the highest levels of the Department of Justice and that all decisions had to be reviewed by the Attorney General himself."[211] He further testified that evidence leading to the White House did not appear to have been fully investigated, even though "[d]uring the course of the criminal conspiracy, [plot organizer] James Tobin made literally hundreds of calls to the political office of the White House."[212] Mr. Twomey also described how "the Republican National Committee had paid several million dollars for the [plotters'] legal fees" and had done so "in consultation with the White House."[213] One of the key implementers of the scheme, Republican operative Allen Raymond, who later wrote the book "How To Rig An Election" documenting his role in this and other Republican vote suppression tactics, also testified and stated his view that the senior most officials and attorneys of the Republican Party apparatus would likely have known about a scheme such as this.[214]

The second matter explored at the May 14th hearing was the Department's apparent failure to take meaningful action in response to reports that Republican-connected voter registration firm named Sproul and Associates had engaged in serious misconduct. The allegations included declining to register Democratic voters and actually destroying registration cards collected from Democratic voters in several states prior to the national elections in 2004.[215] Evidence of such misconduct was widely broadcast in the month prior to those elections, when a television news program in Nevada obtained destroyed registration cards from the trash and a former Sproul employee described in an affidavit being trained to register only Republicans and to tear up Democratic registrations in that state.[216] An investigative reporter in Las Vegas obtained destroyed registration cards and contacted the registrants who reported being "shocked to learn" that their forms had not been filed.[217]

At the hearing, a letter to Committee staff from Holly McCullough, a library manager in Pittsburgh, Pennsylvania was entered into the record. Ms. McCullough described her contacts with Sproul employees and how she had received complaints from her staff that Sproul employees would ask patrons who they planned to vote for in the 2004 presidential election and then would only register people who said that they planned to vote to re-elect President Bush.[218] Ms. McCullough further reported that, although she was easily located by the media seeking information about the activities of Sproul, she had never been contacted by any state or federal law enforcement investigator about the matter. Ms. McCullough further stated that, as a result of Sproul's misconduct, she would no longer allow any voter registration activities to occur at her facilities.[219]

On July 24, 2008, the Constitution Subcommittee held a hearing titled "Lessons Learned from the 2004 presidential Election." The hearing examined the voting problems that were encountered during the 2004 presidential election in order to glean key lessons that could be applied to prevent recurring voting problems before the 2008 general election. The hearing also included a discussion about proactive measures that could be taken by the Department of Justice, Election Assistance Commission, and local and state election officials to effectively address potential voting problems. Two key witnesses who testified during the Subcommittee hearing were J. Kenneth Blackwell, former Secretary of State of Ohio, who appeared only after the Subcommittee voted to authorize a subpoena in February 2008,[220] and Hans von Spakovsky, Visiting Scholar at the Heritage Foundation, who had significant involvement in the Department's decision to approve the Georgia photo identification requirement.

Mr. Blackwell was the focus of many of the questions during the hearing. He gained national prominence for his dual roles as Chief Elections Official of Ohio and co-chair of the "Committee to re-elect George W. Bush" during the 2004 election. Allegations of conflict of interest and voter disenfranchisement led to the filing of at least sixteen election related lawsuits naming Mr. Blackwell as a defendant.[221] Until this point, he had refused to respond to a series of letters from Chairman Conyers and other Members of the Committee concerning the 2004 election, as described in a 102-page report produced in 2005 at Mr. Conyers' request.[222] In questioning Mr. Blackwell, Congresswoman Debbie Wasserman Schultz noted, "what is disturbing to me is it appears as though you spent more time as secretary of state in the 2004 election reducing or suppressing voter participation as opposed to expanding it." She cited several examples: "you created new standards on the use of provisional ballots which disfranchised thousands of voters in predominantly Democratic or minority areas. You rejected thousands of new voter applications simply because they were not printed on the correct weight of paper."[223]

In discussing suggestions to prevent voting problems during the 2008 election, Gilda Daniels, former Deputy Voting Section Chief, testified, "In 2004, in my estimation, DOJ's perspective was too retrospective and not preventive. An inordinate amount of resources went into election day activities. In order to protect the fundamental right to vote, the government must act prior to election day."[224] Expounding on the steps that had been taken by the Department, Mr. von Spakovsky stated that the Bush Administration officials met with civil rights organizations. Mr. Hebert countered that the Department should move beyond meeting. He said, "I would agree that it's important obviously for the Justice Department to meet with civil rights organizations and voting groups and others. But you have to do more than just meet. You have to agree on what the procedures are going to be at the Department of Justice when you encounter a real problem, say like vote caging."[225]

Finally, on September 24, 2008, the Subcommittee on the Constitution and the Committee on House Administration's Subcommittee on Elections held a joint oversight hearing to examine federal, state, and local efforts to prepare for the 2008 election. Several state and local election officials and voting rights experts testified. Witnesses acknowledged the significant increase in the number of voters – more than 3.5 million new voters, up 64% from the same period four years ago. The witnesses discussed the proactive and preemptive steps that will and should be taken by federal, state, and local official to address election administration and voting rights issues likely to arise during the 2008 presidential election in order to ensure a fair election. Witnesses addressed a range of issues, from early voting, machine allocation and military voting and provisional ballots and voter suppression.

In urging the Department to take proactive, preemptive steps to prepare for the upcoming election Paul Hancock, Partner, K&L Gates and former Justice Department Acting Deputy Assistant Attorney General for Civil Rights, cautioned that there is no "re-run" in presidential elections. "So when we talk about preparing for this election, what we need to do is have a procedure in place, a program in place, for identifying the problems before the day of the election and correcting those problems before the day of the elections, or at least promptly as the election is taking place."[226]

More recently, in the run up to the 2008 presidential election, Chairman Conyers and other members took action in response to apparent efforts to suppress votes by targeting groups such as Association of Community Organizations for Reform Now (ACORN) which work to register and turn out voters. Republican animosity towards ACORN was well-known to the Committee from the investigation into the U.S. Attorney removals, as David Iglesias appears to have been targeted for removal in part because he resisted Republican pressure to bring a frivolous indictment of the group.[227] And Bradley Schlozman – who replaced U.S. Attorney Todd Graves in Missouri after Mr. Graves resisted a flawed lawsuit proposed by Mr. Schlozman that unduly burdened the right to vote – himself brought several highly questionable (and widely publicized) indictments against ACORN workers in the days before the 2006 elections.[228]

Thus, when a supposed nationwide investigation into ACORN was launched and improperly leaked in the weeks just before the 2008 presidential election, Chairman Conyers immediately questioned the Attorney General and the Director of the FBI on the matter, writing that "it is simply unacceptable that such information would be leaked during the very peak of the election season" and pointing out that the leak likely violated Department regulations as well as "valuable Department traditions regarding the need for cautious and sensitive handling of election-related matters during the run up to voting (or, as here, while early voting is underway)."[229] Several days later, Chairman Conyers and Subcommittee Chairs Nadler and Sánchez wrote again on this subject, decrying reports of violence and intimidation against election workers around the country, including threats that had been made against ACORN after the leak of information about the supposed investigation of the group.[230] In response to these communications, the Department has referred the matter to its Offices of the Inspector General and Professional Responsibility.[231]

The Committee continued to keep a watchful eye on charges of voter suppression around the country in the run up to the 2008 elections. For example, Chairman Conyers along and Subcommittee Chairman Nadler sent a letter to Attorney General Muskasey on September 18, 2008 requesting an investigation into reports that the Republican Party in Macomb County, was planning to use a list of foreclosed homes as a basis to challenge voters and block them from participating in the November 2008 election.[232] In addition, on October 29, 2008, Chairman Conyers and Subcommittee Chairmen Nadler and Bobby Scott wrote a letter to the Department to inform them of and call for an appropriate investigation of a fraudulent flyer claiming that state law required Democrats to vote on Wednesday, November 5, 2008.[233]

III.   Findings

Politicization of the Prosecution Function

1.   United States Attorneys were removed from office based on improper partisan political considerations. In some cases, the removals were based on overt political reasons such as a desire to satisfy Republican operatives or politicians or displeasure with the U.S. Attorney's approach to politically sensitive matters such as voter fraud prosecutions. In other cases, the role of politics was more indirect, such as where U.S. Attorneys were removed to create an open job for a favored Republican political operative.

- Former United States Attorney David Iglesias appears to have been removed from his position for improper political reasons, including complaints by New Mexico Republicans regarding his handling of voter fraud and political corruption cases.[234]

- Former United States Attorney Todd Graves appears to have been removed from his position for improper political reasons, including his refusal to intervene in a political disagreement among Missouri Republicans.[235] Mr. Graves may also have been removed because his approach to voting cases was not helpful to Republican political interests.[236]

- Former United States Attorney John McKay may have been removed from his position for improper political reasons, such as Republican complaints about his refusal to bring voter fraud charges in connection with the extremely close 2004 gubernatorial election in Washington state.[237]

- Former United States Attorney Bud Cummins appears to have been improperly removed to create a position for former Karl Rove aide Tim Griffin to fill. Some other firings remain unsatisfactorily explained (such as the removal of former United States Attorney Dan Bogden) and may also have been intended to create openings for young Republican to enhance their future employment and political prospects.[238]

2. Because the Administration and its allies have refused to cooperate with either the congressional investigation or the Department of Justice's own internal investigation into this matter, critical facts about the reasons for the firings or the broader issues of the politicization of the Department of Justice remain unknown. While the Committee's investigation was extensive (as was the Inspector General's), thousands of documents remain hidden inside the White House and no White House officials have provided sworn testimony about their role in these matters. The Justice Department too has refused to provide subpoenaed documents on this subject. Examples of the stonewalling by the Administration on this subject include the following:

- Karl Rove, Harriet Miers, and other White House figures refused to speak with the Committee or with other investigators and White House documents have been withheld.[239]

- Senator Domenici and his staff have refused to speak with Department investigators.[240]

- The Republican National Committee has refused to produce subpoenaed documents about the firings.[241]

- The Justice Department has refused to produce documents about the Siegelman case or other instances of alleged selective prosecution.[242]

3. The removal of some of the United States Attorneys may have violated the law. While the full facts are not yet known, it appears that at least some of the removals may have violated federal laws against public corruption, fraud, and obstruction of justice.

- The pressure placed on David Iglesias to make charging and prosecutorial decisions based on partisan political considerations may have violated federal statutes regarding obstruction of justice (18 U.S.C. §1503), wire fraud (18 U.S.C. § 1343), provision of honest services (18 U.S.C. §1346), and conspiracy (18 U.S.C. § 1349, 18 U.S.C. §371).[243]

64

- Removing federal prosecutors such as David Iglesias, John McKay, or Todd Graves based on their refusal to use their public offices to affect elections may have violated the criminal Hatch Act's prohibition on retaliation against employees who refuse to aid a political campaign (18 U.S.C. § 606).[244]

- Removing federal prosecutors such as David Iglesias, John McKay, or Todd Graves to influence the outcome of future elections or as part of a broader-based effort to hinder citizens' exercise of their constitutional right to vote may have violated the civil Hatch Act (5 U.S.C. § 7332) and the federal criminal prohibition on depriving citizens of the constitutional rights under color of law (18 U.S.C. § 242).[245]

4. **Then-Attorney General Alberto Gonzales made inaccurate or misleading statements to Congress and the public, including:**

- Alberto Gonzales' statement that he "was not involved in seeing any memos, was not involved in any discussions about what was going on" appears to have been false.[246] Just a few months before he made this statement, Mr. Gonzales participated in the key meeting on November 27, 2006, where he received a memorandum detailing the plan and personally approved the removals.[247]

- At least one of Alberto Gonzales' contradictory statements about the role of the Deputy Attorney General, some of which were given under oath, appears to have been false.[248] At one point, Mr. Gonzales testified that the Deputy's views were of paramount importance to him in approving the removals and at another point he testified that the Deputy was not sufficiently involved in the matter.[249]

- Mr. Gonzales' testimony that "I would never, ever make a change in a United States attorney position for political reasons... I just would not do it" was false; at a minimum, it is clear that U.S. Attorney Bud Cummins was removed so that a former aide to Karl Rove could bolster his political resume with service as a U.S. Attorney.[250]

- Mr. Gonzales' testimony about his conversations with Senator Domenici in late 2005 and early 2006 concerning David Iglesias appears to have been false, as these conversations do not appear to have involved complaints by Senator Domenici about Mr. Iglesias' job performance and instead appear to have focused on the Senator's belief that Mr. Iglesias should be given more resources.[251]

- Mr. Gonzales' statement that he did not discuss the matter with potential witnesses appears to have been false in light of Monica Goodling's testimony that he reviewed his recollections with her.[252]

- Mr. Gonzales' statements to Department investigators that he had "no present recollection" of approving a sweeping order delegating personnel authority to Kyle Sampson and Monica Goodling may have been inaccurate in light of his testimony before the House Judiciary Committee on May 10, 2007, describing the creation of this order in which Mr. Gonzales' did not profess any lack of recollection on the subject.[253]

5.   Then-Deputy Attorney General Paul McNulty and then-Principal Associate Deputy Attorney General Will Moschella made several inaccurate or misleading statements, including:

- Testimony by Deputy Attorney General McNulty and Principal Associate Deputy Attorney General Moschella that minimized the role of the White House in the U.S. Attorney firings was misleading.[254] The White House did not play merely a perfunctory or "final approval" role at the end of the process in Fall 2006, as Mr. McNulty and Mr. Moschella testified, but was substantially involved in the matter from its inception in early 2005. Indeed, White House officials Harriet Miers and Karl Rove appear to have originally proposed the idea of removing U.S. Attorneys and Ms. Miers' office received multiple drafts of the firing list over a two year period. In addition, while these documents have not yet been made available, the Department of Justice has confirmed that internal White House documents discuss the plan, including "specific U.S. Attorneys who could be removed."[255]

- Mr. McNulty and Mr. Moschella's failure to inform the Committee of Sen. Domenici's October 2006 call to Mr. McNulty regarding Mr. Iglesias was a significantly misleading omission, because that call appears to have played a material role in the decision to remove Mr. Iglesias from his position.[256]

6.   Former Chief of Staff to the Attorney General Kyle Sampson made inaccurate or misleading statements to Congress and the public, including:

- Kyle Sampson's written statement to Senate counsel that only 8 U.S. Attorneys were removed from their positions in 2006 was false.[257] In fact, 9 U.S. Attorneys were removed in 2006: Daniel Bogden, Paul Charlton, Margaret Chiara, Bud Cummins, Todd Graves, David Iglesias, Carol Lam,

John McKay, and Kevin Ryan.[258]

- Kyle Sampson's claim that the removals were based on poor performance appears to have been false.[259] Most of the removed U.S. Attorneys were top performers as reflected in their Department performance evaluations.[260]

- Kyle Sampson's testimony regarding the addition of David Iglesias to the removal list as part of a "group" of United States attorneys added together at the end of the removal process was inaccurate, as there was no such group added at the end and David Iglesias was placed on the list on his own, not as part of a larger set of additions.[261]

- The Department's written statement, drafted by Mr. Sampson and reviewed by White House officials, that Karl Rove had no role in the firing of Bud Cummins appears to have been false, as Mr. Rove appears to have been involved in the matter.[262]

- Kyle Sampson's repeated professed lack of memory was also highly suspicious given the seriousness of the issues and the length of time he worked on the replacement process.[263]

7. Then-Chief of Staff to the Deputy Attorney General Michael Elston made apparently inaccurate or misleading statements, including:

- Mr. Elston made statements about telephone calls he placed to the removed U.S. Attorneys that may have been inaccurate or misleading. The U.S. Attorneys who received these calls considered them threatening or intimidating, but Mr. Elston denied this.[264]

- Mr. Elston's testimony about a November 1, 2006, e-mail listing the names of U.S. Attorneys that he transmitted to Kyle Sampson may have been incomplete or inaccurate. Mr. Elston testified that he was not actually recommending that any of the U.S. Attorneys named on this e-mail be removed from their positions, but sitting U.S. Attorney Mary Beth Buchanan has accused Mr. Elston of lying to her and, by extension, to the Committee about this subject.[265]

- Several of the inaccurate or misleading statements described above may have violated the federal False Statements statute, 18 U.S.C. § 1001. A criminal investigation of this matter is underway, and press reports indicate that at least one Department official has been referred to a grand jury.[266]

8.   White House officials played a significant role in the removal of United States Attorneys and subsequent inaccurate or misleading statements on this subject._ Although the full extent of this involvement is not known due to the Administration's withholding of documents and testimony, it is clear even on the current record that the White House played a significant role in instigating, planning, and executing the removal of U.S. Attorneys.

- The idea to remove U.S. Attorneys originated with Karl Rove and Harriet Miers in early 2005, when Mr. Rove asked attorneys in the White House Counsel's office if U.S. Attorneys would be "selectively replace[d]" and Ms. Miers raised the idea of replacing all 93 U.S. Attorneys at that time.[267]

- White House officials reviewed multiple drafts of the firing list between early 2005 and December 2006.[268]

- White House officials in the legal, political, and communications offices gave final approval for the removals.[269]

- White House officials participated in developing and approving the Department of Justice's response to the controversy that arose after the removals.[270]

- White House documents subpoenaed by the Committee discuss "the wisdom of [the] proposal, specific U.S. Attorneys who could be removed, potential replacement candidates, and possible responses to congressional and media inquiries about the dismissals."[271]

- Because the President and former White House officials have refused to cooperate with either the congressional investigation or the Department of Justice investigation into this matter, critical facts about the role of White House officials in this matter remain unknown.[272]

9.   Other Department personnel appear to have been hired or fired based on improper or unlawful partisan political considerations._ After Monica Goodling testified before the House Judiciary Committee that she had "crossed the line" in basing hiring decisions on political considerations, the Department of Justice's Offices of the Inspector General and Professional Responsibility concluded that there had been extensive consideration of such factors for a range of career and non-political Department posts in violation of Department policies and regulations, and in some cases contrary to federal statutes.

- Improper or unlawful partisan political considerations were taken into account in the selection of summer interns and Department Honors program attorneys.[273] The problem was most severe in 2006 when,

68

according to the Department's Offices of the Inspector General and Professional Responsibility, "the Screening Committee inappropriately used political and ideological considerations to deselect many candidates."[274]

- Improper or unlawful partisan political considerations were taken into account in the hiring of career prosecutors and immigration judges, and the selection of detailees for placement in senior Department offices.[275] In particular, Monica Goodling "improperly subjected candidates for certain career positions to the same politically based evaluation she used on candidates for political positions, in violation of federal law and Department policy" and "considered political or ideological affiliations when recommending and selecting candidates for other permanent career positions, including a career SES position in the Executive Office for U.S. Attorneys (EOUSA) and AUSA positions. These actions violated federal law and Department policy, and also constituted misconduct."[276]

- This conduct was harmful to the operations of the Department "because it resulted in high-quality candidates for important details being rejected in favor of less-qualified candidates. For example, an experienced career terrorism prosecutor was rejected by Goodling for a detail to EOUSA to work on counter terrorism issues because of his wife's political affiliations. Instead, EOUSA had to select a much more junior attorney who lacked any experience in counter terrorism issues and who EOUSA officials believed was not qualified for the position."[277]

- "[T]he most systematic use of political or ideological affiliations in screening candidates for career positions occurred in the selection of [Immigration Judges] who work in the Department's Executive Office for Immigration Review (EOIR)."[278]

10.   Partisan politics may have influenced federal criminal prosecutions around the country. A number of federal criminal matters such as the politically-charged prosecutions of former governor of Alabama Donald Siegelman, former Wisconsin civil servant Georgia Thompson, former Allegheny County Coroner Cyril Wecht, Mississippi Supreme Court Justice Oliver Diaz and Mississippi trial attorney Paul Minor may have been tainted by politics, but the House Judiciary Committee has been refused access to information needed to reach conclusions on this issue.[279]

Politicization of the Civil Rights Division and Voting Rights Enforcement

11.   Partisan politics appears to have influenced Justice Department pre-clearance determinations to the detriment of minority voters.

69

- There are three specific voting cases where politics appear to have influenced the enforcement decisions of the Department: (i) In 2001, the Justice Department unnecessarily delayed its determination on whether a Mississippi redistricting plan met the requirements of the Voting Rights Act which resulted in the implementation of a redistricting the favored the Republican Party and harmed minority voters; (ii) in 2003, CRT career professional staff (attorneys and analysts) concluded that the Texas congressional redistricting plan spearheaded by Rep. Tom DeLay violated the Voting Rights Act because it illegally diluted the votes of blacks and Hispanics in order to ensure a Republican majority in the state's congressional delegation, however Justice Department political appointees overruled the lawyers and approved the plan; and (iii) in 2005, CRT staff attorneys and analysts who reviewed a Georgia voter-identification law recommended the law's rejection, because they determined that the law was likely to discriminate against black voters, however, political officials[280] overruled the team's recommendation.[281]

- In its report, "The Erosion of Rights," the Citizens Commission on Civil Rights found that current and former Justice Department attorneys stated that political considerations led senior officials to delay the Mississippi redistricting case and overrule the staff in the Georgia photo ID and Texas redistricting case.[282]

- The Department's analysis in these cases was illustrated by then-Voting Right Division Chief John Tanner who said in defending Department's decision to approve the Georgia Photo ID voting law that "minorities don't become elderly the way white people do: They die first."[283]

- After overruling the career professionals in the Voting Section in both the Georgia and Texas matters, the Justice Department barred staff attorneys from offering recommendations in major Voting Rights Act cases, marking a significant change in the procedures meant to insulate such decisions from politics.[284]

12.   <u>Partisan politics appears to have led to the decline of discrimination cases involving voting rights brought by the Justice Department.</u>

- In 2007, former senior Civil Rights Division attorneys testified that "since 2001, the Civil Rights Division has brought only two cases alleging voting discrimination against African Americans. One, in Crockett County, Tennessee, was authorized under the previous Administration, with the complaint finally filed in April 2001. The other was in 2006 in Euclid, Ohio. No cases involving voting discrimination against African

Americans voters have been brought in the Deep South throughout the entire Administration."[285]

- During the Bush Administration, the Department took a series of positions adverse to the right of minority voters, such as advising states to deny provisional ballots to voters without IDs, and asking a federal judge in Ohio shortly before the 2004 presidential election to permit challenges to minority voters based on "caging" tactics banned in other jurisdictions.[286]

- The Department modified the Federal Prosecution of Election Offenses manual in a manner that increases the opportunity for partisan political consideration to influence an election by allowing voting fraud investigations and prosecutions cases to be initiated immediately before an election, and allowing such cases to be brought on an isolated rather than a systemic basis.[287]

- Political appointees in the Department's Civil Rights Division also took unprecedented steps to change performance evaluations of career attorneys based on political considerations. Joe Rich, a former Voting Rights Chief from 1999 to 2005, testified that he "was ordered to change standard performance evaluations of attorneys under his supervision to include critical comments of those who had made recommendations that were counter to the political will of the front office and to improve evaluations of those who were politically favored."[288]

Section 2 – Assault on Individual Liberty: Detention, Enhanced Interrogation, Ghosting and Black Sites, Extraordinary Rendition, Warrantless Domestic Surveillance, and National Security and Exigent Letters

[T]he state of war is not a blank check for the President when it comes to the rights of the nation's citizens.[289]

– Supreme Court Justice Sandra Day O'Connor,
in *Hamdi v. Rumsfeld*

A few days after the 9/11 attacks, Vice President Dick Cheney appeared on *Meet the Press*, where he was interviewed by Tim Russert. One part of the interview went as follows

<u>Mr. Russert:</u>   When Osama bin Laden took responsibility for blowing up the embassies in Kenya and Tanzania, U.S. embassies, several hundred died, the United States launched 60 tomahawk missiles into his training sites in Afghanistan. It only emboldened him. It only inspired him and seemed even to increase his recruitment. Is it safe to say that that kind of response is not something we're considering, in that kind of minute magnitude?

<u>Mr. Cheney:</u>   I'm going to be careful here, Tim, because I – clearly it would be inappropriate for me to talk about operational matters, specific options or the kinds of activities we might undertake going forward. We do, indeed, though, have, obviously, the world's finest military. They've got a broad range of capabilities. And they may well be given missions in connection with this overall task and strategy.

We also have to work, though, sort of the dark side, if you will. We've got to spend time in the shadows in the intelligence world. A lot of what needs to be done here will have to be done quietly, without any discussion, using sources and methods that are available to our intelligence agencies, if we're going to be successful. **That's the world these folks operate in, and so it's going to be vital for us to use any means at our disposal, basically, to achieve our objective.**[290]

For years, it was not clear what the "dark side" consisted of, what was meant by the "shadows of the intelligence world," and what were the "sources and methods" that the Vice

President considered to "available to our intelligence agencies" that were among the "any means at our disposal." Over time, however, at least some of the facts have emerged. The Administration engaged in a series of unilateral actions at the direction of the President through his subordinates in connection with detention, interrogation, and intelligence collection that were characterized by the assertion of unreviewable executive power and the rejection of ongressional and judicial limitations on this power.

The facts that have emerged have come from various sources. Some documents, such as certain of the Department of Justice Office of Legal Counsel memoranda, have been disclosed by the White House and the Department of Justice. Other information, such as certain facts associated with the President's decision to implement his own foreign intelligence collection system outside of FISA, was uncovered and disclosed by the press. In numerous cases, congressional oversight hearings were critical in obtaining the public disclosure of facts associated with some of the conduct at issue – such as public confirmation of the facts associated with the attempts by then-White House Counsel Alberto Gonzales to obtain the signature of then-Attorney General Ashcroft on orders extending the President's surveillance program at a time when Mr. Ashcroft was in intensive care at the hospital, or testimony in which the Director of the CIA acknowledged the use of water-boarding on certain detainees. In other instances, Inspector General Reports were critical in detailing misconduct, such as with respect to the FBI's misuse of national Security and Exigent Letters, or confirming instances of harsh treatment of detainees at Guantanamo.

After the initiation of hostilities in Afghanistan, the Bush Administration had to make decisions as to what to do with persons captured as suspected enemy fighters or terrorists. There were several interrelated issues: what procedures should be used to determine whether the detainees should be held in custody, and for how long; where should the detainees be held and under what conditions; and what limitations, if any, existed on the techniques used to interrogate them. These decisions presented numerous legal issues, such as whether federal court jurisdiction extends to Guantanamo Bay, Cuba, for purposes of the application of the *habeas corpus* statutes; if so, whether foreign detainees were entitled to pursue *habeas corpus* remedies in the federal courts; whether a military commissions system may be implemented at the direction of the President – even where Congress has legislated on this topic; and whether the congressionally enacted torture or war crimes statutes constrained the conduct of U.S. Government employees in interrogating detainees.

Though each of these policy decisions presented its own legal issues, as a matter of policy-making they can also be seen as intertwined. For the Administration's policy decision to hold detainees where they would have no access to the courts was devised precisely to permit the Executive Branch – through the military or the intelligence community – to interrogate them under rules set by that Branch, without interference by the Congress or the courts, without the constraints of either the criminal laws or the Constitution.

Three critical decisions were made in the first months after the 9/11 attacks to effectuate these goals:

1.   to implement a military commission system for the purposes of determining the status of the detainees – built from scratch – so as to avoid the procedures related to military commissions already enacted by Congress in the Code of Military Justice;

2.   to hold the detainees in Guantanamo Bay, Cuba – in the hopes this would be outside the reach of U.S. courts; and

3.   to decide as a legal matter that the detainees would not be entitled to treatment as prisoners of war under the Geneva Conventions, and also would not qualify for the protections of Common Article 3 of the Conventions – which meant that the criminal prohibitions under the federal War Crimes statute would not apply to the U.S. interrogators.

This Section details the nature of those decisions as they relate to detention and interrogation policy, as well as probing the Administration's policies with regard to extraordinary rendition, black sites and ghosting, warrantless surveillance and National Security and Exigent Letters.

I.   Detention

A.   Factual Background

October 2001 Domestic War Powers Memorandum

On October 23, 2001, Deputy Assistant Attorney General John Yoo and Special Counsel Robert Delahunty in the Department of Justice's Office of Legal Counsel (OLC) prepared a memorandum entitled: "Authority for Use of Military Force to Combat Terrorist Activities Within the United States."[291] This unclassified memorandum suggests broad power of the president as Commander in Chief to use military force inside the United States, contemplating even seizure and detention of United States citizens (or lawfully admitted aliens) in some circumstances. As such, the memorandum – though it does not squarely address detention policy -- is consistent with the September 25, 2001, War Powers Memorandum which claimed for the president domestic war powers, anticipates the assertions of presidential power in the domestic detention context just a few months later, and anticipates the November 2001 conclusion that the president has the power to subject United States citizens to military commissions.

The memorandum, which was directed to White House Counsel Alberto Gonzales and Defense Department General Counsel William J. Haynes, addresses whether the president has constitutional or statutory authority to use military force inside the United States in terrorism-related situations and, if so, whether such domestic military operations would be barred by either the Fourth Amendment or the federal Posse Comitatus statute. Examples of the type of force considered for purposes of the analysis include, but are not limited to: (1) destroying civilian aircraft that are believed to have been hijacked; (2) deploying troops to control traffic in and out of a major American city; (3) seizing or attacking civilian property, such as apartment buildings, office complexes, or ships, believed to contain terrorism suspects; and, (4) using military-level eavesdropping and surveillance technology on domestic targets.

Mr. Yoo and Mr. Delahunty concluded that both Article II of the Constitution and the 9/11 use of force resolution would authorize these types of domestic military operations (even though Congress had expressly *rejected* language proposed by the Administration for the AUMF that would have authorized domestic military operations).[292] The memorandum also contains extended discussion of a hypothetical example which posits that a domestic military commander has received information, not rising to the level of probable cause, suggesting that a terrorist has hidden inside an apartment building and may possess weapons of mass destruction. According to the memorandum, not only does the Constitution permit the commander to seize the building, detain everyone found inside, and then interrogate them – all without obtaining any sort of warrant – but information gathered by military commanders in this way could used for criminal prosecution purposes as long as the primary reason for the seizure was the military fight against terrorism and not law enforcement. This memorandum was referenced in a subsequent OLC memorandum for the legal conclusion "that the Fourth Amendment had no application to domestic military operations."[293]

November 2001 Decision to Try Detainees, Including U.S. Citizens, in Military Commissions

Originally, the issue of what to do with the detainees was assigned to a task force composed of representatives of several agencies, under the direction of Ambassador Pierre-Richard Prosper, a career prosecutor who worked for Secretary of State Colin Powell. Ambassador Prosper described that initial process as follows:

> A week after September 11th, I was in the White House, meeting with the then- White House counsel, Alberto Gonzales, and David Addington... And because of my background, having been a war crimes prosecutor in Rwanda and having dealt with these issues, it was decided that I would lead an interagency group to look at this question... **I put the problem on the table. How are we going to deal with them? How can we prosecute them? What can we prosecute them for? And ultimately, where will they be detained?**[294]

The legal rationale for the use of military commissions was set forth in an OLC memorandum dated November 6, 2001, which provided that "under 10 U.S.C. § 821 and his inherent powers as Commander in Chief, the president may establish military commissions to try and punish terrorists apprehended as part of the investigation into, or the military and intelligence operations in response to, the September 11 attacks."[295] Notably, as in other contexts, the OLC opinion recognizes no limitation on the president's power to establish such commissions – Congress's prior actions or inactions in this sphere of activity were irrelevant: "Even if Congress had not sanctioned the use of military commissions to try all offenses against the laws of war, the President, exercising his authority as Commander in Chief, could order the creation of military commissions to try such offenses."[296]

Just as any limitations on the president's war-making powers in the Authorization for Use of Military Force Against Terrorists (AUMF) were dismissed, so were any limitations in section 821: "[Section] 821 simply gives sanction to the existing practice of the Executive in making use of military commissions, it does not on its face place any restriction on the use of commissions."[297] The memorandum asserted that "if § 821 were read as restricting the use of military commissions... it would infringe on the President's express constitutional powers as Commander in Chief."[298] The memorandum also asserted that U.S. citizens could be tried by military commissions: "[I]n the context of the current conflict, any actions by U.S. citizens that amount to hostile acts against the United States or its citizens... would make a person a 'belligerent' subject to trial by military commission..."[299] And finally, the memorandum asserted, since aliens enjoyed even fewer protections than U.S. citizens (especially in times of war), enemy aliens – including those lawfully admitted into the United States – seized in the United States would likewise be subject to trial by military commission.[300]

On November 13, 2001, President Bush signed an order establishing the framework for the trial of detainees by military commission.[301] According to press reports, this order was prepared by David Addington and Deputy White House Counsel Tim Flanigan, at Vice President Cheney's direction, in secret.[302] As one reporter described:

> Three days after the Ashcroft meeting, Cheney brought the order for military commissions to Bush. **No one told [White House Counsel John B.] Bellinger, [Condoleeza] Rice or [Colin] Powell, who continued to think that Prosper's working group was at the helm**.

> After leaving Bush's private dining room, the vice president took no chances on a last-minute objection. He sent the order on a swift path to execution that left no sign of his role. After Addington and Flanigan, the text passed to Berenson, the associate White House counsel. Cheney's link to the document broke there: Berenson was not told of its provenance.

> Berenson rushed the order to deputy staff secretary Stuart W. Bowen Jr., bearing instructions to prepare it for signature immediately -- without advance distribution to the president's top advisers. Bowen objected, he told colleagues later, saying he had

handled thousands of presidential documents without ever bypassing strict procedures of coordination and review. He relented, one White House official said, only after "rapid, urgent persuasion" that Bush was standing by to sign and that the order was too sensitive to delay.[303]

Both the State Department and the Justice Department had been kept out of the loop on the decision, and both were upset. Ambassador Prosper, in an interview for PBS's *Frontline*, confirmed that he and Secretary of State Colin Powell had been kept in the dark about this decision.[304] *The Washington Post* described the secrecy of the process, as well as the angry reaction by Attorney General John Ashcroft to the decision to use military commissions instead of civilian courts, a decision which effectively excluded the Justice Department from the role of trying terrorists, as follows:

> The attorney general [sic] found Cheney, not Bush, at the broad conference table in the Roosevelt Room. According to participants, Ashcroft said that he was the president's senior law enforcement officer, supervised the FBI and oversaw terrorism prosecutions nationwide. The Justice Department, he said, had to have a voice in the tribunal process. **He was enraged to discover that [John] Yoo, his subordinate, had recommended otherwise -- as part of a strategy to deny jurisdiction to U.S. courts.**
>
> Raising his voice, participants said, Ashcroft talked over Addington and brushed aside interjections from Cheney. "The thing I remember about it is how rude, there's no other word for it, the attorney general was to the vice president," said one of those in the room. Asked recently about the confrontation, Ashcroft replied curtly: "I'm just not prepared to comment on that."[305]

Because the order establishing military commissions was silent as to the procedures to be used by the commissions, its potential scope was ominous, and it drew immediate criticism. As one rights organization warned:

> Under President Bush's November 13th Military Order on military commissions, **any foreign national designated by the President as a suspected terrorist or as aiding terrorists could potentially be detained, tried, convicted and even executed without a public trial, without adequate access to counsel, without the presumption of innocence or even proof of guilt beyond reasonable doubt, and without the right to appeal**.
>
> The U.S. State Department has repeatedly criticized the use of

military tribunals to try civilians and other similar limitations on due process around the world. Indeed, its annual Country Reports on Human Rights Practices evaluate each country on the extent to which it guarantees the right to a "fair public trial" – which it defines to include many of the due process rights omitted by the President's Military Order. The Order may make future U.S. efforts to promote such standards appear hypocritical. Indeed, even if its most egregious failings are corrected in subsequent regulations, the text of the Order may become a model for governments seeking a legal cloak for political repression.[306]

Conservative *New York Times* columnist William Safire derided the military commissions as "Star Chamber tribunals" and "kangaroo courts." He noted:

> The [Uniform Code of Military Justice] demands a public trial, proof beyond reasonable doubt, an accused's voice in the selection of juries and right to choose counsel, unanimity in death sentencing and above all appellate review by civilians confirmed by the Senate. Not one of those fundamental rights can be found in Bush's military order setting up kangaroo courts for people he designates before "trial'" to be terrorists. **Bush's fiat turns back the clock on all advances in military justice, through three wars, in the past half-century.**[307]

The decision to use military commissions thus was designed to exclude both Congress and the courts from a role in determining the circumstances under which persons should be detained and remain detained.

December 2001 Decision to Hold Detainees at Guantanamo

The next decision was where to detain those captured in Afghanistan, to keep them from potential judicial oversight or other scrutiny. In December 2001, the decision was announced to hold the detainees at the military prison in Guantanamo Bay, Cuba, a place described by Secretary of Defense Rumsfeld as "the least worst place we could have selected. It has disadvantages, as you suggest. Its disadvantages, however, seem to be modest relative to the alternatives."[308] Central to the decision to use Guantanamo was John Yoo's legal conclusion that the Guantanamo detainees would not enjoy access to U.S. courts. According to Mr. Yoo, "a district court cannot properly entertain an application for a writ of *habeas corpus* by an enemy alien" who was detained there.[309] In short, Guantanamo was selected as a "law free" zone, where the detainees enjoyed no legal protections.

The Administration's Public Defense of Its Guantanamo Policies

The Administration's public defense of its Guantanamo policies has consisted largely of stressing the evil nature of the detainees and overstating their intelligence value. In January 2002, President Bush characterized the detainees as "killers" and "terrorists" and "parasite[s],"[310] and Vice President Cheney described them in similarly harsh terms:

> **These are the worst of a very bad lot. They are very dangerous. They are devoted to killing millions of Americans, innocent Americans, if they can, and they are perfectly prepared to die in the effort.**[311]

Admiral John Stufflebeam described them as "the worst of the worst and if let out on the street, they will go back to the proclivity of trying to kill Americans and others";[312] Defense Secretary Rumsfeld, as "among the most dangerous, best-trained, vicious killers on the face of the earth";[313] and General Richard Myers, as "people that would gnaw through hydraulic lines in the back of a C-17 to bring it down."[314]

Despite these sweeping descriptions, however, more than two-thirds of those detained at Guantanamo Bay have been released. In May 2006, the Department of Defense issued a list of 759 individuals who had been detained at Guantanamo.[315] Defense Department press releases indicate that approximately 19 other persons have since been brought there[316] – for a total of about 780. As of December 2008, approximately 250 remained there.[317]

What has happened to the released detainees? In 2006, the Associated Press reported that it had located 245 of the 360 men who had been freed as of that time. Of that group, "205 of the 245 were either freed without being charged or were cleared of charges related to their detention at Guantanamo. Forty either [stood] charged with crimes or continue to be detained."[318] The report continued:

> **Only a tiny fraction of transferred detainees have been put on trial**. The AP identified 14 trials, in which eight men were acquitted and six are awaiting verdicts. Two of the cases involving acquittals – one in Kuwait, one in Spain – initially resulted in convictions that were overturned on appeal.
>
> **The Afghan government has freed every one of the more than 83 Afghans sent home**. Lawmaker Sibghatullah Mujaddedi, the head of Afghanistan's reconciliation commission, said many were innocent and wound up at Guantanamo because of tribal or personal rivalries.
>
> At least 67 of 70 repatriated Pakistanis are free after spending a year in Adiala Jail. A senior Pakistani Interior Ministry official said investigators determined that most had been "sold" for

bounties to U.S. forces by Afghan warlords who invented links between the men and al-Qaida. "We consider them innocent," said the official, who declined to be named because of the sensitivity of the issue.

All 29 detainees who were repatriated to Britain, Spain, Germany, Russia, Australia, Turkey, Denmark, Bahrain and the Maldives were freed, some within hours after being sent home for "continued detention."[319]

Even as recently as June 2005, Vice President Cheney asserted: "We had some 800 people down there. We've screened them all, and we've let go those that we've deemed not to be a continuing threat. But the 520 some that are there now are serious, deadly threats to the United States. For the most part, if you let them out, they'll go back to trying to kill Americans."[320] About 270 of those 520 have since been released.

It likewise appears that the Administration may have overstated the intelligence value of the detainees to publicly justify their prolonged detention. Again, numerous reports suggested that the intelligence value was limited to a few individuals, and the lack of results from the initial interrogation of the detainees – prompting the use of harsher methods – had less to do with the methods being used than with the essential fact that the detainees had little to offer. As summarized in one report:

> Senior military officials, like Steve Rodriguez, the Head of Interrogations at Guantánamo, have questioned the intelligence value of the majority of Guantánamo prisoners. In 2004, Rodriguez maintained that "20, 30, 40, maybe even 50 [of the Guantánamo detainees] are providing critical information today." Lt. Col. Anthony Christino stated in 2004 "that there is a continuing intelligence value... for [s]omewhere a[round] a few dozen, a few score at the most" of the Guantánamo prisoners.[321]

These detention policies were implemented as intended. As noted, hundreds of individuals were captured overseas and brought to Guantanamo. The Administration sought to have them subject to the military commission system established by the Executive Branch to determine the validity of their detention and vigorously defended this policy and the denial of the detainees of access to the federal courts. Even in the domestic United States, a United States citizen (Jose Padilla) and a lawfully admitted alien (Ali Saleh Kahlal al-Marri) were arrested in the United States by civilian law enforcement authorities and then transferred to military custody at the order of the President. For years, they were held in military custody, and during substantial periods of their detentions, they were deprived of access to counsel to challenge the bases of their detentions. All the while, the Administration vigorously defended the prerogative of the president, as Commander-in-Chief, to exercise this power over individual liberty, inside the

United States, and to insist that this exercise of discretion was not subject to meaningful review by the courts.

B.   The Bush Administration's Detention Policies in the Courts

The Administration's detention policies were rooted in views as to the scope of the president's inherent, uncheckable powers as Commander in Chief. In 2002, once persons were captured in Afghanistan or in other foreign countries, or were taken into custody in the United States, the lawfulness of the Administration's detention policies – and the scope of the president's claimed powers – came under challenge in federal courts.

The cases are discussed in some detail below, for several reasons. First, they raised profound issues as to the power of the president as Commander in Chief under the Constitution, including whether actions taken under that claimed power could be checked by Congress or reviewed by the courts. Second, they also raised profound issues as to the statutory and constitutional rights, if any, to which the detainees were entitled, including whether those rights could be infringed by the president acting alone, or acting with the authorization of Congress. Third, the Administration's conduct of the litigation, including steps it took in connection with the actual circumstances of confinement of the given plaintiffs during the course of the litigation to influence the facts subject to review, reveals the intensity of the Administration's determination to have its views of presidential power accepted by the courts. Fourth, the cases are an important part of the narrative of how the detention policies evolved, as, for example, the Supreme Court's decision invalidating the president's military commission system in 2006 led to Congress's enactment of the Military Commissions Act, which itself contained terms implicating the *habeas corpus* rights of the Guantanamo detainees, thus occasioning yet further Supreme Court litigation.

Finally, the cases reveal the near unanimous rejection by the courts of the president's broad claims of Commander in Chief powers, or other inherent powers, to undertake actions without congressional authorization – a rejection that can best be understood by an appreciation of exactly what the Administration argued, the persistence and the repetition of those arguments in a variety of settings, and other actions associated with its conduct of the litigation.

The President's Power to Detain an American Citizen Captured in Afghanistan Without Judicial Review (*Hamdi*)

The first case involved U.S. citizen Yaser Esam Hamdi, who was captured in Afghanistan in 2001 and taken to Guantanamo in 2002. When it became apparent that he was an American citizen, Mr. Hamdi was transferred to the Norfolk Naval Station Brig. On May 10, 2002, Mr. Hamdi's father, as a "next friend," filed a petition for *habeas corpus* with the U.S. District Court for the Eastern District of Virginia. The issue was whether the federal courts could review the President's basis for Mr. Hamdi's detention, and if so, what would be the nature of that review.

First, in May and June 2002, the District Court ordered that Mr. Hamdi be permitted access to his attorney. The Government appealed these rulings to the Fourth Circuit Court of Appeals. In addition, the Government advanced a sweeping assertion of presidential power, arguing the petition should be dismissed in its entirety and that the federal court "may not review at all [the President's] designation of an American citizen as an enemy combatant – that [the President's] determinations on this score are the first and final word."[322]

In rejecting the government's contentions, the Court of Appeals in July 2002 concisely described the implications of dismissing the case on the grounds asserted by the Government:

> In dismissing, we ourselves would be summarily embracing a sweeping proposition – namely **that, with no meaningful judicial review, any American citizen alleged to be an enemy combatant could be detained indefinitely without charges or counsel on the government's say-so.**[323]

On remand to the district court, the Government submitted an affidavit dated July 24, 2002, to support the Administration's position that Mr. Hamdi was an enemy combatant. The affidavit represented that Mr. Hamdi had been a Taliban fighter who had surrendered to the Northern Alliance. The affidavit did not claim that Mr. Hamdi had fought against the United States, or that he was affiliated with al Qaeda.[324] In an opinion dated August 16, 2002, the district court held that due process required a more detailed and specific showing than was set forth in the affidavit.[325]

The Government immediately appealed to the Fourth Circuit. In January 2003, the Fourth Circuit reversed, holding that Mr. Hamdi's concession that he was seized in the battlefield was sufficient to justify his being held as an enemy combatant, and that the trial court went too far in seeking more information as to the facts justifying Mr. Hamdi's detention.[326] After the Fourth Circuit denied rehearing by the full panel in July of 2003,[327] the case was taken to the Supreme Court.

From the time Mr. Hamdi was captured until the Supreme Court decided to hear his case, Mr. Hamdi – a U.S. citizen incarcerated by the United States – was not permitted access to an attorney. The Supreme Court agreed to hear the case on January 3, 2004. On February 3, 2004, more than two years after this U.S. citizen was detained, the Government for the first time permitted Mr. Hamdi to consult with an attorney.[328]

Again, in front of the Supreme Court, the Government argued that the decision to label Mr. Hamdi an enemy combatant was solely for the president to make, and that the bases for that decision were not subject to judicial review.

In an opinion issued June 28, 2004, Justice Sandra Day O'Connor, writing for a four-Justice plurality, avoided deciding the question whether the president, under the

Constitution and solely relying on his Article II Commander- in-Chief powers, had the power to designate a U.S. citizen an enemy combatant and thereby order his detention. Justice O'Connor did conclude, however, that Congress, by way of the AUMF, had granted the president that power.[329] Significant to Justice O'Connor's conclusion was that Mr. Hamdi was seized in the shooting battlefield. To this end, Justice O'Connor stressed that "[b]ecause detention to prevent a combatant's return to the battlefield is a fundamental incident of waging war, in permitting the use of 'necessary and appropriate force,' Congress has clearly and unmistakably authorized detention in the narrow circumstances considered here."[330]

In interpreting the scope of the AUMF, Justice O'Connor acknowledged that this "war" was unlike other wars, and that the AUMF could not be read as sanctioning the "indefinite" detention of Mr. Hamdi for purposes of interrogation:

> Hamdi contends that the AUMF does not authorize indefinite or perpetual detention. **Certainly, we agree that indefinite detention for the purpose of interrogation is not authorized.** Further, we understand Congress' grant of authority for the use of "necessary and appropriate force" to include the authority to detain for the duration of the relevant conflict, and our understanding is based on longstanding law-of-war principles.[331]

Even though the president had the power granted by Congress to seize an American as an enemy combatant, as a procedural matter, the Court held, the factual grounds for the detention were subject to judicial review.[332] The plurality squarely concluded that "due process demands that a citizen held in the United States as an enemy combatant be given a meaningful opportunity to contest the factual basis for that detention before a neutral decisionmaker,"[333] and that Mr. Hamdi – a citizen – possessed "core rights to challenge meaningfully the Government's case and to be heard by an impartial adjudicator."[334]

The four-Justice plurality explicitly warned of the threat to liberty posed by a broad interpretation of the president's Commander in Chief powers, and stressed the Constitutional role of Congress and the courts in protecting individual liberties: that "the state of war is not a blank check for the President when it comes to the rights of the Nation's citizens"; that "unless Congress acts to suspend it, the Great Writ of *habeas corpus* allows the Judicial Branch to play a necessary role in maintaining this delicate balance of governance, serving as an important judicial check on the Executive's discretion in the realm of detentions"; and that "it would turn our system of checks and balances on its head to suggest that a citizen could not make his way to court with a challenge to the factual basis for his detention by his Government, simply because the Executive opposes making available such a challenge."[335]

The unlikely pair of Justices Antonin Scalia and John Paul Stevens dissented altogether, finding that the President had acted outside the limits of his Constitutional powers. For Mr. Hamdi's detention in this manner to be lawful, Congress would have to have first suspended the writ of *habeas corpus* – which it certainly had not done.[336] As Justice Scalia wrote in dissent:

> If the situation demands it, the Executive can ask Congress to
> authorize suspension of the writ – which can be made subject to
> whatever conditions Congress deems appropriate, including even
> the procedural novelties invented by the plurality today. To be
> sure, suspension is limited by the Constitution to cases of rebellion
> or invasion. But whether the attacks of September 11, 2001,
> constitute an "invasion," and whether those attacks still justify
> suspension several years later, are questions for Congress rather
> than this Court [citations omitted]. **If civil rights are to be
> curtailed during wartime, it must be done openly and
> democratically, as the Constitution requires, rather than by
> silent erosion through an opinion of this Court.**[337]

Another two Justices (Souter and Ginsburg) believed that Congress had not provided the president the authority to designate detainees enemy combatants, but concurred in the holding that further judicial review of the bases of Mr. Hamdi's detention was required.[338]

So, even though not all the Constitutional issues were resolved by this decision, six of the Justices agreed that due process required that Mr. Hamdi, a U.S. citizen, have an opportunity to challenge the factual bases underlying his detention – notwithstanding the Administration's claims that either under the Constitution or under the AUMF, the president on his unreviewable word alone could order his detention as an enemy combatant.

As a result of the Supreme Court's decision, Mr. Hamdi, after spending close to three years in custody, a great portion of it in solitary confinement without access to an attorney, would finally obtain the hearing he had been seeking, where he could contest the legal basis for his detention, albeit under evidentiary standards broadly favorable to the Government. And for its part, the Executive Branch, which had announced to the world that only the "worst of the worst" had been seized and brought to Guantanamo, would have the opportunity (and obligation) to prove its case, demonstrating the dangerousness of at least one Guantanamo detainee and thereby helping vindicate the President's military detention policy.

But this did not happen; and what happened instead is telling: By way of an agreement between Mr. Hamdi and the United States dated September 17, 2004 – less than 90 days after the Supreme Court ruled – the United States agreed to send Mr. Hamdi back to Saudi Arabia.[339] The terms of the agreement did not require that Mr. Hamdi be detained in Saudi Arabia – to the contrary, the United States specifically agreed "to make no request that Hamdi be detained by the Kingdom of Saudi Arabia based on information as to Hamdi's conduct known to the United States."[340] In exchange for the various promises of the United States, including that of permitting his return to Saudi Arabia,[341] Mr. Hamdi agreed to renounce terrorism, not to travel to specific locations, including Pakistan and Afghanistan, to renounce his U.S. citizenship, and to dismiss the *habeas* petition.[342]

The President's Power to Establish Military Commissions to Determine Validity of Detention (*Hamdan*)

In the case of Salim Hamdan, the Supreme Court again recognized an essential role for Congress in establishing certain military policies, rejecting the President's claims of uncheckable Commander-in-Chief powers. Once again, the issue was the extent of presidential power – this time to implement the "military commission" procedures – where such procedures were not authorized by Congress, and where Congress had provided alternative procedures.[343]

Salim Hamdan, Osama bin Laden's driver, was captured by American forces in Afghanistan in 2001, and was transferred to Guantanamo in 2002. In July of 2003, the President designated Mr. Hamdan for trial by a military commission.[344] Counsel was appointed in December 2003 and, in April of 2004, Mr. Hamdan filed a *habeas corpus* petition, which was transferred to the U.S. District Court for the District of Columbia. Mr. Hamdan challenged the President's order establishing the military commission as a violation of separation of powers – arguing that Congress, and not the President, had the power to prescribe the rules of war.[345] The Administration's position was described by the district court as follows: "The major premise of the Government's argument that the President has untrammeled power to establish military tribunals is that his authority emanates from Article II of the Constitution and is inherent in his role as commander-in-chief."[346] The district court rejected this argument, citing Supreme Court precedent establishing that "the authority to appoint military commissions is found, not in the inherent power of the presidency, but in the Articles of War (a predecessor of the Uniform Code of Military Justice) by which *Congress* provided rules for the government of the army."[347]

The trial court found that the military commissions prescribed for the Guantanamo detainees were defective on due process grounds, as the accused could be excluded from his trial under rules that could prevent him from being informed of the evidence against him. The district court held that "in this critical respect[,] the rules of the Military Commission are fatally 'contrary to or inconsistent with' the statutory requirements for courts-martial convened under the Uniform Code of Military Justice, and thus unlawful."[348]

On appeal, the Government again argued that the President, as Commander in Chief, possessed "inherent authority to establish military commissions," as to which Congress had no proper role: "That Congress also has powers that may be relevant to the prosecution of terrorists, such as the power to establish inferior Article III courts and the power to define and punish offenses against the law of nations... in no way undermines the President's authority, as Commander in Chief, to exercise the traditional functions of a military commander by using military commissions to punish enemies who violate the laws of war."[349] The Government urged the court of appeals to abstain from judicial review;[350] but it reversed the lower court on the issue of the legal validity of the military commissions, concluding they were valid – not because of inherent presidential powers under Article II, but because *Congress*, by way of the AUMF and other laws, had authorized the president to establish them.[351]

On petition to the Supreme Court, the Government repeated its contentions:

> The President's war power under Article II, Section 2, of the
> Constitution includes the inherent authority to create military
> commissions even in the absence of any statutory authorization,
> because that authority is a necessary and longstanding component
> of his war powers.[352]

In a 5-3 June 2006 decision, the Supreme Court squarely rejected the Government's contentions, holding that the power to create alternate military tribunals was entrusted by the Constitution to Congress:

> The Constitution makes the President the "Commander in Chief"
> of the Armed Forces, Art. II, § 2, cl. 1, but vests in Congress the
> powers to "declare War... and make Rules concerning Captures on
> Land and Water," Art. I, § 8, cl. 11, to "raise and support Armies,"
> id., cl. 12, to "define and punish... Offences against the Law of
> Nations," id., cl. 10, and "To make Rules for the Government and
> Regulation of the land and naval Forces," id., cl. 14. The interplay
> between these powers was described by Chief Justice Chase in the
> seminal case of *Ex parte Milligan*:

> "The power to make the necessary laws is in Congress; the power
> to execute in the President. Both powers imply many subordinate
> and auxiliary powers. Each includes all authorities essential to its
> due exercise. But neither can the President, in war more than in
> peace, intrude upon the proper authority of Congress, nor Congress
> upon the proper authority of the President... Congress cannot
> direct the conduct of campaigns, **nor can the President, or any
> commander under him, without the sanction of Congress,
> institute tribunals for the trial and punishment of offences**,
> either of soldiers or civilians, unless in cases of a controlling
> necessity, which justifies what it compels, or at least insures acts of
> indemnity from the justice of the legislature."[353]

Thus, in *Hamdan*, the Supreme Court rejected the assertions of uncheckable presidential power that were set forth in Mr. Yoo's September 25, 2001, War Powers Memorandum and November 6, 2001, Military Commissions Memorandum, including, implicitly, the broader assertion in those memoranda that the president's powers in the Constitution could be read far more expansively than Congress's. The Court's opinion marked a significant repudiation of the Bush-Cheney conception of expansive, uncheckable war powers for the president.

In the wake of *Hamdan*, Congress enacted the Military Commissions Act of 2006, establishing a military commission system for trying the Guantanamo detainees.[354] (That Act is described in the Interrogation Section of this Report.) Mr. Hamdan was ultimately tried by this military commission; in the summer of 2008, he was convicted of providing material support for terrorism, but acquitted of more serious charges.[355] Despite a request by the prosecutors for a sentence of at least 30 years, the military panel sentenced Mr. Hamdan to 66 months.[356] Mr. Hamdan received credit for the 61 months he had been held prior to trial. He was released and returned to Yemen in late November 2008 to serve the remaining few months of his sentence.[357]

The President's Power to Order Detention of Persons Without Access to Federal Courts – *Rasul* and *Boumediene*

In *Rasul v. Bush*,[358] the Supreme Court decided a narrow but significant legal issue of statutory interpretation relating to the scope of federal court jurisdiction over detainees held in Guantanamo. As framed by the Court, the issue was "whether the *habeas* statute confers a right to judicial review of the legality of executive detention of aliens in a territory over which the United States exercises plenary and exclusive jurisdiction, but not 'ultimate sovereignty.'"[359] Mr. Rasul argued that Guantanamo Bay was part of the United States for purposes of the *habeas* statute; the Bush Administration argued to the contrary. The Court, noting that "[b]y the express terms of its agreements with Cuba, the United States exercises 'complete jurisdiction and control' over the Guantanamo Bay Naval Base, and may continue to exercise such control permanently if it so chooses,"[360] concluded that "[the *habeas* statute] confers on the District Court jurisdiction to hear [Mr. Rasul's and other] *habeas corpus* challenges to the legality of their detention at the Guantanamo Bay Naval Base."[361] The Court did not address what it meant by the "legality of their detention," nor did it prescribe the nature of the factual review a district court should undertake to determine whether the detention was lawful. *Rasul*, unlike *Hamdi* and *Hamdan*, did not explicitly involve a clash as to the limits of presidential power vis-à-vis the power of Congress – it involved the reach of federal judicial power.

Subsequently, in the *Boumediene* case, the Supreme Court faced a series of issues relating to the rights of the Guantanamo detainees to seek *habeas* relief in the U.S. courts.[362] The threshold issue for the Court was whether the Military Commissions Act (MCA) – enacted in the aftermath of *Hamdan* – was intended to deprive the courts of their jurisdiction to hear *habeas* claims filed by the Guantanamo detainees, and if so, whether that deprivation was constitutional.[363]

The Court held that the MCA did, in fact, purport to "den[y] the federal courts jurisdiction to hear *habeas corpus* actions pending at the time of its enactment."[364] but that the Constitution provided the Guantanamo detainees a right to have their *habeas* petitions heard, and that the MCA thus worked an unconstitutional "suspension" of that right.[365] The procedures previously provided in the Detainee Treatment Act (DTA) for reviewing the validity of an individual's detention were not an adequate substitute for *habeas* review, the Court stated. In particular, the DTA procedures did not permit the federal courts to engage in adequate fact-finding, or to release prisoners:

> Although we do not hold that an adequate substitute must duplicate
> § 2241 in all respects, it suffices that the Government has not
> established that the detainees' access to the statutory review
> provisions at issue is an adequate substitute for the writ of *habeas
> corpus*. [The MCA] thus effects an unconstitutional suspension of
> the writ.[366]

The Court stressed that the *habeas* writ was an essential check on governmental power –
in this case, presidential power: "The Framers' inherent distrust of governmental power was the
driving force behind the constitutional plan that allocated powers among three independent
branches. This design serves not only to make Government accountable but also to secure
individual liberty."[367]

Thus, the Court concluded that the right to seek a *habeas* writ was available to the
Guantanamo detainees, notwithstanding their status as non-citizens, and, picking up on Justice
O'Connor's concerns in *Hamdi* about indefinite detention, specifically alluded to the fact that the
detainees had now spent years in custody, with no end in sight:

> It is true that before today the Court has never held that noncitizens
> detained by our Government in territory over which another
> country maintains de jure sovereignty have any rights under our
> Constitution. But the cases before us lack any precise historical
> parallel. **They involve individuals detained by executive order
> for the duration of a conflict that, if measured from September
> 11, 2001, to the present, is already among the longest wars in
> American history**. *See* Oxford Companion to American Military
> History 849 (1999). The detainees, moreover, are held in a
> territory that, while technically not part of the United States, is
> under the complete and total control of our Government. Under
> these circumstances the lack of a precedent on point is no barrier to
> our holding.[368]

Though the Court did not address the legal standards that governed the detention, or the
nature of the fact-finding proceeding to which the detainees were entitled, the Court did make
clear that the lower federal courts were to engage in a substantive review of the evidence, that
exculpatory material must be considered, and that an essential component of the power of the
reviewing court was the power to order release of the detainee if the evidence did not support the
detainee's continued detention.

The reaction of the Bush Administration was swift. Attorney General Mukasey made a
speech calling upon Congress"to resolve the difficult questions left open by the Supreme Court,"

a request that many critics felt would have the effect of only further delaying court review of the Guantanamo cases.[369] Mr. Mukasey desired legislation based on six principles, a number of which would have greatly limited the ability to address Guantanamo cases or to fashion an appropriate remedy where detention was found to have been improper: 1) that the federal courts "may not order the government to bring enemy combatants into the United States; 2) that national security information be protected; 3) that the Military Commission trials proceed, with the *habeas* petitions permitted only after the commission trials; 4) that "the legislation should acknowledge again and explicitly that this Nation remains engaged in an armed conflict with al Qaeda, the Taliban, and associated organizations, who have already proclaimed themselves at war with us and who are dedicated to the slaughter of Americans, soldiers and civilians alike... [C]ongress should reaffirm that for the duration of the conflict the United States may detain as enemy combatants those who have engaged in hostilities or purposefully supported al Qaeda, the Taliban, and associated organizations";[370] 5) that Congress establish sensible procedures for *habeas* challenges going forward, such as providing that one court have exclusive jurisdiction over those cases; and 6) that "Congress should provide a single means to challenge detention."

The President's Power to Order the Military Detention of an American Citizen Seized by Civilian Authorities in the United States (*Padilla*)

Perhaps the most troubling of all the detention cases is that involving U.S. citizen Jose Padilla. On May 8, 2002, Mr. Padilla was arrested in Chicago on a material witness warrant issued out of the Southern District of New York. In June 2002, the Government withdrew the subpoena on which the arrest warrant had been based, and the President issued an order directing that the Secretary of Defense take custody of Mr. Padilla as an enemy combatant. Pursuant to the November 2001 military commission order then in place, this meant that Mr. Padilla would be held in military custody and, presumably, tried by a military commission.[371] Mr. Padilla was then moved to military custody and held at the Navy Brig in South Carolina.[372]

The *Padilla* litigation was taking place at the same time as the *Hamdi* litigation, with perhaps the key difference being the fact that Mr. Padilla was arrested by civilian law enforcement authorities inside the United States, whereas Mr. Hamdi, also a U.S. citizen, was taken into custody in Afghanistan – a detention upheld by the Court.

> *1.   June-December 2002 – initial litigation in Southern District of New York; Chief Judge Mukasey orders Government to permit Mr. Padilla access to counsel.*

After Mr. Padilla was transferred to South Carolina, his attorney filed a writ of *habeas corpus* with the Southern District of New York, and the case was assigned to then-Chief Judge Michael Mukasey. Mr. Padilla, like Mr. Hamdi, was denied access to counsel in connection with this *habeas* claim. The critical issues raised by the initial litigation were the scope of the president's power to designate Mr. Padilla– like Mr. Hamdi, a U.S. citizen – an enemy combatant and transfer him to military custody, the nature of judicial review (if any) of that decision, and whether the conditions of confinement, including the denial of access to counsel, were permissible. There were also venue issues as to whether the petition was properly brought in the Southern District of New York, where Mr. Padilla was seized, as opposed to South Carolina, where he was being held.

In its initial brief before Chief Judge Mukasey, the Government argued that the president had essentially unreviewable "core Commander in Chief" powers to determine that Mr. Padilla was an enemy and place him in military custody – that "[t]he capture and detention of enemy combatants during wartime falls within the president's core constitutional powers as Commander in Chief, which, in the present conflict, are exercised with the specific support of Congress"[373] – and that the U.S. military may constitutionally "seize and detain enemy combatants or other enemy belligerents for the duration of an armed conflict."[374] It was not "significant that an enemy combatant is captured within United States territory in civilian dress rather than in uniform or on a foreign battlefield."[375] Mr. Padilla's status as an American citizen "does not affect the authority of the military to detain [him]."[376]

On December 4, 2002, Chief Judge Mukasey held that the President did have the power to order Mr. Padilla's detention: "[T]he President is authorized under the Constitution and by law to direct the military to detain enemy combatants in the circumstances present here, such that Mr. Padilla's detention is not per se unlawful."[377] As to the scope of judicial review, Chief Judge Mukasey held that "to resolve the issue of whether Mr. Padilla was lawfully detained on the facts present here, the court will examine only whether the President had some evidence to support his finding that Mr. Padilla was an enemy combatant, and whether that evidence has been mooted by events subsequent to his detention."[378] Chief Judge Mukasey further ruled that Mr. Padilla had a right to counsel in connection with such a proceeding.[379]

2.   *December 2002 to March 2003 – Government refuses to provide counsel*

The Government refused to comply with the part of Chief Judge Mukasey's order requiring that Mr. Padilla have access to an attorney, and on January 9, 2003 asked him to amend that part of the order.[380] The Government argued it was crucial in the interrogation process for Mr. Padilla to believe circumstances were hopeless and that permitting Mr. Padilla to consult with an attorney would interfere with the interrogation and thus endanger national security.[381] The Government submitted an affidavit from the Defense Intelligence Agency (DIA) (the "Jacoby Declaration") that represented:

> Permitting Padilla any access to counsel may substantially harm our national security interests. As with most detainees, Padilla is unlikely to cooperate if he believes that an attorney will intercede in his detention. DIA's assessment is that Padilla is even more inclined to resist interrogation than most detainees. DIA is aware that Padilla has had extensive experience in the United States criminal justice system and had access to counsel when he was being held as a material witness. These experiences have likely heightened his expectations that counsel will assist him in the interrogation process. Only after such time as Padilla has

perceived that help is not on the way can the United States reasonably expect to obtain all possible intelligence information from Padilla.[382]

Chief Judge Mukasey held a hearing in which he castigated the Government's counsel Paul Clement (who would later serve as Solicitor General under Mukasey at the Department of Justice) for the Government's refusal to grant Mr. Padilla access to counsel – an act which appeared on its face to be contumacious. Though the Government had filed a motion to amend the terms of his order, Chief Judge Mukasey perceived that the Government was seeking simply to reargue its position that Mr. Padilla should not have counsel. And as Mukasey made clear, if the Government's motion to amend the order was in substance a "motion to reargue," the Government had not complied with certain procedural requirements. At the argument on the Government's motion, the following interchange occurred:

> The Court: Good morning. This conference, as it was initially conceived, was supposed to be for the purpose of discussing what steps had been taken voluntarily by the parties to arrange for counsel to see Mr. Padilla. It appears, or I gather from the papers that have been submitted, that the government has no intention of allowing that to happen, at least not voluntarily.
>
> * * * * * * *
>
> The Court: You decided this really wasn't a reargument motion so you didn't have to mention the law at all on the subject, right? That's what your telling me?
>
> Mr. Clement: Well –
>
> The Court: Is that what you're telling me?
>
> Mr. Clement: I certainly apologize that –
>
> The Court: I'm not looking for an apology; I'm looking for an explanation. Is that what you're telling me?
>
> Mr. Clement: What I'm telling you is that because the motion was not directed at a traditional reconsideration but was directed at the terms –
>
> The Court: Then why did you apologize for leaving facts out?[383]

After some additional give and take, with Chief Judge Mukasey challenging the Government's conduct and its legal position, Mr. Clement turned the discussion toward the substantive issue of permitting Mr. Padilla access to an attorney:

Mr. Clement: ... And I think in fairness, as we read your Honor's opinion, we felt that we had not done our job in apprising you of the nature of our concerns [relating to right to counsel]. You seemed to read our concern about interrupting interrogation in the sense that we were somehow suggesting that the attorney would be there for every interrogation on an ongoing basis and that was our concern, and the concern that we wanted your Honor to be aware of was the concern and the potential for interference –

The Court: Okay. Are there any other facts that you have that you haven't apprised me of?

Mr. Clement: No...

* * * * * * *

The Court: I want you to be clear first about the things that I'm asking you about. Would you please be clear about whether you have any additional facts, either relating to Mr. Padilla specifically or relating to people in Mr. Padilla's category, that you think I ought to take into account before deciding the motion?

Mr. Clement: The only thing I would say, your Honor, what I was about to say, is that as the Jacoby declaration says on its first page --

The Court: I've seen the declaration. Do you have anything else?

Mr. Clement: What the Jacoby declaration says is that it's not based on ongoing interrogations with Padilla because we've been sensitive to the concerns.

The Court: What the answer to my question, do you have additional facts or not?

Mr. Clement: If the Court would like to order us to provide --

The Court: I'm not ordering anything. You're the lawyer. What I want to know is whether if I decide this motion now I'm going to get another submission that says, judge, we've got some additional fact or additional facts to the additional facts. Do you understand the question?

Mr. Clement: I understand the question.

The Court: What's the answer?

Mr. Clement: The answer to that would be no.

<u>The Court:</u>   Thank you. You may take your seat...[384]

In an order dated March 11, 2003, Judge Mukasey declined to reverse his initial order that Mr. Padilla be permitted to consult with counsel.[385]

3.   *March-December 2003 – Appeal to Second Circuit*

The case was appealed to the Second Circuit.[386] In an opinion dated December 18, 2003 – about 21 months after Mr. Padilla's detention – the Second Circuit concluded that the power to define circumstances justifying seizure and detention of American citizens seized in this country was squarely allocated by the Constitution to Congress – not the president – and thus rejected the President's claims that his Commander-in-Chief powers permitted him to detain Mr. Padilla:

> **[C]ongress, not the Executive, should control utilization of the war power as an instrument of domestic policy**... Thus, we do not concern ourselves with the Executive's inherent wartime power, generally, to detain enemy combatants on the battlefield. Rather, we are called on to decide whether the Constitution gives the President the power to detain an American citizen seized in this country until the war with al Qaeda ends.[387]

The Second Circuit arrived at this conclusion from its reading of the powers granted Congress and those granted the President by the Constitution:

> The level of specificity with which the Framers allocated these domestic powers to Congress and the lack of any even near-equivalent grant of authority in Article II's catalogue of executive powers compels us to decline to read any such power into the Commander-in-Chief Clause. **In sum, while Congress – otherwise acting consistently with the Constitution – may have the power to authorize the detention of United States citizens under the circumstances of Padilla's case, the President, acting alone, does not.**[388]

This holding was the complete opposite of Mr. Yoo's assertion that the President's enumerated powers were a limitation on congressional power.

The Second Circuit ordered the Secretary of Defense:

> to release Padilla from military custody within 30 days. The government can transfer Padilla to appropriate civilian authorities who can bring criminal charges against him. Also, if appropriate, Padilla can be held as a material witness in connection with grand

jury proceedings. In any case, Padilla will be entitled to the constitutional protections extended to other citizens.[389]

4.   *December 2003 to June 2004 – appeal to Supreme Court; Government permits Mr. Padilla access to counsel*

The Government sought Supreme Court review and, as it had in the courts below, defended its decision to hold Mr. Padilla as an enemy combatant as a proper exercise of the President's Commander-in-Chief powers, supported by the authority granted to him by Congress under the AUMF. As argued in the Government's March 2004 brief to the Supreme Court:

> The President, explicitly invoking Congress's [AUMF], as well as his authority as Commander in Chief, made a determination that Jose Padilla "is, and at the time he entered the United States in May 2002, was, an enemy combatant," that Padilla is "closely associated with al Qaeda" and has engaged in "hostile and war-like acts," and that "it is in the interest of the United States that" he be detained "as an enemy combatant." ....The President's determination represents a core exercise of the authority both conferred by Congress and granted him by Article II, and it makes clear that Padilla... squarely fits this Court's definition of an enemy combatant subject to military seizure and detention. [390]

On the same day that it filed its brief in the Supreme Court, the Government permitted Mr. Padilla– 18 months after his seizure – to consult with an attorney,[391] and by so doing removed this issue from Supreme Court review.

On June 28, 2004, in a 5-4 decision, the Supreme Court reversed the Second Circuit on venue, holding that the litigation should have been brought where Mr. Padilla was in custody – that is, where his "custodian" was located – namely, South Carolina and not New York.[392] This sent the case to the federal courts in the Fourth Circuit.

5.   *July 2004 to February 2005 – litigation resumes before the district court in South Carolina*

Mr. Padilla had to start over again in the Fourth Circuit. In February 2005 – now over two-and-a-half years after his seizure – the District Court in South Carolina, for largely the same reasons that were set forth by the Second Circuit, ruled that Mr. Padilla's detention was illegal. The court held that the President did not have the inherent power to order the detention, and that Congress had not authorized it in the AUMF.

6.   *February-September 2005 – Appeal to Fourth Circuit; Clement announces that the United States is a "battlefield"*

94

The case was then appealed to the Fourth Circuit, where both sides repeated their earlier arguments. At oral argument July 19, 2005, Mr. Clement, still counsel for the Government, and recently confirmed as Solicitor General, argued that Mr. Padilla's seizure was legally equivalent to Mr. Hamdi's, and thus that Mr. Padilla's detention was authorized under the AUMF, as was Mr. Hamdi's. The only way the two seizures could be equivalent, however, was if Chicago and New York (where citizen Padilla was seized, transferred, and then turned over to the military) were considered the legal equivalent of the "battlefield" of Afghanistan where Mr. Hamdi had been seized.

If accepted by the court, such an equivalency would mean that the president had the power to designate any person in the United States – even one who had never taken up arms – as an "enemy combatant," and order him or her thrown into the Navy brig without any meaningful judicial review. It also had broader implications for other military powers the president might claim for use in the United States – such as the power to call out troops to search buildings, or use military personnel to spy on U.S. citizens.

Mr. Clement, apparently aware of the legal and political ramifications of claiming the United States was a battlefield, initially seemed to attempt to avoid making this claim, even though it was the position that the Administration had secretly developed in 2001 and had acted on the basis of ever since. Rather, Mr. Clement noted that Mr. Padilla had come to Chicago from Afghanistan, and argued that he was fittingly designated as an "enemy combatant" for his activities there. In a colloquy with the Fourth Circuit judges, Clement initially attempted to avoid being pinned down on the "battlefield" point, instead trying to broaden the ruling of *Hamdi* to non-battlefield seizures. Judge Michael asked Mr. Clement to cite legal authority for such a seizure.

Judge Luttig: If the facts of [*Hamdi*] are that it involves a battlefield detention, is it not your understanding that the holding of the case is limited to that set of facts, even if the reasoning could be read broader? The holding is limited to that set of facts?

Mr. Clement: Again, that is not how I would read it your honor...

* * * * * * *

J. Michael: **What in the Laws of War allows you to undertake a non-battlefield capture and hold someone for the duration**? I don't think you cite to anything, in the Laws of War.

Mr. Clement: Your honor, I think... if one wants to talk about the Laws of War I think there are two principles that I would start with. One is the Laws of War that *Hamdi* recognized, it doesn't focus solely on capture on the battlefield, it's the activities on the battlefield that makes somebody an

95

enemy combatant. If they're picked up in town or the battle or something, that doesn't limit the authority...

J. Michael: Well that may make some sense but what, you've got people in the Defense Department that ought to be studying the Laws of War all the time, you've got the Laws of Warfare, **I don't see that you've cited us to anything out of the Laws of War that would authorize a non-battlefield capture and detention.** If you can cite us chapter and verse I think that would be helpful.

Eventually, under forceful questioning by Judge Luttig, Clement made the assertion, with increasing conviction, that the United States was, in fact, a "battlefield" for purposes of assessing the reach of the president's Commander-in-Chief powers

Judge Luttig: **In effect, Mr. Clement, doesn't the United States have to be arguing that, at least in the War on Terror, the battlefield includes the United States?**

Mr. Clement: **Your honor, I think that is certainly true...**

Judge Luttig: **Is that the position of the United States?**

Mr. Clement: **That is the position of the United States.**

Judge Luttig: That the United States of America is a battleground in the War on Terror[?]

Mr. Clement: That is our position and I don't see how it could be otherwise if one understands the context.

Judge Luttig: You keep referring, in fairness, in response to our questions, that we have nonbattlefield detention here. So the import of the question is this: do we not in effect have a battlefield detention?

Mr. Clement: I think that you can characterize it in that way and I think that's accurate, and again, in fairness to the questions that were asked of me, I think that there is language in the *Hamdi* plurality that is talking about foreign battlefield and so, I mean...

Judge Luttig: Well? That drives you right back into my threshold question whether *Hamdi* as a precedent would control. And if, as your point there suggests, it was limited to foreign battlefields, then *a fortiori* it would not govern here unless you are prepared to say that this is a battlefield.

<u>Mr. Clement:</u>	Well, I am prepared to say that this is a battlefield, I am not prepared to say it is a foreign battlefield….

* * * * * * *

<u>Judge Luttig:</u>	Why would you go surveying the universe of possible battlefields to the seeming exclusion of the United States? Is it just a reluctance to represent on behalf of the United States that the President believes that this is a battlefield on the War on Terror?
<u>Mr. Clement:</u>	No its not your honor, it's a simple…
<u>Judge Luttig:</u>	Well then why wouldn't you say that's it? And then you're covered by *Hamdi*, you're covered by the Laws of War, relied upon in *Hamdi*, and you don't have to resort to this more attenuated argument that, "Well, take for instance the battlefield on terrorism moves to London, our concern is that Padilla may fly to London." Well that's okay, but it's hardly persuasive.
<u>Mr. Clement:</u>	Well, your honor with all respect, I think, I color my reluctance to the advocate's unwillingness to rest on a single argument when he has two. And I think that the fact…
<u>Judge Luttig:</u>	The question is, the advocate usually rests on his best argument and not his second best if he only has one.
<u>Mr. Clement:</u>	Well I haven't had any resistance to resting on both your honor[.]

* * * * * * *

<u>Judge Luttig:</u>	Don't you see all of these niceties don't get you very far unless you are prepared to boldly say that the United States of America is a battlefield in the War on Terror? And don't you see that if you are prepared to say that and you can successfully defend that position, it cuts a wide swath through everything that you have been challenged on here today?
<u>Mr. Clement:</u>	**Your honor, I can say that, I can say it boldly**[.][393]

On September 9, 2005, the Fourth Circuit ruled for the Government and against Mr. Padilla, holding that pursuant to the AUMF, the President had the power to order Mr. Padilla detained in military custody, and specifically referencing the need for interrogation – intelligence gathering – as a basis for detention.[394] The court rejected Mr. Padilla's contention that the Government was required either to charge him in the criminal courts or let him go, and ultimately concluded that these aspects of Mr. Padilla's detention were authorized by Congress under the

AUMF:

> Equally important, in many instances criminal prosecution would impede the Executive in its efforts to gather intelligence from the detainee and to restrict the detainee's communication with confederates so as to ensure that the detainee does not pose a continuing threat to national security even as he is confined – impediments that would render military detention not only an appropriate, but also the necessary, course of action to be taken in the interest of national security.

> The district court acknowledged the need to defer to the President's determination that Padilla's detention is necessary and appropriate in the interest of national security... However, we believe that the district court ultimately accorded insufficient deference to that determination, effectively imposing upon the President the equivalent of a least-restrictive-means test. To subject to such exacting scrutiny the President's determination that criminal prosecution would not adequately protect the Nation's security at a very minimum fails to accord the President the deference that is his when he acts pursuant to a broad delegation of authority from Congress, such as the AUMF.[395]

The Fourth Circuit, in upholding Mr. Padilla's detention, relied on the AUMF, and did not consider whether the President could order the detention based on Article II powers.

7. *September-December 2005 – Government seeks to transfer Mr. Padilla to Florida to moot Supreme Court review*

Within days of the Fourth Circuit's ruling in favor of the United States – and while the parties were awaiting the Supreme Court's decision whether to accept the case for review – the Government requested approval for Mr. Padilla to be transferred from military custody to a civilian jail, to face federal criminal prosecution – evidently intending to moot Supreme Court review of the Fourth Circuit's decision upholding his military confinement.

That the Government could, after holding Mr. Padilla in military custody for three and half years, abruptly find that the need to do so had come to an end, so soon after it had obtained a favorable ruling from the Fourth Circuit, and perhaps just days prior to a decision from the Supreme Court as to further review, stunned the Fourth Circuit and strained its credulity, as evidenced in its December 21, 2005 order denying Mr. Padilla's transfer:

> Because of their evident gravity, we must believe that the consequences of the actions that the government has taken in this

98

important case over the past several weeks, not only for the public perception of the war on terror but also for the government's credibility before the courts in litigation ancillary to that war, have been carefully considered. But at the same time that we must believe this, we cannot help but believe that those consequences have been underestimated.

For, as the government surely must understand, although the various facts it has asserted are not necessarily inconsistent or without basis, its actions have left not only the impression that Padilla may have been held for these years, even if justifiably, by mistake – an impression we would have thought the government could ill afford to leave extant. **They have left the impression that the government may even have come to the belief that the principle in reliance upon which it has detained Padilla for this time, that the President possesses the authority to detain enemy combatants who enter into this country for the purpose of attacking America and its citizens from within, can, in the end, yield to expediency with little or no cost to its conduct of the war against terror – an impression we would have thought the government likewise could ill afford to leave extant. And these impressions have been left, we fear, at what may ultimately prove to be substantial cost to the government's credibility before the courts, to whom it will one day need to argue again in support of a principle of assertedly like importance and necessity to the one that it seems to abandon today.** While there could be an objective that could command such a price as all of this, it is difficult to imagine what that objective would be.[396]

The Supreme Court approved Mr. Padilla's transfer,[397] and ultimately declined to review the Fourth Circuit's opinion.[398] The Government, in arguing against Supreme Court review, claimed that in light of Mr. Padilla's transfer to civilian custody the case was moot;[399] but the Court declined to reach the mootness question.

The Fourth Circuit's opinion in *Padilla* stands as the ruling of the highest court to consider the power of the President – albeit under the AUMF – to order the military detention of an American seized in the United States. It is one of the few instances where the Administration has succeeded in persuading a court to adopt any of its expansive views of the President's Commander-in-Chief powers. Its potential precedential significance is undermined by: 1) the Government's effort to moot Supreme Court review; 2) the Fourth Circuit's hindsight suggestion that the opinion was procured by representations that were no longer credible, and 3) the Government's request, once its conduct in the litigation was called into question, that the Fourth Circuit vacate the opinion.[400] Nevertheless, it sits in the caselaw for the proposition that an

American can be seized in the United States by civilian law enforcement personnel, handed over to the military, and interrogated for years at the direction of the President, with only limited recourse to the courts to challenge the basis for the detention.

8.   *Mr. Padilla's allegations that he was subjected to harsh treatment*

Mr. Padilla's treatment while in custody was not at issue in the *habeas* litigation, but it sheds light on the conduct of the litigation and the relationship between the U.S. military and the Justice Department in formulating litigation policy.

After Mr. Padilla was transferred to Florida to face federal terrorism charges, he filed a motion, through his attorney, requesting that the prosecution be dismissed because of "outrageous government misconduct." In a lengthy pleading, Mr. Padilla described at length his treatment while in captivity, characterizing it as torture:

On June 9, 2002, President George W. Bush declared Mr. Padilla an Enemy combatant and directed Secretary of Defense Donald H. Rumsfeld to take custody of Mr. Padilla from the Attorney General. Mr. Padilla was transferred to the Naval Consolidated Brig at the Naval Weapons Station in Charleston, South Carolina (hereinafter "Naval Brig"), where he was denied all access to counsel. The government argued that Mr. Padilla should not be allowed to see a lawyer because he might pass illicit communications through his attorney. The government also asserted that allowing Mr. Padilla access to counsel or to learn that a court was hearing his case could provide him with the expectation that he would some day be released.

Only after such time as Padilla has perceived that help is not on the way can the United States reasonably expect to obtain all possible intelligence information from Padilla... Providing him access to counsel now... would break – probably irreparably – the sense of dependency and trust that the interrogators are attempting to create. [Jacoby Declaration].

In an effort to gain Mr. Padilla's "dependency and trust," he was tortured for nearly the entire three years and eight months of his unlawful detention. The torture took myriad forms, each designed to cause pain, anguish, depression and, ultimately, the loss of will to live. The base ingredient in Mr. Padilla's torture was stark isolation for a substantial portion of his captivity. For nearly two

100

years – from June 9, 2002, until March 2, 2004, when the Department of Defense permitted Mr. Padilla to have contact with his lawyers – Mr. Padilla was in complete isolation. Even after he was permitted contact with counsel, his conditions of confinement remained essentially the same. He was kept in a unit comprising sixteen individual cells, eight on the upper level and eight on the lower level, where Mr. Padilla's cell was located. No other cells in the unit were occupied. His cell was electronically monitored twenty-four hours a day, eliminating the need for a guard to patrol his unit. His only contact with another person was when a guard would deliver and retrieve trays of food and when the government desired to interrogate him.

His isolation, furthermore, was aggravated by the efforts of his captors to maintain complete sensory deprivation. His tiny cell -- nine feet by seven feet -- had no view to the outside world. The door to his cell had a window, however, it was covered by a magnetic sticker, depriving Mr. Padilla of even a view into the hallway and adjacent common areas of his unit. He was not given a clock or a watch and for most of the time of his captivity, he was unaware whether it was day or night, or what time of year or day it was.

In addition to his extreme isolation, Mr. Padilla was also viciously deprived of sleep. This sleep deprivation was achieved in a variety of ways. For a substantial period of his captivity, Mr. Padilla's cell contained only a steel bunk with no mattress. The pain and discomfort of sleeping on a cold, steel bunk made it impossible for him to sleep. Mr. Padilla was not given a mattress until the tail end of his captivity. Mr. Padilla's captors did not solely rely on the inhumane conditions of his living arrangements to deprive him of regular sleep. A number of ruses were employed to keep Mr. Padilla from getting necessary sleep and rest. One of the tactics his captors employed was the creation of loud noises near and around his cell to interrupt any rest Mr. Padilla could manage on his steel bunk. As Mr. Padilla was attempting to sleep, the cell doors adjacent to his cell would be electronically opened, resulting in a loud clank, only to be immediately slammed shut. Other times, his captors would bang the walls and cell bars creating loud startling noises. These disruptions would occur throughout the night and cease only in the morning, when Mr. Padilla's interrogations would begin.

101

Efforts to manipulate Mr. Padilla and break his will also took the form of the denial of the few benefits he possessed in his cell. For a long time Mr. Padilla had no reading materials, access to any media, radio or television, and the only thing he possessed in his room was a mirror. The mirror was abruptly taken away, leaving Mr. Padilla with even less sensory stimulus. Also, at different points in his confinement Mr. Padilla would be given some comforts, like a pillow or a sheet, only to have them taken away arbitrarily. He was never given any regular recreation time. Often, when he was brought outside for some exercise, it was done at night, depriving Mr. Padilla of sunlight for many months at a time. The disorientation Mr. Padilla experienced due to not seeing the sun and having no view on the outside world was exacerbated by his captors' practice of turning on extremely bright lights in his cell or imposing complete darkness for durations of twenty-four hours, or more.

Mr. Padilla's dehumanization at the hands of his captors also took more sinister forms. Mr. Padilla was often put in stress positions for hours at a time. He would be shackled and manacled, with a belly chain, for hours in his cell. Noxious fumes would be introduced to his room causing his eyes and nose to run. The temperature of his cell would be manipulated, making his cell extremely cold for long stretches of time. Mr. Padilla was denied even the smallest, and most personal shreds of human dignity by being deprived of showering for weeks at a time, yet having to endure forced grooming at the whim of his captors.

A substantial quantum of torture endured by Mr. Padilla came at the hands of his interrogators. In an effort to disorient Mr. Padilla, his captors would deceive him about his location and who his interrogators actually were. Mr. Padilla was threatened with being forcibly removed from the United States to another country, including U.S. Naval Base at Guantanamo Bay, Cuba, where he was threatened his fate would be even worse than in the Naval Brig. He was threatened with being cut with a knife and having alcohol poured on the wounds. He was also threatened with imminent execution. He was hooded and forced to stand in stress positions for long durations of time. He was forced to endure exceedingly long interrogation sessions, without adequate sleep, wherein he would be confronted with false information, scenarios, and documents to further disorient him. Often he had to endure multiple interrogators who would scream, shake, and otherwise assault Mr. Padilla. Additionally, Mr. Padilla was given drugs against his will, believed to be some form of lysergic acid diethylamide (LSD) or phencyclidine (PCP), to act as a sort of truth serum during his interrogations.

Throughout most of the time Mr. Padilla was held captive in the Naval Brig he had no contact with the outside world. In March 2004, one year and eight months after arriving in the Naval Brig, Mr. Padilla was permitted his first contact with his attorneys. Even thereafter, although Mr. Padilla had access to counsel, and thereby some contact with the outside world, those visits were extremely limited and restricted. Significantly though, it was not until Mr. Padilla was permitted to visit with counsel that one of his attorneys, Andrew Patel, was able to provide Mr. Padilla with a copy of the Quran. Up until that time, for a period of almost two years, Mr. Padilla was [denied] the right to exercise his religious beliefs.[401]

The motion was denied.

Mr. Padilla was convicted at trial of conspiracy charges. The Government sought a life sentence, but Judge Marcia Cooke, noting that "[t]here is no evidence that these defendants personally maimed, kidnapped [sic] or killed anyone in the United States or elsewhere," sentenced him to 17 years. Significantly, Judge Cooke said that she took into account the "harsh" conditions to which Mr. Padilla was subjected while in the brig.[402] He remains in custody.[403]

The President's Power to Order Military Detention of Lawfully Admitted Alien Seized by Civilian Authorities in the United States (*al-Marri*)

Another case presenting some of the same features as *Padilla* is that of Ali Saleh Kahlal al-Marri. Mr. al-Marri was arrested as a material witness December 12, 2001, at his home in Peoria, Illinois. He was a Qatari citizen, in the United States lawfully, with his family, on a student visa pursuing a masters degree at Bradley University, where he had previously received a bachelors degree in 1991. He was indicted in February 2002 on various credit card fraud offenses. A year later, in January of 2003, he was indicted on additional charges relating to identification fraud and false statements to the FBI. These charges were dismissed in the Southern District of New York for improper venue, but identical charges were filed in the Central District of Illinois, where Mr. al-Marri was transferred for trial. On May 29, 2003, the district judge set a July 21, 2003 trial date, and on June 20, 2003, the court scheduled a suppression hearing for July 2, 2003.

On June 23, 2003, the Government moved *ex parte* to dismiss the indictment based on a declaration signed by President Bush setting forth his determination that Mr. al-Marri was an "enemy combatant." President Bush ordered the Attorney General to transfer Mr. al-Marri to military custody at the Charleston brig, where Mr. al-Marri has since remained, in solitary confinement, without charge or trial.

Mr. al-Marri's conditions of confinement, as described by his attorneys in his September 2008 petition for Supreme Court review of his detention, are markedly similar to the treatment alleged by Mr. Padilla:

> **For the first sixteen months of al-Marri's military confinement, he was held incommunicado.** His attorneys, his wife and five children, and the International Committee for the Red Cross ("ICRC") all were denied access. The government ignored al-Marri's counsel's repeated requests to communicate with him. During that time, al-Marri was repeatedly interrogated in ways that bordered on, and sometimes amounted to, torture, including sleep deprivation, painful stress positions, extreme sensory deprivation, and threats of violence or death.
>
> Only in October 2004 was al-Marri again allowed access to counsel. Al-Marri, however, remains in virtual isolation in the brig. Other than his attorneys and ICRC officials, al-Marri is not permitted to see anyone from the outside world. To date, he has been allowed only two phone calls with his family, both earlier this year, and then only after the government faced litigation challenging his conditions of confinement.[404]

Over the years during his detention, Mr. al-Marri has sought to challenge the bases of his incarceration. Initially, in July of 2003, shortly after he was turned over to the military, his attorney filed a petition on his behalf for a writ of *habeas corpus* in Illinois, where his criminal charges had been pending. This petition was dismissed on venue grounds, because he was by then being held in South Carolina.[405]

In July of 2004, Mr. al-Marri's counsel filed a subsequent *habeas* petition in South Carolina, initiating a round of litigation that involved many of the same issues as those in the *Padilla* case. Mr. al-Marri maintained that he was entitled to know the factual bases for his detention, and to challenge them in a real court proceeding, where he would not only be informed of the specific charges but would have the opportunity to challenge the evidence and present evidence on his behalf. The Government, in response, asserted that the President had the constitutional power as Commander in Chief, or power granted him under the AUMF, to designate Mr. al-Marri an "enemy combatant," that the court must defer to those assertions of power, and that the court should affirm Mr. al-Marri's detention on the basis of an affidavit

104

executed by an official of the Executive Branch, portions of which were secret, and nearly all of which consisted of hearsay.

In further support for its right to continue Mr. al-Marri's detention, potentially indefinitely, the Government submitted a "Declaration of Jeffrey N. Rapp of the Joint Intelligence Task Force for Combating Terrorism." The "Rapp Declaration" sets forth serious allegations, including, for example, that Mr. al-Marri had met with Osama bin Laden, had researched the use of cyanide, and intended to be involved in deadly terrorist events in the United States. It did not allege that Mr. al-Marri was ever on or near a "battlefield."

In considering the positions of the parties, the district court found that the Rapp Declaration was sufficient on its face to justify the continued military detention of Mr. al-Marri, and placed the burden on Mr. al-Marri to rebut the allegations set forth in the Rapp Declaration. Mr. al-Marri responded that he was not required to rebut the allegations, some of which were secret and unknown to him; rather, it was for the Government to prove them, and that Mr. al-Marri was entitled to certain basic due process rights, such as the disclosure of exculpatory evidence. In August of 2006, Mr. al-Marri's *habeas* petition was dismissed,[406] and Mr. al-Marri appealed the dismissal to the Fourth Circuit.

In June of 2007, a three-judge panel of the Fourth Circuit reversed the district court and concluded that Mr. al-Marri's military detention must end.[407] The Government then sought and obtained rehearing by the full court.

Over a year later, on July 15, 2008, the Fourth Circuit *en banc* reversed the panel decision and ruled, in a 5-4 decision, that the AUMF granted the President the power to detain Mr. al-Marri as an enemy combatant, but that Mr. al-Marri had the right to challenge the allegation that he was an enemy combatant.[408] As to this latter point, the court held that the district court's placing the burden on Mr. al-Marri to respond to secret and hearsay allegations, and denying him access to essential evidence did not accord with constitutional due process protections to which he was entitled. Notably, no member of the panel agreed that the President had the inherent authority as Commander in Chief to order Mr. al-Marri's military detention inside the United States.

The *al-Marri* case, like the *Padilla* case, has the following features: the civilian arrest of a person lawfully in the United States; the order by the President that the person be turned over to military custody for potentially indefinite incarceration; the subjection of that individual to harsh interrogation techniques such as sleep deprivation; the denial to that individual of legal counsel and other essential aspects of due process to permit him to challenge the bases of his detention; the claim that the President enjoys such powers over the individual's liberty as Commander in Chief, or, in the alternative, that such power were granted by Congress in the AUMF. The implications of the President's view of his power are obvious and ominous: "This intolerable reading of the law would leave a president free to suspend the rights of anyone, including American citizens."[409]

Judge Motz, writing for the 4 judges who believed the Executive did not have authority to subject Mr. al-Marri to military detention as an "enemy combatant," either inherently under the Constitution, or under the AUMF, made it clear she was not suggesting that Mr. al-Marri be freed, but that the Government comply with the law:

> We would also grant al-Marri *habeas* relief. **Even assuming the truth of the Government's allegations, they provide no basis for treating al-Marri as an enemy combatant or as anything other than a civilian.** This does not mean that al-Marri, or similarly situated American citizens, would have to be freed. Like others accused of terrorist activity in this country, from the Oklahoma City bombers to the convicted September 11th conspirator, they could be tried on criminal charges and, if convicted, punished severely. But the Government would not be able to subject them to indefinite military detention.
>
> With regret, we recognize that this view does not command a majority of the court. **Our colleagues hold that the President can order the military to seize from his home and indefinitely detain anyone in this country – including an American citizen – even though he has never affiliated with an enemy nation, fought alongside any nation's armed forces, or borne arms against the United States anywhere in the world. We cannot agree that in a broad and general statute, Congress silently authorized a detention power that so vastly exceeds all traditional bounds.** No existing law permits this extraordinary exercise of executive power. [footnote omitted] Even in times of national peril, we must follow the law, lest this country cease to be a nation of laws. For "[l]iberty and security can be reconciled; and in our system they are reconciled within the framework of the law."[410]

Mr. al-Marri sought Supreme Court review of the Fourth Circuit decision, urging the Court to resolve "the scope of the government's domestic military detention power granted by the AUMF and permitted under the Constitution."[411] The Bush Administration urged the Court not to grant review, arguing, among other reasons, that review was not yet appropriate because Mr. al-Marri had not yet availed himself of the expanded protections ordered by the Fourth Circuit: "If petitioner's challenge is successful, there will be no need for this Court to consider the purely legal question of the President's authority. If it is not successful, petitioner will be able to reassert his claims at that time."[412] In addition, the Government argued that the military detention of Mr. al-Marri based upon facts set forth in the Rapp Declaration was authorized by the AUMF, because Mr. al-Marri was an "enemy combatant" within those facts.[413]

On December 5, 2008, the Supreme Court agreed to hear the case.[414]

When subjected to judicial scrutiny, the Administration's claims of vast uncheckable Commander-in-Chief powers supposedly provided the President under the Constitution have largely disintegrated. In *Hamdi*, the Supreme Court declined to endorse the Government's claim that those powers inherently authorized him to keep Hamdi in military detention simply because he was seized on the battlefield, though a four-Justice plurality held that Congress had granted him that authority in the AUMF. In *Hamdan*, the Supreme Court held that those powers did not authorize the President to establish military trial commissions in violation of the Uniform Code of Military Justice (enacted by Congress) and the Geneva Conventions. Even in *Padilla* and *al-Marri*, the Fourth Circuit, in upholding the two detentions, held that they were lawful only because Congress had given the President the requisite power. Further, the ability of the Executive Branch to avoid jurisdiction of the courts by holding the detainees at Guantanamo was foreclosed by the Supreme Court's decisions in *Rasul* and *Boumediene*. As a last resort, the Administration turned to efforts to moot judicial review, by belatedly providing access to counsel or transferring to civilian custody after prolonged military detention.

One of the most emphatic rejections of this Administration's expansive assertions of presidential military power came from Justice Scalia, in his dissent in *Hamdi*: "The very core of liberty by our Anglo-Saxon system of separated power has been freedom from indefinite imprisonment at the will of the Executive."[415]

C. Committee Action

The House Committee on the Judiciary engaged in a number of hearings and oversight activities with regard to the Bush Administration's detention policies and related issues.

An oversight hearing on detention-related issues, titled "Habeas Corpus and Detentions at Guantanamo Bay," was held by the Subcommittee on the Constitution, Civil Rights, and Civil Liberties, on June 26, 2007. At that time, the due process landscape for the detainees was bleak. This hearing focused on the Administration's Guantanamo detention polices that placed all decisions related to detention in the hands of the military components of the Executive Branch. Moreover, the Administration had scrapped traditional military justice procedures for adjudicating the status of detainees and, through the passage of the Military Commissions Act of 2006,[416] not only implemented a military commission process with evidentiary rules stacked against the detainees but sought to deprive them of their ability to seek *habeas corpus* relief in the federal courts. The Administration was, at that time, arguing in the federal courts that the detainees had no right to judicial review of those decisions.

Subcommittee Chairman Jerrold Nadler described the situation as follows:

This Administration seems to believe that it has greater wisdom and virtue than governments of the last 800 years, that it can be trusted to make correct and just determinations about who should be locked up without any independent review.

The President claims the power to point his finger at anybody who is not an American citizen and say, "you are an enemy combatant because I say so. And because I say so, we are going to keep you in jail forever, with no hearing, no writ of *habeas corpus*, no court proceeding, no confrontation of witnesses, no probable cause, no due process of any kind."[417]

One of the witnesses, Jonathan Hafetz of the ACLU's National Security Project, bluntly described the Combatant Status Review Tribunal – the military body established by the Administration to make decisions about a detainee's status – as having been "created deliberately to avoid *habeas* review." He further described it as follows:

> [a] summary proceeding that lacks all the hallmarks of due process: denying detainees attorneys, relying on secret evidence, preventing detainees from calling witnesses or presenting evidence, using evidence gained by torture and other abuse, and **rubber-stamping detentions based on what higher-up have said and political influence.**[418]

He characterized Guantanamo as a "failure" and stated that "a principal reason is that the United States has denied *habeas corpus* to Guantanamo detainees; it has prevented any lawful or meaningful process to determine whether we are detaining people in accordance with law."[419]

Subcommittee Chairman Nadler challenged former Administration lawyer Bradford Berenson on the Administration's legal theory in *Padilla*:

Mr. Nadler: The President claims the power, for example, in the Padilla case, to seize someone in the United States, some who we don't know to be an enemy combatant – there may be information to that effect,... and throw them in a military brig forever.

How is that not a new tyrannical power?

Mr. Berenson: I think that is a misunderstanding of the power that the President claimed with respect to Mr. Padilla.

I was working in the White House at the time that Padilla was first captured, and the United States never took the position that Mr. Padilla did not have right of access to U.S. courts and did not have the ability to file a writ of *habeas corpus*.

* * * * * * *

[T]he dispute was really over what the *habeas* court could do. The administration took a very restrictive view of the right mode of judicial review for the *habeas* court; that is, it was extremely deferential review, which essentially amounted to a review of the record on which the administration had based its conclusion that Padilla was a combatant. The administration did not want trial-type adversary proceedings, with lawyers on both sides duking it out –

Mr. Nadler: How can the characterization of the accusation deprive me of rights?

Mr. Berenson: Because it is a fundamentally different thing to take up arms against this Nation –

* * * * * * *

Mr. Nadler: **The position you are taking is that, because they are accused of being an enemy combatant, they should have fewer rights than someone accused of different crimes but even more serious crimes.**

Mr. Berenson: Well, the evidence on which the President certified that Mr. Padilla was an enemy combatant included very good intelligence about his meetings with Osama bin Laden –

Mr. Nadler: It may or may not be wonderful intelligence. It may or may not be true. That is not the question.[420]

Other witnesses at that hearing stressed the numerous problems with the Military Commissions Act and the Administration's determined efforts to deny detainees the right to seek *habeas* relief. They made the following points:

- Permitting *habeas* review would impose a very modest burden on the courts.[421]

- As a policy matter, "[f]or the very reason that the law of war allows us to detain persons without charging them with criminal conduct for extended periods, it is all the more important to be sure that the process for determining who those people are is beyond reproach."[422]

- The "global war on terror" has "no identifiable enemies, no recognizable

109

battlefields and no foreseeable end. It is precisely the indeterminate, open-ended nature of the fight against terrorism that increases the risk that government officials will inadvertently detain the wrong people based upon suspicion, innuendo or mistake. In other words, the very nature of what the Administration calls a global war on terror makes *habeas corpus* more, not less, important."[423]

- The Guantanamo detention polices have shaken the trust that the world had in America's justice system, and undermined the faith that is necessary to fight terrorism.[424]

In addition, the Committee has specifically sought public release of the Memorandum dated October 23, 2001, that addressed the lawfulness of the use of military powers inside the United States[425] – a topic that appears to address or implicate the president's ability to exercise military powers in connection with detention policy of Americans inside the United States.

II. Interrogation

A. Factual Background

December 2001toFebruary 2002 – Determinations That the Protections of the Geneva Conventions, Including Common Article III, Do Not Apply to Guantanamo Detainees

The decision announced in December 2001 that the Administration intended to detain captives at Guantanamo – based on the private legal conclusion that "a district court cannot properly entertain an application for a writ of *habeas corpus* by an enemy alien" who was detained there[426] – reflected its desire to, among other things, interrogate the detainees without interference from the courts.

At about the same time, the Defense Department General Counsel's Office began soliciting information from the "Joint Personnel Recover Agency"(JPRA) regarding detainee "exploitation."[427] One of the functions of JPRA is to train American personnel to resist interrogation techniques considered illegal under the Geneva Conventions. In particular, the JPRA oversaw "Survival Evasion Resistance and Escape (SERE) training. As described by the Senate Armed Services Committee:

> **The techniques used in SERE school, based, in part, on Chinese Communist techniques used during the Korean war to elicit false confessions,** include stripping students of their clothing, placing them in stress positions, putting hoods over their heads, disrupting their sleep, treating them like animals, subjecting them to loud music and flashing lights, and exposing them to extreme temperatures. It can also include face and body slaps and until recently, for some who attended the Navy's SERE school, it

110

included waterboarding.[428]

Over the next two years, the JPRA would consult with and assist the Department of Defense in the formulation of interrogation techniques.

On January 9, 2002, Deputy Assistant Attorney General Yoo signed a memorandum that concluded that detainees from the war in Afghanistan were not entitled to the protections of the Geneva Conventions, particularly the right to protections as prisoners of war and the even more fundamental protections of the Conventions' Common Article 3.[429] These legal conclusions were not only necessary to ensure that U.S. military personnel at Guantanamo could use coercive interrogation on the detainees – a practice not permitted if the detainees were protected by the Conventions – but, more significantly, to assure that the U.S. military personnel would not be subject to the limitations on their conduct under the War Crimes Act of 1996. That Act defined "war crime" as either a "grave breach" of the Conventions, or any violation of Common Article 3,[430] and provided for fines, life imprisonment, and even execution for criminal violations, whether perpetrated inside or outside of the United States.

Mr. Yoo concluded that al Qaeda was not eligible to claim the protections of the Geneva Conventions because, among other reasons, al Qaeda was a "non-State actor," and because the "nature of the conflict" – that is, a conflict between a "nation State and a non-governmental organization" – was not a conflict covered by Common Article 3 of the Conventions.[431] Similarly, the Taliban militia was not entitled to those protections because, among other reasons, Afghanistan was a "failed state" that "was without the attributes of statehood necessary to continue as a party to the Geneva Conventions," or was otherwise "functionally indistinguishable from al Qaeda."[432]

On January 25, 2002, White House Counsel Alberto Gonzales, in a memorandum to President Bush, endorsed Yoo's analysis in the January 9, 2002 memorandum, and advised President Bush to declare the Taliban and Al Qaeda exempt from Geneva Convention protections.[433]

On February 2, 2002, State Department Legal Advisor William H. Taft IV authored a memorandum to White House Counsel Gonzales warning that rejection of the Geneva Conventions would raise serious concerns. "A decision that the conventions do not apply to the conflict in Afghanistan in which our armed forces are engaged deprives our troops there of any claim to the protection of the conventions in the event they are captured."[434]

On February 7, 2002, President Bush signed a Memorandum titled "Humane Treatment of al Qaeda and Taliban Detainees" that resolved the internal debate regarding the treatment of detained individuals. This Memorandum provided that the protections enumerated in the Conventions would not apply to the detainees. The President's memo stated there was a need for "new thinking in the law of war," though it did call for humane treatment for the detainees "in a manner consistent with the principles of Geneva" – "to the extent appropriate and consistent with military necessity."[435]

Having determined that key provisions of international law (and hence the War Crimes Act) did not constrain the interrogators, the next question was whether other domestic criminal statutes – such as the federal criminal torture statute – constrained them. There were evidently separate interrogation policies for the military (at Guantanamo) and for the CIA, though the precise roles of these agencies, and the precise evolution of policies for these different agencies, are not always clear from the information obtained to date.

The August 1, 2002 Torture Memorandum

Having decided that persons seized in the conflict with al Qaeda and the Taliban would be detained at Guantanamo, where it was believed they would have no access to the courts to challenge their detentions, and having decided that the detainees were not were not to be treated as POWs or protected by Common Article 3 of the Geneva Conventions, the next issue for the Administration was the limits of interrogation – what was meant by "torture," and the potential application of the federal criminal torture statutes to the conduct of the interrogators.[436] In a memorandum to Alberto Gonzales (then White House Counsel) dated August 1, 2002, the Justice Department's OLC provided advice to the White House as to the legal meaning of "torture" under the federal criminal statutes that prohibited it.[437] The memorandum did not distinguish between acts of the military and acts of the CIA.[438]

Recognizing that torture involves the infliction of "severe pain," one controversial aspect of the opinion was its conclusion that "severe pain ... as used [in the federal criminal statute prohibiting torture] must rise to ... the level that would ordinarily be associated with a sufficiently serious physical condition such as death, organ failure, or serious impairment of body functions."[439] This would appear to allow, for example, crushing the little toe or water-boarding or drilling through a tooth.[440]

Even aside from minimizing the "pain" aspect of what was meant by torture, this memorandum set forth other bases whereby torture would be permitted. For example, in one instance, Mr. Yoo argued that torture could be justified in the name of national defense. This is how one law professor dissected that claim:

> The analysis of self-defense, for example, inverts a doctrine permitting last-resort defensive violence against assailants into a rationale for waterboarding helpless prisoners. OLC cites no conventional legal authority for this inversion, for the simple reason that there is none. Although OLC claimed to base its analysis on the teachings of "leading scholarly commentators" ... in fact this is only one such commentator, and OLC flatly misrepresents what he says. [footnote omitted].[441]

112

The memorandum further concluded that the President could not be constrained from ordering torture, even under a broad definition of that term, because neither Congress nor a treaty could limit the President in the exercise of his Commander-in-Chief powers:

> **In light of the President's complete authority over the conduct of war, without a clear statement otherwise, we will not read a criminal statute as infringing on the President's ultimate authority in these areas.**

* * * * * * *

> In order to respect the President's inherent constitutional authority to manage a military campaign against al Qaeda and its allies, [18 U.S.C. 2340A] must be construed as not applying to interrogations undertaken pursuant to his commander-in-chief authority. As our Office has consistently held during this Administration and previous Administrations, Congress lacks authority under Article I to set the terms and conditions under which the President may exercise his authority as Commander in Chief to control the conduct of operations during a war... [T]he President's power to detain and interrogate enemy combatants arises out of his constitutional authority as Commander in Chief... Congress may no more regulate the President's ability to detain and interrogate enemy combatants than it may regulate his ability to direct troop movements ion the battlefield. Accordingly, we would construe Section 2340A to avoid this constitutional difficulty, and conclude that it does not apply to the President's detention and interrogation of enemy combatants pursuant to his Commander-in-Chief authority.[442]

Under the logic of Deputy Assistant Attorney General Yoo's view of presidential power, the president, as Commander in Chief, could direct the torture of a detainee's innocent child in order to obtain his cooperation, and no law can stop him. This is no exaggeration, nor is it a proposition from which Mr. Yoo would retreat. In a December 1, 2005, debate with Notre Dame Professor Doug Cassel, Mr. Yoo stated the president could lawfully order "crushing the testicles of a person's child":

> Mr. Cassel: If the President deems that he's got to torture somebody, including by crushing the testicles of the person's child, there is no law that can stop him?

> Mr. Yoo: No treaty.

Mr. Cassel: Also no law by Congress. That is what you wrote in the August 2002 memo.

Mr. Yoo: I think it depends on why the President thinks he needs to do that.[443]

After the August 1, 2002 Torture Memorandum was leaked, it came under a barrage of criticism – particularly for its assertions regarding the scope of presidential power. In December 2004, the OLC, now under Acting Assistant Attorney General Daniel Levin, issued another opinion superseding the earlier memorandum in its entirety, and specifically rejecting the "organ failure" definition of torture.[444] The new opinion did not address the President's supposed power to order torture (notwithstanding federal law that prohibited torture) – an issue deemed "unnecessary" because the President had directed that U.S. personnel not torture.

August 1, 2002 – Waterboarding Approved for CIA Use

In March 2002, a senior al Qaeda operative, Abu Zubaydah, was captured, and the CIA sought guidance on how it could interrogate him. As reported by the Senate Armed Services Committee:

> Secretary of State Condoleezza Rice, who was then the National Security Advisor, said that, "in the spring of 2002, CIA sought policy approval from the National Security Council (NSC) to begin an interrogation program for high-level al-Qaida terrorists." Secretary Rice said that she asked Director of Central Intelligence George Tenet to brief NSC Principals on the program and asked Attorney General John Ashcroft "personally to review and confirm the legal advice prepared by the Office of Legal Counsel." She also said that Secretary of Defense Donald Rumsfeld participated in the NSC review of CIA's program.[445]

On August 1, 2002, the same day that the Torture Memorandum was issued, the Justice Department OLC, in a separate memorandum signed by Jay Bybee, approved the CIA's use of waterboarding.[446] This memorandum is heavily redacted, and the publicly disclosed portions do not specifically mention waterboarding. However, its contents are described in an undated memorandum from the CIA to OLC, referring to CIA interrogators having been informed that the Justice Department had in a classified August 1, 2002 opinion concluded that certain interrogation techniques, "including the waterboard," did not violate the torture statute.[447] Moreover, in context, it appears that the redacted August 1, 2002, Justice Department OLC memorandum was written to authorize the waterboarding of Abu Zubaydah, who was captured in March of 2002.[448] It is not publicly known what, if any, other interrogation techniques were approved in that second August 1, 2002 memorandum.[449]

The full extent of the CIA's interrogation program has not been disclosed. Vice President

114

Cheney has recently taken credit for it, however, in an ABC News interview:

> Mr. Karl: Did you authorize the tactics that were used against Khalid Sheikh Mohammed?
>
> Mr. Cheney: I was aware of the program, certainly, and involved in helping get the process cleared, as the agency in effect came in and wanted to know what they could and couldn't do. And they talked to me, as well as others, to explain what they wanted to do. **And I supported it.**[450]

October 2002 to March 2003 – Development of Techniques for Use at Guantanamo

It has been reported that throughout 2002, there was a growing sense within the Administration that the interrogation policies at Guantanamo were not yielding the desired intelligence, and a corresponding desire that more aggressive interrogation techniques be used to extract information from the detainees. In September 2002, David Addington, with others, went to Guantanamo.[451] One of the purposes of the visit was to address issues associated with the limits on interrogation. The reaction of one of the JAG officers there, Diane Beaver, was described as follows:

> [Addington, Gonzales, and Department of Defense General Counsel Jim Haynes] met with the intelligence people and talked about new interrogation methods. They also witnessed some interrogations. **Beaver spent time with the group... She recalled the message they had received from the visitors: Do "whatever needed to be done." That was a green light from the very top – the lawyers for Bush, Cheney, Rumsfeld, and the C.I.A.**[452]

On October 11, 2002, the head of the Military Intelligence Task Force, General Michael Dunlavey, requested that his superior officers approve the use of certain "counter resistance techniques" for interrogation. Lieutenant Colonel Diane Beaver provided the supporting legal advice. In the letter, Dunlavey divided the "counter-resistance strategies" into three categories. Category I techniques include yelling and deceiving. Category II techniques include stress positions, forcing individuals to stand for up to four hours, for example; isolation for up to 30 days; hooding during transportation and questioning; 20-hour interrogations; removal of "comfort items (including religious items)"; nudity; forced grooming; and the use of "detainee's individual phobias (such as fear of dogs) to induce stress." Category III techniques – which, in General Dunlavey's scheme, only a commanding general could approve, included:

(i)   The use of scenarios designed to convince the detainee that death or severely painful consequences are imminent for him and/or his family.

(ii)   Exposure to cold weather or water (with appropriate medical monitoring).

(iii)   Use of a wet towel and dripping water to induce the perception of suffocation, or waterboarding.

(iv)   Use of mild, non-injurious physical contact (such as grabbing and light pushing).[453]

As the Senate Armed Services Committee reported, some of these techniques – "including stress positions, exploitation of detainee fears (such as fear of dogs), removal of clothing, hooding, deprivation of light and sound, and the so-called wet towel treatment or the waterboard"– were patterned after those associated with the Armed Forces SERE training.[454]

On October 25, 2002, General James Hill sent General Dunlavey's request to the Defense Department with his own letter stating, "I desire to have as many options as possible at my disposal and therefore request that Department of Defense and Department of Justice lawyers review the third category of techniques. I believe we should provide our interrogators with as many legally permissible tools as possible."[455]

During the October-November 2002 time-frame, numerous voices from components of the military expressed their opposition to or concerns with the enhanced interrogation techniques being urged.[456]

On November 27, 2002, Department of Defense General Counsel Jim Haynes requested that Secretary Rumsfeld approve the counter-resistance techniques.[457] On December 2, 2002, Secretary Rumsfeld approved Haynes's request for the use of Category I and II techniques. He additionally approved the use of the "mild, non-injurious" Category III techniques. Beside his approval, Rumsfeld wrote, "**However, I stand for 8-10 hours a day. Why is standing limited to 4 hours? D.R.** "[458]

The response of the Guantanamo investigators was swift. According to the Senate Armed Services Committee Report:

> Following the Secretary's December 2, 2002 authorization, senior staff at GTMO began drafting a Standard Operating Procedure (SOP) specifically for the use of SERE techniques in interrogations. The draft SOP stated that "The premise behind this is that the interrogation tactics used at U.S. military SERE schools are appropriate for use in real-world interrogations. These tactics and techniques are used at SERE school to 'break' SERE detainees. The same tactics and techniques can be used to break real detainees during interrogation." The draft "GTMO SERE SOP" described how to slap, strip, and place detainees in stress

116

positions. It also described other SERE techniques, such as "hooding," "manhandling," and "walling" detainees.

On December 30, 2002, two instructors from Navy SERE school arrived at GTMO. The next day, in a session with approximately 24 interrogation personnel, the two SERE instructors demonstrated how to administer stress positions, and various slapping techniques. According to two interrogators, those who attended the training even broke off into pairs to practice the techniques.

Exemplifying the disturbing nature of the training, the SERE instructors explained "Biderman's Principles" – which were based on coercive methods used by the Chinese Communist dictatorship to elicit false confessions from U.S. POWs during the Korean War – and left with GTMO personnel a chart of those coercive techniques. Three days after they conducted the training, the SERE instructors met with GTMO's Commander, Major General Geoffrey Miller. According to some who attended that meeting, Major General Miller stated that he did not want his interrogators using the techniques that the Navy SERE instructors had demonstrated. That conversation, however, took place after the training had already occurred and not all of the interrogators who attended the training got the message.[459]

On January 15, 2003, in response to concerns raised by the General Counsel for the Department of Navy, Alberto Mora, Secretary Rumsfeld rescinded his December 2 instructions, disallowed the use of the Category II and III interrogation techniques, and required that the Secretary approve the use of these techniques.[460] He also set up a "working group" to address the interrogation policies.

On March 6, 2003, the working group issued a "Working Group Report on Detainee Interrogations in the Global War on Terrorism." The report adopted what was in essence the Yoo-Gonzales conclusions from 2002 – that the President, as Commander in Chief, was not bound by international treaties prohibiting torture, or the federal anti-torture statutes:

In order to respect the President's inherent constitutional authority to manage a military campaign, [the statutory prohibitions against torture] must be construed as inapplicable to interrogations undertaken pursuant to his authority as Commander-in-Chief. **Congress lacks authority under Article I to set the terms and conditions under which the President may exercise his authority as Commander-in-Chief to control the conduct of operations during a war**.

117

The Report concluded that Executive Branch officials, including those in the military, could be immune from domestic and international prohibitions against torture for a variety of reasons, including a belief by interrogators that they were acting on orders from superiors "except where the conduct goes so far as to be patently unlawful."[461]

John Yoo's March 14, 2003, Torture Memorandum

In a March 14, 2003, memorandum, Mr. Yoo again opined on the issue of torture.[462] The legal aspects of the memorandum generally track the same expansive views of presidential power set forth in prior memoranda, including his reliance on the presumed reach of the AUMF.[463] Significantly, as with the September 25, 2001, War Powers Memorandum described in the Preface to this Report, this memorandum intimated but did not explicitly state that the President enjoyed the latitude to exercise Commander-in-Chief powers inside the United States. Mr. Yoo noted that "the Government has engaged in a broad effort at *home and abroad* to counter terrorism."[464] The memorandum cites newspaper articles for the proposition that "al Qaeda continues to enjoy information and resources that allow it to organize and direct active hostile forces against this country, both *domestically* and abroad,"[465] and therefore that "information is perhaps the most critical weapon for defeating al Qaeda."[466] And he asserts that the "[o]ne of the core functions of the Commander in Chief is that of capturing, detaining, and interrogating members of the enemy."[467]

Mr. Yoo spends significant efforts explaining that neither the Fifth Amendment (due process) or Eighth Amendment (cruel and unusual punishments) provide rights to captured enemy soldiers, and, in a footnote, further noting that "the Fourth Amendment ha[s] no application to domestic military operations."[468] Mr. Yoo would have had at least two reasons to insert this qualification as to the applicability of the Fourth Amendment: First, he certainly knew that Jose Padilla, a U.S. citizen, had been seized in the United States, had been turned over to the military, without a judge ever passing on the military detention, and was then being subject to the sort of coercive interrogation that Yoo would further discuss in the memorandum, Second, he would likely have known that the United States was engaging in electronic surveillance in the United States that was not permitted under FISA and arguably violated the Fourth Amendment.

Mr. Yoo's discussion of the President's war power is again couched in extreme and sweeping terms: "The President enjoys complete discretion in the exercise of his Commander-in-Chief authority... "; "[the President has] complete authority over the conduct of war;" "[the] President [is placed] in the dominant constitutional position due to his authority as Commander in Chief ..."; "the conduct of war is a matter that is fundamentally executive in nature, the power over which the Framers vested in a unitary executive." In light of those war powers, he reasons, federal criminal law involving assault, maiming, stalking and torture cannot be applied to the military, for to do so would "infring[e] on the President's ultimate authority [over the conduct of war]"[469] and that those statutes should therefore be interpreted so as not to create a Constitutional conflict.

In his effort to make the point that the torture statute is ambiguous, Mr. Yoo points out, for example, that criminal statutes against murder do not explicitly provide an exception to permit the military forces to kill an enemy in combat – yet clearly the homicide statutes would not be applied to the military in that context. By this logic, he reasons that the torture statute, which does not specifically set forth its applicability to military personnel, would also not apply to the military.[470] He compares applying criminal torture laws against service personnel who torture in the performance of their duties with, for example, applying criminal drug laws against undercover law enforcement officers who possess drugs in the performance of their duties, or applying speeding laws against an ambulance driver.[471] According to Mr. Yoo, "the legislative history indicates no intent to apply [the torture prohibition] to the conduct of military personnel."[472]

The application of the torture statute to the military, however, would appear evident from the statute. When Congress enacted the statute, it explicitly stated it was implementing the Convention Against Torture, and that Convention explicitly contemplates that the torture prohibitions were to apply to the military in wartime.[473] For example, Article 2 provides:

1. Each State Party shall take effective legislative, administrative, judicial or other measures to prevent acts of torture in any territory under its jurisdiction.

2. No exceptional circumstances whatsoever, **whether a state of war or a threat or war, internal political instability or any other public emergency, may be invoked as a justification of torture**.

3. An order from a superior officer or a public authority may not be invoked as a justification of torture.[474]

Similarly, Article 10 provides:

1. Each State Party shall ensure that education and information regarding the prohibition against torture are fully included in the training of law enforcement personnel, civil or military, medical personnel, public officials **and other persons who may be involved in the custody, interrogation or treatment of any individual** subjected to any form of arrest, detention or imprisonment.

2. Each State Party shall include this prohibition in the rules or instructions issued in regard to the duties and functions of any such persons.[475]

Further, the prohibition in the torture statute explicitly reaches acts of torture committed "outside the United States,"[476] again contemplating that it would reach actors (such as the military) that operate in the international arena. Moreover, the notion that Congress enacted a ban against torture that would not apply to the circumstances when torture would appear to be the most likely – when used by the military (of any country) against enemies, external and internal – makes no sense.[477]

Again, Mr. Yoo brandished his trump card: if his interpretation of the torture or war crimes statute was wrong, and it was interpreted as applying to the military, then, he claimed, it would be unconstitutional.[478]

On April 16, 2003, Secretary Rumsfeld approved 24 techniques laid out in a memo to General Hill. Four of the techniques were considered stressful enough to require Rumsfeld's explicit approval.[479]

On December 30, 2004, Acting Assistant Attorney General Dan Levin, head of the Justice Department's Office of Legal Counsel, issued a new memorandum that superceded the Yoo-Bybee memorandum. The Levin memorandum stated that "torture is abhorrent," but stated in a footnote that the OLC "[did] not believe that any of their conclusions [in the prior memorandum] would be different under the standards set forth in this memorandum."[480]

Use of Harsh Interrogation at Guantanamo

The techniques set forth in the various memoranda issued in late 2002 and early 2003 were, in fact, used at Guantanamo. Already previously documented in various contexts, this was confirmed by Department of Justice Inspector General Glenn Fine, whose report describing observations of FBI agents visiting Guantanamo, summarized the techniques observed being used on one detainee, Muhammad al-Khatani:

- Tying a dog leash to the detainee's chain, walking him around the room, and leading him through a series of dog tricks

- Repeatedly pouring water on his head

- Stress positions

- 20-hour interrogations

- Stripping him naked in the presence of a female

- Holding him down while a female interrogator straddled the detainee without placing weight on him

- Women's underwear placed over his head and a bra placed over his clothing

- A female interrogator massaging his back and neck region over his clothing

- Describing his mother and sister to him as whores

- Showing him pictures of scantily clothed women

- Discussing his repressed homosexual tendencies in his presence

- A male interrogator dancing with him

- Telling him that people would tell other detainees that he got aroused when male guards searched him

- Forced physical training

- Instructing him to pray to an idol shrine.[481]

Inspector General Fine's report also described the technique of "short-shackling":

> Prolonged short-shackling, in which a detainee's hands were shackled close to his feet to prevent him from standing or sitting comfortably, was another of the most frequently reported techniques observed by FBI agents at Guantanamo. This technique was sometimes used in conjunction with holding detainees in rooms where the temperature was very cold or very hot in order to break the detainees' resolve.

> A DOD investigation, discussed in the Church Report, described the practice of short-shackling prisoners as a "stress position." **Stress positions were prohibited at Guantanamo under DOD policy beginning in January 2003. However, these FBI agents' observations confirm that prolonged short-shackling continued at Guantanamo for at least a year after the revised DOD policy took effect.**[482]

The use of these interrogation techniques at Guantanamo has also been confirmed by other sources.[483]

Migration of Guantanamo Interrogation Techniques to Abu Ghraib

It has been established that the Guantanamo techniques "migrated" to Abu Ghraib. An internal Department of Defense report stated:

In August 2003, [Major General] Geoffrey Miller [then Commander of Guantanamo] arrived [in Iraq] to conduct an assessment of DoD counterterrorism interrogation and detention operations in Iraq.... **He brought to Iraq the Secretary of Defense's April 16, 2003 policy guidelines for Guantanamo – which he reportedly gave to CJTF-7[484] as a potential model – recommending a command-wide policy be established. He noted, however, the Geneva Conventions did apply to Iraq**.... [T]here was also a store of common lore and practice within the interrogator community circulating through Guantanamo, Afghanistan and elsewhere.[485]

Indeed, although the Administration had acknowledged that the Geneva Conventions applied to the treatment and interrogation of detainees in Iraq,[486] Air Force interrogator Steve Kleinman testified before the Senate Armed Services Committee that he had observed interrogations in Iraq that would clearly violate the Conventions.[487] Mr. Kleinman further testified that, when he complained of these apparent violations of Geneva Convention obligations, he was told that Department of Defense Counsel William "Jim" Haynes had approved the interrogation methods and that "terrorists" detained in Iraq were not entitled to Geneva convention protections.

Though the Administration has attempted to lay the blame for abuses at Abu Ghraib on a "few bad apples,"[488] according to a bipartisan report by the Senate Armed forces Committee, the record indicates that the actions there were rooted in the decisions associated with the use of harsh interrogation techniques at Guantanamo – including techniques developed from SERE training – and in particular, the decision by Secretary Rumsfeld to implement those techniques in December of 2002. The Senate Armed Service Committee concluded:

> The abuse of detainees at Abu Ghraib in late 2003 was not simply the result of a few soldiers acting on their own. Interrogation techniques such as stripping detainees of their clothes, placing them in stress positions, and using military working dogs to intimidate them appeared in Iraq only after they had been approved for use in Afghanistan and at GTMO. **Secretary of Defense Donald Rumsfeld's December 2, 2002 authorization of aggressive interrogation techniques and subsequent interrogation policies and plans approved by senior military and civilian officials conveyed the message that physical pressures and degradation were appropriate treatment for detainees in U.S. military custody.** What followed was an erosion in standards dictating that detainees be treated humanely. [489]

Role of High-level Officials

It has also been reported that the decisions as to which techniques were to be used on which detainees were made by a "Principals Group" consisting of the most senior officials in the Bush Administration, including Vice President Cheney, former National Security Advisor Condoleezza Rice, Defense Secretary Donald Rumsfeld, and Secretary of State Colin Powell, as well as CIA Director George Tenet and Attorney General John Ashcroft. ABC News reported, for example:

> The so-called Principals who participated in the meetings also approved the use of "combined" interrogation techniques – using different techniques during interrogations, instead of using one method at a time – on terrorist suspects who proved difficult to break, sources said.
>
> **Highly placed sources said a handful of top advisers signed off on how the CIA would interrogate top al Qaeda suspects – whether they would be slapped, pushed, deprived of sleep or subjected to simulated drowning, called waterboarding.**
>
> The high-level discussions about these "enhanced interrogation techniques" were so detailed, these sources said, some of the interrogation sessions were almost choreographed – down to the number of times CIA agents could use a specific tactic.
>
> The advisers were members of the National Security Council's Principals Committee, a select group of senior officials who met frequently to advise President Bush on issues of national security policy.
>
> **At the time, the Principals Committee included Vice President Cheney, former National Security Advisor Condoleezza Rice, Defense Secretary Donald Rumsfeld and Secretary of State Colin Powell, as well as CIA Director George Tenet and Attorney General John Ashcroft.**[490]

ABC News further reported that Attorney General Ashcroft, for one, was less than comfortable in that role: "Then-Attorney General Ashcroft was troubled by the discussions. He agreed with the general policy decision to allow aggressive tactics and had repeatedly advised that they were legal. But he argued that senior White House advisers should not be involved in the grim details of interrogations, sources said."[491]

The Congress and the President Battle over Interrogation Techniques

In June of 2004, the August 1, 2002, Torture Memorandum was leaked and published by

The Washington Post,[492] and over the next year additional details emerged concerning the Administration's interrogation practices.

In December 2005, Congress passed the Detainee Treatment Act of 2005, which President Bush signed into law in January 2006.[493] This Act addressed permissible interrogation practices for both the Armed Forces and the intelligence community:

- As to the Armed Forces, section 1002(a) provided that "[n]o person in the custody or under the effective control of the Department of Defense or under detention in a Department of Defense facility shall be subject to any treatment or technique of interrogation not authorized by and listed in the United States Army Field Manual on Intelligence Interrogation."

- Recognizing that persons were held not only by the Armed Forces but by the intelligence community, section 1003(a) provided that "[n]o individual in the custody or under the physical control of the United States Government, regardless of nationality or physical location, shall be subject to cruel, inhuman, or degrading treatment or punishment."[494]

- Section 1004(a) provided an affirmative defense – retroactive as well as prospective – for those who may have engaged in what otherwise might be considered to have been criminal conduct in connection with interrogation, providing that in civil or criminal actions against government personnel, it shall be a defense that "a person of ordinary sense and understanding would not know the practices were unlawful," and that "[g]ood faith reliance on advice of counsel should be an important factor, among others, to consider in assessing whether a person of ordinary sense and understanding would have known the practices to be unlawful."[495]

After its enactment, however, the President issued a signing statement declaring that: (i) the Act's scope was unclear, and that he would "construe it" consistent with his Commander-in-Chief powers, and (ii) he did not accept that under the Constitution he was bound by any strictures of the Act:

> The executive branch shall construe Title X in Division A of the Act, relating to detainees, **in a manner consistent with the constitutional authority of the President to supervise the unitary executive branch and as Commander in Chief and consistent with the constitutional limitations on the judicial power**, which will assist in achieving the shared objective of the Congress and the President, evidenced in Title X, of protecting the American people from further terrorist attacks.[496]

124

Following the Supreme Court's June 2006 decision in *Hamdan* invalidating the military commission system set up by the President – among other reasons, because it had not been authorized by Congress, it conflicted with the procedures Congress had established in the Uniform Code of Military Justice, and its procedures did not comply with the Geneva Conventions – the President sought and obtained legislation from Congress that purported to address the defects identified by the Court. (*Hamdan* is discussed in the Interrogation Section in this Report.) In October 2006, the President signed the "Military Commissions Act of 2006" (MCA) into law.[497]

The MCA was designed to remove the chief legal obstacles that the Administration's detention and interrogation policies were facing in the courts. First, the Act provided congressional authorization for a military commission system, in which "unlawful enemy combatants" would be tried, leaving it to the Executive Branch to say who was an unlawful enemy combatant. It permitted the use of evidence obtained by coercion in certain circumstances.[498] It also stripped from Guantanamo detainees their right to seek *habeas* relief in the federal courts.[499]

Second, the Act imposed a new interpretation of how the Geneva Conventions applied. It gave the President the principal role in determining what kinds of conduct would constitute a violation of Common Article 3, also a crime under U.S. law, or would constitute a violation of the prohibition against "cruel, inhuman and degrading" treatment in violation of the Conventions, a "grave breach" of which would also constitute a crime under U.S. law:

> As provided by the Constitution and by this section, the President has the authority for the United States to interpret the meaning and application of the Geneva Conventions and to promulgate higher standards and administrative regulations for violations of treaty obligations which are not grave breaches of the Geneva Conventions.

During debate on the bill in the Senate, Senator John Warner understood this to be a virtue of the bill:

> [T]his bill acknowledges the President's authority under the Constitution to interpret the meaning and application of the Geneva Conventions, and to promulgate administrative regulations for violations of our broader treaty obligations which are not grave breaches of the Geneva Conventions.[500]

But Senator Patrick Leahy saw it in precisely the opposite light:

> In fact, the new legislation muddies the waters. It saddles the War Crimes Act [which criminalizes certain violations of the Geneva

Convention] with a definition of cruel or inhuman treatment so
oblique that it appears to permit all manner of cruel and extreme
interrogation techniques. Senator McCain said this weekend that
some techniques like waterboarding and induced hypothermia
would be banned by the proposed law. But Senator Frist and the
White House disavowed his statements, saying that they preferred
not to say what techniques would or would not be allowed. That is
hardly clarity; it is deliberate confusion.

**Into that breach, this legislation throws the administration's
solution to all problems: more presidential power.** It allows the
administration to promulgate regulations about what conduct
would and would not comport with the Geneva Conventions,
though it does not require the President to specify which particular
techniques can and cannot be used. This is a formula for still fewer
checks and balances and for more abuse, secrecy, and
power-grabbing. It is a formula for immunity for past and future
abuses by the Executive.[501]

The Act did not specify whether "waterboarding" was prohibited. But Senators John
McCain and Lindsey Graham, in a joint statement the following year, said it clearly was:
"Waterboarding is clearly outlawed by several statutes, including both the Detainee Treatment
Act and the Military Commissions Act."[502]

Upon the Senate's passage of the MCA, President Bush quickly asserted that the MCA
would not be interpreted as impacting the CIA's interrogation programs:

The Military Commissions Act of 2006 will allow the continuation
of a CIA program that has been one of America's most potent tools
in fighting the War on Terror. Under this program, suspected
terrorists have been detained and questioned about threats against
our country. Information we have learned from the program has
helped save lives at home and abroad.[503]

The 110th Congress responded to this loophole President Bush sought to create seeking to
give legislative guidance as to the range of permissible conduct of intelligence agency
interrogation, this time by limiting the intelligence community to the techniques in the Army
Field Manual. Section 327(a) of the Intelligence Authorization Act for Fiscal Year 2008 that was
passed by Congress on February 13, 2008, provided:

No individual in the custody or under the effective control of an
element of the intelligence community or instrumentality thereof,
regardless of nationality or physical location, shall be subject to

any treatment or technique of interrogation not authorized by the
United States Army Field Manual on Human Intelligence Collector
Operations.[504]

President Bush vetoed this Act on March 8, 2008. In doing so, he stressed the need for a
separate CIA interrogation program, and specifically noted that "waterboarding" was no longer
part of that program..

> Section 327 of the bill would harm our national security by
> requiring any element of the Intelligence Community to use only
> the interrogation methods authorized in the Army Field Manual on
> Interrogations. It is vitally important that the Central Intelligence
> Agency (CIA) be allowed to maintain a separate and classified
> interrogation program...
>
> My disagreement over section 327 is not over any particular
> interrogation technique; for instance, it is not over waterboarding,
> which is not part of the current CIA program. Rather, my concern
> is the need to maintain a separate CIA program that will shield
> from disclosure to al Qaeda and other terrorists the interrogation
> techniques they may face upon capture. In accordance with a clear
> purpose of the "Military Commissions Act of 2006," my veto is
> intended to allow the continuation of a separate and classified CIA
> interrogation program that the Department of Justice has
> determined is lawful and that operates according to rules distinct
> from the more general rules applicable to the Department of
> Defense. While I will continue to work with the Congress on the
> implementation of laws passed in this area in recent years, I cannot
> sign into law a bill that would prevent me, and future Presidents,
> from authorizing the CIA to conduct a separate, lawful intelligence
> program, and from taking all lawful actions necessary to protect
> Americans from attack.[505]

Destruction of CIA Waterboarding Videotapes

In December 2007, the news media reported that two years earlier, the CIA had destroyed
at least two videotapes documenting the 2002 interrogation of two senior al Qaeda operatives in
the agency's custody.[506] The videotapes depicted CIA operatives subjecting the two terrorism
suspects, Abu Zubaydah (the first detainee in CIA custody) and Abd al-Rahim as-Nashiri, to
severe interrogation techniques, including waterboarding.[507] They were destroyed around
November 2005, in the midst of judicial scrutiny of the CIA's detention program, and as
Congress was debating standards for interrogation practices, and insulating them from judicial
review, in what became the Detainee Treatment Act.

In a December 6, 2007, statement to CIA employees, CIA Director Michael Hayden said that the decision to destroy the tapes was made "within the CIA," and that the tapes were destroyed in an effort to protect the safety of undercover officers. General Hayden said that the tapes posed a "serious security risk," and that if they had become public, they would have exposed CIA officials "and their families to retaliation from al Qaeda and its sympathizers." General Hayden further claimed that the tapes no longer had intelligence value.[508] He added that the tapes were mainly used as an "internal check," and that they were destroyed only after the agency's Office of General Counsel and Office of the Inspector General had examined them and determined that they showed lawful methods of questioning.[509] It was reported that the ultimate decision to destroy the tapes was made by Jose Rodriguez, Jr., head of the Directorate of Operations, and that the CIA's own lawyer, John Rizzo, was not notified beforehand.[510]

Although General Hayden claimed that congressional oversight committees had been fully briefed about the existence of the tapes, and told in advance of the decision to destroy them, Congressman Peter Hoekstra (the House Intelligence Committee's chairman from 2004-2006) later said he was "never briefed or advised that [the] tapes existed, or that they were going to be destroyed."[511] Furthermore, Congresswoman Jane Harman (the Ranking Member of that Committee from 2002-2006), said she had told CIA officials several years ago that destroying any interrogation tapes would be a "bad idea."[512]

On December 19, 2007, *The New York Times* revealed that at least four top White House lawyers had taken part in discussions with the CIA between 2003 and 2005 about whether to destroy the videotapes.[513] According to that report, White House officials who participated in those discussions included then-White House counsel Alberto Gonzales; David Addington; John Bellinger III, who until January 2005 was the senior lawyer at the National Security Council; and Harriet Miers, then-Deputy White House Counsel, who succeeded Mr. Gonzales in 2005.[514] The accounts further detail that there were conflicting sentiments among White House officials regarding whether or not to destroy the tapes, with some officials expressing "vigorous sentiment" to destroy them.

B.   Committee Action

During the 110th Congress, the House Judiciary Committee conducted over a dozen hearings that either focused exclusively or touched on the problems raised by interrogation policy under the Bush Administration. These included hearings concerning the effectiveness of physically coercive interrogation techniques, potential legal liability relating to destruction by the CIA of harsh interrogation tapes; and a series of hearings concerning the various OLC opinions dealing with interrogation and potential legal liability relating thereto.

Effectiveness of Enhanced Interrogation

On November 8, 2007, the Subcommittee on Constitution, Civil Rights, and Civil Liberties held a hearing titled: "Torture and the Cruel, Inhuman and Degrading Treatment of

Detainees: The Effectiveness and Consequences of 'Enhanced' Interrogation.'" This hearing explored claims that aggressive interrogation – beyond the standards set forth in the Army Field Manual – is necessary and effective when questioning detainees in the Administration's war on terror. Chairman Nadler posed the following questions in his opening: "Does betraying our values make us safer? Do we need to do these terrible things in order to survive in this dangerous world?"[515]

One of the witnesses, a former instructor at the U.S. Navy Survival, Evasion, Resistance and Escape (SERE) School, described waterboarding as follows:

> The SERE [curriculum] was designed over 50 years ago to show that, as a torture instrument, waterboarding is a terrifying, painful and humiliating tool that leaves no physical scars and which can be repeatedly used as an intimidation tool. Waterboarding has the ability to make the subject answer any question with a truth, a half-truth, or outright lie in order to stop the procedure. Subjects usually resort to all three, often in rapid sequence.
>
> Most media representations or recreations of the waterboarding are inaccurate, amateurish, and dangerous improvisations which do not capture the true intensity of the act. Contrary to popular opinion, it is not a simulation of drowning. It is drowning.
>
> In my case, the technique was so fast and professional that I didn't know what was happening until the water entered my nose and throat. It then pushes down into the trachea and starts to process a respiratory degradation. **It is an overwhelming experience that induces horror, triggers a frantic survival instinct. As the event unfolded, I was fully conscious of what was happening: I was being tortured.**[516]

Colonel Steven Kleinman, an expert interrogator and human intelligence officer, testified that the conclusion that coercion is an effective means of obtaining reliable intelligence information "is, in my professional opinion, unequivocally false."[517] Witnesses discussed further the lack of reliability of information gained through aggressive, coercive interrogation, and how using such techniques has damaged the U.S. moral and legal standing in the world.

Witnesses also stressed the following points:

- excessive stress, insufficient sleep, and other environmental influences can result in substantial memory deficit, increasing the unreliability of intelligence gathered from a detainee such conditions;[518]

- official authorization of harsh techniques opens the door to widespread abuse and torture of detainees, as illustrated by the widespread abuse of prisoners at Abu Ghraib, with photographs showing use of techniques that had been approved by high-ranking Administration officials for use on detainees at Guantanamo Bay;[519]

- "enhanced" interrogation has devastating physical and mental consequences, with government documents revealing, for example, that a detainee who had been left in a room with a temperature over 100 degrees was found "almost unconscious on the floor, with a pile of hair lying next to him. He had apparently literally been pulling his own hair out throughout the night.";[520]

- the standards of conduct for interrogation contained in the Army Field Manual are sufficiently flexible to allow for fully effective interrogation;[521]

- lowering the standard on how the United States treats its detainees sets a harmful and dangerous standard for treatment of its own servicemen and women by other countries;

- the reported torture and cruel treatment of detainees by the United States has increased anti-American feelings in the Middle East.[522]

Potential Criminal Liability for Destruction of Videotapes

Following reports that the CIA had destroyed videotapes depicting the harsh interrogation of "high value" al Qaeda detainees, the full Committee held the first public hearing on this matter on December 20, 2007.[523] That hearing focused on the possible legal liability related to conduct depicted on interrogation tapes and destruction of the tapes. Despite repeated invitations, the Department of Justice did not appear at the hearing. Other witnesses, including Professor Steven Saltzburg, and Elisa Massimino of Human Rights Watch, explained the need for independent congressional oversight of Administration interrogation policy, and highlighted the following points:

- the apparent purpose for the destruction of tapes was to prevent any review – by any judicial tribunal or Congress – of the interrogation techniques depicted on those tapes, which reportedly included waterboarding;[524]

- with regard to congressional review, the November 2005 destruction of tapes reportedly occurred after discussion with White House lawyers and as Congress was considering imposing additional restrictions on interrogations. At this same time, Vice President Cheney was aggressively lobbying Congress to exempt the CIA from any such restrictions; therefore, the destruction was intended to deprive Congress of information relevant to its oversight role;[525]

- as for judicial review, destruction of the tapes may have violated court orders requiring preservation of evidence of detainee interrogations;[526]

- destruction of the tapes also may jeopardize prosecution of detainees;[527]

- Congress should conduct independent oversight of the issue, particularly given its passage of standards for detainee treatment in the DTA, and its decision to exempt the CIA from those standards.

Chairman Conyers called for Attorney General Mukasey to appoint a truly independent special prosecutor to investigate this matter, and to investigate harsh interrogation methods generally.[528] While Mr. Mukasey did appoint a Department employee to investigate the matter, he refused to appoint an independent prosecutor under the relevant DOJ regulations. That investigation remains ongoing.

OLC Opinions Concerning Enhanced Interrogation and Potential Legal Liability Thereto

The Judiciary Committee held a series of hearings concerning the range of issues stemming from the controversial legal opinions justifying waterboarding and other enhanced interrogation techniques. The issues included potential legal liability relating to such acts, as well as the FBI's involvement.

The first of these hearings took place February 7, 2008 – two days after CIA Director Michael Hayden informed the Senate Select Committee on Intelligence that the CIA had waterboarded three detainees.[529] Chairman Conyers questioned Attorney General Mukasey at an oversight hearing as to whether the Department of Justice would launch a criminal investigation concerning the CIA's use of waterboarding:

Mr. Conyers: **Well, are you ready to start a criminal investigation into whether this confirmed use of waterboarding by United States agents was illegal?**

Mr. Mukasey: ...**No, I am not**, for this reason: Whatever was done as part of a CIA program at the time that it was done was the subject of a Department of Justice opinion through the Office of Legal Counsel and was found to be permissible under law as it existed then.

For me to use the occasion of the disclosure that that technique was one part of the CIA program – an authorized part of the CIA program, would be for me to tell anybody who relied, justifiably, on a Justice Department opinion that not only may they no longer rely on that Justice Department opinion, but that they will now be subject to criminal investigation for having done so.

131

That would put in question not only that opinion, but also any other opinion from the Justice Department.

Essentially, it would tell people: "You rely on a Justice Department opinion as part of a program, then you will be subject to criminal investigation when, as and if the tenure of the person who wrote the position changes or, indeed, the political winds change." And that is not something that I think would be appropriate and it is not something I will do.[530]

Unanswered was the implicit question as to how the Attorney General could know the waterboarding was done in good faith reliance on the OLC opinions and within whatever limits had been set by the Justice Department without first investigating the facts.[531]

Next, at an April 23, 2008, oversight hearing on the FBI, in response to questioning pertaining to his decision to remove his agents from situations in which the CIA was engaging in enhanced interrogation techniques, Director Mueller explained that "our protocol is not to have been – not to use coercion in any of our interrogations or our questioning, and we have abided by our protocol."[532] He also mentioned that the FBI follows its protocol of alerting the proper authorities and determining whether certain interrogation techniques are illegal. When asked whether the FBI followed that protocol in the context of the CIA's interrogation techniques, Director Mueller stated that "we followed our own protocols"[533] and "reached out to DOD and DOJ in terms of activity that [the FBI was] concerned might not be appropriate.[534]

Director Mueller further described the FBI's practices as follows: "[W]e do not engage in coercion in any form, and my saying that meaning, quite obviously, [we] do not engage in torture, but coercion in any form in the course of our interrogations. Our protocol and our policy is to generally develop rapport as the mechanism of obtaining the information we need in the course of an investigation, and I will say it has served us well."[535] Though there was some ambiguity on the matter, it appears that Director Mueller was unaware of, and that the FBI was not involved in, the harsh interrogations inflicted on Mr. al-Marri and Mr. Padilla.[536]

The Committee also explored the question of possible legal liability stemming from the apparent fact that one of the three men who were waterboarded – Abu Zubaydah – was captured in March 2002, and presumably interrogated prior to the August 1, 2002 memorandum authorizing waterboarding, which Attorney General Mukasey alluded to in his testimony.[537] In subsequent hearings, former Attorney General Ashcroft and Attorney General Mukasey were each questioned about the potential criminal responsibility for waterboarding that may have occurred prior to the issuance of that memorandum – that is, at a time when such conduct could not be defended or excused as having occurred in conformance with Justice Department OLC guidance. Neither of them was knowledgeable of the pertinent facts:

On July 17, 2008, former Attorney General Ashcroft testified as follows:

Mr. Nadler: Attorney General Ashcroft, in your testimony you mentioned Abu Zubaydah, who was captured in March 2002. The Inspector General report on the FBI's role in interrogation makes clear that the was interrogated beginning in march of that year. The Yoo-Bybee legal memo [i.e., the "torture memorandum"] was not issued until August 2002. So was the interrogation of Abu Zubaydah before August 2002 done without DOJ legal approval?

Mr. Ashcroft: I don't know.

Mr. Nadler: Well, did you offer legal approval of interrogation methods used at that time?

Mr. Ashcroft: At what time, sir?

Mr. Nadler: Prior to August of 2002, [in] March 2002.

Mr. Ashcroft: I have no recollection of doing that at all.

Mr. Nadler: ...Do you know if waterboarding was used on Abu Zubaydah before the DOJ approved it?

Mr. Ashcroft: I do not.[538]

Attorney General Mukasey was no more responsive at an oversight hearing the following week:

Mr. Nadler: [W]hen you last appeared before this committee [in February 2008], sir, you stated that you could not order an investigation into interrogation practices that have been authorized by the OLC opinions because it would not be fair to infer any possibility of criminal intent to someone who is following an OLC legal opinion. But it is now clear that one of the detainees, Abu Zubaydah, for example, was interrogated for months in the spring and summer of 2002, before the first OLC opinion on the issue we know of, the August 1, 2002, legal memo by John Yoo was issued.

Attorney General Ashcroft testified last week he did not recall providing legal advice on interrogation methods at that time and did not recall whether anyone else at the Department had provided such advice. Now given the uncertainty about whether any legal advice had been provided before these interrogations, have you or anyone at the Department investigated the legality of the interrogation methods used before the August 1 Yoo memo was issued?

Mr. Mukasey: I have not investigated that myself. I think part of that question involves whether the methods employed were consistent with that memo or not, and I don't know whether they were or they were not.

Mr Nadler: Do you think someone should take a look at that?

Mr. Mukasey: I think a look at that may very well be taken or have been taken. I am not specifically aware of it as I sit here.

Mr. Nadler: Can you let us know?

Mr. Mukasey: I will take a look.[539]

On February 14, 2008, the Constitution Subcommittee convened a hearing with the author of some of the memoranda that permitted harsh interrogation practices, the acting head of the Office of Legal Counsel Steven Bradbury.[540] At this hearing, Mr. Bradbury provided detailed information about the Administration's legal analysis of waterboarding, and confirmed that the interrogation program had been derived from military SERE training.[541] Mr. Bradbury sought to deflect Members' concern about the waterboarding practice by arguing that the U.S. form of waterboarding was not the same as that perpetrated during the Spanish Inquisition.

The Committee also pressed the Department of Justice for access to these secret legal memoranda, described in press reports as so disturbing that then-Deputy Attorney General James Comey "told colleagues at the department that they would all be 'ashamed' when the world eventually learned" of them.[542] The Central Intelligence Agency vigorously resisted Committee efforts on this matter, but eventually Committee staff succeeded in obtaining limited access to the documents.

The Committee's interest in the secret work of the Department's Office of Legal Counsel was heightened when the Defense Department declassified and released John Yoo's March 14, 2003, Torture Memorandum. That memorandum referenced nearly a dozen additional non-public legal memoranda, prompting Chairman Conyers and Constitution Subcommittee Chair Nadler to write the Attorney General seeking information about what appeared to be a growing catalog of secret Department opinions on War on Terror issues.[543] The Committee has attempted to obtain all the pertinent memoranda that address the Administration's claimed war powers in areas that touch detention, interrogation, and other areas impacting civil liberties.

On June 27, 2008, after efforts to obtain the memoranda through cooperative means had proven unavailing, the Committee issued a subpoena to the Attorney General seeking, among other documents:

> Complete and unredacted versions... of any and all non-classified, non-public Office of Legal Counsel opinions addressing issues

related in any way to national security, war, terrorism interrogations, civil or constitutional rights of U.S. citizens, or presidential, congressional, of judicial power that the Office of Legal Counsel has issued since January 20, 2001.[544]

While some of these documents have been provided, the Department's refusal to provide a full list of the relevant memoranda makes it impossible to assess how many are still being improperly withheld.

In Spring and Summer 2008, the Committee, largely through the Subcommittee on the Constitution, Civil Rights, and Civil Liberties, held a series of further hearings exploring the origin of and legal rationalization for the Administration's interrogation programs.

At the first of those hearings, on May 6, 2008, Professor Phillipe Sands described the findings of his investigation into these matters and his conclusion that, contrary to Administration assertions, the push to employ the harsh interrogation techniques did not originate on the front lines, but was instead a top-down initiative, approved and pressed at the highest levels of government.[545] Professor Sands also described the key role in this matter played by senior Administration officials such as David Addington at the White House, Jim Haynes and Douglas Feith at the Department of Defense, and John Yoo at the Department of Defense.

Legal ethics expert David Luban of Georgetown University discussed the extraordinary substantive flaws in the John Yoo legal opinions, and raised significant concerns about the process used to draft them.[546] Under questioning, Professor Luban addressed another issue that often comes up during discussion or investigation of interrogation methods, testifying that, in his years of study, including a detailed look at the Bush Administration's claims, he has *never* come across any actual "ticking bomb" scenario of the type often used to justify extreme interrogation measures.[547]

On June 18, 2008, the Subcommittee heard from former Office of Legal Counsel head Daniel Levin and former Chief of Staff to Secretary of State Powell Lawrence Wilkerson.[548] Mr. Levin described his concerns about the substance of and the process used to draft the OLC torture memoranda and his efforts to draft a more responsible replacement memo.[549] Mr. Levin further confirmed that he was forced out of the Office of Legal Counsel by Attorney General Gonzales, at a time when he was preparing additional legal opinions that would impose constraints on the use of harsh interrogation practices such as waterboarding.[550] Mr. Levin was thus never able to complete those opinions; instead, they were finished by Mr. Bradbury, and became the memos that so troubled Jim Comey that he said the Nation would be "ashamed" when they became public.

Colonel Wilkerson testified regarding his own investigation into the Administration's interrogation program, and his concerns about the great harm to the Nation's security that the Administration's policies had wrought. Colonel Wilkerson also described his understanding of

Secretary Powell's views on this matter, stating that Secretary Powell had been very upset with Donald Rumsfeld's approach to these issues, which Secretary Powell believed had harmed the nation. According to Col. Wilkerson, Secretary Powell had also been troubled by the President's role in authorizing these harsh interrogation techniques; in Secretary Powell's view, Mr. Bush was "complicit" in these abuses.[551]

Pursuant to subpoenas issued by the Subcommittee, John Yoo and David Addington, two key architects of the Administration's interrogation policies, appeared before the Subcommittee on June 26, 2008, giving their only public testimony on this subject.[552] Mr. Yoo distanced himself from responsibility for the contents of the August 1, 2002, Torture Memorandum, testifying that "I did not draft it by myself" and that he merely "contributed to the drafting of it."[553] This effort to deny responsibility for the memo was quite striking, considering that in his own book he quite directly states that he was the "drafter" of such opinions.

Mr. Yoo was unwilling to state that *any* interrogation method would be unlawful if the President believed it necessary, even refusing, under questioning by Chairman Conyers, to rule out burying a suspect alive.[554] When asked whether it would constitute torture if an enemy were to use the same interrogation techniques on U.S. personnel that he had approved for use on the enemy, he had trouble providing a direct answer, saying that "it would depend on the circumstances" but that he was "not saying it would never – that it would always not be torture."[555]

Mr. Addington likewise minimized his role in these matters, despite extensive press reports that he was an active and aggressive advocate for the Administration's harsh interrogation program. He stated that he was merely a "client" (or possibly a representative of the White House client) of John Yoo and that he simply approved Mr. Yoo's plan to analyze these legal issues.[556] That testimony is at odds with the numerous reports of his extensive role in advancing and enforcing the Administration's views of presidential power. Furthermore, although Mr. Addington acknowledged being substantially involved in the CIA's interrogation program, he denied that, if aspects of the program were found unlawful, he personally would bear any legal or moral responsibility.[557]

Douglas Feith, former number three official at the Defense Department, also appeared before the Subcommittee as part of this series of hearings. Mr. Feith generally testified that he supported humane treatment of detainees;[558] however, his concept of "humane treatment" included the techniques authorized by Secretary Rumsfeld, at Mr. Feith's urging, in December 2002, including methods such as 20-hour interrogation sections, stress positions, nudity, manipulation of phobias, and unlimited deprivation of light and sound.[559]

Attorney General Ashcroft, in testimony before the House Judiciary Committee on July 17, 2008, was clear that he perceived that Mr. Yoo did not approach the weighty tasks with appropriate independence. Mr. Ashcroft was asked by Rep. Brad Sherman about former OLC head Jack Goldsmith's statement that Mr. Yoo "took instructions" from White House Counsel

Alberto Gonzales "without running the matters by his superiors in the Department of Justice," and that "when the White House wanted to elevate Yoo to lead the office of OLC, [Mr. Ashcroft] put [his] foot down and vetoed Yoo for the job."[560] In response, Mr. Ashcroft stated:

Mr. Ashcroft: Let me say what I can say here. I think it is very important, and this is consistent with the traditions and responsibility of OLC to have independent, detached, fully vetted advice provided by the OLC, the Office of Legal Counsel, to the President of the United States.

During this time in the Justice Department there were key individuals in the Department that served me and served the Department, served America, that expressed to me reservations that related to the proximity that characterized the relationship that he had with various individuals in the administration...

Mr. Sherman: **So you were opposed to Mr. Yoo getting the job as Chief of OLC?**

Mr. Ashcroft: **I felt that the United States of America and the President would both best be served, especially as it related to the characteristics I previously mentioned, if there would be an OLC Chief that would emphasize those characteristics more profoundly.**[561]

Indeed, in some instances Mr. Yoo took positions contrary to those of Attorney General Ashcroft, and in others, he advanced such extreme positions that his successors, Jack Goldsmith and Daniel Levin, had to retract Mr. Yoo's memoranda regarding torture, Mr. Goldsmith, former Deputy Attorney General James Comey, and FBI Director Robert Mueller had to disavow interpretations of law associated with FISA (precipitating the March 4, 2004 hospital confrontation discussed in Part IV of this Section), and Attorney General Mukasey ultimately disavowed Mr. Yoo's conclusion that the Fourth Amendment did not apply to domestic military operations.

III.   Extraordinary Rendition, Ghosting and Black Sites

A.   Factual Background for Legal Memoranda

Subsequent to the September 11th terrorist attacks, press reports and court cases have shed some light on the U.S. government's practice of "extraordinary rendition": the covert transfer of individuals to foreign states in circumstances where torture or cruel, inhuman, or degrading treatment is likely.[562] While defending rendition as a valuable tool in the war on terror,[563] the Bush Administration has kept the specifics of this practice shrouded in secrecy. As a result, it remains unknown how many individuals have been subjected to the Administration's extraordinary rendition program; but U.S. officials have indicated that the practice has been used frequently following the 9/11 attacks.[564] Estimates range from 100-150 to several thousand renditions of terror suspects, to countries including Egypt, Syria, Saudi Arabia, Jordan, and Pakistan.[565] And the facts that have emerged about the program paint a picture, according to *The Washington Post* of a "CIA-sponsored operation... in which terrorism suspects are forcibly taken for interrogation to countries where torture is practiced."[566] As described by one Administration official directly involved in rendering suspects to foreign countries: "We don't kick the [expletive] out of them. We send them to other countries so they can kick the [expletive] out of them."[567]

According to former U.S. government officials, rendition has been used by several administrations, primarily by or at the request of a receiving state and for the purpose of bringing individuals to answer criminal charges in that state.[568] Involvement in these renditions to "justice" has been widely acknowledged;[569] but news reports and individual cases suggest that the purpose of rendition shifted following the 9/11 terrorist attacks from rendition to "justice" to rendition for the purpose of interrogation, often in circumstances indicating that torture was foreseeable.[570]

The transfer of an individual to a country where torture is foreseeable violates U.S. and international law.[571] The U.N. Convention Against Torture and Cruel, Inhuman and Degrading Treatment (Torture Convention) prohibits torture and the transfer of individuals to countries where it is likely that they will be tortured.[572] The Federal Torture Statute criminalizes torture committed outside the United States and the conspiracy to commit torture outside the United States[573] If a U.S. official rendered an individual to another country with the agreement or mutual understanding that the individual would be tortured, the official would be criminally liable under the Federal Torture Statute.[574]

The Administration has taken the position that, to the extent any of these laws apply to its extraordinary rendition program,[575] U.S. officials comply with laws prohibiting transfers in circumstances where torture is likely, by, "when appropriate, obtaining assurances from a foreign government that an individual will not be tortured if transferred to that country."[576] However, press reports, congressional testimony, and the experience of individuals who have apparently been rendered to foreign countries and tortured, indicate that such assurances are insufficient at best, and – at worst – may be a cynical attempt to defeat criminal liability. A March 2005 *Washington Post* article quoted one unnamed CIA officer involved in renditions as describing assurances from other countries as "a farce," while another U.S. government official took the position that "it's beyond that. It's widely understood that interrogation practices that would be illegal in the U.S. are being used."[577] That article reported that the CIA's general counsel requires only a "verbal assurance" from a receiving country's security service that a detainee will be treated humanely before a rendition can take place.[578]

A related component of the CIA rendition program is the agency's use of secret overseas prisons – "black sites" – and its "ghosting" of detainees. According to press reports, six days after the 9/11 attacks, President Bush issued a classified directive authorizing the CIA for the first time to capture, detain, and interrogate terrorism suspects. This directive, which remains secret, allowed the CIA to hold individuals without any official record of doing so, thus avoiding any accountability for or monitoring of their identities, whereabouts, or treatment. Individuals held at these secret "black sites"overseas were held incommunicado – without access to the International Committee of the Red Cross, much less their government officials, families, or lawyers – and subject to aggressive interrogation procedures approved by Department of Justice lawyers for use by the CIA, including waterboarding.[579]

In addition to holding detainees at secret "black sites," according to a Defense Department internal report, the CIA also detained and interrogated individuals at prison facilities in Iraq, without officially acknowledging or registering them as detainees, a practice referred to as holding "ghost" detainees, or "ghosting."[580] Because these detainees were not processed as prisoners, and there are no records or identifying information for them, "the audit trail of personnel responsible for capturing, medically screening, safeguarding and properly interrogating the 'ghost detainees' cannot be determined."[581]

Through use of secret "black sites" and the ghosting of detainees within or among prison facilities in Iraq, the CIA has reportedly engaged in a sustained practice of "enforced disappearance," thereby placing individuals outside the protection of the law, in possible contravention of U.S. and international law.[582] It has been estimated that the CIA "disappeared" at least 100 prisoners subsequent to the 9/11 attacks, with the whereabouts of as many as two to three dozen still unknown.[583]

President Bush finally confirmed the existence of the CIA secret detention program on September 6, 2006 – five years after he secretly authorized it. This revelation came shortly before the fifth anniversary of the 9/11 attacks, and in response to the Supreme Court's decision in *Hamdan v. Rumsfeld*. *Hamdan* held that Common Article 3 of the Geneva Conventions applied to individuals detained in the Administration's war on terror, and that the Administration's military commissions system at Guantanamo violated the Conventions and U.S. law. According to President Bush, the *Hamdan* decision jeopardized the future of the CIA secret detention program, and required the transfer of 14 detainees, previously held secretly by the CIA and subject to an "alternative set" of interrogation procedures, to military detention at Guantanamo Bay, Cuba.[584] That group of detainees included Khalid Sheikh Mohammed, identified by President Bush as "the mastermind behind the 9/11 attacks."

On October 17, 2006, President Bush signed into law the Military Commissions Act (described in Section II of this Chapter) – which he had called for in his September 6, 2006 speech – emphasizing that it would allow the CIA to continue its program of secret detention and interrogation:

> The Military Commissions Act of 2006 is one of the most important pieces of legislation in the war on terror. This bill will allow the Central Intelligence Agency to continue its program for questioning key terrorist leaders.[585]

On July 20, 2007, President Bush issued an executive order interpreting Common Article 3 of the Geneva Conventions as it applies to interrogation programs operated by the CIA.[586] U.S. officials have taken the position that the order authorizes "what the administration calls 'enhanced' interrogation techniques" and have confirmed that the CIA "again is holding prisoners in 'black sites' overseas."[587]

There appears to be considerable evidence with respect to both previous and ongoing use of black sites/ghosting as well as extraordinary rendition. With regard to black sites and ghosting we have the following evidence:

- In February 2008, ABC New reported that the Administration had continued to admit that "alternative" interrogation procedures were used on detainees held in the CIA's black sites (and that at least three of these detainees were waterboarded).[588]

- In 2007 Amnesty International released a Report titled "Off the Record, U.S. Responsibility for Enforced Disappearances in the 'War on Terror,'" describing detainees claiming to have been held and interrogated in secret (and also alleging that they had been tortured). [589]

- Earlier press accounts describing the practice of black sites; [590] the President's own admission regarding black sites in his September 6, 2006, speech, along with the transfer of 14 detainees from such cites to Guantanamo Bay; and Inspector General Reports describing ghosting in Iraq.[591]

And with regard to the practice of extraordinary rendition, we have the following evidence:

- Khaled El-Masri, a German citizen, allegedly was rendered by U.S. agents because he was mistaken for a terror suspect with a similar name from Macedonia, where he was vacationing, to a detention center in Afghanistan, where he was allegedly tortured for several months.[592]

- Binyam Mohammed, an Ethiopian student, was rendered by U.S. agents to prisons in Morocco and Afghanistan, where he was reportedly held and tortured before being transferred to the U.S. detention facility at Guantanamo Bay, Cuba.[593] Mr. Mohammed has alleged that he was held at CIA "black sites" overseas for nearly three years and that, during this time, he was regularly interrogated by a CIA agent and subject to regular beatings, hung for hours from his wrists, and cut with a small scalpel on his chest and penis.[594]

- Mamdouh Habib, an Egyptian-born citizen of Australia, was detained in Pakistan in October 2001, and claims to have been brutally interrogated and placed in the custody of Americans who rendered him to Egypt. Mr. Habib was held in Egypt for six months, where he was reportedly beaten with blunt instruments, threatened with rape, shackled and forced to stand on tiptoe for hours with water up to his chin, and forced into prolonged, painful stress positions.[595] Under brutal interrogation, Mr. Habib made multiple false confessions. He was then returned to U.S. custody and flown to the U.S. detention facility in Guantanamo Bay, Cuba, where he remained until released, without charge, in January 2005.[596]

- Bisher al-Rawi, a British permanent resident, was reportedly kidnaped in Gambia in November 2002 and flown to a CIA site in Afghanistan where he was reportedly imprisoned, interrogated and tortured – including being subject to extreme cold temperatures and beaten – before being transferred to the U.S. detention facility in Guantanamo Bay, Cuba in February 2003.[597] He was imprisoned there until his release, without charge, in March 2007.[598]

- Osama Mustafa Hassan Nasr (Abu Omar), an Egyptian cleric and legal resident of Italy, was abducted in Milan in February 2003, flown to Egypt, and turned over to Egyptian intelligence services, where he was interrogated and allegedly tortured.[599] After nearly four years in custody, Mr. Omar was released in 2007.[600]

- Muhammad Saad Iqbal, a Pakistani, was arrested early in 2002 in Indonesia and flown by the CIA to Egypt, where he was imprisoned for three months, interrogated, and allegedly tortured – including being beaten, tightly shackled, covered with a hood and given drugs, subjected to electric shocks, and denied sleep.[601] After several months, Mr. Iqbal was flown by the CIA to Bagram, the American air base in Afghanistan, where he was held and interrogated for nearly a year – sometimes shackled and handcuffed in a small cage with other detainees – before being transferred to Guantanamo Bay. Mr. Iqbal was released without charge in 2008, after more than six years in American custody.

- Maher Arar, a Canadian citizen, was stopped by U.S. immigration officials as he was changing planes at the JFK Airport in New York City in September 2002 on his way home to Canada from a family vacation. Federal agents and officials detained and interrogated Mr. Arar for nearly two weeks on suspicion that he had ties to al Qaeda and then transferred him to Syria where he was imprisoned for a year and reportedly tortured.

Other countries – including some of our strongest allies – have condemned the Administration's extraordinary rendition of terror suspects, and have taken steps to ensure that they are not cooperating in this practice.[602] In February 2008, Members of Parliament in the United Kingdom accused Administration officials of lying regarding rendition flights, after U.S. officials admitted that prior assurances that British airspace or airfields were not being used for rendition flights had proven false.[603]

German Chancellor Angela Merkel openly disapproved of CIA rendition flights. In December 2005, after she said that Secretary of State Condeeleezza Rice had admitted that mistakes had been made in Mr. El-Masri's case, "aides to Ms. Rice scrambled to deny that, saying instead that Ms. Rice had said only that if mistakes were made, they would be corrected."[604] In June 2007, German authorities issued arrest warrants against ten U.S. agents for their alleged involvement in Mr. El-Masri's rendition.[605]

Similarly, Italian authorities have pursued criminal charges against twenty-six U.S. agents involved in the extraordinary rendition of terror suspect Abu Omar, who was taken from Italy to Egypt, where he was allegedly tortured. And the United Kingdom currently is investigating whether to bring criminal charges against the American CIA agents allegedly responsible for the rendition and torture of Binyam Mohamed.[606]

B.   Committee Action

The Subcommittee on Constitution, Civil Rights, and Civil Liberties, working jointly with the Subcommittee on International Organizations, Human Rights, and Oversight of the House Committee on Foreign Affairs, conducted two hearings focused on rendition. At the first of these hearings, on October 18, 2007, Fred Hitz, the first CIA Inspector General, and a retired career intelligence officer, described what appeared to be the Administration's extraordinary rendition policies as "unwise if not illegal."

> The concept of renditions mutated after 9/11, when "the gloves were taken off" law enforcement and intelligence [and]... instead of snatching the suspected terrorists for trial in the U.S., we delivered them to allied nations for interrogation under rules and circumstances that resulted in the use of interrogation methods beyond what would have been permitted to U.S. authorities.
>
> In some instances, we sought to protect ourselves against blowback by writing a letter to the foreign liaison contact seeking assurances that the methods used would be congruent with international law, but the letter was exchanged at such a low level diplomatically and in such boilerplate language that it was really meaningless as a restraint on the practices of nations with poor human rights records.
>
> **I believe this is doing indirectly what U.S. officials would be prohibited from doing directly and is unwise, if not illegal.**[607]

The particular focus of these hearings was the case of Maher Arar, the Canadian citizen who was seized by U.S. agents and sent to Syria, where he was imprisoned for a year and reportedly tortured.

Mr. Arar testified by satellite that he was stopped by U.S. immigration officials while transiting through JFK airport in New York, detained for nearly two weeks, and then sent to Syria, against his wishes, and despite telling U.S. officials that he would be tortured there. Mr. Arar described his year in a Syrian jail cell as being held "in a grave," and described how, during interrogations, he was blindfolded, punched, and beaten with a shredded electrical cable.[608] He also recalled being placed outside other interrogation rooms, where he could hear other prisoners screaming in pain during interrogations, telling the Subcommittee that "the women's screams haunt me the most."[609]

Other hearing witnesses, law professors Kent Roach and David Cole, described Canada's response to Mr. Arar's case. After Mr. Arar returned to Canada in October 2003, the Canadian government agreed to convene a commission (the "Arar Commission") to investigate his case. The Arar Commission spent two-and-a-half years looking into his case, interviewed 83 witnesses, and subpoenaed approximately 21,000 documents.[610] It ultimately concluded that there was no evidence that Mr. Arar had ever been linked to terrorist groups, or had ever posed a security threat. It further concluded that the Canadian government had shared inaccurate information with the United States, which had led to Mr. Arar's detention by the United States while he was transiting through JFK airport on his way home to Canada.[611]

Following issuance of the Arar Commission's report, Canadian Prime Minister Stephen Harper apologized to Mr. Arar and his family, and announced that the Canadian government would compensate Mr. Arar in the amount of $10.5 million (Canadian). Royal Canadian Military Police Commissioner Giuliano Zaccardelli also apologized to Mr. Arar and his family for RCMP's role in the "terrible injustices" they had endured, and later resigned after admitting that he gave incorrect testimony to the Arar Commission.[612] Mr. Arar has never been charged with wrongdoing by Canada, Syria, or the United States.

As Professor Cole testified, Canada's response "demonstrates how a democracy should respond when such a wrong has been done... By contrast, the United States argues that Arar's claims cannot even be heard in court, claiming that its interest in secrecy trumps even the prohibition on torture."[613] Professor Cole, along with Fred Hitz, former Inspector General and Legislative Counsel of the CIA, and Daniel Benjamin, former National Security Council advisor, also discussed the problematic evolution of the use of rendition following the 9/11 attacks. Their points included:

- Rendition has evolved from a means of bringing suspects from foreign countries to the United States in order to stand trial, into a means for transferring suspects to foreign countries to be interrogated harshly, through the use of methods that violate U.S. and international law.[614]

- The United States's rendition of terror suspects to countries where they have been tortured has undermined the legitimacy of U.S. policy, harmed U.S. relationships with foreign allies, and put future cooperation from foreign allies at risk.[615]

- Rendition to torture violates U.S. and International laws,[616] including the Substantive Due Process Clause of the Fifth Amendment to the U.S. Constitution, the Federal Torture Statute,[617] the Torture Victim Protection Act (TVPA),[618] the Foreign Affairs Reform and Restructuring Act of 1998 (FARRA),[619] the United Nations Convention Against Torture and Other Cruel, Inhuman or Degrading Treatment or Punishment (CAT),[620] and the International Convention on Civil and Political Rights (ICCPR).[621]

- "Assurances" from a receiving country, promising that a suspect will not be tortured, are insufficient. Such assurances are inherently unreliable, because countries that torture generally deny that they do so, and because there is no effective means to monitor the assurances once a suspect has been transferred and is out of the control of the sending state.[622]

During this hearing, both Chairs and both Ranking Members of the Subcommittees apologized to Mr. Arar for his mistreatment at the hands of U.S. officials, with Chairman Nadler further apologizing for the failure of the Administration to remove Mr. Arar from its terror watchlists:

> On behalf of my fellow citizens, I want to apologize to you, Mr. Arar, for the reprehensible conduct of our Government for kidnapping you, for turning you over to Syria, a nation that our own State Department routinely recognizes as routinely practicing torture. I also want to apologize for the continued and, from everything I have seen, some of which I am not at liberty to discuss, baseless decision to maintain the fiction that you are a danger to this country.[623]

Following this hearing, in December 2007, the DHS Office of Inspector General (OIG) finally produced a classified report that had been requested by Mr. Conyers in December, 2003.[624] The report was accompanied by a one-page unclassified summary, which contained a brief recitation of facts already admitted publicly by the Administration, but omitted any conclusions reached or recommendations.

After receiving the classified report and one-page unclassified summary, Chairman Conyers objected to classification of the entire report as "SECRET," noting concerns that "there appears to be significant over-classification" of information, and that there was no explanation of the claim that additional, unclassified information in the report was protected by "legal privileges." Chairman Conyers asked DHS to explain, paragraph-by-paragraph, the basis for its classification and other asserted privileges.[625] In follow-up discussions with Committee staff, the DHS General Counsel agreed to release additional portions of the report, and to identify and explain the specific privileges being claimed for the remaining restricted, but unclassified, information.

Delays in release of a revised report prompted the Constitution Subcommittee to announce another joint hearing. On the eve of this hearing, held June 5, 2008, the DHS General Counsel agreed to release additional portions of the report publicly at the hearing. DHS General Counsel still has not addressed the concerns about significant over-classification with respect to a number of paragraphs designated as "SECRET."

The publicly released version of the DHS OIG report reveals troubling facts suggesting possible criminal misconduct. For example, the Inspector General concluded that, after finding that it was "more likely than not" that Mr. Arar would be tortured if sent to Syria,[626] INS officials still decided that the United States could send Mr. Arar there even though the "assurances upon which INS based Arar's removal were ambiguous regarding the source or authority purporting to bind the Syrian government to protect Arar,"[627] and their "validity" "appears not to have been examined."[628] The Inspector General also expressed concern with the speed with which U.S. officials rushed to remove Mr. Arar, and their possible interference with his access to counsel:

> **The method of the notification of the [Convention Against Torture protection] interview to Arar's attorneys and the notification's proximity to the time of the interview [a phone message left at a work number at 4:30 p.m. on a Sunday for an interview that started at 9:00 p.m. that same Sunday night] were questionable**. INS attorneys believed that Arar and his attorney would have had the opportunity to review the I-148 after its issuance and INS attorneys expected the 'inevitable *habeas*' to be filed at any time. However, that opportunity was never realized as Arar was removed immediately after service of the I-148."[629]

Indeed, Mr. Arar was not served with the I-148 removal order until he was being transported to an airport in New Jersey, where he was the sole passenger boarded on a private plane that ultimately took him to Amman, Jordan via Washington, D.C. He was then transferred to the custody of Syrian officials.[630]

At the June 5, 2008, hearing addressing the Arar rendition, under questioning from Constitution Subcommittee Chairman Jerrold Nadler, current DHS Inspector General Richard L. Skinner, former DHS Inspector General Clark Ervin, and International law expert Scott Horton all testified that they believed the removal of Mr. Arar to Syria may have violated criminal laws, including the Convention Against Torture and Federal Torture Statute.[631] As Mr. Ervin explained:

[t]here is no question but that given everything we know, the intention here was to render him to Syria, as opposed to Canada, because of the certainty that he would be tortured in Syria and he would not be in Canada.[632]

Inspector General Skinner and Professor Horton agreed that, if it could be demonstrated that high-ranking U.S. officials intentionally deprived Mr. Arar of the means to challenge his detention and transfer to Syria with the knowledge that he would likely be tortured there, that would constitute a prima facie case of criminal misconduct.[633]

Following the hearing, Chairmen Conyers, Nadler, and Delahunt called upon Attorney General Mukasey to appoint an outside special counsel to investigate whether criminal laws were violated in Mr. Arar's case because of concerns, in particular, about possible obstruction with Mr. Arar's efforts to obtain legal counsel and the apparent ambiguity regarding the validity of the alleged assurances received from Syria.[634] The Attorney General refused that request.[635]

IV.   Warrantless Surveillance

A.   The Genesis of the Bush Administration's Warrantless Surveillance Program

On or about October 4, 2001, the Bush Administration commenced a program of warrantless foreign intelligence wiretapping – wiretapping not authorized by The Foreign Intelligence Surveillance Act (FISA).[636] This program – referred to as the "President's surveillance program" or the "Terrorist Surveillance Program" (TSP)[637] – was described by Attorney General Gonzales in February 2006 as permitting interceptions "where one party to the communication is outside the U.S. and the government has 'reasonable grounds to believe' that at least one party to the communication is a member or agent of al Qaeda, or an affiliated terrorist organization," and the Program was reviewed and reauthorized by the President approximately every 45 days."[638]

According to Director of National Intelligence (DNI) Michael McConnell, the surveillance program was not static; the "details of the activities [of this program] changed in certain respects over time."[639] Public reporting indicates that the program not only involved the collection of the contents of targeted communications, but also the interception of a large volume of information to collect and analyze "meta-data"such as identifying or routing information for social network analysis[640] without penetrating the content of the communications (hereinafter, "the data-base program").[641] The legal rationale for this program was based, like other parts of the Imperial Presidency, on the Administration's theory of uncheckable presidential power as Commander in Chief, or on the claim that the program was implicitly authorized by Congress in the Authorization for the Use of Military Force (AUMF).

As with the other expansive powers claimed by the Administration in the weeks after 9/11, it appears that the legal justification was obtained from then-Deputy Assistant Attorney

General John Yoo, working closely with Vice President Cheney's staff. *The Washington Post* has reported that "Yoo wrote a memo that said the White House was not bound by a federal law prohibiting warrantless eavesdropping on communications that originated or ended in the United States."[642]

As with other sensitive issues regarding the President's claimed war powers, an extraordinary line of communication was set up between the Department of Justice and the White House, through the Department's Office of Legal Counsel. This alternative line of communication was directly between Mr. Yoo and Mr. Addington in the Office of the Vice President, rather than through Departmental structures that had been developed specifically to prevent abuses of power. Indeed, Mr. Addington was so fiercely protective of the program that he refused to allow even the NSA to know the legal basis for it: it has been reported that when, in late 2003, the NSA's General Counsel and Inspector General sought access to Mr. Yoo's memoranda, which underlay the Attorney General's certification of the form and legality of the President's authorizations, Mr. Addington angrily rebuffed them and sent them away empty-handed.[643]

According to former OLC head Jack Goldsmith, it was Mr. Addington who was the "chief legal architect of the Terrorist Surveillance Program,"[644] and who famously boasted, "[w]e're one bomb away from getting rid of that obnoxious [FISA] court."[645]

The Vice President did not try to conceal his leadership of the program – indeed, it was his office that took the lead in briefing the few Senators and Representatives who were read in to the program. According to *The New York Times*:

> After the special program started, Congressional leaders from both
> political parties were brought to Vice President Dick Cheney's
> office in the White House. The leaders, who included the chairmen
> and ranking members of the Senate and House intelligence
> committees, learned of the N.S.A. operation from Mr. Cheney, Lt.
> Gen. Michael V. Hayden of the Air Force, who was then the
> agency's director and is now a full general and the principal deputy
> director of national intelligence, and George J. Tenet, then the
> director of the C.I.A., officials said.[646]

The Washington Post reported the Vice President's involvement as well. "We met in the Vice President's office [to be briefed on the warrantless surveillance],' recalled former Senator Bob Graham (D-FL). Bush had told Graham already, when the Senator assumed the intelligence panel chairmanship, that 'the Vice President should be your point of contact in the White House.' Cheney, the president said, 'has the portfolio for intelligence activities.'"[647]

This approach continued when Senator Graham was replaced as the leading Democrat on the Intelligence Committee by Senator Jay Rockefeller (D-WV). When Senator Rockefeller was alarmed about information he received in a briefing about the surveillance activities, he was forbidden to follow up with expert staff, but required to present his concerns in a hand-written note to the Vice President.[648] This tight rein was not limited to congressional oversight committees. All secret documents pertaining to the program were kept in the Office of the Vice President, and David Addington had the power within the Administration to reject the NSA's request to review the Yoo memoranda providing the legal justification for the secret program they were being tasked to undertake, and to block for some time attempts to read the Deputy Attorney General into the program.[649]

At some point after the establishment of the initial NSA warrantless surveillance program, the Administration informed Chief Judges Royce Lamberth, and later Colleen Kollar-Kotelly, of the Foreign Intelligence Surveillance Court (FISC) about the program. Both Chief Judges expressed concerns about the program's legality, and sought to ensure that FISA warrants were not issued based on affidavits that contained information from the NSA warrantless surveillance programs.[650] According to government sources, "[b]oth judges expressed concern to senior officials that the president's program, if ever made public and challenged in court, ran a significant risk of being declared unconstitutional... Yet the judges believed they did not have the authority to rule on the president's power to order the eavesdropping... and focused instead on protecting the integrity of the FISA process."[651]

For instance, Chief Judge Royce Lamberth reached a compromise agreement with the Administration on FISA warrant applications involving information developed through the warrantless surveillance program. These applications were to be carefully "tagged." They were to be presented only to the presiding judge. And information obtained through warrantless NSA surveillance could not form the basis for obtaining the FISA warrant; instead, independently gathered information would have to provide the justification for FISA monitoring.[652] Both Chief Judges Lamberth and Kollar-Kotelly were given personal assurances that no information obtained in the warrantless surveillance program would be used to gain warrants from their court.

Despite these assurances, and the existence of minimization procedures to protect Americans' information that might have been inadvertently acquired, information was not as well segregated as intended. For instance, according to *Newsweek*, "although the NSA is supposed to follow data minimization procedures that protect the identities of its intelligence targets, the agency ... apparently revealed the names of more than 10,000 U.S. citizens that it has monitored."[653]

B. Internal Disagreements as to the Program's Legality; Disclosure of the Program by *The New York Times* in December 2005

In late 2003, frustrations with the program within the legal teams at the Justice Department and NSA began to bubble over. John Yoo had left the Department. Jack Goldsmith, the new Assistant Attorney General for the Office of Legal Counsel, was shutting down the informal channels through which David Addington had for so long directed the legal justification for the Administration's interrogation, detention, and surveillance policies. Attorneys became increasingly concerned that the FISC would begin to assert itself. This led to a high-stakes showdown in which the President, confronted by the imminent resignation of the higher levels of the Department of Justice and FBI, blinked. It also appears to have caused such disruption within the Department that a whistleblower was moved to contact *The New York Times*, which eventually revealed the existence of the program.

By early 2004, James A. Baker, Counsel for Intelligence Policy in Justice Department's Office of Intelligence Policy and Review (OIPR), was forced to acknowledge to the FISC that NSA was not providing the Justice Department with the information needed to implement the tagging system, and that the Department may have inadvertently provided the court "tainted" information (that is, information obtained from the President's surveillance programs) to obtain FISA warrants. It seemed that the government's agreement with Judge Kollar-Kotelly and Judge Lamberth had been breached.[654]

Judge Kollar-Kotelly complained to Attorney General Ashcroft, which apparently led to a review of the program.[655] Eventually, the Department agreed that a high-level official would certify that the information provided to the FISC was accurate, or face possible perjury charges. It has been reported that, once the program was disclosed to the public, one of the judges on the court – District Court Judge James Robertson – became so concerned about the program's legality that he resigned his position in protest.[656]

It was not until December 2005 – more than four years after the surveillance program commenced – that aspects of its existence were disclosed publicly. In early 2004, Thomas Tamm, an attorney in OIPR who was not read into the program, became concerned as parts of his workload bumped up against the information that was being segregated per the agreement with the Chief Judges. As he inquired further about what appeared to be a back-door process that was not authorized by FISA, he was warned off. When he asked a supervisor directly if there was a secret program, he was told "I assume what they are doing is illegal." He was told by one of Baker's deputies that the office was in trouble with the Chief Judge of the FISC, and that the special process was being shut down. The deputy told him "[t]his may be [a time] the Attorney General gets indicted."

Shocked by the prospect of illegal activity going on within the Justice Department, Tamm contacted a reporter for *The New York Times*[657] and relayed what little he knew about the program.[658] While a team of *Times* reporters began to investigate the story into the Fall of 2004, initial reporting was suspended after *Times* editors concluded that sourcing was too thin to justify an election-eve bombshell about an illegal surveillance program.[659]

Over a year later, *The New York Times* finally reported on the program, despite an unprecedented last-minute intervention by the Administration, in which President Bush summoned the publisher and editor to the Oval Office to try to dissuade them from running the story.[660] On December 16, 2005, the paper disclosed that the NSA had conducted warrantless wiretaps on certain international communications that may have involved individuals in the United States:

> While many details about the program remain secret, officials familiar with it say the N.S.A. eavesdrops without warrants on up to 500 people in the United States at any given time. The list changes as some names are added and others dropped, so the number monitored in this country may have reached into the thousands since the program began, several officials said.[661]

The salient features of the program, as they emerged, revealed that the various authorizations for the surveillance program had apparently been counter-signed by Attorney General Ashcroft, seemingly with little enthusiasm and through a truncated process that cut out his normal intelligence advisors. As *The New York Times* reported, Mr. Ashcroft initially signed off on the program without formal legal review and without the concurrence of Deputy Attorney General Larry Thompson. Mr. Ashcroft was reported to have complained to associates that the White House "just shoved it in front of me and told me to sign it."[662]

As time went by and he could not bring in his full national security team to discuss the authorizations, Attorney General Ashcroft reportedly became increasingly concerned about the legal underpinnings of the surveillance program. These concerns came to a head in early 2004, as the relationship between the Department and the FISC became strained over the segregated information obtained by non-FISA warrantless electronic surveillance, and as the Vice President's back-door channel into the Department closed.

With John Yoo having departed the Department of Justice, newly appointed OLC chief Jack Goldsmith reviewed the secret wiretapping program, and concluded it was legally flawed and could not withstand legal scrutiny. Deputy Attorney General James Comey agreed with Mr. Goldsmith's legal conclusions. In March of 2004, Attorney General Ashcroft was hospitalized as one of the 45-day authorizations for the program was coming due. The day that Mr. Ashcroft was stricken with pancreatitis, he and Mr. Comey had discussed Jack Goldsmith's findings. In light of that conversation, Mr. Comey refused to certify the periodic authorization for legality in his role as Acting Attorney General.[663]

Mr. Comey was called to the White House and confronted by the Vice President and his lawyers. He refused to back down from the Department's legal concerns. Mr. Comey argued to the Vice President that "[i]f I can't find a lawful basis for something, your telling me you really, really need to do it doesn't help me." He was direct with the Vice President and the intelligence community leaders who Vice President Cheney had assembled to pressure him – the legal reasoning that John Yoo and David Addington had used to create the program was "facially flawed."[664]

That night, a high-stakes incident unfolded. Mr. Comey and FBI Director Robert Mueller had to race to the hospital to shield the prostrate Attorney General from an attempt by White House Counsel Alberto Gonzales and Chief of Staff Andrew Card to pressure him into certifying the program in a weakened state from his intensive-care unit sickbed. Mr. Comey's Senate testimony about this incident dramatically describes the events:

Mr. Comey: In the early part of 2004, the Department of Justice was engaged – the Office of Legal Counsel, under my supervision – in a reevaluation both factually and legally of a particular classified program. And it was a program that was renewed on a regular basis, and required signature by the attorney general certifying to its legality.

And the – and I remember the precise date. The program had to be renewed by March the 11th, which was a Thursday, of 2004. And we were engaged in a very intensive reevaluation of the matter.

And a week before that March 11th deadline, I had a private meeting with the attorney general for an hour, just the two of us, and I laid out for him what we had learned and what our analysis was in this particular matter.

And at the end of that hour-long private session, he and I agreed on a course of action. And within hours he was stricken and taken very, very ill.

Mr. Schumer: (inaudible) You thought something was wrong with how it was being operated or administrated or overseen.

Mr. Comey: We had – yes. We had concerns as to our ability to certify its legality, which was our obligation for the program to be renewed.

The attorney general was taken that very afternoon to George Washington Hospital, where he went into intensive care and remained there for over a week. And I became the acting attorney general.

And over the next week – particularly the following week, on Tuesday – we communicated to the relevant parties at the White House and elsewhere our decision that as acting attorney general I would not certify the program as to its legality and explained our reasoning in detail, which I will not go into here. Nor am I confirming it's any particular program. That was Tuesday that we communicated that.

The next day was Wednesday, March the 10th, the night of the hospital incident. And I was headed home at about 8 o'clock that evening, my security detail was driving me. And I remember exactly where I was – on

151

Constitution Avenue – and got a call from Attorney General Ashcroft's chief of staff telling me that he had gotten a call.

* * * * * * *

[The call was from] Mrs. Ashcroft from the hospital. She had banned all visitors and all phone calls. So I hadn't seen him or talked to him because he was very ill.

And Mrs. Ashcroft reported that a call had come through, and that as a result of that call Mr. Card and Mr. Gonzales were on their way to the hospital to see Mr. Ashcroft.

* * * * * * *

So I hung up the phone, immediately called my chief of staff, told him to get as many of my people as possible to the hospital immediately. I hung up, called Director Mueller and – with whom I'd been discussing this particular matter and had been a great help to me over that week – and told him what was happening. He said, "I'll meet you at the hospital right now."

* * * * * * *

And so I raced to the hospital room, entered. And Mrs. Ashcroft was standing by the hospital bed, Mr. Ashcroft was lying down in the bed, the room was darkened. And I immediately began speaking to him, trying to orient him as to time and place, and try to see if he could focus on what was happening, and it wasn't clear to me that he could. He seemed pretty bad off.

Spoke to Director Mueller by phone. He was on his way. I handed the phone to the head of the security detail and Director Mueller instructed the FBI agents present not to allow me to be removed from the room under any circumstances. And I went back in the room.

* * * * * * *

I sat down in an armchair by the head of the Attorney General's bed. The two other Justice Department people stood behind me. And Mrs. Ashcroft stood by the bed holding her husband's arm. And we waited.

And it was only a matter of minutes that the door opened and in walked Mr. Gonzales, carrying an envelope, and Mr. Card. They came over and

152

stood by the bed. They greeted the attorney general very briefly. And then Mr. Gonzales began to discuss why they were there – to seek his approval for a matter, and explained what the matter was – which I will not do.

And Attorney General Ashcroft then stunned me. He lifted his head off the pillow and in very strong terms expressed his view of the matter, rich in both substance and fact, which stunned me – drawn from the hour-long meeting we'd had a week earlier – and in very strong terms expressed himself, and then laid his head back down on the pillow, seemed spent, and said to them, "But that doesn't matter, because I'm not the Attorney General."[665]

* * * * * * *

And as he laid back down, he said, "But that doesn't matter, because I'm not the attorney general. There is the attorney general," and he pointed to me, and I was just to his left.

The two men did not acknowledge me. They turned and walked from the room. And within just a few moments after that, Director Mueller arrived. I told him quickly what had happened. He had a brief – a memorable brief exchange with the Attorney General and then we went outside in the hallway.

* * * * * * *

While I was talking to Director Mueller, an agent came up to us and said that I had an urgent call in the command center, which was right next door. They had Attorney General Ashcroft in a hallway by himself and there was an empty room next door that was the command.

And he said it was Mr. Card wanting to speak to me.

I took the call. And Mr. Card was very upset and demanded that I come to the White House immediately.

I responded that, after the conduct I had just witnessed, I would not meet with him without a witness present.

He replied, "What conduct? We were just there to wish him well."

And I said again, "After what I just witnessed, I will not meet with you without a witness. And I intend that witness to be the Solicitor General of the United States.

* * * * * * *

> I was very upset. I was angry. I thought I just witnessed an effort to take advantage of a very sick man, who did not have the powers of the attorney general because they had been transferred to me. I thought he had conducted himself, and I said to the attorney general, in a way that demonstrated a strength I had never seen before. But still I thought it was improper.
>
> And it was for that reason that I thought there ought to be somebody with me if I'm going to meet with Mr. Card.[666]

The crisis that this scene triggered cannot be overstated. The White House was willing to circumvent the legal chain of command at the Justice Department to try to pressure a man in intensive care to certify a form that he knew was inaccurate. In the wake of the hospital visit, the Acting Attorney General of the United States – an attorney of unquestioned ethics – was unwilling to meet with the White House Chief of Staff without a witness present. The Director of the FBI posted agents to the Attorney General's sickbed not to guard against terrorists or other threats, but to guard him and his deputy from the White House Counsel and Chief of Staff.[667] As Director Mueller's contemporaneous notes recount, he posted a Attorney General, who he observed to be "feeble, barely articulate, [and] clearly stressed"in the wake of the incident.[668]

The next day, the Vice President forced through – over the Justice Department's objections – an Addington-drafted reauthorization of the program that substituted the White House Counsel for the Attorney General as the official certifying the legality of the program. Immediately, the Acting Attorney General, the Director of the FBI, the General Counsel of the FBI, the General Counsel of the CIA, the Assistant Attorney General for the Office of Legal Counsel, the Assistant Attorney General for the Criminal Division, and other Justice Department officials began to prepare to resign *en masse*.[669] In fact, Attorney General Ashcroft's Chief of Staff asked that Mr. Comey delay his resignation until Mr. Ashcroft's medical condition improved, so that he could join the group in resigning.[670]

As is recounted by Barton Gellman in his Pulitzer-prizewinning series on Vice President Cheney, on March 12, 2004, President Bush countermanded the authorization that he had signed the day before when he realized that Mr. Comey and FBI Director Mueller were planning to resign that afternoon. In pulling back from the brink, President Bush allowed the Justice Department to not only reassess the legal underpinnings of the program, but to demand modifications to the program as well. Some of the changes that were made as a result of the near-rebellion are public. For instance, by the end of the summer of 2004, the Justice Department and the NSA had promulgated an internal checklist to determine whether probable cause existed to monitor conversations under the program, rather than trying to legally justify

154

undifferentiated dragnet surveillance.[671]

C. Bush Administration's Public Statements Concerning Warrantless Surveillance

Despite all of the internal questions that were being raised as to the legality of the warrantless surveillance program, President Bush publicly made statements that implied that all wiretaps involved court orders. For instance, on April 19, 2004, in arguing for renewal of the PATRIOT Act, the President stated:

> I'll tell you another good thing that happened. Before September the 11th, investigators had better tools to fight organized crime than to fight international terrorism. That was the reality. For years, law enforcement used so-called roving wire taps to investigate organized crime. **You see, what that meant is if you got a wire tap by court order – and, by the way, everything you hear about requires court order, requires there to be permission from a FISA court, for example.**[672]

The next day, as he continued to press for reauthorization of the PATRIOT Act, the President again made a statement implying that the foreign intelligence collection system was one that depended on wiretaps: **"When we're talking about chasing down terrorists, we're talking about getting a court order before we do so."**[673]

President Bush made similar statements throughout 2005. For instance, in June 2005, President Bush told the Ohio State Highway Patrol that "Law enforcement officers need a federal judge's permission to wiretap a foreign terrorist's phone, a federal judge's permission to track his calls, or a federal judge's permission to search his property."[674] Similarly, in an event at the Port of Baltimore in July, 2005, President Bush tried to rebut concerns about civil liberties in anti-terrorist activities, stating "Law enforcement officers need a federal judge's permission to wiretap a foreign terrorist's phone, or to track his calls, or to search his property."[675]

Once the warrantless wiretapping program became public, the Administration's denials switched to attempts at justification. In December 2005, after *The New York Times* ran the story that the Aministration had engaged in various warrantless wiretapping programs, President Bush admitted to at least portions of the program.[676] Under one description, the NSA targeted international communications when there was cause to believe that at least one party to the communication was outside of the United States and was a member or agent of al Qaeda or an associated terrorist organization.[677]

The notion that collection was permissible when only one party to the conversation was outside of the United States ("one-end-foreign") directly contradicted the common understanding that collection of communications within the United States was covered by the Fourth

Amendment and FISA. FISA *specifically* applied to the "interception of international wire communications to or from any person (whether or not a U.S. person) within the United States without the consent of at least one party."[678] And yet, in defending the President's surveillance program, the Administration claimed that such interceptions were legal, and acted as though this had never been in question. For instance, in a speech in January 2006, Vice President Cheney brushed aside the firestorm of criticism that followed *The New York Times* piece, stating

> [Y]ou frequently hear this called a "domestic surveillance program." It is not. We are talking about international communications, one end of which we have reason to believe is related to al Qaeda or to terrorist networks affiliated with al Qaeda.

> * * * * * * *

> This is a wartime measure, limited in scope to surveillance associated with terrorists, and conducted in a way that safeguards the civil liberties of our people.[679]

In that speech, Cheney not only ignored the requirements of FISA, but brushed off attacks on the program; in his view, a "vital requirement in the war on terror is that we use whatever means are appropriate to try to find out the intentions of the enemy," and only through "round the clock efforts" and "decisive policies" had major terrorist attacks been averted since those of September 11.

D. Concerns About Legality and Effectiveness of the President's Warrantless Surveillance

As details emerged, the President's surveillance program engendered widespread opposition across the political spectrum. The legal and constitutional underpinnings of the program were questioned by a broad range of observers, including conservatives and non-partisan groups such as: "then-Senate Judiciary Chairman Arlen Specter (R-PA), Senators Chuck Hagel (R-NE), Olympia Snowe (R-ME), Richard Lugar (R-IN), Susan Collins (R-ME), John Sununu (R-NH), Larry Craig (R-ID), Lindsey Graham (R-SC), and John McCain (R-AZ); former GOP Congressman Bob Barr; conservative activists Grover Norquist, David Keene, and Paul Weyrich; former Republican officials such as Judge and former Reagan FBI Director William Sessions, former Reagan Associate Deputy Attorney General Bruce Fein, and former Nixon White House Counsel John Dean; conservative legal scholars such as CATO's Robert Levy and University of Chicago Professor Richard Epstein, noted conservative columnists William Safire, George Will, and Steve Chapman; the American Bar Association; the Congressional Research Service; and numerous current and former members of the Bush Administration."[680]

Among other things, Senator Specter stated that the Administration's legal interpretation "just defies logic and plain English."[681] Numerous government officials who were familiar with the warrantless surveillance program considered it to be "unlawful and possibly unconstitutional, amounting to an improper search."[682] Other officials were quoted as stating that "an investigation should be launched into the way the Bush Administration has turned the intelligence community's most powerful tools against the American people, while officials at the NSA indicated they wanted nothing to do with the program and were fearful that it was an illegal operation.[683]

The consensus that the President's warrantless surveillance activities and the arguments set forth in its defense were a radical departure from accepted FISA law was expressed in detail by David Kris, the former Associate Deputy Attorney General for national security, who issued a 23-page legal analysis finding that the Administration's arguments were "weak" and unlikely to be supported by the court.[684] Thomas H. Kean, Chairman of the 9/11 Commission, counted himself among those who doubted the legality of the program. He said in an interview that the Administration did not inform his commission about the program and that he "wished it had."[685]

One government official involved in the operation of the President's surveillance program said that he had privately complained to a congressional official about his doubts as to the program's legality, but that nothing had come of his inquiry.[686] Another former senior intelligence official at the NSA explicitly stated that "there was apprehension, uncertainty in the minds of many about whether or not the President did have that constitutional or statutory authority."[687]

The Bush Administration has implicitly acknowledged that the President's surveillance program did not meet then-existing FISA requirements. In a letter to the Intelligence Committees in December 2005, the Department of Justice explained to Congress that "FISA could not have provided the speed and agility required for the early warning detection system."[688] As details of the program began to emerge, the Administration issued a public justification of it,[689] claiming that the President had the power to implement it either pursuant to his inherent Article II authority as Commander in Chief, or pursuant to implicit authorization by Congress when it enacted the AUMF.[690]

In a press conference in December 2005, Attorney General Gonzales was asked why the Administration did not seek legislation for the President's surveillance program:

> Q. [Reporter]: If FISA didn't work, why didn't you seek a new statute that allowed something like this legally?

> Mr. Gonzales: That question was asked earlier. We've had discussions with members of Congress, certain members of Congress, about whether or not we could get an amendment to FISA, and **we were advised that that was not likely to be – that was not something we could likely get,** certainly now without jeopardizing the existence of the program, and therefore, killing the

program. And that – and so a decision was made that because we felt that the authorities were there, that we should continue moving forward with this program."[691]

Thus, the Administration asserted on the one hand that Congress authorized the NSA program in the AUMF, and at the same time, said it did not ask Congress for such authorization because it feared Congress would say no. Moreover, the Administration's reliance on the AUMF is belied by the legislative history of the AUMF – Congress specifically *rejected* the Administration's request that the AUMF be written to give the president authority to "use all necessary and appropriate force *in the United States*" as well as "against those nations, organizations, or persons he determines planned, authorized, committed, or aided the terrorist attacks that occurred on September 11, 2001."[692]

Not only did the AUMF not explicitly amend FISA; it is not even clear that the AUMF constitutes a "statute" within the meaning of FISA. As Professor Jonathan Turley explained in a 2006 briefing before House Judiciary Committee Democrats, "the Force Resolution is not a statute for the purpose of Section 1809 [of FISA]."[693] The Congressional Research Service also concluded that, "[a]lthough section 109(a) of FISA does not explicitly limit the language "as authorized by statute" to refer only to Title III and to FISA, the legislative history suggests that such a result was intended."[694]

The Bush Administration was willing to violate FISA, to risk a Constitutional crisis, to put at risk prosecutions, and tie up law enforcement resources in order to pursue its warrantless wiretapping programs. However, there is little indication that the President's surveillance program was beneficial in the war against terrorism, in no small part because the flood of undifferentiated information was so massive as to be meaningless, from an intelligence standpoint. One Pentagon consultant admitted, "[t]he vast majority of what we did with the [NSA] intelligence was ill-focused and not productive. It's intelligence in real time, but you have to know where you're looking and what you're after."[695]

Government sources told *The Washington Post* that the program had had little discernible impact on the government's ability to prevent terrorist plots by al Qaeda, and that fewer than ten U.S. persons per year aroused sufficient suspicion to justify seeking a full-fledged FISA warrant – a "washout" rate so low as to make it doubtful whether the President's program could be deemed reasonable under the Fourth Amendment.[696] In December 2005, *The Washington Times* reported that:

> ... more than four years of surveillance by the National Security
> Agency has failed to capture any high-level al Qaeda operative in
> the United States. They said al Qaeda insurgents have long
> stopped using the phones and even computers to relay messages.
> Instead, they employ couriers. 'They have been way ahead of us in
> communications security,' a law enforcement source said. 'At

most, we have caught some riff-raff. But the heavies remain free and we believe some of them are in the United States.'[697]

According to *The New York Times*, "[L]aw enforcement and counterterrorism officials said the program had uncovered no active Qaeda networks inside the United States planning attacks. 'There were no imminent plots – not inside the United States,' the former FBI official said."[698] On February 2, 2006, FBI Director Mueller testified that the warrantless surveillance program had not identified a single al Qaeda representative in the United States since the September 11 attacks.[699]

The limited usefulness of the President's surveillance program seems to have cut across its various aspects. For instance, *The Washington Post* reported that "[i]ntelligence officers who eavesdropped on thousands of Americans in overseas calls under authority from President Bush have dismissed nearly all of them as potential suspects after hearing nothing pertinent to a terrorist threat, according to accounts from current and former government officials and private-sector sources with knowledge of the technologies in use.[700] So too, there is little evidence that the NSA's domestic data base program aided in the apprehension of terrorists. *Newsweek* reported that "administration officials [they] interviewed … questioned whether the fruits of the NSA [database] program – which they doubted, though not publicly at the risk of losing their jobs – have been worth the cost to privacy."[701]

A former senior prosecutor stated that "[t]he information was so thin, and the connections were so remote, that they never led to anything, and I never heard any follow-up," and FBI resources were sidetracked on fruitless investigations of "dead ends or innocent Americans."[702] Indeed, the leads from the President's surveillance program were seen as so unproductive within the FBI that agents joked that "a new bunch of tips meant more calls to Pizza Hut," even after the NSA began ranking its tips in response to FBI complaints.[703] FBI Director Mueller testified to the Senate that "most leads [received by the FBI], whether it be from the NSA or overseas from the CIA, ultimately turn out not to be valid or worthwhile."[704] And when interviewed by Wolf Blitzer on May 14, 2006, then-Senate Majority Leader Bill Frist (R-TN), while defending the program's lawfulness, refused to identify or even acknowledge any specific successes against terrorism, even though he was asked three separate times whether "there has been one success story that you can point to."[705]

When the Administration sought to amend FISA in the 110th Congress, it had no problem revealing details of the President's non-FISA wiretapping, or broadly characterizing surveillance activities – often inaccurately. After years in which the Administration denied access to Congress about these activities, Director of National Intelligence McConnell revealed certain aspects of the program to the *El Paso Times* in an attempt to explain his actions in negotiating the Protect America Act of 2007.[706] Minority Leader John Boehner was also reported to have perhaps revealed classified information on television about the FISA Court ruling that rejected the Bush Administration's attempts to bring the President's program under the court's imprimatur.[707]

Thereafter, the Administration and its supporters seemingly mischaracterized surveillance activities, and perhaps publicly revealed classified information, inaccurately claiming that TSP-style programs had been used in a terrorism case in Germany, and arguing that traditional FISA standards undercut the military's ability to respond to the kidnaping and murder of soldiers from the 10th Mountain Division in Iraq. Both of these claims were revealed as false when the facts were made public.[708]

In the wake of the December 2005 public disclosure of the Program's existence, the Department of Justice's Office of Professional Responsibility (OPR), at the request of Representative Maurice Hinchey (D-NY), attempted to conduct an internal investigation into the program. This effort died in early 2006, after the President himself denied OPR investigators the necessary security clearances to learn about the program's workings.[709] Immediately after Michael Mukasey was confirmed as Attorney General in November 2007, the investigation was re-opened – a decision that suggested to many that Mukasey "wanted to remedy what many in Congress saw as an improper decision by the President to block the clearances."[710] As this Report is written, we are still awaiting results of that investigation.

In January 2006, the Electronic Frontier Foundation (EFF) filed a federal class-action lawsuit alleging that AT&T had collaborated with the NSA in a massive illegal program to wiretap and data-mine communications. Cases from around the country alleging similar violations were consolidated before Chief Judge Vaughn Walker of the Northern District of California,[711] who declined to dismiss the cases on "state secrets" grounds as urged by the Administration.[712] In January 2009, Judge Walker again refused to dismiss one of the consolidated cases, *Al Haramain Islamic Foundation v. Bush*, holding that the plaintiffs in that case had alleged sufficient facts for their case to proceed, even though the Government had used "state secrets"grounds to withhold classified information the plaintiffs believed would help establish that they were aggrieved parties entitled to sue under FISA.[713]

Another federal lawsuit, filed in January 2006 by the ACLU in the Eastern District of Michigan, alleged both a secret warrantless program to intercept Americans' communications with persons overseas, and a massive data-mining project in which the e-mails call records of Americans were sifted through indiscriminately.[714] In that case, Judge Anna Diggs Taylor granted summary judgment for the ACLU on the issues concerning the President's surveillance program, ruling that warrantless interception within the United States of "international telephone and internet communications of numerous persons and organizations" was illegal.[715]

First, Judge Diggs Taylor ruled, the program violated FISA. "In this case, the President has acted, undisputedly, as FISA forbids. FISA is the expressed statutory policy of our Congress. The presidential power, therefore ... cannot be sustained."[716] Second, it violated the Constitution. "[T]he Office of the Chief Executive has itself been created, with its powers, by the Constitution. There are no hereditary Kings in America and no powers not created by the Constitution. So all 'inherent powers' must derive from that Constitution."[717]

Subsequently, the Sixth Circuit overturned Judge Diggs Taylor's decision, on jurisdictional grounds – without rejecting her substantive reasoning – ruling that the plaintiffs did not have standing to bring the case because they had no evidence with which to establish that they were targets of the warrantless surveillance of which they complained.[718]

E.   Additional Scrutiny and Legislative Activity in the 110th Congress

Following the elections of 2006, in which Democrats gained control of Congress, the Bush Administration brought the President's program under FISC review.[719] According to a public letter from Attorney General Gonzales, on January 10, 2007, the Administration decided to bring these activities (referred to by the Attorney General as the "Terrorist Surveillance Program") within the scrutiny of the FISC.

According to that letter, a judge of the FISC issued an order "authorizing the Government to target for collection international conversations into or out of the United States where there is probable cause to believe that one of the communicants is a member or agent of al Qaeda or an associated terrorist organization." Further, "any electronic surveillance that was occurring as part of the Terrorist Surveillance Program will now be conducted subject to the approval of the Foreign Intelligence Surveillance Court."[720] That judicial oversight soon posed problems, as the Administration's strained theories of presidential power were put to the test by a neutral adjudicator.[721] The court's opportunity to fully examine the program quickly revealed that the President's program was not a simple recasting of existing FISA, but was a dramatically new approach to foreign intelligence surveillance. In May 2007, the FISC rejected the use of administratively-issued programmatic authorizations for the interception of foreign communications which were acquired within the United States.[722]

On June 7, 2007, the Judiciary Committee held its first FISA hearing in the 110th Congress: "Oversight Hearing on the Constitutional Limitations on Domestic Surveillance," under the auspices of the Subcommittee on the Constitution, Civil Rights, and Civil Liberties. At this time, the Administration did not notify the Committee that certain OLC memos written by John Yoo had been repudiated, or that changes to the program had resulted as a consequence of a revitalized FISC. Rather, the Administration characterized the involvement of the FISC as their own "achievement" that allowed the President to decide not to continue the program.[723]

At that hearing, Principal Deputy Assistant Attorney General Steven Bradbury, who was then acting as head of the Office of Legal Counsel, tried to defend the legality of the President's program by simply repeating the justifications set forth in the Justice Department's White Paper of January 2006. Bradbury argued that the President had "full authority" to authorize the TSP in order to carry out his duty "to protect the Nation from armed attack,"and in the alternative, that the AUMF allowed such surveillance, notwithstanding the law that FISA is the exclusive means of electronic surveillance.[724]

In the summer of 2007, the Administration suddenly and urgently called on Congress to enact FISA revisions before its imminent August recess, to close what the Administration termed "pressing gaps" in the surveillance regime. Director McConnell publicly characterized these gaps as having been created by different rulings concerning the surveillance program by different judges of the FISC after the program was brought under its supervision in January 2007, leaving the intelligence community "*in extremis*" after May 31, 2007.[725] According to Director McConnell, this created an "intelligence gap," as the intelligence community worked to prepare FISA warrant applications for countless acquisitions of foreign-to-foreign communications that happened to flow through switches in the United States.

These claims, and the insistence that there was no time for a more deliberative consideration of the important Constitutional issues at stake, that the country was at grave risk, provided the impetus for FISA legislation that was passed on August 4, 2007, and signed into law the following day – the "Protect America Act" (PAA).[726] Congress insisted, however, that the legislation be short-term, to expire in 180 days, so that a more careful examination could be undertaken before any changes became permanent.

The PAA was immediately criticized for lacking prior court approval of the procedures by which Americans' communications would be filtered, for allowing broad collection of information from libraries, landlords, and businesses, and for lacking protections for Americans swept up in overseas dragnets.

Following the passage of the PAA, House Speaker Nancy Pelosi tasked Chairman Conyers and his Intelligence Committee counterpart Silvestre Reyes with immediately revisiting FISA reform to address the weaknesses of the PAA. As those efforts began, Director McConnell, in an interview with the *El Paso Times*, explained details of the program enacted in the PAA, defending the program, and his actions in the legislative effort to pass the PAA. While making his case, Director McConnell may have inadvertently confirmed some of the parameters of the President's program:

> There are a couple of issues to just be sensitive to. There's a claim of reverse targeting. Now what that means is we would target somebody in a foreign country who is calling into the United States and our intent is to not go after the bad guy, but to listen to somebody in the United States. **That's not legal, it's, it would be a breach of the Fourth Amendment. You can go to jail for that sort of thing.**
>
> And if a foreign bad guy is calling into the United States, if there's a need to have a warrant, for the person in the United States, you just get a warrant. And so if a terrorist calls in and it's another terrorist, I think the American public would want us to do surveillance of that U.S. person in this case. So we would just get a warrant and do that.

162

It's a manageable thing. On the U.S. persons side it's 100 or less. And then the foreign side, it's in the thousands. Now there's a sense that we're doing massive data mining. In fact, what we're doing is surgical. A telephone number is surgical. So, if you know what number, you can select it out. So that's, we've got a lot of territory to make up with people believing that we're doing things we're not doing.[727]

On September 5, 2007, the Full Committee began to examine the issue, through the hearing "Warrantless Surveillance and the Foreign Intelligence Surveillance Act: The Role of Checks and Balances in Protecting Americans' Privacy Rights." The hearing continued on September 18, 2007. In that hearing, civil liberties and national security experts Suzanne Spaulding, Mort Halperin, and former Congressmen Bob Barr urged the Committee to draft FISA legislation that preserved the oversight role of the FISC, rather than leaving the wiretapping in the unsupervised hands of the Executive Branch. They also urged that any bill contain protections against reverse targeting, and robust minimization standards to prevent the indiscriminate dissemination of intercepted communications.

Suzanne Spaulding cautioned that oversight and judicial review were necessary not just to protect against abuse, but also to ensure that any surveillance program actually worked. According to Ms. Spaulding, secret programs that mock the rule of law actually hinder our ability to confront the real threats posed by international terrorism, as such cynical exercises weaken our moral authority in the world: "[T]he best way to be strong on terrorism is not to defer to the avaricious accumulation of power by the executive branch but to better understand the true nature of the long-term struggle against violent extremism. We can only defeat this threat by building upon the strengths of our system, including its checks and balances."[728]

A witness called by the Minority, University of Virginia law professor Robert Turner, argued that the president had the power to engage in surveillance without court oversight or congressional sanction, and that even the original FISA statute was an unconstitutional infringement on those powers.[729] For their part, Director McConnell and Assistant Attorney General for National Security Ken Wainstein argued for maximum flexibility for surveillance programs going forward, and for immunity for telecommunications carriers who had cooperated with the President's surveillance program.

In the wake of those hearings, and companion hearings held by the Select Committee on Intelligence,[730] a new bill, H.R. 3773, the "RESTORE Act," was introduced jointly by Chairman Conyers and Select Committee Chairman Silvestre Reyes, which passed the House of Representatives by a 227-189 vote in November 2007. That bill set forth a surveillance program that responded to the expressed needs of the intelligence community while also including important FISC review procedures and civil liberties protections, such as a prohibition on reverse targeting, that were not included in the PAA. The RESTORE Act did not provide the telecommunications carrier immunity for which the Administration had been pressing. The

Senate passed its version of FISA reform legislation in February 2008. Unlike the House bill, the Senate bill provided immunity for the carriers, and had less court review and other protections than did the House bill.

The Committee finally obtained access to the highly-classified documents it had been seeking in January 2008, after months of negotiations[731] and attempts by the Administration to severely limit the access.[732] These documents included the President's authorization for the warrantless wiretapping program, legal opinions underlying the President's program, and the requests sent to the telecommunications companies.[733] Following review of the classified President's surveillance program, the Judiciary Committee conducted lengthy and extensive classified hearings on February 28 and March 5, 2008, to hear testimony from Administration officials and from the telecommunications carriers that had participated in the warrantless surveillance program. A key focus was the issue of retroactive immunity for the carriers.

In the wake of the classified hearings, Democratic Members of the Committee issued an unclassified report concluding that the Bush Administration had not credibly established a justification for Congress to take the extraordinary action of enacting blanket retroactive immunity for the carriers.[734] In their unclassified statement, the Democratic Members indicated that the case for retroactive immunity might have been stronger if the carriers had responded consistently to the Administration's requests; instead, there appeared to be a variety of responses at various times, with differing justifications. The statement also explained that the Members' review of classified information "reinforced serious concerns about the potential illegality of the Administration's actions in authorizing and carrying out its warrantless surveillance program."[735]

Following the classified hearings and issuance of the Democratic report, the House passed a response to the Senate bill. Representing a compromise with the Senate version, the new House bill addressed the issue of telecommunications carrier liability, but not through a grant of immunity. Rather, it responded to concerns that the carriers were hamstrung in their defense by allowing the court access to classified information to enable it to determine whether the carrier's justifications were valid, effectively overruling the Administration's assertion of the state secrets privilege that had blocked the companies from establishing their right to immunity under FISA. Even this provision drew a veto threat from the White House.

In June of 2008, after many months of negotiations between House Democrats and House Republicans, the Senate, and the Administration, a final bill was passed that represented an improvement over the PAA, though it continued to fall short on a number of key issues.

Some of the key positive provisions in the FISA Amendments Act of 2008 (FAA), H.R. 6034, include:

- Requiring prior FISC approval of procedures for overseas surveillance.

- Closing a loophole in FISA that for thirty years had left Americans totally unprotected from surveillance when out of the country, by now requiring a prior showing of probable cause.

- Requiring the Executive Branch to promulgate guidelines for appropriate targeting, for minimization, and to prevent reverse targeting.

- Mandating reports on a number of features of the collection systems authorized by the Act, and these reports must be disclosed to the House and Senate Judiciary Committees, not simply the Intelligence Committees.

- Tasking the Inspectors General of the agencies with intelligence responsibilities to investigate the President's warrantless wiretapping program, and release a public version of their findings. While private litigation can play an important role in uncovering the truth, such a strategy is currently hampered by the state secrets privilege, classification, and other restrictions on information. It is expected that the oversight provisions of the FAA will supplement private efforts to uncover and redress surveillance abuses by the Bush Administration, and to protect Americans in the future.

- Reiterating that FISA is *the only* legal means of electronic surveillance, and that no novel legal theories of presidential power can support additional programs.[736]

- Requiring all future requests to telecommunications carriers or others for assistance to name the specific statutory basis for the request.

Some of the key concerns with the FAA include:

- The omission of the more stringent reverse targeting prohibitions and programs of the alternative bills, such as the RESTORE Act. Most notably, the FAA does not require that the reverse targeting guidelines the FISC must approve define reverse targeting as listening to a foreigner when *a significant purpose* is to target an American; instead, targeting is not reverse targeting unless a *primary* purpose is to target an American.

- The failure of the FAA to mandate the specific criteria of earlier versions of FISA reform, through which reverse targeting could be inferred from a telltale pattern of multiple disseminations of a U.S. person's communications.

- The weakening of emergency provisions of earlier versions of FISA reform, in which the government had to show that the intelligence would be "lost" if they did not act immediately. The FAA allows an exception for exigent circumstances in which surveillance can occur for up to a week before an application is submitted to the FISC. Exigent circumstances are defined broadly, including a circumstance when intelligence might not be "timely acquired."

- The inclusion of provisions allowing for a retroactive grant of telecommunications carrier immunity. While the FAA did provide the courts slightly greater access to information about the program, and did not engage in court-stripping in favor of the secret FISC, the final bill does not provide for effective judicial review of the lawfulness of the President's secret wiretapping program or the lawfulness of the actions of the carriers.

V.   National Security Letters (NSLs) and Exigent Letters

A.   The Increased use of NSLs Subsequent to 9/11 and the Enactment of the PATRIOT Act and PATRIOT Reauthorization Act

National Security Letters (NSLs) are written directives from the FBI to provide information, issued directly to third parties, such as telephone companies, financial institutions, Internet service providers, and consumer credit agencies, without judicial review.[737] Over the last 20 years, Congress has enacted a series of laws authorizing the FBI to use NSLs to obtain information in terrorism, espionage, and classified information leak investigations without obtaining warrants from the FISC or from any other court.[738] The PATRIOT Act substantially expanded the FBI's preexisting authority to obtain information through NSLs, by broadening the scope of entities that could use the authority and the scope of the parties subject to NSLs, and relaxing the preconditions for seeking NSLs.

A November 6, 2005, *Washington Post* article reported that the FBI was at that time issuing 30,000 NSLs per year, a hundredfold increase over historical practices.[739] The article also suggested that the FBI was using NSLs to spy on ordinary Americans – in contrast with the Justice Department's assurances to the Committee a year earlier that the Department was "unaware of any case where any provision of the USA PATRIOT Act has been abused."[740] The Department wrote a letter to then-Chairman F. James Sensenbrenner accusing *The Washington Post* of presenting a "materially misleading portrayal" of the FBI's use of NSLs.[741]

The disclosures in *The Washington Post* article increased congressional concern regarding the potential abuse of NSLs. As a result, in the USA PATRIOT Improvement and Reauthorization Act (PATRIOT Reauthorization Act), enacted on March 9, 2006, Congress directed the Justice Department's Office of the Inspector General (OIG) to review "the effectiveness and use, including any improper or illegal use, of national security letters issued by the Department of Justice."[742] Congress also directed the OIG to review and report on the use of NSLs for two time periods: calendar years 2003 through 2004, and calendar years 2005 through 2006. The first report was provided to Congress in March 2007. The second report, due on December 31, 2007, was not finalized until March 2008.[743]

The PATRIOT Reauthorization Act included requirements that the Attorney General submit to Congress the total number of NSL requests issued under each of the NSL statutes.[744] However, President Bush rebuffed these reporting requirements in a signing statement, declaring that he did not consider himself bound to tell Congress how these authorities were being used and that, despite the law's requirements, he could withhold the information at his discretion. He wrote: "The executive branch shall construe the provisions...that call for furnishing information to entities outside the executive branch... in a manner consistent with the president's constitutional authority to supervise the unitary executive branch and to withhold information."[745]

B. March 2007 Justice Department Inspector General Report and Subsequent Committee Hearings

The March 2007 Justice Department Inspector General report on the FBI's use of NSLs[746] identified a variety of FBI abuses of the expanded NSL authority that Congress had granted the FBI post 9/11. Many of these abuses included gathering vast amounts of irrelevant private information about individuals, uploading and indefinitely retaining it in FBI databases; inaccurate reporting to Congress regarding the number and use of NSLs; issuing NSLs without proper authorization and outside statutory and regulatory requirements; and widespread abuse in the use of so-called "exigent letters" – "emergency" requests for telephone and other data – in non-emergencies, without even a pending investigation, as a means to bypass normal NSL procedures.[747]

In particular, the OIG found that on over 700 occasions, the FBI had obtained telephone toll billing records or subscriber information from three telephone carriers without first issuing NSLs or grand jury subpoenas.[748] Instead, the FBI had issued "exigent letters," signed by FBI Headquarters Counterterrorism Division personnel not authorized to sign NSLs.[749] The FBI Communications Analysis Unit (CAU) contracted with three telephone carriers between May 2003 and March 2004.[750] In order to justify funds for these contracts, the CAU had explained in memoranda that "[p]revious methods of issuing subpoenas or National Security Letters (NSL) and having to wait weeks for their service... is insufficient to meet the FBI's terrorism prevention mission."[751] The exigent letters typically stated that "[d]ue to exigent circumstances, it is requested that records for the attached list of telephone numbers be provided. Subpoenas requesting this information have been submitted to the U.S. Attorney's Office who will process and serve them formally... as expeditiously as possible."[752] However, the OIG learned that, contrary to those assertions, the FBI had obtained the telephone records prior to serving NSLs or grand jury subpoenas, and that the subpoenas had actually not been provided to the U.S. Attorney's Office before the FBI sent the letters to the telephone carriers.[753]

Furthermore, there was often no pending investigation associated with the request at the time the exigent letter was sent, much less any exigent circumstances.[754] Moreover, the FBI was unable to determine which letters were sent in true emergency situations due to inadequate record-keeping.[755] To attempt to cover for these violations, the FBI issued NSLs after-the-fact, sometimes months later;[756] and CAU officials would ask FBI field offices to open new investigations, so the after-the-fact NSLs could be issued, without telling them that the requested documents had already been obtained.[757]

FBI attorneys in the National Security Law Branch (NSLB) became aware of the use of exigent letters in 2004, after FBI field offices complained. In late 2004, an NSLB assistant general counsel advised CAU officials that the practice did not comply with the ECPA NSL statute. The NSLB still recommended the use of exigent letters in true emergencies,[758] however, and offered to dedicate personnel to expedite the issuance of CAU NSL requests, but the CAU never pursued that offer.[759] As of March 2007, the FBI had discontinued the use of exigent letters, but was still unable to determine the extent to which NSLs or grand jury subpoenas were issued to cover the documents requested with "exigent letters."[760]

The OIG concluded that the FBI had "made factual misstatements in its official letters to the telephone companies either as to the existence of an emergency justifying shortcuts around lawful procedures or with respect to steps the FBI supposedly had taken to secure lawful process."[761] The OIG further concluded that the FBI's acquisition of this telephone information circumvented the ECPA NSL statute, and also violated the Attorney General's Guidelines and internal FBI policy.[762]

The OIG also found that the FBI had sent at least 19 "certificate letters" to a Federal Reserve Bank seeking financial records concerning 244 named individuals, instead of issuing NSLs pursuant to the Right to Financial Privacy Act (RFPA).[763] Although most of the individuals whose records were sought were subjects of FBI investigations, not all were.[764] The assistant general counsel discovered by accident in 2004 that these letters had actually requested records from the Federal Reserve Bank, as opposed to merely requesting that a search for records be conducted, as FBI personnel had represented to FBI attorneys.[765]

According to the OIG, the FBI also did not report possible Intelligence Oversight Board violations. OIG reviewed NSL violations that the FBI was required to report to the President's Intelligence Oversight Board (IOB). Executive Order 12863 directs the IOB to inform the president of any activities that the IOB believes "may be unlawful or contrary to Executive Order or presidential directive."[766] The FBI has developed an internal process for self-reporting possible IOB violations to its General Counsel's office.[767]

The FBI identified 26 possible violations involving the use of NSL authorities from 2003 through 2005, of which it reported 19 to the IOB. These 19 violations involved the issuance of NSLs without proper authorization, improper requests under the statutes cited in the NSLs, and unauthorized collection of telephone or Internet e-mail transactional records, including records containing data beyond the time period requested in the NSL itself.[768] Twenty-two of the 26 possible IOB violations were due to FBI errors, while four were due to third-party errors.[769]

In addition to the violations that the FBI reported, the OIG also found possible violations in documents it reviewed relating to NSLs in a sample of FBI investigative files in four FBI field offices. In that review, the OIG found that 17 of these files (or 22%) contained one or more possible violations that the FBI had not identified. These possible violations included infractions that were similar to those that the FBI had identified, but also included instances in which the FBI issued NSLs for different information than what had been approved by the field supervisor. Based on this sample, the OIG concluded that a significant number of possible NSL-related violations are not being identified or reported by the FBI.[770]

The OIG found that the data regarding NSLs issued by the FBI from 2003 through 2005 were incomplete and inaccurate during the relevant review period.[771] The Justice Department was required to file semi-annual classified reports to Congress describing the total number of NSL requests issued pursuant to three of the five NSL authorities.[772] In those reports, the Justice Department provided the number of requests for records and the number of investigations of different persons or organizations that generated NSL requests.[773] These numbers were each broken down into separate categories for investigations of "U.S. persons or organizations" and "non-U.S. persons or organizations."[774]

According to unclassified data that the FBI reported to Congress, the number of NSL requests has increased since 2000. The FBI claimed it issued approximately 8,500 NSL requests in 2000, approximately 39,000 in 2003, approximately 56,000 in 2004, and approximately 47,000 in 2005.[775] However, the OIG concluded that these numbers were inaccurate, due to three flaws in the manner in which the FBI records, forwards, and accounts for information about its use of NSLs, including incomplete and inaccurate information in the Office of General Counsel's National Security Letter database (OGC); the failure of FBI special agents or support personnel to consistently enter the NSL approval Electronic Communications into its Automated Case Support system in a timely manner;[776] and incorrect data entries found when the OIG examined the OGC database.[777]

The OIG also determined that during the period 2003 through 2005, FBI Headquarters Counterterrorism Division had generated over 300 NSLs exclusively from administrative "control files," rather than from "investigative files," in violation of FBI policy as reflected in the FBI's National Foreign Intelligence Program Manual.[778] Less rigorous documentation requirements apply to control files, and the OIG found that the practice of generating NSLs from them made it difficult for FBI supervisors who reviewed the NSLs to determine if the required statutory predicate had been satisfied and whether the information sought was relevant to an authorized investigation.[779]

There was also a concern regarding the retention of information acquired in violation of NSL authorities. According to the report, neither the Attorney General's National Security Investigation Guidelines nor internal FBI policies required the purging of information derived from NSLs in FBI databases, regardless of the outcome of the investigation.[780] Therefore, once information is obtained in response to a NSL, it is indefinitely retained and retrievable by the plethora of authorized personnel who have access to various FBI databases.[781]

On March 20, 2007, the House Judiciary Committee convened a hearing to explore NSL issues including those raised in the Inspector General's report. In his opening statement, Chairman Conyers noted that "in the immediate aftermath of September 11th, the Department of Justice told us that they needed significantly enhanced authority, while promising the members of this committee in no uncertain terms that these new tools would be carefully and appropriately used... [O]ne week ago, the Inspector General told us that the exact opposite was true of the promise that had been made that there was not a single instance, when the PATRIOT Act was being reauthorized, that the law had been abused."[782]

Justice Department Inspector General Glenn Fine and FBI General Counsel Valerie Caproni were the only witnesses. Mr. Fine recounted the 7 instances found in the small sampling from the FBI field office audit in which the FBI had engaged in illegal uses of NSLs, specifically when the FBI obtained information to which it was not entitled via the use of an NSL.[783] Those instances included using NSLs to acquire educational records or full credit reports in a counterintelligence case.[784] Given the small sample size of the audit, Mr. Fine noted that "I think there are possible violations of either law, the attorney general guidelines or the FBI's policies several thousand times, if you statistically extrapolate."[785]

During much of her testimony, FBI General Counsel Valerie Caproni was pressed to respond to the most troubling aspect of the OIG report: the improper use of exigent letters. Ms. Caproni testified that, while the use of the exigent letters had stopped, they "were undoubtedly an inappropriate shortcut to the [statutory] process."[786] Recognizing that the use of exigent letters, among other identified abuses of NSLs, was an indictment on the FBI's ability to police itself, Ms. Caproni testified that "I think this report has told us we internally have to do a far better job at making sure that we are maintaining internal controls over the use of the [NSL] tool."[787] In addressing the issue of accurate congressional reporting, Ms. Caproni said that "[t]he responsibility to gather the data for congressional reporting lies with my division, and we did not do an acceptable job. The processes we put in place for tabulating NSLs were inadequate, and we had no auditing process in place to catch errors."[788] The report had also exposed that, in many of the FBI field offices, the files did not contain signed copies of NSLs that had already been issued. When specifically questioned about this, Ms. Caproni acknowledged that it was a problem but could not explain why it was the case.[789]

Republican Congressman Jim Sensenbrenner, who chaired the Committee when the PATRIOT Act passed in 2001 and when it was reauthorized in 2006, explained during the hearing that "I just make the observation that one of the things that gets people in this town in big trouble is overreaching. I think that, given your report, Mr. Fine, the FBI has had a gross overreach. What this does is it erodes support for the function that the FBI does to protect all of us from future terrorist attacks."[790]

C.   March 2008 Justice Department IG "Assessment of Corrective Action" Report and Subsequent Committee Hearings

In March 2008, the Justice Department OIG released its second report, "A Review of the

FBI's Use of National Security Letters: Assessment of Corrective Actions and Examination of NSL Usage in 2006."[791] The 2008 report found that while top-level FBI officials had shown a commitment to correcting the deficiencies, but that their efforts had not always adequately filtered down to the FBI field offices.[792] The report made several recommendations to address this problem.[793]

The OIG found that the FBI's own reviews had not only confirmed deficiencies identified in OIG reports, it had found additional problems:[794] Among the findings:

- The FBI's own reviews confirmed that the types of deficiencies identified in OIG's 2007 report had occurred throughout the FBI from 2003 through 2006.[795]

- The FBI's field review found a higher overall possible Intelligence Oversight Board (IOB) violation rate (9.43%) than OIG found (7.5%) in the sample that OIG examined in the 2007 report.[796]

- The FBI's review did not capture all NSL-related possible intelligence violations in the files it reviewed.

- FBI inspectors were unable to locate information provided in response to a significant number of NSLs chosen for review in its sample, leading the OIG to conclude that the results of the FBI field review likely understated the rate of possible intelligence violations.[797]

- 11 blanket NSLs issued by Headquarters officials in 2006, seeking telephone data on 3,800 telephone numbers, did not comply with PATRIOT Reauthorization Act requirements, internal FBI policy, or both.[798]

OIG noted that in 2006 the FBI issued 49,425 NSL requests, a 4.7% increase over NSL 2005.[799] And it reconfirmed the finding in its 2007 report that NSL requests generally, and those involving U.S. persons specifically, had increased during the period from 2003 through 2006.[800]

OIG acknowledged that because only one year had passed since the last report, some corrective measures had not been fully implemented, and it might be too early to definitively state whether the corrective measures hade appropriately addressed the problems OIG identified in the 2007 report.[801] The report found that while the majority of NSLs and approval memoranda complied with the PATRIOT Reauthorization Act certification requirements and FBI policy, 17 NSL approval memoranda (5% of the random sample) contained insufficient explanations to justify imposition of these obligations.[802] As a result, OIG suggested that Special Agents in Charge and Chief Division Counsel were not careful in reviewing and approving relevant documents.[803]

OIG also identified Intelligence Oversight Board violations, many of which had been unreported: These included:

- 84 possible intelligence violations involving the use of NSLs, of which the FBI had determined that 34 needed to be reported to the President's Intelligence Oversight Board (IOB).[804]

- Of the 34 intelligence violations, 20 were the result of FBI errors, while 14 resulted initially from mistakes by recipients of the NSLs.[805]

As a result of these findings, OIG ultimately suggested 17 recommendations for the FBI, ranging from improved review of NSL authorities prior to their issuance to the provision of timely reports of possible intelligence violations.[806]

On April 15, 2008, the House Judiciary's Subcommittee on the Constitution, Civil Rights, and Civil Liberties held a second hearing concerning NSLs.[807] The first panel of witnesses at the hearing consisted of OIG Glenn Fine and FBI General Counsel Valerie Caproni. Inspector General Fine's testimony was consistent with the findings in his office's 2008 report. He explained that the FBI had made some progress in implementing the recommendations from the 2007 report,[808] like developing a new data system to facilitate the issuance and tracking of NSLs, issuing guidance memoranda and providing mandatory training to agents, prohibiting the use of exigent letters, and creating a new Office of Integrity and Compliance,[809] but said that "additional work remains to be done."[810] A working group established to examine how NSL-derived information is used and retained by the FBI had not adequately addressed measures to label or tag NSL-derived information, or to minimize the retention and dissemination of such information. The FBI still needed to implement several key recommendations from the 2007 report, including reevaluating the reporting structure for the chief division counsel in each FBI field office. The FBI's own reviews of its field case files found a higher rate of NSL violations than the Inspector General's review. The number of intelligence violations identified by the field reviews was 640, a substantial number, and the number of violations the field offices reported in 2006 was significantly higher than in prior years.[811]

In responding to concerns about the FBI's use of NSLs, Ms. Caproni, while highlighting some of the progress the FBI had made, acknowledged that "there were clearly failures of internal controls, as well as instances in which [the FBI] had inadequate controls and training."[812] While attempting to minimize the FBI's actions, Ms. Caproni said that "the vast majority of [NSL] errors involved third-party errors, that is, the recipient of the NSL giving us more information than we asked for, or inattention to detail..."[813] She acknowledged that the discussion of exigent letters in the Inspector General's 2007 report was "the single most troubling discovery by the inspector general," and that the FBI was already beginning to take corrective actions to remedy the problems that the use of exigent letters produced.[814]

The second panel of witnesses at the hearing included Jameel Jaffer, director of the ACLU's National Security Project; Bruce Fein, adjunct scholar with the American Enterprise

Institute, resident scholar at the Heritage Foundation, lecturer at the Brookings Institution, and adjunct professor at George Washington University; Michael Woods, former chief of the FBI's National Security Unit (1997-2002); and David Kris, former Associate Deputy Attorney General (2000-2003) and currently adjunct professor at Georgetown University Law Center.

Mr. Jaffer explained that, because of changes made by the PATRIOT Act, "the FBI can compile vast dossiers about innocent people – dossiers that could include financial information, credit information and even information that is protected by the First Amendment."[815] He noted that the "inspector general's audits confirm that the FBI is collecting information about people two and three times removed from actual suspects."[816] He also asserted that the problem of gag orders needed to be addressed, and that a potential solution would place time limits on them, and allow NSL recipients to challenge them in court.[817]

Inspector General Fine emphasized that the use of NSLs naturally raises questions about the need for customary checks and balances.[818] In that context, he discussed the fact that with a grand jury, unlike the FBI and NSLs, there "are citizens who decide whether to issue a subpoena for records that are sought in NSLs. And the grand jury is overseen by a judge, an Article III judge."[819] Mr. Woods testified that while NSLs must be flexible and efficient, they need to be controlled, and it is necessary to have "effective minimization rules, effective retention rules."[820] He continued to explain that "beyond the sort of legal effectiveness or legal elegance of [rules governing NSLs], they have to be rules that inspire confidence in the American public, confidence that this authority is under control, confidence that it is being used correctly."[821]

Mr. Kris advocated for the enactment of "a single statute providing for national security subpoenas to replace all of the current NSL provisions."[822] Doing this, he explained, "would streamline and simplify current law, which is both intricate and idiosyncratic, to the detriment of both our liberty and our security."[823]

VI.   Findings

Detention

1.   The President claimed and asserted powers in connection with detainees that, under the Constitution, were not his to claim and assert.

- The President, through the Department of Defense, ordered that detainees be held at Guantanamo Bay for potentially indefinite duration, and sought to deny them access to the U.S. courts or to other procedures required by the Geneva Conventions pursuant to which they could challenge the factual and legal bases of their detention.[824] The Supreme Court held that the Constitution provided the detainees the right to seek *habeas corpus*, that these rights could not be denied by the President, and that only the Congress could suspend the right of *habeas corpus* for them.[825]

- To try the detainees, the President, through others in the Executive Branch, implemented a military commission system that was unlawful because, among other reasons, it had not been authorized by Congress (to whom the Constitution gives the authority to provide for the rules of war), it violated the Uniform Code of Military Justice (duly enacted by Congress), and violated the Geneva Conventions.[826]

2. <u>The President used extreme and unprecedented legal theories to order the detention of Americans or persons detained in America, and, through subordinates, detained them in military custody.</u>

- The President, claiming power as Commander in Chief, ordered that a United States citizen (Jose Padilla), arrested in the United States, be turned over to military custody, where he was then held without counsel, placed in solitary confinement, and subjected to harsh interrogation.[827]

- To frustrate Mr. Padilla's ability to obtain judicial review of the bases for his detention, the Government refused to permit Mr. Padilla access to an attorney, refused to comply with an order of the district court ordering Mr. Padilla to have access to an attorney (instead appealing the order), and only permitted Mr. Padilla access to an attorney 20 months after his turnover to military custody to avoid the prospect of Supreme Court scrutiny of this refusal.

- To avoid Supreme Court review of the Fourth Circuit's opinion upholding Mr. Padilla's military detention, and to preserve that opinion as favorable precedent, the Government transferred him to civilian custody. In the face of a critical reaction from the Fourth Circuit that the Government's litigation positions and tactics undermined the credibility of its representations, the Government said it would not object to the Fourth Circuit's vacating the opinion.

- The President ordered that a lawfully admitted alien, Ali Saleh Kahlah Al-Marri, arrested in the United States, be turned over to military custody, held without counsel, and subjected to harsh interrogation; and the Department of Justice defended these actions by claiming that the President had, in addition to powers granted by the Authorization to Use Military Force, essentially unreviewable power to undertake such actions pursuant to power granted him by the Constitution as Commander in Chief.

- The Department of Justice has opined in other contexts that the President has certain unreviewable powers as Commander in Chief, not subject to check by Congress, that he could exercise to detain persons in the United States – even U.S. citizens. In October 23, 2001, an OLC memorandum asserted that the Fourth

Amendment did not apply to military operations in the United States – a legal position that Attorney General Mukasey has apparently withdrawn. The November 6, 2001, Military Commissions Memorandum similarly concluded that the President, as Commander in Chief, could direct that U.S. citizens be tried by military commissions.

Interrogation

3.   The President, through the Central Intelligence Agency and Department of Defense, has subjected detainees to waterboarding, extreme temperature manipulation, stress positions, sleep deprivation, and other harsh interrogation techniques. There are serious questions whether these actions constitute torture, or a "grave breach" of the prohibition against cruel, inhuman, and degrading treatment, in violation of the Geneva Conventions and U.S. criminal law. These techniques appear to have been approved by the highest officials within the Bush Administration.

- Commencing in late 2001, at about the time the decisions were made to bring detainees to Guantanamo, the Department of Defense "reverse engineered" the SERE interrogation techniques which had been designed to severely test U.S. service personnel as a way of training them to withstand harsh interrogation by the enemy – to use them instead as interrogation techniques *against* Guantanamo Bay detainees.[828]

- The Justice Department Office of Legal Counsel, working with and at the direction of the President's and Vice President's lawyers Alberto Gonzales and David Addington, advanced and relied on flawed and discredited legal rationales in support of the use of these interrogation techniques, including: (i) asserting that al Qaeda and Taliban prisoners were not entitled to the baseline protections of Common Article 3 of the Geneva Conventions, which prohibits torture, and cruel and degrading treatment[829] – a contention subsequently rejected by the Supreme Court in *Hamdan v. Rumsfeld*;[830] and, (ii) advancing legal opinions – in a January 2002 memorandum dealing with the application of the War Crimes Act, an August 1, 2002, Torture Memorandum, and a March 14, 2003, Torture Memorandum – that the President, as Commander in Chief, can order harsh interrogation techniques that might otherwise violate the War Crimes Act or other criminal law, and that any laws or treaties that would constrain him would be unconstitutional. The legal conclusions set forth in the August 1, 2002, Torture Memorandum as to the scope of this presidential power have been withdrawn.

- In another August 1, 2002, Memorandum, the Justice Department OLC specifically approved the use of "waterboarding" by the CIA. Three al Qaeda individuals were waterboarded by U.S. government personnel.

- It is unknown whether waterboarding was initiated prior to the August 1, 2002, Justice Department OLC memorandum that, on its face, would have permitted it. No investigation appears to have been conducted as to potential criminal conduct associated with pre-August 1, 2002, waterboarding or other interrogation practices used at that time.[831]

- In late 2002, Secretary of Defense Donald Rumsfeld approved a list of interrogation techniques that included stress positions, isolation, hooding, nudity, changes in temperature, and exploitation of individual phobias such as fear of dogs, for use on detainees at Guantanamo.[832] Pursuant to this approval, numerous Guantanamo detainees were subjected to harsh interrogation techniques that were not authorized by the Code of Military Justice. [833]

- The use of the harsh interrogation techniques migrated from Guantanamo to Iraq, where they were employed by inexperienced soldiers on the detainees at Abu Ghraib – conduct which has caused severe damage to the United States's reputation and credibility.[834]

- The persons identified with the use of harsh interrogation techniques include Vice President Cheney, then-National Security Advisor Condoleezza Rice, then-Defense Secretary Donald Rumsfeld, then-Secretary of State Colin Powell, then-CIA Director George Tenet, and then-Attorney General John Ashcroft.[835]

- These principals reportedly approved the use of "combined" interrogation techniques – using multiple methods at one time – and the waterboarding of "high value" detainees. Vice President Cheney has publicly associated himself with the CIA's use of these harsh techniques, including waterboarding.[836]

Extraordinary Rendition, Ghosting and Black Sites

4.   President Bush granted the CIA unprecedented authority to detain and interrogate terror suspects, resulting in a secret program in apparent violation of U.S. and International law.

- Six days after the 9/11 attacks, President Bush issued a classified directive, which remains secret, that allowed the CIA for the first time to capture, detain, and interrogate terrorism suspects. Under this authority, the CIA used several methods – including the rendition of suspects to other countries where torture was likely and the use of secret prisons – to avoid legal limits and oversight mechanisms that prevent the torture and other inhumane treatment of detainees.[837]

- The President acknowledged the existence of this secret program – and that detainees had been held secretly by the CIA and subject to an "alternative set" of interrogation procedures – only after the Supreme Court rejected the

Administration's argument that it was not legally bound by the humane treatment requirements in Common Article 3 of the Geneva Conventions.[838]

- Individuals who were subject to the CIA's secret program have reported that they were interrogated using techniques – including beatings, threats of rape, shackling in painful stress positions, extreme sleep and temperature manipulation – that violate prohibitions on torture and other cruel, inhuman, or degrading treatment.[839]

5.   <u>The President's classified directive resulted in the unlawful "extraordinary rendition" of an unknown number of individuals in possible contravention of United States and International Law.</u>

- By or with the assistance of the CIA, anywhere from 100-150 to several thousand terror suspects were abducted and transferred to countries known to practice torture for the apparent purpose of avoiding legal limits – or criminal liability for – harsh interrogation.[840]

- In an apparent effort to avoid legal liability for transferring suspects to torture in violation of U.S. and International law, the Administration has argued that it obtains "assurances" from foreign government that individuals will not be tortured. But press reports, congressional testimony, and the experience of individuals rendered to torture indicate that such assurances are insufficient, and raise troubling questions about whether these assurances have been obtained and relied upon in good faith by U.S. officials.[841]

- Foreign allies have condemned the Administration's "extraordinary rendition" program and have filed criminal charges against U.S. agents involved in renditions in their countries.[842]

- The Inspector General of the Department of Homeland Security has concluded that further investigation is warranted to determine whether criminal laws were violated when U.S. officials rendered Maher Arar to Syria even after finding that it was "more likely than not" that he would be tortured. In that case, the Inspector General concluded that alleged assurances that he would not be tortured "were ambiguous" and their "validity" appeared not to have been examined.[843]

- The Inspector General's investigation into Maher Arar's case was not completed until late 2007 – over four years after it was requested. That investigation was delayed by, among other things, the Administration's use of legal privileges and classification to block even the inspector general's access to information.[844] In half that time, Canada convened and completed a public inquiry into Mr. Arar's case and issued a public 1,600-page, three-volume report with factual background, analysis, and recommendations.

- The Administration has sought to avoid judicial review of its extraordinary rendition program by raising the state secret privilege as a complete bar to suit, arguing that any case involving extraordinary rendition must be dismissed outright and without any effort to determine whether the case can be litigated without disclosure of information harmful to national security.[845]

6.   The President's classified directive resulted in the enforced disappearance of detainees through use of CIA secret overseas prisons – "black sites" – or by the "ghosting" of detainees in possible violation of United States and International Law.

- The CIA appears to have created and maintained a system of secret overseas prisons – "black sites" – that allowed it to detain and interrogate individuals without any official record of doing so. The CIA also "ghosted" detainees, holding them at prison facilities in Iraq without officially acknowledging or registering them as detainees.[846]

- The CIA apparently used these "black sites" or "ghosted" detainees in order to avoid accountability for or monitoring or their identities, whereabouts, or treatment. By placing these detainees outside the protection of the law – denying them access to the International Committee of the Red Cross, government officials, families, or lawyers – the CIA engaged in a sustained practice of "enforced disappearance." [847]

- While the CIA's program of secret detention and interrogation was suspended by President Bush in 2006, following the Supreme Court's *Hamdan* decision that Common Art. 3 of the Geneva Convention applies to detainees in the war on terror, the President's subsequent July 20, 2007 executive order appears to have revived it. The whereabouts of as many as two to three dozen of the estimated 100 or more detainees "disappeared" by the CIA are still unknown.[848]

FISA/Warrantless Surveillance

7.   The Bush Adminstration pursued a warrantless wiretapping program in apparent violation of the Foreign Intelligence Surveillance Act.

- The Administration – through the direction of the Office of the Vice President – conducted warrantless electronic surveillance contrary to the express provisions of the Foreign Intelligence Surveillance Act of 1978 ("FISA") that mandated that FISA shall be the "exclusive means by which electronic surveillance...and the interception of wire and oral communication may be conducted."[849]

- The Administration justified wiretapping outside of FISA by way of a spurious claim that the president had the inherent powers as Commander in Chief to exercise military powers (including spying) inside the domestic United States, and that the Authorization for the Use of Military Force enacted in the wake of the September 11th Attacks had implicitly modified FISA.[850]

- The AUMF did not override FISA's status as the exclusive legal means of foreign intelligence surveillance. Nor did the AUMF override the requirement that statutes be amended through legislative action, rather than implicitly. While FISA certainly is subject to amendment, it is clear that the AUMF does not come close to being an "implicit" amendment.[851] In the January 2006 White Paper that attempted to justify a domestic surveillance program, the Bush Administration was dismissive of clear congressional intent that authorization for expanded surveillance authority would have to take the form of a particularized amendment, relegating this position to one held by "some Members of Congress" at the time FISA was adopted[852] The White Paper failed to note that those "some Members" were actually the committees of jurisdiction who issued the report on the bill.[853]

- The only court to rule on the lawfulness of the program found it unlawful, and among other things rejected the Administration's inherent authority argument, finding that "**There are no hereditary Kings in America and no power not created by the Constitution.**"[854] (The decision was overturned on jurisdictional, not substantive, grounds)

- The Administration admits that it undertook, within the United States and without a warrant from the FISA Court, the widespread collection of international calls and e-mail even when one party to the communications was in the United States.[855] The program also is reputed to have involved the bulk interception and storage of communications in order to sift for patterns and "meta-data."[856]

8.   Legal and policy procedures were circumvented as part of the warrantless surveillance program, to put a legal gloss the Administration's activities.

- The Administration set up secret channels outside of the chain of command, through which the Office of the Vice President and an attorney in the Justice Department's Office of Legal Counsel set surveillance law and policy. This caused the Attorney General to certify the legality of a warrantless surveillance program without full counsel of his national security and intelligence advisors.[857]

- When the Justice Department and the FISA Court began to question the legality of the secret program justified by John Yoo and David Addington, the Administration overrode the concerns of the Acting Attorney General, the Director of the FBI, and senior Justice Department officials. Rather, the

Administration had the White House Counsel certify to the program's lawfulness, on the theory that the president was the ultimate arbiter of what the law is for the Executive Branch.

- The abrogation of long-established processes that ensure sound legal policymaking had the result of the President both authorizing the program and certifying that what had been done was lawful, removing even the thinnest veneer of legal oversight from the extra-legal program.[858]

9.   <u>The Administration tried to conceal its actions by shielding from liability those private companies who cooperated in intercepting communications without a warrant.</u>

- Telecommunications companies willingly participated in warrantless wiretapping, without insisting on FISA warrants or other statutorily-mandated directives or requests. Despite the lack of judicial authorization or a statutory basis for surveillance, the Administration insisted on shielding the companies from lawsuit, so as to prevent a full understanding of the extent of any illegal activities and a full accounting for how those activities came to occur. As reflected in the Democratic House Judiciary Committee Members' public report following review of the secret wirepapping memoranda, there appeared to be a variety of actions at various times with differing justifications in response to Administration requests.[859]

- President Bush and Attorney General Gonzales had a direct conflict of interest when they asserted the state secrets privilege in privacy lawsuits against telecommunications carriers, when they insisted upon immunity for the carriers in FISA reform legislation, and when they denied the Justice Department's Office of Professional Responsibility the ability to investigate a domestic surveillance program. These actions had the effect of shielding their apparently illegal activity from legal scrutiny. Any consideration of the lawfulness of the conduct of the telecommunications carriers would have naturally entailed a consideration of the lawfulness of the Administration's own conduct.

- On this issue, the Administration was on shaky legal ground notwithstanding the secret justifications obtained from John Yoo, and had to know that there would be serious problems if the Justice Department's internal re-evaluation and near rebellion were to ever come to light. The courts had already held that the Administration could not implement military commissions in Guantanamo, Cuba, based on presidential assertions of Commander in Chief power.[860] Here, the Administration would have to maintain that the President enjoyed the power to engage in domestic warrantless surveillance inside the United States even though Congress had specifically enacted a statutory scheme – FISA – to limit him in the exercise of that power. If the AUMF did not authorize the President to exercise certain military powers *outside* of the United States against aliens, it is difficult to imagine any court concluding the AUMF authorized him to conduct warrantless electronic surveillance *inside* the United States against civilians.

10. <u>The President and Vice President misled the public about domestic surveillance programs.</u>

- On many occasions while the warrantless wiretapping program was operating, the President and Vice President made misleading statements to give the impression to the public and to Congress that all foreign surveillance was being conducted through established FISA principles and methods. For instance, just weeks after the crisis in which the leadership of the Justice Department almost resigned en masse over the program, the President gave a speech in which he claimed "everything you hear about requires court order, requires there to be permission from a FISA court. "[861] These public claims contrast with the Administration's arguments – internally, to the FISA Court, and to select congressional intelligence oversight members (conveniently sworn to secrecy).

- These claims are also contradicted by the development, administration, and constant reauthorization of a program which was specifically designed to conduct surveillance without a court order – that is, without a warrant or "permission from a FSIA court." While certain legalities and forms were observed, court orders were specifically *not* required. Indeed, the entire point of the President's non-FISA foreign intelligence surveillance program was to avoid obtaining such orders.

<u>NSLs and Exigent Letters</u>

11. <u>The FBI collected and uploaded personal information on individuals who were innocent and irrelevant to FBI investigations.</u>

- In a few instances, documents reflecting receipt of responsive records specifically incorporated Social Security numbers and date of birth information on individuals who were not relevant to the underlying investigation were electronically uploaded into FBI databases by the field office that served the NSL.[862]

- Neither the Attorney General's National Security Investigation Guidelines nor internal FBI policies required the purging of information derived from NSLs in FBI databases, regardless of the outcome of the investigation.[863] Therefore, once information is obtained in response to a NSL, it is indefinitely retained and retrievable by the plethora of authorized personnel who have access to various FBI databases.

12. <u>The FBI tried to or actually obtained information that it was not entitled to obtain through NSLs.</u>

- The FBI issued an NSL to obtain educational records from a university, even though the particular NSL statute specifically did not authorize the acquisition of education records.[864]

- The FBI acquired full credit reports in a counterintelligence investigation, when full credit reports are only permissible in counterterrorism cases.[865]

- After the FISA Court had denied an FBI request in 2006 for a Section 215 business record order seeking "tangible things" as part of a counterterrorism case – citing First Amendment concerns -- the FBI then circumvented the court's oversight and pursued the investigation using three NSLs based on the same information contained in the Section 215 application, despite the fact that NSLs are subject to the same First Amendment constraints.[866]

- The FBI sent at least 19 "certificate letters" to a Federal Reserve Bank seeking financial records concerning 244 named individuals, instead of issuing NSLs pursuant to the Right to Financial Privacy Act.[867] Although most of the individuals whose records were sought were subjects of FBI investigations, some were not.[868]

13. <u>The FBI was not fully forthcoming with the American public and Congress regarding its use and abuse of national security letters.[869]</u>

- From 2003 through 2005, the FBI identified 26 possible intelligence violations involving its use of NSLs.[870] When the Department of Justice's OIG visited four FBI field offices and reviewed a sample of 77 investigative case files and 293 NSLs, it found 22 possible violations that the FBI had not been identified or reported.[871]

- Given that the Department of Justice's OIG had no reason to believe that the number of violations it identified in the field offices was skewed or disproportionate to the number of violations in other files, the Inspector General Fine concluded that the evidence suggests that the large number of NSL-related violations throughout the FBI had not been identified or reported by FBI personnel.[872]

- According to unclassified data that the FBI reported to Congress, the number of NSL requests has increased since 2000. The FBI claimed it issued approximately 8,500 NSL requests in 2000, approximately 39,000 in 2003, approximately 56,000 in 2004, and approximately 47,000 in 2005.[873] However, the Department of

Justice's Inspector General concluded that these numbers were inaccurate due to three flaws in the manner in which the FBI records, forwards, and accounts for information about its use of NSLs, including incomplete and inaccurate information in the Office of General Counsel's National Security Letter database; the failure of FBI special agents or support personnel to consistently enter the NSL approval Electronic Communications into its Automated Case Support system in a timely manner;[874] and incorrect data entries when it examined the OGC database.[875]

- FBI General Counsel Valerie Caproni acknowledged that "[t]he responsibility to gather the data for congressional reporting lies with my division, and we did not do an acceptable job. The processes we put in place for tabulating NSLs were inadequate, and we had no auditing process in place to catch errors."[876]

14. <u>Through the improper use of exigent letters, the Administration circumvented statutory NSL procedures, Attorney General Guidelines, and FBI policies by collecting telephone toll billing records or subscriber information from three telephone companies without first issuing NSLs or grand jury subpoenas.</u>[877]

- The FBI used these exigent letters in non-emergency circumstances and failed to ensure that there were authorized investigations to which the requests could be tied.[878]

- The exigent letters also inaccurately represented that the FBI had already requested subpoenas for the information when in fact it had not.[879]

- The FBI failed to ensure that NSLs were issued promptly to telephone companies after the exigent letters were sent; instead, after obtaining the records from telephone companies, the FBI often issued NSLs *months* after the fact to cover the information it had already obtained.[880]

- The exigent letters were signed by FBI Headquarters Counterterrorism Division personnel who were not authorized to sign NSLs.[881]

- National Security Law Branch (NSLB) FBI attorneys became aware of the use of exigent letters as early as 2004, after FBI field offices complained to them.[882]

- In late 2004, although an NSLB Assistant General Counsel counseled FBI officials that the practice of using exigent letters did not comply with the NSL statute, the NSLB office still recommended their use in true emergencies.[883]

- The FBI issued 11 "blanket NSLs" in 2006 seeking data on 3,860 telephone numbers. The Department of Justice's Inspector General found that none of these "blanket NSLs" complied with FBI policy and eight imposed non-disclosure requirements on recipients that did not comply with the law. The "blanket NSLs" were written to "cover information already acquired through exigent letters and other informal requests."[884]

Section 3 – Misuse of Executive Branch Authority

*Our Constitution is very clear...in making the President an
overseer of all the varied duties the Congress creates for
government agencies to perform. Yet our Constitution is equally
clear in permitting Congress to assign these duties to them and not
the President. He is not "the decider," but the overseer of
decisions by others. When the President fails to honor that
admittedly subtle distinction, he fails in his constitutional
responsibility to "take Care that the Laws be faithfully executed."
The assignment of decisional responsibility to others is a part of
those laws to whose faithful execution he must see.*[885]

– Professor Peter L. Strauss, Columbia Law School

Serious concerns have been raised about the Bush Administration's efforts to override or contradict congressional authority in several respects, including through the use of presidential signing statements and the agency rulemaking process. President Bush has used signing statements – formal statements issued by a president when he signs legislation – to claim the power to nullify, without a veto, parts of more than 100 laws passed by Congress, based on assertions of executive authority and the theory of the "unitary executive." These include assertions of the power to violate legislation concerning such matters as the treatment of detainees, whistleblower protections, affirmative action, and censorship of scientific data. Specific examples include the McCain Amendment, which explicitly outlawed cruel, inhuman, and degrading treatment of detainees held by the United States; provisions of the 2005 Energy Policy Act protecting whistleblowers at the Department of Energy; and provisions in the 2004 Intelligence Reform and Terrorism Prevention Act that directed the national intelligence director to recruit and train more women and minorities in order to diversify the intelligence community.

The Bush Administration's aggrandized control over the rulemaking process may be the strongest assertion of presidential power in this area in decades, to the detriment of the public interest. A most notable example is President Bush's Executive Order 13422, which substantially changes how regulations are promulgated. Some fear that it is a "power grab" that can be used to undermine public protections and that it represents "an attempt to bypass Congress by establishing standards for regulatory initiation that are not consistent with statutory requirements."[886] In addition, certain rules protecting public health and the environment have been delayed or weakened because of intervention by the Bush Administration. The Administration used directives and other alternative processes as a means to circumvent formal rulemaking and override congressional intent.

I. Presidential Signing Statements

The first oversight hearing held by the House Judiciary Committee in the 110th Congress, on January 31, 2007, concerned the use of presidential signing statements by the Bush Administration.[887] Although presidents have often issued signing statements when enacting legislation to explain their interpretation of the law, significant controversy had arisen because President Bush's statements often challenged or indicated a possible intent to disregard specific statutory provisions. In 2006, the issue attracted significant press attention, a Senate Judiciary Committee hearing,[888] and a report by an American Bar Association Task Force. The Task Force concluded that the use of signing statements to claim the power to disregard legislation is "contrary to the rule of law and our constitutional system of separation of power" and recommended additional congressional oversight on the subject.[889]

A.   Historical Background

Presidents have used signing statements since the Monroe Administration,[890] and the first controversies regarding signing statements arose during the Jackson and Tyler Administrations.[891] Presidents Polk and Pierce appeared to move away from signing statements, and President Grant, while using them, admitted that it was an unusual practice.[892]

Signing statements, particularly those used to voice constitutional objections, became somewhat more common by 1950.[893] They reached a new prominence, however, during the Reagan Administration. President Reagan issued 276 signing statements, 71 of which (26%) questioned the constitutionality of a statutory provision.[894] The Reagan Administration's goal, as articulated by then-Office of Legal Counsel lawyer Samuel Alito, was to establish the signing statement as part of a statute's legislative history that courts would use in interpretation.[895] This met with limited success; while the Supreme Court referenced signing statements in two major cases, there is no indication that it granted them any significant weight.[896] In one particularly contentious case, President Reagan used a signing statement to state that he was specifically instructing the Attorney General not to comply with portions of a law he considered unconstitutional.[897] However, after unfavorable judicial rulings that upheld the underlying law and after the House took steps to eliminate funds for the Attorney General's office, the Administration agreed to comply with the law.[898]

President George H.W. Bush and, to a lesser extent, President Bill Clinton continued to expand the use of signing statements. Out of the 214 signing statements issued by the first President Bush, 146 (68%) raised constitutional objections, and out of the 391 issued by President Clinton, 105 (27%) raised constitutional objections.[899] Both used the statements as ways to object to perceived encroachment by Congress on the president's executive powers. Clinton Assistant Attorney General Walter Dellinger argued that signing statements could theoretically be used to make "substantive legal, constitutional, or administrative pronouncements,"[900] and that the president – after careful and explicit weighing of the circumstances and where he believes that the Supreme Court would agree with him – could refuse to enforce statutes he believes to be unconstitutional.[901] At a White House briefing on February 9, 1996, Assistant Attorney General Dellinger elaborated:

When the president's obligation to execute laws enacted by
Congress is in tension with his responsibility to act in accordance
to the Constitution, questions arise that really go to the very heart
of the system, and the president can decline to comply with the
law, in our view, only where there is a judgment that the Supreme
Court has resolved the issue.[902]

B.   The Bush Administration's Use of Signing Statements

As Chairman Conyers explained in his opening statement at the January 31, 2007,
hearing, the Committee's concern focused on presidential signing statements as symptomatic of
the "growing abuse of power within the Executive Branch" under the George W. Bush
Administration.[903] The Committee leaned that, as of January 2007, President Bush had issued
150 signing statements challenging over 1,100 provisions of law, more than all previous
presidents combined. These have included statements challenging the McCain amendment
explicitly outlawing the cruel, inhuman, and degrading treatment of detainees, reporting
requirements of the USA PATRIOT Act, affirmative action provisions, and whistleblower
protections. These statements often claimed that challenged legal provisions improperly
interfered with Executive Branch authority or violated the "unitary executive" theory, under
which all Executive Branch-related power is controlled solely by the president.

President Bush's signing statements have differed from those of President Clinton and his
other predecessors in several key respects. First, an overwhelming number of them (100 out of
128 or 86% as of September 20, 2006) have raised constitutional objections, and without specific
indication that the Supreme Court had addressed or resolved the issue in the President's favor.[904]
Second, each statement typically challenged multiple provisions of a statute. The American Bar
Association (ABA) Task Force found:

From the inception of the Republic until 2000, Presidents produced
signing statements containing fewer than 600 challenges to the
bills they signed. According to the most recent update, **in his one
and a half terms so far, President George W. Bush (Bush II)
has produced more than 800.**[905]

According to signing statement expert Professor Christopher Kelley, as of January 12, 2007,
President Bush had issued 150 signing statements challenging 1,149 provisions of law.[906]

In challenging the constitutionality of portions of the USA PATRIOT Act and other high-
profile laws, President Bush's signing statements have essentially asserted that the President
does not believe that he is bound by key provisions of the legislation.[907] Finally, they have
sought to further a broad view of executive power and President Bush's view of the "unitary
executive."[908] In general, President Bush's signing statements have not contained specific
refusals to enforce particular provisions or analysis of specific legal objections, but instead have

been broad statements asserting that the president will enforce a particular law or provision consistent with the president's constitutional authority, making their true intentions and scope unclear and rendering them difficult to challenge.[909]

Several examples of controversial Bush Administration signing statements illustrate this inclination:

The McCain Amendment on Treatment of Detainees

The McCain Amendment, which was part of the 2005 Department of Defense Authorization bill, explicitly outlawed cruel, inhuman, and degrading treatment of detainees held in United States custody anywhere in any part of the world.[910] After significant negotiations between Congress and the White House, the McCain Amendment passed by veto-proof margins in both houses, including a 90-9 margin in the Senate.[911] Despite the apparent agreement between the White House and Congress, President Bush issued a signing statement suggesting that the government could ignore the McCain Amendment in certain circumstances.[912] A senior Administration official told a *Boston Globe* reporter that the President, pursuant to the signing statement, might use interrogation techniques banned under the legislation in "special" national security-related situations.[913]

USA PATRIOT Act

After the reauthorization of the USA PATRIOT Act, President Bush on March 9, 2006, issued a signing statement suggesting he could disregard the legislation's requirement that the President report to Congress on the steps he was taking to implement the Act's provisions.[914] Senator Leahy, then the ranking member of Senate Judiciary Committee, called the President's action "nothing short of a radical effort to re-shape the constitutional separation of powers and evade accountability and responsibility for following the law." [915]

Affirmative Action

Signing statements on the Export-Import Bank Reauthorization Act of 2002 and on 14 other Acts during President Bush's first term indicated that the Executive Branch would carry out affirmative action provisions "in a manner consistent with the requirements of equal protection under the Due Process Clause of the Fifth Amendment."[916] This phrase raised concerns that, since many Bush Administration officials regard affirmative action programs as a violation of equal protection, the Administration might refuse to carry out affirmative action programs in the affected statutes.[917] In the Intelligence Reform and Terrorism Prevention Act of 2004, Congress required the national intelligence director to recruit and train women and minorities in order to diversify the intelligence community.[918] The President's signing statement for that Act was issued with the same caveat despite the Supreme Court's ruling in *Grutter v. Bollinger*,[919] upholding affirmative action as consistent with the Equal Protection Clause.

<u>Whistleblower Protections</u>

In 2002, President Bush issued a signing statement accompanying the Sarbanes-Oxley law combating corporate fraud. The statement was read by many as attempting to narrow a provision protecting corporate whistleblowers in a way that would have left them with very little protection.[920] Senators Leahy and Grassley wrote a letter to the President stating that his narrow interpretation was at odds with the plain language of the statute, and the Administration appeared to back away.[921]

As part of the Energy Policy Act of 2005, Congress included another provision protecting whistleblowers at the Department of Energy and the Nuclear Regulatory Commission, reportedly "because lawmakers feared that Bush appointees were intimidating nuclear specialists so they would not testify about safety issues related to a planned nuclear waste repository at Yucca Mountain in Nevada."[922] Notwithstanding the previous exchange with Senators Leahy and Grassley, President Bush once again claimed, in a signing statement on August 8, 2005, that the Executive Branch does not have to comply with these whistleblower protections. As discussed below, later Government Accountability Office (GAO) analysis undertaken at the Judiciary Committee's request revealed that some of these provisions have in fact not been followed.

C.   Committee Actions

These facts and concerns about the Bush Administration's use of signing statements were thoroughly explored at the Judiciary Committee's January 31, 2007, hearing. Testimony at the hearing also revealed strong bipartisan opposition to such abuse of signing statements, as expressed by Republican former Representative Mickey Edwards and ABA President Karen Mathis. As Professor Charles Ogletree of Harvard Law School explained, moreover, the Bush Administration not only has claimed the right to refuse to implement parts of legislation through signing statements, in violation of law and the Constitution, but also has failed to identify those provisions it has improperly disregarded in practice. Professor Ogletree pointed out that "[w]hen the president refuses to enforce a law on constitutional grounds without interacting with the other branches of government, it is not only bad public policy, but also creates a unilateral and unchecked exercise of authority in one branch of government without the interaction and consideration of the others." Chairman Conyers made clear that the Committee would continue its efforts to "get to the bottom" of the Administration's abuse of signing statements.

On March 2, 2007, following up on the January 31 hearing, Chairman Conyers and Constitution, Civil Rights, and Civil Liberties Subcommittee Chairman Nadler wrote to the Attorney General asking detailed questions about 17 particularly troubling signing statements in which President Bush claimed the authority to disregard provisions of law. A partial response on May 30, 2007, indicated that the Administration had in fact properly implemented five of these challenged statutes. The Department declined, however, to answer the remainder of the Committee's questions.

Chairman Conyers proceeded to work with Senator Robert Byrd to engage the help of the GAO to pursue the Committee's concerns. In general, the GAO found that the use of presidential signing statements was increasing and that federal courts have cited or referred to such statements "only infrequently" and "have only in rare instances relied on them as authoritative interpretations of the law."[923] For the first time, moreover, the GAO reports specifically examined the question of whether federal agencies were carrying out portions of federal statutes to which the President objected in signing statements. In consultation with Chairman Conyers and Senator Byrd, the GAO selected for review a number of signing statements in which the President claimed the ability to disregard selected provisions of federal law. These included signing statements issued with respect to fiscal year 2006 appropriations acts and signing statements challenging ten provisions of law that were raised by Chairman Conyers and Chairman Nadler in their March 2, 2007, letter to the Justice Department. The GAO issued two reports, in June and December 2007, examining a total of 22 signing statements in which the President claimed the ability to disregard selected provisions of federal law.[924]

The GAO determined that in 9 of the 22 instances (over 40%), federal agencies had failed to fully execute legal provisions to which the President had objected in signing statements. These included, for example, the failure of the Defense Department to include separate budget justification documents explaining how Iraq War funding was to be spent in its 2007 budget request as required by Congress, and the failure of the Department of Energy to comply with all the whistleblower protections mandated by Congress, as discussed above.[925] Although in several instances the agencies indicated that they were not intentionally defying the law and did plan to achieve compliance, both Chairman Conyers and Senator Byrd expressed concern and called for continued oversight. As Chairman Conyers explained, "[T]his Administration's power grabbing attitude should be checked and balanced with more congressional oversight of the use and abuse of presidential signing statements."[926]

Partly because of the negative attention focused on signing statements and the increased use by President Bush of the veto pen, 2008 witnessed a decrease in the use of signing statements to challenge legislation. Serious concerns were raised, however, when a presidential signing statement concerning the National Defense Authorization Act for 2008 claimed the authority to disregard several provisions of law, including expanding protections for whistleblowers who work for government contractors and limiting the Administration's ability to set up permanent bases in Iraq without congressional approval. Judiciary Committee staff worked closely with the staff of the House Armed Services's Subcommittee on Oversight and Investigations, which conducted a hearing on the issue on March 11, 2008. At the hearing, Chairman Vic Snyder announced that the Defense Department had assured him that it intended to implement the Act as written.[927]

Finally, in October 2008, President Bush used signing statements to challenge parts of a military authorization act and a statute giving inspectors general greater independence from White House control. Specifically, the signing statements took exception to provisions forbidding funding from being used to exercise control over Iraq oil resources, requiring negotiations for an agreement for Iraq to share some of the costs of American military operations, and strengthening legal protections against possible political interference with agency inspectors general. Although there has been no indication that agencies would in fact disobey these provisions and President Bush will be leaving office in January, the author of several of these sections commented that such signing statements "create uncertainty in the law that should not be there."[928]

Perhaps reflecting the continued congressional and public scrutiny and skepticism concerning the Bush Administration's abuse of signing statements, both presidential candidates in this year's election made clear their opposition to this practice and pledged to end it if elected.[929] In particular, President-elect Obama has pledged not to "use signing statements to nullify or undermine congressional instructions as enacted into law," explaining that:

> While it is legitimate for a president to issue a signing statement to
> clarify his understanding of ambiguous provisions of statutes and
> to explain his view of how he intends to faithfully execute the law,
> it is a clear abuse of power to use such statements as a license to
> evade laws that the president does not like or as an end-run around
> provisions designed to foster accountability. I will not use signing
> statements to nullify or undermine congressional instructions as
> enacted into law. The problem with this Administration is that it
> has attached signing statements to legislation in an effort to change
> the meaning of the legislation, to avoid enforcing certain
> provisions of the legislation that the president does not like, and to
> raise implausible or dubious constitutional objections to the
> legislation.[930]

This critique, and this pledge, correspond closely to the views of congressional, academic, and professional critics of the Bush Administration's abuse of signing statements.

II.   Rulemaking Process

A.   Factual Background

"Federal regulation, like taxing and spending, is one of the basic tools of government used to implement public policy."[931] Impacting on nearly every aspect of our lives, regulations[932] have significant benefits and costs as aptly summarized in the following:

> Agencies issue thousands of rules and regulations each year to
> implement statutes enacted by Congress. The public policy goals
> and benefits of regulations include, among other things, ensuring
> that workplaces, air travel, foods, and drugs are safe; that the
> Nation's air, water and land are not polluted; and that the

appropriate amount of taxes is collected. The costs of these regulations are estimated to be in the hundreds of billions of dollars, and the benefits estimates are even higher. Given the size and impact of federal regulation, it is no surprise that Congresses and Presidents have taken a number of actions to refine and reform the regulatory process within the past 25 years. One goal of such initiatives has been to reduce regulatory burdens on affected parties, but other purposes have also played a part. Among these are efforts to require more rigorous analyses of proposed rules and thus provide better information to decision makers, to enhance oversight of rule making by Congress and the President, and to promote greater transparency and participation in the process.[933]

The Administrative Procedure Act (APA),[934] enacted in 1946, establishes minimum procedures to be followed by federal administrative agencies when they conduct business that affects the public and requires judicial review of certain administrative acts. Many agency actions, however, are not subject to the APA. As one academic noted, "the American administrative system, by evolution and design, is characterized by a considerable degree of informality, agency discretion and procedural flexibility."[935] With federal agencies issuing "more than 4,000 final rules each year on topics ranging from the timing of bridge openings to the permissible levels of arsenic and other contaminants in drinking water,"[936] the current federal regulatory process faces many significant challenges. President John F. Kennedy in 1961 observed that "the steady expansion of the Federal administrative process during the past several years has been attended by increasing concern over the efficiency and adequacy of department and agency procedures."[937]

Within the Executive Office of the President, the Office of Management and Budget (OMB) is charged with the responsibility to oversee and coordinate Executive Branch agencies. The Office works with agencies "to help improve administrative management, to develop better performance measures and coordinating mechanisms, and to reduce any unnecessary burdens on the public."[938] Since the 1930s, OMB has been involved in "questions of management and organization of the Executive Branch" and the level of its involvement has fluctuated over time.[939]

With regard to the regulatory processes of Executive Branch agencies, OMB's Office of Information and Regulatory Affairs (OIRA) reviews significant proposed and final rules from federal agencies before they are published in the Federal Register.[940] As a result of OIRA's review, draft rules may be revised before publication, withdrawn before a review is completed, or returned to the agencies "because, in OIRA's analysis, certain aspects of the rule need to be reconsidered."[941] According to the Judiciary Committee's bipartisan Administrative Law, Process and Procedure Project for the 21st Century,[942] "OIRA can have a major influence on the direction of a wide range of public policies."[943]

OMB's participation in rulemaking during some Administrations can be problematic. Academics, such as Georgetown University Law Center Professor David Vladeck, state that OMB can cause "an agency to take action that is contrary to the statutory directive that the agency is required to enforce, or is otherwise arbitrary or irrational."[944] He explains:

> **OMB's participation is a one-way ratchet – OMB presses agencies to do less to protect the public health, not more, and to focus on lower cost options, not more protective ones.** OMB's job is to ensure that rules meet a cost/benefit litmus test, and many experts claim that cost/benefit analysis is inherently anti-regulatory... While the anticipated *costs* of regulation are generally easier to estimate (and easy to overstate), the *benefits* of regulation – avoided cancers, miscarriages, genetic damage that might cause infertility or birth defects, kidney failures requiring dialysis and transplant, to name just a few – are notoriously difficult to quantify and are often downplayed or ignored by OMB.[945]

B.   Executive Control by the Bush Administration

Executive Order 13422: Expanding White House Political Control Over Rulemaking

"With little fanfare,"[946] President Bush issued Executive Order 13422 on January 18, 2007.[947] Executive Order 13422 substantively amended the procedures and requirements that agencies must follow to promulgate rules that had been in place since 1993 pursuant to Executive Order 12866, a directive issued by President Clinton.[948]

President Bush's order "gives the White House much greater control over the rules and policy statements that the government develops to protect public health, safety, the environment, civil rights and privacy."[949] Critics of this order question whether it is an attempt to establish standards for rulemaking that are inconsistent with statutory requirements.[950] For example, a *New York Times* commentator noted that Executive Order 13422 "will make it even easier for political appointees to overrule the professionals, tailoring government regulations to suit the interests of companies that support the G.O.P."[951]

Shortly after Executive Order 13422 was issued, the House Judiciary Committee's Subcommittee on Commercial and Administrative Law held an oversight hearing on the order.[952] Witnesses who testified at this hearing included: Steven D. Aitken, Acting Administrator Office of Information and Regulatory Affairs, Office of Management and Budget; Professor Sally Katzen, University of Michigan Law School; Dr. Curtis W. Copeland, Specialist in American National Government, Congressional Research Service; Paul R. Noe with C&M Capitolink LLC; and Professor Peter L. Strauss, Columbia University School of Law. The hearing focused on four general concerns presented by the order as follows:

<u>Greater Specificity and Market Analysis Requirements</u>

Executive Order 13422 revises Executive Order 12866's first principle of regulation. Under the prior order, each agency was required to identify the problem (including where applicable, failures of public markets or public institutions that warrant new agency action) as well as assess the significance of such problem. As revised, the agency must now "identify in writing the specific market failure (such as externalities, market power, lack of information) or other specific problem that it intends to address (including where applicable, the failures of public institutions) that warrant new agency action, as well as assess the significance of that problem, to enable assessment of whether any new regulation is warranted."[953] CRS explains:

> The new language appears to (1) elevate "market failure" to greater prominence as a rulemaking rationale (removing the "where applicable" caveat and placing it before and on par with the more general statement of problem identification); (2) more clearly define what constitutes a market failure (e.g., "externalities, market power, lack of information"); (3) require a more precise delineation of why the agency is issuing the rule (the "specific" market failure or the "specific" problem); (4) require that the delineation be in writing; and (5) make clear that the purpose of this requirement is to facilitate a determination of whether the rule is needed.[954]

As a result of this revision, it appears that agencies may have to meet a much higher threshold before they can promulgate regulations with a greater likelihood of "paralysis by analysis."[955] A greater concern is that Executive Order 13422 may be "an attempt to bypass Congress by establishing standards for regulatory initiation that are not consistent with statutory requirements."[956] As Chairman Conyers observed:

> **Executive Order 13422's requirement that a "market failure" or problem be identified to justify governmental intervention also marks a serious increase of regulatory control by the White House.** It is often at the request of the industry that the agencies issue best practices and policies. To make them more complicated only seems to further interfere in the regulatory process.[957]

<u>Heightened Scrutiny of Significant Guidance Documents</u>

Agencies, from time to time, issue guidance documents intended to provide nonbinding information regarding their regulations. Issued often at the request of industry, these documents "interpret key policy and technical questions."[958] Executive Order 13422 makes several substantive amendments to Executive Order 12866 with respect to guidance documents.[959] First, it adds a definition of "guidance document," which is defined as "an agency statement of general applicability and future effect, other than regulatory action, that sets forth a policy on a statutory, regulatory, or technical issue or an interpretation of a statutory or regulatory issue."[960] Second, it defines a "significant guidance document."[961] Third, and perhaps most importantly, it extends certain requirements that pertain to rulemaking to guidance documents issued by agencies[962] which, as a result, will "allow the White House to create a bureaucratic bottleneck that would slow down agencies' ability to give the public the information it needs."[963]

CRS notes that the implications of these new requirements "are potentially significant."[964] It explains:

> Agencies issue thousands of guidance documents each year that are intended to clarify the requirements in related statutes and regulations. Therefore, **the requirement that agencies provide OIRA with advance notification of significant guidance documents may represent a major expansion of the office's (and, therefore, the President's) influence**, particularly when coupled with the ability of OIRA to determine which guidance documents are "significant" and the ability of OIRA to conclude that "additional consultation will be required" before a document is issued. Also, the requirement that presidentially appointed regulatory policy officers ensure compliance with this requirement arguably represents another extension of the President's authority in regulatory agencies.[965]

Greater Emphasis on Cost-Benefit Analysis

Executive Order 13422 now requires an agency, as part of its regulatory plan, to include, in addition to its estimate of the anticipated costs and benefits of each rule that the agency reasonably expects to issue in the upcoming fiscal year, its best estimate of the combined aggregate costs and benefits of all of its regulations planned for the calendar year to assist with the identification of priorities.[966] This requirement may be problematic as Sally Katzen, OIRA Administrator under the Clinton Administration explained at a hearing held by the Judiciary Subcommittee on Commercial and Administrative Law in 2007:

> [T]o try to estimate either costs or benefits at the notice of inquiry stage or before the agency has made even tentative decisions is like trying to price a new house before there is even an option on the land and before there are any architects plans. The numbers may be interesting, but hardly realistic, and to aggregate such numbers would likely do little to inform the public but could do much to inflame the opponents of regulation.[967]

And, because certain certain aspects of this new requirement are unclear, CRS notes that it may

195

"prove difficult to implement in a meaningful fashion."[968] For example, CRS pointed out that agencies typically would not have developed cost or benefit information at the time that the regulatory plan is developed, and that some regulations in the plan are never promulgated.

<u>Greater Role for Political Appointees in the Rulemaking Process</u>

As issued in 1993, Executive Order 12866 required agencies to establish regulatory policy officers, but left to the agencies who those individuals would be and how much influence the would have over the rulemaking process. In contrast, Executive Order 13422 mandates that an agency designate a presidential appointee to be a regulatory policy officer.[969] It also says that this officer must approve every proposed regulation before the agency may commence the rulemaking process and before such regulation may be included in the agency's regulatory plan.[970] In response to these new requirements, Representative Henry A. Waxman (D-CA), Chair of the Committee on Oversight and Government Reform, observed, "'The executive order allows the political staff at the White House to dictate decisions on health and safety issues, even if the government's own impartial experts disagree. This is a terrible way to govern, but great news for special interests."[971]

Ultimately, however, it may be difficult to determine what effect these changes have had on the rulemaking process. As CRS explained, it is currently unclear whether agency regulatory policy officers have stopped any agency regulatory initiatives before they became draft rules, or, if so, whether there has been an increase in such stoppages since the officers' authority was enhanced by Executive Order 13422.."[972] Nevertheless, CRS noted that certain of these new requirements appear "to significantly enhance the role of the agency regulatory policy officer as part of the regulatory planning process."[973] CRS also pointed out that Executive Order 13422 is "silent as to whether the designated presidential appointee would be subject to Senate confirmation," which provides a means to strengthen congressional "influence over agency decision making."[974] CRS concluded that, "Given the enhanced power and authority of the policy officer to control day-to-day rulemaking activities within federal agencies ("no rulemaking shall commence"), the policy officer could be considered to be an officer of the United States under the appointments clause of the Constitution."[975] Therefore, Congress could require the policy officers to be subject to Senate confirmation. As Chairman Conyers observed:

> [T]he policies and regulations that are created to protect public
> health, safety, the environment, civil rights, and privacy and should
> be created by experts in the field and not by a political appointees.
> **Such a deviation from past process only serves to compromise**
> **the protection of the public while enhancing the president's**
> **political power.**[976]

C.   Efforts by OIRA to Control Rulemaking

During the Clinton Administration, the OIRA Adminstration saw her roles as collegial.

Over the course of the George W. Bush Administration, however, OIRA has returned to the role it had during the Reagan Administration, even describing itself in an annual report as the "gatekeeper for new rulemakings."[977] The Administrator of OIRA explained that one of his office's functions is "to protect people from poorly designed rules," and that OIRA review is a way to "combat the tunnel vision that plagues the thinking of single-mission regulators."[978] This "return to the gatekeeper perspective of OIRA's role has implications for an array of OIRA's functions."[979]

It has been argued that "OIRA's increasingly aggressive role in controlling agency action" may be "the biggest administrative law story of the new century."[980] Manifestations of OIRA's heightened role in the rulemaking process, as identified by the GAO[981] and CRS,[982] include the following:

- the development of a detailed economic analysis circular and what agency officials described as a perceptible "stepping up the bar" in the amount of support required from agencies for their rules, with OIRA reportedly more often looking for regulatory benefits to be quantified and a cost-benefit analysis for every regulatory option that the agency considered, not just the option selected;

- the issuance of 21 letters returning rules to the agencies between July 2001 and March 2002 — three times the number of return letters issued during the last six years of the Clinton Administration;[983]

- the issuance of 13 "prompt letters" between September 2001 and December 2003 suggesting that agencies develop regulations in a particular area or encouraging ongoing efforts. However, OIRA issued two prompt letters in 2004, none in 2005, one in 2006, and none in 2007[.]

According to CRS, these and other initiatives "represent the strongest assertion of presidential power in the area of rulemaking in at least 20 years."[984]

Direct Intervention by the Administration to Control Rulemaking

In addition to the ways in which the Bush Administration has exerted control over the rulemaking process discussed above, the Administration has informally intervened in this process by either overriding agency action or delaying its review of rules. For example, it came to light earlier this year that the U.S. Environmental Protection Agency (EPA) weakened some of its regulatory limits on smog-forming ozone "after an unusual last-minute intervention by President Bush, according to documents released by the EPA."[985] Although the EPA's Clean Air Scientific Advisory Committee supported the EPA's proposed ozone standard rule, OIRA Administrator Dudley "urged the EPA to consider the effects of cutting ozone further on 'economic values and on personal comfort and well-being.'"[986] President Bush intervened and he "decided on a requirement weaker than what the EPA wanted."[987]

At an oversight hearing that examined the aftermath of Executive Order 13422, Chairman Conyers explained the problematic aspects of when politics trump public safety:

> I am concerned that the Administration's unprecedented control over the rulemaking process serves as yet another barrier to against consumer protection, specifically against exposure to harmful environmental pollutants and other safety and health requirements. This is most recently illustrated by the controversy over the air quality regulations issued by the EPA for ozone standards. Notwithstanding that agency's sage advice about the need for tougher standards, the President personally intervened to ensure that lower standards would be used.
>
> **We have seen in other contexts that this President has tried to take unto himself absolute authority on issues such as surveillance, privacy, torture, enemy combatants, and rendition, and signing statements. The issue of public health and safety that we are looking at today, as protected by our administrative agencies, is no less important.**[988]

Another means by which the Administration has directly controled agency rulemaking is to delay its review of rules. For example, Executive Order 12866 requires OIRA's reveiws to be completed within 90 days of when a rule is submitted, unless such period is extended by no more than 30 days at the request of the agency head.[989] According to data available from the General Services Administration, however, OIRA failed to complete its review of various rules within these limits.[990] As of early 2008, one EPA draft rule (on radiation protection guidance for the general public) had been under OIRA review for two and one-half years (since October 2005), and another EPA rule (on standards for radioactive waste disposal in Yucca Mountain, Nevada) had been under review for fifteen months (since December 2006). Until OIRA's review is completed, these rules cannot be formally promulgated.

Using Directives and Other Means to Circumvent Formal Rulemaking

The Congressional Review Act[991] serves to keep "Congress informed of the rulemaking activities of federal agencies"[992] by requiring agencies to submit to each chamber of Congress and the Comptroller General a copy of the rule and certain other materials before the rule may take effect.[993] Once a rule is submitted, Congress has 60 legislative or session days to complete its review and, if necessary, disapprove the rule.[994]

In an apparent effort to avoid the Act's requirement, the Bush Administration sought to avoid congressional review by issuing directives instead of rules. For example, the Centers for Medicare & Medicaid Services (CMS) issued a letter on August 17, 2007 to state health officials concerning the State Children's Health Insurance Program for the purpose of "clarifying" how

CMS will apply existing statutory and regulatory requirements in its review of requests by states to extend eligibility under the Program to children from lower-income families.[995] CMS established new requirements and stated in the letter that it could take corrective action against states that fail to adopt the identified measures within 12 months.[996] Although both CRS and GAO concluded that this letter was a "rule" within the meaning of the Congressional Review Act and must therefore be submitted to Congress before it could take effect,[997] CMS stated that "'GAO's opinion does not change the department's conclusion that the Aug. 17 letter is still in effect.'"[998] Because the letter was never submitted to Congress, the Congressional Review Act's disapproval process was not initiated.

Midnight Rulemaking

The term "midnight rule" refers to a final (Executive Branch) administrative agency rule promulgated at the very end – usually between the November presidential election and inauguration day – of an outgoing administration's term of office.[999] Empirical evidence shows that, at least since the Carter Administration, outgoing administrations have increased the rate at which they have issued final rules following the November presidential election.[1000] The rate of increase has been the greatest when the new president and the former president have hailed from different parties.[1001]

There are a number of reasons why an outgoing administration will increase the rate at which it issues final rules during the midnight period. The most commonly cited reason is the administration's desire to set long-term regulatory policy that will survive its departure.[1002] Another oft-cited reason is the administration's desire to await the conclusion of the November elections before issuing controversial rules that may cost its party votes.[1003]

In the last months of the Bush Administration, there have been heightened efforts to push through final regulations.[1004] In October 2008, *The Washington Post* warned:

> **The new rules would be among the most controversial deregulatory steps of the Bush era and could be difficult for his successor to undo.** Some would ease or lift constraints on private industry, including power plants, mines and farms.
>
> Those and other regulations would help clear obstacles to some commercial ocean-fishing activities, ease controls on emissions of pollutants that contribute to global warming, relax drinking-water standards and lift a key restriction on mountaintop coal mining.[1005]

At the request of Chairman Conyers, the nonpartisan CRS conducted its own independent analysis of this phenomenon. It concluded that "federal agencies appear to be issuing an increasing number of rules at the end of the Bush Administration" and identified a 33.6% increase in the number of final rules submitted to the GAO each month pursuant to requirements of the Congressional Review Act from June through October 2008 when compared to the first five months of the year.[1006] CRS also found that the number of major rules submitted by the agencies to the GAO between June and October 2008 was 119% higher than the number of such rules submitted during the same period in 2007.[1007]

Some of these last-minute rules were controversial[1008] and have been described as "'last-minute' policymaking."[1009] For example, CRS said that the following regulations had been identified by Members of Congress and others as problematic as of November 18, 2008:[1010]

- a Department of the Interior (DOI) rule that, in the words of the proposal, requires that surface coal mining operations "minimize the creation of excess spoil and the adverse environmental impacts of fills," but that some observers have said would allow deposits of waste mountaintop material within 100 feet of certain streams.

- a DOI proposed rule that would, among other things, give federal agencies greater responsibility in determining when and how their actions may affect species under the Endangered Species Act. Several Members of Congress have expressed concerns about the draft rule, contending that it eliminates key protections of the Act.

- a Department of Justice rule that would "clarify and update" the policies governing criminal intelligence systems that receive federal funding, but that some contend would make it easier for state and local police to collect, share, and retain sensitive information about Americans, even when no underlying crime is suspected.

- a Department of Labor rule that would change the way that occupational health risk assessments are conducted within the Department. Legislation was introduced during the 110th Congress, H.R. 6660 and S. 3566, that would have prohibited the issuance or enforcement of this rule."

Previous presidents have imposed regulatory moratoria "to control rulemaking at the start of their administrations" and to give them more time to implement new regulatory oversight processes.[1011] For example, President Reagan issued a memorandum to his Cabinet and the Environmental Protection Agency asking them, to the extent permitted by law, to postpone for 60 days the effective date of all final rules scheduled to take effect in the next 60 days and to refrain from issuing any new final rules.[1012] Similarly, the Director of OMB, under the Clinton Administration, asked the heads of executive departments and independent agencies to not send proposed or final rules to be published in the Federal Register until they were approved by an agency head appointed by the President and confirmed by the Senate.[1013]

Shortly after President George W. Bush assumed office, his chief of staff directed all executive departments and agencies to not send proposed or final rules to the *Federal Register*, withdraw from publication rules that had not yet been published, and postpone for 60 days the effective date of rules that had been published, but not yet taken effect.[1014] This directive imposed a blanket, 60-day delay of all regulations without allowing for any notice or comment.

While the delay of the effective date of a rule subject to the Administrative Procedure Act (APA) may require notice and comment,[1015] the Bush Administration invoked the APA's "good cause" exception to required notice-and-comment procedures. At least one successful lawsuit was filed challenging the invocation of the exception.[1016]

D. Lack of Transparency

Patrick Henry warned more than 300 years ago, "The liberties of a people never were, nor ever will be, secure when the transactions of their rulers may be concealed from them."[1017] In the absence of oversight, those liberties can be jeopardized particularly if the Executive Branch is not checked by Congress. Without transparency, it is impossible to know the extent, for example, that special interests or inappropriate factors play in official action.

Although the extent these factors play in rulemaking is critical, the nonpartisan CRS observes, "[I]t is difficult for anyone outside the agencies or OIRA to determine the impact of most of the Bush Administration's regulatory management initiatives."[1018] For example, the Committee, through the Subcommittee on Commercial and Administrative Law, sought to consider the impact and ramifications of Executive Order 13422 one year after it was promulgated at an oversight hearing held on May 6, 2008.[1019] The hearing also examined other aspects of the Administration's role in the rulemaking process. Dr. Curtis Copeland, a Specialist in American National Government at CRS, testified at this hearing that it was unclear whether:

- agency RPOs [regulatory policy officers] have stopped any agency regulatory initiatives before they became draft rules, or, if so, whether there has there been an increase in such stoppages since the RPOs' authority was enhanced by Executive Order 13422;

- OIRA has declared certain scientific information "highly influential," therefore requiring the rulemaking agencies to use detailed peer review procedures;

- OIRA is using the general principles for risk assessment (e.g., that agencies use the "best reasonably obtainable scientific information") to stop agency rules;

- OIRA has used its authority in Executive Order 13422 to require "additional consultation" before agencies can issue significant guidance documents; and

- the January 2007 "good guidance practices" bulletin has changed the nature of the guidance that agencies give to regulated entities.[1020]

Likewise, Dr. Copeland observed that it was "unclear how many 'significant guidance documents' OIRA has reviewed since Executive Order 13422 was issued in January 2007."[1021] In addition, he noted that "[a]lthough OIRA is required to disclose when agency rules are submitted for review, when the reviews are complete, and the results of the reviews, no such requirements pertain to agency guidance documents."[1022]

In 2003, GAO reached a similar conclusion regarding the opaqueness of OIRA's reviews.[1023] Specifically, GAO said that:

- OIRA interpreted the transparency requirements in Section 6 of Executive Order 12866 as applying only to formal reviews (which can be as short as one day), not to informal OIRA reviews that can go for months, and which OIRA has described as the period when it can have its greatest impact on agency rules;

- OIRA interpreted a requirement that OIRA disclose documents exchanged between OIRA and the agencies as not applying to documents exchanged by OIRA desk officers;

- OIRA's meeting log did not clearly indicate which regulatory action was being discussed or the affiliations of the participants in those meetings; and

- OIRA's database did not clearly indicate which rules had been changed at the direction of OIRA, or the significance of those changes.

"Federal regulations are among the most important and widely used tools for implementing the laws of the land – affecting the food we eat, the air we breathe, the safety of consumer products, the quality of the workplace, the soundness of our financial institutions, the smooth operation of our businesses,"although it is extremely difficult to follow the regulatory process.[1024] And, while e-rulemaking "has transformative potential to increase the comprehensibility, transparency and accountability of the regulatory process,"[1025] a report prepared under the auspices of the American Bar Association concluded that the Administration's efforts to promote this initiative has not been "entirely successful." The report noted basic deficiencies with respect to how the Administration's e-rulemaking system is structured and funded and with respect to the public's ability to access the system.[1026]

Equally problematic is the concern that the Administration may have advised agencies to not cooperate with Congress with respect to the conduct of congressionally-sanctioned empirical studies done as part of the Administrative Law, Process and Procedure Project for the 21st Century. The Project, which was originally approved on January 26, 2005, by the Judiciary Committee as part of its Oversight Plan for the 109th Congress[1027] and continued as part of the Committee's Oversight Plan for the 110th Congress,[1028] was intended to undertake a nonpartisan, academically credible analysis of administrative law, process and procedure.[1029] As part of this Project, seven hearings were held on this subject matter, three symposia were held,[1030] and the

Project sponsored three empirical studies.[1031]

Over the course of the Project, however, it came to light that the Administration apparently instructed certain agencies to not cooperate with two of these empirical studies. An academic researcher contracted by the CRS to study public participation at the development stage of a rulemaking proceeding encountered reluctance by most agencies to provide information vital to one of these studies. According to CRS, his "requests for information were often met with reluctance and suspicion and his most valuable contacts with knowledgeable officials were on deep background."[1032] Similarly, a comprehensive study of science advisory panels in federal agencies encountered little cooperation among the agencies, even though the Administration was provided letters of introduction from the Director of CRS and the Chairman and Ranking Member of the Subcommittee on Commercial and Administrative Law.[1033]

The failure of the Project to secure cooperation with the Administrative underscores the need to reauthorize and appropriate funding for the Administrative Conference of the United States (ACUS or Conference). Established as a permanent independent agency in 1964 (which became operational three years later),[1034] the Conference was created to develop recommendations for improving procedures by which federal agencies administer regulatory, benefit, and other government programs.[1035] It served as a "private-public think tank" that conducted "basic research on how to improve the regulatory and legal process"[1036] and served as a consultative resource for Congress.[1037] The organization and independence of ACUS encouraged cooperative involvement from all three branches of government. As a result, ACUS-sponsored empirical research generally garnered support and cooperation from all sectors of government. This may explain why the Conference's recommendations were well-founded, effective, and generally accepted. After failing to be appropriated funds for fiscal year 1996, ACUS ceased operations as of October 31, 1995.[1038] The statutory provisions establishing ACUS, however, were not repealed and, in 2008, ACUS was reauthorized for an additional three years.[1039]

III.   Findings

<u>Abuse of Presidential Signing Statements</u>

1.   <u>President Bush has improperly used signing statements to attempt to nullify, without a veto, more than 1100 provisions in over 100 laws passed by Congress, based on assertions of executive authority and the theory of the "unitary executive."</u> These have included, for example:

> • The McCain Amendment, which explicitly outlawed cruel, inhuman, and degrading treatment of detainees held by the U.S.[1040] In signing the Defense appropriations legislation to which the Amendment was attached, however, President Bush claimed the authority to construe it in accord with his asserted authority to "supervise the unitary Executive Branch and as

Commander in Chief," in order to help in "protecting the American people from further terrorist attacks."[1041] As several scholars and analysts have pointed out, this effectively amounts to a claim that the president can "waive the torture ban if he decides that harsh interrogation techniques will assist in preventing terrorist attacks."[1042] In fact, a senior Administration official reportedly stated that pursuant to the signing statement, the president might authorize interrogation techniques banned under the legislation in "special" national security-related situations.[1043]

- Provisions of the 2005 Energy Policy Act protecting whistleblowers at the Department of Energy and the Nuclear Regulatory Commission who provide information to Congress.[1044] When the President signed this legislation, he issued a statement asserting that he would interpret these provisions "in a manner consistent with the President's constitutional authority to supervise the unitary Executive Branch" which, analysts have pointed out, claims that the president, not Congress, "will determine whether" such employees "can give information to Congress."[1045]

- Provisions in the 2004 Intelligence Reform and Terrorism Prevention Act that directed the national intelligence director to recruit and train more women and minorities in order to diversify the intelligence community.[1046] Yet when the President signed this law, he asserted that he would interpret it " consistent with the requirement that the Federal Government afford equal protection of the laws under the Due Process Clause of the Fifth Amendment," raising concerns that since some Administration officials regard affirmative action program as a violation of equal protection, the Administration could refuse to carry out this and similar provisions[1047].

2.   <u>The Bush Administration has failed to fully execute a number of public law provisions – 9 of 22 studied by the GAO – to which the President has objected in signing statements.</u> For example:

- In its FY2006 appropriations legislation, Congress required that the Department of Defense include separate budget justification documents concerning its 2007 budget requests explaining how funding for contingency operations would be spent. As with other signing statements asserting Executive Branch authority, President Bush issued a signing statement claiming that these provisions would be applied "in a manner consistent with the President's constitutional authority to... recommend for congressional consideration such measures as the President shall judge necessary and expedient." In fact, the GAO found that the Department failed to submit a budget justification document with respect to contingency operations in Iraq, as required by law. The GAO concluded that the

Executive Branch "did not execute this provision as written."[1048]

- As discussed above, the President objected under the "unitary executive" theory to provisions of the Energy Policy Act of 2005 that provided additional protections to whistleblowers at the Nuclear Regulatory Commission and the Department of Energy. One specific provision required the agencies to notify their employees that they are covered by specific whisteblower protections. The GAO found that despite acknowledging this requirement, the Energy Department had not so notified its employees more than two years after the statute was enacted and "did not state when it plans" to do so. The GAO thus concluded that the Energy Department "has not implemented" the law as required by Congress.[1049]

3.   <u>In contrast to his predecessors, an overwhelming number of President Bush's signing statements have raised constitutional objections to multiple provisions of statutes he has signed and asserted that he is not bound by them.</u>[1050] Such claims would violate Article II, section 3, of the Constitution, which requires the president to "take care that the laws be faithfully executed," as well as Article I, section 7, which requires the president to either sign or veto legislation. As interpreted by the Supreme Court, Article I, section 7, does not permit a partial veto of legislation, although that is arguably what the Administration has done in issuing signing statements objecting to parts of legislation and then, in at least some cases, failing to implement them.[1051]

Rulemaking Process

4.   <u>The Administration's greatly enhanced control over the rulemaking process has been to the detriment of the public interest and has served to circumvent legislative intent.</u> As noted by the nonpartisan CRS, this Administration's regulatory and rulemaking initiatives represent the strongest assertion of presidential power in this area in at least 20 years.[1052] This enhanced presidential control over rulemaking has been manifested in various ways.

- One of the most egregious examples of this excessive control is Executive Order 13422, which substantially changed how rules are promulgated by agencies. Issued by President Bush without any prior consultation, Executive Order 13422 made the most significant changes to the presidential review process since its predecessor was issued in 1993. According to the nonpartisan CRS, the executive order represents "a clear expansion of presidential authority over regulatory agencies" that is "consistent with the President's view of the 'unitary executive.'"[1053]

- Under President Bush, the role of the Office of Information and Regulatory Affairs (OIRA) within OMB has changed from serving as a counselor for agencies to a self-described "gatekeeper" of agency rulemaking. As a result

205

of this changed role, the Administration has undermined legislative intent. OIRA's enhanced control over rulemaking has been manifested in numerous respects.[1054]

- Contrary to the public interest, the Bush Administration has directly and indirectly intervened in the rulemaking process to weaken or delay rules. Specific examples include: (i) efforts by the Environmental Protection Agency (EPA) to weaken some of its limits on smog-forming ozone after an unusual last-minute intervention by President Bush, who wanted a requirement weaker than what the EPA advised. Congress delegated rulemaking authority with regard to ozone to the EPA, not the president. This action represents a usurpation of congressionally delegated rulemaking authority from the EPA to the president;[1055] and (ii) the Administration has delayed its review of a time-sensitive regulation intended to protect a seriously endangered species.[1056]

- The Bush Administration has sought to circumvent the requirements of the Congressional Review Act, which mandates that agencies submit rules to Congress before they become effective. Notwithstanding opinions issued by the GAO and CRS finding that a "directive" issued by the Department of Health & Human Services constitutes a "rule" within the meaning of the Act, the agency refused to rescind its "directive" until just days before the states would have lost funding for their failure to comply.[1057]

- The Bush Administration promulgated a series of "midnight regulations," some of which were "among the most controversial deregulatory steps of the Bush era" and involved easing controls on emissions of pollutants that contribute to global warming, relaxing drinking-water standards and lifting a key restriction on mountaintop coal mining.[1058]

- Serious concerns have been raised that, in its rush to regulate, the Bush Administration has given the public insufficient time to submit comments, conducted hasty and perfunctory reviews of important public comments, and otherwise deviated from accepted rulemaking practices.[1059] In the case of one controversial midnight rule, for example, an executive-branch agency asked its experts to review 200,000 public comments in just 32 hours.[1060] In another, the agency required staff to review 300,000 comments disapproving of a rule in only a week.[1061]

5. <u>Under the Bush Administration, the rulemaking process has become less transparent and less accountable to the public and to Congress.</u> Key parts of the rulemaking review process are not transparent. As a result, it is unclear to what extent outside entities and the Administration influence rulemaking and subvert legislative intent.

- The Administration's influence on agency rulemaking is difficult to discern even after the proposed or final rule is published because key parts of the OIRA review process and other Administration initiatives are not transparent.[1062]

- President Bush's Executive Order 13422 made rulemaking even less transparent by requiring political appointees to pre-approve agencies' proposed regulations.[1063]

- On two occasions, this Administration thwarted efforts by the House Judiciary Committee to conduct a nonpartisan empirical analysis of the early stages of the rulemaking process and with respect to an analysis of the role of federal advisory committees by instructing agencies not to cooperate with these studies.[1064]

Section 4 – Retribution Against Critics

*The critic of the war [Joseph F. Wilson] comes out. He points
fingers at the White House... He is fair game. Anything goes... His
wife [Valerie Plame Wilson] had a job with the CIA. She worked in
the counterproliferation division... She gets dragged into the
newspapers. Some may think that's okay. It isn't.*[1065]

– Special Counsel Patrick Fizgerald
Closing Argument in *United States v. Libby*

The Bush Administration has been repeatedly charged with employing improper and even unlawful means to discredit – and, in some cases, retaliate against – both internal and external critics. No act of retribution against its critics, though, has attracted more public attention than the 2003 leak of Valerie Plame Wilson's covert CIA identity following the publication of an op-ed by her husband, Ambassador Joseph F. Wilson, criticizing the Administration, and the subsequent criminal conviction of Vice President Cheney's Chief of Staff I. Lewis Libby for obstructing the investigation of the leak.

Although the most notable victims of Administration's retribution against critics, Ambassador Wilson and his wife were not the only ones. The Administration retaliated against numerous other critics. Notable victims have included former General Eric Shinseki, former Secretary of the Treasury Paul O'Neill, former White House counter-terrorism czar Richard Clarke, Richard Kay and other prominent CIA officials, and Department of Justice whistleblowers Thomas Tamm and Jesselyn Radack to name only a few.

I.   The Leak of Valerie Plame Wilson's Covert CIA Identity and Its Aftermath

A.   The July 2003 Disclosure by the Press

The event that set in motion the unauthorized leak of Valerie Plame Wilson's covert CIA identity in June and July of 2003 was the publication of Nicholas Kristof's May 6, 2003, article in *The New York Times* titled "Missing in Action: Truth."[1066] The article concerned President Bush's by-then-disproved claim that Iraq had tried to purchase uranium from Niger to build nuclear weapons. Mr. Kristof reported that he had been "told by a person involved in the Niger caper that more than a year ago the Vice President's office asked for an investigation of the uranium deal, so a former ambassador to Africa was dispatched to Niger. In February 2002, according to someone present at the meeting, that envoy reported to the C.I.A. and State Department that the information was unequivocally wrong."[1067] Mr. Kristoff did not identify the former ambassador by name.

On June 12, 2003, reporter Walter Pincus published a follow-up article in *The Washington Post*. He reported that, in response to an inquiry made by the Vice President, the CIA had sent an unnamed "retired ambassador" to Niger to investigate the claim that Iraq had sought to procure uranium from that country and that, at the conclusion of the trip, the Ambassador reported to the CIA that the "'uranium-purchase story was false.'"[1068]

Five days after Mr. Pincus' article appeared, a still more critical article titled "The First Casualty: The Selling of the Iraq War" appeared in the *The New Republic* online.[1069] Like the Kristof and Pincus articles, *The New Republic* article reported that, following a request for information by the Vice President, the CIA had dispatched an unnamed ambassador to Niger to investigate the allegation that Iraq had sought uranium from Niger to build nuclear weapons. The article included a statement by the unnamed ambassador that, by early 2002, Administration officials "knew the Niger story was flat-out false."[1070] The article was especially critical of the Administration's (and, in particular, Vice President Cheney's) handling of intelligence.

On July 6, 2003, Ambassador Joseph F. Wilson published an op-ed in the *The New York Times* in which he identified himself as the unnamed ambassador in the earlier press accounts.[1071] (He also discussed his trip during a July 6 appearance on NBC's *Meet the Press* and a July 8 appearance on NBC News.) [1072] Ambassador Wilson revealed that, in February 2002, the CIA had sent him on a trip to Niger to investigate the allegations regarding Iraq's nuclear activities, that he doubted the veracity of the allegation, and that he believed the Vice President had been briefed on his conclusions.[1073] Ambassador Wilson's disclosure generated extensive media coverage.[1074]

On July 14, 2003, Mr. Novak revealed Ms. Wilson's name and identity in a column that appeared in *The Chicago Sun Times*. He wrote: "Wilson never worked for the CIA, but his wife, Valerie Plame, is an agency operative on weapons of mass destructions. Two senior officials told me his wife suggested sending Wilson to Niger..."[1075] Other public disclosures in the press soon followed.[1076] Accusations that White House officials had retaliated against Ambassador Wilson surfaced immediately. At least one high-ranking White House official, Karl Rove, was apparently undisturbed. It has been widely reported that he informed Chris Matthews of MSNBC that Ambassador Wilson's "wife" was "fair game."[1077]

As of the date Mr. Novak published his article, Ms. Wilson was an "under cover" (that is, covert) CIA "operative on weapons of mass destruction." Her employment status with the CIA was "classified information prohibited from disclosure under Executive Order 12958,"[1078] which governs the handling and disclosure of classified information.[1079]

With the publication of Mr. Novak's article, Ms. Wilson's then-classified and covert CIA identity was blown and her career at the CIA over.[1080] The effect of the disclosure was not only to destroy Ms. Wilson's career in intelligence, but also to hinder U.S. intelligence efforts working oversees, as well as others who may have interacted with Ms. Wilson or her cover organization for many years.[1081] Any reliable assessment of the damage, though, would require review of the classified "damages assessment" that the CIA conducted after Mr. Novak's column appeared.[1082]

B.   The Bush Administration's Response to the Leak

Immediately after Mr. Novak's column appeared, the CIA contacted the Justice Department four times in the span of three weeks to notify it that the disclosure of Ms. Wilson's name and covert status likely violated the law and to request a criminal investigation.[1083] Months passed without the commencement of an investigation. In late September 2003, over a month after the first CIA notification, the Justice Department finally confirmed it had authorized the FBI to begin an investigation (though without the supervision of an independent special counsel).[1084] Even then, the Department waited three days before notifying the White House of the investigation, and the White House in turn waited eleven hours before asking all White House staff to preserve evidence.[1085] Adding to the delay was the White House counsel's decision to screen all evidence for "relevance" before turning it over to the Justice Department.[1086]

Other aspects of the Justice Department's handling of the investigation have come under scrutiny. Of particular concern is that then-Attorney General Ashcroft was privately briefed on the FBI's interview of Karl Rove.[1087] Mr. Ashcroft had personal and political connections to Mr. Rove: Mr. Rove was an adviser to Mr. Ashcroft during the latter's political campaigns for the U.S. Senate, for which he earned almost $750,000.[1088] Mr. Rove was also instrumental in securing Mr. Ashcroft's appointment as Attorney General after Mr. Ashcroft lost his Senate seat.

On December 30, 2003, Attorney General Ashcroft finally recused himself from the investigation. Then-Deputy Attorney General James Comey became the acting Attorney General with respect to the leak investigation. He appointed Patrick Fitzgerald, the Bush-appointed U.S. Attorney for the Northern District of Illinois, as a special counsel to lead the investigation.[1089]

From the outset, though, Mr. Fitzgerald encountered numerous problems. Among them was the failure of senior White House officials to execute waivers so that reporters with whom they had spoken could submit to interviews and provide testimony without breaching their confidentiality obligations.[1090] In a March 2005 court filing, Mr. Fitzgerald stated he could not close the matter because of *New York Times* reporter Judith Miller's inability to testify about conversations with senior White House officials.[1091] Mr. Fitzgerald later noted that the failure to execute the waivers delayed the conclusion of the investigation (and the Libby indictment) by over a year.[1092]

While the FBI was investigating the leak allegations, Press Secretary Scott McClellan was denying any wrongdoing by the President's aides. He insisted during a September 29, 2003, press conference that he had personally spoken with Karl Rove, and that Mr. Rove had denied any involvement in the leak. He also represented that the President "kn[ew] that Karl Rove wasn't involved," but he did not say how the President knew, contenting himself with the observation that the allegations against Mr. Rove were "ridiculous."[1093]

Mr. McClellan reaffirmed Mr. Rove's innocence at an October 7, 2003, press conference held soon after the Justice Department's investigation began. This time, though, Mr. McClellan "categorically" denied not only Mr. Rove's involvement in the leak, but also Mr. Libby's (just as he had privately done with reporters several days earlier).[1094,1095] Mr. McClellan later revealed during testimony before the House Judiciary Committee that the "President and Vice President directed me to go out there and exonerate Scooter Libby"[1096] and that "the top White House officials who knew the truth – including Rove, Libby, and the Vice President – allowed [him], even encouraged [him], to repeat a lie." He also told the Committee that he "regret[ed] the role he played in "relaying false information."[1097] Anticipating a promise that the President would soon make, Mr. McClellan also promised that any White House official found to have leaked classified information would be fired.[1098] Mr. McClellan repeated the denials of White House involvement in the leak during an October 10 press conference.[1099]

Mr. Rove also publicly denied his involvement in the leak. Asked by an ABC News reporter whether he leaked the name or identity of Ms. Wilson, Mr. Rove answered unequivocally "no."[1100] He gave this assurance even though several months earlier, just after news of the leak broke, he had told Chris Matthews of MSNBC's *Hardball* that Ambassador Wilson's wife was "fair game."

President Bush, for his part, responded to the investigation by promising to fire any leakers. On September 30, 2003, when asked about Mr. Rove's involvement in the leak, the President declared: "Listen, I know of nobody – I don't know of anybody in my Administration who leaked classified information... If somebody did leak classified information, I'd like to know it, and we'll take the appropriate action. And this investigation is a good thing."[1101] The President was even more definitive during a June 10, 2004, exchange with the press when he answered the question, "Do you stand by your pledge to fire anyone found to have done so," with an unqualified "yes."[1102] On July 18, 2005, however, the President appeared to back off his earlier promises when, in response asked at a press conference, he promised to fire only any White House officials who had actually "committed a crime."[1103] The President's press secretary, Scott McClellan, would later acknowledge in testimony before the House Judiciary Committee that the President had "changed the threshold" for accountability among his aids.[1104]

C.   The Libby Indictment and Trial: Evidence of a White House Leak

On October 28, 2005, special counsel Fitzgerald held a press conference at which he announced that, although his investigation would continue, the grand jury convened to investigate the leak of Ms. Wilson's identity had returned a five-count indictment against Scooter Libby.[1105] The indictment did not charge Mr. Libby with violating any laws governing the disclosure of Ms. Wilson's identity, but instead with obstructing the special counsel's investigation by lying both to FBI investigators (during interviews held in October and November of 2003) and to the grand jury convened to investigate the leak (during testimony given in March 2004).[1106]

A six-week trial was held during January and February of 2007 in the U.S. District Court for the District of Columbia. On March 6, 2007, the jury found Mr. Libby guilty all but one of the counts set forth in the indictment, including the indictment's main count – obstruction of justice.[1107] The trial evidence, though focused on the issue of obstruction of justice, necessarily revealed important facts about the circumstances under which Ms. Wilson's CIA identity was leaked. The evidence received into evidence at trial (including Mr. Libby's grand jury testimony) conclusively established the following facts[1108]:

After Nicholas Kristof's *New York Times* article appeared in early May 2003, Vice President Cheney and Mr. Libby immediately began investigating the circumstances of Ambassador Wilson's Niger trip.[1109] Five key events came to light at the trial:

(i)   *Libby's Contacts with the Department of State. – May 29, 2003.* On May 29, 2003, Mr. Libby asked Marc Grossman, the Undersecretary of State for Political Affairs, for information about the travel of the unnamed retired ambassador referenced in the Kristoff *New York Times* article. That same day Mr. Grossman called Mr. Libby with information about the trip (which he had acquired from e-mails received from the Assistant Secretary of State for Intelligence and the Assistant Secretary of State for African Affairs). Mr. Grossman informed Mr. Libby that the former ambassador was Joseph F. Wilson and that he would report back upon concluding his investigation. He then commissioned an internal report.[1110]

(ii)   *Mr. Libby's Communications with the Vice President – June 11, 2003.* On June 11, 2003, Mr. Libby and the Vice President spoke by phone in anticipation of a *Washington Post* article by reporter Walter Pincus – an article about which Mr. Pincus had contacted the Vice President's press office seeking comment and information. The Vice President dictated several talking points to share with Mr. Pincus. Chief among them was that the Vice President had not requested Ambassador Wilson's mission to Niger. It was during this conversation that Vice President informed Mr. Libby, as Mr. Libby's own notes clearly reveal, that Ambassador Wilson's wife, Valerie Plame Wilson, worked in the CIA's Counterproliferation Division.[1111] (How Vice President Cheney learned of Ms. Wilson's identity has never been definitively established.[1112] He may have learned it from, among others, CIA Director George Tenet.[1113]) Mr. Libby thereafter shared the talking points with Mr. Pincus prior to the publication of Mr. Pincus' June 12 article.[1114]

(iii)   *Mr. Libby's Communications with the CIA – June 11, 2003.* On June 11, 2003, following his conversation with Vice President Cheney, Mr. Libby called Robert Grenier, Associate Deputy Director of Operations at the CIA. Mr. Libby told Mr. Grenier that Ambassador Wilson was telling people that he had been sent to Niger at the request of the Vice President. Mr. Libby asked Mr. Grenier whether the CIA had sent Ambassador Wilson to Niger and, if so, whether it was done in response to inquiries made by the Vice President about the Iraq-Niger nuclear weapons allegations. After consulting with the CIA's Counterproliferation Division, Mr. Grenier called Mr. Libby back that day. He informed Mr. Libby, among other things, that Ambassador Wilson's wife (whom Mr. Grenier did not identity by

212

name) was a CIA employee in the Counterproliferation Division and played a role in sending him to Niger. Mr. Libby responded by asking Mr. Grenier if the CIA's Director of Public Affairs, William Harlow, would make public Mr. Grenier's finding that the Department of State and Defense were "interested" in Ambassador Wilson's trip. (Mr. Libby and the Vice President wanted the information relayed to the public before the publication of Mr. Pincus' forthcoming June 12 article to dispel the notion that the Vice President was behind the trip.[1115]) After consulting with Mr. Harlow, Mr. Grenier called back Mr. Libby and told him that the CIA could probably make that information public.[1116]

(iv)   *The Vice President's and Mr. Libby's Communications with Cathie Martin of the Vice President's Staff – June 11, 2003.* Also on June 11, 2003, Cathie Martin, then Assistant to the Vice President for Public Affairs and later Director of Communications for Policy and Planning at the White House, spoke with Mr. Harlow by way of follow up to Mr. Libby's above-referenced conversation with Mr. Grenier. She learned from Mr. Harlow that Ambassador Wilson's wife worked at the CIA. As soon as she received this information, she relayed it to both the Vice President and Mr. Libby during a meeting in the Vice President's office.[1117]

(v)   *Mr. Grossman's Report to Mr. Libby – June 12, 2003.* On June 10 or 11, 2003 (most likely the latter), Mr. Grossman received a memo dated June 10 from the State Department's Intelligence and Research Branch prepared in response to Mr. Libby's May 29 inquiry. The next day (probably June 12) Mr. Grossman reported to Mr. Libby on the memo's findings. After giving Mr. Libby background on Ambassador Wilson's trip, Mr. Grossman told him that "there was one other thing that I thought he needed to know, which was that Mrs. Wilson, or that Joe Wilson's wife worked at the Agency" (that is, the CIA). (As a matter of "protocol," Mr. Grossman supplied a copy of the memo Deputy Secretary of State Richard Armitage. He also told Secretary of State Colin Powell about his conversation with Mr. Libby.)[1118] Two days later (June 14), Mr. Libby revealed Ms. Wilson's name along to his CIA briefer, Craig Schmall, during his daily intelligence briefing.[1119]

On June 23, 2003, Mr. Libby met with *New York Times* reporter Judith Miller.[1120] According to Ms. Miller, Mr. Libby was "agitated and frustrated," and "angry" with the CIA for the way it had handled the Niger matter. He explained that the Vice President had not sent Ambassador Wilson to Niger; the CIA had done so unbeknownst to the Vice President. During this conversation, Mr. Libby also informed Ms. Miller that Ambassador Wilson's wife worked at the CIA's "non-proliferation bureau."[1121] This was the first known leak of Ms. Wilson's identity outside the Administration.

By the time his July 6 op-ed appeared in *The New York Times*, Ambassador Wilson had become (in the words of Special Counsel Patrick Fitzgerald) an "obsession" for Mr. Libby, the Vice President, and other White House officials.[1122] Mr. Libby himself admitted that he and the Vice President were "upset" over the op-ed.[1123] The Vice President clipped the article using a pen knife and, in his own hand, wrote the following rhetorical note consciously above its title: "Have they [i.e., the CIA] done this sort of thing before. Send an ambassador to answer a question... *Or did his wife send him on a junket.*"[1124] Mr. Libby likewise clipped the article and underlined its key passages.[1125]

Just a day after the op-ed appeared, Mr. Libby had lunch with White House Press Secretary Ari Fleischer. Mr. Fleischer informed Mr. Libby that he had been questioned by reporters about Ambassador Wilson's trip to Niger. Mr. Libby replied that the Vice President had not sent Ambassador Wilson on the trip; it was his wife who had. Mr. Libby then informed Mr. Fleischer – on the "Q.T.," as Mr. Fleischer testified – that Ambassador Wilson's wife (whom Mr. Fleischer recalls Mr. Libby identifying by name) worked at the "counter proliferation division" of the CIA. Mr. Fleischer did not ask Mr. Libby whether Ms. Wilson's identity was covert or classified. Evidence introduced during the Libby trial strongly suggests that Mr. Libby shared this information with the hope that Mr. Fleischer would pass it along to White House reporters.[1126]

Also on July 7, 2003, the Vice President's Special Assistant for Public Affairs, Cathie Martin, e-mailed Mr. Fleischer with talking points on the Niger trip personally dictated by the Vice President. The key talking point was again that the Vice President had not sent Ambassador Wilson on the trip. Mr. Fleischer repeated the talking points during his July 7 press briefing.[1127] The very next day, July 8, the Vice President dictated a revised set of talking points to Ms. Martin for dissemination to the press by Mr. Fleischer.[1128] The revised talking points began with the following sentence: "It is not clear who authorized Joe Wilson's trip to Niger." [1129] The addition of this talking point raises important questions, for it is undisputed that the Vice President knew (1) that the CIA had authorized the trip and (2) that, during his July 7 press briefing, Mr. Fleischer had so informed the press. Journalists have speculated that Vice President Cheney included the new July 8 talking point to lead "reporters in the direction of asking about Plame."[1130] An anonymous source who has apparently reviewed the confidential report of the FBI's interview with the Vice President has reported that the Vice President "was at a loss to explain how the change of the talking points focusing attention on who specifically sent Wilson to Niger would not lead ... to exposure" of Ms. Plame Wilson's identity.[1131]

While traveling with the President in Africa aboard Air Force One on July 11, 2003, Mr. Fleischer heard from yet another high-ranking White House official – this time White House Communications Director Dan Bartlet – that Ambassador Wilson was sent to Niger by his wife, a CIA employee, not the Vice President. (How exactly Mr. Bartlett knew was not revealed at trial; Mr. Fleischer indicated that Mr. Bartlett was reading off an unidentified document.) Soon thereafter Mr. Fleischer had informal conversations with three journalists traveling with the President in Africa – Tamara Lipper of *Newsweek*, David Gregory of NBC News, and John Dickerson of *Time Magazine* – about Ambassador Wilson's Niger trip. He informed them that the Ambassador's wife, a CIA employee, was responsible for sending him on the Niger trip.[1132]

On July 12, 2003, Mr. Fleischer and Mr. Bartlett, while on board a return Air Force One flight from Africa, agreed to contact several reporters to address negative press surrounding the President's state-of-the-union claim of a Iraq-Niger uranium connection. Mr. Fleischer followed up by contacting, among others, Walter Pincus of *The Washington Post*. Mr. Fleischer did not recall at trial disclosing Ms. Wilson's identity to Mr. Pincus,[1133] but Mr. Pincus testified with certainty that, in the context of disclaiming any involvement by the Vice President in arranging Ambassador Wilson's Niger trip, Mr. Fleischer did so. Mr. Pincus' contemporaneous notes reflect that Mr. Fleischer told him that "Wilson's wife" handled "WMD" (weapons of mass destruction).[1134] Mr. Pincus added that it was Mr. Fleischer who brought up the subject; Mr. Pincus did not solicit the information.[1135] As for Mr. Bartlett, it was not revealed at trial to whom, if anyone, he disclosed Ms. Wilson's identity.

Mr. Libby, for his part, disclosed Ms. Wilson's identity to at least two reporters following the appearance of the Wilson op-ed on July 6, 2003 – first to Judith Miller (for a second time) on July 8, 2003, and then to Matt Cooper of *Time Magazine* on July 11 or 12, 2003. As for Ms. Miller, Mr. Libby arranged the July 8 meeting with her at the Vice President's behest. (Mr. Libby also spoke with NBC News' Andrea Mitchell at the Vice President's behest to pass along the talking points he had drafted for Cathie Martin.[1136]) The main purpose of the meeting was for Mr. Libby to leak portions of the National Intelligence Estimate – which the President had declassified (a fact then known only to the President, the Vice President, and Mr. Libby) – in order to support the White House's position that the Administration's statements about the alleged Iraq-Niger connection had been well-founded.[1137] The Vice President told Mr. Libby to "get everything out" during his meeting with Ms. Miller. (Mr. Libby denied during his grand jury testimony the Vice President's directive included leaking Ms. Wilson's CIA identity.[1138]) Mr. Libby and Ms. Miller spoke for two hours. Ms. Miller testified that Mr. Libby again told her (this time on "deep background") that Ms. Wilson worked for a CIA division he called "WINPAC" (Weapons Intelligence Non-Proliferation and Arms Control). (Significantly, July 8 was the same date that, as noted above, the Vice President revised the press talking points for Cathie Martin so as to focus the press' attention on the question of who authorized Ambassador Wilson's trip.) Mr. Libby repeated the information during a follow-up telephone conversation with Ms. Miller.[1139]

A revealing trial exhibit at least raises the possibility that the Vice President had directed Mr. Libby to leak Ms. Wilson's identity to Ms. Miller and reporters. It consists of notes the Vice President wrote to himself in the early fall of 2003 when Mr. Libby was lobbying Press Secretary Scott McClellan to issue a statement, as Mr. McClellan had done for Mr. Rove, exonerating him from the accusations that White House officials had leaked Ms. Wilson's classified CIA identity. The Vice President noted the unfairness of Mr. Libby, alone among White House staffers, having been asked to "stick his neck in the meat grinder" after the Ambassador Wilson story broke and then having been denied the same support that Mr. Rove received from the White House Press Secretary.[1140] Other testimony, noted below, is in accord.

As for Mr. Cooper, Mr. Libby spoke to him four days later (July 12), also at the direction of the Vice President. The Libby-Cooper conversation occurred immediately after Mr. Libby conferred with the Vice President about how to deal with the press regarding Ambassador Wilson's claims about the Iraq-Niger matter.[1141] (During an interview with the FBI, Mr. Libby conceded the possibility that, during their July 12 conversation, the Vice President directed him to discuss Ms. Wilson's CIA affiliation with the press in order to counter Ambassador Wilson's claims. Here again, though, Mr. Libby attributed his knowledge about Ms. Wilson's identity to reporters.[1142]) Mr. Cooper testified that, during their July 12 meeting, Mr. Libby confirmed for him what Mr. Cooper had already heard from another White House source the day before (July 11, 2003) – that Ambassador Wilson's trip was arranged by his wife, a CIA employee.[1143] (Mr. Libby admitted during his grand jury testimony that he discussed Ms. Wilson with Mr. Cooper, although he attributed his knowledge of her identity entirely to other reporters.[1144])

Mr. Cooper's other White House source was none other than key presidential advisor (and later Deputy Chief of Staff) Karl Rove. It is not publicly known who told Mr. Rove that Ambassador Wilsons's wife worked at the CIA.[1145] It is undisputed, however, that on July 11 Mr. Rove told Mr. Cooper that Ms. Wilson (whom he did not identify by name – only as Ambassador Wilson's wife) worked on weapons of mass destruction at the CIA and had arranged the 2002 Niger trip. At the end of their conversation, Mr. Rove told Mr. Cooper not to "get too far out on Mr. Wilson." He also told Mr. Cooper that he had "already said too much." Mr. Cooper testified that, following his call with Mr. Rove, he perceived that a campaign to discredit Ambassador Wilson was afoot.[1146]

Mr. Cooper was not the only reporter, though, to whom Mr. Rove disclosed Ms. Wilson's CIA employment during early July 2003. Of more significance for obvious reasons, Mr. Rove also disclosed it to journalist Robert Novak – a subject that Mr. Rove and Mr. Libby privately discussed on July 10 or 11.[1147] Mr. Novak testified that he first learned of Ms. Wilson's CIA employment from Deputy Secretary of State Richard Armitage. Mr. Rove independently confirmed that information.[1148] Defending his public disclosure of Ms. Plame's name and CIA identity in his July 14 *Chicago Sun Times* column, Mr. Novak would later observe: "I didn't dig it out, it was given to me [by Secretary Armitage and Mr. Rove]... They thought it was significant, they gave me the name and I used it."[1149]

D.   Mr. Libby's Conviction, Sentence, and Presidential Grant of Clemency

On March 6, 2007, after a six-week trial, a federal jury found Mr. Libby guilty of obstruction of justice, perjury, and related felony offenses arising from his late 2003 statements to FBI agents during two investigatory interviews conducted in late 2003 and his testimony before the grand jury convened to investigate the leak in early 2004. Special Counsel Patrick Fitzgerald observed in a post-trial court submission that "Mr. Libby lied about nearly everything that mattered."[1150] The following facts (which are drawn from the undisputed evidence introduced at trial and narrated so as to comport with the jury's verdict) underlay Mr. Libby's conviction[1151]:

During the Justice Department's investigation, Mr. Libby told the FBI that, at the end of a conversation with Tim Russert of NBC News on July 10, 2003, Mr. Russert asked him if he "was aware that Wilson's wife worked for the CIA." Mr. Libby responded by telling Mr. Russert that "he did not know, and Russert replied that all the reporters knew." Mr. Libby further claimed that Mr. Russell's disclosure was news to him: He did not at the time recall that, just a few weeks early on June 12, 2003, the Vice President had told him that Ambassador Wilson's wife worked at the CIA. (Mr. Libby had no choice but to admit to the FBI that the Vice President had shared this information. The FBI had in its possession Mr. Libby's handwritten notes reflecting his conversation with the Vice President and the disclosure of Ms. Wilson's CIA employment.) Mr. Libby also told the FBI that "he did not discuss Wilson's wife" with *New York Times* reporter Judith Miller during their lengthy meeting on July 8, 2003.[1152]

During his March 2004 testimony before the grand jury, Mr. Libby repeated in sum and substance the above statements about his conversation with Mr. Russert. He made several additional statements to similar effect. Among them was that, during conversations with other reporters during July 2003, Mr. Libby advised them that he had heard from reporters that Ms. Wilson worked at the CIA, but that he himself did not know whether Ms. Wilson worked there.[1153]

As the undisputed facts establish, however, none of these statements were true. When Mr. Libby spoke with Mr. Russert and other reporters, he was "well aware" that Ms. Wilson worked at the CIA. To highlight only the key facts set forth in the preceding section: Mr. Libby was informed several times in early June 2003 – that is, well before Ambassador Wilson published his July 6 op-ed in *The New York Times* and Mr. Novak published his July 14 article disclosing Ms. Wilson's identity – of Ms. Wilson's employment at the CIA: on June 11 by the Vice President himself; sometime in June by the Vice President's Assistant for Public Affairs, Cathie Martin; on June 11 by a CIA official; and on June 12 by an Undersecretary of State. He then had several conversations about the matter during June, including a June 14 conversation with his CIA briefer and, more importantly, a June 23 conversation with Judith Miller of *The New York Times* during which he disclosed Ms. Wilson's CIA affiliation (but not her name). Several key conversations predating his July 10 discussion with Mr. Russert followed in July: On July 7, Mr. Libby informed the White House Press Secretary Ari Fleischer, and then on July 8 informed Ms. Miller for a second time, that Ms. Wilson worked at the CIA. On July 12, Mr. Libby had yet another conversation with Ms. Miller during which he discussed Ms. Wilson's employment at the CIA. He also had a conversation on July 8 with David Addington, the Vice President's counsel and himself a former CIA lawyer, about what internal paperwork would exist if a person whose spouse worked at the CIA had been sent on an oversees trip.[1154]

As for Mr. Libby's key statements and testimony concerning his conversation with Mr. Russert on July 10, 2003, they were proved to be a complete fabrication. Mr. Russert and Mr. Libby did speak on July 10. But Mr. Russert neither asked Mr. Libby if he knew that Ambassador Wilson's wife worked at the CIA nor told Mr. Libby that all reporters knew it. In fact, they did not even discuss Ms. Wilson, let alone her employment at the CIA. The discussed only Mr. Libby's complaints about MSNBC's television coverage of the Vice President.[1155]

On June 5, 2007, the U.S. District Court for the District of Columbia sentenced Mr. Libby to prison term of 30 months to be followed by two years of supervised release and imposed a $250,000 fine. Mr. Libby asked the court to release him on bond pending the resolution of his then-pending appeal. The court denied his request, finding that Mr. Libby had not satisfied the statutory requirement for release pending appeal – namely, that his appeal "raise[d] a substantial question of law or fact likely to result... in reversal"[1156] of his conviction.[1157] On July 2, 2007, the U.S. Court of Appeals for the DC. Circuit affirmed the district court's order.

President Bush immediately responded by commuting Mr. Libby's prison sentence in its entirety. He left intact Mr. Libby's conviction, as well as the fine and supervised release. President Bush did not question Mr. Libby's guilt. To the contrary, he praised the special counsel's integrity, acknowledged that he "respected" the jury's verdict, and emphasized the importance of holding "accountable" high government officials who breached the public trust by perjuring themselves. (It has been reported that White House Counsel Fred Fielding privately told the President how overwhelming the evidence was against Mr. Libby.) President Bush cited as the sole basis for granting clemency his determination that Mr. Libby's 30-month prison sentence was "excessive." He pointed out that, despite the sentence commutation, Mr. Libby remained subject to a "harsh punishment" in the form of a fine and supervised release. The President also noted in this regard that the "reputation" Mr. Libby had "gained through his years of public service and professional work in the legal community" would be "forever damaged" and that the "consequences of his felony conviction on his former life as a lawyer, public servant, and private citizen will be long-lasting."[1158]

During a press conference held the next day, White House Press Secretary Tony Snow (who had replaced Mr. McLellan) reiterated that the basis of the President's clemency decision was the excessiveness of Mr. Libby's sentence. (Mr. Snow added in a *USA Today* op ed published the next day that the President sought to "rectify an excessive punishment."[1159]) Mr. Snow, though, refused to answer several important questions about the President's decision, including whether the President had consulted with Vice President Cheney. Mr. Snow even refused to disclose whether the President had consulted with any Justice Department officials.[1160] He did acknowledge, however, that the President had not consulted the U.S. Pardon Attorney,[1161] whose recommendations presidents "usually" seek before making clemency decisions.[1162]

E.   Committee Actions

The Leak

The special counsel's investigation and the Libby trial confirmed and, in some cases revealed to the public for the first time, important facts about the circumstances of the Valerie Plame Wilson leak. But other key facts eluded the special counsel as a result of Scooter Libby's lies to the FBI and grand jury. As the special counsel explained at a press conference announcing the indictment, Mr. Libby's lies prevented him from answering with sufficient certainty to justify criminal charges such critical questions as what White House officials knew about Ms. Wilson's classified status when they leaked her identity, what motivated them to do so, and whether they

218

acted with the requisite criminal intent. He also explained, both during this press conference and during his closing argument during the trial, that Mr. Libby's lies had left "cloud" over the Vice President's office.[1163] The special counsel declined to say whether he thought a crime was committed – insisting that he could comment only within the "four corners of the indictment" – and declined the House Committee on Oversight and Government Reform's subsequent request to be interviewed.[1164]

Both the House Judiciary Committee and the House Oversight Committee sought answers to the questions left unanswered by the Libby trial. Beginning in 2007, after the Democratic party regained control of the House,[1165] both committees made repeated letter requests of the Administration to disclose one key category of documents that might well answers those questions: reports of FBI interviews of President Bush, Vice President Cheney, and key White House officials alleged to have participated in the leak.[1166]

Citing "confidentiality interests," the White House responded by allowing the Oversight Committee staff to review only redacted versions of the reports of interviews with White House officials (though it initially declined to allow the House Judiciary Committee staff even that inadequate access, relenting only in the face of a Committee subpoena),[1167] and it refused altogether to allow any access to the reports of the interviews with President Bush and Vice President Cheney. That left the committees with no choice but to serve subpoenas on Attorney General Mukasey – the Oversight Committee on June 16, 2008, and the Judiciary Committee on June 27, 2008 – compelling the production of the reports.[1168]

Again citing "confidentiality interests," the Attorney General refused to comply with the subpoenas. The Oversight Committee responded by informing Attorney General Mukasey that, on July 16, 2008, it would meet to consider a resolution holding him in contempt if he did not produce the subpoenaed documents (except for the report of President Bush's interview, which the Committee was willing to forego if the subpoenas were otherwise honored) or the President did not raise a *valid* claim of executive privilege by that date.[1169] The Attorney General responded on July 16, 2008, by raising an unprecedented and belated claim of executive privilege on the President's behalf.[1170] The dispute between Congress and the Bush Administration remains unresolved.[1171]

As for President Bush and Vice President Cheney, the redacted portions of FBI interviews with high-ranking White House officials raised "significant questions" about their involvement in the leak.[1172] A letter from House Oversight and Government Reform Committee Chairman Waxman to the Attorney General noted that, in "his interview with the FBI, Mr. Libby stated that it was 'possible' that Vice President Cheney instructed him to disseminate information about Ambassador Wilson's wife to the press."[1173]

The White House's Response to the Leak

On March 16, 2007, the House Oversight and Government Reform Committee held a hearing to address, among other things, whether the Administration took "the appropriate investigative and disciplinary steps" following the public disclosure of Ms. Wilson's CIA identity in July 2003.[1174] Much of the hearing focused on the Administration's apparent failure to comply with Executive Order 12958,[1175] which "prescribes a uniform system for classifying, safeguarding, and declassifying national security information,"[1176] and the "Classified Information Nondisclosure Agreement,"[1177] which all Bush Administration officials who leaked Ms. Wilson's identity signed at the outset of their employment.[1178] The Committee heard from two witnesses on these questions: James Knodell, Chief Security Office for the Office of Security and Emergency Preparedness, Office of Administration, Executive Office of the President, and William Leonard, Director, Information Security Oversight Office, National Archives and Records Administration.

During the March 16 hearing, the Oversight Committee established that Executive Order 12958 requires administration officials who learn that classified information has been compromised – whether intentionally or unintentionally – to report promptly whatever they know to the White House Office of Security and Emergency Preparedness. That office *must* then conduct an investigation and, upon finding that any classified information was disclosed to an unauthorized person, *must* take necessary corrective action, which may include rescinding the security clearance of any official found to have been responsible for the disclosure.[1179] Of equal importance, Executive Order 12958 *requires* that executive-branch officials who disclose classified information to unauthorized recipients – whether the disclosure is made "knowingly, willfully, or negligently" – be "subject to appropriate sanctions." Sanctions include "reprimand, suspension...removal...[and] loss or denial of access to classified information."[1180]

As for the "Classified Information Nondisclosure Agreement" (which Executive Order 12958 requires White House employees to sign), it (i) requires the signatory to comply with Executive Order 12958 and other specifically designated laws prohibiting the disclosure of classified information (including the above-noted Intelligence Identities Protection Act); (ii) prohibits the signatory from divulging classified information "to anyone" not authorized to receive it; (iii) requires the signatory, whenever he or she is in doubt about the classification status of information, to confirm that it is not classified before disclosing it and to "verify" that anyone to whom he or she discloses classified information is authorized to receive it; (iv) informs the signatory of the damage to national security that may attend the unauthorized disclosure of classified information; and (v) warns him or her that breach of the agreement (whether or not intentional) may result in disciplinary action, including the rescission of any security clearances he holds and the termination of his employment.[1181] Signatories to the agreement acknowledge, upon signing it, they have "received a security indoctrination" on its contents.[1182] All of the White House officials involved in the Plame Wilson leak investigation signed the agreement.

Mr. Knodell confirmed that all signatories to "Nondisclosure Agreement" have an "affirmative responsibility, ... if there is any question in their mind as to the true classification status of information they are provided, ... to seek clarification before the disclosure."[1183] (They also have a responsibility to disclose its classified status to any authorized recipient.[1184]) That obligation appears not only in the agreement but also in an accompanying briefing booklet that signatories receive.[1185] A closely related obligation appearing in the booklet (which is of particular relevance to Karl Rove's disclosure to Mr. Novak) is that a signatory may not confirm classified information obtained by a reporter without first "confirm[ing] through an unauthorized official that the information...has been declassified."[1186]

Principally through Mr. Knodell's testimony, the Committee on Oversight and Government Reform established three important, undisputed facts. *First*, no White House official (including Karl Rove) reported the public disclosure of Ms. Wilson's classified identity to the White House Office of Security and Emergency Preparedness. *Second*, neither that office nor any other office within the White House conducted any investigation into the leak – including how Karl Rove learned of Ms. Wilson's covert CIA identity – let alone a prompt investigation as required by the executive order. (The only executive-branch investigation was special counsel Patrick Fitzgerald's criminal investigation, and that did not begin until months after the public disclosure of Ms. Plame's identity.) Neither the President nor the Vice President or any White House official even broached the subject of an investigation. *And third,* no White House official was disciplined for failing to report the leak of Ms. Wilson's classified CIA identity or for actually leaking her identity – even following the Libby trial, which conclusively proved the leak of the information. None even had his security clearance rescinded or restricted.[1187]

A year after the Oversight Committee hearing, the Judiciary Committee held a hearing during which it heard from former White House Press Secretary Scott McClellan about his September and October 2003 statements to the press that neither Karl Rove nor Scooter Libby played any role in leaking Ms. Wilson's covert CIA identity. Most revealing was Mr. McClellan's testimony that, after he made an unequivocal public statement exonerating Mr. Rove, Mr. Libby asked Mr. McClellan to issue an exonerating statement for him too. Mr. McClellan initially refused. Several days later, after a successful lobbying campaign by Mr. Libby, White House Chief of Staff Andrew Card directed Mr. McClellan to issue a statement exonerating Mr. Libby. (That Mr. Libby lobbied the Vice President for such a statement is confirmed by a set of proposed talking points he prepared for the Vice President and Mr. Libby's own grand jury testimony.[1188] Mr. Libby's own testimony also confirms that he did not disclose to Mr. McLellan the numerous conversation he had with reporters during which Ms. Wilson's identity was discussed.[1189]) Mr. McClellan told the Committee that Mr. Card admitted that he was acting at the direction of the President and Vice President.[1190] (A handwritten note from Vice President Cheney to himself introduced during the Libby trial and referenced at this hearing confirms Mr. McClellan's testimony. It says that the press office "has to... call out to key press saying same thing about Scooter as Karl."[1191]) Though reluctant to issue a statement exonerating Mr. Libby given that the criminal investigation was then underway, Mr. McClellan called Mr. Libby and asked him if had been involved in the leak. Mr. Libby "assured" him in "unequivocal terms that he was not." Mr. McClellan then contacted reporters and issued a statement exonerating Mr. Libby.[1192]

The President's Grant of Clemency

On July 17, 2008, the Judiciary Committee held a hearing on the Libby commutation to address why the President commuted Mr. Libby's prison sentence and whether the President misused his clemency power.[1193] Several weeks before the hearing, the Committee asked the President to provide relevant documents and allow White House officials involved in the commutation decision to testify. (The press had reported that the President had given the Libby situation an unusually high degree of his personal attention.[1194]) The Committee asked the President to follow the example of President Ford, who testified about his pardon of President Nixon, and later President Clinton, who allowed his aides to testify about several of his controversial end-of-term pardons by declining to invoke executive privilege and honoring the Committee's request for information.[1195] President Bush refused to do so. In a letter from White House Counsel Fred Fielding to the Committee, the President even questioned the Committee's authority to hold an oversight hearing[1196]

Without access to the relevant documentation or the testimony of the President's key aides, the Committee was unable to learn why the President commuted Mr. Libby's prison sentence.[1197] But the evidence the Committee did receive at least raised question as to whether the cited reason – i.e., the "excessiveness" of the Mr. Libby's sentence – was the real reason that underlay the President's decision. As one expert witness testified, the "President's stated reasons for commuting all of Mr. Libby's prison [term] are hard to understand and even harder to justify."[1198]

Expert testimony offered at the hearing established that, by any objective measure, Mr. Libby's 30-month prison sentence was not excessive and, as one expert testified, may even have been "merciful."[1199] The statue under which Mr. Libby was properly sentenced allowed the district court judge,[1200] in the exercise of his discretion, to impose a prison term as long as 25 years, and required the judge to consider the sentencing range set forth in the federal guidelines established by the U.S. Sentencing Commission. Those guidelines provided for a sentencing range of 30 to 37 months in Mr. Libby's case.[1201] The 30-month prison term to which the judge sentenced Mr. Libby was thus at the very "*bottom* of the sentencing range suggested by" the guidelines.[1202] A sentence even at the top of the range would have been considered "presumptively reasonable" under the Supreme Court's decision in *Rita v. United States*,[1203] which was handed down just days before the President announced the Libby clemency decision.[1204] In fact, one expert informed the Committee that, despite "thousands" of appeals, "no federal appellate court has declared a single within-guideline sentence to be unreasonably long." He added that, "[a]gainst this legal backdrop, the President's conclusion that Mr. Libby's prison term was 'excessive' is curious, to say the least."[1205]

As for Mr. Libby's government service, which President Bush suggested might be a mitigating factor justifying a prison term shorter than 30 months, the expert witnesses from whom the Committee heard testified that it provided no grounds for downward departure from the sentencing guidelines. They pointed to the Supreme Court's holding in *Rita* that a within-guidelines sentence is presumptively reasonable no matter the defendant's record of public service. In *Rita*, the Court affirmed a lower court's ruling that no downward departure was warranted for white-collar defendant convicted of perjury despite his 25 years of decorated military service (and, on top of that, his ailing health.).[1206]   The Bush Administration of course argued in favor of the reasonableness of the sentence in *Rita*.[1207]

A still more compelling reason to question Mr. Bush's cited reason for his grant of clemency, though, is that he commuted Mr. Libby's sentence altogether rather than reducing it (as he was certainly authorized to in the exercise of his constitutional clemency power). As one expert witness testified at the hearing, "Even if one accepts the President's assertion that a 30-month prison term for Mr. Libby was excessive, it is hard to justify or understand the President's decision to commute Mr. Libby's prison sentence in its entirety."[1208]

Witnesses at the hearing pointed to several other reasons to question President Bush's explanation. They included:

- President Bush did not follow the usual procedures governing the exercise of presidential clemency power. He did not, in particular, consult with the U.S. Pardon Attorney.   Nearly all clemency requests are first considered by that office, which reviews them in accordance with Department of Justice regulations and guidelines.[1209]

- The exercise of the clemency power in Mr. Libby's case was unusual to say the least. As the Pardon Attorney testified, "a commutation of sentence is an extraordinary form of clemency that is rarely granted." None of the factors that might justify a sentence commutation under the Justice Department's own internal pardon manual – including a physical disability or "unrewarded cooperation with the government" – was present in Mr. Libby's case.[1210]

- Sentence commutations are usually only granted after a convicted defendant has served a substantial period of time in prison. Inmates are not even eligible to apply for a commutation under the Justice Department guidelines until they have first reported to prison.[1211] Mr. Libby had served no time in prison when the President commuted his sentence.

- President Bush himself stated that the crimes of which Mr. Libby were convicted were serious felonies for which Mr. Libby had to be held accountable.[1212] The decision to spare Mr. Libby even a single day in prison runs counter to the President's statement.

- President Bush has granted fewer pardons than any president in recent history (just as he granted comparatively few pardons while serving as Governor of Texas).[1213] One reporter has characterized the President as being "stingy" when it comes to pardons.[1214] He has been stingier still with respect to sentence commutations. At the time of the hearing, the President had granted only three commutations during his entire presidency.[1215] The President's commutation of Mr. Libby's prison sentence, before Mr. Libby had served even a single day of his 30-month prison sentence, ran counter to the President's past practice.

- The Bush Administration has consistently argued that white collar offenders should receive no sentencing leniency and urged courts to sentence white collar offenders within federal sentencing guidelines.[1216] President Bush's grant of clemency to Mr. Libby was inconsistent with his own Administration's position.

If the President did not commute Mr. Libby's prison sentence because he believed it to be excessive, then why did he do so? The President's refusal to honor the Committee's request for documents and testimony prevented the Committee from answering that question.

There are, however, a number of possible answers. One possibility, of course, is that the President's commutation decision was a simple act of loyalty as a reward for Mr. Libby's service. But at least three more unsettling possibilities surfaced at the hearing:

First, the President may have delivered on an agreement to spare Mr. Libby jail time if, at trial, he declined to implicate Vice President Cheney and White House officials in the leak of Ms. Wilson's identity. That possibility is suggested by, among other things, Mr. Libby's refusal to testify at his trial despite his lawyer's emphatic statement to the jury at the outset of the trial that Mr. Libby would testify and claim that Mr. Libby had been scapegoated to protect Mr. Rove.[1217] Was Mr. Libby reminding the President that his silence came at a price? One witness suggested that the promise of testimony was a "shot across the bow."[1218]

Second, the President may have sought to prevent Mr. Libby from cooperating with investigators following his conviction. The commutation of Mr. Libby's prison sentence deprived investigators of the ability to offer Mr. Libby a meaningful incentive – namely, a reduced prison term – in exchange for cooperating with the investigation.[1219]

And third, the President may have sought to prevent Congress from uncovering the facts underlying the Plame Wilson leak. At the time the President granted clemency to Mr. Libby, the House Committee on Oversight and Government Reform was investigating the leak of Ms. Plame's identity. The decision to commute Mr. Libby's prison sentence rather than pardon him outright while Mr. Libby's appeal was pending left Mr. Libby free to invoke the Fifth Amendment in response to a congressional inquiry.[1220]

II.   Retaliation Against Other Administration Critics

The leak of Valerie Plame Wilson's covert identity was the most notable, serious, and troubling act of retribution undertaken by the Bush Administration against its critics, but it was by no means the only one. Journalists, congressional committees, and inspectors general have compiled a long list of others who suffered much the same fate at the hands of the Bush

Administration. In *The Constitution in Crisis*, Chairman Conyers and the Democratic staff of the House Judiciary Committee provided numerous examples of retribution against critics.[1221] The following examples highlighted in *The Constitution in Crisis* remain of particular concern:

Military Officers – Including Former General Eric Shinseki

Former General Eric Shinseki, Chief of Staff of the United States Army, was punished and undermined for contradicting Donald Rumsfeld's pre-war assessment of troop needs in Iraq. In February 2003, General Shinseki presciently testified before the Senate Armed Services Committee that the Defense Department's troop estimate for occupying Iraq was too low and that "something on the order of several hundred thousand soldiers" would be needed. He further stated, "We're talking about post-hostilities control over a piece of geography that's fairly significant, with the kinds of ethnic tensions that could lead to other problems."[1222] He continued: "It takes a significant ground force presence to maintain a safe and secure environment, to ensure that people are fed, that water is distributed all the normal responsibilities that go along with administering a situation like this."[1223]

This, however, was very different from what the Defense Department had been telling Congress and the American public, as it had put the figure for occupation troop needs closer to 100,000 troops. Deputy Defense Secretary Paul Wolfowitz called General Shinseki's estimate "wildly off the mark" and Defense Secretary Rumsfeld, similarly stated that "[t]he idea that it would take several hundred thousand U.S. forces I think is far off the mark"[1224] It was also reported that in a semi-private meeting, the Pentagon's civilian leadership told the Village Voice newspaper that General Shinseki's remark was "bullshit from a Clintonite enamored of using the army for peacekeeping and not winning wars."[1225]

General Shinseki refused to back down from his honest – and, ultimately correct – estimate. A spokesman for the General, Col. Joe Curtin, stated, "He was asked a question and he responded with his best military judgment."[1226] And, in another congressional hearing, General Shinseki stated that the number "could be as high as several hundred thousand....We all hope it is something less."[1227]

In the aftermath of these comments, Defense Department officials leaked the name of Shinseki's replacement 14 months before his retirement, rendering him a lame duck commander and "embarrassing and neutralizing the Army's top officer."[1228] As one person who engaged in high-level planning for both wars said, "There was absolutely no debate in the normal sense. There are only six or eight of them who make the decisions, and they only talk to each other. And if you disagree with them in public, they'll come after you, the way they did with Shinseki."[1229] General Shinseki "dared to say publicly that several hundred thousand troops would be needed to occupy Iraq [and] was ridiculed by the administration and his career was brought to a close."[1230]

Former Treasury Secretary Paul O'Neill and Economic Advisor Lawrence Lindsey

Former Secretary of Treasury Paul O'Neill was punished twice by the Administration, once for opposing President Bush's tax policy, for which he was forced to resign in January 2003,[1231] and later for providing a first hand account of the Administration's decision-making process in the lead up to the Iraq War. In "The Price of Loyalty," written by former *Wall Street Journal* reporter Ron Suskind, Mr. O'Neill recounts how the Administration was discussing plans for going to war in Iraq well before the September 11 attacks. He stated that Iraq was discussed at the first National Security Council meeting after President Bush was inaugurated in January 2001. "From the very beginning, there was a conviction that Saddam Hussein was a bad person and that he needed to go," Mr. O'Neill told *60 Minutes*.[1232] The only task was "finding a way to do it."[1233] He also stated that he never saw any credible intelligence indicating that Saddam Hussein had weapons of mass destruction.[1234]

Before the book was published, Donald Rumsfeld called Secretary O'Neill and tried to persuade his longtime friend not to go through with the project. Rumsfeld labeled it a "sour grapes" book.[1235] But when Mr. O'Neill went through with the book, the Administration sought to discredit him by launching an investigation into his use of classified documents and whether he shared them with *60 Minutes* in his interviews.[1236] As Paul Krugman of the *New York Times* pointed out, the Administration "opened an investigation into how a picture of a possibly classified document appeared during Mr. O'Neill's TV interview. This alacrity stands in sharp contrast with their evident lack of concern when a senior Administration official, still unknown, blew the cover of a C.I.A. operative because her husband had revealed some politically inconvenient facts."[1237]

The investigation did not uncover any improprieties.[1238] The Treasury Department's inspector general reported that although Mr. O'Neill received the classified material after his resignation, the lapse was the fault of the Department, not Mr. O'Neill.[1239]

The Administration also sought to minimize Mr. O'Neill's role as a high-level official and painted him to be completely out of step with reality. As one writer observed, "O'Neill's revelations have not been met by any factual rebuttal. Instead, they have been greeted with anonymous character assassination from a 'senior official': 'Nobody listened to him when he was in office. Why should anybody now?'"[1240]

The Administration also went after former senior White House economic adviser Larry Lindsey. Mr. Lindsey angered the White House in September 2002 when he made a prescient prediction that a war with Iraq would cost between $100 billion and $200 billion, an estimate Administration officials at the time insisted was too high. In December 2002, the White House requested Mr. Lindsey resign from his post.[1241] Mr. Lindsey's estimate, of course, has proved to be on the far low side. As Frank Rich wrote, "Lawrence Lindsey, the President's chief economic adviser, was pushed out after he accurately projected the cost of the Iraq War."[1242]

<u>Counter-terrorism Czar Richard Clarke</u>

The Administration personally attacked Richard Clarke, the former counter-terrorism czar, for publishing a book in which he recounted how the Bush Administration was fixated on invading Iraq. Mr. Clarke's book, *Against All Enemies: Inside the White House's War on Terror–What Really Happened*, was published in March of 2004. Mr. Clarke, who worked for both Democratic and Republican administrations and helped shape U.S. policy on terrorism under President Reagan, the first President Bush, and President Clinton, suggests in his book that President George W. Bush was overly fixated on Saddam Hussein and Iraq. Mr. Clarke stated that President Bush's top aides wanted to use the terrorist attacks of 9/11 as an excuse to remove Saddam from power.[1243] In an interview with CBS, Mr. Clarke recalled: "Rumsfeld was saying we needed to bomb Iraq... We all said, 'but no, no, al-Qaeda is in Afghanistan.'"[1244] Mr. Rumsfeld responded: "There aren't any good targets in Afghanistan. And there are lots of good targets in Iraq."[1245]

Mr. Clarke also stated that his team substantively examined whether there was a connection between Iraq and the 9/11 attacks. "We got together all the FBI experts, all the C.I.A. experts. We wrote the report. We sent the report out to C.I.A. and found FBI and said, 'Will you sign this report?' They all cleared the report. And we sent it up to the President and it got bounced by the National Security Advisory or Deputy. It got bounced and sent back saying, 'Wrong answer... Do it again.'"[1246]

The Bush Administration went into attack mode in an attempt to discredit and smear Mr. Clarke. Dan Bartlett, White House communications director, dismissed Mr. Clarke's accounts as "politically motivated," "reckless," and "baseless."[1247] Scott McClellan, President Bush's spokesman, portrayed Mr. Clarke as a disgruntled former employee: "Mr. Clarke has been out there talking about what title he had... He wanted to be the deputy secretary of the Homeland Security Department after it was created. The fact of the matter is, just a few months after that, he left the Administration. He did not get that position. Someone else was appointed."[1248] Even Republican Majority Leader Bill Frist went after Mr. Clarke, saying "In his appearance before the 9/11 commission, Mr. Clarke's theatrical apology on behalf of the nation was not his right, his privilege or his responsibility. In my view it was not an act of humility, but an act of supreme arrogance and manipulation."[1249]

The Bush Administration's smear campaign against Mr. Clarke was widely discussed. As Joe Conason, a political commentator and journalist, stated, "[A]dministration officials have been bombarding him with personal calumny and abuse. They have called him an embittered job-seeker, a publicity-seeking author, a fabricator, a Democratic partisan and, perhaps worst of all, a friend of a friend of John Kerry. The Administration's attacks were seriously questioned by those who were aware of Mr. Clarke's qualifications. One journalist described the White House's attacks as "desperate" because "for the first time since the September 11 attacks, [President] Bush's greatest accomplishments have been credibly recast as his greatest failures."[1250]

<u>Army Core of Engineers Chief Contracting Office Bunnatine Greenhouse</u>

227

Bunnatine Greenhouse was the chief contracting officer at the Army Corps of Engineers, the agency that has managed much of the reconstruction work in Iraq. In October 2004, Ms. Greenhouse came forward and revealed that top Pentagon officials showed improper favoritism to Halliburton when awarding military contracts to Halliburton subsidiary Kellogg Brown & Root (KBR).[1251] Mr. Greenhouse stated that when the Pentagon awarded Halliburton a five-year $7 billion contract, it pressured her to withdraw her objections, actions which she claimed were unprecedented in her experience.[1252]

In June 27, 2005, Ms. Greenhouse testified before Congress, detailing that the contract award process was compromised by improper influence by political appointees, participation by Halliburton officials in meetings where bidding requirements were discussed, and a lack of competition.[1253] She stated that the Halliburton contracts represented the "most blatant and improper contract abuse I have witnessed during the course of my professional career."[1254] Days before the hearing, the acting general counsel of the Army Corps of Engineers had reportedly let Ms. Greenhouse know that it would not be in her best interest to appear voluntarily.[1255]

On August 27, 2005, the Bush Administration demoted Ms. Greenhouse, removing her from the elite Senior Executive Service and transferring her to a lesser job in the corps' civil works division. As Frank Rich of the *New York Times* described the situation, "[h]er crime was not obstructing justice but pursuing it by vehemently questioning irregularities in the awarding of some $7 billion worth of no-bid contracts in Iraq to the Halliburton subsidiary Kellogg Brown & Root. "They went after her to destroy her."[1256]

III. Findings

<u>The Leak of Valerie Plame Wilson's Covert CIA Identity</u>

1. <u>In June and July of 2003, White House officials, likely acting in concert, leaked Valerie Plame Wilson's classified covert CIA identity, thereby ruining Ms. Wilson's CIA career, endangering the lives of covert agents working overseas, and setting back intelligence efforts involving the proliferation of weapons of mass destruction.</u>

- As of July 14, 2003, Valerie Plame Wilson was a covert agent of the CIA whose identity was classified under Executive Order 12958.[1257] Ms. Wilson was also a "covert agent" under the Intelligence Identities Protection Act.[1258]

- At least three White House officials – the Vice President's Chief of Staff Scooter Libby, the White House Press Secretary Ari Fleischer, and presidential adviser (and later Deputy White House Chief of Staff) Karl Rove – leaked Ms. Wilson's identity to at least seven different journalists: Walter Pincus of *The Washington Post*, David Gregory of NBC News, John Dickerson of *Time Magazine*, Judith Miller of *The New York Times*, Matt

Cooper of *Time Magazine*, Robert Novak of *The Chicago Sun Times*, and Bob Woodward of *The Washington Post*) during 2003.[1259]

- Another administration official, Deputy Secretary of State Richard Armitage, leaked Ms. Wilson's identity to Bob Woodward of *The Washington Post* and Robert Novak of *The Chicago Sun Times*.[1260]

- The disclosures may well have been coordinated among White House officials.[1261]

- Soon after the leaks, Ms. Wilson's name and CIA affiliation appeared in the press. Her CIA cover was blown and her CIA career over. The disclosure likely hindered U.S. intelligence efforts and endangered the lives of covert CIA agents working overseas.[1262]

2.   Vice President Cheney himself may have directed or participated in the leak. Several undisputed facts at least raise a strong inference that the Vice President did so.

- Well before Ms. Wilson's identity was leaked, the Vice President informed Mr. Libby that Ambassador "Wilson's wife" worked for the CIA.[1263]

- That June 12, 2003, disclosure occurred in the context of discussions with Mr. Libby about how to respond to press inquiries about Ambassador Wilson.[1264]

- The Vice President specifically directed Mr. Libby to meet with reporter Judith Miller on July 8, 2003, to rebut the allegations set forth in Ambassador Wilson's op-ed in *The New York Times*. It was during this meeting that Mr. Libby disclosed that Ms. Wilson worked at the CIA.[1265]

- A redacted report of the FBI's interview with Mr. Libby reflects that Mr. Libby told the FBI that "it was 'possible' that Vice President Cheney instructed him to disseminate information about Ambassador Wilson's wife to the press."[1266] And a journalist has recently reported that the confidential report of the FBI's interview with Vice President Cheney suggests that the Vice President in fact did so.[1267]

- A handwritten note by the Vice President introduced into evidence includes a notation that Mr. Libby had been sent "into the meat grinder"[1268] to repair the damage from the Niger story.

3.   The leak of Ms. Wilson's covert identity was impermissibly motivated, contravened executive-branch rules governing classified information, and may even have violated

<u>criminal laws governing classified information.</u>

- Karl Rove, Scooter Libby, and Ari Fleischer appear to have leaked Ms. Wilson's identity for the purpose of discrediting Ambassador Wilson following his July 6, 2003, op-ed criticizing the Administration's handling of intelligence during the runup to the 2003 invasion of Iraq. They may also have been motivated by animus toward Ambassador Wilson for criticizing the executive privilege. [1269]

- The Administration officials who leaked Ms. Wilson's covert CIA identity appear to have violated both Executive Order 12958 and the companion terms of the"Classified Non-Disclosure Agreement" that each of them signed.[1270] Executive Order 12958 prohibits any "knowing, willful, or negligent action that could reasonably be expected to result in an unauthorized disclosure of classified information."[1271] The publicly available evidence creates a strong inference that Karl Rove and Scooter Libby actually knew that Ms. Wilson's identity was classified.[1272] If they did not know, they should have inquired about Ms. Wilson's status before leaking her identity.[1273] After all, they knew Ms. Wilson to be a CIA employee who worked in the Counterproliferation Division.

- These White House officials may also have violated criminal laws governing the disclosure of classified information. Chief among them is the Intelligence Identities Protection Act, which prohibits the intentional disclosure of classified information that identifies a "covert agent," if the disclosing party knows "that the information disclose so identifies such covert agent..." and "that the United States is taking measures to conceal such covert agent's" status.[1274] Whether they violated the Act turns principally on whether, at the time of the leaks, they knew that Ms. Wilson was a covert agent within the meaning of this statutory language, what they intended when they disclosed her identity, and whether they acted in concerted.[1275] The public record does not permit a any definitive findings with respect to those questions.[1276]

4.   <u>Numerous improper actions by the President, the Vice President and senior White House officials prevented the public from learning the full truth about the leak of Ms. Wilson's covert identity.</u>

- White House and senior administration officials failed to conduct any investigation into the circumstances of the leak, as required by Executive Order 12958, delayed the appointment of a special counsel, and failed to cooperate adequately with the special counsel's investigation.[1277]

- The President stymied the investigation of both the House Judiciary Committee and the House Oversight Committee by refusing to turn over unredacted versions of copies of FBI reports of interviews with the senior Administration officials, and refused altogether the committees' requests for the interviews of the President and Vice President.[1278]

- The Vice President's Chief of Staff, Scooter Libby, obstructed the Justice Department's investigation into the leak of Ms. Wilson's identity. One juror reported that he and his fellow jurors believed Mr. Libby did so to protect the Vice President.[1279] Whatever Mr. Libby's motivation, his obstruction prevented Special Counsel Fitzgerald from making a "confident determination of what in fact occurred"[1280] – in particular, whether any White House official or the Vice President violated any criminal laws, including the above-cited Intelligence Identifies Protection Act.[1281] Special Counsel Patrick Fitzgerald has likened himself to an umpire who has sand thrown in his eyes.[1282]

- Several White House officials made false and misleading statements to the public about their role in leaking Ms. Wilson's identity. Among them was Karl Rove, who stated that he was not involved in the leak. Conclusive evidence establishes that Karl Rove leaked Ms. Wilson's identity to Robert Novak.[1283]

- Andrew Card, acting at the behest of both the President and Vice President, directed White House Press Secretary Scott McLellan to issue a public statement exonerating Scooter Libby (as he had earlier done for Mr. Rove), despite his reluctance to do so given the pendency of the Justice Department's criminal investigation.[1284] Questions have been raised whether, in so directing Mr. McClellan, Mr. Card, the President, and the Vice President obstructed justice.[1285]

- The grant of clemency to Mr. Libby may have deprived him of any incentive to cooperate with investigators.[1286]

5. <u>The President's failure to honor his promise to fire any leakers, his grant of clemency to Mr. Libby, and his statements about the reasons for the grant of clemency raise serious questions about the propriety of the President's own conduct during the aftermath of the leak.</u>

- President Bush broke his promise to fire anyone in his administration who leaked Ms. Wilson's covert CIA identity. The public record shows the President twice promised in non uncertain terms to fire any leakers.[1287] But on July 18, 2005, when it became clear that Karl Rove and other officials were involved in the leak, the President changed course and raised the accountability bar by declaring that he would fire only leakers found to have violated criminal laws. None of the leakers was ever fired; none was ever disciplined; and none had his security clearance rescinded. Contrary to Executive Order 12958, the President failed even to direct an investigation into the leak.[1288]

- President Bush commuted Mr. Libby's prison sentence even though Mr. Libby criminally obstructed justice the special counsel's investigation into the leak, thereby preventing the grand jury from determining whether a crime had been committed. President Bush's grant of clemency remains subject to the widely leveled criticism that it flouted the rule of law and reflected the President's unwillingness to hold Administration officials accountable for violating the law, even with respect to a matter as important as national security and the safety of U.S. intelligence agents.[1289]

- President Bush may have misled the public when he cited as the reason for the grant of clemency to Mr. Libby the "excessiveness" of Mr. Libby's sentence. Mr. Libby's sentence was not excessive under the Federal Sentencing Guidelines that governed the sentence; even if the President believed it to be excessive, he would presumably have reduced rather than eliminated it.[1290] The Judiciary Committee was unable to determine President's Bush's actual motivation for commuting Mr. Libby's sentence, because the President stonewalled the Committee's request for information.[1291]

Section 5 – Government in the Shadows:
Executive Privilege, Secrecy, and the Manipulation of Intelligence

Executive secrecy is one of the monarchical customs...certainly fatal to republican government.[1292]

– John Taylor
An Inquiry Into the Principles and Policy of the Government of the United States (1814)

The Bush Administration's cloak of secrecy has been interwoven with many of the abuses of executive power recounted in other sections of this Report. This section of the Report considers the Bush Administration's claims of executive privilege; withholding of necessary documents and testimony from Congress without formal executive privilege assertions; use of the state secrets privilege, the president's classification authority, and narrow construction of the Freedom of Information Act. By any measure, this Administration has been extraordinarily secretive. In his first year of office alone, President Bush "delayed the release of presidential papers from the Reagan White House, imposed limits on public access to government documents, refused to share revised data from the 2000 Census, and shielded decades-old FBI records from scrutiny. Advisers even declined to disclose the brand of pretzel that Bush choked on."[1293]

Criticism of the Bush Administration's secrecy has come from across the political spectrum, including would-be allies in Congress and conservative advocacy groups like Judicial Watch. Larry Klayman, former chairman of Judicial Watch, has compared the current Administration to an "Old-World style of government, where the sovereign is considered to be elite and the people are considered to be the rabble, and they have little to no right to know what the government is doing."[1294]

A simple change in administration does not rectify all past harms when some of these expansions of Executive Branch secrecy have been institutionalized. Steven Aftergood, Director of the Project on Government Secrecy at the Federation of American Scientists, points out that, "[o]nce a precedent is set and an administration not sufficiently rebuked, this kind of secrecy becomes a permanent option."[1295]

In examining the Bush Administration's penchant for secrecy, the Iraq War merits particular attention. Beginning shortly after the terrorist attacks on September 11, 2001, the Bush Administration built a case before Congress and the American public for pre-emptive war against Iraq. Investigations by the Judiciary Committee's Democratic Staff, the Senate Intelligence Committee, the House Oversight and Government Reform Committee, and various news agencies subsequently revealed that the Administration had taken the use, misuse, and tailoring of intelligence information to unprecedented lengths in order to bolster support for the war. The

Administration also tried to silence its critics through selective declassification of intelligence assessments and reports by congressional committees.[1296] As Senator Bob Graham wrote in 2003, "[t]he recent scandal over the Bush Administration's manipulation of intelligence data leading up to the war in Iraq is a glaring example of why our government should be open and honest with the American people."[1297]

I.   Executive Privilege

A.   Formal Assertions of Executive Privilege

"Executive privilege" is an assertion made by the president of the United States as grounds for refusing to produce information or documents, or for witnesses refusing to answer questions, in response to a request or subpoena. The concept of "executive privilege" is not mentioned in the Constitution, but is grounded in the separation of powers doctrine. Past presidents have argued that executive privilege is necessary to ensure frank and candid information exchange in the Executive Branch, and have generally used it to protect conversations and information provided to or from the president or, in some very limited circumstances, top presidential advisers.

Pushing the Boundaries Early On

Signs of President Bush's broad interpretation of executive privilege appeared shortly after he first took office, beginning with two assertions of executive privilege blocking requests for Clinton-era documents. The first came in early 2001, when the conservative non-profit Judicial Watch submitted Freedom of Information Act (FOIA) requests to the Department of Justice for documents related to pardon applications considered by President Clinton. The Justice Department withheld approximately 4,300 pages of responsive documents, claiming that they were exempt from production under the presidential communications and deliberative process privileges.[1298] Judicial Watch filed a lawsuit to obtain the documents and, on appeal, the court rebuked the Bush Administration's attempt to expand the presidential communications privilege to documents that were not "solicited and received" by the president.[1299]

Shortly after the Judicial Watch case began, then-Chairman of the House Committee on Government Reform Dan Burton issued a subpoena to the Justice Department for memoranda relating to the Committee's investigation of corruption allegations at the FBI's Boston field office. The Administration resisted the subpoena, and, as characterized by Chairman Burton, "explained to the Chairman and Committee staff that the Administration wished to establish an inflexible policy to withhold from Congress all deliberative prosecutorial documents."[1300] In December 2001, President Bush invoked executive privilege and directed Attorney General John Ashcroft not to produce the subpoenaed documents. Although the dispute was eventually resolved and the documents handed over to the Committee, the Committee report on the matter records that "it was clear that the Administration sought to establish a new restrictive policy regarding prosecutorial documents and that no demonstration of need by the Committee would be sufficient for the Justice Department to produce the documents."[1301]

<u>FBI's Valerie Plame Leak Investigation</u>

In early 2007, the House Oversight and Government Reform Committee opened an investigation into the leak of covert CIA agent Valerie Plame Wilson's identity by White House officials.[1302] The Committee began with a hearing on March 16, 2007, at which it heard testimony from Ms. Wilson and White House Security Office Director James Knodell. Mr. Knodell testified that his office never conducted an investigation into the leak of Ms. Wilson's identity, due to the ongoing criminal investigation; that senior White House officials had failed to report their knowledge of the leak, as required by Executive Order 12958; and that there were no administrative sanctions for White House officials as a result of the leak.[1303] On July 16, 2007, Chairman Henry Waxman wrote to Special Counsel Patrick Fitzgerald and requested documents from his investigation into the leak, including reports from FBI interviews of the President and Vice President.[1304] Mr. Fitzgerald produced many of the requested documents but, at the request of the White House, withheld records of interviews of White House officials.[1305] Chairman Waxman appealed to the Attorney General for an "independent judgment" to produce the documents and, following months of negotiations, the request was fulfilled in part.[1306]

Despite negotiations and repeated requests by Chairman Waxman, however, the Justice Department continued its refusal to produce the interview reports of the President and Vice President. On June 16, 2008, the Oversight Committee issued a subpoena to Attorney General Mukasey for those interview records. The return date was set for June 23, 2008.[1307] In response, the Justice Department wrote to the Committee on June 24, 2008, that it would not provide the subpoenaed documents and mentioned the possible executive privilege implications in the matter.[1308] Chairman Waxman wrote to the Attorney General on July 8, 2008, informing him that the Committee would refrain from seeking the records of the President's interview for the time, but reiterating the request for the Vice President's interview report and informing him that the Committee would meet on July 16 to consider citing the Attorney General with contempt unless the documents were produced or a valid assertion of privilege was made.[1309]

On July 16, 2008, the Department of Justice informed the House Oversight and Government Reform Committee that, at the Attorney General's request, the President had asserted executive privilege in response to that Committee's subpoena for documents related to the FBI's investigation of the leak.[1310] Enclosed with the letter was a legal opinion written by Attorney General Mukasey for the President, arguing that the content of the subpoenaed documents fell "squarely within the presidential communications and deliberative process components of executive privilege," and further contending that because the documents sought were from law enforcement files, the "law enforcement component of executive privilege" also applied.[1311] Chairman Waxman's request for a privilege log describing the withheld documents was also refused.[1312]

In report approved by Oversight and Government Reform Committee Chairman Waxman and former Ranking Member Tom Davis "agreed that the President's assertion of executive privilege over [the report of the FBI interview with the Vice President] was legally unprecedented and an inappropriate use of executive privilege."[1313] The Chairman and Ranking Member explained that the "Vice President had no reasonable expectation of confidentiality regarding the statements he made to Mr. Fitzgerald and the FBI agents,"[1314] and that the presidential communications privilege that has been carved out by the courts does not cover summaries of conversations provided to third parties.[1315] They further rejected the President's privilege claims on the basis that there is "no precedent in which executive privilege has been asserted over communications between a vice president and his staff about vice presidential decision-making,"[1316] pointing out the apparent inconsistency between the privilege claim at hand and the argument of David Addington, the Vice President's Chief of Staff, that "the Vice President belongs neither to the executive nor the legislative branch."[1317]

The Bush Administration's invocation of the presidential communications component of executive privilege was far from surprising given the consistency with which it has defended the broad application of the privilege. However, it was Attorney General Mukasey's argument for the application of a "law enforcement component of executive privilege" that took legal scholars by surprise. Peter Shane, an expert on executive privilege at Ohio State University Moritz College of Law, called the claim "utterly unprecedented," and one that he had never heard of before.[1318] Mark Rozell, executive privilege expert at George Mason University, called the Administration's claim "an argument to protect the White House's own political interests and save it from embarrassment."[1319] The Committee's bipartisan report refuted the notion of a law enforcement executive privilege claim, noting that the Attorney General did not cite any judicial decision recognizing it, and that the Department's opinion memoranda that he cited applied only to open investigations, not the Special Counsel's closed case.[1320]

EPA Investigation

In 2005, California requested that the Environmental Protection Agency (EPA) waive federal standards for greenhouse gas emission standards for cars on the grounds that its own state standards were more stringent.[1321] Section 209(b) of the Clean Air Act requires the EPA to waive federal preemption of California motor vehicle emissions standards if California's standards are, in aggregate, as protective of public health and welfare as federal standards.[1322] After a nearly two-year delay, the EPA rejected the request. The House Oversight and Government Reform Committee began investigating allegations of political interference in the waiver decision in late 2007 and, through interviews with EPA staff and Associate Deputy Administrator Jason Burnett, learned that EPA career staff had unanimously communicated to the Administrator on multiple occasions that the waiver should be granted.[1323] The Committee also learned that EPA Administrator Stephen Johnson was interested in granting the waiver until he communicated with the White House regarding the decision.[1324]

In early 2008, the Bush Administration was separately accused of improperly pressuring the Environmental Protection Agency to weaken certain proposed regulations affecting smog and greenhouse gas levels. The Clean Air Act established a Clean Air Scientific Advisory Committee to advise the EPA Administrator on setting national ambient air quality standards (measured by levels of ozone in the atmosphere). The Advisory Committee and EPA career staff recommended amending the standards to more stringent levels, a recommendation echoed in the draft final rule submitted by EPA Administrator Johnson to the White House Office of Management and Budget (OMB) on February 22, 2008.[1325] On March 11, 2008, just hours before the final rule was to be released, EPA staff learned that the rule was to be rewritten to implement a less stringent standard.[1326] The next day, Susan Dudley, Administrator of the Office of Information and Regulatory Affairs at OMB, explained in a letter to EPA Administrator Johnson that the President had reviewed the proposed standards and concluded that the less stringent standard should be adopted.[1327]

On March 14, 2008, Chairman Waxman of the House Oversight and Government Reform Committee wrote to Administrators Johnson and Dudley to request documents relating to the ozone standards decision.[1328] Although some documents were produced, the EPA and OMB withheld many of the documents responsive to Chairman Waxman's requests. On April 9 and May 5, 2008, Chairman Waxman issued subpoenas to EPA Administrator Johnson for the outstanding documents related to EPA communications with the White House in both cases.[1329] Chairman Waxman also issued a subpoena to Susan Dudley for OMB documents related to the ozone standards regulation decision.[1330] Because the EPA and OMB continued to withhold the majority of documents responsive to the subpoenas, the Oversight and Government Reform Committee scheduled a vote to hold Administrators Dudley and Johnson in contempt of Congress for June 20, 2008. The day of the scheduled vote, Chairman Waxman received letters from the EPA and OMB informing him that President Bush had asserted executive privilege over the disputed documents and the vote was cancelled so the Committee could review the privilege claims.[1331]

The June 20 letters asserting privilege both included a June 19, 2008, letter from Attorney General Michael Mukasey to the President regarding the basis for asserting executive privilege with respect to the Committee's investigations, arguing that the documents "implicate both the presidential communications and deliberative process components of executive privilege."[1332] Upon review of the Attorney General's analysis, the Committee rejected the privilege claims:

> The President's assertion of executive privilege...is expansive. It covers any communications that occurred within the White House, no matter how attenuated the connection between the staff authoring the communications and the presidential decisionmaking process. At the same time, the Administration has barred a key EPA official from responding to Committee questions about these communications and has refused to provide the Committee basic information about the authorship and distribution of the documents that would enable the Committee to assess the merits of the privilege claim and whether further accommodations could be achieved. The assertion of executive privilege under these circumstances has stymied the Committee's investigation of the

waiver and ozone decisions.

For these reasons, the Committee finds that the President's assertion of executive privilege is wrong and an abuse of the privilege.[1333]

On October 23, 2008, the House Oversight and Government Reform approved by voice vote a report rejecting the President's privilege claims. No additional documents were produced by either the EPA or OMB in response to the subpoenas.

Investigation Into the U.S. Attorney Firings by the House and Senate Judiciary Committees

The most arguably protracted fight over executive privilege during the Bush Administration has stemmed from the House and Senate Judiciary Committees' struggle to enforce subpoenas issued in the course of investigations into the U.S. Attorneys firings controversy that began in early 2007.[1334]

Before the Committees had even issued subpoenas, the President and other Administration officials made statements suggesting that executive privilege would be invoked in response to congressional requests for documents or testimony.[1335] In response, the House Judiciary Committee's Commercial and Administrative Law Subcommittee held a hearing on March 29, 2007, titled "Ensuring Executive Branch Accountability." The Subcommittee examined executive privilege claims in the context of the U.S. Attorneys firings controversy and related issues. The discussion among the Subcommittee members and witnesses explored the contours of executive privilege and its potential use to block congressional inquiry, specifically as related to the appearance of presidential advisors for testimony before Congress.

During the hearing, Representative Hank Johnson (D-GA) asked what factors should be taken into account in balancing executive privilege against congressional oversight functions. Panelist Beth Nolan, former White House Counsel to President Clinton, responded as follows:

> First of all, I would like to say that no court has ever addressed this claim that former presidents have made, and this president seems to be making, that White House advisors are immune from being called to testify. There is no judicial decision on that. **The judicial decisions we do have say that executive privilege involves balancing**....We have seen that courts may look, for instance, in a case such as this where I think there is no question that Congress has oversight authority with respect to these matters, then is Congress able to obtain the information in another way. That would be one question that you might look to.[1336]

Subcommittee Chair Sánchez asked the panelists if Congress needed to establish a likelihood of criminal wrongdoing in the case of the U.S. Attorney firings in order to overcome an assertion of the presidential communications privilege, or if "an indication of inefficiency or maladministration" would be sufficient.[1337] Panelist Beth Nolan responded as follows:

> I certainly think so. If you have something that looks like obstruction of justice, an attempt to interfere with individual cases for reasons that really should be outside the authority of officials to do, then I think that is exactly the kind of thing. You are talking then about issues, whether they are criminal obstruction of justice or whether it is simply questions about the administration of justice, impartial execution of prosecutorial discretion, questions that really go to the heart of the rule of law and our criminal justice system, then **I would say that not only does Congress have the right to receive information relevant to that, but it has a responsibility**. That is what the American people look to Congress to do."[1338]

As previously stated, despite numerous attempts to reach a compromise with the Administration and secure the voluntary production of the needed documents and testimony, the Committee was forced to issue subpoenas to former White House Counsel Harriet Miers and White House Chief of Staff and custodian of records Josh Bolten on June 13, 2007. On the same day, the Senate Judiciary Committee also issued subpoenas for the White House documents as well as documents and testimony from Sara Taylor, former Deputy Assistant to the President and Director of Political Affairs. On June 28, 2007, White House Counsel Fred Fielding wrote to Chairmen Conyers and Leahy, informing them that the President had decided to exert executive privilege with respect to the subpoenaed White House documents and had likewise directed Ms. Miers and Ms. Taylor not to produce any documents.[1339] The Committee later learned that the White House also directed Ms. Miers not to appear or testify before the House Judiciary Committee.

In the face of intransigence on the part of Administration officials to comply with the subpoenas as noted in Section 1, the full House passed the Judiciary Committee's resolution to hold Harriet Miers and Josh Bolten in contempt of Congress on February 14, 2008, as well as a resolution authorizing the Judiciary Committee to file a lawsuit to obtain the subpoenaed documents and testimony. As the Committee explained in its report on the Miers-Bolten contempt resolution, the Administration's expansive claims of executive privilege were rejected on four grounds:

(i) The privilege was not properly asserted because, despite requests from Chairman Conyers, there was never a directive personally signed by the President asserting executive privilege. In past privilege cases, the courts have stated that a personal assertion by the president is legally required and this principle has been recognized in previous House contempt proceedings.[1340]

239

(ii)   The courts had previously held that a party asserting executive privilege in response to a subpoena for documents must produce a privilege log describing each document being withheld. Despite requests by Chairman Conyers that the White House produce a privilege log in an effort to reach a compromise in the matter, no such log was ever produced.[1341]

(iii)   The presidential communications privilege – the specific form of executive privilege that covers communications by the president or his immediate advisors – did not apply to the information requested by the Committee. Although one court of appeals has extended executive privilege with respect to communications to or from some White House staff "in the course of preparing advice for the president" for a decision to be made by the president,[1342] the White House itself has maintained that President Bush never received any advice on, and was not himself involved in, the U.S. Attorney firings.[1343]

(iv)   The compelling need of the House of Representatives to obtain the subpoenaed documents and testimony greatly outweighed the claims of executive privilege.

The White House's claims of executive privilege and immunity from subpoena were met with similar disagreement from legal scholars and editorial boards. Constitutional lawyer and former Reagan Justice Department appointee Bruce Fein wrote, "President Bush's assertion of executive privilege to stymie the committee's well-founded investigations is wildly misplaced."[1344] Another expert on constitutional law, Professor Erwin Chemerinsky of Duke University School of Law, wrote to Chairman Conyers:

> From a constitutional perspective, the claims of executive privilege
> are not sufficient to overcome Congress's constitutional
> responsibility to conduct meaningful oversight and to consider
> possible federal legislation. Simply put, this is a situation where the
> claim of executive privilege is weak and the need for congressional
> access to the information is strong.[1345]

In an editorial published on November 16, 2007, after the Committee had filed its report recommending that Harriet Miers and Josh Bolten be held in contempt but before the full House voted on the contempt resolutions, *The New York Times* cautioned:

> The Bush Administration's days are numbered. But the damage it
> has done to the balance of powers could be long-lasting. **If
> Congress wants to maintain its Constitutional role, it needs to
> stand up for itself. A good place to start is by making clear that
> its legitimate investigative authority cannot be defied, and any
> who choose to do so will pay a heavy price.**[1346]

Following the House's passage of the contempt resolutions, Speaker of the House Nancy Pelosi referred the citations to the U.S. Attorney for the District of Columbia, "whose duty," according to the statute that provides for the prosecution of contempt of Congress citations, "it shall be to bring the matter before the grand jury for its action."[1347] On February 29, 2008, Attorney General Michael Mukasey responded to Speaker Pelosi that, "the Department has concluded that the non-compliance by Mr. Bolten and Ms. Miers with the Judiciary Committee subpoenas did not constitute a crime, and therefore the Department will not bring the congressional contempt citations before a grand jury or take any other action to prosecute Mr. Bolten or Ms. Miers."[1348]

In response to the Justice Department's refusal to enforce the contempt citations, the Committee filed a civil action in the District of Columbia federal district court seeking a ruling that the Administration's theories of executive privilege were legally unsound and the enforcement of the Committee's subpoenas. As stated in Section 1, Judge John Bates granted the Committee's motion for partial summary judgement, ruling that the White House's claims that Harriet Miers was immune from the congressional subpoena were invalid, and that the Administration owed the Committee a detailed listing of the documents being withheld.[1349] Although Judge Bates was not asked to rule on the White House's executive privilege claims, he did order the Administration to produce a detailed listing of the documents being withheld.[1350] The Administration appealed the ruling, however, and the matter is now pending before the U.S. Court of Appeals for the District of Columbia. The Administration also successfully petitioned the appellate court for a stay of Judge Bate's ruling pending the appeal, and as of the date of this Report, the White House has still not produced any documents in response to the Committee's subpoena and Harriet Miers has not testified.[1351]

As discussed in Section 1 of this Report, the Judiciary Committee's investigation into the U.S. Attorney firings led to an investigation of allegations of politically selective prosecutions.[1352] On May 22, 2008, the Committee subpoenaed former White House adviser Karl Rove to question him about allegations that he pressured the Justice Department to prosecute former Alabama Governor Don Siegelman and the broader U.S. Attorneys controversy. On July 9, 2008, the day before Mr. Rove was scheduled to appear before the Commercial and Administrative Law Subcommittee, his attorney Robert Luskin informed Chairman Conyers that Mr. Rove would not comply with the subpoena, pursuant to a direction from the President.[1353] In a letter to Mr. Luskin, also sent on July 9, White House Counsel Fred Fielding wrote that the White House had "been advised by the Department of Justice ... that a present or former immediate adviser to the President is constitutionally immune from compelled congressional testimony about matters that arose during his or her tenure as a presidential aide and relate to his or her official duties."[1354] The White House argued that forcing the President to testify before Congress would violate the Executive Branch's status as co-equal to Congress and the separation of powers – essentially that the President's executive privilege protects him from any congressional subpoena. The White House further claimed that a president's advisers are an extension of the president himself – his "alter ego" – and that therefore forcing a close presidential adviser to testify would also violate separation of powers principles.[1355]

The Subcommittee on Commercial and Administrative Law met on July 10, 2008, and considered Karl Rove's claim of executive privilege-related immunity. Subcommittee Chair Sánchez ruled that the claims were invalid because they were not properly asserted; because no court has ever held that presidential advisers are immune from compulsory process in any setting; because the claims contradicted the practice of the Bush Administration and other administrations of allowing presidential advisers to testify before Congress; because Mr. Rove had spoken publicly about the matters the Committee wished to discuss with him; and because the White House had previously stated that the President had no personal involvement in the matter, a critical element in a valid assertion of executive privilege.[1356] The Subcommittee upheld the ruling by a vote of 7-1. On July 30, 2008, the Committee voted 20-14 to approve a report recommending that Karl Rove be cited for contempt of Congress by the full House of Representatives. The Committee filed its report on September 15, 2008.

B.   Withholding Documents or Testimony Without Formally Asserting Executive Privilege

Throughout the two terms of President George W. Bush, the Administration has on numerous occasions used threats of executive privilege or made public statements implying that some facet of executive privilege might apply, in order to stifle requests for information.

One of the Bush Administration's earliest applications of the principles underlying executive privilege without a formal privilege assertion can be found in Vice President Cheney's refusal to comply with a request by the General Accounting Office (GAO) for information related to the National Energy Policy Development Group (NEPDG), consisting of high-level federal officials led by Vice President Cheney, which was charged with recommending a proposal for a national energy policy.[1357] Democrats in Congress were critical of the policy the group developed – worried that it simply called for increased drilling for oil and coal while ignoring the need for renewable energy sources – and also of the secrecy surrounding the NEPDG's deliberative process.[1358] On April 19, 2001, Reps. John Dingell and Henry Waxman, then-Ranking Members of the House Energy and Commerce and Government Reform Committees, respectively, asked the GAO to study the NEPDG; specifically, they wanted to know the extent to which the group consulted with representatives of energy corporations.[1359]

The Vice President's office repeatedly denied attempts by GAO access to information related to the NEPDG, despite numerous attempts at accommodation by the GAO General Counsel and Comptroller General.[1360] On February 22, 2002, the GAO "reluctantly" filed suit against Vice President Cheney, noting that it was "the first time that GAO [had] filed suit against a federal official in connection with a records access issue."[1361] The district court dismissed the case on procedural grounds on December 9, 2002. [1362]

Although the GAO did not appeal the District Court's dismissal, the non-profit groups Sierra Club, Inc. and Judicial Watch filed suit against Vice President Cheney to obtain information related to the NEPDG meetings. The case eventually made its way to the Supreme

242

Court as *Cheney v. U.S. District Court*. As former Massachusetts Special Assistant Attorney General Joan Lukey wrote in *The Washington Post*:

> Throughout the Cheney litigation, the Administration took the novel position that it would not assert "executive privilege" as grounds for withholding the information ... **Instead, the White House insisted on relying on the somewhat amorphous (some might even say squishy) notion that the task force documents were protected because the vice president was operating pursuant to his "executive powers."** The Administration therefore took the position that if it did not assert executive privilege and the vice president was carrying out the duties conferred on the executive by the Constitution, the documents relating to those duties did not have to be turned over -- and the courts did not have the right to review that decision.[1363]

After sending the case back to the appellate court, the Supreme Court advised the lower court to be "mindful of the burdens imposed on the executive branch in any future proceedings," thereby implicitly rejecting the Bush Administration's contention that the Vice President's activities should not be subject to pretrial discovery at all.[1364] Eventually, the appellate court concluded that because sub-groups of the NEPDG were not advisory committees subject to the Federal Advisory Committee Act, the Vice President did not have to disclose information concerning the identities of the energy lobbyists who participated in NEPDG meetings and the extent to which their views shaped the NEPDG's policy recommendations.[1365]

At the same time, another battle raged over the Administration's willingness to allow the testimony of top-level officials at the hearings held by the National Commission on Terrorist Attacks Upon the United States, commonly known as the 9/11 Commission. This dispute came to a head when, in early 2004, then-National Security Adviser Condoleezza Rice refused to testify publicly before the Commission. According to her spokeswoman, Bush Administration attorneys requested that Dr. Rice's testimony before the Commission, a body created by congressional mandate and therefore legislative in the eyes of the White House, would set a precedent for legislative branch oversight over executive branch staff.[1366] Although the Administration did not directly assert executive privilege over the testimony, press reports and public statements by Commission and congressional officials indicated that similar concerns underlay the Administration's resistance.[1367]

The White House's argument in favor of keeping Dr. Rice's conversations with the Commission behind closed doors was no doubt undercut by her frequent appearance in the media discussing subjects that would be covered in her testimony.[1368] The Administration eventually reversed course and allowed Dr. Rice to testify, but in his letter explaining the reversal, White House Counsel Alberto Gonzales insisted, "Dr. Rice's public testimony ... does not set, and should not be cited as, a precedent for future requests for a National Security Adviser or any other

White House Official to testify before a legislative body."[1369]

On the same day as the reversal, the Administration refused to allow Doug Badger, Special Assistant to the President for Health Policy, to testify before the House Ways and Means Committee in a hearing focusing on the cost of Medicare's prescription drug program.[1370] Echoing his earlier letters concerning Dr. Rice's testimony before the 9/11 Commission, then-White House Counsel Alberto Gonzales wrote to Committee Chairman Bill Thomas, "[i]t is longstanding White House policy, applied during administrations of both parties, that members of the White House staff should decline invitations to testify at congressional hearings."[1371] As then-Member Charles Rangel pointed out, however, White House officials from both the Bush and Clinton Administrations had in fact testified before congressional Committees.[1372] Similar to the White House's initial refusal to allow Dr. Rice's testimony, President Bush made no formal assertion of executive privilege, but the argument by Mr. Gonzales was that public testimony by White House staff would have a chilling effect on a president's ability to receive candid advice from his or her staff. Ways and Means Ranking Member Rangel disagreed with the White House:

> **Executive privilege only applies when an official has had conversations directly with the President.** In invoking executive privilege, we must assume that the topic of withholding these estimates was a topic of conversation between Mr. Badger and the President himself. In any event, accounts of conversations or exchanges between White House officials and the drug industry or members of Congress [as was the case with the testimony sought by the Committee from Mr. Badger] are clearly not a place where separation of powers applies.[1373]

In response to the White House's refusal to allow the testimony, Democrats on the Ways and Means Committee attempted to have the Committee subpoena Doug Badger and another witness who was unavailable to testify at the requested time. The Committee vote failed 23 to 16 along party lines and, under Republican leadership, the matter ended there.[1374]

The House Judiciary Committee has also had difficulty obtaining testimony from White House officials in matters over which the President has not formally asserted executive privilege. As noted in Section 4 of this Report, Chairman Conyers wrote to President Bush in advance of a July 12, 2007, Judiciary Committee hearing on the President's July 2 decision to commute former Vice Presidential Chief of Staff Scooter Libby's prison sentence. He informed the President of the upcoming hearing and requested that President Bush decline to assert executive privilege and allow White House officials to testify before the Committee on the Libby clemency. Chairman Conyers cited President Clinton's decision to allow top-level staff to testify before the House Government Reform Committee concerning the pardon of Marc Rich as well as President Ford's testimony before the Judiciary Committee in 1974 about his decision to pardon President Nixon.[1375]

White House Counsel Fred Fielding declined Chairman Conyers's request.[1376] Although Mr. Fielding did not indicate that the President had asserted executive privilege, his letter discussed and cited an opinion memorandum written by Attorney General Janet Reno to advise President Clinton on the legal basis for a decision to exert executive privilege in response to a congressional inquiry on a pardon decision.[1377]

II. Improper Use of State Secrets and Other Authorities

A. Abuse of State Secrets

The state secrets privilege allows the Executive Branch to prevent the release of documents and information in litigation if disclosure would compromise national security. The privilege was first recognized by the Supreme Court in *U.S. v. Reynolds,*[1378] and was derived from the president's constitutional authority to protect the Nation. In the years following *Reynolds*, the state secrets privilege was used sparingly. Courts in turn were respectfully of the Executive's judgment in these areas, and in the few state secrets cases that arose, rarely compelled disclosure over the government's objection.

During the Bush Administration, however, invocation of the privilege has exploded. In its first six years, the Administration raised the privilege in almost 30 percent more cases per year than the prior administrations (and there is no reason to believe that the rate of invocation has slowed).[1379] According to one report, "[t]he government invoked the privilege in only four cases between 1953 and 1976, but it has been invoked more than 20 times since the September 11 terrorist attacks and at least five times" in 2006 alone."[1380] And beyond the simple increase in assertions, the Bush Administration has expanded the purposes for which it invokes the privilege. Prior to the Bush Administration, the privilege was used to justify the government's refusal to disclose information or to bar certain evidence from trial.[1381] Under President Bush, however, the Administration has urged that the privilege requires outright dismissal of sensitive lawsuit. Indeed, the Administration has argued for this sort of total dismissal in over 90 percent more cases than previous administrations.[1382]

Under the Bush Administration, state secrets doctrine has been invoked in seeking dismissal of lawsuits in cases involving: (i) extraordinary rendition; (ii) the warrantless wiretapping program; (iii) post-9/11 detention of American citizens; and (iv) lawsuits brought by former federal employees alleging racial discrimination and retaliation, as discussed below.

Extraordinary rendition

As noted in Section 2, the state secrets doctrine has been invoked in two cases involving extraordinary rendition of terrorism suspects. In the first case, a German national named Khalid El-Masri sought compensation after having been reportedly abducted by a European police force, transferred to the Central Intelligence Agency, and then taken to Afghanistan and tortured.[1383] Mr. El-Masri was eventually released when it became clear that he was an innocent man and this was a case of mistaken identity. A federal judge granted the Administration's request to dismiss Mr. El-Masri's case on state secrets grounds, accepting its assertion that allowing the litigation to proceed would compromise national security. In October 2007, the Supreme Court declined to hear the matter on appeal.[1384] Mr. El-Masri wrote of his experience attending the appellate court's argument in his case:

> Although I did not understand all of the arguments made by the lawyers, I was impressed by the dignity of the proceedings and by the respect for the rule of law that I have always associated with America. I'm deeply disappointed to find that this same legal system denies me the chance to fully present my case...
>
> During my visit in November, many Americans offered me their personal apologies for the brutality that had been perpetrated against me in their name. I saw in their faces the true America, an America that is not held captive by fear of unknown enemies and that understands the strength and power of justice. **That is the America that, I hope, one day will see me as a human being — not a state secret.**[1385]

The state secrets doctrine also formed the basis of the dismissal of a lawsuit brought by Canadian Maher Arar, whose case is also discussed in Section 2.[1386] Mr. Arar's request for civil compensation based on his rendition to Syria, where he was tortured, was dismissed by a New York-based federal court, although the matter has recently been re-argued.[1387]

In comments following the dismissal of his suit, Mr. Arar said, "[i]f the courts will not stop this evil act, who is going to stop this administration?... The court system is what distinguishes the West from the Third World. When a court will not act because of 'national security,' there is no longer any difference between the West and the Third World."[1388]

Warrantless Wiretapping Program

As noted in Section 2, the Bush Administration has used the state secrets doctrine to urge that cases challenging its domestic warrantless surveillance programs be dismissed.[1389]

In the Al-Haramain case,[1390] the Muslim charity Al-Haramain Islamic Foundation argued that it was the subject of illegal warrantless surveillance by the government. The basis for this claim, in part, was a document accidentally produced to the Foundation's lawyers indicating that their conversations with Foundation officials had been monitored by the government.[1391] Because of the accidental production, the FBI later repossessed this document. Then the Administration argued that the Foundation's case should be dismissed because it could not prove that it had been monitored. When the Foundation argued that the repossessed document proved it had been monitored, the Administration then argued that the state secrets privilege barred any mention of the document and refused to release it or confirm its contents.[1392] The Appeals Court hearing the case ultimately dismissed the Foundation's request for the critical document.[1393]

Employee lawsuits

The state secrets doctrine was also relied on by the Bush Administration to prevent whistleblower Sibel Edmonds from challenging her dismissal from the FBI's translation division. Ms. Edmonds, hired for her proficiency in Middle Eastern languages, was fired less than a year after she reported numerous deficiencies in the translation process to her supervisors, including poorly translated documents from before September 11, 2001, that had been relevant to the impending attacks. After raising concerns about these and other issues, Ms. Edmonds was fired. When she sued to recover her job or compensation for what she was alleged was her improper dismissal, the Administration successfully argued that the state secrets privilege barred the suit.[1394] She was also prevented from testifying in a civil suit brought by families of 9/11 victims.[1395] The state secrets doctrine was also invoked to obtain a dismissal of a racial discrimination case brought by former CIA agent Jeffrey Sterling against George Tenet and other CIA officials.[1396]

The Constitution Subcommittee held a hearing on January 29, 2008, concerning the issue of the misuse of the state secrets doctrine. Testimony was received from H. Thomas Wells, Jr., President-Elect, American Bar Association; Judith Loether, daughter of one of the victims of the plane crash at issue in *U.S. v. Reynolds*; the Honrable Patricia Wald, retired Chief Judge for the U.S. Court of Appeals for the D.C. Circuit; Patrick Philbin, partner at Kirkland & Ellis; and Kevin Bankston, Senior Attorney, Electronic Frontier Foundation.

Ms. Loether testified about the death of her father, an RCA engineer working under Air Force contract, when she was just seven years old. She testified that she had not known much about the accident or the lawsuit involving her family's quest for compensation that had ended in the United States Supreme Court. And she explained how, years later, doing a random internet search for information on her father's death, she had come across the supposedly secret report that the Supreme Court had allowed the government to conceal, which actually contained no national security information at all. Ms. Loether explained:

> The more I understood what had happened to my mother and why, the more betrayed I felt. **It seemed that the case that allows the Executive to keep its secrets was, at its very foundation, a gross overstatement by the government to forward its own purposes; to get themselves a privilege.** At what cost? The cost was truth and justice and faith in this government.[1397]

Most of the witnesses agreed that, given the increased use of the state secrets privilege to seek dismissal of cases, it was necessary to craft solutions that would allow for greater judicial review of privilege claims and the requisite flexibility to fashion appropriate orders.[1398] In the words of Dr. Louis Fisher, Specialist in Constitutional Law with the Law Library of the Library of

Congress:

> Assertions are assertions, nothing more. Judges need to look at
> disputed documents and not rely on how the executive branch
> characterizes them. Affidavits and declarations signed by executive
> officials, even when classified, are not sufficient....What is at stake
> is more than the claim or assertion by the executive branch
> regarding state secrets. **Congress needs to protect the vitality of
> a political system that is based on separation of powers, checks
> and balances, and safeguards to individual rights.**[1399]

B.   Abuse of Other Authorities

Above and beyond the misuse of the executive and state secrets privileges, the Bush
Administration has used a variety of other authorities to prevent Congress and the American
public from obtaining access to information regarding its conduct. Although the Judiciary
Committee was not able to conduct a comprehensive review of all of these matters through
oversight hearings, it is useful to briefly inventory some of the more salient concerns that have
come to light with respect to classification authorities, the Freedom of Information Act, the
Presidential Records Act, and the Vice President's Office.

Classification

Since 1940, Executive Orders have governed federal policy on the classification of
documents pertaining to national security. There are generally three levels of classification – "top
secret," "secret," and "confidential," in order of exclusivity. In addition, certain federal agencies
have been allowed to create their own internal classification procedures.[1400] The Clinton
Administration, under Attorney General Janet Reno, favored a policy of transparency. President
Clinton's Executive Order 12958 promoted disclosure by, among other things,

- limiting the duration of classification in most cases to 10 years;

- creating a system for automatically declassifying historical documents of
  significance 25 years or older;

- establishing a system for challenging classification designations, as well as an
  appeals process for those decisions;

- instilling a presumption towards lower classification or non-classification in
  situations where there was doubt as to the proper level of classification.

As a result, under the Clinton Administration, the Executive Branch declassified nearly ten times
as many documents as the historical average.[1401]

On March 25, 2003, President Bush issued Executive Order 13292, revising the Clinton order and reversing many of its key policies in ways that encouraged excessive classification and discouraged appropriate declassification.[1402] Some of the key differences between the two orders include:

- The Bush order deleted the sections in the Clinton order resolving doubtful classifications in favor of lower or non-classification, allowing federal officials to classify documents with a dubious need for secrecy.

- Where the Clinton order used 10 years as a default duration for most documents, the Bush Administration allowed for an initial classification period of 25 years. While the Clinton order limited extensions to ten-year periods, the Bush order has no limit on extensions.[1403]

- Under the Clinton order, documents 25 years old or more deemed by the Archivist of the United States to be of historic value were automatically declassified, unless the controlling agency head determined that their release "should" result in one of several specific harms. The Bush order changed the operative standard from "should" to "could," thus dramatically weakening the standard.[1404]

- The Bush order strengthened other standards in favor of withholding. Portions of the Clinton order which had stated that information in specified substantive categories "may" be classified were revised to read that such information "shall be" classified.

In addition to developing general rules favoring classification, the Bush Administration has used its classification authority in numerous instances to protect against disclosure of potentially unlawful or inappropriate activities. For example, the White House attempted to retroactively classify parts of the Joint Congressional Intelligence Committee's report on its inquiry into the 9/11 attacks that had already been made public, including excerpts from the FBI's July 2001 Phoenix flight-school memo previously published elsewhere, the names of senior Administration officials, and information on anti-terror intelligence previously disclosed in public testimony.[1405] The Bush Administration also sought to block the release of the Joint Congressional Intelligence Committee's report.[1406] Senator Bob Graham, Chairman of the Senate Intelligence Committee at the time of the report's release, also alleged that the Bush Administration made politically-motivated classification decisions when it shielded portions of the Joint Committee's report that raised suspicions of possible support for some of the 9/11 hijackers by officials in Saudi Arabia.[1407]

The Bush Administration also attempted to limit the access Members of Congress had to classified information needed to carry out their oversight and legislative duties. On October 5, 2001, President Bush issued a memorandum to the heads of the State, Treasury, Defense and Justice Departments, as well as the Directors of the FBI and CIA, instructing that the only

Members who could receive briefings regarding classified or sensitive law enforcement information were the Speaker of the House, the House Minority Leader, the Senate Majority and Minority Leaders, and the Chairs and Ranking Members of the two Intelligence Committees–a group that is commonly known as the "gang of eight."[1408] Members of both parties in both houses of Congress decried the new policy as too restrictive and the House Defense Appropriations Subcommittee postponed a scheduled markup of a $318 billion defense spending bill until the new directive was reversed.[1409] Although the President responded to the outcry by easing the restrictions and allowing additional members to receive classified briefings, disputes between Congress and the Executive Branch over the release of classified information continued.[1410]

The same pattern followed with other classified information needed for effective congressional oversight of the Administration's national security operations. Key legal memoranda and other documents were withheld from Members and cleared staff regarding the domestic warrantless surveillance program, even while Members were being pressed by the Administration to review and revise that program.[1411] As noted in Section 2 of this Report, these materials were eventually provided, but only when it became clear that Congress would not provide the Administration with desired legislation without gaining this access.[1412] Similarly, numerous Office of Legal Counsel legal opinions and memoranda dealing with issues of presidential power, including those regarding the Administration's interrogation programs and its legal views on the hostilities in Iraq were withheld despite requests and subpoenas from both House and Senate Committees, even where the memoranda were not classified and even were they had been superceded or revoked. Eventually, some access was gained to these materials, but only after burdensome negotiations and the scheduling of possible contempt votes in the House Judiciary Committee and the issuance of a subpoena for Attorney General Mukasey's personal testimony on the withholding before the Senate Judiciary Committee.[1413]

In addition, on May 9, 2008, the White House issued a "Memorandum for the Heads of Executive Departments and Agencies on the Sharing of Controlled Unclassified Information." This memorandum introduced "Controlled Unclassified Information" as a new government category that replaced "Sensitive but Unclassified." Although the memorandum explicitly states that the use of the "controlled unclassified information" label "may inform but [does] not control" the decision to disclose under FOIA, lower-level staff, seeing the label on responsive documents, may instinctively treat it as protected and withhold it from disclosure.[1414]

The Bush Administration also used classification to hide the facts of potentially illegal activities in its terrorist detention and interrogation programs. The Executive has apparently classified all statements made by terrorism suspects in detention, however innocuous. Thus, conversations between prisoners and their attorneys were presumptively classified, even if the information would assist in preparing the client's defense.[1415] The Defense Department has also classified a variety of innocuous information from conversation and correspondence with prisoners, including poetry.[1416]

Classification procedures have also been used to withhold critical information from defense counsel in cases involving suspected terrorists. In military commission proceedings against Omar Khadr, the commission reportedly issued secret orders preventing Mr. Khadr's counsel from learning the names of the witnesses against him, thereby limiting his counsel's ability to provide a full and vigorous defense.[1417] In a terrorism prosecution case against Dr. Ali al-Tamimi, a D.C.-area professor convicted of inciting terrorism as part of the Virginia Jihad Network, federal intelligence agencies have made a series of filings secret from both prosecution and defense, prompting the judge in the case, Leonie M. Brinkema, to state, "I am no longer willing to work under circumstances where both the prosecuting team and defense counsel are not getting any kind of access to these materials."[1418]

In addition, *The Washington Post* obtained an order issued by Judge Stephen R. Henley, the Army colonel tasked with overseeing the proceedings against five men accused of orchestrating the terrorist attacks of September 11, 2001, that imposed broad classification rules on information related to the 9/11 trials. In a story published January 7, 2009, the newspaper reported that the order, which remains unavailable to the public, in part states:

> ...any document or information including but not limited to any
> subject **referring** to the Central Intelligence Agency, National
> Security Agency, Defense Intelligence Agency, Department of
> State, National Security Council, Federal Bureau of Investigation, or
> intelligence agencies of any foreign government, or similar entity,
> or information in the possession of such agency, **shall be presumed
> to fall within the meaning of 'classified national security
> information or document'** unless and until the [senior security
> adviser] or Prosecution advises otherwise in writing.[1419]

The order also presumptively classifies "any statements made by the accused" and allows the court to classify information that is already publicly available, such as testimony regarding the CIA's acknowledged waterboarding of Khalid Sheik Mohammed, one of the defendants in the case.[1420] Jennifer Daskal, senior counter-terrorism counsel at Human Rights Watch, called the rules, "little more than a thinly disguised attempt to classify evidence simply because it might be embarrassing or unlawful," and warned, "[i]f these rules applied in all cases, there would be no such thing as an open trial in America."[1421]

FOIA Requests

The Freedom of Information Act (FOIA) was enacted on the premise that every citizen has the right to access federal agency records or information.[1422] The Bush Administration has sought to limit its exposure under FOIA in several respects:

- An October 12, 2001, directive from then-Attorney General Ashcroft issued new guidelines for responding to FOIA requests.[1423] It was a reversal of the Clinton Administration's policy, which instructed agencies to take a broad view of their obligations under FOIA – to favor release of information unless harm would result from disclosure. In contrast, the Ashcroft directive instructed heads of federal agencies to identify reasons to deny access to information by invoking one of the Act's exemptions, even if no harm would result from disclosure.

- On March 19, 2002, Andrew Card, then-White House Chief of Staff, issued a memorandum advising executive departments and agencies to use FOIA exemptions to withhold "sensitive but non-classified" information.[1424] The memo also encouraged its recipients to re-classify certain types of unclassified or previously declassified information.

- In contravention of the OPEN Government Act of 2007, President Bush, in his proposed 2009 budget, transferred the office of the FOIA Ombudsman from the National Archives, an independent federal entity, to the Department of Justice, which is part of the Executive Branch and ultimately supervised by the Attorney General, a presidential appointee. Congress had created the position in response to the Administration policies designed to limit the volume of documents produced in response to FOIA requests. The transfer was initiated by the Vice President's office after it had engaged in an escalating series of confrontations with the National Archives over the Vice President's obligations to report his possession of classified information.[1425]

Presidential Records Act

The Bush Administration has moved to curtail its exposure under the Presidential Records Act, which changed the legal ownership of presidential records from private to public and established a new statutory framework under which presidents must manage their records:[1426]

- On March 23, 2001, then-White House Counsel Alberto Gonzales directed the National Archives not to release to the public 68,000 pages of records from the Reagan Administration that academic scholars had requested and that archivists had determined posed no threat to national security or personal privacy. The Presidential Records Act required those documents to become available January 20, 2001–twelve years after President Reagan left office.

- When historians objected to the Gonzales directive, stating that it undermined the Presidential Records Act, President Bush issued Executive Order 13233.[1427] This order allows former presidents and vice presidents, or their representatives, to bar release of documents by claiming one of numerous privileges. Contrary to prior law, the order prohibits the Archivist of the United States from rejecting a former president's claim of privilege. The order also allows the current president to attempt to block release of a former president's records even if such action subverts the former president's wishes.[1428]

252

The Vice President's office has sought to limit its obligations to accountability and transparency:[1429]

- After declining to provide reports on his office's possession of classified data to the National Archives and Record Administration in compliance with President Bush's 2003 executive order,[1430] Vice President Cheney had his staff block an attempt by the Archives' Information Security Oversight Office to perform an on-site audit. Vice President Cheney then attempted to have the executive order amended and have the investigating office at the National Archives eliminated.[1431]

- Vice President also took the position that, given his duties as tiebreaker in the Senate, the Office of the Vice President is actually part of the legislative branch, and not subject to executive orders.[1432]

- In response to a Senate Judiciary subpoena for documents relating to the warrantless wiretapping program, the Office of the Vice President again drew a distinction between it and the Executive, responding that the "Committee authorized the chairman to issue subpoenas to the Executive Office of the President and the Department of Justice, but did not authorize issuance of a subpoena to the Office of the Vice President."[1433]

- In a December 8, 2008, filing as part of a lawsuit over enforcement of the Presidential Records Act requirements, Vice President Cheney asserted that he "alone may determine what constitutes vice presidential records or personal records, how his records will be created, maintained, managed and disposed, and are all actions that are committed to his discretion by law."[1434]

III. Manipulation and Misuse of Intelligence

Considerable evidence exists in the public record indicating that President Bush and senior members of his Administration sought to manipulate and misuse intelligence in the lead-up to the Iraq War. Much of this information is included in the previous report prepared for Mr. Conyers, *The Constitution in Crisis*. As a threshold matter, as noted in that report, the 2000 presidential election focused on many issues relating to domestic and foreign policy.[1435] However, the topic of Iraq was virtually unmentioned in the campaign. In a presidential debate with then-Vice President Al Gore, then-presidential candidate George W. Bush emphasized that he would be careful about using troops for "nation-building" purposes and that he would not launch a pre-emptive war because he believed the role of the military was to "prevent war from happening in the first place."[1436] At the same time, some future members of the Bush Administration, including high-ranking officials such as Vice President Richard Cheney, Defense Policy Board Advisory Committee Chairman Richard Perle and Deputy Defense Secretary Paul Wolfowitz were part of this group, were waiting for war with Iraq.[1437]

Immediately after the September 11 attacks, President Bush and members of his Administration displayed an immediate inclination to blame Iraq – the President asked counter-terrorism adviser Richard Clarke to determine if Saddam Hussein is "linked in any way;"[1438] White House officials instructed General Wesley Clark to state that the attack was "connected to Saddam Hussein;"[1439] and Undersecretary of Defense Douglas Feith proposed that the U.S. select a "non al-Qaeda target like Iraq."[1440] Just a few months after the attacks and over a year prior to the U.S. invasion of Iraq, the Vice President appeared on *Meet the Press* on December 9, 2001, and made a connection to the American public: "Well, what we now have that's developed since you and I last talked, Tim [Russert], of course, was that report that's been pretty well confirmed, that [Mohammed Atta, one of the hijackers]... did go to Prague and he did meet with a senior official of the Iraqi intelligence service in Czechoslovakia last April, several months before the attack."[1441]

In his January 29, 2002, State of the Union Address, the President remarked that countries like Iraq, Iran and North Korea "constitute an axis of evil" and "pose a grave and growing danger."[1442] The President continued, "I will not wait on events, while dangers gather.[1443] On June 1, 2002, during a speech at West Point, President Bush formally enunciated a doctrine of preemptive military action that would soon be used against Iraq.[1444]

It was also around this time that Vice President Cheney and his then-Chief of Staff Scooter Libby began making a series of unusual trips to the Central Intelligence Agency (CIA) to discuss Iraq intelligence.[1445] As early as October 2002, various U.S. military officials, intelligence employees, and diplomats charged that the Bush Administration put intelligence analysts under intense pressure to produce reports supporting the White House's argument that Saddam Hussein posed an immediate threat and that preemptive military action was necessary. One anonymous official stated at the time, "[a]nalysts at the working level in the intelligence community are feeling very strong pressure from the Pentagon to cook the intelligence books."[1446]

At the same time, the President's public statements asserted a reluctance to use military force in Iraq. He assured the public that he had not made up his mind to go to war with Iraq and that war was a last resort.[1447] However, contrary to these public statements, the Bush Administration formed the White House Iraq Group (WHIG) in August 2002 in an apparent effort to bolster public support for war with Iraq.[1448] Then, in an August 26, 2002 speech to the Veterans of Foreign Wars National Convention, Vice President Cheney began to make the case for war against Iraq when he declared, "[t]he Iraqi regime has in fact been very busy enhancing its capabilities in the field of chemical and biological agents. And they continue to pursue the nuclear program they began so many years ago." In this speech Vice President Cheney went on to say "we know Saddam has resumed his efforts to acquire nuclear weapons."[1449]

The Bush Administration buttressed their claim that Iraq had a vigorous nuclear weapons program based on statements that Saddam Hussein had sought to acquire aluminum tubes for use as centrifuges to enrich uranium. On September 8, 2002, – after leaked, classified, and misleading information about the aluminum tubing had been reported in the media – Vice President Cheney and National Security Advisor Condoleezza Rice both appeared on television to argue and confirm that the tubes were part of Iraq's aggressive nuclear weapons program.[1450] The claims concerning the tubes appear to have been based on the views of a single CIA analyst known in press accounts as "Joe." As *The New York Times* reported, "[s]uddenly, Joe's work was ending up in classified intelligence reports being read in the White House. Indeed, his analysis was the primary basis for one of the agency's first reports on the tubes, which went to senior members of the Bush Administration on April 10, 2001."[1451]

Shortly thereafter, the Administration made further alarming and sensational claims about the danger posed to the United States by Iraq, including in a September 12, 2002, address by President Bush to the United Nations, and began to press forward publicly with preparations for war, calling Iraq a "grave and gathering danger."[1452] President Bush implied that the Iraqi government would supply WMDs to terrorist when he said, "[a]nd our greatest fear is that terrorist will find a shortcut to their mad ambitions when an outlaw regime supplies them with the technologies to kill on a massive scale. In one place – in one regime – we find all these dangers."[1453] The President reiterated Vice President Cheney's declarations that Iraq had an ongoing nuclear weapons program as well as statements about the countries capacity to produce chemical weapons.[1454] In the days following the President's speech to the United Nations, Iraq delivered a letter to U.N. Secretary-General Kofi Annan stating that it would allow the return of U.N. weapons inspectors without conditions.[1455] But on September 18, President Bush discounted Hussein's offer to let U.N. inspectors back into Iraq as a ploy.[1456] President Bush commented on September 25, 2002, "[y]ou can't distinguish between al Qaeda and Saddam when you talk about the War on Terror."[1457] On September 27, 2002, Defense Secretary Rumsfeld claimed that he had "bulletproof" evidence of ties between Saddam and al Qaeda.[1458]

Shortly before the congressional vote on authorization for the war in Iraq in October, 2002, Members of Congress sought and obtained a National Intelligence Estimate (NIE), the coordinated assessment of the Intelligence Community on Iraq. The NIE was made available to Members of Congress, but not released to the public until July 18, 2003, and then only in part.[1459] Regarding the NIE, Senator Richard Durbin of Illinois subsequently stated the classified information he had seen did not support the Bush Administration's portrayal of the Iraqi threat. "It's troubling to have classified information that contradicts statements made by the Administration," Durbin said. "[t]here's more they should share with the public."[1460]

In an October 7, 2002, speech in Cincinnati, shortly before the congressional vote to authorize military action, the President stated: "We've learned that Iraq has trained al Qaeda members in bomb-making and poisons and deadly gases... We know that Iraq and al Qaeda have had high-level contacts that go back a decade."[1461] On October 11, 2002, Congress approved a joint resolution for the use of force in Iraq.[1462] Based on the intelligence findings in the National

Intelligence Estimate provided to Congress by the Administration, the resolution stated that Iraq posed a continuing threat to the United States by, among other things, actively seeking a nuclear weapons capability.[1463]

The President's focus then moved on to the United Nations in an effort to persuade the U.N. to approve renewed weapons inspections in Iraq and sanctions for noncompliance. Once again, the President asserted his reluctance to take military action. Upon signing the resolution, the President stated, "I have not ordered the use of force. I hope the use of force will not become necessary."[1464] On November 8, 2002, the United Nations Security Council adopted U.N. Resolution 1441, which stipulated that Iraq was required to readmit U.N. weapons inspectors under more stringent terms than required by previous U.N. Resolutions.[1465]

On January 27, 2003, the International Atomic Energy Agency (IAEA) indicated that the Bush Administration's claim that aluminum tubes being delivered to Iraq were part of an Iraqi nuclear weapons program was likely false.[1466] In the wake of this claim being discredited, President Bush informed the country in his State of the Union address on January 28, 2003, "[t]he British government has learned that Saddam Hussein recently sought significant quantities of uranium from Africa."[1467]

On February 5, 2003, Secretary of State Colin Powell took the Bush Administration's case to the United Nations Security Council. In a presentation to the United Nations, Secretary Powell charged, among other things, that Iraq had mobile production facilities for biological weapons.[1468] Secretary of State Powell stated: "I can trace the story of a senior terrorist operative telling how Iraq provided training in these weapons to al Qaeda."[1469] Secretary Powell also said that, "[w]e are not surprised that Iraq is harboring Zarqawi and his subordinates. This understanding builds on decades-long experience with respect to ties between Iraq and al Qaeda."[1470] Following the visit to the United Nations, the Administration indicated its readiness and enthusiasm for going to war. Vice President Cheney made an appearance on *Meet the Press* and stated that the war would not be long, costly or bloody because the U.S. would "be greeted as liberators."[1471]

On March 18, 2003, the President submitted a letter to the Speaker of the House of Representatives and the President Pro Tempore of the Senate informing the Congress of his determination that diplomatic and peaceful means alone would not protect the Nation or lead to Iraqi compliance with United Nations demands.[1472] Two days later, the President launched the preemptive invasion.

A little more than a month into the invasion, President Bush landed aboard the USS Abraham Lincoln and, standing beneath a massive banner reading "Mission Accomplished," he stated that major combat operations in Iraq had ended. However, it became immediately evident that this declaration of victory was premature.

On January 28, 2004, head of the Iraq Survey Group David Kay testified before the Senate Armed Services Committee that there was no evidence of participation by either Saddam Hussein or his principal henchmen in the WMD-sharing with al Qaeda or any other terrorist organizations.[1473] Dr. Kay also reported the Iraq Survey Group did not find evidence that the aluminum tubes were intended for nuclear use and that "based on the evidence that was collected... it's more probable that those tubes were intended for use in a conventional missile program, rather than in a centrifuge program."[1474]

Amid growing evidence that the case for war was faulty, the Administration sought to pre-empt inquiries into the manipulation of intelligence by launching limited internal investigations. On February 6, 2004, President Bush created the Robb-Silberman Commission, which later found that the intelligence community was wrong in almost all of its pre-war judgments about Iraq's weapons of mass destruction.[1475] However, this Commission was specifically prohibited from examining the use or manipulation of intelligence by policymakers.[1476]

On March 16, 2004, the Democratic staff of the U.S. House Committee on Government Reform submitted a report to Ranking Member Henry A. Waxman. This report, titled "Iraq on the Record: the Bush Administration's Public Statements on Iraq," details public statements made by senior Bush Administration officials regarding policy toward Iraq. The report indicates that "five officials made misleading statements about the threat posed by Iraq in 125 public appearances. The report and an accompanying database identify 237 specific misleading statements by the five officials."[1477]

In May 2004, Bryan Burrough wrote in "The Path to War," an article published in *Vanity Fair* magazine, that Bush Administration officials used repeated questioning of analysts' work and re-tasking of the same assignments to obtain intelligence assessments that would fit the Administration's policy goals.[1478] This dynamic was corroborated by Richard Kerr, a former high-level CIA analyst who was brought out of retirement to conduct the agency's classified internal review of pre-war intelligence on Iraq and how it was used by the White House. Mr. Kerr reported, "There were people who felt there was too much pressure. Not that they were being asked to change their judgments, but they were being asked again and again to re-state their judgments – do another paper on this, repetitive pressures. Do it again."[1479] Eventually the CIA Ombudsman reported that several analysts he spoke with in the preparation of a June 2002 report on the CIA's analysis of connections between Iraq and al Qaeda "mentioned pressure and gave the sense that they felt the constant questions and pressure to reexamine issues were unreasonable."[1480]

On June 16, 2004, the National Commission on Terrorist Attacks Upon the United States (9-11 Commission) held the first session of it its twelfth and final hearing, focusing on the September 11th plot. At that hearing, Commission staff reported on its investigation into the Vice President's allegations of meetings between Mohammed Atta and an Iraqi intelligence official in Prague, concluding, "we do not believe that such a meeting occurred."[1481] The Commission cited FBI photographic and telephone evidence; Czech and U.S. investigations; and reports from detainees, including the Iraqi official with whom Atta was alleged to have met.[1482] Douglas MacEachin, a member of the 9/11 Commission staff and former Deputy Director of Intelligence at the CIA, also testified that contacts between Iraq and al Qaeda did not constitute a "collaborative relationship," and that the staff had "found no credible evidence that Iraq and al Qaeda cooperated on attacks against the United States."[1483] These findings were repeated in the final report of the 9/11 Commission, published on July 22, 2004.[1484]

On July 7, 2004, the Senate Select Committee on Intelligence released its first report in a series on intelligence in the lead-up to the Iraq War. The Committee's investigation reviewed over 30,000 pages of intelligence assessments and source data as well interviews with over 200 officials in the Intelligence Community (IC).[1485] Among other things, the Senate Select Committee's 2004 Report on Pre-War Intelligence confirmed CIA assessments that "there was no evidence proving Iraqi complicity or assistance in an [al Qaeda] attack" and that contacts between the two "did not add up to an established formal relationship."[1486] This report, along with other available information, largely rebutted Bush Administration claims that Iraq had acquired aluminum tubes for use in developing nuclear weapons. The Senate Intelligence report revealed that "the information available to the intelligence community indicated that these [aluminum] tubes were intended to be used for an Iraqi conventional rocket program and not a nuclear program."[1487] The report found that the Energy Department's contradictory conclusions to the CIA were published on May 9, 2001, in the Energy Department's Daily Intelligence Highlight on Intelink, a website used by the American intelligence community and the White House.[1488] Senate Intelligence further found that Defense Department experts also relayed their findings that the aluminum tubes corresponded to the tubes required for rocket use and not nuclear weapon production prior to the Administration's September 2002 public statements.[1489]

As the war continued into 2005, with U.S. casualties approaching 1,500, Iraq held elections on January 30. The Administration heralded the elections as a symbol of freedom and as an event which validated the initial invasion. By that point, however, the reason for attacking Iraq had shifted from an imminent threat of weapons of mass destruction; to combating terrorism after the September 11, attacks; to regime change; and eventually to promoting democracy.

While evidence and accounts of Administration insiders strongly suggested a predetermination to go to war and the manipulation of intelligence to justify it, that evidence and those accounts were attacked by Administration officials as inaccurate or biased. Then, on May 1, 2005, the *Sunday London Times* published the first in a series of important documents known as the "Downing Street Minutes." The Downing Street Minutes (DSM) are a collection of classified documents, written by senior British officials during the spring and summer of 2002, which recounted meetings and discussions of such officials with their American counterparts focusing on the U.S. plan to invade Iraq. The Downing Street Minutes provide documentary evidence that in the spring and summer of 2002, it was understood by the Blair government that the Bush Administration had irrevocably decided to invade Iraq. These documents indicate that President Bush had told Prime Minister Blair, "when we have dealt with Afghanistan, we must come back to Iraq" (Fall, 2001)[1490]; that "Condi's enthusiasm for regime change is undimmed" (March 14, 2002)[1491]; that the U.S. has "assumed regime change as a means of eliminating Iraq's WMD threat" (March 25, 2002)[1492]; that "Bush wanted to remove Saddam through military action, justified by the conjunction of terrorism and WMD" and that "the intelligence and facts were being fixed around the policy" (July 23, 2002).[1493]

The Downing Street Minutes generated significant media coverage in Great Britain in the lead up to the British elections, but initially received very little media attention in the United States. This circumstance began to change when, on May 5, 2005, Congressman Conyers – then the Ranking Member of the House Judiciary Committee – along with 87 other Members of Congress (eventually 121), wrote to the President demanding answers to the allegations presented in the DSM. In his letter, Representative Conyers questioned the President on whether there "was there a coordinated effort with the U.S. intelligence community and/or British officials to 'fix' the intelligence and facts around the policy." On June 16, 2005, Rep. Conyers convened the first proceeding in the United States Congress to address the serious charges raised in the Minutes. When the Republican leadership of the House refused to allow a formal hearing room for this proceeding, the meeting was held in the Capitol basement.

Four witnesses appeared at this proceeding: Ambassador Joseph C. Wilson, activist Cindy Sheehan, who lost her son Casey in the Iraq War and founded the Gold Star Families for Peace, former CIA analyst Ray McGovern, and attorney John Bonifaz. Ambassador Wilson explained the importance of the matter:

> [T]he most solemn decision a government in our democracy ever has to make is that decision to send our soldiers to die and to kill in the name of our country. In making that decision, we deserve a debate based on facts, not on information that is thrown into the debate, not because it is true, but because it supports a political decision that has already been made.[1494]

After this hearing, Mr. Conyers and other Judiciary Committee Members personally delivered to the White House a letter asking President Bush when he decided to attack Iraq and a petition signed by over 500,000 Americans.[1495] The President's refusal to answer the Members' questions prompted the Judiciary Committee Democratic staff's investigation, culminating in the publication of *The Constitution in Crisis* in August, 2006.

The following Congress, on June 5, 2008, the Senate Select Committee on Intelligence (SCCI) completed the second phase of its investigation into the manipulation of intelligence in the lead-up to the March 2003 invasion of Iraq. That day, the Committee released its report detailing prewar statements by Bush Administration officials misrepresenting intelligence on Iraq and the threat it represented to the U.S. on numerous occasions.[1496]

The Senate Intelligence Committee concentrated its analysis on "statements that were central to the nation's decision to go to war."[1497] The report examined five important speeches by President George W. Bush and top Administration officials[1498] and selected elements that fall into the following categories: nuclear weapons, biological weapons, chemical weapons, weapons of mass destruction, methods of delivery, links to terrorism, regime intent, and assessments about consequences of U.S. invasion on Iraq post-war. Also, to support its analysis, the Committee gathered information from intelligence reports that were produced prior to March 19, 2003, to better "understand the state of intelligence analysis at the time of various speeches and statements."[1499] By concentrating on inter-agency intelligence reports, the Committee highlighted some of the "disagreements with the intelligence community and where different reporting could substantiate different interpretations." In addition, the report focuses on the selective use of intelligence information and the ability of the Administration to declassify and divulge intelligence information.[1500]

The Committee report concluded that a number of public statements made by high-ranking members of the Bush Administration in the lead-up to the Iraq War were not supported by the available intelligence, including:

- Statements and implications by the President and Secretary of State suggesting that Iraq and al Qaeda had a partnership, or that Iraq had provided al Qaeda with weapons training were not substantiated by the intelligence.[1501] In particular, the Intelligence Committee noted that on several occasions, the CIA and the DIA expressed doubts that there was any collusion between Hussein and bin Ladin because "Saddam views bin Ladin's brand of Islam as a threat to his regime and bin Ladin is opposed to those Muslim states that do not follow his version of Islam."[1502] With regarding to weapons training, by February 2002, the Intelligence Committee had questioned the credibility of al-Libi, the former bin Laden aide who had sought to link Iraq with al Qaeda and weapons trainings.[1503]

- Statements by the President Bush and Vice President Cheney indicating that Saddam Hussein was prepared to give weapons of mass destruction to terrorist groups for attacks against the U.S. were contradicted by available intelligence information.[1504] In particular, the Committee found intelligence assessments before and after the President's September 2002 address consistently expressed the difficulty of trying to gauge Saddam's intentions with accuracy, and ultimately concluded that Saddam Hussein would not likely want to risk his regime's survival by using WMDs against the United States.[1505]

- Statements by President Bush and Vice President Cheney regarding the postwar situation in Iraq, in terms of the political, security and economic, did not reflect the concerns and uncertainties expressed in the intelligence products.[1506]

- Statements by the President and Vice President prior to the October 2002 NIE regarding Iraq's production of chemical weapons omitted uncertainties as to whether such production was ongoing.[1507] In particular the Senate Intelligence Committee found Bush Administration officials ignored disagreements within the IC with regard to assessments of Iraq's capabilities to use unarmed aerial vehicles

(UAVs) as delivery systems for chemical and biological weapons. Although the October 2002 NIE indicated that Iraq intended to outfit UAVs for such purposes, the Air Force intelligence agency dissented.[1508] Statements by Bush Administration officials prior to the release of the 2002 NIE also omitted IC uncertainties with regard to Iraq's chemical weapons capabilities,[1509] and could not confirm ongoing production of chemical weapons.[1510]

- The statement by Defense Secretary Donald Rumsfeld in testimony before Congress that the Iraqi government operated WMD facilities that were not vulnerable to conventional airstrikes because they were buried deeply underground was not substantiated by available intelligence information.[1511]

- The Vice President's repeated claims that Muhammad Atta met an Iraqi intelligence officer in Prague in 2001 were not confirmed by the Intelligence Community.[1512] The Committee found that by May 2002, the CIA found that there was contradictory reporting on this trip and that it was again unable to verify Atta's reported trip through other channels; the CIA also found "no conclusive indication of Iraqi complicity or foreknowledge" of the September 11th attacks;[1513] and that in July 2002, the Defense Intelligence Agency (DIA) indicated that there were "significant information gaps in this reporting [regarding a April 2001 Atta meeting in Prague] that render the issue impossible to prove or disprove."[1514]

- With regard to President Bush's 2003 State of the Union remarks indicating Saddam Hussein had sought uranium from Africa, the Senate Intelligence Committee identified three important warnings that President Bush omitted. The CIA had warned him not to use that claim because of uncertainty as to its validity[1515]; the National Intelligence Estimate of October 2002 (NIE) did not include this claim in its "Key Judgements" summary of important points on which its conclusion of a current nuclear weapons program was based[1516]; and the State Department found the claim "highly dubious."[1517]

On July 25, 2008, Chairman Conyers convened a formal Judiciary Committee hearing, titled "Executive Power and Its Constitutional Limitations." The purpose of the hearing was to further explore the Bush Administration's abuse of executive authority, including allegations of manipulating pre-war intelligence. The testimony from many of the witnesses, including Representative Dennis Kucinich of Ohio and former Los Angeles county prosecutor Vincent Bugliosi, centered around the Bush Administration's use of intelligence in making the case for war. Representative Kucinich's testimony focused on the role that fabricated intelligence played in justifying the war to Members of Congress and the American public at large, arguing that the President and Vice President knowingly misled Members of Congress in order to convince them to authorize the 2003 invasion of Iraq.[1518]

Mr. Bugliosi discussed the incomplete state of a declassified intelligence assessment in

October 2002, which became known as the "White Paper." The White Paper portrayed Hussein's Iraq as an imminent threat to the United States, but, as Mr. Bugliosi testified, "the conclusion of U.S. Intelligence that Hussein would only be likely to attack us if he feared we were about to attack him was completely deleted."[1519] The omission made Prime Minister Hussein appear much more dangerous. Former Judiciary Committee member Elizabeth Holtzman also testified, and described her conclusion that "[t]he deceptions, exaggerations and misstatements made by high level Administration officials to drive the country into the tragically mistaken Iraq War subvert the constitution."[1520]

In his book released August 5, 2008, *The Way of the World: A Story of Truth and Hope in an Age of Extremism*, author Ron Suskind reported that White House officials had directed the fabrication of a letter in the name of Saddam Hussein's former Intelligence Chief Tahir Habbush that suggested a link between Iraq and Mohammed Atta.[1521] On August 20, 2008, Chairman Conyers wrote the key Administration insiders alleged to be involved in the matter: George Tenet, former Director of the CIA; Rob Richer, former CIA Deputy Director of Clandestine Operations and Chief of the Near East Division; John Maguire, one of the heads of the CIA's Iraq Operations Group in the Near East Division; A.B. "Buzzy" Krongard, former Executive Director of the CIA; John Hannah, Assistant to the Vice President for National Security Affairs; and Lewis I. "Scooter" Libby, former Chief of Staff to the Vice President.[1522] No information was obtained in response to these letters that confirmed the recipients' knowledge of the forgeries.[1523] Accordingly, the Administration figures who ordered and authored the apparent forgery – and their involvement in leaking it through foreign intelligence channels – remain unidentified.

In December 2008, Representative Henry A. Waxman, Chairman of the Committee on Oversight and Government Reform, released a memorandum revealing that, in apparent contrast to assurances given by Attorney General Alberto Gonzales to the Senate Select Committee on Intelligence in a 2004 letter, the CIA had in fact objected to the statement by President Bush in his 2003 State of the Union speech regarding Saddam Hussein seeking uranium from Africa.[1524] John Gibson former Director of Speechwriting for Foreign Policy at the National Security Council (NSC) indicated that he attempted to insert the claim about African uranium in a September 12, 2002, speech being written for President Bush to give to the United Nations.[1525] Mr. Gibson stated that he was never able to clear the language with the CIA because the agency was concerned about the information's reliability. Similarly, a few weeks later, a high level CIA official had contacted then-National Security Advisor Condoleezza Rice personally to express the CIA's position that the statement was not credible and should be taken out of a speech that President Bush was preparing to deliver on September 26, 2002.[1526]

In the final weeks of 2008 and of their second term, President Bush and Vice President Cheney gave a series of interviews in which they have discussed the lead-up to and execution of the war in Iraq. Speaking with Jonathan Karl of *ABC News*, Vice President Cheney disagreed with the assessment Karl Rove that had the pre-war intelligence been correct, the U.S. would not have invaded Iraq. Vice President Cheney insisted that "what they got wrong was that there weren't any stockpiles."[1527] In an interview with Martha Raddatz of *ABC News*, President Bush spoke of the relationship between al Qaeda and Iraq:

> Mr. Bush: Clearly, one of the most important parts of my job because of 9/11 was to defend the security of the American people. There have been no attacks since I have been president, since 9/11. One of the major theaters against al Qaeda turns out to have been Iraq. This is where al Qaeda said they were going to take their stand. This is where al Qaeda was hoping to take ...

> Ms. Raddatz: But not until after the U.S. invaded.

> Mr. Bush: Yeah, that's right. So what?[1528]

President Bush went on to insist that he "did not have the luxury of knowing [Saddam Hussein] did not have [weapons of mass destruction], neither did the rest of the world until after we had come and removed him."[1529]

IV.   Findings

Expansion of Executive Privilege

1.   On numerous occasions, the Bush Administration has significantly delayed or entirely refused the production of documents or congressional testimony by Executive Branch officials by claiming that such productions would infringe upon executive privilege. President Bush has not only vastly expanded the notion of executive privilege and its applications, but also has used executive privilege claims as a means of stonewalling congressional investigations. Subpoenas not complied with include:

- An April 25, 2007, House Oversight and Government Reform Committee subpoena for the testimony of the Secretary of State regarding alleged Niger document forgeries;[1530]

- A June 13, 2007, House Judiciary Committee subpoena for the testimony of former White House Counsel Harriet Miers and documents concerning the U.S. Attorneys firings investigation;[1531]

- A June 13, 2007, Senate Judiciary Committee subpoena for the testimony of White House Chief of Staff Joshua Bolten and documents concerning the U.S. Attorneys firings investigation;[1532]

- A June 13, 2007, House Judiciary Committee subpoena to Robert Duncan, RNC Chairman, as custodian of record, for documents;

- A June 26, 2007, Senate Judiciary Committee subpoena for documents and testimony of White House Deputy Chief of Staff Karl Rove concerning the U.S. Attorneys firings investigation;[1533]

- A March 13, 2008, House Oversight and Government Reform Committee subpoena for unredacted copies of documents in the possession of the Environmental Protection Agency;[1534]

- An April 16, 2008, House Oversight and Government Reform to Susan Dudley, Administrator, Office of Information and Regulatory Affairs in the White House Office of Management and Budget (OMB) for documents concerning the EPA's denial of California's request for a waiver to impose stricter greenhouse gas emission standards;[1535]

- The April 9, 2008, and May 5, 2008, House Oversight and Government Reform Committee subpoenas for the testimony of EPA Administrator Stephen L. Johnson regarding the EPA's denial of California's request for a waiver to impose stricter greenhouse gas emissions;[1536]

- A May 22, 2008, House Judiciary Committee subpoena for the testimony of White House Deputy Chief of Staff Karl Rove concerning the U.S. Attorneys firings investigation;[1537]

- A June 16, 2008, House Oversight and Government Reform Committee subpoena to Attorney General Mukasey concerning FBI interview reports with President Bush and Vice President Cheney regarding the outing of CIA agent Valerie Plame;[1538]

- A June 27, 2008, House Judiciary Committee subpoena to Attorney General Mukasey for documents previously requested from the Department of Justice concerning withheld OLC opinions, FBI interviews of President Bush and Vice President Cheney regarding the outing of Valerie Plame, and internal Justice Department documents concerning the Siegelman and Wecht prosecutions.[1539]

- An October 21, 2008, Senate Judiciary Committee subpoena to Attorney General Mukasey for documents pertaining to legal analysis and advice provided by the Department of Justice's Office of Legal Counsel regarding the Bush Administration's terrorism policies, including detention and interrogation polices and practices.[1540]

State Secrets Privilege

2.   **In contrast to assertions of state secrets privilege under previous administrations, the Bush**

264

Administration invoked the privilege to dismiss cases challenging specific ongoing government programs and prevented disclosure of potentially unlawful conduct by the Administration itself.[1541] These assertions have prevented disclosure of potentially unlwaful conduct by members of the Bush Administration, including:

- Invocation of the state secrets privilege resulted in the dismissal of a wrongful termination lawsuit brought by former FBI agent and whistleblower Sibel Edmonds. In an investigation taking place at the same time, the FBI's Inspector General determined that Sibel Edmonds had been improperly dismissed and that her charges had never been properly investigated.[1542]

- Invocation of the state secrets privilege resulted in the dismissal of a lawsuit brought by Khalid el-Masri, preventing judicial review of the legality of the Administration's rendition programming.[1543]

- Invocation of the state secrets privilege resulted in the dismissal of a lawsuit brought by Maher Arar, preventing judicial review of the legality of the Administration's rendition programming.[1544]

- Invocation of the state secrets privilege resulted in the dismissal of a lawsuit brought by the Al-Haramain Islamic Foundation, preventing judicial review of the legality of the Administration's warrantless wiretapping program.[1545]

- Invocation of the state secrets privilege resulted in the dismissal of a lawsuit brought by the ACLU, preventing judicial review of the legality of the Administration's warrantless wiretapping program.

- Invocation of the state secrets privilege resulted in the dismissal of a lawsuit brought by the Electronic Frontier Foundation, preventing judicial review of the legality of the Administration's warrantless wiretapping program.

- Invocation of the state secrets privilege resulted in the dismissal of a lawsuit brought by the Center for Constitutional Rights, preventing judicial review of the legality of the Administration's warrantless wiretapping program.

Abuse of Classification and Other Authorities

3.   The Bush Administration has misused authority with regard to the classification of documents under the Freedom of Information Act, the Presidential Records Act, and the Vice

- Executive Order 13292 issued by President Bush reversed many key policies mitigating in favor of declassification, including providing for longer periods of time for declassification and weakening the standards for declassification.[1546]

- FOIA was significantly weakened under the Bush Administration as a result of (i) a 2001 directive by then-Attorney General Ashcroft encouraging agency heads to deny FOIA requests even if no harm would result from disclosure; (ii) 2002 and 2008 White House memoranda which encouraged denying FOIA claims for "sensitive but unclassified information" and using the newly-created "controlled unclassified information" designation to "inform" (but not control) the decision whether to release information to the public; and (iii) the transfer in the Administration's proposed fiscal year 2009 budget of the newly-created FOIA Ombudsman position from the independent National Archives to the Department of Justice, which is part of the Executive Branch.[1547]

- Executive Order 13233 issued by President Bush weakens the Presidential Records Act by allowing former presidents and vice presidents to bar release of documents by claiming one of numerous privileges.[1548]

- The Vice President's Office sought to treat itself as an entity not subject to Executive Branch disclosure obligations, and denied information to the Archivist and tried to have the Archivist's investigating office eliminated.[1549]

Manipulation and Misuse of Intelligence

4. <u>A decision had been made to invade Iraq while President Bush and senior members of his Administration continued to make statements that a decision had not been made to invade.</u>

- President Bush and senior members of his Administration made numerous statements to the effect that no decision had been made to go to war with Iraq. For example, as early as September 8, 2002, Vice President Cheney insisted that "no decision's been made yet to launch a military operation,"[1550] and as late as March 6, 2003, President Bush declared "I've not made up our mind about military action."[1551]

- The Downing Street Minutes provided unrebutted documentary evidence that by the spring and summer of 2002, the Blair government had reason to believe that the

266

Bush Administration had made an irrevocable decision to invade Iraq. Among other things, the leaked documents revealed that President Bush had told Prime Minister Blair "when we have dealt with Afghanistan, we must come back to Iraq" (Fall, 2001)[1552]; "Condi's enthusiasm for regime change is undimmed" (March 14, 2002)[1553]; the U.S. has "assumed regime change as a means of eliminating Iraq's WMD threat" (March 25, 2002)[1554]; and "Bush wanted to remove Saddam through military action, justified by the conjunction of terrorism and WMD" and "the intelligence and facts were being fixed around the policy" (July 23, 2002).[1555]

5.   President Bush and senior members of his Administration made unsubstantiated, if not false, claims linking Saddam Hussein and al Qaeda.

- Members of the Bush Administration, including the President, made a number of statements linking Saddam Hussein to the events of September 11 and to al Qaeda. For example, President Bush commented on September 25, 2002, "You can't distinguish between al Qaeda and Saddam when you talk about the War on Terror;"[1556] and on September 27, 2002, Secretary Rumsfeld claimed that he had "bulletproof"evidence of ties between Saddam and al Qaeda.[1557] However, the 2008 Senate Intelligence Committee Report found that on several occasions, the CIA and the DIA expressed doubts that there was any collusion between Hussein and bin Ladin because "Saddam views bin Ladin's brand of Islam as a threat to his regime and bin Ladin is opposed to those Muslim states that do not follow his version of Islam."[1558] Moreover, the 9-11 Commission concluded that it had found no "collaborative" relationship between Iraq and al Qaeda and that "[w]e have no credible evidence that Iraq and al Qaeda cooperated on attacks against the United States."[1559]

- Vice President Cheney made unsubstantiated, if not false, claims specifically linking Iraq with the September 11 hijacker Muhammad Atta. Vice President Cheney appeared on *Meet the Press* on December 9, 2001, and stated: "Well, what we now have that's developed since you and I last talked, Tim [Russert], of course, was that report that's been pretty well confirmed, that [Mohammed Atta, one of the hijackers]... did go to Prague and he did meet with a senior official of the Iraqi intelligence service in Czechoslovakia last April, several months before the attack."[1560] Subsequently, the 9-11 Commission addressed the Vice President's allegations of meetings between Atta and Iraqi intelligence, concluding, "We do not believe that such a meeting occurred."[1561]

- Both President Bush and Secretary of State Powell made unsubstantiated, if not false, claims that Iraq had trained al Qaeda members to use chemical and biological weapons. In his October 7, 2002, speech in Cincinnati, the President stated: "We've learned that Iraq has trained al Qaeda members in bomb-making and poisons and deadly gases,"[1562] and in his February 5, 2003, speech before the UN,

Secretary of State Powell stated: "I can trace the story of a senior terrorist operative telling how Iraq provided these weapons to al Qaeda."[1563] These allegations were based on disclosures by Ibu al-Shaykh al-Libi, an aide to bin Laden in U.S. custody. However, the 2008 Senate Intelligence Committee reported noted that by February of 2002, intelligence sources began to question al-Libi's credibility, with a DIA defense intelligence report finding, "It is possible [al-Libi] does not know any further details; it is more likely this individual is intentionally misleading debriefers."[1564]

- President Bush made unsubstantiated, if not false, claims that Iraq would supply weapons to terrorist groups. During his September 12, 2002, speech to the United Nations General Assembly, President Bush indicated that the Iraqi government would supply WMDs to terrorist when he said "our greatest fear is that terrorist will find a shortcut to their mad ambitions when an outlaw regime supplies them with the technologies to kill on a massive scale. In one place – in one regime – we find all these dangers..."[1565] However, according to the 2008 Senate Intelligence report, intelligence assessments before and after the President's September 2002 address consistently expressed the difficulty of trying to gauge Saddam's intentions with accuracy.[1566]

6.   <u>President Bush and senior members of his Administration made unsubstantiated, if not false, claims concerning Iraq's alleged nuclear weapons program.</u>

- President Bush and other senior members of his Administration made unsubstantiated, if not false, claims that Iraq had acquired uranium from Africa. In his 2003 State of the Union Address, President Bush told the country, "the British Government has learned that Saddam Hussein recently discussed significant acquisition of uranium from Africa."[1567] However, in their 2008 report, the Senate Intelligence Committee disclosed that the CIA had warned the President not to use that claim because of uncertainty as to its validity,[1568] and the State Department found the claim "highly dubious."[1569] In addition, in December of 2008, the Oversight and Government Reform Committee disclosed a memorandum indicating that the President's statement regarding uranium had not been cleared by the CIA.[1570]

- President Bush and senior members of his Administration made unsubstantiated, if not false, claims that Iraq was using aluminum tubes to assist in making nuclear weapons. On September 8, 2002, Vice President Cheney and National Security Advisor Condoleezza Rice both appeared on television to argue and confirm that the tubes were part of Iraq's aggressive nuclear weapons program.[1571] President Bush would later state in his 2003 State of the Union Address that Saddam Hussein was trying to buy tubes "suitable for nuclear weapons production."[1572] However, the July 2004 report by the Senate Intelligence Committee revealed that, at the time, "the information available to the intelligence community indicated that these [aluminum] tubes were intended to be used for an Iraqi conventional rocket program and not a nuclear program."[1573]

7.   Senior members of the Bush Administration placed undue pressure on intelligence officials in order to obtain intelligence assessments that aided their efforts to make the case for invading Iraq.

- As early as October 2002, an anonymous intelligence official stated, "Analysts at the working level in the intelligence community are feeling very strong pressure from the Pentagon to cook the intelligence books."[1574] Richard Kerr, a former high-level CIA analyst who conducted the agency's classified internal review of pre-war intelligence on Iraq and how it was used by the White House, reported, "There were people who felt there was too much pressure. Not that they were being asked to change their judgments, but they were being asked again and again to re-state their judgments-do another paper on this, repetitive pressures. Do it again."[1575]

Section 6 – Policy Recommendations

Discussed below is a comprehensive set of 47 recommendations designed to respond to the abuses and excesses of the Bush Imperial Presidency. They correspond to the topics discussed in more detail in sections one through five of this report, although a short explanation of the reasons for each recommendation is included below. Some of these recommendations will require congressional action, while others can and should be implemented promptly by executive action by the incoming Obama Administration.

General

1.   **The Congress and the Judiciary Committee should pursue document and witness requests pending at the end of the 110th Congress, including subpoenas, and the incoming Administration should cooperate with those requests.** The Committee's outstanding requests include: (i) subpoenas to Harriet Miers and Josh Bolten for testimony and documents relating to the politicization of the Department of Justice and the U.S. Attorney firings; (iii) a subpoena to Karl Rove for testimony relating to the politicization of the Department of Justice and the U.S. Attorney firings; (iii) a subpoena to the Republican National Committee for documents relating to the politicization of the Department of Justice and the U.S. Attorneys firings; (iv) a subpoena to Attorney General Mukasey for documents regarding selective prosecution, undisclosed OLC memoranda concerning national security and related issues, and unredacted FBI reports of interviews with President Bush, Vice President Cheney, and other White House officials concerning the unauthorized disclosure of Valerie Plame Wilson's identity; (v) the unredacted notes of FBI Director Mueller relating to the 2004 hospital visit at Attorney General Ashcroft's bedside and the Terrorist Surveillance Program; (vi) information regarding the Justice Department's arrangements to pay for former Attorney General Gonzales' legal fees stemming from the pending class action lawsuit relating to allegations of politicized hiring; and (vii) e-mails and documents pertaining to the FBI whistleblower claims of Bassem Youssef and Michael German.[1576]

    <u>Reason:</u> The Bush Administration has relied on excessively broad claims of executive privilege and immunity from subpoena to obstruct congressional oversight of the Administration's operations and activities. While a new Administration is soon to take office, critical questions about the matters under investigation remain unanswered. No president should be allowed to run out the clock on important congressional oversight in this fashion. While executive confidentiality may be necessary in limited circumstances to protect the content and candor of counsel to the president, the principle has been abused. Left unresolved, this dispute involving the Judiciary Committee and the Congress could set a dangerous precedent whereby future administrations could avoid congressional inquiry simply by refusing to provide documents and waiting out the end of the presidential term. The executive would then effectively be able to erase one of the checks held over it by the legislative branch.[1577]

2.   **Congress should establish a Blue Ribbon Commission or similar panel to investigate**

the broad range of policies of the Bush Administration that were undertaken under claims of unreviewable war powers, including detention, enhanced interrogation, ghosting and black sites, extraordinary rendition, and warrantless domestic surveillance. This Commission should have subpoena power, the power to take depositions, and the right to compel testimony or seek access to the courts to enforce subpoenas for hearing or deposition testimony or for documents. The president should order full cooperation by all present and past federal employees with requests for information from this Commission, and, to the extent possible, waive privileges, including privileges that may be asserted by prior Administration officials, that would otherwise impede the fact-finding process.[1578] Chairman Conyers introduced H.R. 104 on the first day of the 111th Congress, January 6, 2009, to provide for such a commission.

Reason: At present, information concerning the Bush Administration's policies that have impacted civil liberties – such as its detention, interrogation, ghosting, rendition, and warrantless domestic surveillance policies – has emerged in somewhat limited internal investigations, a few press articles and some self-serving public statements or publications, and the disclosure of a limited set of documents. While there have been some important Committee investigations on particular matters of controversy, there has been no systematic effort to ascertain the pertinent facts as to the formulation and implementation of these policies. The American people and Congress must have a more comprehensive understanding of the facts and circumstances that resulted in the policies and practices of the Bush Administration by which it asserted that the president could exercise uncheckable and unreviewable powers as Commander in Chief in spheres of action that directly impacted the Constitutional rights of United States citizens.

Previous blue-ribbon panels, such as the "National Commission on Terrorist Attacks Upon the United States" (the "9/11 Commission") have helped inform and educate the public and the Congress, as have congressional "select committees" such as the Select Committee to Study Government Intelligence Activities (the "Church Committee"), the respective "House Select Committee to Investigate Covert Arms Transactions with Iran" and the "Senate Select Committee on Secret Military Assistance to Iran and the Nicaraguan Opposition" (the congressional "Iran/Contra Committees"), and the Senate Select Committee on Presidential Campaign Activities (the Senate "Watergate" Committee, chaired by Senator Sam Ervin).

3.   The Attorney General should appoint a Special Counsel, or expand the scope of the present investigation into CIA tape destruction, to determine whether there were criminal violations committed pursuant to Bush Administration policies that were undertaken under unreviewable war powers, including enhanced interrogation, extraordinary rendition, and warrantless domestic surveillance. This criminal investigation should, for the first time, ascertain and critically examine the facts to determine whether federal criminal laws were violated. It may be appropriate for certain aspects of the factual investigation by the prosecutor to await pertinent reports by the Inspectors General or information developed by any Blue Ribbon Commission or Select Committee. As part of this process, the incoming Administration should provide all relevant information and all necessary resources to outstanding Justice Department investigations, including with respect to the U.S. Attorney removals, the politicization of the Civil

Rights Division, and allegations of selective prosecution. Congress should also consider extending the statute of limitations for potential violations of the torture statute, war crimes statute, laws prohibiting warrantless domestic surveillance, or for crimes committed against persons in United States military custody or CIA custody to ten years.

Reason: Among other things, documented incidents of grave abuse of detainees at various detention facilities including Abu Ghraib and Guantanamo Bay and the extraordinary rendition of terror suspects to countries where they have been tortured, and the implementation of warrantless surveillance inside the United States, raise credible concerns that criminal laws may have been violated.[1579] At present, the Attorney General has agreed only to appoint a special U.S. Attorney to determine whether the destruction of videotapes depicting the waterboarding of a detainee constituted violations of federal law.[1580] Despite requests from Congress, that prosecutor has not been asked to investigate whether the underlying conduct being depicted – the waterboarding itself or other harsh interrogation techniques used by the military or the CIA – violated the law.[1581] Thus far the Attorney General has similarly refused to appoint a special counsel to investigate whether the practice of extraordinary rendition and, in particular whether the extraordinary rendition of Canadian citizen Maher Arar, violated the law. Similarly, there remains a serious question as to whether the warrantless domestic surveillance engaged in as part of the so-called "Terrorist Surveillance Program" prior to January 2007, violated the law.[1582]

It would seem that all or part of the above-described conduct meets the relevant requirements under federal regulations for the appointment of a special counsel (28 CFR 600.1), in that (i) a criminal investigation is warranted (e.g., waterboarding and warrantless domestic surveillance appear to violate criminal laws); (ii) the investigation would present a conflict of interest for the Justice Department (e.g., some of the potentially culpable parties have worked for or with the Department); and (iii) appointment of a special counsel would be in the public interest (e.g., it would help dispel a cloud of doubt over our law enforcement system).

Politicization of the Department of Justice

4. The incoming Administration should review and consider strengthening the policy limiting contacts concerning prosecution and enforcement matters. The incoming Administration should review and strengthen as appropriate the current policy limiting contacts between the White House, the Department of Justice, and Members of Congress regarding prosecution and civil enforcement matters.

Reason: Attorney General Mukasey deserves credit for revising the Ashcroft/Gonzales policy under which a broad range of individuals within the White House were authorized to communicate with Department personnel about criminal prosecution or civil enforcement matters. Further review is warranted, however, to assess whether the current policy has appropriately limited these channels of communication. In addition, at present, this policy appears to be contained solely in a memorandum from Attorney General Mukasey to Department of Justice officials, including United States Attorneys.[1583] In past administrations, however, Department policy regarding contacts with the White House or members of Congress on prosecution and civil enforcement has additionally been stated in formal communications to congressional Committee Chairs and the White House Counsel,[1584] and the incoming Administration should consider whether such additional steps are warranted.

5. **The incoming Administration should continue the customary practice of replacing U.S. Attorneys at the outset of the Administration.** The Administration should accept the resignation of current U.S. Attorneys, as has been customary for incoming administrations when a change of party occurs, and should promptly appoint new U.S. Attorneys to all positions nationwide except where traditional recommenders urge that retaining current U.S. Attorneys would be in the public interest.

Reason: The Bush Administration's politicization of the United States Attorney corps has shaken the public's faith in the fairness of our federal criminal justice system. The Administration's refusal to provide a full public accounting of these issues to Congress or to the public has exacerbated the problem and cast an unfortunate cloud over the entire U.S. Attorney corps. In these circumstances, it is imperative to have a clean break and appoint a new slate of respected federal prosecutors through an appropriately thorough and professional process. In particular cases where traditional recommenders urge that current U.S. Attorneys be retained and the president concludes that doing so would be in the public interest, exceptions to this process may be appropriate. The Bush Administration, it should be noted, has already facilitated this process by requesting all political appointees to submit such letters of resignation "consistent with past practice." [1585]

6. **Congress should expand Justice Department Inspector General jurisdiction.**
Congress should consider legislation that would clarify and expand the jurisdiction of the Department of Justice's Office of the Inspector General to allow investigation of misconduct by senior Justice Department officials and United States Attorneys, such as the Amendment to H.R. 928 on this subject offered by Chairman Conyers and passed by the House during the 110th Congress.[1586]

Reason: Under current law, charges of political interference with prosecution decisions fall within the jurisdiction of the Department's Office of Professional Responsibility (OPR) and may not be investigated by the Department's Inspector General. Thus, the highly controversial Siegelman case and other matters raising concerns about political interference with prosecutorial decision-making are being investigated solely by OPR. Because OPR is answerable to the Attorney General, while the Inspector General has statutory independence, such matters are often better investigated by OIG. Accordingly, the next Administration and the Congress should support legislation allowing OIG to investigate allegations of misconduct by senior Department officials and United States Attorneys. This would strengthen the Department's ability to address such matters internally and enhance the credibility of Department investigations of these sensitive issues.

7.   The incoming Administration should improve the Executive Office of Immigration Review (EOIR) and the functioning of the immigration courts. The next Administration should ensure the professionalism and quality of the immigration courts, including the review process, by: increasing the number of immigration judges and law clerks; filling judicial vacancies promptly; providing meaningful and ongoing education and training for judges; addressing technology issues; and engaging in a review of Board of Immigration Appeals practices, such as affirmances without opinion and the implementation of the 2002 "streamlining" regulations.[1587] An expert roundtable to consider further administrative and legislative improvements should be convened.

Reason: A Joint Report by the Department's Inspector General and Office of Professional Responsibility found substantial and "systematic" politicization in the selection of immigration judges, in violation of the law.[1588] The recommended improvements would minimize the substantive impact of this improper politicization and enhance the performance of EOIR and the immigration courts.[1589]

8.   The Department of Justice should rescind the policy prohibiting career voting section employees from making recommendations as to whether the Department should object to proposed voting changes. The Attorney General should reinstate the policy followed prior to 2005 and allow recommendations from career staff as to whether the Department should object to proposed voting changes from state and local jurisdictions under Section 5 of the Voting Rights Act. It should also be made clear that career staff need not artificially limit their written analysis to the facts surrounding specific Section 5 submissions.

Reason: Under Section 5 of the Voting Rights Act, the Department of Justice reviews proposed changes to voting practices and procedures in jurisdictions with a history of voting discrimination, and can object to and make difficult to enact changes that have the purpose or effect of harming minority voting rights. As discussed in Section 1, in response to significant controversy concerning the Department's decision not to object to a Georgia law requiring photo identification to vote, a decision that some charged had involved political considerations, it was reported that the Department's political leadership instituted a new policy in 2005 requiring that staff members who review Section 5 submissions limit their written analysis to the facts of specific cases and refrain from making any recommendations as to whether the Department should object to the change.[1590] Informal reports indicate that ths policy remains in effect. In addition to the concern about politicization of Justice Department decisions, such a policy impairs the ability of the Justice Department to effectively analyze proposed voting changes and protect minority voting rights and should therefore be eliminated.

9.   The Department of Justice should revise the Federal Prosecution of Election Offenses Manual. The Attorney General should reinstate language contained in the "Policy and Procedural Considerations" section of the January 1995 manual designed to prevent partisan abuse of election law enforcement by the Department. The Department should restore language warning against investigating allegations of voter fraud shortly before an election, reinstate the earlier cautionary policy against pursuing isolated instances of individual voter fraud (as compared to large scale cases of voter suppression), and reinstate the list of pre-election investigatory precautions (including those with respect to voter fraud) to be followed by prosecutors.

Reason: A federal criminal investigation initiated close to an election runs the risks of chilling legitimate voting participation and campaign activities, particularly in jurisdictions where there is a history of disfranchisement efforts targeting racial and ethnic minorities. As discussed in Section 1, moreover, actual and attempted politicization of voter fraud cases during the Bush Administration, such as the cases brought in 2006 by acting U.S. Attorney Brad Schlozman in Missouri, clearly warrant the reinstatement of language designed to help prevent partisan abuse of election law enforcement by federal prosecutors. In addition, federal election fraud prosecutions should involve a systemic and organized pattern of abuse, since individual cases typically have a minimal impact on the integrity of the voting process and generally represent an unwise use of Departmental resources.

10. **Congress should enact comprehensive election reform legislation.** Among other things, the legislation should: (i) prohibit deceptive practices and voter intimidation;[1591] (ii) prohibit the practice of voter caging (including caging based on mortgage foreclosure lists) and establish circumstances under which voters can properly be challenged at the polls;[1592] (iii) establish a uniform system for counting provisional ballots; (iv) clarify that non-matches between a registration list and drivers license or Social Security information under HAVA is not an automatic trigger for removing voters from voter registration rolls; (v) make clear that voters without photo identification can vote if they sign an affidavit confirming their identity; (vi) eliminate disparities in the allocation of voting machines and poll workers among a state's precincts; (vii) mandate early voting and election day registration procedures; (viii) provide uniform standards for vote recounts; and (ix) prohibit voting machine companies that manufacture or sell voting equipment to state and local governments from engaging in political activities.[1593] Chairman Conyers introduced a comprehensive election reform bill, H.R. 105, the Voter Opportunity and Technology Enhancement Rights (VOTER) Act of 2009 on the first day of the 111th Congress, January 6, 2009.

Reason: Voting irregularities and improprieties were reported throughout the country during the 2000 and subsequent presidential elections. As discussed in Section 1, actions of the Justice Department since then have weakened voting rights. Many barriers prevented thousands of people from voting. Voter registration was made more difficult. Officials misconstrued, misapplied and abused identification and provisional-ballot rules. In some areas, there were few voting machines in heavily populated minority areas, leading to unacceptable wait times, and there were suspicious voting-machine "errors." There were also numerous allegations of voter intimidation, voter deception, and vote suppression. Attempts were made to improperly challenge voters based on mass mailing or "caging" tactics, and to disqualify voters because of non-matches between information on registration lists and other data bases, contrary to the law.[1594] On the positive side, experience with early voting and same day registration has demonstrated that these methods can help prevent a number of these voting difficulties. Numerous reports have documented these problems and potential solutions.[1595] Comprehensive federal legislation including the specific reforms listed above, most of which have been included in previous federal election reform proposals, would promote uniformity of procedures and help ensure that all voters who are eligible to vote are able to vote, and have their vote properly counted in Federal elections.

Assault on Individual Liberty: Detention, Enhanced Interrogation, Ghosting and Black Sites, Extraordinary Rendition, Warrantless Domestic Surveillance, and National Security and Exigent Letters

11.   The Department of Justice should reform its Office of Legal Counsel. The Attorney General should adopt rules to ensure that the Office of Legal Counsel provides the high quality, professional and independent legal advice that has long been its hallmark. Accordingly, the incoming Administration should formally adopt the well-stated "Principles to Guide the Office of Legal Counsel," proposed on December 21, 2004, by 19 former OLC attorneys.[1596] These principles address matters such as the appropriate standards of professionalism and independence that should guide OLC attorneys, the importance of considering and addressing alternative legal arguments, the importance of conducting an effective interagency review of sensitive policy opinions, and related matters. They require public disclosure of opinions that conclude that the executive branch may disregard a federal statutory requirement, and call for timely disclosure of most OLC opinions. Furthermore, all current legal opinions should be reviewed, flawed opinions should be withdrawn, and non-classified opinions should be publically disclosed as appropriate. In the future, classified opinions should be made available to the House and Senate Judiciary Committees, to ensure effective oversight of the Department of Justice. Finally, if necessary, Congress should consider legislation such as H.R. 6929, the "Office of Legal Counsel Reporting Act of 2008," introduced by Representative Brad Miller in the 110th Congress, which would specifically require that OLC opinions be disclosed to Congress and that the Comptroller General review OLC practices.

Reason: The Department of Justice's Office of Legal Counsel has been at the center of providing the legal rationale for unreviewable Commander in Chief powers to justify the Bush Administration's policies regarding torture and interrogation (among other areas), and other executive usurpations of power. Traditional lines of communication between the White House and OLC broke down during the Bush Administration, so that White House aides worked too closely with lower tier OLC officials such as John Yoo to craft legal opinions that were politically or operationally useful to the Administration but which were not legally sound. These actions undermined OLC in a way that has harmed the nation, and in particular has damaged our intelligence services, which received erratic and unreliable guidance on the most sensitive of matters.

It is antithetical to the principles of our Constitution that the president should claim secret powers supported by secret interpretations of the Constitution. In fact. it is not fully known what body of "secret law" sits on the secret books of the Department of Justice and other Executive

Branch offices. Documents such as those advising interpretations of the law that have been found unconstitutional by courts – such as the memoranda which concluded that the Geneva Conventions did not apply to the detainees – should be explicitly revoked.

12.   The incoming Administration should close the U.S. prison at Guantanamo Bay. The President by executive order should close the Guantanamo Bay detention facility and dismantle the existing military commission system. The al Qaeda detainees accused of hostile conduct should, as a general matter, be charged with federal offenses and tried in the United States courts. Every effort should be made to find foreign countries to which other detainees who cannot be tried (either for lack of usable evidence or for other reasons), should be sent.[1597] In rare circumstances and as a last resort, detainees – such as the Chinese Uighurs[1598] – may be released into the United States.[1599] The statute of limitations for terrorism related offenses should be increased from 8 to 10 years to minimize the prospect that the fact that the individuals have been held in Guantanamo (or elsewhere in military custody) would impede the ability to prosecute. Finally, Congress should conduct oversight and consider repealing the Military Commissions Act if necessary.

Reason: The actions of the United States in taking into military custody persons from around the world and sending them blind-folded and shackled to a remote island prison, where they have been subjected to harsh interrogation, has brought world-wide condemnation, especially where the processes for determining whether they should be so detained lacked procedural fairness. Indeed, the Bush Administration chose to hold the detainees at Guantanamo Bay on the assumption that there would be no institutions (such as the courts) to second-guess decisions as to who should be detained, for how long, and under what conditions. Even though the Supreme Court has required the Administration to use procedures that permit judicial review of the detention determinations and has permitted the detainees access to federal courts to pursue *habeas corpus* claims, approximately 250 prisoners are still held at Guantanamo.

The prisoners at Guantanamo cannot be neatly categorized. Some are al Qaeda fighters who can and should be prosecuted and tried for criminal terrorist acts, including their involvement in terrorist conspiracies. Others, like the Chinese Uighurs, do not pose a threat to the United States. The majority are alleged to have fought against the United States in Afghanistan, and of this group, many appear to have been low-level fighters – and may not have committed prosecutable war crimes. Some were turned over to the United States by bounty hunters or others seeking rewards. David Hicks and Salim Hamdan have already been returned to Australia and Yemen respectively, and hundreds of others have been freed. Every diplomatic effort should be made to repatriate or find countries willing to accept prisoners who cannot be tried. In rare circumstances, the United States should be willing to accept some of the Guantanamo detainees. This is a small but necessary step as part of a process of convincing other allies to accept some of them as well.[1600]

The costs of shutting down Guantanamo include the intense diplomatic efforts necessary to find countries willing to accept the prisoners upon their release and the devotion of judicial resources to try the al Qaeda prisoners or others for whom criminal prosecution is appropriate. However, the costs of maintaining Guantanamo are profound, and include the fact that its very existence serves as a recruiting motivation for future terrorists. Thus, notwithstanding the difficulties involved in closing Guantanamo, and recognizing that there are risks inherent in that process, the incoming Administration should do what is necessary to close Guantanamo.

13.   The incoming Administration should require that all persons arrested in the United States be subject to civilian law enforcement procedures with requisite due process guarantees. This should include immediately taking steps to effectuate the transfer of Ali Saleh Kahlah al-Marri from military to civilian custody in order to charge him with federal terrorism-related offenses.[1601] If Mr. al-Marri were to object to that transfer - for such act would moot out Supreme Court review - the Government should seek approval from the Supreme Court to move him, or seek a remand from the Supreme Court to the Fourth Circuit so that the Fourth Circuit can rule on its request to move him. At the same time, the Justice Department should request that the Fourth Circuit vacate its July 2008 opinion, in light of the fact that the litigation has been mooted by events, and, in particular, so that the Fourth Circuit opinion that upheld Mr. al-Marri's military detention does not remain "good law" on this issue.[1602]

Reason: The detentions of Jose Padilla (an American citizen) and Ali Saleh Kahlah al-Marri (a lawfully admitted alien), each of whom was arrested in the United States and turned over to military custody upon the order of the President, constitute among the most extreme assertions of presidential power undertaken by the Bush Administration, and involve the Administration's claim that the United States itself is a "battlefield" on which the president can exercise full military power. As a practical matter, this means the incoming President, through the Department of Justice, should take a dramatically different legal position on the issues associated with the on-going detention of Mr. al-Marri. That case is presently before the Supreme Court, where the Bush Justice Department has maintained that the president, either under powers granted him directly by the Constitution as Commander in Chief or granted by Congress under the AUMF, may order the indefinite military detention of Mr. al-Marri.[1603] Mr. Al-Marri, with support of numerous *amici*, has challenged his detention in federal court, and maintained that the president has no such power under either authority.

14.   The incoming Administration should end torture and abuse. The President should issue an executive order that ends the use of torture or cruel, inhuman or degrading treatment of persons in U.S. custody or control and prohibits the use – by any agency, including the Central Intelligence Agency – of any practice not authorized by the Army Field Manual on Intelligence Interrogations, including but not limited to waterboarding. One concrete step that the President should take toward that end is to formally rescind President Bush's Memorandum of February 7, 2002, in which he concluded that as Common Article 3 of the Geneva Conventions does not apply to either al Qaeda or Taliban detainees.[1604] If necessary, Congress should consider enactment of a bill that embodies the principles of H.R. 4114, the "American Anti-Torture Act of 2007," introduced by Rep. Jerrold Nadler in the 110th Congress, which provided, among other provisions: "No person in the custody or under the effective control of the United States shall be subject to any treatment or technique of interrogation not authorized by and listed in the United States Army Field Manual on Intelligence Interrogation."[1605]

Reason: Among the actions taken by President Bush that has most damaged the United States standing and credibility as a moral leader in the world, his decisions – through Vice President Cheney, David Addington, and others – to permit waterboarding of detainees and to subject them to cruel, inhuman and degrading treatment stands at or near the top. Former Secretary of State Powell has stated that "The world is beginning to doubt the moral basis of our fight against terrorism."[1606]

To be clear, torture is currently banned under United States laws (under the anti-torture statute, the War Crimes Act, the Geneva Conventions, and the Detainee Treatment Act). It is an unfortunate state of affairs that these prohibitions have been called into doubt by the Bush Administration and its insistence that it may avoid these laws simply by redefining the term "torture." For the incoming President to reassert America's commitment to recognizing the prohibitions against torture and cruel, inhuman and degrading treatment should not suggest that there is any ambiguity in those prohibitions. Nonetheless, actions by the United States to again foreswear its intent to use torture or cruel, inhuman or degrading treatment will constitute an important first step to permit the United States to regain its international standing as a leader in the advocacy for human rights.

15. **The incoming Administration should end the CIA program of secret detention and abusive interrogation.** The incoming President should revoke Executive Order 13440 (issued July 20, 2007) and bring an immediate end to the CIA's secret detention and interrogation program. Consistent with military guidelines and international law, the President should restore accurate accounting and reporting of all detainees, ensure that the International Committee of the Red Cross (ICRC) be notified of and granted access to all detainees,[1607] publicly disclose the identities, fate, and whereabouts of all detainees currently or previously held in secret, and ensure that detainees are afforded the baseline substantive right to be free from torture or cruel, inhuman, and degrading treatment. Finally, Congress should conduct oversight and consider legislation if necessary.

Reason: In September 2006, five years after he first secretly authorized it, President Bush admitted the existence of a secret CIA detention and interrogation program. Under this program, detainees were held incommunicado at secret prison sites – so-called "black sites" – and subject to aggressive interrogation, including waterboarding. In addition to holding detainees at secret facilities, the CIA also reportedly "ghosted" detainees within or among prison facilities in Iraq. Ghost detainees were not registered or processed as prisoners, allowing the CIA to avoid accountability for and documentation of their identity, whereabouts, and treatment. To date, the number of individuals held secretly remains unknown, but it is estimated that at least 100 individuals were held secretly by the CIA and that the whereabouts of two to three dozen remain unknown. While this program was suspended by President Bush in September 2006, a subsequent July 20, 2007, executive order appears to have revived it.[1608] Holding prisoners in secret allows for torture and abusive detention and interrogation practices. It also undermines future efforts by the U.S. to demand ICRC access to U.S. personnel being held abroad and further undermines our moral standing in the world.

16.   The incoming Administration should end the Bush Administration's practice of the extraordinary rendition of terror suspects. The President should halt the rendition of terror suspects in circumstances where torture is likely and should direct a comprehensive, interagency review of U.S. rendition practices, including the use of assurances from receiving countries that a detainee will not be tortured. This should include ensuring that relevant agencies promulgate regulations to implement the legal obligation that the U.S. not transfer persons to countries where it is more likely than not that they will be tortured. Congress should conduct oversight hearings on the policy and consider legislation to limit the transfer of suspects from U.S. custody based in part on aspects or principles of H.R. 1352, the "Torture Outsourcing Prevention Act," introduced by Rep. Edward Markey in the 110th Congress, which would make it illegal for the government to transfer detainees to countries that the State Department has substantial grounds to believe engage in torture or other cruel or degrading treatment, and S. 1876, the "National Security with Justice Act of 2007," introduced by Sen. Joe Biden in the 110th Congress, which prohibits extraterritorial detention and rendition except in limited circumstances.

Reason: Following the September 11th terrorist attacks, the Bush Administration rendered individuals to countries – including Syria, Egypt, Jordan, and Morocco – where torture of persons identified as having ties to al Qaeda or terrorism was likely. These "extraordinary renditions" – the covert transfer of individuals to foreign states in circumstances where torture is likely – violate U.S. and international law.[1609] While the exact number of individuals subjected to the Administration's extraordinary rendition program remains unknown, the cases that have come to light have generated concern that the Administration has used the practice frequently,[1610] and as a tool to avoid legal limits on – or criminal liability for – harsh interrogation.[1611]

The Bush Administration's extraordinary rendition program has been condemned by some of the U.S.'s strongest allies, and U.S. agents have been indicted in Italy and Germany for their involvement in renditions from those countries.[1612] The Administration asserts that it has met any obligation to prevent transfers in circumstances where torture is foreseeable because it has gotten assurances from foreign governments that individuals will not be tortured.[1613] But press reports, congressional testimony, and the experience of individuals rendered to foreign countries indicate that such assurances are insufficient protection against torture and also raise troubling questions about whether these assurances have been obtained and relied upon in good faith by U.S. officials.[1614] Any such assurances should comply with applicable legal and human rights standards, and appropriate federal agencies should carry out their obligations under the Foreign Affairs Reform and Restructuring Act of 1998 to adopt regulations that individuals should not be transferred to countries where it is more likely than not that they will be tortured.[1615]

17.   The President, the Director of National Intelligence, the Director of the Central Intelligence Agency, and the Director of the National Security Agency should implement

policies to ensure that there is no "reverse targeting" used under authorities created by the FISA Amendments Act of 2008. Such policies, whether resulting from legislation, amendments to Executive Order 12333 or internal guidelines and procedures, should make it clear that it is impermissible to acquire the communications of a U.S. person (who is protected by FISA) by targeting their acquaintances overseas (for whom a FISA warrant is not necessary). Such guidelines should prohibit reverse targeting when a significant purpose of the interception is to acquire an American's communications. Moreover, the guidelines should require a warrant from the Foreign Intelligence Surveillance Court if the intercepted communications of a known U.S. person are disseminated outside of the collecting agency repeatedly, as this is an indication that the U.S. person may in fact be the target. Congress should conduct oversight and consider legislation if necessary.

Reason: The 110th Congress enacted the FISA Amendments Act of 2008 (FAA). This Act, while an improvement on the Protect America Act which had been enacted to update FISA in 2007, still lacks certain key protections against "reverse targeting" by members of the intelligence community (the intelligence components of the Director of National Intelligence, Central Intelligence Agency, National Security Agency, Department of Homeland Security, Department of Defense, Department of State, and Department of Justice). When Congress allowed the Executive Branch the ability to go to the FISC to obtain broad authorizations for overseas communications, concerns were raised that such broad powers could be used to engage in reverse targeting. Although the Administration had claimed that it would not engage in such practices, and recognized that reverse targeting would be illegal if it occurred,[1616] guidelines and training programs are necessary to ensure that reverse targeting does not happen.

18.   The President, the Director of National Intelligence, the Director of the Central Intelligence Agency, and the Director of the National Security Agency should implement policies to ensure that foreign intelligence surveillance is limited to targeted collection. The President should promulgate regulations and Executive Orders to dispel any concern that the FISA Amendment Act or other surveillance activities would allow bulk collection – the indiscriminate collection of *all* international communications into and out of the United States. Congress should conduct oversight and consider legislation if necessary.

Reason: It has been reported that the Bush Administration's secret wiretapping program involved not just the interception of foreign communications within the United States, but also the seizure and storage of masses of e-mail and other electronic traffic for future analysis.[1617] During the debates on the FAA, Director of National Intelligence Mike McConnell denied that the United States had the capacity – let alone the desire – to engage in bulk collection, but he would not rule out bulk collection should technology develop to make such a dramatic seizure feasible.[1618] Limitation of acquisitions – to circumstances in which a significant purpose of the acquisition of the communication is to obtain foreign intelligence information and in which at least one party is a specific individual target who is reasonably believed to be located outside of the United States – should serve to prevent such wholesale collection while preserving the ability to target persons overseas under the flexible authorities of the FAA. The method of the collection should not be broader than the parameters under which the interception is authorized. That is, if the intelligence community is only authorized to acquire communications of "a specific individual target," it is unreasonable to undertake such an acquisition through the wholesale seizure of communications traffic.

19.   The incoming Administration should ensure full implementation of Inspector General recommendations concerning the FBI's use of NSLs. The FBI Director should complete implementation of the Inspector General's 2007 recommendations, including adequately accounting for information acquired from NSLs; training agents in all 56 field offices; ensuring that agents continue to abide by Attorney General Guidelines to use the least intrusive techniques during their investigations; and fully addressing the problems pertaining to the hierarchical issues in the field offices between Special Agents in Charge (SACs) and Chief Division Counsel. [1619] Congress should conduct careful oversight in this area and, if necessary, consider legislation addressing the current problems with NSL usage, incorporating at minimum the pre-PATRIOT Act NSL issuance standard requiring "specific and articulable facts giving reason to believe that the information or records sought... pertain to a foreign power or agent of a foreign power;" providing the recipient of an NSL the right to challenge the NSL and its nondisclosure requirement; providing a cause of action to any person aggrieved by the illegal provision of records pertaining to that person as a result of an NSL issued contrary to law, placing a time limit on an NSL gag order and allowing for a court approved extension; and providing for minimization procedures to ensure that information obtained pursuant to an NSL regarding persons who are no longer of interest in an authorized investigation is destroyed, along the lines of H.R. 3189, the "National Security Letters Reform Act," introduced by Rep. Jerrold Nadler in the 110th Congress.

Reason: In 2007 and 2008, reports from the Justice Department's Inspector General documented problems and abuses with the FBI's use of national security letters, including: the use of exigent letters,[1620] inaccurate and incomplete congressional reporting regarding the use of NSLs,[1621] inaccurate reporting of possible Intelligence Oversight Board violations,[1622] circumventing NSL statutes by issuing NSLs in impermissible contexts,[1623] and indefinitely retaining personal information on individuals even if they were irrelevant to terrorism investigations.[1624] In its 2008 report, the IG found that the FBI had made some progress in implementing its recommendations from the 2007 report, but that several recommendations were not yet implemented.[1625] The incoming Justice Department and the Inspector General should ensure that the FBI adequately and fully implements the remaining recommendations and does not backtrack on any progress to date.[1626]

Legislation restoring the pre-PATRIOT Act NSL issuance standard would help eliminate the problems highlighted in the Inspector General's reports pertaining to the acquisition and indefinite retention of information on American citizens who are not reasonably suspected of being involved in terrorism. Legislation could also help address concerns identified under Patriot Act provisions authorizing the FBI to impose blanket, indefinite, prior restraints on speech, strictly confining an NSL recipient's ability to challenge the gag in court, and limiting judicial review of a gag order (making it difficult to determine whether the order violates NSL statutes, the

Constitution, or other legal rights and privileges).[1627] Statutory changes regarding minimization rules may also be needed to reduce the potential for the misuse of information acquired through NSLs and to ensure that NSLs capture information only on individuals who actually are the subjects of terrorism investigations.

20. **The incoming Administration should withdraw the proposed Justice Department rule on criminal intelligence system operating policies and carefully review and revise as needed the Attorney General's guidelines for FBI operations.** The proposed Criminal Intelligence Systems Operating Policies rule, published in the summer of 2008, should be withdrawn and the process started from scratch because of serious concerns about its potential to improperly invade Americans' privacy and other rights. Similar concerns warrant a careful re-examination of the Attorney General FBI guidelines to ensure that they strike the appropriate balance between effective law enforcement and the respect for civil liberties and individual rights.

Reason: The Department of Justice's proposed rule on Criminal Intelligence Systems Operating Policies has generated significant controversy.[1628] This rule appears to permit the collection of information by state and local law enforcement agencies regarding non-criminal (and constitutionally protected) activities and sharing that information with non-law enforcement agencies. The rule would also allow for the collection of information about organizations and individuals, resulting in potential violations of individuals' First Amendment rights and the creation of McCarthy era-type "blacklists." Additionally, the regulation would extend the retention period for information in criminal intelligence systems from five years to ten years and would allow for the tolling of the retention period during a person's incarceration. This could lead to the retention of inaccurate, obsolete, and otherwise unreliable information in the systems that could be used to wrongly accuse someone of a crime. The incoming Administration should withdraw the proposed rule and restart the rulemaking process so that a final rule in this area does not have these defects.

In late 2008, the Bush Administration also issued FBI Domestic Investigation and Operations Guidance regarding the Attorney General Guidelines for Domestic FBI Operations, issued September 29, 2008. These Guidelines have generated significant concern, both as to their timing just before the end of the Bush Administration and their authorization of potentially intrusive techniques against Americans. For example, critics have raised significant questions about provisions that could give FBI field agents the authority to conduct some forms of physical surveillance and interviews without getting approval from or filing specific reports with their supervisors.[1629] The FBI has indicated that the guidelines are to be reviewed in the fall of 2009. As part of that review, the incoming Administration should consider modifying the guidelines and the accompanying guidance as appropriate to ensure that they protect civil rights and civl liberties as well as promoting effective law enforcement.

21. **The President should nominate and bring into operation the Privacy and Civil Liberties Oversight Board.** The incoming President should appoint all members to the Privacy and Civil Liberties Oversight Board created by Congress and urge the Senate to hold prompt confirmation hearings for the candidates. Further, the President's first budget proposal should contain sufficient funds to actually bring the board into existence as an effective entity.

Reason: This Board was created by the Intelligence Reform and Terrorism Prevention Act of 2004.[1630] It was originally part of the White House but was made an independent agency in the Executive Branch pursuant to the Implementing Recommendations of the 9/11 Commission Act of 2007.[1631] The Board's mandate is to monitor the impact of U.S. government actions on civil liberties and privacy interests, and to advise Executive Branch officials to help ensure that such interests are appropriately considered in executive actions undertaken to protect against terrorism. It has five members who are appointed by the president and subject to confirmation by the Senate. The terms of its original members expired in January 2008. However, President Bush failed to nominate candidates for all seats on the board, and none have been confirmed by the Senate. As a result, the revised Board has never gone into operation.

22. <u>The President should renew efforts to implement U.S. obligations under human rights treaties.</u> The incoming President should reactivate the Interagency Working Group on Human Rights Treaties (replaced under the Bush Administration by the Policy Coordinating Committee on Democracy, Human Rights, and International Operations), which would create an open and transparent process for treaty reporting and consider compiling a comprehensive human rights compliance report on the U.S., similar to that compiled by the State Department on other countries.

Reason: The incoming Administration needs to reassert its commitment to the rule of law as well as send a clear message to the world that the United States will take a leadership role in promoting human rights at home and abroad. Since 1992, the United States has ratified only three major human rights treaties.[1632] However, little oversight and few legislative initiatives have focused on codifying the rights and obligations under these treaties. Official U.S. action has been primarily limited to periodic reporting and review process activities by Geneva-based committees who monitor treaty compliance.

23. <u>The incoming Administration should review and consider modifications to Bureau of Prisons use of authority under Special Administrative Measures.</u> The incoming Administration should review how the Special Administrative Measures (SAM) authority has been used, including mental health screening of prisoners subjected to extreme isolation under the SAM rules, and consider appropriate modifications, which may include modifying SAM rules. The review should additionally ensure attorney-client privileges to prisoners in federal custody.

Reason: Under the Bush Administration, an interim rule drastically expanded the Bureau of Prisons (BOP) authority under the Special Administrative Measures (SAMs).[1633] The regulation became effective immediately without the usual opportunity for prior public comment. The rules now give the Attorney General virtually unlimited and unreviewable discretion to strip any person in federal custody of the right to communicate with counsel confidentially.

Misuse of Executive Branch Authority

24. <u>**The President should end abuse of presidential signing statements.**</u> President Obama should fulfill his pledge that he will "not use signing statements to nullify or undermine congressional instructions as enacted into law"[1634] as has occurred under the Bush Administration. He should also make clear that, despite his predecessor's signing statements, he intends to fully execute existing laws.

Reason: A presidential signing statement is not part of the enactment process.[1635] Yet President Bush has issued signing statements unilaterally claiming the power to refuse to implement parts of laws enacted by Congress, and has in fact done so in a number of instances. As recognized on a bipartisan basis, the pattern and practice of signing statements by the Bush Administration has represented a major abuse of power, undermining the authority of the Congress and the intent of the Framers of the Constitution. By executive action fulfilling his pre-election pledge, and by making clear that he will fully execute laws as to which President Bush issued signing statements, President Obama can end this abuse, as some of the most severe critics of the Bush Administration's use of signing statements have recognized.[1636] If necessary, Congress should consider possible legislation, such as some of the proposals in the 110th Congress, to prevent future misuse of signing statements.[1637]

25. <u>**The incoming Administration should restore rulemaking from the White House to traditional agency authority consistent with congressional intent and the public interest.**</u> As a threshold matter, the President should take two initial steps to restore this traditional authority to the relevant agency: (i) clarify that the role of the Office of Information and Regulatory Affairs (OIRA) within the Office of Management and Budget (OMB) is to facilitate the rulemaking process rather than to serve as a gatekeeper on rulemaking; and (ii) rescind Executive Order 13422, which by substantially enhancing the Executive Branch's control over agency rulemaking, has undermined congressional intent.

Reason: Under President Bush's leadership, OIRA's role has changed from serving as a counselor for agencies to a self-described "gatekeeper" of agency rulemaking. OIRA's current gatekeeping role conflicts with the fact that Congress delegates rulemaking authority to the agencies, not to OMB.[1638] Issued without any prior consultation in January 2007, Executive Order 13422 undermines congressional intent in several respects. For example, the Order's requirement that an agency identify a specific "market failure" establishes standards for regulatory initiation that are not consistent with statutory requirements and that can be used to deter congressionally-intended regulatory actions.[1639] A diverse group of 17 regulatory experts supports this recommendation.[1640]

26. <u>**The incoming Administration should make rulemaking more transparent, understandable, and informative, thereby permitting greater accountability to Congress and the public.**</u> The President should: (i) amend Executive Order 12866 to mandate that the rulemaking process be transparent and subject to greater accountability consistent with recommendations made by GAO;[1641] and (ii) require agencies to use electronic rulemaking.[1642] In addition, Congress should: (i) fund the Administrative Conference of the United States (ACUS); and (ii) enact legislation to clarify the applicability of the Congressional Review Act with respect to what constitutes a "rule" within the meaning of the Act.

Reason: The Administration's influence on agency rulemaking is difficult to discern even after the proposed or final rule is published because key parts of the OIRA review process and other Administration initiatives are not transparent. The only transparency required by OMB is during the formal review process. Accordingly, it is unclear whether outside entities have exercised undue influence and whether the Administration has directly or indirectly intervened in the rulemaking process to weaken or delay rules contrary to the public interest.[1643] In addition, OIRA discloses neither how many "significant" guidance documents it has reviewed since the issuance of Executive Order 13422 nor whether any changes were made to those documents as a result of those reviews. Further, agency regulatory policy officers do not disclose how many rules they changed or completely prevented from being published in the *Federal Register*.[1644] The need for greater transparency was also cited by a diverse group of 17 regulatory experts.[1645]

Other ways to promote greater transparency include implementing an effective electronic rulemaking process, as the current system makes it very difficult to track rulemaking.[1646] This recommendation is supported by various regulatory experts.[1647] In addition, ACUS could conduct empirical analyses with the cooperation of all three branches of government and make recommendations to the Administration and Congress on how the rulemaking process can be improved.[1648] Further, the Congressional Review Act should be clarified with respect to what constitutes a "rule" within the meaning of the Act in light of the fact that the Bush Administration has sought to circumvent the requirements of the Congressional Review Act, which mandates that agencies submit rules to Congress before they become effective.[1649]

27. **The incoming Administration should rein in "Midnight" rulemaking, which implements the priorities of a lame-duck administration even though a new President has been elected.** The President should: (i) impose a 60-day moratorium on regulations not yet finalized or in effect; and (ii) prohibit Executive Branch agencies from unilaterally issuing "midnight regulations" – regulations issued during the last several months of an outgoing president's term of office – except in compelling or exigent circumstances. If necessary, Congress should consider legislative restrictions on the practice, such as H.R. 34, the "Midnight Rule Act," introduced by Rep. Nadler at the beginning of the 111th Congress.

Reason: While many outgoing administrations attempt to expedite the rulemaking process to ensure their priorities are addressed, such an expedited process may shortcut meaningful agency review and public participation processes. A recent spate of controversial midnight regulations issued by the Bush Administration relating to the environment, civil liberties, the preemption of state consumer safety laws, and other important matters of public policy, present serious concerns about midnight regulations. Such rules can be particularly problematic if they have been rushed through the review and comment process.[1650] As recommended by a diverse group of regulatory experts, a moratorium would allow time for the incoming Administration to review problematic regulations not yet finalized or in effect.[1651]   Regulations required by court order, statute, or necessity to meet regulatory emergencies could be exempt from the moratorium.[1652]

Other Incursions by the Executive Branch

In addition to the above recommendations concerning the misuse of signing statements and regulatory authority, over the last eight years we have witnessed a number of additional instances of misuse of Executive Branch authority or unaccountable abuses of power which warrant a Legislative or Executive Branch response. Several of these additional recommendations were worked on by the Committee over the last two years and are set forth below.

28.   The incoming Administration and Congress should restore the full protection of the attorney-client privilege. The Obama Administration should issue an executive order or memorandum requiring application to all agencies of the August 28, 2008, Justice Department guidelines on corporate prosecutions, which recognized the importance of the attorney-client privilege and work-product doctrine. Congress should also consider legislation to prohibit federal prosecutors from considering a corporation's willingness to "waive" its attorney-client privilege and work-product protections in making charging and leniency decisions. H.R. 3013, the "Attorney-Client Privilege Protection Act of 2007," which passed the House on November 13, 2007, by voice vote, would restore judicial oversight to these protections, while preserving prosecutorial discretion necessary to fight corporate crime.

Reason: The centuries-old common law and constitutional protections of the attorney-client privilege and attorney work-product doctrine are fundamental to our nation's system of justice. Unfortunately, past governmental policies gave rise to a "culture of waiver" that placed the continuing vitality of these crucial protections in serious jeopardy. Specifically, the Department of Justice had previously adopted policies that placed defendants at greater risk of prosecution if they claimed any of the fundamental protections embodied in the attorney-client privilege or work-product doctrine. The genesis of these policies was a series of Justice Department memoranda, which include a 2006 memorandum from then-Deputy Attorney General Paul McNulty, permitting prosecutors to demand a privilege waiver after receiving Department approval, and granting corporate defendants credit from criminal charges for "voluntarily" waiving without being formally asked. In a laudatory change of direction, the Department, on August 28, 2008, issued new guidelines on corporate prosecutions, specifically recognizing the importance of the attorney-client privilege and work-product doctrine.[1653]   Because the guidelines follow the spirit of H.R. 3013, the Obama Administration should take immediate steps to replicate the Justice Department guidelines by executive order for all agencies. Legislation may also be necessary if certain independent regulatory agencies (such as the Securities and Exchange Commission) fail to follow the President's lead and to ensure that these standards apply under future administrations.

29.   Congress should enact press shield legislation. Congress should pass legislation that provides a qualified privilege that prevents a reporter's source material from being revealed except under certain narrow circumstances, such as where it is necessary to prevent an act of terrorism or other significant and specified harm to national security or imminent death or significant bodily harm. H.R. 2102, the "Free Flow of Information Act," which passed the House on October 16, 2007, by a vote of 398-21, will restore the independence of the press while balancing the legitimate and important interests that society has in maintaining public safety.

Reason: One of the most fundamental principles enshrined by the Founding Fathers in the First Amendment of the Constitution is freedom of the press. This freedom is one of the cornerstones of our democracy; without it, we cannot have a well-informed electorate and a government that truly represents the will of the people. The Bush Administration has repeatedly assaulted the press by imprisoning or threatening imprisonment of reporters. As noted by the *Washington Post*, "40 reporters have been hauled into federal court and questioned about their sources, notes and reports in civil and criminal cases."[1654]

Many stories would not have been published without a promise of confidentiality to sources, such as Watergate, the Pentagon Papers, and Iran-Contra. More recent news stories brought to light based on confidential sources include the conditions at the Walter Reed Army Medical Center, the Abu Ghraib prison scandal, and the abuse of steroids by baseball players. At present, 49 States and the District of Columbia have some form of a shield law. The lack of a corresponding federal reporter's privilege undercuts these state laws. Because the privilege is not absolute, a federal law will prevent law enforcement officials from using journalists and the results of their fact-gathering as a shortcut to a proper investigation but will not obstruct truly appropriate and necessary inquiries. With the reporter shield law, law enforcement will be forced to pursue other sources of information before being able to turn to journalists for their notes.

30.   The incoming Administration should limit the ability of Executive Branch officials to prevent victims of terrorism from recovering for their losses. The President should seek to resolve a dispute between victims of torture and the government of Iraq committed during the Gulf War. If not, Congress should consider enacting legislation, such as H.R. 5167, the "Justice for Victims of Torture and Terrorism Act," which passed the House on September 15, 2008, by voice vote. This legislation will enable American POWs and civilians to hold the Government of Iraq liable for the physical and emotional injuries they sustained while held captive by Iraqi officials during the Gulf War.[1655]

Reason: In 1998, Congress passed the "Flatow Amendment" to specify that a cause of action existed against the officials, employees, and agents of foreign states who commit a terrorist act "while acting within the scope of" their employment if a U.S. government official would be liable for similar actions.[1656] Unfortunately, in conjunction with the 2003 Iraq War, President Bush took a series of actions that, in combination, had the effect of making Iraq's assets in the U.S. unavailable to terrorism victims who, after March 20, 2003, obtained terrorism-related judgments against Iraq.[1657] In 2008, Congress sought to amend the Foreign Sovereign Immunities Act (FSIA) of 1978 to enable victims whose claims were dismissed for lack of a federal cause of action to re-file their claims under new 28 U.S.C. §1605A – a new FSIA terrorism exception and explicit cause of action against terrorist states – and enforce judgments by attaching a defendant state's assets.[1658] However, President Bush vetoed the FY08 National Defense Authorization Act, solely on the basis of this provision.[1659]

31. Congress should pass legislation holding Administration-designated contractors in Iraq and elsewhere responsible for their criminal misconduct. Congress should pass legislation to explicitly address the inadequacies of our criminal law in war zones. H.R. 2740, the "MEJA Expansion and Enforcement Act of 2007," which passed the House on October 4, 2007, by a vote of 389-30, would make contractors and contract personnel under Federal contracts criminally liable for crimes committed overseas. It would amend the Military Extraterritorial Jurisdiction Act ("MEJA"),[1660] which criminalizes offenses committed outside the United States by members of the Armed Forces and certain Defense Department contractors, but does not cover all contractors providing services in an overseas military operation.[1661]

Reason: An estimated 180,000 contractors are currently working in Iraq, and thousands more are working in Afghanistan and elsewhere.[1662] Unfortunately, the current law does not clearly specify that these contractors are accountable for their criminal conduct.[1663] For example, contractors hired through the Defense Department are subject to both the Uniform Code of Military Justice and MEJA, while contractors who commit crimes on Federal property may be prosecuted under the USA PATRIOT Act. The vast majority of armed contractors performing security functions overseas, however, may not be subject to any of these laws. Thus, although the Justice Department has recently brought five indictments against contractors involved in the Iraq Nisour square shooting where at least 17 Iraqis were killed, lawyers for the defendants have already stated that they will contest whether the Justice Department has jurisdiction under MEJA to bring the case.[1664]

In another example, Jamie Leigh Jones, a young woman working for Halliburton/KBR in Iraq, testified before the Judiciary Committee that she was drugged and raped by fellow employees in 2005.[1665] Almost four years later, we have yet to hear of the status of the investigation or prosecution.

32. The Department of Justice should issue guidelines to require transparency and uniformity of corporate deferred and non-prosecution agreements. The Attorney General should revise guidelines regarding the Justice Department's use of deferred prosecution agreements (DPAs) and non-prosecution agreements (NPAs) in order to provide greater transparency and consistency in their use and in the selection and compensation of independent corporate monitors. DPAs and NPAs are agreements between the federal government and individual corporations in which the government agrees to not prosecute or defer criminal prosecution in exchange for the corporation agreeing to specific actions such as changes in corporate policies and payment of monetary penalties. If necessary, Congress should consider enacting legislation such as H.R. 6492, the "Accountability in Deferred Prosecution Act of 2008," which would require the Attorney General to take steps to ensure that the process is fair for all parties to the agreement and that prosecutors award contracts to corporate monitors pursuant to a process that is open, public and competitive.[1666]

Reason: DPAs and NPAs often impose significant obligations on corporations, including the payment of substantial monetary penalties, the implementation of stringent corporate governance and compliance measures, mandatory cooperation with the government's ongoing investigation (often requiring waiver of the corporation's attorney-client and work-product privileges), waiver of speedy trial rights and statute of limitations defenses, and agreement to external oversight by an independent corporate monitor approved by the government.[1667] The Justice Department, however, has provided minimal guidance to United States Attorneys with respect to how these agreements should be structured, how independent monitors should be selected, and what are appropriate duties for these monitors.[1668] The absence of meaningful guidance has led to inconsistent use of these agreements among the jurisdictions, unequal treatment of corporations that choose to enter into such agreements, and abuse in the appointment of independent corporate monitors.[1669]

Retribution Against Critics

33. __Congress should consider legislation concerning the exercise of clemency involving government officials.__ Congress should consider legislation that would require the president, upon granting clemency to a current or former Executive Branch official, to report to Congress (1) whether the official was involved in any ongoing or contemplated criminal or civil investigation; (2) whether the president sought the recommendation of the federal official responsible for the investigation as to the implication of the clemency grant on the investigation and, if so, the nature of the official's recommendation; and (3) whether the responsible official communicated to the president his or her belief that the grant of clemency would interfere with any ongoing or contemplated investigation into possible misconduct by the president, vice president, or administration officials. Those and similar procedural requirements appear in H.R. 5961, the "Integrity and Accountability in Administration Pardons Act of 2006," which then-Ranking Member John Conyers, Jr. introduced in the House during the 109th Congress. Congress should also consider legislation that would require lobbyists to disclose pardon-relating lobbying activities directed at the Executive Branch.[1670]

Reason: The president's clemency power can too easily be used to interfere with or hinder a civil or criminal investigation into malfeasance by the president, vice president, and Executive Branch officials. A pardon can even shut down an investigation altogether by immunizing the subjects of the investigation from prosecution. That concern arose most notably at the end of George H. W. Bush's Administration, when the President pardoned former Defense Secretary Casper Weinberger and Assistant Secretary of State Elliott Abrams with respect to their actions during the Iran-Contra scandal of the mid-1980s The prosecution of Secretary Weinberger and Assistant Secretary Abrams might well have brought the President's own actions under public scrutiny.[1671] President George W. Bush's 2007 grant of clemency to Vice President Cheney's chief of staff, Scooter Libby, raised similar concerns, as did President's Clinton's end-of-term pardons of his brother, Roger Clinton, and Clinton friend and partner in the Whitewater real-estate venture, Susan McDougal. Legislation along the lines of H.R. 5961 would render the president more publicly accountable when granting clemency to Executive Branch officials,[1672] while leaving the President's constitutional clemency authority undisturbed.[1673] As for lobbying-disclosure legislation, it may be needed to expose pardon-lobbying by wealthy and influential pardon applicants of the sort the public witnessed during the final days of the Clinton Administration.[1674]

34.   Congress should enhance and strengthen protection for Executive-Branch whistleblowers. Congress should pass legislation to enhance and strengthen existing legal protection for whistleblowers. Needed changes of particular importance include according protection to federal employees who report high-level misconduct directly to Congress (rather than requiring them to "report up the chain of command"), reversing court decisions that have largely gutted existing legal protections against retaliation, and enhancing legal remedies for successful claimants. Congress should also extend whistleblower protections to CIA, FBI, and other employees who work on national security matters. Most are currently unprotected under existing federal laws. Legislation introduced during the 110th Congress that passed the House but failed to become law (including H.R. 985, the "Whistleblower Protection Enhancement Act of 2007," and S. 274, the "Federal Employee Protection Disclosure Act") offers a starting point for future legislation.

Reason: A key component to government accountability is protecting the employees who are on the inside and decide to report wrongdoing. Federal employees are often the first, and perhaps the only, people to see signs of corruption, government misinformation, and political manipulation. They are in a distinct position to alert Congress or other authorities when officials put political agendas ahead of facts or sound policy. Unfortunately, as seen in cases involving the Bush Administration, whistleblowers often are the victims of retaliation by their superiors. The threat of such retaliation can have a chilling effect on federal employees' willingness to blow the whistle. Enhanced legal protections would help insulate whistleblowers from the threat of retaliation. National security officials particularly deserve whistleblower protections. They are federal government employees who have undergone extensive background investigations, obtained security clearances, and handled classified documents. They are in the unique position of handling the most sensitive law enforcement and intelligence projects, but they currently receive no protection when they come forward to identify abuses that are undermining our national security.

Government in the Shadows: Executive Privilege, Secrecy, and the Manipulation of Intelligence

35.   Congress should enact changes in statutes and rules to strengthen Congress' contempt power. Congress should pass legislation that would establish a clear and expeditious mechanism to enforce congressional subpoenas civilly against current and former Executive Branch officials. Congress should also adopt legislation creating a process for the appointment of a special counsel to prosecute current or former Executive Branch employees held in contempt of Congress for refusing to testify or produce documents in response to a congressional subpoena, such as Representative Miller's H.R. 6508, the "Special Criminal Contempt Procedures Act." In addition, the House should consider adopting a rule providing for procedures to go forward with inherent contempt as necessary.

Reason: While the Committee's lawsuit to enforce subpoenas against Harriet Miers and Josh Bolten has established that Congress may enforce its subpoenas in federal court under the Declaratory Judgment Act, the procedures required can be burdensome and time consuming. The established remedy of statutory criminal contempt has proven ineffective because the Justice Department has refused to prosecute despite the House's finding of contempt. Any use of Congress' recognized power of inherent contempt has been frustrated by the absence of specific procedures in the House. A law specifically authorizing civil contempt proceedings to enforce subpoenas would avoid problems of delay and create an orderly, streamlined, non-criminal mechanism to resolve these disputes. Legislation should also make clear that when Congress determines that a present or former Executive Branch official is in contempt for refusing to comply with a subpoena, enforcement cannot simply be stopped by the Administration's refusal to go forward (as occurred in the Miers-Bolten case), but would be turned over to a special counsel because of the obvious conflict of interest. The Miers-Bolten situation also highlighted the need for clarification of the process for exercising Congress' inherent contempt power to penalize an individual who defies a subpoena, and specific rules to address questions such as how inherent contempt proceedings would be initiated, what House entities would prosecute and initially rule on such charges, and what and how penalties can be imposed.

36.   The incoming Administration should establish procedures for asserting Executive Privilege. The President should issue an executive order establishing procedures for asserting executive privilege, including a commitment to personally invoke the privilege and to provide adequate descriptive information to Congress if documents are withheld. Congress should engage in oversight concerning the efficacy of any proposed procedures and determine whether additional action in the form of legislation is necessary.

Reason: During the 110th Congress, the Administration withheld subpoenaed documents from Congress on the basis of executive privilege on multiple occasions.[1675] However, some of these invocations of privilege were stated in communications from the White House Counsel; no personal assertion of the privilege by President Bush, as caselaw and prior executive practice require, was ever presented.[1676] Accordingly, the incoming Administration should establish clear guidelines for the assertion of privilege that include provision of an unambiguous personal claim of privilege by the president.

In addition, the interbranch accommodation process under the Bush Administration suffered because of a consistent refusal of the White House to provide adequate information about documents being withheld, which would have allowed Congress to consider possible compromises in an informed manner. As Judge Bates recognized in the Judiciary Committee's lawsuit against Harriet Miers and Josh Bolten, "a more detailed description of the documents withheld and the privileges asserted would be a tremendous aid during the negotiation and accommodation process."[1677]

37.   The incoming Administration and Congress should prevent abusive assertion of the state secrets privilege. The President should issue an Executive Order specifying that (i) the state secrets privilege should be invoked narrowly to challenge the admissibility of particular pieces of evidence, not to dismiss entire cases, and (ii) when invoked, the government should make a reasonable attempt to provide a non-privileged substitute – such as a redacted version or a summary – instead. The next Congress should also pass legislation that sets out the substantive standards and procedural framework for meaningful judicial review of state secret claims, and requires judges to review the information that the government seeks to withhold and determine whether its disclosure would be harmful to national security using procedures that safeguard classified and other potentially sensitive information. These provisions were included in H.R. 5607, the "State Secret Protection Act," introduced by Reps. Nadler and Conyers in the 110th Congress.

    Reason: Although there are valid reasons for recognizing a state secrets privilege, preventing the sort of broad abuses of the privilege perpetrated by the Bush Administration requires action in both the Legislative and Executive Branches. The state secrets privilege was used by the Bush Administration to broadly escape judicial review of a number of potentially illegal actions, including rendition, warrantless domestic surveillance, and post-9/11 detention of American citizens, and in discrimination and retaliation claims brought by former federal employees.   Corrective measures are needed from the Executive to limit the circumstances and manner in which state secrets privilege is asserted. Corrective measures are needed from the Legislative branch to standardize the process and provide uniform substantive standards by which courts may fairly evaluate whether the state secrets privilege, when challenged, was properly invoked.

38.   The incoming Administration and Congress should improve the system for classification and declassification. The President should issue an Executive Order that (i) rescinds Executive Order 13292, thereby restoring the previous presumptions for declassification, (ii) requires each Executive Branch agency that classified information during the Bush administration to perform a detailed review of its classification guides in order to eliminate obsolete requirements and to reduce the total amount of classification to a minimum, (iii) modifies military and intelligence classification rules to reduce unnecessary classification, (iv) adds a balancing test that requires that the public value of the information be considered when determining if it is to be declassified, and (v) ends the practice of reclassifying declassified documents. Congress should also consider legislation to prohibit political manipulation of the classification/declassification process in the future. The legislation should incorporate the recommendations of the Moynihan Commission,[1678] among them, (i) the establishment of a national declassification center to declassify material (with guidance from the originating agencies) and make it available to the public, (ii) establishing a single, independent Executive

Branch office for coordinating classification and declassification practice, (iii) requiring classification officials to weigh a variety of factors, including costs and benefits of secrecy, in arriving at their initial classification decision, and (iv) having the Director of National Intelligence issue a directive outlining the appropriate scope of protection for methods and sources as a rationale for classification.

Reason: As a general matter, government documents should be declassified in all but the most necessary of circumstances, in order to promote the widest distribution of government information. The Bush Administration has largely operated under a veil of secrecy, not only seeking to keep existing classified information out of the public domain, but also attempting to re-classify documents that have already been declassified and released to the public. The consequences of using classification to keep potentially damaging revelations out of the public eye can be grave. For example, the Bush Administration used classification in order to embellish the 2002 National Intelligence Estimate on Iraq's weapons of mass destruction capabilities and its ties to al Qaeda.[1679] The public version omitted major caveats, uncertainties, and dissents contained in the classified version, thus leading the public to believe that the threat posed by Iraq was far more certain and immediate than the intelligence agencies actually believed.

39. **Congress should consider legislation requiring the President to publicly announce the declassification of classified materials.** Congress should consider legislation whereby the Executive Office of the President is required to provide public notice whenever it declassifies documents, with the notices to be published on the White House website and other selected locations. The legislation should require the president to inform the congressional intelligence committees within a reasonable time frame whenever intelligence has been declassified, as provided in S. 2660, introduced by Sen. Diane Feinstein in the 109th Congress. Her legislation provided a 15-day time period in which to give congressional intelligence committees notice of declassification.

Reason: The Administration appears to have selectively leaked numerous items of classified information to buttress their case for war. The President himself appears to have secretly authorized the declassification of information without notice in an effort to neutralize Ambassador Wilson's op-ed concerning the Administration's uranium claims. The public would have better access to information were the White House to issue public notices upon declassification.

40. **The Department of Justice should restore the presumption of disclosure under FOIA.** The Attorney General should rescind the October 2001 Ashcroft directive that reversed the presumption of disclosure under FOIA and restore the principle that information should be released unless it is both exempt from disclosure and it would be harmful to release it.[1680]

Reason: The October 2001 directive issued by then-Attorney General Ashcroft reversed the presumption of disclosure under FOIA. Explicitly superseding the Department of Justice's FOIA Memorandum of October 4, 1993, the directive imposed a high threshold for disclosure, permitting the heads of all federal departments and agencies to make discretionary decisions to disclose information protected under the FOIA "only after full and deliberate consideration of the institutional, commercial, and personal privacy interests that could be implicated." Adopted as Administration policy, the directive has resulted in a lack of transparency by the federal government. Indeed, 2007 witnessed the lowest percentage of FOIA requests granted in full, 35.6%, since data collection started in1998.[1681] The previous presumption in favor of disclosure should be restored. Conflicts in balancing the public interest in information about its government with legitimate needs for secrecy should be decided in favor of disclosure.

41.   The President should rescind Bush White House memoranda that significantly restrict the use and disclosure of non-classified information.   In particular, the memoranda that should be revoked include White House Chief of Staff Andrew Card's Memorandum for the Heads of Executive Departments and Agencies on "Action to Safeguard Information Regarding Weapons of Mass Destruction and Other Sensitive Documents Related to Homeland Security,"(March 19, 2002) and President Bush's Memorandum for the Heads of Executive Departments and Agencies on the Sharing of Controlled Unclassified Information" (May 9, 2008).

Reason: While national security concerns may legitimately require preventing the disclosure of certain classified information, those arguments fall away when that information is already declassified and in the public domain. The 2002 memo staked out broad Executive authority and encouraged agencies to reclassify information that was no longer classified and, similar to the Ashcroft memo on the Freedom of Information Act, encouraged the use of various FOIA exemptions to withhold disclosure of sensitive but unclassified information, which was not defined. The 2008 memo introduced "Controlled Unclassified Information" as a new government category that replaced "Sensitive but Unclassified." Rescinding the memos would promote greater transparency of government records by reducing the avenues by which documents could be withheld from the public for classification reasons.

Similarly, while the Bush Administration claims that the purpose of the 2008 memo is to standardize practices and improve information sharing, it effectively continues an expansion of secrecy in government by adding an unnecessary level of uncertainty for government employees deciding which documents may be released in response to public inquiry. Although the Memorandum explicitly states that the use of the "controlled unclassified information" label "may inform but [does] not control" the decision to disclose under FOIA, lower-level staff, seeing the label on responsive documents, may instinctively treat it as protected and withhold it from disclosure.[1682] Poorly-trained or ill-informed junior staff, unfamiliar with these new designations, may be overly cautious in withholding documents, which is currently the norm in cases of uncertainty as a result of the memos described above. Because of the threat of under-disclosure, the incoming Administration should reduce potential room for error by minimizing the number of classification designations (in addition to mandating a presumption of disclosure, as described above).

42.   The President should place the Office of FOIA Ombudsperson in the National

Archives. The President should resolve the impasse created by the Bush Administration and place the office of FOIA ombudsperson in the National Archives and Records Administration rather than in the Department of Justice, in compliance with the OPEN Government Act of 2007.[1683] This would situate the entity in a neutral forum to aid requesters with their FOIA requests without potential interference from a party in possession of requested documents, and provide impartial oversight over compliance.

Reason: In enacting the OPEN Government Act of 2007, Congress created an ombudsperson responsible for FOIA requests. The position was created in response to Bush Administration policies designed to limit the volume of documents produced in response to FOIA requests. The position was created in the National Archives, and was designed to both assist requesters by providing informal guidance and reviewing agency compliance. In contravention of the enacting law, in 2008, the Bush Administration administratively transferred the office of FOIA ombudsperson from the National Archives, an independent federal entity, to the Department of Justice, which is part of the Executive Branch and ultimately supervised by the Attorney General, a presidential appointee. This change occurred before the office even began functioning. The transfer was initiated by the Vice President's office after it had engaged in an escalating series of confrontations with the National Archives over the Vice President's obligations to report his possession of classified information. As the ombudsperson's superior, the Attorney General could directly and indirectly influence the ombudsperson's actions and limit the guidance provide and disclosures authorized.

43. **The incoming Administration should restore the accessibility of presidential records.**
The President should issue an Executive Order rescinding Executive Order 13233 and restoring the requirements of Executive Order 12667. Such an order should have the effect of making presidential records generally available to the public twelve years after the president has left office, and preventing former presidents and vice presidents from indefinitely claiming privilege over such documents.[1684]

Reason: President Bush issued Executive Order 13233, concerning the Presidential Records Act, which superseded Executive Order 12667. Under the old Executive Order, presidential documents were made public 12 years after the custodial president left office. Under President Bush's Order, former presidents and vice presidents and their representatives may seek to bar the release of such documents by claiming one of numerous privileges, allowing the president and vice president to enshroud numerous historical documents in a permanent secrecy.

44. **Congress should modernize the Presidential Records Act.** Congress should consider legislation that would modernize the Presidential Records Act and clarify its application to a modern White House using multiple and overlapping communications systems, such as blackberries and personal digital assistants. The legislation should enact criminal penalties for intentional destruction of presidential records or deliberate circumvention of official record-keeping mechanisms when conducting presidential business.

296

Reason: The Bush Administration's widespread use of political communications equipment to conduct official business has led to a number of challenges in investigating allegations of official misconduct such as the U.S. Attorney removals. Other investigations have been hampered by the loss of e-mail communications and inconsistency within backup and archiving mechanisms. Investigation by the Oversight and Government Reform Committee revealed that, in some instances, personnel intentionally and knowingly diverted official business to outside communication systems to avoid White House recordkeeping systems.[1685]

45. **The incoming Administration should clarify the applicability of rules of access to the Office of the Vice President.** The President should issue an Executive Order clarifying that the rules of secrecy applicable to the Executive Branch apply equally to the Office of the Vice President and that the Office of the Vice President is subject to the same document preservation requirements as the president.

Reason: Vice President Cheney has consistently refused to comply with information disclosure mandates applicable to the entire Executive Branch.[1686] He has justified his noncompliance on the grounds that the secrecy rules which bind the Executive are not applicable to the Office of the Vice President. The Office of the Vice President cited this alleged ambiguity in declining to comply with the National Archives' request for the preservation of documents, a request with which even the Office of the President has complied. The dispute led to unnecessary litigation between the two offices. The political nature of the Vice President's position became evident when his chief of staff David Addington attempted to have the Archivist's office eliminated. There is no proper policy or constitutional basis for excluding the Vice President's office from general rules of access.

46. **The incoming Administration should eliminate overly restrictive "Gang of 8" briefings in favor of more effective mechanisms.** To the extent possible, the President should avoid using "Gang of 8" briefings, as the system leads to abuses. If necessary, Congress should consider amending the National Security Act to (i) expand 50 U.S.C. §413b(c)(2) to permit staff members of the Gang of 8 with suitable security clearances to participate, (ii) make clear that the Gang of 8 can discuss the contents of these briefings with their congressional colleagues under suitable protections, and (iii) clarify the meaning of the word "covert" within the statute.

Reason: The National Security Act of 1947 requires the president to keep all members of the congressional intelligence committees fully and currently informed of all of the intelligence activities of the United States.[1687] However, where covert actions are involved, the president is statutorily permitted to limit notification to the so-called "Gang of 8," the leaders of the House and Senate and the chairs of the House and Senate intelligence committees.[1688] "Gang of 8" briefings exclude staff, regardless of their levels of security clearance; moreover, the debriefed members are forbidden from taking notes or discussing the substance of these briefings with their colleagues. Despite the express limitation spelled out in the statute, the Bush Administration has used "Gang of 8" briefings to brief a limited number of Members on a wider variety of issues not provided for within the law, such as warrantless domestic surveillance; the Congressional

Research Service specifically found that the program "would appear to fall more closely under the definition of an intelligence collection program, rather than qualify as a covert action program as defined by statute."[1689] On one occasion in October 2001, the Bush White House went so far as to say that any congressional briefing involving classified information should be limited to the "Gang of 8" and no one else in Congress. This undermines the express purpose of the National Security Act, which was to keep the intelligence committees fully informed of the federal government's intelligence activities. In addition, no legislation should be able to limit the ability of any Members of Congress to share information with other Members when necessary to carry out their constitutional responsibilities, and amendments to the rules of both Houses would be appropriate to make this clear.

47. **The incoming Administration mandate steps to avoid manipulation and misuse of intelligence.** The President should issue an Executive Order that ensures that (i) versions of National Intelligence Estimates ("NIEs") and other documents made public adequately indicate dissents or caveats, (ii) only official components of the intelligence community can produce intelligence assessments, and (iii) senior officials not make public assertions inadequately supported by intelligence, and there be procedures for corrective action should that occur. In addition, by executive action or by statutory mandate if necessary, an unclassified version of National Intelligence Estimates and comparable assessments, including important caveats and dissents, should be publicly released.

Reason: The "hands-on" approach of the Bush Administration in directly reviewing raw intelligence data that had not been vetted through appropriate channels led to improper assumptions, incorrect assessments, and a diminution in independent recommendations, all of which led to misguided policies with devastating long-term consequences.

Senior Defense Department executives established the Office of Special Plans (OSP), which purported to produce intelligence reports and assessments about alleged Iraqi WMDs and links to al Qaeda. Working with the Office of the Vice President, OSP sent its products directly to the White House, without their being subject to review and comment by the intelligence community. At the same time, the Vice President, his staff and other senior Executive officials made repeated trips to the CIA to press analysts to conform their evaluations on Iraq to predetermined positions.

Rather than provide unbiased independent assessments to the White House, the intelligence community effectively came under the Office of the Vice President, which then filtered the intelligence to comport with the policy positions of the Executive. For example, the Bush Administration cited an intelligence community estimate that aluminum tubes imported by Iraq were intended for centrifuges to enrich uranium to weapons grade. Department of Energy (DOE) scientists, who were the Americans most expert on uranium enrichment, were confident that the tubes were not intended for use as centrifuge. They had vehemently dissented from the majority Community view that the tubes were intended for centrifuges. Moreover the State Department intelligence experts on nuclear proliferation agreed with the DOE experts.

Although NIEs, which are authoritative assessments by the intelligence community on intelligence related to specific national security issues, are under the possession and control of the president, the misuse of NIEs by the President in the Iraq War illuminates why publishing declassified versions is so important. The Bush Administration made public a declassified version of the 2002 National Intelligence Estimate about the WMD threats posed by Iraq. However, the published version omitted major caveats, acknowledgment of poor information, expressions of low probability, and dissenting views. It also omitted the Intelligence Community consensus that there was little likelihood that Saddam would give whatever WMD he might have had to terrorists, as President Bush had suggested. It is crucial to ensure that Congress and the public can consider the facts and assumptions relied upon in fashioning some of the Executive's most grave policy decisions.

Endnotes

1. *United States v. Hamdi*, 542 U.S. 507, 568-69 (2004) (Scalia, J., dissenting).

2. David Addington, who was at the time Counsel to the Vice President, shows up on virtually no documents. But he had a pervasive and dominant presence within the Administration in forcefully advocating the expansive use of power in the Imperial Presidency. A *New Yorker* profile describes what it was like to be in one of these internal debates with Mr. Addington:

> Richard Shiffrin, the former Pentagon lawyer, said that during a tense White House meeting held in the Situation Room just a few days after September 11th "all of us felt under a great deal of pressure to be willing to consider even the most extraordinary proposals. The CIA, the N.S.C., the State Department, the Pentagon, and the Justice Department all had people there. Addington was particularly strident. He'd sit, listen, and then say, 'No, that's not right.' He was particularly doctrinaire and ideological. He didn't recognize the wisdom of the other lawyers. He was always right. He didn't listen. He knew the answers." The details of the discussion are classified, Shiffrin said, but he left with the impression that Addington "doesn't believe there should be co-equal branches."

Meyer, "The Hidden Power," *The New Yorker*, July 3, 2006, *available at* http://www.newyorker.com/archive/2006/07/03/060703fa_fact1?currentPage=6 .

An article on the formulation of the interrogation policies described the September 2002 visit to Guantanamo by Mr. Addington, White House Counsel Gonzales, Defense Department General Counsel Jim Haynes, and CIA General Counsel John Rizzo made it clear that Mr. Addington was perceived as "definitely the guy in charge." Sands, "The Green Light," *Vanity Fair*, May 2008, *available at* http://www.vanityfair.com/politics/features/2008/05/guantanamo200805?currentPage=1.

In an interview with PBS, Jack Goldsmith, who succeeded John Yoo in the Justice Department's Office of Legal Counsel (OLC), described Mr. Addington as "very sarcastic and aggressive against people with whom he disagreed, and dismissive oftentimes."

> Q: What was he like to work with?

> A: He was many things. He had a lot of experience, so he could always make arguments from precedent or the way things had been done before, which was very powerful in these arguments. He was very tough in making his

arguments. He was very sarcastic and aggressive against people with whom he disagreed, and dismissive oftentimes. He was learned. He knew a lot about precedents and practices, and he acted with the implicit blessing of the Vice President. All of these things made him a very, very forceful presence.

Q: How did you know he had the "implicit blessing" of the Vice President?

A: I say implicit because it was never explicit... I don't ever recall him invoking the Vice President's authority. But everyone understood that... he and the Vice President were on the same page, and everyone understood that the arguments that Addington was making in these meetings were the arguments that the Vice President was going to be making to the President...

Q: What was it like to argue with Addington?

A: David could be very, very aggressive in his arguments, sometimes personal and ad hominem, often mixed with precedents, arguments, knowledge, directions from the President. It was a bombastic mixture of argumentative strategies...

There were two questions that Addington always asked: "Do you think we have the power on our own to do what we're doing?" And the answer was yes, there were good legal arguments for it.

The second question was: "Is it possible that if we go to Congress the President might not get what he wants, and the Congress might place restrictions on the President, and the President might conceivably be left in a weaker position, thereby making it harder for him to protect Americans?" And the answer to that question was always yes. Those two questions usually ended the argument.

Interview with Jack Goldsmith re: David Addington, *Frontline: Cheney's Law* (PBS television broadcast), *available at* http://www.pbs.org/wgbh/pages/frontline/cheney/themes/addington.html.

3. Addington, *quoted in* Goldsmith, *The Terror Presidency* 124 (W. W. Norton & Co. 2007).

4. Goldsmith, *The Terror Presidency* 126 (W. W. Norton & Co. 2007).

5. *Id.* at 126.

6. *Const.* art. II, § 3. Congress's initial response to President Bush's extraordinary assertions and assumptions of power is noteworthy. For the first six years of the Bush Presidency, when both

Houses of Congress were, except for a brief period, controlled by the President's own political party, Congress was apparently often kept in the dark about presidential actions that infringed on Congress's assigned Constitutional responsibilities. Even when it was made aware of such action, all to often it stood silent or, in a few instances in the area of national security, largely accepted and enacted the President's legislative proposals and in so doing ratified actions he had already taken. During these years, Congress provided scant oversight, and largely abandoned its Constitutionally assigned role to make the laws of the United States in national security matters. It was, to an astonishing extent, compliant, some might even say complicit, in the aggrandizement of the president's power.

A *New York Times* reporter quoted Senator Lindsey Graham as giving the following response to the question why he and his fellow senators waited so long to try to reclaim their place in the constitutional order: "'The Congress was intimidated after 9/11,' [Graham] answered. 'People were afraid to get in the way of a strong executive who was talking about suppressing a vicious enemy, and we were AWOL for a while, and I'll take the blame for that. We should have been more aggressive after 9/11 in working with the executive to find a collaboration, and I think the fact that we weren't probably hurt the country. I wish I had spoken out sooner and louder." Mahler, "After the Imperial Presidency," *N.Y. Times Mag.*, Nov. 7, 2008, *available at* http://www.nytimes.com/2008/11/09/magazine/09power-t.html?_r=2&hp&oref=slogin&oref=slogin .

Senator Arlen Specter made similar comments to the reporter: "[I] asked Specter, who was chairman of the Judiciary Committee from 2005 to January 2007, how he thought Congress had fared vis-à-vis the Executive Branch during the Bush Administration. 'Decades from now,' he answered, 'historians will look back on the period from 9/11 to the present as an era of unbridled executive power and congressional ineffectiveness.'" *Id.*

7.*Const.* art. II, § 2.

8.Other examples from 18th Century Europe include Louis XIV of France, whose view of monarchical power was famously expressed: "Le etat, c'est moi." (In English, "I am the State.")

9.*See* discussion in Section 3.

10.Interview with Jonathan Karl, ABC News, Dec. 15, 2008, *available at* http://a.abcnews.com/Politics/story?id=6464697&page=1.

11.The text of the original White House draft joint resolution is found at *Cong. Rec.*, 107th Cong., 1st sess. Oct. 1, 2001, pp. S9949-S9951 (daily ed.). *See also* , Grimmett, CRS Report RS 22357, *Authorization for Use of Military Force in Response to the 9/11 Attack (P.L. 107-40): Legislative History*. The resolution proposed by the White House provided: "That the President is authorized to use all necessary and appropriate force against those nations, organizations or persons he determines planned, authorized, harbored, committed, or aided in the planning or commission of the attacks against the United States that occurred on September 11, 2001, *and to deter and pre-empt any future acts of terrorism or aggression against the United States.*" *Id.* at 5-6 (emphasis added).

12. Holmes, "John Yoo's Tortured Logic," *The Nation,* May 1, 2006, *available at* http://www.thenation.com/doc/20060501/holmes/2 [hereinafter *John Yoo's Tortured Logic*].

13. Daschle, "Power We Didn't Grant," *Wash. Post,* Dec. 23, 2005 at A21, *available at* http://www.washingtonpost.com/wp-dyn/content/article/2005/12/22/AR2005122201101.html (emphasis added). In hindsight, it appears the Administration may also have been seeking this additional phrase to cite as congressional authorization for conducting warrantless surveillance inside the United States, without regard to the legal requirements of FISA.

14. Pub.L. No. 107-40, 115 Stat. 224, 224 (2001). *See also* Grimmett, CRS Report RS 22357, *Authorization for Use of Military Force in response to the 9/11 Attack (P.L. 107-40): Legislative History* (emphasis added).

15. Section 2 of the AUMF provided:

> (b) WAR POWERS RESOLUTION REQUIREMENTS —
>
> > (1) SPECIFIC STATUTORY AUTHORIZATION — Consistent with section 8(a)(1) of the War Powers Resolution, the Congress declares that this section is intended to constitute specific statutory authorization within the meaning of section 5(b) of the War Powers Resolution.
> >
> > (2) APPLICABILITY OF OTHER REQUIREMENTS- Nothing in this resolution supercedes any requirement of the War Powers Resolution.

16. It is unknown who else in addition to Mr. Yoo may have worked on the September 25, 2001, Memorandum or reviewed it before it was made final. Over the next several months, nearly all the legal opinions asserting as Administration policy broad and unreviewable presidential war powers came from this one 35-year-old lawyer, toiling in relative obscurity in the Justice Department. In certain aspects, Mr. Yoo was a law-maker unto himself.

17. Memorandum, The President's Constitutional Authority to Conduct Military Operations Against Terrorists and Nations Supporting Them, by Dep. Asst. Att'y. Gen'l. John C. Yoo, Dept. of Justice, OLC, Sept. 25, 2001, *available at* http://www.usdoj.gov/olc/warpowers925.htm [hereinafter September 25 2001 War Powers Memorandum] (emphasis added).

18. The evidence on this score is overwhelming. For example, Secretary of Defense Rumsfeld made comments at 2:40 on the afternoon of September 11 about the possibility of retaliating

against Iraq. The notes of Rumsfeld's staffer, Stephen Cambone, the Principal Deputy Under Secretary of Defense for Policy, document Donald Rumsfeld's 2:40 p.m. instructions to General Myers to find the "[b]est info fast . . . judge whether good enough [to] hit S.H. [Saddam Hussein] at same time - not only UBL [Usama Bin Laden]." The notes are available on-line at http://www.outragedmoderates.org/2006/02/dod-staffers-notes-from-911-obtained.html. See also Borger, "Blogger Bares Rumsfeld's Post 9/11 Orders," *The Guardian*, Feb. 24, 2006, *available at* http://www.guardian.co.uk/world/2006/feb/24/freedomofinformation.september11.

Richard Clarke has written and spoken publicly about receiving pressure in the days following 9/11 to find a link between Saddam Hussein and the terrorists and about Rumsfeld's desire to attack Iraq. In his book, Clarke wrote:

> I expected to go back to a round of meetings [after September 11] examining what the next attacks could be, what our vulnerabilities were, what we could do about them in the short term. Instead, I walked into a series of discussions about Iraq. At first I was incredulous that we were talking about something other than getting al Qaeda. Then I realized with almost a sharp physical pain that Rumsfeld and Wolfowitz were going to try to take advantage of this national tragedy to promote their agenda about Iraq. They were talking about Iraq on 9/11. They were talking about it on 9/12.

Clarke, *Against All Enemies: Inside America's War on Terror* 30, (Free Press 2004).   Clarke also described his interactions with President Bush on this topic on "60 Minutes." "Clarke's Take on Terror," CBS News, Mar. 21, 2004, *available at* http://www.cbsnews.com/stories/2004/03/19/60minutes/main607356.shtml.

In a Meet the Press interview, General Wesley Clark said he had been asked to find a link between al Qaeda and Saddam Hussein:

> Mr. Clark: There was a concerted effort during the fall of 2001, starting immediately after 9/11, to pin 9/11 and the terrorism problem on Saddam Hussein.
>
> Mr. Russert: By who? Who did that?
>
> Mr. Clark: Well, it came from the White House, it came from people around the White House. It came from all over. I got a call on 9/11. I was on CNN, and I got a call at my home saying, "You got to say this is connected. This is state-sponsored terrorism. This has to be connected to Saddam Hussein." I said, "But--I'm willing to say it, but what's your evidence?" And I never got any evidence.

304

Interview of Wesley Clark by Tim Russert, Meet the Press, June 15, 2003, *reported in* "Media Silent on Clark's 9/11 Comments," *Fairness and Accuracy in Reporting*, June 20, 2003, *available at* http://www.fair.org/index.php?page=1842.

Deputy Secretary of Defense Paul Wolfowitz confirmed in an interview with Vanity Fair magazine that in the immediate days following the 9/11 attacks there were discussions about attacking Iraq. Wolfowitz stated:

> There was a long discussion during [meetings at Camp David after the 9/11 attacks] about what place if any Iraq should have in a counterterrorist strategy. On the surface of the debate it at least appeared to be about not whether but when. There seemed to be a kind of agreement that yes it should be, but the disagreement was whether it should be in the immediate response or whether you should concentrate simply on Afghanistan first.

Deputy Secretary Wolfowitz Interview with Sam Tannenhaus, *Vanity Fair*, May 15, 2003, *available at* http://www.defenselink.mil/transcripts/transcript.aspx?transcriptid=2594. On September 20, 2001, a group calling itself "People for a New American Century" sent a letter to President Bush, signed by William Kristol and Richard Perle among others, that called for attacking Iraq even if Iraq were not implicated in the 9/11 attacks. *See* Letter from William Kristol et al to President Bush, September 20, 2001, *available at* http://zfacts.com/p/165.html.

19. The National Commission on Terrorist Attacks Upon the United States, *The 9/11 Commission Report*, W.H. Norton, authorized ed. (2004), pp. 334-36 (footnotes omitted). The Report also noted:

> Within the Pentagon, Deputy Secretary Wolfowitz continued to press the case for dealing with Iraq. Writing to Rumsfeld on September 17 in a memo headlined "Preventing More Events," he argued that if there was even a 10 percent chance that Saddam Hussein was behind the 9/11 attack, maximum priority should be placed on eliminating that threat. Wolfowitz contended that the odds were "far more" than 1 in 10, citing Saddam's praise for the attack, his long record of involvement in terrorism, and theories that Ramzi Yousef was an Iraqi agent and Iraq was behind the 1993 attack on the World Trade Center.

Id.

20. September 25 2001 War Powers Memorandum.

21. Although Mr. Yoo, as a lawyer, may have believed that Congress had no constitutional role in authorizing the use of military force, or that the War Powers Act was unconstitutional, he

certainly knew that the AUMF as enacted did not "demonstrate Congress's acceptance" of his assertions as to the nature of the president's "unilateral war powers." As Mr. Yoo as well aware, in enacting the AUMF, Congress had *rejected* the pre-emption language sought by the President, had included provisions citing to the War Powers Act, and had narrowed the scope of the AUMF from that requested by the President insofar as he had sought authorization to use military power inside the United States. By no fair interpretation of events did the AUMF – in which Congress insisted on basing its authorization on the War Powers Act – reflect Congress's "acceptance of the President's unilateral war powers."

22. September 25, 2001 War Powers Memorandum (emphasis added).

23. September 25, 2001 War Powers Memorandum (emphasis added). The sentence is susceptible to a less controversial interpretation – that the president could lawfully use military power against targets around the world to protect Americans citizens at home or abroad. The more natural reading, however, is that the "battlefield" where military force could be used included locations in the United States. In light of the Administration's subsequent reliance on the president's Commander-in-Chief power as justification for actions such as the seizure of Jose Padilla in Chicago and the warrantless surveillance inside the United States, it is fairly clear that the latter interpretation was intended.

Indeed, that interpretation is consistent with later assertions by the Administration. In a November 7, 2001, memorandum regarding the president's power to use military commissions to try terrorists, the Office of Legal Counsel specifically included using such commissions "to try U.S. citizens seized in the United States." In defending a court challenge to the military detention of a U.S. citizen, the Government characterized the United States as a "battlefield." Jackman, "U.S. a Battlefield, Solicitor General Tells Judges," *Wash. Post,* July 20, 2005, p. A09, *available at* http://www.washingtonpost.com/wp-dyn/content/article/2005/07/19/AR2005071901023.html. And in a December 17, 2005 radio address, President Bush described fighting the war on terror on the "home front": "We're fighting these enemies across the world. Yet in this first war of the 21st century, one of the most critical battlefronts is the home front. And since September the 11th, we've been on the offensive against the terrorists plotting within our borders." President Bush's Radio Address, Dec. 17, 2005, *available at* http:/www.whitehouse.gov/news/releases/2005/12/20051217.html.

24. "Interview with John Yoo," *Frontline*, July 19, 2005, *available at* http://www.pbs.org/wgbh/pages/frontline/torture/interviews/yoo.html (emphasis added).

25. In one of the Government's briefs in the *Padilla* case, for example, the Government specifically argued that "[t]he President's exercise of his Commander in Chief powers [to seize Padilla, a U.S. citizen, in the United States] comes with 'full statutory authorization from Congress,' and his constitutional authority therefore is at its broadest." *Padilla v. Bush, et al*, 02 Civ. 4445 (MEM) (S.D.N.Y), Respondents' Reply In Support of Motion to Dismiss the Amended Petition for a Writ of Habeas Corpus (Oct. 11, 2002) at 13. Mr. Yoo would similarly

306

argue that "Congress also implicitly authorized the President to carry out electronic surveillance to prevent further attacks on the United States in the [AUMF] passed on September 18, 2001." Yoo, *War by Other Means, An Insider's Account of the War on Terror* 115 (New York, 2006). And similarly, as to military commissions: "Congress's AUMF implicitly included the power to detain enemy combatants." *Id*. at 149.

26.President's Letter to Congress on American Response to Terrorism, Oct. 9, 2001, *available at* http://www.whitehouse.gov/news/releases/2001/10/20011009-6.html (emphasis added). The President's speech to the Nation announcing the initiation of hostilities made no reference to the AUMF: "On my orders, the United States military has begun strikes against al Qaeda terrorist training camps and military installations of the Taliban regime in Afghanistan." Presidential Address to the Nation, Oct. 7, 2001, *available at* http://www.whitehouse.gov/news/releases/2001/10/20011007-8.html.

27.Memorandum for Alberto R. Gonzales, Counsel to the President, *Legality of the Use of Military Commissions to Try Terrorists*, from Patrick F. Philbin, Deputy Assistant Attorney General (Nov. 6, 2001), at 1, 5 (emphasis added).

28.Memorandum for William J. Haynes, General Counsel, Department of Defense, from John Yoo, Dep. Asst Att'y Gen., and Robert J. Delahunty, Special Counsel, *Re: Application of Treaties and Laws to al Qaeda and Taliban Detainees* (Jan. 9, 2002) at 11(emphasis added; footnote omitted).

29.Memorandum for Alberto R. Gonzales, Counsel to the President, from Jay S. Bybee, Asst Att'y Gen., *Re: Standards of Conduct for Interrogation under 18 U.S.C. §§ 2340-2340A* (Aug. 1, 2002) at 31 (emphasis added).

30.Memorandum for William J. Haynes, II, General Counsel, Department of Defense, from Department of Justice, OLC, *Re: Military Interrogation of Alien Unlawful Combatants Held Outside the United States* (Mar. 14, 2003) (emphasis added). The pertinent memoranda authorizing the non-FISA warrantless surveillance have not been released. Presumably, they set forth similar justifications. As Mr. Yoo stated in an interview: "If it's part of the president's power as a constitutional matter to gather intelligence, including intercepting communications, then that's a power that's included and Congress can't seize it just because it wants to." *Frontline: Cheney's Law* (PBS television broadcast), available at http://www.pbs.org/wgbh/pages/frontline/cheney/view/main.html (transcript available at http://www.pbs.org/wgbh/pages/frontline/cheney/etc/script.html).

31."Congress, [the Administration's critics] say, should pass a law on every aspect of the use of force, not in the AUMF's general terms, but only in declared specifics..." Mr. Yoo, *War by Other Means, An Insider's Account of the War on Terror* 149 (New York, 2006).

32."Padilla's complaints mirror the left's campaign against the war. To them, the 9/11 attacks did not start a war, but instead were simply a catastrophe, like a crime or even a natural disaster.

They would limit the U.S. response only to criminal law enforcement managed by courts, not the military. Every terrorist captured away from the Afghanistan battlefield would have the right to counsel, Miranda warnings, and a criminal trial that could force the government to reveal its vital intelligence secrets." Mr. Yoo, "Terrorist Tort Travesty," *Wall St. J.*, Jan. 19, 2008, available at http://online.wsj.com/article/SB120070333580301911.html. Mr. Yoo does not indicate which critics from "the left" advance this position.

33. As New York University Law Professor Stephen Holmes explains in a review of one of Mr. Yoo's books on the president's war powers:

> To make his contrarian claim ring true, Yoo whites out contrary
> evidence and draws dubious conclusions on the basis of
> fragmentary and carefully selected facts. He disregards the main
> thrust of the historical record and misrepresents the parts he
> acknowledges. He ferrets out (and exaggerates the importance of)
> scattered shreds of evidence that, at first glance, seem to back up
> his predetermined narrative. . . .

John Yoo's Tortured Logic.

34. September 25, 2001 War Powers Memorandum (emphasis added).

35. Notably, the Declaration of Independence lists, among the grievances against King George III:

> He has kept among us, in times of peace, Standing Armies without
> the Consent of our legislatures.

> He has affected to render the Military independent of and superior
> to the Civil Power.

36. John Jay wrote in a slightly different context about the "human nature" that moves monarchs to war:

> It is too true, however disgraceful it may be to human nature, that
> nations in general will make war whenever they have a prospect of
> getting anything by it; nay, absolute monarchs will often make war
> when their nations are to get nothing by it, but for the purposes and
> objects merely personal, such as thirst for military glory, revenge
> for personal affronts, ambition, or private compacts to aggrandize
> or support their particular families or partisans. These and a variety
> of other motives, which affect only the mind of the sovereign, often
> lead him to engage in wars not sanctified by justice or the voice
> and interests of his people...

308

The Federalist No. 4, "Concerning Dangers From Foreign Force and Influence (continued)," Nov. 7, 1787 (John Jay).

37. *The Federalist* No. 69, at 470 (J. Cooke ed., Wesleyan University Press 1961).

38. *Const.* art. I, § 8. Professor Holmes stresses this point in his book review:

> Yoo repeatedly asserts that the Framers gave Congress only two checks on the executive's foreign-policy powers: namely, the power to impeach and the power to cut off supplies. This is prima facie implausible, given the impressive arsenal of foreign-policy powers assigned to Congress by the Constitution, including the powers to define violations of the law of nations, to issue letters of marque and reprisal, to make rules concerning captures on land and water, to raise and support an army and navy, to make rules for their governance and to regulate international commerce–not to mention the Senate's powers to accept or reject ambassadorial appointments and to approve or reject treaties, and, of course, Congress's power to declare war.

John Yoo's Tortured Logic.

39. *Const.* art. II, § 2.

40. *United States v. Hamdi*, 542 U.S. 507, 568-69 (2004) (Scalia, J., dissenting) (emphasis added).

41. "Thus, a declaration of war served the purpose of notifying the enemy, allies, neutrals, and one's own citizens of a change in the state of relations between one nation and another." Yoo, "The Continuation of Politics by Other Means: The Original Understanding of War Powers," 84 *Cal. L. Rev.* 167, 207 (1996).

42. Madison, "Helvidius No. 1," *Philadelphia Gazette*, Aug. 31, 1793, *reprinted in The Mind of the Founder*, rev. ed., ed. Marvin Meyers (Indianapolis: Bobbs-Merrill Co., 1981), 206-207, *quoted in* Savage, *Takeover, The Return of the Imperial Presidency and the Subversion of American Democracy* 19 (Little Brown & Co., 2007) (emphasis in original).

43. Madison, *The Writings of James Madison* 132 (Gaillard Hunt ed., 1906), *quoted in* Fisher, "Lost Constitutional Moorings: Recovering the War Power," 81 *Ind. L.J.* at 1205. *See also* Cole, "What Bush Wants to Hear," *N.Y. Review of Books*, Nov. 17, 2005, *available at* http://www.nybooks.com/articles/18431:

> Many of the Framers passionately defended the decision to deny the President the power to involve the nation in war. When Pierce

Butler, a member of the Constitutional Convention, proposed giving the President the power to make war, his proposal was roundly rejected. George Mason said the President was "not to be trusted" with the power of war, and that it should be left with Congress as a way of "clogging rather than facilitating war." James Wilson, another member, argued that giving Congress the authority to declare war "will not hurry us into war; it is calculated to guard against it. It will not be in the power of a single man, or a single body of men, to involve us in such distress; for the important power of declaring war is vested in the legislature at large." Even Alexander Hamilton, one of the founders most in favor of strong executive power, said that "the Legislature alone can interrupt [the blessings of peace] by placing the nation in a state of war." As John Hart Ely, former dean of Stanford Law School, has commented, while the original intention of the Founders on many matters is often "obscure to the point of inscrutability," when it comes to war powers "it isn't."

44. *John Yoo's Tortured Logic* at 3.

45. Delahunty and Yoo, "The President's Constitutional Authority to Conduct Military Operations Against Terrorist Organizations and the Nations That Harbor or Support Them," 25 *Harv. J. of Law and Pub. Pol.* 487, 494 (Spring 2002) (footnote omitted). Mr. Yoo makes a similar assertion in a March 2003 OLC memorandum: "That sweeping grant [in Article II] vests in the President the 'executive power' and contrasts with the enumeration of the powers – those 'herein' – granted to Congress in Article I." Memorandum for William J. Haynes, II, General Counsel, Department of Defense, from Department of Justice, OLC, *Re: Military Interrogation of Alien Unlawful Combatants Held Outside the United States* (Mar. 14, 2003), at 5.

46. September 25, 2001 War Powers Memorandum.

47. *Const.* art. I, § 8.

48. Yoo, "The Continuation of Politics by Other Means: The Original Understanding of War Powers," 84 *Cal. L. Rev.* at 290-94.

49. Fisher, "Lost Constitutional Moorings: Recovering the War Power," 81 *Ind. L.J.* 1199, 1235-36 (2005).

50. *Id.* at 1237-38. As Fisher wryly notes, "There was room [in Mr. Yoo's law review article] for 625 footnotes but not for that one." *Id.* at 1238. Another early court decision Fisher discusses is *United States v. Smith*, 27 F. Cas. 1192, 1230 (C.C.N.Y. 1806) (No. 16,342), where the court addressed, and rejected, the argument that the president could ignore and countermand the Neutrality Act of 1794: "The [P]resident cannot control the statute, nor dispense with its

execution, and still less can he authorize a person to do what the law forbids." The court noted there was a "manifest distinction between our going to war with a nation at peace, and a war being made against us by an actual invasion, or a formal declaration. In the former case, it is the exclusive province of [C]ongress to change a state of peace into a state of war." *Id*.

51.*Youngstown Sheet & Tube Co. v. Sawyer*, 343 U.S. 579, 640 (1952).

52.In *Dames & Moore v. Regan*, 453 U.S. 654, 661(1981), the entire Supreme Court embraced Justice Jackson's view as "bringing together as much combination of analysis and common sense as there is in this area."

53.*Executive Nomination: Hearing before the S. Judiciary Comm.*, 109th Cong. (Jan. 6, 2006) (statement of Alberto Gonzales on his nomination to serve as Attorney General).

54.Bowermaster, "Charges may result from firings, say two former U.S. Attorneys," *Seattle Times*, May 9, 2007, http://seattletimes.nwsource.com/html/localnews/2003699882_webmckayforum09m.html (reported remarks to assembled United States Attorneys at Scottsdale, Arizona.).

55."Ex-Aide Insists White House Puts Politics Ahead of Policy," *N.Y. Times*, Dec. 2, 2002, http://query.nytimes.com/gst/fullpage.html?res=9A03E2DA1E38F931A35751C1A9649C8B63.

56.Fonda & Healy, "How Reliable Is Brown's Resume?," *Time Magazine*, Sept. 8, 2005, http://www.time.com/time/nation/article/0,8599,1103003,00.html.

57.Eilperin & Leonning, "Top scientist rails against hirings," *Wash. Post*, Nov. 22, 2008, at A3.

58.*See, e.g.*: Draft Committee Report, "The Activities of the White House Office of Political Affairs," *H. Comm. on Oversight and Govt. Reform*, 110th Cong., Oct. 2008, http://oversight.house.gov/documents/20081015105434.pdf; Majority Staff Report prepared for Chairman Henry A. Waxman, "FDA Career Staff Objected to Agency Preemption Policies," *H. Comm. on Oversight and Govt. Reform*, 110th Cong, Oct. 2008, at http://oversight.house.gov/documents/20081029102934.pdf; Memorandum to Oversight and Government Reform Committee Members from the Majority Staff, "EPA's Denial of the California Waiver," *H. Comm. on Oversight and Govt. Reform*, 110th Cong, May 19, 2008, http://oversight.house.gov/documents/20080519131253.pdf; Memorandum to Oversight and Government Reform Committee Members from the Majority Staff, "Supplemental Information on the Ozone NAAQS," *H. Comm. on Oversight and Govt. Reform*, 110th Cong, May 20, 2008, http://oversight.house.gov/documents/20080520094002.pdf.

59.*See, e.g.*, Thornton & Soto, "Lam Asked to Step Down," San Diego Union Tribune, Jan. 12, 2007, http://www.signonsandiego.com/news/metro/20070112-9999-1n12lam.html.

60.*See, e.g.*, Rood, "White House Pushes Out Another Prosecutor," *TPMMuckracker.com*, Jan. 15, 2007, http://tpmmuckraker.talkingpointsmemo.com/archives/002340.php. As Rood's opening sentences reads, "Strange days? Less than a week after news broke that the Bush Administration has forced the resignation of San Diego U.S. Attorney Carol Lam, we learn that it has done the same to Daniel Bogden, U.S. Attorney for Nevada."

61.H. Rep. No. 110-423, at 24 (2007). *Available at* http://frwebgate.access.gpo.gov/cgi-bin/getdoc.cgi?dbname=110_cong_reports&docid=f:hr423.1 10.pdf.

62.*Id.* at 44-47 (2007).

63.E-mail from Kyle Samspon, Chief of Staff to Att'y Gen. Alberto Gonzales, to David Leitch, Deputy White House Counsel (Jan. 9, 2005, 7:34 PM EST) (OAG 180); Krugman, "Department of Injustice," *N.Y. Times*, March 9, 2007, http://select.nytimes.com/2007/03/09/opinion/09krugman.html?_r=1&scp=1&sq=Department%2 0of%20INjustice&st=cse.

64.*Id.* Updated data based on a larger sample that was presented at a joint hearing of two Judiciary Subcommittees in October 2007 indicated that Democrats were five times as likely to be investigated as Republicans. *See* H. Rep. No. 110-423, at 35 (2007).

65.H. Rep. No. 110-423, at 30-31 (2007). In its written opinion, the three judge appeals court labeled the prosecution's theory of the case "preposterous." *United States v. Thompson*, 484 F.3d 877 (7th Cir. 2007).

66.H. Rep. No. 110-423, at 30-31 (2007).

67.*Id.* at 35.

68.Rosenbaum, "Justice Department Accused of Politics in Redistricting," *N. Y. Times*, May 31, 2002, at A14.

69.McCaffrey, "U.S. Backs off Discrimination Cases," *Detroit Free Press*, Dec. 11, 2003, at 15A.

70.Savage, "Civil Rights Hiring Shifted in Bush Era: Conservative Leaning Stressed," *Boston Globe*, July 23, 2006, at A1.

71.*Oversight Hearing on the Employment Section of the Civil Rights Division of the U.S. Department of Justice: Hearing Before Subcomm. on the Const., Civil Rights, and Civil Liberties of the H. Comm. on the Judiciary*, 110th Cong. (2007) (statement of Richard Ugelow, Practitioner in Residence, Washington College of Law, American University).

72.Eggen, "Civil Rights Focus Shift Roils Staff At Justice; Veterans Exit Division as Traditional Cases Decline," *The Washington Post*, Nov. 13, 2005, at A1.

73.*Id.*

74.Savage, "Civil Rights Hiring Shifted in Bush Era: Conservative Leaning Stressed," *Boston Globe*, July 23, 2006, at A1.

75.*Id.*

76.*Id.*

77.Subpoenas issued by H. Judiciary Comm. Chairman John Conyers, Jr. to David Iglesias, Carol Lam, Bud Cummins, and John McKay (March 1, 2007).

78.Alexander, *Machiavelli's Shadow* (St. Martin's Press) (June 1998).

79.*See, e.g.*, Thornton & Soto, "Lam Asked to Step Down," San Diego Union Tribune, Jan. 12, 2007, http://www.signonsandiego.com/news/metro/20070112-9999-1n12lam.html.

80.Letter from H. Judiciary Comm. Chairman John Conyers, Jr. and Rep. Howard Berman to Attorney General Alberto Gonzales (Jan. 17, 2007).

81.*Dept. of Justice Oversight: Hearing Before the S. Comm. on Judiciary*, 110th Cong. 22 (2007) (statement of Alberto Gonzales, Att'y Gen. Of the United States).

82.*H.R. 580, Restoring Checks and Balances in the Confirmation Process of U.S. Attorneys: Hearing before the Subcomm. on Commercial and Administrative Law of the H. Comm. on the Judiciary.*, 110th Cong. *passim* (2007) (statement of William E. Moschella, Principal Associate Deputy Attorney General). *A transcript of the hearing is available at* http://judiciary.house.gov/hearings/printers/110th/33809.PDF.

83.*Id.* at 13-14 (statement of William E. Moschella, Principal Assoc. Dep. Att'y Gen.).

84.*Id.* (statements of former United States Att'ys Carol Lam, David Iglesias, Daniel Bogden, John McKay, Bud Cummins, and John McKay).

85.*Id.* at 10 (statement David Iglesias, former United States Att'y).

86.*Id.* at 10 (statement David Iglesias, former United States Att'y).

87.*Id.* at 24 (statement John McKay, former United States Att'y).

88.*Id.* at 258-261 (responses to Questions for the Record submitted by Bud Cummins, former United States Att'y).

89.*Id.* at 268, 276-277 (responses to Questions for the Record Submitted by former U.S. Att'ys Paul Charlton and John McKay).

90. Letter from House Judiciary Committee Chairman John Conyers, Jr. and Subcommittee Chair Linda Sánchez to Alberto Gonzales, Att'y Gen. of the United States, Mar. 8, 2007 (*available at* http://judiciary.house.gov/hearings/pdf/Conyers-Sanchez070308.pdf); Letter from House Judiciary Committee Chairman John Conyers, Jr. and Subcommittee Chair Linda Sánchez to Fred Fielding, White House Counsel, Mar. 9, 2007 (*available at* http://judiciary.house.gov/hearings/pdf/Conyers-Sanchez070309.pdf).

91. *Subcommittee Meeting to Consider Subpoena Authorization Concerning the Recent Termination of United States Attorneys and Related Subjects: Meeting of the Subcomm. on Commercial and Administrative Law of the H. Comm. on the Judiciary,* 110th Cong. (2007).

92. Subpoena issued by H. Judiciary Comm. Chairman John Conyers, Jr. to Attorney General Alberto Gonzales (Apr. 10, 2007).

93. E-mail from Kyle Sampson, Chief of Staff to Att'y Gen. Alberto Gonzales, to Harriet Miers, White House Counsel (Jan. 9, 2006, 10:09 AM EST) (OAG 20-21); E-mail from Harriet Miers, White House Counsel, to Kyle Sampson, Chief of Staff to Att'y Gen. Alberto Gonzales (Sept. 17, 2006, 3:15 PM) (OAG 34-35); E-mail Kyle Sampson, Chief of Staff to Att'y Gen. Alberto Gonzales, to Harriet Miers, White House Counsel, and William Kelley, Deputy White House Counsel (Nov. 15, 2008 12:08 PM) (DAG 14-17); E-mail from Kyle Sampson, Chief of Staff to Att'y Gen. Alberto Gonzales, to William Kelley, Deputy White House Counsel (Dec. 4, 2006, 6:26 PM EST) (OAG 45-48).

94. E-mail from Kyle Samson, Chief of Staff to Att'y Gen. Alberto Gonzales, to William Kelley, Deputy White House Counsel (May 11, 2006, 11:36 AM EST) (OAG 22).

95. H. Rep. No. 110-423, at 33 (2007).

96. E-mail from Kyle Samspon, Chief of Staff to Att'y Gen. Alberto Gonzales, to David Leitch, Deputy White House Counsel (Jan. 9, 2005, 7:34 PM EST) (OAG 180).

97. H. Rep. No. 110-423, at 43-51 (2007).

98. *Hearing on the Continuing Investigation into the U.S. Attorneys Controversy: Hearing before the Subomm. on Commercial and Administrative Law of the H. Comm. on the Judiciary,* 110th Cong. *passim* (2007) (statement of James Comey, former Deputy Att'y Gen. of the United States).

99. H. Rep. No. 110-423, at 43-51(2007).

100. *Id.* at 29, 48-49 (2007).

101. *Id.* at 36, 49-50 (2007).

102. *Id.* at 36-37 (2007).

103.*Id.* at 24-28 (2007).

104.*Id.* at 29-35 (2007).

105.Interview with Kyle Sampson at 95-96 (July 10, 2007),
http://judiciary.house.gov/hearings/pdf/Interview071107.pdf

106.*The Continuing Investigation into the U.S. Attorneys Controversy and Related Matters: Hearing Before the H. Comm. on the Judiciary*, 110th Cong. 7 (2008) (statement of Glenn Fine, Dept. of Justice Inspector Gen.).

107.*Oversight Hearing on the United States Department of Justice: Hearing Before the H. Comm. on the Judiciary*, 110th Cong. (2007) (statement of Alberto Gonzales, Att'y Gen. of the United States); *Department of Justice Oversight: Hearing Before the S. Comm. on the Judiciary*, 110th Cong. (2007) (statement of Alberto Gonzales, Att'y Gen. of the United States).

108.H. Rep. No. 110-423, at 36-38 (2007).

109.*Id.* at 37 (2007).

110.*Continuing Investigation into the U.S. Attorneys Controversy and Related Matters: Hearing Before the H. Comm. on the Judiciary,* 110th Cong. (2007) (statement of Monica Goodling, former Senior Counsel to Att'y Gen. Alberto Gonzales and White House Liaison, U.S. Dept. of Justice).

111.*Id.* at 34, 81.

112.Joint Report of the U.S. Dep. of Justice Office of Professional Responsibility and Office of the Inspector General, "An Investigation of Allegations of Politicized Hiring in the Department of Justice Honors Program and the Summer Law Intern Program" (June 2008). *Available at* http://www.usdoj.gov/oig/special/s0806/final.pdf; Joint Report of the U.S. Dep. of Justice Office of Professional Responsibility and Office of the Inspector General, "An Investigation of Allegations of Politicized Hiring by Monica Goodling and Other Staff in the Office of the Attorney General" (July 2008). *Available at* http://www.usdoj.gov/oig/special/s0807/final.pdf.

113.*The Continuing Investigation into the U.S. Attorneys Controversy: Hearing Before the Subcomm. on Commercial and Administrative Law of the H. Comm. on the Judiciary*, 110th Cong. 43 (2007) (statement of James Comey, former Dep. Att'y Gen. of the United States).

114.*The Continuing Investigation into the U.S. Attorneys Controversy and Related Matters: Hearing Before the H. Comm. on the Judiciary*, 110th Cong. 106-110 (statement of Monica Goodling, former Senior Counsel to Att'y Gen. Alberto Gonzales and White House Liaison, U.S. Dept. of Justice).

115.*Id.* at 106-110.

116.*Id.* (Prepared Statement of Monica Goodling at 3).

117.Statement of John Conyers, Jr., Chairman of the H. Comm. on the Judiciary, *as quoted in* "Judiciary Chairman Conyers, Leahy Issues Subpoenas for White House Officials, Documents," Press Release of the H. Comm. on the Judiciary (June 13, 2007), *available at* http://www.speaker.gov/blog/?p=482.

118.Subpoenas issued by H. Judiciary Comm. Chairman John Conyers, Jr. to former White House Counsel Harriet Miers and White House Chief of Staff Joshua Bolten (June 13, 2007).

119.Subpoena issued by H. Judiciary Comm. Chairman John Conyers, Jr. to Mike Duncan, Republican National Committee Chair (July 13, 2008).

120.Letter from George T. Manning to H. Judiciary Comm. Chairman John Conyers, Jr. (July 10, 2007).

121.Letter from Fred Fielding, White House Counsel, to Chairman John Conyers, Jr., H. Comm. on the Judiciary, and Chairman Patrick J. Leahy, S. Comm. on the Judiciary (June 28, 2007).

122.Letter from Robert Kelner to H. Judiciary Comm. Chairman John Conyers, Jr. (July 31, 2007).

123.*Meeting to Consider: a Resolution and Report Recommending to the House of Representatives that Former White House Counsel Harriet Miers and White House Chief of Staff Joshua Bolten be Cited for Contempt of Congress: Meeting of the H. Comm. on the Judiciary,* 110th Cong. (2007).

124.Roll Call Vote No. 60, H.Res. 982, U.S. House of Representatives, Feb. 14, 2008, *available at* http://clerk.house.gov/evs/2008/roll060.xml.

125.Letter from Attorney General Michael Mukasey to Speaker of the House Nancy Pelosi (Feb. 29, 2008).

126.*Committee on the Judiciary v. Miers*, Civil Action No. 08-0409 (JDB) (United States District Court for the District of Columbia, July 31, 2008).

127.Memorandum Opinion and Order, *Committee on the Judiciary v. Miers*, Civil Action No. 08-0409 (JDB) (United States District Court for the District of Columbia, July 31, 2008).

128.*Id.* at 78.

129.*Id.*

130.Opinion and Order Granting Motion for Stay Pending Appeal, *Committee on the Judiciary v. Miers*, Appeal No. 08-5357, United States Court of Appeals for the District of Columbia Circuit (October 6, 2008).

131. Joint Report of the Department's Offices of the Inspector General and Professional Responsibility, *An Investigation Into the Removal of Nine US Attorneys,* September 2008.

132. Joint Report of the Department's Offices of the Inspector General and Professional Responsibility, *An Investigation Into the Removal of Nine US Attorneys,* September 2008, at 325-26.

133. *Id.* at 357-58.

134. Joint Report of the U.S. Dept. of Justice Office of the Inspector General and U.S. Dept. of Justice Office of the Professional Responsibility, "An Investigation into the Removal of Nine U.S. Attorneys in 2006," at 338 (Sept. 2008). *Available at* http://www.usdoj.gov/oig/special/s0809a/final.pdf.

135. *Id.* at 358.

136. "Statement by Attorney General Michael B. Mukasey on the Report of an Investigation into the Removal of Nine U.S. Attorneys in 2006," *U.S. Dept. of Justice Office of Public Affairs,* Sept. 29, 2008, *available at* http://www.usdoj.gov/opa/pr/2008/September/08-opa-859.html.

137. E-mail from Kyle Sampson to David Leitch, Deputy White House Counsel, responding to a "Question from Karl Rove," (Jan. 9, 2005). *See also* Krugman, "Department of Injustice," *N.Y. Times,* Mar. 7, 2007 ("The bigger scandal, however, almost surely involves prosecutors still in office. The Gonzales Eight were fired because they wouldn't go along with the Bush Administration's politicization of justice. But statistical evidence suggests that many other prosecutors decided to protect their jobs or further their careers by doing what the Administration wanted them to do: harass Democrats while turning a blind eye to Republican malfeasance.").

138. Shields & Cragan, *The Political Profiling of Elected Democratic Officials: When Rhetorical Vision Participation Runs Amok,* EpluribusMedia.org (Feb. 18, 2007), http://www.epluribusmedia.org/columns/2007/20070212_political_profiling.html.

139. *Joint Hearing on Allegations of Selective Prosecution: The Erosion of Public Confidence in Our Federal Justice System: Joint Hearing Before the Subcomm. on Commercial and Administrative Law and the Subcomm. on Crime, Terrorism, and Homeland Security of the H. Comm. on the Judiciary,* 110th Cong. 16 (2007) (statement of Donald C. Shields, Ph.D.).

140. *Id.* at 16.

141. *See* Editorial, "Time to Vote Contempt," *N.Y. Times,* Feb. 14, 2008, http://www.nytimes.com/2008/02/14/opinion/14thu1.html?scp=1&sq=TimetoVoteContempt&st=cse ("There are people in jail today, including a former governor of Alabama, who have raised credible charges that they were put there for political reasons."); Horton, "A Primer In Political Persecution," *Harper's Magazine,* Oct. 24, 2007, http://www.harpers.org/archive/2007/10/hbc-90001500; Kalson, "The Wecht Indictment: Given the Bushies' record, you have to wonder if it's

all about politics," *Pittsburgh Post-Gazette*, July 22, 2007, http://www.post-gazette.com/pg/07203/803200-149.stm; Cohen, "The United States Attorneys Scandal Comes to Mississippi," *N.Y. Times*, Oct. 11, 2007, http://www.nytimes.com/2007/10/11/opinion/11thu3.html; Letter from 44 Former State Attorneys General to Chairman John Conyers, Jr., H. Comm. on the Judiciary, and Chairman Patrick Leahy, S. Comm. on the Judiciary (July 13, 2007) (The Attorneys General letter specifically addressed the prosecution of former Alabama Governor Don Siegelman).

142.*Joint Hearing on Allegations of Selective Prosecution: The Erosion of Public Confidence in Our Federal Justice System: Joint Hearing Before the Subcomm. on Commercial and Administrative Law and the Subcomm. on Crime, Terrorism, and Homeland Security of the H. Comm. on the Judiciary*, 110th Cong. (2007) (statement of Richard Thornburgh, former Att'y Gen. of the United States).

143.Majority Staff Report Prepared for Chairman John Conyers, Jr., "Allegations of Selective Prosecution in Our Federal Criminal Justice System," *H. Comm. on the Judiciary*, 110th Cong. (Apr 2008), *available at* http://judiciary.house.gov/hearings/pdf/SelPros/Report080417.pdf

144.Letters from Chairman John Conyers, Jr., H. Comm. on the Judiciary, to Michael Mukasey, Att'y Gen. of the United States (Sept. 23, 2008, and Oct. 22, 2008).

145.*Id.*

146.Interview with Mary Beth Buchanan at 149-51 (June 15, 2007), *available at* http://judiciary.house.gov/hearings/pdf/Interview071107.pdf.

147.*Joint Hearing on Allegations of Selective Prosecution: The Erosion of Public Confidence in Our Federal Justice System: Joint Hearing Before the Subcomm. on Commercial and Administrative Law and the Subcomm. on Crime, Terrorism, and Homeland Security of the H. Comm. on the Judiciary*, 110th Cong. (2007).

148.*Id.* (statement of G. Douglas Jones, former United States Att'y).

149.*Id.* (statement of G. Douglas Jones, former United States Att'y).

150.Letter from Chairman John Conyers, Jr. and other Members of the H. Comm. on the Judiciary to Alberto Gonzales, Att'y Gen. of the United States (July 17, 2007).

151.Letter from Brian A. Benczkowski, Principal Deputy Assistant. Att'y Gen. of the United States, to Chairman John Conyers, Jr., H. Comm. on the Judiciary (Sept. 4, 2007).

152.*Id.*

153.*Id.*

154. Letter from Chairman John Conyers, Jr. and other Members of the H. Comm. on the Judiciary to Alberto Gonzales, Att'y Gen. of the United States (Sept. 10, 2007).

155. *See* Rosenberg, "Statement Concerning the History of and Basis for Congressional Access to Deliberative Justice Department Documents," *Statement Before the H. Comm. on Govt. Reform*, 107th Cong. (Feb. 6, 2002) (Rosenberg's statement contains a detailed Appendix listing "18 significant congressional investigations of the Department of Justice which involved either open or closed investigations in which the Department agreed to supply documents pertaining to those investigations, including prosecutorial decision-making memoranda and correspondence, and to provide line attorneys and investigative personnel for staff interviews and for testimony before committees").

156. Those documents, which dealt with prosecution decisions in murder cases and related issues, and which the Department claimed were related to ongoing litigation, were produced to Congress despite being subject to a formal claim of executive privilege by President Bush, on terms negotiated by then-Assistant Attorney General Michael Chertoff and the staff of the then-Government Reform Committee. *See* H. Rep. 108-414, at 132-33 (2004) *(Everything Secret Degenerates: The FBI's Use of Murderers As Informants*, Third Report of the Committee on Government Reform).

157. Letter from Keith Nelson, Principal Deputy Assistant Att'y Gen., to Chairman John Conyers, Jr., H. Comm. on the Judiciary (Nov. 14, 2008).

158. Letter from Chairman John Conyers, Jr., H. Comm. on the Judiciary, to Michael Mukasey, Att'y Gen. of the United States (Dec. 10, 2008).

159. *United States v. Siegelman*, et al, Appeal No. 07-13163-B, (11th Cir. Mar. 27, 2008).

160. Letter from Chairman John Conyers, Jr., H. Comm. on the Judiciary, to Michael Mukasey, Att'y Gen. of the United States (Nov. 8, 2008).

161. Chander, "House Judiciary Chairman Conyers says Siegelman Case E-mails Raise Questions," *Birmingham News*, Nov. 14, 2008, *available at* http://www.al.com/news/birminghamnews/statebriefs.ssf?/base/news/1226740555295690.xml&coll=2.

162. Silver, "Many questions surround Wecht retrial, set for May," *Pittsburgh Post-Gazette,* Apr. 9, 2008, *available at* http://www.post-gazette.com/pg/08100/871605-85.stm.

163. Editorial, "It's Over: There is no need for a second Wecht Trial," *Pittsburgh Post-Gazette*, Apr. 9, 2008, http://www.post-gazette.com/pg/08100/871522-35.stm; Cato, "Majority Thought Wecht was Innocent, Juror Says," *Pittsburgh Tribune Review*, Apr. 9, 2008, *available at* http://http://www.pittsburghlive.com/x/pittsburghtrib/s_561365.html.

164. Silver, "Some Jurors Skeptical of Case Against Wecht," *Pittsburgh Post Gazette*, Apr. 10, 2008, *available at* http://www.post-gazette.com/pg/08101/872086-85.stm.

165. Prine & Cato, "FBI's Calls Upset Jurors in Wecht Trial," *Pittsburgh Tribune Review*, Apr. 11, 2008, *available at* http://www.pittsburghlive.com/x/pittsburghtrib/s_561792.html.

166. *Id.*

167. Letter from Citizens of the Western District of Pennsylvania to Michael Mukasey, Att'y Gen. of the United States, and Mary Beth Buchanan, U.S. Att'y for the Western Dist. of Pennsylvania (Apr. 16, 2008).

168. Letter from H. Marshall Jarrett to Chairman John Conyers, Jr., H. Comm. on the Judiciary (May 5, 2008).

169. The Division now enforces the Civil Rights Acts of 1957, 1960, 1964, and 1968; the Voting Rights Act of 1965, as amended through 2006; the Equal Credit Opportunity Act; the Americans with Disabilities Act; the National Voter Registration Act; the Uniformed and Overseas Citizens Absentee Voting Act; the Voting Accessibility for the Elderly and Handicapped Act; and additional civil rights provisions contained in other laws and regulations. These laws prohibit discrimination in education, employment, credit, housing, public accommodations and facilities, voting, and certain federally funded and conducted programs. In addition, the Division enforces the Civil Rights of Institutionalized Persons Act of 1980, which authorizes the Attorney General to seek relief for persons confined in public institutions where conditions exist that deprive residents of their constitutional rights; the Freedom of Access to Clinic Entrances Act, the Police Misconduct Provision of the Violent Crime Control and Law Enforcement Act of 1994; and Section 102 of the Immigration Reform and Control Act of 1986 (IRCA), as amended, which prohibits discrimination on the basis of national origin and citizenship status as well as document abuse and retaliation under the Immigration and Nationality Act. The Division prosecutes actions under several criminal civil rights statutes which were designed to preserve personal liberties and safety. The Division is also responsible for coordinating the civil rights enforcement efforts of federal agencies whose programs are covered by Title VI of the Civil Rights Act of 1964, Title IX of the Education Amendments of 1972, and Section 504 of the Rehabilitation Act of 1973, as amended, and assists federal agencies in identifying and removing discriminatory provision in their policies and programs.

170. *See e.g.*, Rosenbaum, "Justice Department Accused of Politics in Redistricting," *N.Y. Times*, May 31, 2002 at A14; McCaffrey, "U.S. Backs Off Discrimination Cases; Justice Department Files Fewer Job, Housing Suits," *Detroit Free Press*, Dec, 11, 2003 at A15; Eggen, "Civil Rights Focus Shift Roils Staff at Justice; Veterans Exit Division as Traditional Cases Decline," *Wash. Post*, Nov. 13, 2005, at A1.

171. *See* American Civil Liberties Union, *Race & Ethnicity In America: Turning A Blind Eye to Injustice* 15, 22 (2007), *available at* http://www.aclu.org/pdfs/humanrights/cerd_full_report.pdf.

172.*Id.* at 22.

173.Kengle, "Why I Left the Civil Rights Division", *TPMMuckraker.com*, Apr. 30, 2007, http://tpmmuckraker.talkingpointsmemo.com/archives/003120.php.

174.Eggen, "Civil Rights Focus Shift Roils Staff At Justice; Veterans Exit Division as Traditional Cases Decline," *Wash. Post*, Nov. 13, 2005, at A1.

175.Eggen, "Staff Opinions Banned In Voting Rights Cases: Criticism of Justice Dept.'s Rights Division Grows," *Wash. Post*, Dec. 10, 2005, at A3.

176.42 U.S.C. § 1973 (2008).

177.Citizens' Commission on Civil Rights, "The Erosion of Rights: Declining Civil Rights Enforcement Under the Bush Administration" 32 (2007) (*hereinafter "Commission Report"*). *Available at* http://www.americanprogress.org/issues/2007/03/pdf/civil_rights_report.pdf.

178.*Protecting the Right to Vote: Election Deception and Irregularities in Recent Federal Elections: Hearing Before the H. Comm. on the Judiciary*, 110th Cong. (2007) (statement of Ralph G. Neas, president and CEO, People For the American Way).

179.Editorial, "Honesty in Elections," *N.Y. Times*, Jan. 31, 2007, http://www.nytimes.com/2007/01/31/opinion/31wed1.html.

180.*Id.*

181.*Protecting the Right to Vote: Election Deception and Irregularities in Recent Federal Elections: Hearing Before the H. Comm. on the Judiciary*, 110th Cong. (2007) (statement of Sen. Barack Obama).

182.*Id.* (statement of Sen. Barack Obama).

183.Commission Report.

184.Commission Report, Chapter 2.

185.In 2005, the Justice Department precleared a Georgia law requiring voters to present government-issued picture identification in order to vote at the polls on Election Day. According to the Commission's report, the enactment represented one of the leading examples of legislation advocated by some political officials across the country to address alleged problems of fraudulent voting at the polls, but which would erect barriers to voting that particularly would harm minority voters. The Voting Section staff prepared a detailed memorandum recommending an objection. Included in the memo was a reference to an explicitly racial statement by a state legislator who was the sponsor of the legislation who "said that if there are fewer black voters because of this bill, it will only be because there is less opportunity for fraud" and added that "when black voters in her black precincts are not paid to vote, they do not go to the polls." Contrary to the standard operating procedures within the Department that existed for decades, the staff memorandum recommending an objection was not forwarded to the Assistant Attorney General for Civil Rights for consideration prior to him making the final preclearance decision. *See* Commission Report, 37.

186. Under state law, the Mississippi legislature was responsible for enacting a new congressional redistricting plan, but failed to do so. A Mississippi state court then ordered a plan into effect that was favored by the state Democratic Party. In December 2001, the state of Mississippi submitted this plan to the Justice Department for review. In response to the state court drawn plan, the Republican Party brought a lawsuit in federal district court. The federal court held that it would order into effect its plan, drawn by the state Republican Party, if the state court plan was not precleared by the Department of Justice by February 27, 2002. The Voting Section staff attorneys quickly reviewed the state court plan within the 60 day period allotted by statute for review of Section 5 submissions. The staff attorneys concluded that the plan did not adversely affect minority voters and recommended that the Department grant preclearance. Political appointees in the Assistant Attorney General's office rejected the preclearance recommendation and extended the review period beyond the February 27 deadline by asking the State to provide additional information. As a result of this "more information" letter, the February 27th deadline passed without a final preclearance decision by the Justice Department on the state plan, and the federal court ordered its plan into effect. *See* Commission Report, 36.

187. In 2003, the Justice Department precleared a controversial mid-decade congressional redistricting plan enacted by the State of Texas. The plan was drawn in 2003 after an initial post-2000 plan had been implemented by a federal district court in 2001 (following the Texas legislature's failure to adopt a new plan). The 2003 plan resulted in a gain of five congressional districts for Republicans. In order to accomplish this increase, the plan targeted several areas of minority voting strength, which had the effect of both limiting the opportunity of minority voters to elect candidates of their choice to Congress and their opportunity to exert a substantial influence in congressional elections. As a result, the career professional staff of the Voting Section concluded in a detailed, lengthy memorandum that the plan violated Section 5 because it resulted in a retrogression of minority electoral opportunity. Nonetheless, the Department's political appointees precleared the plan. *See* Commission Report, 37.

188. Eggen, "Politics Alleged In Voting Cases Justice Officials Are Accused of Influence," *Wash. Post*, Jan. 23, 2006, at A1.

189. *Id*. at 36-37.

190. *Oversight Hearing on the Civil Rights Division of the Department of Justice: Hearing Before the H. Comm. on the Judiciary*, 110th Cong. (2007) (statement of Joseph Rich, Director of the Fair Housing Community Development, Project Lawyers' Committee for Civil Rights Under Law).

191. *See* Leadership Conference on Civil Rights Education Fund, *The Bush Administration Takes Aim: Civil Rights Under Attack* 4 (Apr. 2003), *available at* http://www.civilrights.org/publications/reports/taking_aim/bush_takes_aim.pdf.

192. Eggen, "Criticism of Voting Law Was Overruled: Justice Dept. Backed Georgia Measure Despite Fears of Discrimination." *Wash. Post*, Nov. 17, 2005, at A1; Eggen, "Justice Staff Saw Texas Districting As Illegal: Voting Rights Finding On Map Pushed by DeLay Was Overruled," *Wash. Post,* Dec. 2, 2005, at A1.

193. *Protecting the Right to Vote: Election Deception and Irregularities in Recent Federal Elections: Hearing Before the H. Comm. on the Judiciary*, 110th Cong. (2007) (statement of Wade Henderson, Leadership Conference on Civil Rights).

194. Kiel, "DoJ Vote Chief Argues Voter ID Laws Discriminate Against *Whites,*" *TPMMuckraker.com*, Oct. 9, 2007, http://tpmmuckraker.talkingpointsmemo.com/archives/004414.php.

195. *Oversight Hearing on the Voting Section of the Civil Rights Division of the U.S. Department of Justice: Hearing Before the Subcomm. on the Const., Civil Rights, and Civil Liberties*, 110th Cong. (2007) (statement of Rep. Artur Davis).

196. *Id.* (statement of Toby Moore, Former Geographer/Social Science analyst, CRT Voting Section).

197. *Id.* (statement of Laughlin McDonald, Director, American Civil Liberties Voting Rights Project). Because of Georgia's history of voting discrimination, the state is covered by Section 5 of the 1965 Voting Rights Act and was therefore required to get federal approval before implementing a photo identification requirement for voting. The ACLU's Voting Rights Project and several other voting rights advocates filed a lawsuit after the U.S. Department of Justice granted preclearance to the Georgia measure on August 26, 2005. In addition to its constitutional and legal claims, the lawsuit claimed that the "stated purpose of Georgia's photo ID requirement – to deter voter fraud – was a pretext intended to conceal the true purpose of the amendment, which was, and is to suppress voting by the poor, the elderly, the infirm, African-American, Hispanic and other minority voters by increasing the difficulty of voting. *See* American Civil Liberties, "Voting Rights Advocates Challenge Georgia Photo ID Law in Federal Court," Sept. 19, 2005, *available at* http://www.aclu.org/votingrights/gen/21247prs20050919.html.

In ruling on the case, the U. S. District Court disagreed with the Department and sided with the ACLU and blocked the controversial new law. The District Court concluded that the plaintiffs would have a substantial likelihood of succeeding on their claims that the Photo ID requirement unduly burdened the right to vote and was tantamount to a poll tax. Further the Court found that the plaintiffs and their constituents would "suffer irreparable harm " if the Court did not grant a preliminary injunction in the case. *See Common Cause/Georgia v. Billups*, 504 F. Supp. 2d (N.D. Ga. 2007).

198.*United States v. Ike Brown and Noxubee County*, Not Reported in F.Supp.2d, 2006 WL 3360746 (S.D. Miss.). The case Ms. Fernandes cites where the Department filed a lawsuit on behalf of white voters was *United States v. Brown* (2006). Interestingly, the court in Noxubee noted in its judgment that "the court does not doubt that similar discrimination against blacks continues to occur throughout this state, perhaps routinely. And it may be true, though the court makes no judgment about this, that the Justice Department has not been responsive, or fully responsive, to complaints by black voters. But, the politics of the decision to prosecute this case, while foregoing intervention in other cases cannot be a factor in the court's decision."

199.Letter from Sheldon T. Bradshaw, Principal Deputy Assistant Att'y Gen. of the United States, Civil Rights Division, to Janice K. Brewer, Arizona Sec'y of State (Apr. 15, 2005).

200.Letter from Joseph D. Rich, Former Voting Section Chief, Civil Rights Division, U.S. Department of Justice, to the Chairwoman Dianne Feinstein, S. Comm. on Rules and Administration (June. 18, 2007).

201.Letter from R. Alexander Acosta, Assistant Att'y Gen., Civil Rights Division, U.S. Department of Justice, to Susan J. Dlott, Judge of the United States District Court for the Southern District of Ohio (Oct. 29, 2004).

202.42 U.S.C. 1973(a) (2008).

203.*DNC v RNC*, C.A. No. 86-3972, U.S. District Court for the District of New Jersey (July 29, 1987). Four days before the 2004 election, the Justice Department's Civil Rights Division Chief sent an unusual letter to U.S. District Judge Susan Dlott of Cincinnati who was weighing whether to let Republicans challenge the credentials of 23,000 mostly African-American voters. It is unusual for the Department of Justice to participate in pre-election eve lawsuits, particularly when it has not been invited to do so. The Ohio case was triggered by allegations that Republicans had sent a mass mailing to mostly Democratic-leaning minorities and used undeliverable letters to compile a list of voters potentially vulnerable to eligibility challenges. In his letter to Judge Dlott, Assistant Attorney General Alex Acosta argued that it would "undermine" the enforcement of state and federal election laws if citizens could not challenge voters' credentials.

204.*Oversight Hearing on Voter Suppression: Hearing Before the Subcomm. on the Const., Civil Rights, and Civil Liberties of the H. Comm. on the Judiciary*, 110th Cong. (2008) (statement of Hilary Shelton, Director, Washington Bureau of the NAACP).

205.*Id.* (statement of Lorraine C. Minnite, Barnard College).

206.*Id.* (statement of Lorraine C. Minnite, Barnard College).

207.*Id.* (statement of Lorraine C. Minnite, Barnard College).

208. Letter from J. Gerald Hebert, The Campaign Legal Center, to Alice S. Fisher, Assistant Att'y Gen. of the United States (Aug. 23, 2007) (*available at* http://www.campaignlegalcenter.org/press-2849.html).

209. Letter from Chairman John Conyers, Jr., H. Comm. on the Judiciary, to Brian A. Benczkowski, Principal Deputy Assistant Att'y Gen. of the United States (May 7, 2008).

210. Opinion No. 2008 DNH 042, *United States v. Tobin*, Crim No. 04-cr-216-1-SM (Feb. 21, 2008). The defendant's convictions on the telephone harassment charges were reversed on appeal due to erroneous jury instructions. *See United States v. Tobin*, 480 F. 3d 53 (1st Cir. 2007).

211. *Joint Hearing on Allegations of Selective Prosecution Part II: The Erosion of Public Confidence in Our Federal Justice System: Hearing Before the Subomm. on Commercial and Administrative Law and the Subcomm. on Crime, Terrorism, and Homeland Security of the H. Comm. on the Judiciary*, 110th Cong. (2008) (statement of Paul Twomey).

212. *Id.* (statement of Paul Twomey).

213. *Id.* (statement of Paul Twomey).

214. *Id.* (statement of Allen Raymond).

215. *See* Manjoo, "Sproul Play," *Salon*, Oct. 21, 2004, http://dir.salon.com/story/news/feature/2004/10/21/sproul/.

216. Knapp, "Investigation Into Trashed Voter Registrations," *KLAS TV News*, Oct. 13, 2004, http://www.klas-tv.com/global/story.asp?s=2421595; Ritter, "Nevada Judge Declines to Reopen Voter Registration in Vegas Area," *Las Vegas Sun*, Oct. 15, 2004, http://www.lasvegassun.com/sunbin/stories/text/2004/oct/15/10150497.html.

217. Knapp, "Investigation Into Trashed Voter Registrations," *KLAS TV News*, Oct. 13, 2004, http://www.klas-tv.com/global/story.asp?s=2421595.

218. Letter from Holly McCullough, Carnegie Library of Pittsburgh, to Sam Sokol, Oversight Counsel, H. Comm. on the Judiciary (Apr. 29, 2008).

219. *Id.*; Despite this serious evidence of potentially criminal violations of federal election laws, no charges were ever brought against any Sproul employee or entity. In fact, the firm head Mr. Nathan Sproul continues as a Republican political operative in good standing and was most recently employed by the McCain-Palin 2008 presidential campaign; Stein, "McCain Employing GOP Operative Accused Of Voter Registration Fraud," *Huffington Post*, Oct. 20, 2008, *available at* http://www.huffingtonpost.com/2008/10/20/mccain-employing-gop-oper_n_136254.html?page=39.

220.On February 26, 2008, the Subcommittee on the Constitution, Civil Rights, and Civil Liberties met for the purpose of considering whether to authorize the Chairman of the Committee to issue a subpoena to for Ohio Secretary of State J. Kenneth Blackwell.

221."Ken Blackwell," *Wikipedia*, Jan. 5, 2008, http://en.wikipedia.org/wiki/Ken_Blackwell.

222.Status Report of the House Committee on the Judiciary Democratic Staff, "Preserving Democracy: What Went Wrong in Ohio?," *H. Comm. on the Judiciary*, 109th Cong. (Jan. 2005). *Available
at* http://www.openelections.org/lib/downloads/references/house_judiciary/final_status_report.pd f.

223.*Lessons Learned from the 2004 Presidential Election: Hearing Before the H. Comm. on the Judiciary*, 110th Cong. (2008) (statement of Rep. Debbie Wasserman Schultz).

224.*Id.* (statement of Gilda Daniels, University of Baltimore Law School).

225.*Id.* (statement of J. Gerald Hebert, The Campaign Legal Center).

226.*Federal, State and Local Efforts to Prepare for the 2008 Election: Joint Hearing Before Subcomm. on the Const., Civil Rights, and Civil Liberties of the H. Comm. on the Judiciary and the Subcomm. on Elections of the H. Committee on House Administration*, 110th Cong. (2008) (statement of Paul Hancock).

227.*See* H. Rep. No. 110-423, at 27-27 (2007).

228.*Id.* 31-32. Mr. Scholzman later provided apparently misleading testimony about these ACORN indictments before the Senate Judiciary Committee, which he was later compelled to formally "clarify" in correspondence with that Committee. *Id.* at 32.

229.Letter from Chairman John Conyers, Jr., H. Comm. on the Judiciary, to the Michael Mukasey, Att'y Gen. of the United States, and Robert Mueller, Director of the Federal Bureau of Investigation (Oct. 16, 2008).

230.Letter from Chairman John Conyers, Jr., Rep. Jerrold Nadler, and Rep. Linda Sánchez of the H. Comm. on the Judiciary to the Michael Mukasey, Att'y Gen. of the United States, and Robert Mueller, Director of the Federal Bureau of Investigation (Oct. 20, 2008).

231.Letter from Keith Nelson, Principle Deputy Assistant Att'y Gen. of the United States, to Chairman John Conyers, Jr., H. Comm. on the Judiciary (Oct. 28, 2008).

232. Mezler, "Lose Your House, Lose Your Vote," *Michigan Messenger*, Sept. 10, 2008.

233.Letter from Chairman John Conyers, Jr., Rep. Jerrold Nadler, and Rep. Bobby Scott of the H. Comm. on the Judiciary to Michael Mukasey, Att'y Gen. of the United States (Oct. 29, 2008).

234. Joint Report of the U.S. Dept. of Justice Office of the Inspector General and U.S. Dept. of Justice Office of the Professional Responsibility, "An Investigation into the Removal of Nine U.S. Attorneys in 2006," at 332 (Sept. 2008); H. Rep. No. 110-423, at 24-28 (2007).

235. Joint Report of the U.S. Dept. of Justice Office of the Inspector General and U.S. Dept. of Justice Office of the Professional Responsibility, "An Investigation into the Removal of Nine U.S. Attorneys in 2006," at 331-32 (Sept. 2008).

236. H. Rep. No. 110-423, at 31-32 (2007).

237. *Id.* at 29.

238. Joint Report of the U.S. Dept. of Justice Office of the Inspector General and U.S. Dept. of Justice Office of the Professional Responsibility, "An Investigation into the Removal of Nine U.S. Attorneys in 2006," at 332 (Sept. 2008); H. Rep. No. 110-423, at 36-37 (2007).

239. Joint Report of the U.S. Dept. of Justice Office of the Inspector General and U.S. Dept. of Justice Office of the Professional Responsibility, "An Investigation into the Removal of Nine U.S. Attorneys in 2006," at 2-4, 153-54 (Sept. 2008); H. Rep. No. 110-423, at 43-54 (2007).

240. Joint Report of the U.S. Dept. of Justice Office of the Inspector General and U.S. Dept. of Justice Office of the Professional Responsibility, "An Investigation into the Removal of Nine U.S. Attorneys in 2006," at 3, 154 (Sept. 2008).

241. Letter from Robert Kelner to Chairman John Conyers, Jr, H. Comm. on the Judiciary (July 31, 2007).

242. Letter from Keith Nelson, Principal Deputy Assistant Att'y Gen., to Chairman John Conyers, Jr, H. Comm. on the Judiciary (Nov. 14, 2008).

243. Joint Report of the U.S. Dept. of Justice Office of the Inspector General and U.S. Dept. of Justice Office of the Professional Responsibility, "An Investigation into the Removal of Nine U.S. Attorneys in 2006," at 199-200 (Sept. 2008).

244. H. Rep. No. 110-423, at 26-32 (2007).

245. *Id.* at 26-32.

246. *Id.* at 36; Joint Report of the U.S. Dept. of Justice Office of the Inspector General and U.S. Dept. of Justice Office of the Professional Responsibility, "An Investigation into the Removal of Nine U.S. Attorneys in 2006," at 341-42 (Sept. 2008). at 341-42.

247. Joint Report of the U.S. Dept. of Justice Office of the Inspector General and U.S. Dept. of Justice Office of the Professional Responsibility, "An Investigation into the Removal of Nine U.S. Attorneys in 2006," at 48-49 (Sept. 2008).

248.H. Rep. No. 110-423, at 36 (2007).

249.*Id.* at 36.

250.*Id.* at 36-37. One of the fired U.S. Attorneys, John McKay of Washington, wrote this after watching then-Attorney General Gonzales' testimony before the Senate Judiciary Committee: In my case, I believe that silence in the face of a lie is a form of complicity; despite my initial belief that it was my duty to leave office quietly, I could not be a part of Alberto Gonzales' false and misleading testimony to the Senate." *See* McKay, "Trainwreck at the Justice Department: An Eyewitness Account," *Seattle U. L. Rev.*, 265, 271 (2008), available at http://ssrn.com/abstract=1028545.

251.H. Rep. No. 110-423, at 37 (2007).

252.*Id.* at 37; Joint Report of the U.S. Dept. of Justice Office of the Inspector General and U.S. Dept. of Justice Office of the Professional Responsibility, "An Investigation into the Removal of Nine U.S. Attorneys in 2006," at 342-44 (Sept. 2008).

253.*Compare* Joint Report of the U.S. Dep. of Justice Office of Professional Responsibility and Office of the Inspector General, "An Investigation of Allegations of Politicized Hiring by Monica Goodling and Other Staff in the Office of the Attorney General" (July 2008) with the Testimony by Attorney General Alberto Gonzales during *Oversight Hearing on the Department of Justice: Hearing Before the H. Comm. on the Judiciary*, 110th Cong. 61 n.43 (2007) (statement by Alberto Gonzales, Att'y Gen. of the United States).

254.H. Rep. No. 110-423, at 38 (2007); Joint Report of the U.S. Dept. of Justice Office of the Inspector General and U.S. Dept. of Justice Office of the Professional Responsibility, "An Investigation into the Removal of Nine U.S. Attorneys in 2006," at 345-46 (Sept. 2008).

255.H. Rep. No. 110-423, at 52-53 (2007); Letter of Paul Clement, Acting Att'y Gen. of the United States, to the President, at 2 (June 27, 2007).

256.H. Rep. No. 110-423, at 38 (2007); Joint Report of the U.S. Dept. of Justice Office of the Inspector General and U.S. Dept. of Justice Office of the Professional Responsibility, "An Investigation into the Removal of Nine U.S. Attorneys in 2006," at 34-35 (Sept. 2008).

257.H. Rep. No. 110-423, at 39 (2007).

258.Joint Report of the U.S. Dept. of Justice Office of the Inspector General and U.S. Dept. of Justice Office of the Professional Responsibility, "An Investigation into the Removal of Nine U.S. Attorneys in 2006," at 1 (Sept. 2008).

259.H. Rep. No. 110-423, at 39-40 (2007); Joint Report of the U.S. Dept. of Justice Office of the Inspector General and U.S. Dept. of Justice Office of the Professional Responsibility, "An Investigation into the Removal of Nine U.S. Attorneys in 2006," at 325, 346-50 (Sept. 2008).

260. H. Rep. No. 110-423, at 43-51 (2007).

261. *Id.* at 25 n.8; Joint Report of the U.S. Dept. of Justice Office of the Inspector General and U.S. Dept. of Justice Office of the Professional Responsibility, "An Investigation into the Removal of Nine U.S. Attorneys in 2006," at 198 (Sept. 2008).

262. H. Rep. No. 110-423, at 39, 349 (2007).

263. *Id.* at 347.

264. *Id.* at 40-41.

265. *Id.* at 40-41.

266. Johnson, "Federal Prosecutor Is Making Inquiries in the Investigation of the Dismissal of U.S. Attorneys," *Wash. Post*, Dec. 3, 2008, at A15; Jordan, "Ex-Justice Official May Face Grand Jury," *Associated Press*, June 17, 2008, *available at* http://findarticles.com/p/articles/mi_qn4188/is_20080617/ai_n26688038.

267. H. Rep. No. 110-423, at 52-54 (2007).

268. *Id.* at 52-54.

269. *Id.* at 52-54.

270. *Id.* at 52-54.

271. *Id.* at 52-54.

272. Joint Report of the U.S. Dept. of Justice Office of the Inspector General and U.S. Dept. of Justice Office of the Professional Responsibility, "An Investigation into the Removal of Nine U.S. Attorneys in 2006," at 2-4, 153-54 (Sept. 2008); H. Rep. No. 110-423, at 43-54 (2007).

273. Joint Report of the U.S. Dep. of Justice Office of Professional Responsibility and Office of the Inspector General, "An Investigation of Allegations of Politicized Hiring in the Department of Justice Honors Program and the Summer Law Intern Program" (June 2008).

274. *Id.* at 98.

275. Joint Report of the U.S. Dep. of Justice Office of Professional Responsibility and Office of the Inspector General, "An Investigation of Allegations of Politicized Hiring by Monica Goodling and Other Staff in the Office of the Attorney General" (July 2008).

276. *Id.* at 135.

277. *Id.* at 136.

278. *Id.* at 137.

279. The Department did make United States Attorney Biskupic and certain documents available regarding the Georgia Thompson matter, and this information dispelled many, although not all, concerns about the case. *See* Majority Staff Report Prepared for Chairman John Conyers, Jr., "Allegations of Selective Prosecution in Our Federal Criminal Justice System," *H. Comm. on the Judiciary*, 110th Cong. (Apr 2008), *available at* http://judiciary.house.gov/hearings/pdf/SelPros/Report080417.pdf.

280. The Voting Section chief at the time, John Tanner, was not a political appointee, but he played a pivotal role in the Department's decision to approve the Georgia voter ID, overruling his own staff. Tanner has since been replaced.

281. *See* "II. Politicization of the Civil Rights Division's Voting Section" within this section.

282. Commission Report, 36-37.

283. Kiel, "DoJ Vote Chief Argues Voter ID Laws Discriminate Against *Whites*," *TPMMuckraker.com*, Oct. 9, 2007, http://tpmmuckraker.talkingpointsmemo.com/archives/004414.php.

284. Eggen, "Staff Opinions Banned In Voting Rights Cases: Criticism of Justice Dept.'s Rights Division Grows," *Wash. Post*, Dec. 10, 2005, at A3.

285. *Oversight Hearing on the Voting Section of the Civil Rights Division of the U.S. Department of Justice: Hearing Before the Subcomm. on the Const., Civil Rights, and Civil Liberties of the H. Comm. on the Judiciary*, 110th Cong. (2007) (statement of Julie Fernandes, Leadership Conference for Civil Rights). *Available at* http://judiciary.house.gov/hearings/pdf/Fernandes071030.pdf.

286. *See* "II. Politicization of the Civil Rights Division's Voting Section" within this section.

287. *See* "II. Politicization of the Civil Rights Division's Voting Section" within this section.

288. *Oversight Hearing on the Civil Rights Division of the Department of Justice: Hearing Before the Subcomm. on the Const., Civil Rights, and Civil Liberties of the H. Comm. on the Judiciary*, 110th Cong. 59 (statement of Joseph D. Rich, Director, Fair Housing Community Development Project, Lawyers' Committee for Civil Rights Under Law).

289. *Hamdi v. Rumsfeld*, 542 U.S. 507, 535 (2004).

290. *Interview by Tim Russert, NBC News, with Vice President Cheney at Camp David, Md*, (NBC television broadcast Sept. 16, 2001), *available at* http://www.whitehouse.gov/vicepresident/news-speeches/speeches/vp20010916.html (emphasis added).

291.This unclassified memorandum has never been publicly released, despite repeated requests by Congress, although Committee staff have been given limited access to the memorandum at Department premises with no ability to make copies or to take detailed notes. From that limited review, it is clear that this is a very troubling memorandum which should immediately be released.

292.*See* extended discussion of this issue in the Preface.

293.This October 23, 2001, "Domestic War Powers" Memorandum is referenced in Yoo's March 14, 2003 Torture Memorandum in the following context: "[O]ur Office [the Office of Legal Counsel] recently concluded that the Fourth Amendment had no application to domestic military operations. *See* Memorandum for Alberto R. Gonzales, Counsel to the President, and William J. Haynes, II, General Counsel, Department of Defense, from John C. Yoo, Deputy Assistant Attorney General, and Robert J. Delahunty, Special Counsel, *Re: Authority for Use of Military Force to Combat Terrorist Activities Within the United States* at 25 (Oct 23, 2001)," cited in Memorandum for William J. Haynes, II, General Counsel, Department of Defense, from Department of Justice, OLC, *Re: Military Interrogation of Alien Unlawful Combatants Held Outside the United States*, Mar. 14, 2003.

294.*Frontline: Cheney's Law* (PBS television broadcast), *available at* http://www.pbs.org/wgbh/pages/frontline/cheney/view/main.html (transcript *available at* http://www.pbs.org/wgbh/pages/frontline/cheney/etc/script.html) (emphasis added).

295.Memorandum for Alberto R. Gonzales, Counsel to the President, *Legality of the Use of Military Commissions to Try Terrorists*, from Patrick F. Philbin, Deputy Assistant Attorney General (Nov. 6, 2001) (hereinafter referred to as the "November 6, 2001 Military Commissions Memorandum"), at 1.

> 10 U.S.C. § 821 at that time provided:
>
> > § 821. Art. 21. Jurisdiction of courts-martial not exclusive
> >
> > The provisions of this chapter conferring jurisdiction upon
> > courts-martial do not deprive military commissions, provost courts,
> > or other military tribunals of concurrent jurisdiction with respect to
> > offenders or offenses that by statute or by the law of war may be
> > tried by military commissions, provost courts, or other military
> > tribunals.

The Military Commissions Act of 2006, Pub. L. No. 109-366, revised section 821 to exempt any military commissions created under that Act.

296.November 6, 2001 Military Commissions Memorandum at 3.

297.*Id.* at 6.

298.*Id.* at 5.

299.*Id.* at 15.

300.*Id.* at 16-19.

301."Military Order - Detention, Treatment and Trial of Certain Non-Citizens in the War Against Terrorism." Executive Order dated November 13, 2001, 66 Fed. Reg. 57833 (Nov. 16, 2001). A copy of this Order may also be found at http://www.whitehouse.gov/news/releases/2001/11/20011113-27.html.

302.See, *e.g.*, Savage, *Takeover, The Return of the Imperial Presidency and the Subversion of American Democracy* 134 *et seq* (Little Brown & Co., 2007); *Frontline: Cheney's Law* (PBS television broadcast), *available at* http://www.pbs.org/wgbh/pages/frontline/cheney/view/main.html (transcript *available at* http://www.pbs.org/wgbh/pages/frontline/cheney/etc/script.html).

303.Gellman and Becker, "Angler – The Cheney Vice Presidency," *Washington Post*, June 24, 2007, at A1, *available at* http://blog.washingtonpost.com/cheney/chapters/chapter_1/ (emphasis added).

304.According to the *Frontline* piece:

> Barton Gellman [*Washington Post* reporter]: The news breaks on cable television. Colin Powell happens to be watching. He's astonished by what he's just seen. He picks up the phone to Prosper and he says, "What the hell just happened?"
>
> Amb. Pierre-Richard Prosper: We did have a conversation, and I let him know I was in the dark.

Frontline: Cheney's Law (PBS television broadcast), *available at* http://www.pbs.org/wgbh/pages/frontline/cheney/view/main.html (transcript *available at* http://www.pbs.org/wgbh/pages/frontline/cheney/etc/script.html).

305.Gellman and Becker, "Angler – The Cheney Vice Presidency," *Washington Post*, June 24, 2007, at A1, *available at* http://blog.washingtonpost.com/cheney/chapters/chapter_1/ (emphasis added).

306."Human Rights Watch, "Fact Sheet: Past U.S. Criticism of Military Tribunals" (2001), *available at* http://www.hrw.org/press/2001/11/tribunals1128.htm (emphasis added).

307.Safire, "Seizing Dictatorial Power," *N.Y. Times*, Nov. 15, 2001, *available at* http://query.nytimes.com/gst/fullpage.html?res=9802E6DF163BF936A25752C1A9679C8B63

(emphasis added).

308.Department of Defense News Briefing, Secretary of Defense Donald Rumsfeld and Gen. Richard Myers, Chairman, Joint Chiefs of Staff, Dec. 27, 2001, *at* http://www.globalsecurity.org/military/library/news/2001/12/mil-011227-dod01.htm.

309.Memorandum from John Yoo, Deputy Assistant Attorney General, and Patrick F. Philbin, Deputy Assistant Attorney General, *Possible Habeas Jurisdiction Over Aliens Held in Guantanamo Bay*, to William J. Haynes, General Counsel, Department of Defense (Dec.28, 2001), at 9.

310.President Bush stated:

> And yesterday, the Secretary of Defense went down to Guantanamo Bay with United States senators from both political parties. The senators got to see the circumstances in which these detainees were being held. They – I don't want to put words in their mouth, but according to the Secretary of Defense – I'll let him puts words in their mouth – they felt like, one, that our troops were really valiant in their efforts to make sure that these killers – these are killers – were held in such a way that they were safe. I noticed one of our troops last night was commenting that they are receiving very good medical care. But I'll make my decision about – on how to legally interpret the situation here pretty soon.
>
> * * * * * * *
>
> These are killers. These are terrorists. They know no countries. The only thing they know about countries is when they find a country that's been weakened and they want to occupy it like a parasite.

President George W. Bush, President Meets With Afghan Interim Authority Chairman, Remarks by the President and Chairman of the Afghan Interim Authority Hamid Karzai, Jan. 28, 2002, *available at* http://www.whitehouse.gov/news/releases/2002/01/20020128-13.html (emphasis added). In that same set of remarks, President Bush went so far as to state that the detainees would be "well-treated." In his State of the Union Address a few days prior to the cited statements, President Bush stated: "Terrorists who once occupied Afghanistan now occupy cells at Guantanamo Bay." President George W. Bush, State of the Union Address, Jan. 29, 2002, transcript *available at* http://www.whitehouse.gov/news/releases/2002/01/20020129-11.html.

311.*Interview by Brit Hume with Vice President Cheney in Washington, DC*, (Fox News television broadcast Jan. 27, 2002), *available at* http://www.foxnews.com/story/0,2933,44082,00.html (emphasis added).

312.*Bush Meets Karzai on U.S. Soil, Lateline Broadcast*, (Australian Broadcasting Corporation television broadcast Jan. 29, 2002) *available at* http://www.abc.net.au/lateline/stories/s469211.htm (emphasis added).

313.Smith, "Rumsfeld Visits, Thanks U.S. Troops at Camp X-Ray in Cuba,*" American Forces Press Service News Articles*, Jan. 27,. 2002, *available at* http://www.defenselink.mil/news/newsarticle.aspx?id=43817 (emphasis added). Rumsfeld voiced similar words in 2005: "If you think of the people down there, these are people all of whom were captured on a battlefield. They're terrorists, trainers, bomb makers, recruiters, financiers, UBL's body guards, would-be suicide bombers, probably the 20th hijacker, 9/11 hijacker." *Interview by Jerry Agar KMBZ News Radio, with Secretary Rumsfeld,* (KMBZ radio broadcast June 27, 2005), *available at* http://www.defenselink.mil/transcripts/transcript.aspx?transcriptid=3246.

314.*Secretary Rumsfeld Briefs Reporters* (CNN television broadcast Jan. 11, 2002), *available at* http://transcripts.cnn.com/TRANSCRIPTS/0201/11/se.02.html. There are other examples as well. In November 2004, Press Secretary Scott McClellan stated: "You know, these are enemy combatants that were picked up on the battlefield who are being detained at Guantanamo Bay. They are enemy combatants who were seeking to do harm to America, or plotting to carry out attacks against Americans." Press Gaggle by Scott McClellan, Nov. 30, 2004, *available at* http://www.whitehouse.gov/news/releases/2004/11/20041130-1.html . In December of 2004, McClellan similarly stated: "The President designated individuals again Guantanamo as unlawful enemy combatants who do not share -- they are people who do not share our values, who do not respect the rule of law, and who have no regard for innocent – [Interruption]... * * * But these are people who have no regard for innocent civilian life[.]" Press Briefing by Scott McClellan," Dec. 10, 2004, *available at* http://www.whitehouse.gov/news/releases/2004/12/20041210-9.html.

315."List of Individuals Detained by the Department of Defense at Guantanamo Bay, Cuba from January 2002 through May 15, 2006," (May 15, 2006), *available at* http://www.dod.mil/pubs/foi/detainees/detaineesFOIArelease15May2006.pdf.

316.These numbers are also consistent with those reported in *The Economist*, which reported in February of 2008: "Of the 778 prisoners kept in Guantánamo, fewer than 300 now remain: most of the rest have been repatriated, after long detention, without facing charges." "Seeking the Death Penalty," *The Economist*, Feb. 12, 2008, *available at* http://www.economist.com/displayStory.cfm?story_id=10677748&fsrc=RSS .

317.*See* "Guantanamo Bay Detainees," *available at* http://www.globalsecurity.org/military/facility/guantanamo-bay_detainees.htm.

In a December 2007 press release announcing the transfer of ten detainees to Saudi Arabis, the Department of Defense stated: "Since 2002, approximately 500 detainees have departed Guantanamo for other countries including Albania, Afghanistan, Australia, Bangladesh,

Bahrain, Belgium, Denmark, Egypt, France, Iran, Iraq, Jordan, Kuwait, Libya, Maldives, Mauritania, Morocco, Pakistan, Russia, Saudi Arabia, Spain, Sweden, Sudan, Tajikistan, Turkey, Uganda, United Kingdom and Yemen." Press Release, Dept. of Defense, Detainee Transfer Announced, (Dec. 28, 2007), *available at* http://www.defenselink.mil/Releases/Release.aspx?ReleaseID=11591. Similarly, in its October 2007 brief in the <u>Boumediene</u> case, the Government represented:

> In addition to the CSRT review process, the Department of
> Defense also conducts an annual administrative examination of
> whether it is appropriate to release or repatriate an enemy
> combatant. The 328 administrative reviews conducted in 2006
> resulted in determinations that 55 detainees (roughly 17%) should
> no longer be detained at Guantanamo Bay.   (citation omitted).
> Since 2002, about 390 detainees have been transferred or released
> through this or other processes. See ibid. Today, approximately
> 340 detainees remain at Guantanamo Bay.

"Brief for Respondents [United States]," *Boumediene v. United States*, Sup. Ct., Nos. 06-1195 and 06-1196 (Oct. 2007) at 4, *available at* http://www.abanet.org/publiced/preview/briefs/pdfs/07-08/06-1195_Respondent.pdf .

318.Selsky, "'Vicious Killers' From Guantanamo Routinely Freed Elsewhere," *Associated Press*, Dec. 15, 2006, *available at* http://www.usatoday.com/news/world/2006-12-15-gitmo-freed_x.htm.

319.*Id.*

320.*Interview of the Vice President by Wolf Blitzer*, (CNN television broadcast June 23, 2005), *available at* http://www.whitehouse.gov/news/releases/2005/06/20050623-8.html .

321.*See, e.,g*, Center for Constitutional Rights, "Report on Torture and Cruel, Inhuman, and Degrading Treatment of Prisoners at Guantanamo Bay, Cuba" (2006), *available at* http://ccrjustice.org/files/Report_ReportOnTorture.pdf .

322.*Hamdi v. Rumsfeld*, 296 F.3d 278, 282 (4th Cir. 2002).

323.*Id.* (emphasis added).

324."Declaration of Michael H. Mobbs, Special Advisor to the Under Secretary of Defense for Policy," filed in *Hamdi v. Rumsfeld*, No. 2:02CV439 (E.D.Va), *reprinted at* http://www.pbs.org/wgbh/pages/frontline/shows/sleeper/tools/mobbshamdi.html.

325.*Hamdi v. Rumsfeld*, 243 F.Supp. 2d 527 (E.D. Va. 2002).

326.*Hamdi v. Rumsfeld*, 316 F.3d 450 (4th Cir. 2003).

327.*Hamdi v. Rumsfeld*, 337 F.3d 335 (4th Cir. 2003) (denying rehearing en banc).

328.*See* Brief for Petitioner [Hamdi], *Hamdi v. Rumsfeld*, Sup. Ct., No. 03-6696 (Feb. 23, 2004), reported at 2004 WL 378715 at *4 at fn. 2 ("Hamdi has been forbidden any contact with fellow prisoners and the outside world, with the exception of a visit by a representative of the International Red Cross and the infrequent exchange of censored letters with his family. On February 3, 2004, Hamdi was allowed to meet counsel for the first time. Restrictions imposed by the military on the conditions under which this meeting was permitted did not allow confidential communications."). *See also Hamdi v. Rumsfeld*, 542 U.S. 507, 539 (2004) ("Hamdi asks us to hold that the Fourth Circuit also erred by denying him immediate access to counsel upon his detention and by disposing of the case without permitting him to meet with an attorney. Brief for Petitioners 19. Since our grant of certiorari in this case, Hamdi has been appointed counsel, with whom he has met for consultation purposes on several occasions, and with whom he is now being granted unmonitored meetings. He unquestionably has the right to access to counsel in connection with the proceedings on remand. No further consideration of this issue is necessary at this stage of the case.").

329.Addressing the Government's arguments as to the president's unreviewable powers, Justice O'Connor wrote: "The Government maintains that no explicit congressional authorization is required, because the Executive possesses plenary authority to detain pursuant to Article II of the Constitution. We do not reach the question whether Article II provides such authority, however, because we agree with the Government's alternative position, that Congress has in fact authorized Hamdi's detention, through the AUMF." *Id*. at 516-17.

330.The significance of the fact that Mr. Hamdi was seized in Afghanistan was underscored by Justice O'Connor's response to Justice Scalia's dissent. Justice Scalia stated that Mr. Hamdi's petition for *habeas corpus* should have been granted, in response to which Justice O'Connor stressed that Mr. Hamdi was seized in a fighting zone:

> Further, Justice Scalia largely ignores the context of this case: a United States citizen captured in a foreign combat zone. Justice Scalia refers to only one case involving this factual scenario – a case in which a United States citizen-prisoner of war (a member of the Italian army) from World War II was seized on the battlefield in Sicily and then held in the United States. The court in that case held that the military detention of that United States citizen was lawful...
>
> [J]ustice Scalia can point to no case or other authority for the proposition that those captured on a foreign battlefield (whether detained there or in U.S. territory) cannot be detained outside the criminal process.

Id. at 523-24. There is at least some irony in the fact that the AUMF, which the Administration

336

had to a great extent treated either as irrelevant or as an potential limitation on the president's authority, was relied upon by the plurality as the source of the president's power to designate an American citizen as an enemy combatant.

331. *Id*. at 521 (emphasis added).

332. The four-Justice plurality (Justice O'Connor, writing for herself, Chief Justice Rehnquist, and Justices Breyer and Kennedy) was joined by Justices Souter and Ginsburg, for the part of the decision requiring that Mr. Hamdi be given a meaningful opportunity to challenge his detention

333. *Hamdi v. Rumsfeld*, 542 U.S. 507, 509 (2004). The plurality opinion was authored by Justice O'Connor, and joined by Chief Justice Rehnquist, and Justices Kennedy and Breyer.

334. *Id*. at 535 (citations omitted).

335. *Id*. at 535-37.

336. *Id*. at 573 (Scalia, J., dissenting) ("It follows from what I have said that Hamdi is entitled to a *habeas* decree requiring his release unless (1) criminal proceedings are promptly brought, or (2) Congress has suspended the writ of *habeas* corpus. A suspension of the writ could, of course, lay down conditions for continued detention, similar to those that today's opinion prescribes under the Due Process Clause. Cf. Act of Mar. 3, 1863, 12 Stat. 755. But there is a world of difference between the people's representatives' determining the need for that suspension (and prescribing the conditions for it), and this Court's doing so.")

337. *Id*. at 573 (Scalia, J., dissenting).

338. *Id*. at 539 (Ginsburg, J., and Souter, J., concurring).

339. *Hamdi v. Rumsfeld*, "Agreement," Sept. 17, 2004, *available at* http://news.findlaw.com/wp/docs/hamdi/91704stlagrmnt.html.

340. *Id*. at p. 2, para. 3.

341. The second paragraph of the agreement committed the Government to agreeing to transport Mr. Hamdi "unhooded and in civilian clothes." *Id*. at 2, para. 2.

342. It is difficult to imagine that Mr. Hamdi would not have accepted these precise terms (involving his release to Saudi Arabia conditioned on his promise not to commit new terrorist acts) years earlier, so it is difficult to conceive of any reason for the Government's accession to these terms in September 2004 other than as a means of avoiding the need to comply with the decision of the Supreme Court and provide evidence to support his detention. An even more disturbing possibility is that the Administration had been so determined to see its legal position vindicated in the courts, and so concerned about "precedent" or appearing to yield in the face of litigation, that it had fought for its right to detain Mr. Hamdi – a United States citizen – even

when the Government had reason to conclude that he posed no significant danger.

343.A November 13, 2001, Presidential Order announced that certain individuals seized as part of the war on terror would be detained by the military and be subject to trial by military commissions. "Detention, Treatment, and Trial of Certain Non-Citizens in the War Against Terrorism," 66 Fed. Reg. 57833 (hereinafter "November 13, 2001 Detention Order").

344.The procedural background is set forth in *Hamdan v. Rumsfeld*, 344 F.Supp. 2d 152, 155-56 (D.D.C. 2004). Mr. Hamdan was charged with conspiracy to commit the following offenses: "attacking civilians; attacking civilian objects; murder by an unprivileged belligerent; destruction of property by an unprivileged belligerent; and terrorism." Dept. of Defense, Military Commission List of Charges for Salim Ahmed Hamdan, *available at* http://www.defenselink.mil/news/Jul2004/d20040714hcc.pdf.

345.*Hamdan v. Rumsfeld*, 344 F.Supp. 2d 152 (D.D.C. 2004).

346.*Id*. at 158. The trial judge also quoted from *Application of Yamashita*, 327 U.S. 1 (1946):

> *Congress*, in the exercise of its constitutional power to define and punish offenses against the law of nations, of which the law of war is a part, has recognized the 'military commission' appointed by military command... as an appropriate tribunal for the trial and punishment of offenses against the law of war.

Id. at 16 (emphasis added by trial court).

347.*Id*. at 158 (emphasis added; citation omitted).

348.*Id*. at 168. In addition, if Mr. Hamdan were a prisoner of war, he could not be tried by a military commission except for violations of the laws of war. The trial court found that there needed to be procedures for determining the status of Mr. Hamdan.

349.*See* "Reply Brief for Appellants [The United States]," *Hamdan v. Rumsfeld*, Ct. App., D.C. Cir., No. 04-5393 (Jan. 10, 2005), reported at 2005 WL 189857 at ** 1-10.

350.*See* "Reply Brief for Appellants [The United States]," *Hamdan v. Rumsfeld*, Ct. App., D.C. Cir., No. 04-5393 (Jan. 10, 2005), reported at 2005 WL 189857 at *29.

351.*Hamdan v. Rumsfeld*, 415 F.3d 33, 37-38 (D.C. Cir. 2005). Further, the court of appeals rejected the Administration's claims that the circumstances associated with the detention of Mr. Hamdan were unreviewable or that the courts should abstain. *Id*. at 36-37.

352.*See* Brief for Respondents [The United States], *Hamdan v. Rumsfeld*, No. 05-0184 (Feb. 23, 2006), 2006 WL 460875, at 21 (citing *Johnson v. Eisentrager*, 339 U.S. 763, 788 (1950)). The United States also relied on the claim that Congress, by operation of the AUMF, had granted the president the power to implement military commissions.

353.*Hamdan v. Rumsfeld*, 548 U.S.557, 591-92 (2006) (footnote omitted) (citing *Ex Parte Milligan*, 4 Wall. 2, 139-40 (1866)) (emphasis added).

354.The Military Commissions Act of 2006 (MCA), Pub. L. No. 109-366, 120 Stat. 2600. *See* discussion in Section 2.B.

355.Glaberson, "Bin Laden's Former Driver Is Convicted in Split Verdict," *N.Y. Times*, Aug. 6, 2008, http://www.nytimes.com/2008/08/06/washington/07gitmo.html?hp.

356.Glaberson, "Bin Laden Driver Sentenced to a Short Term," *N.Y. Times*, Aug. 7, 2008, *available at* http://www.nytimes.com/2008/08/08/washington/08gitmo.html?ref=nationalspecial3.

357.R. Worth, "Bin Laden Driver to Be Sent to Yemen," *N.Y. Times*, Nov. 26, 2008, *available at* http://www.nytimes.com/2008/11/26/washington/26gitmo.html?fta=y.

358.*Rasul v. Bush*, 542 U.S. 466 (2004).

359.*Rasul v. Bush*, 542 U.S. 466, 475 (2004), referring to 28 U.S.C. § 2241, which at the time provided, in pertinent part:

> § 2241. Power to grant writ
>
> > (a) Writs of *habeas corpus* may be granted by the Supreme Court, any justice thereof, the district courts and any circuit judge within their respective jurisdictions. The order of a circuit judge shall be entered in the records of the district court of the district wherein the restraint complained of is had.
>
> > * * * * * * *
>
> > (c) The writ of *habeas corpus* shall not extend to a prisoner unless–
>
> > * * * * * * *
>
> > (3) He is in custody in violation of the Constitution or laws or treaties of the United States[.]

360.*Id.* at 480.

361.*Id.* at 484.

362.*Boumediene v. Bush*, __ U.S. __ , 128 S.Ct. 2229 (2008).

363. *Boumediene v. Bush*, __ U.S. __ , 128 S.Ct. 2229 (2008). Section 7(a) of the MCA, 120 Stat. 2635, amends 28 U.S.C. 2241(e) to provide that "[n]o court, justice, or judge shall have jurisdiction to hear or consider an application for a writ of *habeas corpus* filed by or on behalf of an alien detained by the United States who has been determined by the United States to have been properly detained as an enemy combatant or is awaiting such determination."

364. *Boumediene v. Bush*, 128 S.Ct. 2229, 2242 (2008).

365. The "Suspension Clause" of the Constitution, Art. I, sec. 9, cl. 3., provides: "The privilege of the writ of *habeas corpus* shall not be suspended, unless when in cases of rebellion or invasion the public safety may require it."

366. *Boumediene v. Bush*, __ U.S. __ , 128 S.Ct. 2229, 2274 (2008).

367. *Id*. at 2246.

368. *Id*. at 2261 (emphasis added).

369. Transcript of Remarks by Attorney General Michael B. Mukasey at the American Enterprise Institute for Public Policy Research, Jul. 21, 2008, *available at* http://www.usdoj.gov/opa/pr/2008/July/08-opa-633.html

370. Whatever other purposes this fourth principle was intended to accomplish, it would have bolstered the Administration's litigation posture in the *al-Marri* case, discussed in the text, and pending at the time the Attorney General made his comments; it would have provided after-the-fact vindication for the *Padilla* detention; and it would have helped the Administration in other contexts where it was relying on the AUMF to support its contentions as to the lawfulness of presidential acts claimed to be undertaken as Commander in Chief. It also would have had Congress on record supporting detention "for the duration of the conflict" – thus addressing the concerns articulated by the Supreme Court with the Administration's potentially "indefinite" detentions.

371. The Order, as reported by the Second Circuit, stated:

> TO THE SECRETARY OF DEFENSE:
>
> Based on the information available to me from all sources,
>
> REDACTED
>
> In accordance with the Constitution and consistent with the laws of the United States, including the Authorization for Use of Military Force Joint Resolution (Public Law 107-40);
>
> I, GEORGE W. BUSH, as President of the United States and

Commander in Chief of the U.S. armed forces, hereby DETERMINE for the United States of America that:

(1) Jose Padilla, who is under the control of the Department of Justice and who is a U.S. citizen, is, and at the time he entered the United States in May 2002 was, an enemy combatant;

(2) Mr. Padilla is closely associated with al Qaeda, an international terrorist organization with which the United States is at war;

(3) Mr. Padilla engaged in conduct that constituted hostile and war-like acts, including conduct in preparation for acts of international terrorism that had the aim to cause injury to or adverse effects on the United States;

(4) Mr. Padilla possesses intelligence, including intelligence about personnel and activities of al Qaeda, that, if communicated to the U.S., would aid U.S. efforts to prevent attacks by al Qaeda on the United States or its armed forces, other governmental personnel, or citizens;

(5) Mr. Padilla represents a continuing, present and grave danger to the national security of the United States, and detention of Mr. Padilla is necessary to prevent him from aiding al Qaeda in its efforts to attack the United States or its armed forces, other governmental personnel, or citizens;

(6) it is in the interest of the United States that the Secretary of Defense detain Mr. Padilla as an enemy combatant; and

(7) it is REDACTED consistent with U.S. law and the laws of war for the Secretary of Defense to detain Mr. Padilla as an enemy combatant.

Accordingly, you are directed to receive Mr. Padilla from the Department of Justice and to detain him as an enemy combatant.

Reprinted in *Padilla v. Rumsfeld*, 353 F.3d 695, 724-725 (2d Cir. 2004).

372. It is not known why he was moved to South Carolina or if that decision was made with a view to bringing all litigation to the Fourth Circuit – broadly considered a more favorable venue for the Government.

373. *Id.* at 9 (citations omitted). Note the choice of words: The Administration did not say that is was "authorized" by Congress – the actual term used in the "*Authorization* for the Use of Military Force" – only that Congress "supported" the use of force.

374. *Id.* at 18. The Government misleadingly represented that the enemy combatants in detention "receive protection from harm, medical care, and humane treatment." *Id.* at 18-19.

375. *Padilla v. Bush*, 02 Civ. 4445 (MEM) (S.D.N.Y.), Respondents' [the United States'] Response to, and Motion to Dismiss, the Amended Petition for a Writ of Habeas Corpus, at 20.

376. *Id.* at 19 (citations omitted).

377. *Padilla ex rel. Newman v. Bush*, 232 F. Supp. 2d 564, 610 (S.D.N.Y. 2002).

378. *Id.*

379. Mukasey rejected the Government's claim that providing Mr. Padilla access to counsel would impermissibly interfere with the questioning of him or otherwise constitute a security risk: "Padilla's statutorily granted right to present facts to the court in connection with this petition will be destroyed utterly if he is not allowed to consult with counsel." *Id.* at 604.

380. Respondents' Motion for Reconsideration in Part, *Padilla v. Rumsfeld*, 02 Civ. 4445 (MEM) (S.D.N.Y Jan. 9, 2003), *available at* http://www.pegc.us/archive/Padilla_vs_Rumsfeld/Jacoby_Gov_mot_reconsider.doc.

381. The Government may have also believed that if an attorney had access to Mr. Padilla, and learned of the nature of the interrogation techniques being used on him and publicly disclosed those facts, they would be offensive to the Court and to the public.

382. *Padilla ex rel. Newman v. Rumsfeld*, 243 F. Supp.2d 42, 49 (S.D.N.Y. 2003) (quoting Declaration of Vice Admiral Lowell E. Jacoby, Director, Defense Intelligence Agency). In addition, the Government argued that in light of the relaxed and deferential standard of review that will be required of the President's determination of Mr. Padilla's status, the appointment of counsel was unnecessary.

383. *Padilla v. Bush*, 02 Civ. 4445 (Mem.) (S.D.N.Y.) (Transcript of Conference, Jan. 15, 2003).

384. *Id.*

385. *Padilla ex rel. Newman v. Rumsfeld*, 243 F.Supp.2d 42 (S.D.N.Y 2003).

386. To give a sense of the interrelated legal issues, Judge Mukasey certified the following questions for the Second Circuit Court of Appeals:

> 1.   Is the Secretary of Defense, Donald Rumsfeld, a proper respondent in this

case?

2. Does this court have personal jurisdiction over Secretary Rumsfeld?

3. Does the President have the authority to designate as an enemy combatant an American citizen captured within the United States, and, through the Secretary of Defense, to detain him for the duration of armed conflict with al Qaeda?

4. What burden must the government meet to detain petitioner as an enemy combatant?

5. Does petitioner have the right to present facts in support of his *habeas corpus* petition?

6. Was it a proper exercise of this court's discretion and its authority under the All Writs Act to direct that petitioner be afforded access to counsel for the purpose of presenting facts in support of his petition?

Padilla ex rel. Newman v. Rumsfeld, 256 F.Supp.2d 218, 223 (S.D.N.Y. 2003) (footnote omitted). The first two questions involve jurisdiction. The next three go to the core issue: the power of the president to order a U.S. citizen held in military custody and the power of the court to review that decision (and the procedures for such a review). The final relates to whether the court could order that Mr. Padilla receive assistance of counsel.

387. *Padilla v. Rumsfeld*, 352 F.3d 695, 713 (2d Cir. 2003) (citing *Youngstown Sheet & Tube Co. v. Sawyer*, 343 U.S. 579 (1952) (Jackson, J., concurring) and *United States v. Curtiss-Wright Export Corp.*, 299 U.S. 304 (1936)).

388. *Padilla v. Rumsfeld*, 352 F.3d at 715.

389. *Id.*, 352 F.3d and 624.

390. *See* "Brief for Petitioner," *Rumsfeld v. Padilla*, Sup. Ct., No. 03-1027 (Mar. 17, 2004), reported at 2004 WL 378715 at *27.

391. Mr. Padilla, in connection with his criminal case, represented that he first was able to consult with counsel March 2, 2004. *See* "[Defendant Padilla's] Motion to Dismiss for Outrageous Government Conduct," *United States v. Padilla*, Case No. 04-60001-Cr-COOKE/BROWN (S.D. Fl., Oct. 4, 2006) at 5, *available at* http://www.discourse.net/archives/docs/Padilla_Outrageous_Government_Conduct.pdf .

392. Justice Stevens, in dissent, expressed his concern with the detention policy the Government was defending:

At stake in this case is nothing less than the essence of a free society. Even more important than the method of selecting the people's rulers and their successors is the character of the constraints imposed on the Executive by the rule of law. Unconstrained executive detention for the purpose of investigating and preventing subversive activity is the hallmark of the Star Chamber. . . . Access to counsel for the purpose of protecting the citizen from official mistakes and mistreatment is the hallmark of due process.

Executive detention of subversive citizens, like detention of enemy soldiers to keep them off the battlefield, may sometimes be justified to prevent persons from launching or becoming missiles of destruction. It may not, however, be justified by the naked interest in using unlawful procedures to extract information. Incommunicado detention for months on end is such a procedure. Whether the information so procured is more or less reliable than that acquired by more extreme forms of torture is of no consequence. For if this Nation is to remain true to the ideals symbolized by its flag, it must not wield the tools of tyrants even to resist an assault by the forces of tyranny.

Rumsfeld v. Padilla, 542 U.S. 426, 465 (2004) (Stevens, J., dissenting) (footnote omitted).

393. Clement's concession, on Judge Luttig's insistent prompting, that the Government's position was that the American homeland was now a battlefield on which the President had the authority to exercise military power, was apparently the first time any Administration official had ever publicly stated this profound legal proposition, although it was a linchpin of the expansive view of the president's Commander-in-Chief powers on which the Administration had been operating for three-and-a-half years, secretly, and in disregard of Congress's pointed refusal in the AUMF to authorize use of war powers within the United States.

394. *Padilla v. Hanft*, 423 F.3d 386 (4th Cir. 2005).

395. *Id*. 386, 395.

396. *Id*. 582, 587 (4th Cir. 2005) (emphasis added).

397. *Hanft v. Padilla*, 546 U.S. 1084 (Jan. 4, 2006).

398. *Padilla v. Hanft*, 547 U.S. 1062 (April 3, 2006).

399. *See* "Brief for Respondent [United States] ," *Padilla v. Hanft*, Sup. Ct., No. 05-533 (Dec. 16, 2005), reported at 2005 WL 3514331 at *3 ("The fact that the case is now moot itself calls

for denial of certiorari."), * 13 ("Because petitioner has been charged with criminal offenses and ordered released from that military detention, the case is moot and further review would be inconsistent with the jurisdictional requirements of Article III. Indeed, the mootness of this case may be further underscored if the court of appeals vacates its September 9, 2005, opinion.").

400.The Government, in a brief to the Fourth Circuit, suggested that the court might vacate its opinion in light of the fact that Supreme Court review was no longer possible: "Because the mooting events are not attributable to petitioner, the Executive has no objection to this Court's vacatur of its opinion . . .." *See* "Supplemental Brief for the Appellant [United States]," *Padilla v. Hanft*, Fourth Cir. No. 05-6396 (Dec. 9, 2005) at 14, *available at* http://www.wiggin.com/db30/cgi-bin/pubs/Government%20Supplemental%20Brief%2012%201 2%202005.pdf .

> Yoo, in describing the *Padilla* litigation, writes:

>> Eventually, a court of appeals unanimously found in late 2005 that "[u]nder the facts presented here, Padilla unquestionably qualifies as an 'enemy combatant'" . . . even though he had been detained in the United States, not in Afghanistan. While Padilla's case was on appeal to the Supreme Court, the Justice Department concluded it had enough evidence to prosecuted Padilla for crimes. . . . The Supreme Court dismissed the appeal as moot since he was now in criminal court.

Yoo, *War By Other Means: An Insider's Account of the War on Terror* 158 (2006). Mr. Yoo is simply not correct that the Supreme Court dismissed the case on mootness grounds; and his selective description of the opinion ans surrounding events makes not even passing reference to these factors that undermine the decision's its precedential value.

401."[Defendant Padilla's] Motion to Dismiss for Outrageous Government Conduct," *United States v. Padilla*, Case No. 04-60001-Cr-COOKE/BROWN (S.D. Fl., Oct. 4, 2006) at 1-5, *available at* http://www.discourse.net/archives/docs/Padilla_Outrageous_Government_Conduct.pdf.

> The Government did not deny these allegations. As noted in Mr. Padilla's reply brief:

>> In his motion to dismiss for outrageous government conduct, Mr. Padilla made specific and detailed allegations of the conditions of his confinement and the torture he endured. These allegations include isolation; sleep and sensory depravation; hoodings; stress positions; exposure to noxious fumes; exposure to temperature extremes; threats of imminent execution; assaults; the forced administration of mind-altering substances; denial of religious practices; manipulation of diet; and other forms of mistreatment.

Despite these specific allegations, the government does not make any effort to deny or confirm that Mr. Padilla was subjected to the conditions he has alleged. If Mr. Padilla's allegations were false it would be a simple matter for the government to deny that Mr. Padilla was ever deprived of sleep or sensory stimuli, or assert that he was never assaulted or administered mind-altering substances against his will. The government's silence on these issues speaks volumes of Mr. Padilla's allegations of torture. Mr. Padilla asserts that he was not treated humanely, but instead was tortured and that the government's conduct was outrageous.

"Mr. Padilla's Reply to the Government's Response to the Motion to Dismiss for Outrageous Government Conduct," *United States v. Padilla*, Case No. 04-60001-Cr-COOKE/BROWN (S.D. Fl., Oct. 4, 2006) at 6, *available at* http://i.a.cnn.net/cnn/2006/images/12/04/padilla.695.pdf.

402. Whoriskey and Eggen, "Judge Sentences Padilla to 17 Years, Cites His Detention," *Wash. Post*, Jan. 23, 2008, at A3, *available at* http://www.washingtonpost.com/wp-dyn/content/article/2008/01/22/AR2008012200565.html .

403. The *Padilla* litigation raises numerous troubling questions. Is it true, as U.S. citizen Jose Padilla alleged, that he was subjected to harsh interrogation techniques, including sleep deprivation and mind-altering drugs, while in military custody? If so, who approved that he be treated in this fashion, and who – the military, or the intelligence community – conducted the interrogation? When Justice Department attorney (and future Solicitor General) Paul Clement argued in front of then- Chief Judge Mukasey that Mr. Padilla should not be permitted an attorney, did Clement or others in the Department of Justice know the nature of the interrogation techniques to which Mr. Padilla was then being subjected or was intended to be subjected? Was the Government's opposition to Mr. Padilla having access to an attorney designed to keep Chief Judge Mukasey and the public from knowing how Mr. Padilla was being treated – for fear that those facts would have aroused public reaction and influenced the court's interpretation of the law? Who made the decision to transfer Mr. Padilla from the brig in South Carolina to Florida to face federal terrorism charges? Was that decision made to moot out Supreme Court review, so that the Fourth Circuit opinion would remain the law in this case, thus purporting to vindicate the Administration's detention policies?

404. "Petition for Writ of Certiorari," *Al-Marri v. Pucciarelli* (Sep. 19, 2008) at 4-5. As Rep. Melvin Watt said at a 2007 hearing on *habeas corpus* issues at which Mr. al-Marri's lawyer, Jonathan Hafetz, was a witness:

And I guess the most difficult question – even if your client, Mr. Hafetz, turns out to be an enemy combatant – is how one could be basically in a courtroom on a credit card matter in 2003 and then all of a sudden be in a military brig simply because the President of the United States said, 'You are not a credit card common thief;

you are an enemy combatant,' and then to have your client charged – really no charge brought against your client and he be held for 4 years without a charge against him and without any indication of when the detention would end, including 16 months when he was held incommunicado.

Habeas Corpus and Detentions at Guantanamo Bay: Hearing Before the Subcomm. on the Constitution, Civil Rights, and Civil Liberties, H. Comm. on the Judiciary, 110th Cong. (2007) (statement of Rep. Melvin Watt).

405. *Al-Marri v. Bush,* 274 F. Supp. 2d 1003 (C.D. Ill. 2003).

406. *Al-Marri v. Wright,* 443 F. Supp. 2d 774 (D.S.C. 2006).

407. *Al-Marri v. Wright,* 487 F.3d 160 (4th Cir. 2007).

408. There was no consensus as to what was meant by the term "enemy combatant."

409. Editorial, "Tortured Justice," *N.Y. Times,* Dec. 8, 2008, *available at* http://www.nytimes.com/2008/12/08/opinion/08mon1.html?_r=1.

410. *Al-Marri v. Pucciarelli,* 534 F.3d 213, 217-18 (4th Cir. 2008) (Motz, J., conc.) (quoting *Boumediene v. Bush,* ___U.S.___-, 128 S.Ct. 2229, 2278 (2008)) (emphasis added).

411. Petition for Writ of Certiorari, *Al-Marri v. Pucciarelli,* 08-268 (Sep. 19, 2008) at 14.

412. Brief for the Respondent in Opposition [to al-Marri's Petition for Writ of Certiorari], *Al-Marri v. Pucciarelli,* 08-268 (Oct. 2008) at 14.

413. Brief for the Respondent [United States] in Opposition [to al-Marri's Petition for Writ of Certiorari], *Al-Marri v. Pucciarelli,* 08-268 (Oct. 2008) at 17-29.

414. *Al-Marri v. Pucciarelli,* ___ S.Ct.___, 2008 WL 4326485 (Mem) (Dec. 5, 2008) (granting certiorari).

415. *Hamdi v. Rumsfeld,* 542 U.S. 507, 554-55 (2004) (Scalia, J., dissenting). Scalia also quoted from Blackstone's admonition that it would constitute a "notorious act of despotism, as must at once convey the alarm of tyranny" were the Executive to have the power to "imprison arbitrarily":

> Of great importance to the public is the preservation of this personal liberty: for if once it were left in the power of any, the highest, magistrate to imprison arbitrarily whomever he or his officers thought proper.... there would soon be an end of all other rights and immunities... To bereave a man of life, or by violence to

confiscate his estate, without accusation or trial, would be so gross and notorious an act of despotism, as must at once convey the alarm of tyranny throughout the whole kingdom. But confinement of the person, by secretly hurrying him to gaol, where his sufferings are unknown or forgotten; is a less public, a less striking, and therefore a more dangerous engine of arbitrary government...

To make imprisonment lawful, it must either be, by process from the courts of judicature, or by warrant from some legal officer, having authority to commit to prison; which warrant must be in writing, under the hand and seal of the magistrate, and express the causes of the commitment, in order to be examined into (if necessary) upon a *habeas corpus*. If there be no cause expressed, the gaoler is not bound to detain the prisoner. For the law judges in this respect, ... that it is unreasonable to send a prisoner, and not to signify withal the crimes alleged against him.

1 W. Blackstone, Commentaries on the Laws of England 131-133 (1765).

Id.

416. The Military Commissions Act of 2006 (MCA), Pub. L. No. 109-366, 120 Stat. 2600.

417. *Habeas Corpus and Detentions at Guantanamo Bay: Hearing before the Subcomm. on the Constitution, Civil Rights, and Civil Liberties of the H. Comm. on the Judiciary*, 110th Cong. 4-5 (June 26, 2007) (statement of Rep. Jerrold Nadler).

418. *Id.* at 43 (statement of Jonathan Hafetz).

419. *Id.* at 58 (statement of Jonathan Hafetz).

420. *Id.* at 46-49 (testimony of former Associate White House Counsel Bradford Berenson.)

421. *Id.* at 30 (testimony of former State Department Legal Advisor William H. Taft IV).

422. *Id.* at 31.

423. *Id.* at 44 (statement of Jonathan Hafetz).

424. The following colloquy between Rep. Debbie Wasserman Schultz and Lt. Commander Charles Swift, the Judge Advocate General's Corps attorney who represented Mr. Hamdan, is representative of this point:

<u>Ms. Wasserman Schultz:</u>   ...Do you think that the continued detention of   hundreds of

men without charge and without *habeas* rights at
Guantanamo makes us hypocrites?

* * * * * * *

Do you think that this undermines U.S. efforts to
win hearts and minds, an essential component of
any successful counterinsurgency strategy?

And do you not also belief that this puts U.S. troops
at risk, making it harder to credibly object if our
own solders are taken into custody and held
indefinitely without charge and without the ability
to contest the basis of their detention?

Mr. Swift: To me, Guantanamo Bay, as a recruiting magnet and as a cloak for those
who would abuse human rights the world over, does far more damage than
any one person who might be let go by following the rule of law.

Id. at 86-88.

425. In February 2008, Chairman Conyers sent two letters to the White House seeking production
of that document, and again, in a letter co-signed by Reps. Jerrold Nadler and Robert C. "Bobby"
Scott requested its release in an April 2003 letter to Attorney General Mukasey. In that letter,
Chairman Conyers and Reps. Nadler and Scott wrote:

Based on the title of the October 23, 2001 memorandum, and based
on what has been disclosed and the contents of similar memoranda
issued at roughly the same time, it is clear that a substantial
portion of this memorandum provides a legal analysis and
conclusions as to the nature and scope of the Presidential
Commander in Chief power to accomplish specific acts within the
United States. The people of the United States are entitled to know
the Justice Department's interpretation of the President's
constitutional powers to wage war in the United States. There can
be no actual basis in national security for keeping secret the
remainder of a legal memorandum that addresses this issue of
Constitutional interpretation. The notion that the President can
claim to operate under "secret" powers known only to the President
and a select few subordinates is antithetical to the core principles
of this democracy.

Letter from John Conyers, Chairman, H. Comm. on the Judiciary, Rep. Jerrold Nadler, and Rep.
Robert Scott to Michael Mukasey, Attorney General (April 3, 2008), *available at*

http://judiciary.house.gov/news/pdfs/Conyers-Nadler-Scott080403.pdf (emphasis in original).

In April 2008, Mukasey was questioned about this document by Senator Diana Feinstein in a Senate Appropriations Committee Hearing.   The questioning was described in press reports as follows:

> "Is the October 2001 OLC opinion still considered binding by the Department of Justice?" Feinstein asked.
>
> Mukasey at first struggled to answer to Feinstein's satisfaction:
>
> "I can't speak to the October 2001 memo," he said. "We are aware of Congress' oversight interests in this matter…We're trying to work with Congress to meet your legitimate oversight."
>
> "This isn't a question of oversight," Feinstein shot back. "I'm just asking you whether this memo is in force."
>
> "The principle that the Fourth Amendment does not apply in wartime is not in force," Mukasey continued.
>
> "That's not the principle I asked you about," Feinstein countered. "Does it apply to domestic military operations? Is the Fourth Amendment. . . I'm asking you a question. That's not the answer."
>
> "I'm unaware of any domestic military operations being carried out today," he said.
>
> Feinstein tried again: "You're not answering my question. . . . Is this memo binding?"
>
> Mukasey finally replied: "The Fourth Amendment applies across the board regardless of whether it's peace or war time."

"Senators Grill Michael Mukasey at Budget Hearing," The BLT: Blog of the Legal Times, Apr. 10, 2008, *available at* http://legaltimes.typepad.com/blt/2008/04/senators-grill.html.

Finally, on June 27, 2008, the House Judiciary Committee issued a subpoena that specifically demanded production of that Memorandum.   Letter and Subpoena from John Conyers, Jr., Chairman, H. Comm. on the Judiciary to Michael Mukasey, Attorney General (June 27, 2008), *available at* http://judiciary.house.gov/news/pdfs/Conyers080627.pdf. To date, the Administration has refused to release it.

426.Memorandum for William J. Haynes, General Counsel, Department of Defense, *Re: Possible habeas jurisdiction over aliens held in Guantanamo Bay,* from John Yoo, Deputy Assistant Attorney General, and Patrick F. Philbin, Deputy Assistant Attorney General, at 9 (Dec. 28, 2001).

427.*See* "Senate Armed Services Committee Inquiry into the Treatment of Detainees in U.S. Custody," pp. xii-xv, *available at* http://levin.senate.gov/newsroom/supporting/2008/Detainees.121108.pdf .

428."Senate Armed Services Committee Inquiry into the Treatment of Detainees in U.S. Custody," p. xiii, *available at* http://levin.senate.gov/newsroom/supporting/2008/Detainees.121108.pdf. *See also Justice Department's Office of Legal Counsel, Hearing before the Subcomm. on the Constitution, Civil Rights, and Civil Liberties of the H. Comm. on the Judiciary,* 110th Cong., at 17-18 (Feb. 14, 2008) (statement of Steven Bradbury, Principal Deputy Assistant Attorney General, Department of Justice) (describing CIA's use of waterboarding as having been "adapted from the SERE training program").

429.Memorandum for William J. Haynes, General Counsel, Department of Defense, *Re: Application of Treaties and Laws to al Qaeda and Taliban Detainees,* from John Yoo, Deputy Assistant Attorney General, and Robert J. Delahunty, Special Counsel (Jan. 9, 2002).

Within each of Geneva's four Conventions, an identical provision appears in the third section, or article – hence the provision's moniker, "Common Article 3." Article 3 sets forth the fundamental, indissoluble standard to which each signatory nation must adhere: Persons taking "no active part in hostilities" (including those in detention) must be protected from violence to "life and person." Article 3 protects individuals from: murder, mutilation, cruel treatment, and torture; hostage-taking; and outrages against personal dignity, particularly humiliating and degrading treatment. 6 U.S.T. § 3114; 6 U.S.T. § 3217; 6 U.S.T. § 3316; 6 U.S.T. § 3516. The Third Geneva Convention specifically addresses prisoners of war, and guaranteed that these prisoners receive humane treatment at all times, including protection from acts of violence, intimidation, insults, and acts of public curiosity (Article 13). As the Convention entitles every prisoner to respect for their persons and honor in all circumstances (Article 14), it simultaneously expressly forbids any form of torture or cruelty (Article 88).

430.The War Crimes Act of 1996, 18 U.S.C. § 2441 (West 2001 ed.) as in place in 2002 provided, in pertinent part:

§ 2441. War crimes

(a) Offense.--Whoever, whether inside or outside the United States, commits a war crime, in any of the circumstances described in subsection (b), shall be fined under this title or imprisoned for life or any term of years, or both, and if death results to the victim, shall also be subject to the penalty of death.

(b) Circumstances.--The circumstances referred to in subsection (a) are that the person committing such war crime or the victim of such war crime is a member of the Armed Forces of the United States or a national of the United States (as defined in section 101 of the Immigration and Nationality Act).

(c) Definition.--As used in this section the term 'war crime' means any conduct–

(1) defined as **a grave breach in any of the international conventions signed at Geneva** 12 August 1949, or any protocol to such convention to which the United States is a party;

(2) [not applicable]

* * * * * * *

(3) **which constitutes a violation of common Article 3 of the international conventions signed at Geneva**, 12 August 1949, or any protocol to such convention to which the United States is a party and which deals with non-international armed conflict; or

(4) [not applicable].

(emphasis added).

431.Memorandum for William J. Haynes, General Counsel, Department of Defense, *Re: Application of Treaties and Laws to al Qaeda and Taliban Detainees*, from John Yoo, Deputy Assistant Attorney General, and Robert J. Delahunty, Special Counsel, at 11-12 (Jan. 9, 2002).

432.Memorandum for William J. Haynes, General Counsel, Department of Defense, *Re: Application of Treaties and Laws to al Qaeda and Taliban Detainees*, from John Yoo, Deputy Assistant Attorney General, and Robert J. Delahunty, Special Counsel, at 14, 23 (Jan. 9, 2002).

433.Memorandum to President Bush, *Application of the Geneva Convention on Prisoners of War to the Conflict with Al Qaeda and the Taliban*, from Alberto Gonzales, White House Counsel, (Jan. 25, 2002), *available at* http://www.gwu.edu/~nsarchiv/NSAEBB/NSAEBB127/02.01.25.pdf/.

434.Memorandum to Alberto Gonzales, White House Counsel, *Comments on Your Paper on the Geneva Convention*, from William H. Taft IV, State Department Legal Advisor (Feb. 2, 2002), *available at* http://www.nytimes.com/packages/html/politics/20040608_DOC.pdf.

435. Memorandum from President Bush, *Humane Treatment of al Qaeda and Taliban Detainees* (Feb. 7, 2002), *available at* http://www.gwu.edu/~nsarchiv/NSAEBB/NSAEBB127/02.02.07.pdf. The President concluded:

> [O]ur values as a Nation , values that we share with many nations in the world, call for us to treat detainees humanely, including those who are not legally entitled to such treatment... As a matter of policy, the United States Armed Forces shall continue to treat detainees humanely and, to the extent appropriate and consistent with military necessity, in a manner consistent with the principles of Geneva.

Thus, this Memorandum was limited in two significant ways. First it only applied to the Armed Force, not the CIA or other intelligence agencies. And second, it applied only so far as consistent with "military necessity." Subsequently, Attorney General Gonzales would be asked what was meant by "humanely," to which he replied: "As you know, the term 'humanely' has no precise legal definition. As a policy matter, I would define humane treatment as a basic level of decent treatment that includes such things as food, shelter, clothing, and medical care." Written response of Alberto R. Gonzales, Nominee to Be Attorney General, to questions posed by Senator Edward M. Kennedy, question #15, January 2005.

436. 18 U.S.C. § 2340A provides:

> (a) Offense.--whoever outside the United States commits or attempts to commit torture shall be fined under this title or imprisoned not more than 20 years, or both, and if death results to any person from conduct prohibited by this subsection, shall be punished by death or imprisoned for any term of years or for life.

> (b) Jurisdiction.--There is jurisdiction over the activity prohibited in subsection (a) if--

> > (1) the alleged offender is a national of the United States; or

> > (2) the alleged offender is present in the United States, irrespective of the nationality of the victim or alleged offender.

> (c) Conspiracy.--A person who conspires to commit an offense under this section shall be subject to the same penalties (other than the penalty of death) as the penalties prescribed for the offense, the commission of which was the object of the conspiracy.

"Torture" is defined in 18 U.S.C. § 2340, as follows:

> As used in this chapter--

(1) "torture" means an act committed by a person acting under the color of law specifically intended to inflict severe physical or mental pain or suffering (other than pain or suffering incidental to lawful sanctions) upon another person within his custody or physical control;

(2) "severe mental pain or suffering" means the prolonged mental harm caused by or resulting from--

> (A) the intentional infliction or threatened infliction of severe physical pain or suffering;
>
> (B) the administration or application, or threatened administration or application, of mind-altering substances or other procedures calculated to disrupt profoundly the senses or the personality;
>
> (C) the threat of imminent death; or
>
> (D) the threat that another person will imminently be subjected to death, severe physical pain or suffering, or the administration or application of mind-altering substances or other procedures calculated to disrupt profoundly the senses or personality; and

(3) "United States" means the several States of the United States, the District of Columbia, and the commonwealths, territories, and possessions of the United States.

437.Memorandum for Alberto R. Gonzales, Counsel to the President, *Re: Standards of Conduct for Interrogation under 18 U.S.C. §§ 2340-2340A*," By Jay S. Bybee, Assistant Attorney General, Dept. of Justice, Aug. 1, 2002.

This document, by its terms, addresses the applicability of the federal criminal statute prohibiting torture. It has become widely referred to as the "torture memorandum," or "torture memo." *See, e.g.,* Gellman and Becker, "Pushing the Envelope on Presidential Power," *Wash. Post,* June 25, 2007, *available at* http://voices.washingtonpost.com/cheney/chapters/pushing_the_envelope_on_presi/ ("But the "torture memo," as it has become widely known, was not Yoo's work alone."). Consistent with this widespread characterization, this Report refers to this memorandum, which addresses interrogation practices by the CIA, as the August 1, 2002 Torture Memorandum," and refers to the similar memorandum, addressing interrogation practices by Defense Department personnel, as the "March 14, 2003 Torture Memorandum."

Although the memorandum was signed by Assistant Attorney General Jay Bybee, Mr. Yoo was undoubtedly the prime drafter, receiving input from others. In Mr. Yoo's book, *War by Other Means*, he noted that the Department of Justice prohibited specific discussion of the process that produced the memo. Mr. Yoo nonetheless described the preparation of the August

1, 2002, torture memo in terms that reflected his first-hand knowledge of the circumstances associated with its preparation, supporting the conclusion that he was involved:

> Aside from the restricted circle of personnel who could work on it, the opinion went through the normal process of review. No one urged us to make any significant changes in the opinion, and I do not recall anyone disagreeing with the basic conclusions of the opinion. That is not to say that anyone thought it was an easy question to answer; everyone understood that the opinion addressed difficult questions fraught with serious consequences.

Yoo, *War by Other Means, An Insider's Account of the War on Terror* 170. The *Washington Post* reported that Yoo stated Addington had also contributed: "In an interview, Yoo said that Addington, as well as Gonzales and deputy White House counsel Timothy E. Flanigan, contributed to the analysis." Gellman and Becker, "Pushing the Envelope on Presidential Power," *Wash. Post*, June 25, 2007, *available at* http://blog.washingtonpost.com/cheney/chapters/pushing_the_envelope_on_presi/.

438.In fact, in its first sentence, the memorandum seems to contemplate that it would apply to Guantanamo: "As we understand it, this question has arisen in the context of interrogations outside of the United States." August 1, 2002 Torture Memorandum at 1. John Yoo, who was one of the preparers of this document, would later explain that it was written for the CIA, not for the Defense Department. *See, e.g., Department of Justice to Guantanamo Bay: Administration Lawyers and Administration Interrogation Rules (Part III): Hearing before the Subcomm. on the Constitution, Civil Rights, and Civil Liberties, H.Comm. on the Judiciary*, 110th Cong. (June 26, 2008) (written testimony of John Yoo). The same principles set forth in this memorandum would be repeated in a March 2003 memorandum written specifically to respond to a request by the Department of Defense.

439.Memorandum for Alberto R. Gonzales, Counsel to the President, *Re: Standards of Conduct for Interrogation under 18 U.S.C. §§ 2340-2340A*," By Jay S. Bybee, Assistant Att'y Gen.l, Dept. of Justice, Aug. 1, 2002, at 6.

440."Waterboarding" was described in *The Washington Post* as follows:

> The more accurate definition would be "drowning." That term is used to describe several interrogation techniques. The victim may be immersed in water, have water forced into the nose and mouth, or have water poured onto material placed over the face so that the liquid is inhaled or swallowed. The media usually characterize the practice as "simulated drowning." That's incorrect. To be effective, waterboarding is usually real drowning that simulates death. That is, the victim experiences the sensations of drowning: struggle, panic, breath-holding, swallowing, vomiting, taking water

into the lungs and, eventually, the same feeling of not being able to breathe that one experiences after being punched in the gut. The main difference is that the drowning process is halted. According to those who have studied waterboarding's effects, it can cause severe psychological trauma, such as panic attacks, for years.

Wallach, "Waterboarding Used to Be a Crime," *Wash. Post*, Nov. 4, 2007, at B1.

441.Luban, *Legal Ethics and Human Dignity*, excerpt found in *From the Department of Justice to Guantanamo Bay: Administration Lawyers and Administration Interrogation Rules, Part I: Hearing before the Subcommittee on the Constitution, Civil Rights, and Civil Liberties, House Committee on the Judiciary*, 110th Cong. 35-36 (May 6, 2008). In the accompanying footnote, Luban wrote:

> The commentator is Michael S. Moore, *Torture and the Balance of Evils*, 23 Israel L. Rev. 280, 323 (1989). Here is what OLC says: "Leading scholarly commentators believe that interrogation of such individuals that might violate [the anti-torture statute] would be justified under the doctrine of self-defense." [citation to Moore.] And here is what Moore actually says on the page OLC cites: *"The literal law of self-defense is not available to justify their torture*. But the principle uncovered as the moral basis of the defense may be applicable. . . . " [emphasis added by Luban]. OLC states that "the doctrine of self-defense" would justify torture, where Moore says, quite literally, the opposite. Note also the differences between OLC's assertive "would be justified" and Moore's cautious "may be applicable."

Id. at 35 (first brackets in text, second and third brackets added). Similarly, the Torture Memo claimed that the "necessity defense" could be a defense to a torture prosecution, that is, that otherwise criminal conduct (torture) could be justified where undertaken to prevent a greater harm. Professor Luban pointed out the result-oriented and politically self-serving quality to that conclusion by noting that the authors of the Torture Memorandum carefully included language to assure that the "necessity" principles could not be used to justify abortions – hardly the issue.

> [T]he Bybee Memo's authors were not content to argue for the possibility of the necessity defense. They also threw in an argument that even though the necessity defense is available to torturer, it would not necessarily be available in cases of abortion to save a woman's life. [footnote omitted]. **At this point, the partisan political nature of the document becomes too obvious to ignore. It is the moment when the clock strikes thirteen**. Opposition to abortion was an article of faith in the Ashcroft Justice Department, and apparently the OLC lawyers decided to try

for a "two-fer" – not only providing a necessity defense for torture, but throwing in a clever hip-check to forestall any possibility that their handiwork might be commandeered to justify life-saving abortions is a legislature ever voted to outlaw them. Even abortion opponents are likely to balk at the thought that torture might be a lesser evil than abortion to save a mother's life. But this was the conclusion that the OLC aimed to preserve.

Id. at 38 (emphasis added).

442. August 1, 2002 Torture Memorandum at 34-35. This particular principle was directly attributed to Addington. *The Washington Post* reported:

> The vice president's lawyer advocated what was considered the memo's most radical claim: that the president may authorize any interrogation method, even if it crosses the line into torture. U.S. and treaty laws forbidding any person to "commit torture," that passage stated, "do not apply" to the commander in chief, because Congress "may no more regulate the President's ability to detain and interrogate enemy combatants than it may regulate his ability to direct troop movements on the battlefield."

Gellman and Becker, "Pushing the Envelope on Presidential Power," *Wash. Post*, June 25, 2007, *available at* http://blog.washingtonpost.com/cheney/chapters/pushing_the_envelope_on_presi/.

443. This exchange has been widely reported. *See, e.g.*, Hentoff, "Architect of Torture," *The Village Voice*, July 10, 2007, *available at* http://www.villagevoice.com/news/0728,hentoff,77169,6.html, where Hentoff stated that he had discussed the matter with Professor Cassel, who had confirmed the exchange occurred.

There appears to be no limiting principle to Mr. Yoo's view as to the reach of the president's Commander-in-Chief power. If he cannot constrained by law or treaty from ordering the crushing of a child's testicles, then what limit does exist? What is the principled line that Yoo can possibly draw between crushing a child's testicles and ordering summary executions, or the execution of family members, or the execution of U.S. citizens who may be family members, if the president deems it to be part of his Commander-in-Chief powers and necessary as a component of an interrogation program? Could the president suspend the Constitutional amendments that limit him to two terms if he deemed that it was necessary to do so in order to effectively wage a war? Could the president declare a political opponent an "enemy combatant" because that person undermined his ability to wage war – for example, by voting against a weapons program – and order his or her incarceration? If so, what would be the grounds available for the detainee to contest his or her incarceration?

Yale Law School Dean Harold Koh expressed the same concern in his testimony at

Alberto Gonzales's confirmation hearing for Attorney General:

> But if the President has the sole constitutional authority to sanction torture, and Congress has no power to interfere, it is unclear why the President should not also have unfettered authority to license genocide or other violations of fundamental human rights. In a stunning failure of lawyerly craft, the August 1, 2002 OLC Memorandum nowhere mentions the landmark Supreme Court decision in Youngstown Steel & Tube Co. v. Sawyer, where Justice Jackson's concurrence spelled out clear limits on the President's constitutional powers.

Confirmation Hearing on the Nomination Of Alberto R. Gonzales to Be Attorney General of the United States: Hearing Before the S. Comm. on the Judiciary, 109th Cong. (2005) (Statement of Harold Hongju Koh, Dean, Yale Law School), *available at* http://www.law.yale.edu/documents/pdf/KohTestimony.pdf. In a footnote, Koh notes that under the reasoning of the August 1, 2002 Torture Memorandum, "it is hard to explain why Saddam Hussein could not similarly authorize torture under his parallel Commander in Chief power." *Youngstown Steel* is discussed further in the Preface to this Report.

444. Memorandum Opinion for the Deputy Attorney General, *Legal Standards Applicable Under U.S.C. §§ 2340-2340A*, By Daniel Levin, Acting Assistant Att'y Gen., (Dec. 30, 2004), *available at* http://www.justice.gov/olc/18usc23402340a2.htm.

445. *See* "Senate Armed Services Committee Inquiry into the Treatment of Detainees in U.S. Custody," p. xvi, *available at* http://levin.senate.gov/newsroom/supporting/2008/Detainees.121108.pdf.

446. Memorandum for [Redacted], *Interrogation of [Redacted]*, From Jay S. Bybee, Assistant Att'y Gen., Dept. of Justice (Aug. 1, 2002), *available at* http://www.aclu.org/pdfs/safefree/cia_3686_001.pdf.

447. Document Titled "TOP SECRET//[Redacted]," Aug. 4, 2004, *available at* http://www.aclu.org/pdfs/safefree/cia_3685_001.pdf.

448. Zubaydah was waterboarded at a secret location, not Guantanamo.

449. As discussed throughout this report, the Administration had different detention and interrogation rules or "programs" for the CIA and the military, as well as different rules for the military in Guantanamo and in Iraq and Afghanistan. The fact that the CIA operated differently was explicitly acknowledged by the Administration:

> Fewer than 100 terrorists have been detained by the CIA as part of this program....This program has involved the limited use of

alternative interrogation methods judged to be necessary in certain cases because hardened al Qaeda operatives are trained to resist the types of methods approved in the Army Field Manual which governs military interrogations....

These alternative interrogation methods have been used with fewer than one-third of the terrorists who have ever been detained in the program. Certain of the methods have been used on far fewer still. In particular, as General Hayden has now disclosed, the procedure known as waterboarding was used on only three individuals and was never used after March 2003.

Oversight Hearing on the Justice Department's Office of Legal Counsel before the Subcomm. on the Constitution, Civil Rights, and Civil Liberties of the H. Comm. on the Judiciary, 110th Cong. 6, (Feb. 14, 2008) (statement of Steven G. Bradbury, Principal Deputy Assistant Att'y Gen., Office of Legal Counsel, U.S. Dept. of Justice). This difference was also acknowledged in President Bush's Order February 7, 2002, which directed only that the "Armed Forces [*i.e.*, not the CIA]. . . treat the detainees humanely," and in the Administration's interpretation of the Military Commissions Act that, even if understood as constraining the Armed Forces in the use of certain interrogation techniques, was interpreted as not constraining the CIA.

450.*Interview of Vice President Dick Cheney by John Karl* (ABC News television broadcast Dec. 16, 2008) *available at* http://abcnews.go.com/Politics/story?id=6464697&page=1 (emphasis added).

451.The Senate Armed Services Committee reported that the Guantanamo trip occurred a week after a group of Guantanamo interrogators attended training at Fort Bragg, North Carolina conducted by instructors from JPRA's SERE school. "Senate Armed Services Committee Inquiry into the Treatment of Detainees in U.S. Custody," at xvi, *available at* http://levin.senate.gov/newsroom/supporting/2008/Detainees.121108.pdf.

452.Sands, "The Green Light," *Vanity Fair*, May 2008, *available at* http://www.vanityfair.com/politics/features/2008/05/guantanamo200805?currentPage=1.

453.Memorandum for Commander, United States Southern Command, *Counter-Resistance Strategies*, From Maj. Gen. Michael Dunlavey (Oct. 11, 2002), *available at* http://www.torturingdemocracy.org/documents/20021011.pdf.

454."Senate Armed Services Committee Inquiry into the Treatment of Detainees in U.S. Custody," at xviii-xix, *available at* http://levin.senate.gov/newsroom/supporting/2008/Detainees.121108.pdf.

455.Memorandum for Commander, Joint Chiefs of Staff, *Counter-Resistance Techniques*, From Gen. James T. Hill (Oct. 25, 2002).

456. "Senate Armed Services Committee Inquiry into the Treatment of Detainees in U.S. Custody," at xvii-xix, *available at* http://levin.senate.gov/newsroom/supporting/2008/Detainees.121108.pdf.

457. Memorandum for the Secretary of Defense [Donald Rumsfeld], *Counter-Resistance Techniques*, From W. J. Haynes II, General Counsel, Department of Defense (Nov. 27, 2002), *available at* http://www.gwu.edu/~nsarchiv/NSAEBB/NSAEBB127/02.12.02.pdf and http://www.torturingdemocracy.org/documents/20021127-1.pdf.

458. *Id.* (emphasis added)

459. "Senate Armed Services Committee Inquiry into the Treatment of Detainees in U.S. Custody," at xx, *available at* http://levin.senate.gov/newsroom/supporting/2008/Detainees.121108.pdf (emphasis added).

460. Memorandum for Commander, US SOUTHCOM, *Counter-Resistance Techniques*, From Donald Rumsfeld, Secretary of the Defense (Jan. 15, 2003), *available at* http://www.gwu.edu/~nsarchiv/NSAEBB/NSAEBB127/03.01.15.pdf.

461. Memorandum to Secretary of Defense Donald Rumsfeld, *Detainee Interrogations in the Global War on Terrorism: Assessment of Legal, Historical, Policy, and Operational Considerations*, From Pentagon Working Group (Mar. 6, 2003), excerpts available at http://news.findlaw.com/hdocs/docs/torture/30603wgrpt.html> ; *see also* Bravin, "Pentagon Report Set Framework for Use of Torture," *Wall St. J.*, June 7, 2004, at A1.

462. Memorandum for William J. Haynes, II, General Counsel, Department of Defense, *Re: Military Interrogation of Alien Unlawful Combatants Held Outside the United States*, from John C. Yoo, Deputy Assistant Att'y Gen., Dept. of Justice (Mar. 14, 2003) [hereinafter "March 14, 2003 Torture Memorandum"].

463. As to the reach of the AUMF, Yoo noted: "[Congress] has recognized the President's constitutional power to use force to prevent and deter future attacks both within and outside the United States." March 14, 2003 Torture Memorandum at 3. As noted, the AUMF was limited to authorizing force against the perpetrators of the 9/11 attacks, and was certainly not an open-ended authorization to use force anywhere for any purpose, including that of "pre-empting" other terrorist attacks "within and outside the United States." Mr. Yoo himself, in his September 25, 2001, War Powers Memorandum specifically described the limitations of the AUMF.

464. March 14 2003 Torture Memorandum at 3 (emphasis added). One reason that Mr. Yoo may have drafted this particular memo to encompass the president's ability to exercise war powers (including torture) inside the United States was his knowledge that U.S. citizen Jose Padilla had been arrested in Chicago, placed into military custody, and subject to such harsh interrogation.

465. March 14, 2003 Torture Memorandum at 4 (emphasis added).

360

466. National security scholar Deborah Pearlstein of the Woodrow Wilson School of Public Affairs commented on a similar passage in the March 14, 2003 Torture Memorandum:

> Of all the passages in the [March 14, 2003 Torture Memorandum] worthy of dissection, I still can't get past the following:
>
> *Because of the secret nature of al Qaeda's operations, obtaining advance information about the identity of al Qaeda operatives and their plans may prove to be the only way to prevent direct attacks on the United States. Interrogation of captured al Qaeda operatives could provide that information; indeed, in many cases interrogation may be the only method to obtain it.* [citing March 14, 2003 Torture Memorandum at 4] (emphasis added by Pearlstein).
>
> No citation to authority. No offer of any logical or factual support for the claim. No reference to administration policy documents, security analyses, military or intelligence risk assessments, or any particularly evident basis for the statements of any kind. Just Yoo.
>
> Hard to say what bothers me most here. One possibility is just the painful internal contradiction. John Yoo (among others) has devoted so much time to trumpeting the importance of judicial deference to executive expertise. Too bad it turns out that the only "executive" expertise evident here is Yoo's own take on what might be effective in preventing future attacks. Can't particularly think of anything other than torturing captured detainees. So that must be the only way.
>
> Maybe it's that the passage appears not in some foreign policy article or popular op-ed, in which citation to any supporting basis for such assertions wouldn't be expected – but rather in a legal memo, as part of a legal analysis of the president's powers as commander in chief – to which any first-year law firm associate would respond by just hitting the Alt-F8 macro demanding the author "state the basis" of the claim. Or maybe it's the entirely illusory nature of the proposition. We "may be" all about to explode. Or not. Just wanted to throw that out there as a possibility as the reader contemplates whether to buy into the otherwise, uh, unusual, legal analysis that follows.

Pearlstein, "Stuck on Yoo," Slate.com, Apr. 3, 2008, *available at* http://www.slate.com/blogs/blogs/convictions/archive/2008/04/03/stuck-on-yoo.aspx.

467.March 14, 2003 Torture Memorandum at 6.

468.*Id.* at 8 n. 10. Mr. Yoo cited to an October 23, 2001, memorandum for this remarkable proposition. This is typical of the secret law developed within the Department of Justice, where certain legal propositions acquire internal legitimacy by sheer repetition.

469.*Id.* at 11.

470.*Id.* at 14.

471.*Id.* at 16.

472.*Id.* at 16.

473..The torture laws, 18 U.S.C. §§ 2340, 2340A, and 2340B, were enacted as section 506 of "Foreign Relations Authorization Act, fiscal Years 1994 and 1995," Pub. L. 103-236, 108 Stat. 382, Apr. 30, 1994, titled "Torture Convention Implementation."

474.Convention Against Torture and Other Cruel, Inhuman or Degrading Treatment or Punishment, 1465 U.N.T.S. 85, Art. 3, S. Treaty Doc. No. 20, 100th Cong., 2d Sess., (1988) (emphasis added) , *available at* http://www.hrweb.org/legal/cat.html.

475.*Id.*

476.18 U.S.C. § 2340A(a).

477.It is one thing for John Yoo to say that the issue as to whether it applies to the military is "open to question" or "debatable" or some other euphemism to suggest that in his view there may be doubt, but the assertion that Congress displayed no intent to apply the statute to military personnel flies against every reasonable review of the historical record.

478.March 14, 2003 Torture Memorandum at 18-20.

479.Memorandum to Commander, U.S. Southern Command ,*Counter-Resistance Techniques in the War on Terrorism*, from Donald Rumsfeld, Secretary of the Defense,(Apr. 16, 2003), *available at* http://www.gwu.edu/~nsarchiv/NSAEBB/NSAEBB127/03.04.16.pdf.

480. Memorandum Opinion for the Deputy Attorney General, *Legal Standards Applicable Under U.S.C. §§ 2340-2340A*, By Daniel Levin, Acting Assistant Attorney General, (Dec. 30, 2004), *available at* http://www.justice.gov/olc/18usc23402340a2.htm. Footnote 8 of that memorandum reads as follows:

> While we have identified various disagreements with the August
> 2002 Memorandum, we have reviewed this Office's prior opinions
> addressing issues involving treatment of detainees and do not

believe that any of their conclusions would be different under the standards set forth in this memorandum.

481. *The Role of the FBI at Guantanamo Bay: Hearing Before the Subcomm. on International Organizations, Human Rights, and Oversight of the H. Comm. on Foreign Affairs*, 110th Cong. 6 (June 4, 2008) (statement of Glenn A. Fine, Inspector General, Department of Justice), *available at* http://www.usdoj.gov/oig/testimony/t0806/final.pdf. *See also Interrogation Log, Detainee 063*, reprinted by *Time Magazine*, at http://www.time.com/time/2006/log/log.pdf. The Senate Armed Services Committee also described aspects of the al-Khatani interrogation in the context of the issues associated with the adoption of harsh interrogation techniques as follows:

> At about the same time [approximately December 2002], a dispute over the use of aggressive techniques was raging at GTMO over the interrogation of Mohammed al-Khatani, a high value detainee. Personnel from CITF and the Federal Bureau of Investigation (FB) had registered strong opposition, [sic] to interrogation techniques proposed for use on Khatani and made those concerns known to the DoD General Counsel's office. Despite those objections, an interrogation plan that included aggressive techniques was approved. The interrogation itself, which actually began on November 23, 2002, a week before the Secretary's December 2, 2002 grant of blanket authority for the use of aggressive techniques, continued through December and into mid-January 2003.

"Senate Armed Services Committee Inquiry into the Treatment of Detainees in U.S. Custody," at xx, *available at* http://levin.senate.gov/newsroom/supporting/2008/Detainees.121108.pdf. The interrogation was described as follows: "While key documents relating to the interrogation remain classified, published accounts indicate that military working dogs had been used against Khatani. He had also been deprived of adequate sleep for weeks on end, stripped naked, subjected to loud music, and made to wear a leash and perform dog tricks." *Id.* at xxi.

482. *The Role of the FBI at Guantanamo Bay: Hearing Before the House Committee on Foreign Affairs Subcommittee on International Organizations, Human Rights, and Oversight*, 110th Cong. 8 (June 4, 2008) (statement of Glenn A. Fine, Inspector General, Department of Justice), *available at* http://www.usdoj.gov/oig/testimony/t0806/final.pdf.

483. *See*, *e.g.*, Center for Constitutional Rights, "Report on Torture and Cruel, Inhuman, and Degrading Treatment of Prisoners at Guantanamo Bay, Cuba" (July 2006), *available at* http://ccrjustice.org/files/Report_ReportOnTorture.pdf.

484. "CJTF-7" stands for the "Combined Joint Task Force 7," referring to the United States Army in Iraq.

485.Final Report of the Independent Panel to Review Department of Defense Operations, Hon. James R. Schlesinger, Chairman, 37 (Aug. 24 2004) (emphasis added), *available at* http://www.defenselink.mil/news/Aug2004/d20040824finalreport.pdf.

486.Hess, "Iraqi Detainee Interrogations Detailed," *Boston.Globe*, Sep. 26, 2008, *available at* http://www.boston.com/news/nation/washington/articles/2008/09/26/iraqi_detainee_interrogations_detailed/.

487.*Treatment of Detainees in U.S. Custody: Hearing Before the S. Comm. on Armed Services*, 110th Cong. 3, 5 (2008) (statement of Steven M. Kleinman, Colonel, USAFR), *available at* http://media.washingtonpost.com/wp-srv/nation/documents/Kleinman-092508.pdf.

488.*Interview with Deputy Secretary of Defense Paul Wolfowitz* (Pentagon Channel television broadcast May 4, 2004), *transcript available at* http://www.defenselink.mil/transcripts/transcript.aspx?transcriptid=2970. Wolfowitz was asked about the Abu Ghraib scandal:

> Q: Is this going to effect what we're doing over there?
>
> Mr. Wolfowitz: Of course, it has a negative effect. That's why it's such a disservice to everyone else, that a few bad apples can create some large problems for everybody.

489."Senate Armed Services Committee Inquiry into the Treatment of Detainees in U.S. Custody," at xx, xxi, *available at* http://levin.senate.gov/newsroom/supporting/2008/Detainees.121108.pdf.

490.*See, e.g.*, Crawford, "Sources: Top Bush Advisors Approved 'Enhanced Interrogation" Detailed Discussions Were Held About Techniques to Use on al Qaeda Suspects," ABCNews .com, Apr. 9, 2008, *available at* http://abcnews.go.com/TheLaw/LawPolitics/story?id=4583256.

491.*Id.* Ashcroft declined to be interviewed by Justice Department Inspector General Glenn Fine as to issues associated with the FBI's role in interrogation policy.

492.Priest, "Justice Dept. Memo Says Torture 'May Be Justified,'" *Wash. Post,* June 13, 2004, *available at* http://www.washingtonpost.com/wp-dyn/articles/A38894-2004Jun13.html .

493.The Detainee Treatment Act of 2005 was made part of the Defense Department Authorization Act, Title X, Pub. L. 109–148, 119 Stat. 2739.

494.The phrase "cruel, inhuman or degrading treatment" was defined in subsection (d) as "cruel, unusual, and inhumane treatment or punishment prohibited by the Fifth, Eighth, and Fourteenth Amendments to the Constitution of the United States, as defined in the United States Reservations Declarations and Understandings to the United Nations Convention Against Torture and Other Forms of Cruel, Inhuman or Degrading Treatment or Punishment done at New York,

December 10, 1984.

495.As discussed in connection with the discussion of detention policies, the DTA also provided various "combatant status review" procedures to be used with the Guantanamo detainees, and expressly sought to limit the Guantanamo detainees' rights to seek *habeas corpus* in the federal courts.   DTA, §§ 1005(a) and (b) (combatant status review procedures), and 1006(d) (relating to *habeas*).

496."President's Statement on Signing of H.R. 2863, the "Department of Defense, Emergency Supplemental Appropriations to Address Hurricanes in the Gulf of Mexico, and Pandemic Influenza Act, 2006," Dec. 30, 2005, *available at* http://www.whitehouse.gov/news/releases/2005/12/20051230-8.html

497.The Military Commissions Act of 2006 (MCA), Pub. L. No. 109-366, 120 Stat. 2600.

498.*See* MCA, Sec. 3, creating new Title 47, sec. 948r, which provides, in pertinent part:

* * *

(c) Statements Obtained Before Enactment of Detainee Treatment Act of 2005- A statement obtained before December 30, 2005 (the date of the enactment of the Defense Treatment Act of 2005) in which the degree of coercion is disputed may be admitted only if the military judge finds that--

(1) the totality of the circumstances renders the statement reliable and possessing sufficient probative value; and

(2) the interests of justice would best be served by admission of the statement into evidence.

(d) Statements Obtained After Enactment of Detainee Treatment Act of 2005- A statement obtained on or after December 30, 2005 (the date of the enactment of the Defense Treatment Act of 2005) in which the degree of coercion is disputed may be admitted only if the military judge finds that--

(1) the totality of the circumstances renders the statement reliable and possessing sufficient probative value;

(2) the interests of justice would best be served by admission of the statement into evidence; and

(3) the interrogation methods used to obtain the
statement do not amount to cruel, inhuman, or
degrading treatment prohibited by section 1003 of
the Detainee Treatment Act of 2005.

499.The effort to strip *habeas corpus* protections from Guantanamo detainees is discussed in the Detention section of this report.

500.152 Cong. Rec. S10246 (daily ed. Sept. 27, 2006) (statement of Sen. Warner).

501.152 Cong. Rec. S10254 (daily ed. Sept. 27, 2006) (statement of Sen. Leahy) (emphasis added).

502.Press Release, "Senators McCain and Graham Offer Support for Attorney General Nominee [Judge Mukasey],"Nov. 1, 2007, *available at* http://mccain.senate.gov/public/index.cfm?FuseAction=PressOffice.PressReleases&ContentReco rd_id=fca2e817-7e9c-9af9-7d5b-55ef66eeb23f&Region_id=&Issue_id.

503."President Thanks Senate for Passage of Military Commissions Act of 2006," *available at* http://www.whitehouse.gov/news/releases/2006/09/20060928-15.html .

504."Intelligence Authorization Act for Fiscal Year 2008," Enrolled as Agreed to or Passed by Both House and Senate, H.R. 2082, 110th Cong. The Act passed the House by a 222-199 vote on December 13, 2007, passed the Senate by a 51-45 vote on February 13, 2007. The House failed to override the veto, 2/3 being required, by a vote of 225-188 on March 11, 2008.

505."[President George W. Bush's] Message to the House of Representatives," Mar. 8, 2008, *available at* http://www.whitehouse.gov/news/releases/2008/03/20080308-1.html.

506. *See, e.g.*, Mazzetti, "CIA Destroyed Tapes of Interrogations," *N.Y. Times*, December 6, 2007, *available at* http://www.nytimes.com/2007/12/06/washington/06cnd-intel.html.

507.*Id.*

508.*Id.*

509.*Id.*

510.Mazzetti, "C.I.A. Was Urged to Keep Interrogation Videotapes," *N.Y. Times*, Dec. 8, 2007, *available at* http://www.nytimes.com/2007/12/08/washington/08intel.html .

511.*See, e.g.*, Mazzetti, "CIA Destroyed Tapes of Interrogations," *N.Y. Times*, Dec. 6, 2007, *available at* http://www.nytimes.com/2007/12/06/washington/06cnd-intel.html .

512.*Id.*

513. Johnston, "Bush Lawyers Discussed Fate of C.I.A. Tapes," *N.Y. Times*, Dec.19, 2007, available at http://www.nytimes.com/2007/12/19/washington/19intel.html .

514. *Id.*

515. Torture and the Cruel, Inhuman and Degrading Treatment of Detainees: the Effectiveness and Consequences of 'Enhanced' Interrogation, Hearing before Subcomm. on Constitution, Civil Rights, and Civil Liberties of the H. Comm. on the Judiciary, 110th Cong. 2 (2007).

516. *Torture and the Cruel, Inhuman and Degrading Treatment of Detainees: the Effectiveness and Consequences of 'Enhanced' Interrogation, Hearing before Subcomm. on Constitution, Civil Rights, and Civil Liberties of the H. Comm. on the Judiciary*, 110th Cong. 22 (2007) (statement of former SERE instructor Malcolm Nance) (emphasis added).

517. *Id.* at 29 (statement of Col. Steven Kleinman, U.S. Air Force).

518. *Id.* at 30 (statement of Col. Steven Kleinman, U.S. Air Force).

519. *Id.* at 36 (statement of Amrit Singh, Esq., American Civil Liberties Union).

520. *Id.* at 37.

521. *Id.* at 51-52 (testimony of Col. Steven Kleinman, U.S. Air Force).

522. *Id.* at 67 (statement of former SERE instructor Malcolm Nance).

523. *Hearing on the Applicability of Federal Criminal Laws to the Interrogation of Detainees Before the H.Comm. on the Judiciary*, 110th Cong. (Dec. 20, 2007) (unpublished transcript at 110) (testimony of David Addington, Chief of Staff to Vice President).

524. *Id.* unpublished transcript at 20 (statement of Prof. Steve Saltzburg, G.W. University).

525. *Id.* unpublished transcript at 41 (statement of Dir. Elisa Massimino, Human Rights Watch).

526. *Id.* unpublished transcript at 57-59 (statement of Prof. Steve Saltzburg, G.W. University).

527. *Id.* unpublished transcript at 41 (statement of Dir. Elisa Massimino, Human Rights Watch).

528. In a statement issued January 2008, Chairman Conyers stated:

> While I certainly agree that these matters warrant an immediate
> criminal investigation, it is disappointing that the Attorney General
> has stepped outside the Justice Department's own regulations and
> declined to appoint a more independent special counsel in this
> matter. Because of this action, the Congress and the American
> people will be denied – as they were in the Valerie Plame matter –

any final report on the investigation.

Equally disappointing is the limited scope of this investigation, which appears limited to the destruction of two tapes. The government needs to scrutinize what other evidence may have been destroyed beyond the two tapes, as well as the underlying allegations of misconduct associated with the interrogations.

The Justice Department's record over the past seven years of sweeping the Administration's misconduct under the rug has left the American public with little confidence in the Administration's ability to investigate itself. Nothing less than a special counsel with a full investigative mandate will meet the tests of independence, transparency and completeness. Appointment of a special counsel will allow our nation to begin to restore our credibility and moral standing on these issues.

Press Release, H. Comm. on the Judiciary, "Conyers Demands that DOJ Appoint Real Special Counsel," Jan. 2, 2008, *available at* http://judiciary.house.gov/news/010208.html.

529.General Michael Hayden, Director of the CIA, had testified as follows:

[I]n the life of the CIA detention program we've detained fewer than a hundred people. Of the people detained, fewer than a third have had any of what we call the enhanced interrogation techniques used against them. Let me make it very clear and to state so officially in front of this committee that waterboarding has been used on only three detainees. It was used on Khalid Sheikh Mohammed, it was used on Abu Zubaydah, and it was used on [Abd al-Rahim al-Nashiri]. The CIA has not used waterboarding for almost five years. We used it against these three high value detainees because of the circumstances of the time.

Annual Worldwide Threat Assessment: Hearing Before the S. Select Intelligence Comm., 110th Cong. 24-25 (2008) (statement of Gen. Michael Hayden, Director of National Intelligence), *available at* http://www.dni.gov/testimonies/20080205_transcript.pdf .

530.*Hearing on Oversight of the Department of Justice: Hearing Before the House Comm. on the Judiciary*, 110th Cong. (Feb. 7, 2008) (statement of Attorney General Michael Mukasey) (unrevised transcript at 17-18) (emphasis added).

531.Rep. Jan Schakowsky, Rep. Conyers, and 54 other Members of the House subsequently sent a letter to Attorney General Mukasey on June 6, 2008, asking that he "appoint a special counsel to investigate whether the Bush Administration's policies regarding the interrogation of detainees have violated federal criminal laws." That letter referenced confirmed interrogation practices, detainee deaths in custody, and the abuses reported at Abu Ghraib. Letter from Rep. Jan Schakowksy, et al., to Michael Mukasey, Attorney General (June 6, 2008) *available at* http://www.house.gov/schakowsky/Letter%20to%20Mukasey%20Special%20Counsel.pdf.

532.*Hearing on Oversight of the Federal Bureau of Investigation: Hearing before the H. Comm. on the Judiciary*, 110th Cong. (Apr. 23, 2008) (testimony of Dir. Robert S. Mueller) (unrevised transcript at 69).

533.*Id.* (testimony of Dir. Robert S. Mueller) (unrevised transcript at 69).

534.*Id.* (testimony of Dir. Robert S. Mueller) (unrevised transcript at 77).

535.*Id.* (testimony of Dir. Robert S. Mueller) (unrevised transcript at 82).

536.*Id.* (testimony of Dir. Robert S. Mueller) (unrevised transcript at 95-97)

537.See, e.g., Statement by the Press Secretary (Ari Fleischer), April 2, 2002, *available at* http://www.whitehouse.gov/news/releases/2002/04/20020402-2.html. The other two men were captured subsequent to the August 1, 2002 memoranda authorizing waterboarding. Al-Nashiri was captured in the United Arab Emirates in November 2002, and Khalid Sheikh Mohammed was captured in Rawalpindi, Pakistan on March 1, 2003. *See, e.g.*, President George W. Bush, Remarks at signing of National Defense Authorization Act, (Dec. 2, 2002), *available at* http://www.whitehouse.gov/news/releases/2002/12/20021202-8.html (discussing capture of al-Nashiri), and Press Briefing by Ari Fleischer, (Mar. 3, 2003), *available at* http://www.whitehouse.gov/news/releases/2003/03/20030303-3.html (discussing capture of Khalid Sheik Mohammed)).

538.*From the Department of Justice to Guantanamo Bay: Administration lawyers and Administration Interrogation Rules, Part V: Hearing before the H. Comm. on the Judiciary*, 110th Cong. (July 17, 2008) (testimony of former Attorney General John Ashcroft) (unrevised transcript at 15-16).

539.*Hearing on Oversight of the Department of Justice: Hearing before the H. Comm. on the Judiciary*, 110th Cong. (July 23, 2008) (testimony of Att. Gen. Michael Mukasey) (unrevised transcript at 33-34).

540.*Justice Department's Office of Legal Counsel: Hearing before the Subcomm. on the Constitution, Civil Rights, and Civil Liberties of the H. Comm. on the Judiciary*, 110th Cong. (2008).

541.*Id.* at 17-18 (2008) (testimony of Steven Bradbury, Principal Deputy Assistant Attorney General, Department of Justice).

542.Shane, Johnston, and Risen, "Secret U.S. Endorsement of Severe Interrogations," *N. Y. Times*, Oct. 3, 2007. As to the efforts by the Judiciary Committee to obtain access to the documents setting forth the interrogation rules , the following colloquy is instructive:

Mr. Nadler: We're not talking about public disclosure, we're talking about disclosure to this Committee.

Mr. Bradbury: I understand that. And my point today is we recognize your interest, we recognize the unique nature of this issue, the controversial nature of this issue. We do recognize the extraordinary –

Mr. Nadler: But what is– you keep not answering my question. What is the legal basis for your assertion fo your ability to have discretion abut whether to give those document to us?

Mr. Bradbury: Mr. Chairman, I'm not asserting any legal basis.

Mr. Nadler: If there is not legal basis, then you must given them to us.

Mr. Bradbury: It's not a decision for me, but I am saying–I am saying that the Attorney General, in close consultation with the President, are giving careful consideration –

Mr. Nadler: Are you head of the Office of Legal Counsel?

Mr. Bradbury: Yes

* * * * * * *

Mr. Nadler: So you have advised the Attorney General tha t they have the legal right to withhold these documents from this Committee?

Mr. Bradbury: I don't –

Mr. Nadler: Or that they don't have the legal right?

Mr. Bradbury: Mr. Chairman, the Executive Branch does have the legal right to protect the confidentiality of deliberations of the Executive Branch and sensitive documents –

Mr. Nadler: The Executive Branch, you're saying, has the unlimited right, in its own discretion, to withhold any document because of

370

confidentiality?

> Mr. Bradbury: I'm absolutely not saying that . . .

Justice Department's Office of Legal Counsel: Hearing before the Subcomm. on the Constitution, Civil Rights, and Civil Liberties of the H.Comm. on the Judiciary, 110th Cong., at 16 (2008) (testimony of Steven Bradbury, Principal Deputy Assistant Attorney General, Department of Justice).

543.Letter from Rep. John Conyers, Jr., Chairman, H. Comm. on the Judiciary, and Rep. Jerrold Nadler, Chairman, Subcommittee on the Constitution, Civil Rights and Civil Liberties, to Michael Mukasey, Attorney General (April 29, 2008), *available at* http://judiciary.house.gov/news/pdfs/Conyers-Nadler080429.pdf.

544.Letter and Subpoena from John Conyers, Jr., Chairman, H. Comm. on the Judiciary to Michael Mukasey, Attorney General (June 27, 2008), *available at* http://judiciary.house.gov/news/pdfs/Conyers080627.pdf.

545.*Department of Justice to Guantanamo Bay: Administration Lawyers and Administration Interrogation Rules (Part I): Hearing before the Subcomm. on the Constitution, Civil Rights, and Civil Liberties of the H.Comm. on the Judiciary*, 110th Cong. (2008).

546.*See, e.g., Department of Justice to Guantanamo Bay: Administration Lawyers and Administration Interrogation Rules (Part I): Hearing before the Subcomm. on the Constitution, Civil Rights, and Civil Liberties of the H.Comm. on the Judiciary*,110th Cong., at 103-04 (2008) (testimony of Prof. David Luban, Georgetown University Law Center).

547.*Department of Justice to Guantanamo Bay: Administration Lawyers and Administration Interrogation Rules (Part I): Hearing before the Subcomm. on the Constitution, Civil Rights, and Civil Liberties of the H.Comm. on the Judiciary*, 110th Cong., at 120 (2008) (testimony of Prof. David Luban, Georgetown University Law Center).

548.*Id.*

549.*Id.* at 22 (2008) (testimony of Dan Levin, former Acting Assistant Att'y Gen, Dept. of Justice, Office of Legal Counsel).

550.*Id.* at 34-35 (2008) (testimony of Dan Levin, former Acting Assistant Att'y. Gen, Dept.. of Justice, Office of Legal Counsel).

551.*See generally*, Department of Justice to Guantanamo Bay: Administration Lawyers and Administration Interrogation Rules (Part II): Hearing before the Subcomm. on the Constitution, Civil Rights, and Civil Liberties of the H.Comm. on the Judiciary, 110th Cong., at 34-35 (2008) (testimony of Col. Lawrence Wilkinson, former Chief of Staff to Secretary of State Colin Powell) at 46-48.

552.*Department of Justice to Guantanamo Bay: Administration Lawyers and Administration Interrogation Rules (Part III): Hearing before the Subcomm. on the Constitution, Civil Rights, and Civil Liberties of the H.Comm. on the Judiciary*, 110th Cong. (2008).

553.*Id*. at 62 (2008) (testimony of Prof. John Yoo, former Deputy Assistant Attorney General, Dept. of Justice, Office of Legal Counsel).

554.*Department of Justice to Guantanamo Bay: Administration Lawyers and Administration Interrogation Rules (Part III): Hearing before the Subcomm. on the Constitution, Civil Rights, and Civil Liberties of the H.Comm. on the Judiciary*, 110th Cong., at 47 (2008) (testimony of Prof. John Yoo, former Deputy Assistant Attorney General, Dept. of Justice, Office of Legal Counsel).

555.*Id*. at 143-144 (2008) (testimony of Prof. John Yoo, former Deputy Assistant Attorney General, Dept. of Justice Office of Legal Counsel).

556.*Id*. at 31-32 (testimony of David Addington, Chief of Staff to Vice President).

557.*Id*. at 110 (testimony of David Addington, Chief of Staff to Vice President).

558.*See generally From the Department of Justice to Guantanamo Bay: Administration Lawyers and Administration Interrogation Rules (Part IV), Hearing before the Subcomm. on the Constitution, Civil Rights, and Civil Liberties of the H.Comm. on the Judiciary*, 110th Cong. (July 15, 2008) at 29-31 (testimony of Douglas Feith) (describing himself as "receptive to the view that Common Article 3 should bee used").

559.*Id*. at 52-54 (testimony of Douglas Feith).

560.*From the Department of Justice to Guantanamo Bay: Administration Lawyers and Administration Interrogation Rules (Part V): Hearing before the Subcomm. on the Constitution, Civil Rights, and Civil Liberties of the H.Comm. on the Judiciary*, 110th Cong. (July 17, 2008) (unrevised transcript at 127) (testimony of former Attorney General John Ashcroft).

561.*Id*. (emphasis added).

562.*See, e.g.*, Mayer, "Outsourcing Torture, the Secret History of America's "Extraordinary Rendition" program," *The New Yorker*, Feb. 14, 2005, *available at* http://www.newyorker.com/archive/2005/02/14/050214fa_fact6.

563.Condoleezza Rice, Secretary of State, Speech at Andrews Air Force Base, December 5, 2005, *available at* http://usinfo.state.gov/is/Archive/2005/Dec/05-978451.html.

564.Campbell, "September 11: Six Months on: U.S. Sends Suspects to Face Torture," *The Guardian*, Mar. 12, 2002, at 4 (quoting an unnamed U.S. diplomat as acknowledging "[a]fter September 11, [renditions] have been occurring all the time….It allows us to get information from terrorists in a way we can't do on U.S. soil.").

565.Jehl and Johnston, "Rule Change Lets C.I.A Freely Send Suspects Abroad to Jails," *N.Y. Times*, Mar. 6, 2005, at A1 ("former government officials say that since the Sept. 11 attacks, the CIA has flown 100 to 150 suspected terrorists from one foreign country to another, including to Egypt, Syria, Saudi Arabia, Jordan and Pakistan"); Satterthwaite & Fisher, *Beyond Guantanamo: Transfers to Torture One Year After Rasul v. Bush (2005)*, Ctr. For Human Rights & Global Justice, N.Y. Univ. Sch. of Law, *available at* http://www.chrgj.org/docs/Beyond%20Guantanamo%20Report%20FINAL.pdf (quoting Jane Mayer: "one source knowledgeable about the rendition program suggested that the number of renditions since September may have reached as high as several thousand).

566.Whitlock, "Europeans Investigate CIA Role in Abductions," *Wash. Post*, Mar. 13, 2005, at A1.

567.Priest and Gellman, "U.S. Decries Abuse but Defends Interrogations," *Wash. Post*, Dec. 26, 2002, at A1.

568.*See* Garcia, "Renditions: Constraints Imposed by Laws on Torture, No. RL32890" *Congressional Research Service Reports to Congress*, at 3 (Jan. 25, 2008); Mayer, "Outsourcing Torture," *New Yorker*, Feb. 14, 2005, http://www.newyorker.com/archive/2005/02/14/050214fa_fact6.

569.*See* Comm. on Int'l Human Rights of the NY Bar Ass'n and Ctr. For Human Rights and Global Justice, NYU School of Law, *Torture by Proxy: International and Domestic Law Applicable to "Extraordinary Renditions,"* at 15-16 (June 2006), *available at* http://www.chrgj.org/docs/TortureByProxy.pdf (providing examples of statements from FBI and CIA Directors Louis J. Freeh and George Tenet describing renditions to "justice" and their agencies role in this practice).

570.*See, e.g.,* Commission of Inquiry into the Actions of Canadian Officials in Relation to Maher Arar, *Report of the Events Relating to Maher Arar, Factual Background, Vol. I, II and Analysis and Recommendations*, Addendum, at 245 (2006), *available at* http://www.ararcommission.ca/eng/2007-08-08-addendum.pdf (Canadian officials in Washington "spoke of a trend they had noted lately that when the CIA or FBI cannot legally hold a terrorist subject, or with a target questioned in a firm manner, they have them rendered to countries willing to fulfill that role. He said Mr. Arar was a case in point."); Mayer, "Outsourcing Torture," *New Yorker*, Feb. 14, 2005, *available at* http://www.newyorker.com/archive/2005/02/14/050214fa_fact6.

571.For an analysis of the full range of legal constraints on extraordinary rendition, *see* Comm. On Int'l Human Rights of the NY Bar Ass'n and Ctr. For Human Rights and global Justice, NYU School of Law, *Torture by Proxy: International and Domestic Law Applicable to "Extraordinary Renditions,"* at 55-83 (as modified June 2006), http://www.chrgj.org/docs/TortureByProxy.pdf;

Margaret L. Satterthwaite, *Rendered Meaningless: Extraordinary Rendition and the Rule of Law*, 75 Geo. Wash. L.Rev. 1333 (2007); *Rendition to Torture: the Case of Maher Arar*, Joint Hearing before the Subcomm. on Int'l Orgs., Human Rights, and Oversight of the H. Comm. on Foreign Affairs and Subcomm on Constitution, Civil Rights, and Civil Liberties of the H. Comm. on the Judiciary, Serial No. 110-52, at 93-102, 110th Cong. (Oct. 18, 2007) (testimony of Professor David Cole); Michael John Garcia, *Renditions: Constraints Imposed by Laws on Torture*, Congressional Research Service Reports to Congress, No. RL32890, at 3 (Jan. 25, 2008).

572. U.N. Convention Against Torture and Other Cruel, Inhuman or Degrading Treatment or Punishment, opened for signature December 10, 1984, G.A. Res. 39/46, 39 UN GAOR Supp. No. 51, at 197, UN Doc. A/RES/39/708 (1984), entered into force June 26, 1987, 1465 U.N.T.S. 85, 23 I.L.M. 1027 (1984), as modified, 24 I.L.M. 535. Congress implemented U.S. obligations under Art. 3 through the Foreign Affairs Reform and Restructuring Act of 1998 (FARRA). Pub. L. No. 105-277, div. G, Title XXII, § 2242. In FARRA, Congress confirmed the non-refoulement obligation "not to expel, extradite, or otherwise effect the involuntary return of any person to a country in which there are substantial grounds for believing the person would be in danger of being subjected to torture, *regardless of whether the person is physically present in the United States*" (emphasis added).

573. 18 U.S.C. §§ 2340A, B. 18 U.S.C. § 2340A criminalizes torture committed outside the United States when the alleged offender is a U.S. national or is present in the United States Congress did not enact legislation expressly prohibiting torture *inside* the United States, as it presumed that existing federal and State criminal law (*e.g.*, laws prohibiting assault, manslaughter, and murder) would adequately cover acts within the United States.

574. *See* Michael John Garcia, *Renditions: Constraints Imposed by Laws on Torture*, Congressional Research Service Reports to Congress, No. RL32890, at 12, 19 (Jan. 25, 2008).

575. U.S. officials have taken the position that the Torture Convention's prohibition on transfers to countries where torture is likely does not apply extraterritorially (*i.e.*, does not apply to transfers of individuals from one foreign country to another) as a *matter of law* though reiterating that, as a *matter of policy,* the United States does not torture, or send individuals to countries that torture. *See, e.g.*, Letter from Richard A. Hertling, Acting Assistant Attorney General, U.S. Dept. Of Justice, to Rep. Jerrold Nadler, Chairman, Subcomm. on the Constitution, Civil Rights, and Civil Liberties, H. Comm. on the Judiciary (Feb. 26, 2007), at 4. Legal commentators have disagreed with the conclusion regarding the limited, territorial reach of the Torture Convention. *See, e.g.*, Comm. On Int'l Human Rights of the NY Bar Ass'n and Ctr. For Human Rights and global Justice, NYU School of Law, *Torture by Proxy: International and Domestic Law Applicable to "Extraordinary Renditions,"* at 50-54 (as modified June 2006) (concluding that "there appears to be a gap in the implementation of FARRA's policy directive to apply the principle of *non-refoulement* regardless of whether the person is physically present in the United States").

576.*See* Letter from Richard A. Hertling, Acting Assistant Attorney General, U.S. Dept. Of Justice, to Rep. Jerrold Nadler, Chairman, Subcomm. on the Constitution, Civil Rights, and Civil Liberties, H. Comm. on the Judiciary (Feb. 26, 2007), at 4. The Convention Against Torture is silent regarding the use of assurances as a valid means of fulfilling its obligations, but the Committee Against Torture, an independent body that monitors implementation of the Torture Convention, has expressed concern over the United States's use of such assurances and has recommended that the United States accept assurances only from countries who do not practice torture, and only if adequate monitoring can be assured. John Garcia, "Renditions: Constraints Imposed by Laws on Torture, No. RL32890," *Congressional Research Service Reports to Congress*, at 11, n.29 (Jan. 25, 2008).

577.Priest, "CIA's Assurances on Transferred Suspects Doubted," *Wash. Post*, Mar. 17, 2005, at A1.

578.*Id.* It also appears that the CIA is not required to obtain case-by-case approval from the White House or the State or Justice Departments before rendering a suspect to a foreign country. Jehl & Johnston, "Rule Change Lets C.I.A Freely Send Suspects Abroad to Jails," *N.Y. Times*, Mar. 6, 2005, at A1. This would mean that the "verbal" assurance received by a CIA station chief would not be reviewed and validated by the agencies with expertise and responsibility for monitoring and enforcing human rights laws.

579.Johnson, "At a Secret Interrogation, Dispute Flared Over Tactics," *N.Y. Times*, Sept. 10, 2006, *available at* http://www.nytimes.com/2006/09/10/washington/10detain.html?pagewanted=all

580.Office of the Inspector General, Department of Justice, "A Review of the FBI's Involvement in and Observations of Detainee Interrogations in Guantanamo Bay, Afghanistan, and Iraq," 257 (2008) (referencing Vice Adm. Church's investigation into the abuse at Abu Ghraib prison and discovery that, through unwritten agreement, the Coalition Joint Task Force in Iraq provided a number of cells at Abu Ghraib for the CIA's exclusive use in holding ghost detainees).

581."AR 15-6 Investigation of the Abu Ghraib Prison and 205th Military Intelligence Brigade," by LTG Anthony R. Jones, at 23, *available at* http://fl1.findlaw.com/news.findlaw.com/hdocs/docs/dod/fay82504rpt.pdf. *See also* Press Release, Human Rights First, Latest Army Report: More Involved in Abuse Than Previously Reported (August 25, 2004), *available at* http://www.humanrightsfirst.org/media/2004_alerts/0825_b.htm.

582.*See, e.g.*, Amnesty International et al., "Off the Record: U.S. Responsibility for Enforced Disappearances in the 'War on Terror,'" 4 (June 2007), *available at* http://www.hrw.org/backgrounder/usa/ct0607/ct0607web.pdf.

583.*See, e.g.*, Human Rights Watch, "Fighting Terrorism Fairly and Effectively, Recommendations for President-Elect Barack Obama," 14 (November 2008) *available at* http://www.hrw.org/en/reports/2008/11/16/fighting-terrorism-fairly-and-effectively; Amnesty International et al., "Off the Record, U.S. Responsibility for Enforced Disappearances in the 'War on Terror,'" 2 (June 2007) *available at* http://www.hrw.org/backgrounder/usa/ct0607/ct0607web.pdf.

584. President George W. Bush, President Discusses Creation of Military Commissions to Try Suspected Terrorists, Sept. 6, 2006, *available at* www.whitehouse.gov/news/releases/2006/09/20060906-3.html.

585. President George W. Bush, President Bush signs Military Commissions Act of 2006, Oct. 17, 2006, *available at* http://www.whitehouse.gov/news/releases/2006/10/print/20061017-1.html.

586. Exec. Order No. 13,440, 72 Fed. Reg. 40,707 (July 24, 2007), *available at* http://www.fas.org/irp/offdocs/eo/eo-13440.htm.

587. Shane, Johnston, & Risen, "Secret U.S. Endorsement of Severe Interrogations," *N.Y. Times*, Oct. 4, 2007, *available at* www.nytimes.com/2007/10/04/washington/04interrogate.html?_r=1&oref=slogin.

588. *See, e.g.*, Esposito and Ryan, "CIA Chief: We Waterboarded," *ABC News*, Feb. 5, 2008, *available at* http://abcnews.go.com/Blotter/TheLaw/story?id=4244423&page=1.

589. *See, e.g.*, Amnesty International et al., "Off the Record, U.S. Responsibility for Enforced Disappearances in the 'War on Terror,'" 14, 15 (June 2007) *available at* http://www.hrw.org/backgrounder/usa/ct0607/ct0607web.pdf.

590. Johnson, "At a Secret Interrogation, Dispute Flared Over Tactics," *N.Y. Times*, Sept. 10, 2006, *available at* http://www.nytimes.com/2006/09/10/washington/10detain.html?pagewanted=all .

591. Office of the Inspector General, Department of Justice, "A Review of the FBI's Involvement in and Observations of Detainee Interrogations in Guantanamo Bay, Afghanistan, and Iraq" 257 (2008) (referencing Vice Adm. Church's investigation into the abuse at Abu Ghraib prison and his discovery that, through unwritten agreement, the Coalition Joint Task Force in Iraq had provided a number of cells at Abu Ghraib for the CIA's exclusive use in holding ghost detainees).

592. *El-Masri v. U.S.*, 479 F.3d 296 (4th Cir.) (granting defendants' motion to dismiss based on state secret privilege), cert. denied, 128 S.Ct. 373 (2007).

593. Rose, "MI6 and CIA Sent Student to Morocco to be Tortured," *The Observer*, Dec. 11, 2005.

594. *Id.*

595. Mayer, "Outsourcing Torture, the Secret History of America's 'Extraordinary Rendition' Program," *The New Yorker*, Feb. 14, 2005, *available at* http://www.newyorker.com/archive/2005/02/14/050214fa_fact6 (hereinafter "Oursourcing Torture").

596. Bonner, "Detainee Says He Was Tortured While in U.S. Custody," *N.Y. Times*, Feb. 13, 2005.

597. Rose, "A Secret agent's story: 'I helped MI5. My Reward: Brutality and Prison,'" *The Observer*, July 29, 2007.

598. BBC News, "UK man released from Guantanamo," Apr. 1, 2007.

599. Garcia, "Renditions: Constraints Imposed by Laws on Torture, No. RL32890," *Congressional Research Service Reports to Congress*, at 2-3 & n. 6-7 (Jan. 25, 2008).

600. Mariner, "The Trials of Abu Omar," FindLaw, Mar. 12, 2008.

601. Perlez et al., "Ex-Detainee of U.S. Describes a 6-Year Ordeal," *N.Y. Times*, Jan. 6, 2009.

602. *See, e.g.*, European Parliament, *Report on the Alleged Use of European Countries by the CIA for the Transportation and Illegal Detention of Prisoners*, Jan. 30, 2007, *available at* http://www.europarl.europa.eu/comparl/tempcom/tdip/final_report_en.pdf.

603. Burns, "CIA confirms British territory used in rendition flights," *Int'l Herald Tribune*, Feb. 22, 2008.

604. Brinkley, "Rice is Challenged in Europe Over Secret Prisons," *N.Y. Times*, Dec. 7, 2005.

605. Garcia, "Renditions: Constraints Imposed by Laws on Torture, No. RL32890," *Congressional Research Service Reports to Congress*, at 2-3 & n. 6-7 (Jan. 25, 2008).

606. Verhaik, "CIA officers could face trial in Britain over torture allegations," *The Independent*, Oct. 31, 2008.

607. *Rendition to Torture: the Case of Maher Arar, Joint Hearing before the Subcomm. on Int'l Orgs., Human Rights, and Oversight of the H. Comm. on Foreign Affairs and Subcomm. on Constitution, Civil Rights, and Civil Liberties of the H. Comm. on the Judiciary*, 110th Cong., 80 (2007) (testimony of Frederick P. Hitz) (emphasis added).

608. *Id.* at 35.

609. *Id.* at 36.

610. *Id.* at 42.

611.*See, e.g., Rendition to Torture: the Case of Maher Arar, Joint Hearing before the Subcomm. on Int'l Orgs., Human Rights, and Oversight of the H. Comm. on Foreign Affairs and Subcomm on Constitution, Civil Rights, and Civil Liberties of the H. Comm. on the Judiciary*, 110th Cong. 42 (2007); *Commission of Inquiry into the Actions of Canadian Officials in Relation to Maher Arar, Report of the Events Relating to Maher Arar: Analysis and Recommendations*, at 13, 59 (Can.) (2006).

612.CBC News, "RCMP Chief Apologizes to Arar for "Terrible Injustices," September 28, 2006, *available at* http://www.cbc.ca/canada/story/2006/09/28/zaccardelli-appearance.html; CBC News, "RCMP Embattled Chief Quits Over Arar Testimony," December 6, 2006, *available at* http://www.cbc.ca/canada/story/2006/12/06/zaccardelli.html?ref=rss.

613.*Rendition to Torture: the Case of Maher Arar, Joint Hearing before the Subcomm. on Int'l Orgs., Human Rights, and Oversight of the H. Comm. on Foreign Affairs and Subcomm. on Constitution, Civil Rights, and Civil Liberties of the H. Comm. on the Judiciary*, 110th Cong. 96 (2007).

614.*Rendition to Torture: the Case of Maher Arar, Joint Hearing before the Subcomm. on Int'l Orgs., Human Rights, and Oversight of the H. Comm. on Foreign Affairs and Subcomm. on Constitution, Civil Rights, and Civil Liberties of the H. Comm. on the Judiciary*, 110th Cong. 80 (2007) (testimony of Frederick P. Hitz, Center for National Security Law, University of Virginia Law School).

615.*Id.* at 80 (testimony of Frederick P. Hitz, Center for national Security Law, University of Virginia Law School).

616.*Id.* at 89-90 (statement of John Garcia, Esq., Congressional Research Service).

617.18 U.S.C. § 2340A-B.

618.28 U.S.C. § 1350, note.

619.Pub. L. No. 105-277, div. G, Title XXII, § 2242(a).

620.U.N. Convention Against Torture and Other Cruel, Inhuman or Degrading treatment or Punishment, opened for signature December 10, 1984, G.A. Res. 39/46, 39 UN GAOR Supp. No. 51, at 197, UN Doc. A/RES/39/708 (1984), entered into force June 26, 1987, 1465 U.N.T.S. 85, 23 I.L.M. 1027 (1984), as modified, 24 I.L.M. 535.

621.International Covenant on Civil and Political Rights (ICCPR), G.A. Res. 2200A (XXI), UN GAOR, 21st Sess., Supp. No. 16, at 52, UN Doc. A/6316 Dec. 16, 1966, entered into force 23 March 1976, 999 U.N.T.S. 171.

622.*Rendition to Torture: the Case of Maher Arar, Joint Hearing before the Subcomm. on Int'l Orgs., Human Rights, and Oversight of the H. Comm. on Foreign Affairs and Subcomm. on*

Constitution, Civil Rights, and Civil Liberties of the H. Comm. on the Judiciary, 110th Cong. 95 (2007) (testimony of Prof. David D. Cole, Esq., Georgetown University Law Center).

623. *Rendition to Torture: the Case of Maher Arar, Joint Hearing before the Subcomm. on Int'l Orgs., Human Rights, and Oversight of the H. Comm. on Foreign Affairs and Subcomm. on Constitution, Civil Rights, and Civil Liberties of the H. Comm. on the Judiciary*, 110th Cong. 20 (2007); *see also, id.* at 3 (IOHRO Chairman Bill Delahunt (D-MA); *id.* at 4 (IOHRO Ranking Member Dana Rohrabacher (R-CA) ("today we are making sure that we go on the record so that our executive branch is on notice that, yes, we believe that a mistake was made here and that an official apology, as well as perhaps some compensation, is justified"); *id.* at 21 (Constitution Ranking Member Trent Franks (R-AZ))..

624. Letter from John Conyers, Jr., Ranking Member, H. Comm. on the Judiciary, to Clark Kent Ervin, Inspector General, Dept. Of Homeland Security, and John D. Ashcroft, Att'y General (December 16, 2003).

625. Letter from John J. Conyers, Jr, Chairman, H. Comm. on the Judiciary,. to Hon. Michael Chertoff, Secretary, Dep't of Homeland Security, (Jan. 10, 2008).

626. Department of Homeland Security, Office of Inspector General, OIG-08-18, *The Removal of a Canadian Citizen to Syria*, at 22 (March 2008).

627. *Id.* at 5 (March 2008).

628. *Id.* at 22 (March 2008).

629. *Id.* at 30-31 (March 2008) (emphasis added).

630. *Id.* at 30 (March 2008).

631. *U.S. Department of Homeland Security Inspector General Report OIG-08-018, The Removal of a Canadian Citizen to Syria, Joint Hearing before Subcomm. on Int'l Orgs., Human Rights, and Oversight of the H.Comm. on Foreign Affairs the Subcomm. on the Constitution, Civil Rights, and Civil Liberties of the H.Comm. on the Judiciary*, 110th Cong. 74 (2008).

632. *Id.*

633. *Id.*

634. Letter from Rep. John Conyers, Jr., Chairman, H. Comm. on the Judiciary, Rep. Jerrold Nadler, and Rep. William D. Delahunt to Michael Mukasey, Attorney General (July 10, 2008).

635. Letter from Keith B. Nelson, Assistant Att'y Gen. to Rep. John Conyers, Jr., Chairman, H. Comm. on the Judiciary (July 22, 2008) (relying, once again, on the alleged "assurances from Syria that Mr. Arar would be treated in a manner consistent with the CAT" but failing to address

the Inspector General's conclusion that these assurances were ambiguous and that their "validity" was not tested.).

636.The Office of Vice President, in a letter to Sen. Patrick Leahy dated Aug. 20, 2007, lists various "Top Secret/Codeword Presidential Authorization[s]" that would be responsive to an outstanding Senate Judiciary Committee subpoena. The first of these "Authorizations" was dated October 4, 2001, and subsequent authorizations were issued approximately every 6 weeks or so thereafter.

The Foreign Intelligence Surveillance Act of 1978, Pub. L. 95-511("FISA"), governs electronic surveillance of foreign powers or agents of foreign powers in national security investigations. The text makes clear that FISA was to be the "exclusive means by which electronic surveillance . . . and the interception of wire and oral communication may be conducted."

FISA specifically made it a crime to conduct any foreign intelligence electronic surveillance that was not authorized by statute. Furthermore, to ensure against unauthorized electronic surveillance by the telecommunications service providers (and to provide incentive to the carriers to strictly follow the law), FISA provided that telecommunications service providers were entitled to immunity from civil liability for "illegal wiretapping" only where they receive a specific request for assistance from certain officials. The form and purpose of such requests for assistance, and who can issue them, are enumerated in federal law. See, e.g., 18 U.S.C. §2511.

637.Once the existence of the surveillance program became known, the Administration took to referring to it as the "Terrorist Surveillance Program" – or "TSP." This term was used by then-Attorney General Gonzales in February 2006. *See* Prepared Statement of Hon. Alberto R. Gonzales, Attorney General of the United States, *available at* http://www.usdoj.gov/ag/speeches/2006/ag_speech_060206.html. Attorney General Gonzales later explained that "before December 2005, the term 'Terrorist Surveillance Program' was not used to refer to these activities, collectively or otherwise. It was only in early 2006, as part of the public debate that followed the unauthorized disclosure and the President's acknowledgment of one aspect of the NSA activities, that the term Terrorist Surveillance Program was first used." Letter from Alberto Gonzales, Attorney General, to Sen. Patrick J. Leahy, Chairman, S. Comm. on the Judiciary, August 1, 2007.

638.Prepared Statement of Alberto R. Gonzales, Attorney General of the United States, *available at* http://www.usdoj.gov/ag/speeches/2006/ag_speech_060206.html.. *See also* Letter from Office of Vice President to Sen. Patrick Leahy, Chairman, S. Comm. on the Judiciary, August 20, 2007.

639.Letter from J. Michael McConnell, Director of National Intelligence, to Sen. Arlen Specter, Ranking Member, S. Comm. on the Judiciary, July 31, 2007.

640.Klaidman, "Now We Know What the Battle Was About," *Newsweek*, Dec. 13, 2008.

641.Cauley, "NSA Has Massive Database of Americans' Phone Calls," *USA Today*, May 11, 2006, at A1.

642.Slavin, "Scholar Stands by Post-9/11 Writings On Torture, Domestic Eavesdropping, Former Justice Official Says He Was Interpreting Law, Not Making Policy," *Wash. Post.*, Dec. 26, 2005, p A03, *available at*
http://www.washingtonpost.com/wp-dyn/content/article/2005/12/25/AR2005122500570.html.

While any such memorandum remains secret, and Yoo has not confirmed his role, he intimated his involvement in providing legal support for warrantless wiretapping, in his 2006 book about his time in the Bush Administration, *War by Other Means, An Insider's Account of the War on Terror* (New York 2006), at 99-100, where, alluding to press reports that he was responsible for the legal opinions, he said he could neither confirm or deny them, then went on to defend the policies.

And in a 2007 PBS "Frontline" interview, he articulated this expansive view of the President's power: "If it's part of the president's power as a constitutional matter to gather intelligence, including intercepting communications, then that's a power that's included and Congress can't seize it just because it wants to." *Frontline: Cheney's Law* (PBS television broadcast, Oct. 16, 2007), *available at*
http://www.pbs.org/wgbh/pages/frontline/cheney/etc/script.html.

643.Gellman, "Conflict Over Spying Led White House to Brink," *Wash. Post*, Sept. 14, 2008.

644.Goldsmith, *The Terror Presidency*, New York, 2007 at 181.

645.*Id.* (brackets in text).

646.Risen & Lichtblau, "Bush Lets U.S. Spy on Callers Without Courts," *N.Y. Times*, Dec. 16, 2005, *available at* http://www.nytimes.com/2005/12/16/politics/16program.html.

647.Gellman & Becker, "A Different Understanding With the President," *Wash. Post*, June 24, 2007, at A1. The continued role played by the Office of the Vice President is confirmed by its response to a later Senate Judiciary Committee subpoena for documents about the surveillance program, in which the Vice President's counsel confirmed that they possessed responsive documents but declined to produce them. Letter from Shannen W. Coffin, Counsel to the Vice President, to Sen. Patrick J. Leahy, Chairman, S. Comm. on the Judiciary (Aug. 20, 2007), *available at* http://leahy.senate.gov/press/200708/07-08-20%20vp%20letter.pdf.

648.Letter from Sen. John D. Rockefeller IV, Vice Chairman, S. Select Comm. on Intelligence, to Richard Cheney, Vice President (July 17, 2003) *available at*
http://www.fas.org/irp/news/2005/12/rock121905.pdf.

649.Gellman, "Conflict Over Spying Led White House to Brink," *Wash. Post*, Sept. 14, 2008, at A1.

650. Leonnig, "Surveillance Court is Seeking Answers," *Wash. Post*, Jan. 5, 2006, *available at* http:/www.washingtonpost.com/wp-dyn/content/article/2006/01/04/AR2006010401864.html.

651. Leonnig, "Secret Court's Judges Were Warned About NSA Spy Data," *Wash. Post*, Feb. 9, 2006, *available at* http://www.washingtonpost.com/wp dyn/content/article/2006/02/08/AR2006020802511.html.

652. *Id.*

653. Hosenball, "Spying: Giving Out U.S. Names," *Newsweek* (May 2, 2006).

654. Leonnig, "Secret Court's Judges Were Warned About NSA Spy Data," *Wash. Post*, Feb. 9, 2006.

655. *Id.*

656. *Id.*

657. Isikoff, "The Whistleblower Who Exposed Warrantless Wiretaps," *Newsweek*, Dec. 13, 2008.

658. To date, Thomas Tamm has not been prosecuted for whistleblowing, despite the President's use of the language of treason to characterize the leaks: "There is a process that goes on inside the Justice Department about leaks, and I presume that process is moving forward. My personal opinion is it was a shameful act for someone to disclose this very important program in a time of war. The fact that we're discussing this program is helping the enemy." President George W. Bush, White House Press Conference, December 19, 2005, *available at* http://www.whitehouse.gov/news/releases/2005/12/20051219-2.html

659. Calame, "Eavesdropping and the Election: An Answer on the Question of Timing," *N.Y. Times*, Aug. 13, 2006 *available at* http://www.nytimes.com/2006/08/13/opinion/13pubed.html?ex=1313121600&en=804bfc4623ab 003c&ei=5090&partner=rssuserland&emc=rss.

660. Alter, "Bush's Snoopgate," *Newsweek*, Dec. 19, 2005.

661. Risen and Lichtblau, "Bush Lets U.S. Spy on Callers Without Courts," *N.Y. Times*, Dec. 16, 2005, *available at* http://www.nytimes.com/2005/12/16/politics/16program.html.

662. Lichtblau, "Debate and Protest at Spy Program's Inception," *N.Y. Times*, Mar. 30, 2008, *available at* http://www.nytimes.com/2008/03/30/washington/30nsa.html?_r=3&ref=us&oref=slogin&oref=sl ogin&oref=slogin . The article reported: "Deputy Attorney General Larry Thompson refused to sign off on any of the secret wiretapping requests that grew out of the program because of the secrecy and legal uncertainties surrounding it." *Id.* As noted, the need for more formal legal

authorization referenced in the article may have precipitated the October 23 domestic war powers memorandum.

663.This has been attributed by some to a conflict over searching the information within government databases, such as were contemplated by the Pentagon's Total Information Awareness program. *See* Shane and Johnston, "Mining of Data Prompted Fight Over U.S. Spying," *N.Y. Times*, July 29, 2007, *available at* http://www.nytimes.com/2007/07/29/washington/29nsa.html?ex=1343361600&en=6944d332c9 208b3f&ei=5088&partner=rssnyt. "It is not known precisely why searching the databases, or data mining, raised such a furious legal debate. But such databases contain record of the phone calls and e-mail messages of millions of Americans, and their examination by the government would raise privacy issues." *Id.* The particulars of the disagreement have not been confirmed publicly.

664.Gellman, "Conflict Over Spying Led White House to Brink," *Wash. Post,* Sept. 14, 2008, at A1.

665.According to notes written that night by FBI Director Mueller, and a press interview with DAG Comey, Attorney General Ashcroft told Gonzales and Card of his frustration with the extreme compartmentalization surrounding the program, and that having finally been able to get information and legal advice, he felt that "he never should have certified the program in the first place." Gellman, "Cheney Shielded Bush From Crisis," *Wash. Post*, Sept. 15, 2008 at A1

666.*Preserving Prosecutorial Independence: Is the Department of Justice Politicizing the Hiring and Firing of U.S. Attorneys? – Part IV, Hearing Before the S. Comm. on the Judiciary*, May 15, 2007 (testimony of former Deputy Attorney General James B. Comey).

667. Eggen and Kane, "Gonzales Hospital Episode Detailed: Ailing Ashcroft Pressured on Spy Program, Former Deputy Says," *Wash. Post*, May 16, 2007, at A1.

668. Letter from Richard Power, Assistant Director, Federal Bureau of Investigation to Rep. John Conyers, Jr., Chairman, H. Comm. on Judiciary (August 14, 2007)(forwarding notes kept by FBI Director Robert Mueller concerning the hospital incident of March 10, 2004), *available at* http://old.judiciary.house.gov/Media/PDFS/Powers070814.pdf

669.Gellman, "Cheney Shielded Bush From Crisis," *Wash. Post*, Sept. 15, 2008, at A1

670.Eggen and Kane, "Gonzales Hospital Episode Detailed: Ailing Ashcroft Pressured on Spy Program, Former Deputy Says," *Wash. Post*, May 16, 2007, at A1.

671.Thomas and Klaidman, "Full Speed Ahead ," *Newsweek*, Jan. 9, 2006. (Indeed, despite the extensive public discussion of this matter, numerous details about the exchange remain hidden from Congress and the public, including for example the complete contents of FBI Director Mueller's notes regarding the confrontation and subsequent events which the Administration has unjustifiably withheld from the House Judiciary Committee.)

672. "President Bush Calls for Renewing the USA PATRIOT Act," Remarks by the President on the USA PATRIOT Act, Hershey Lodge and Convention Center, Hershey, Pennsylvania (Apr. 19, 2004), *available at* http://www.whitehouse.gov.news/releases/2004/04/print/20040419-4.htm (emphasis added).

673. The President's sought to reassure his audiences that the PATRIOT Act and his surveillance activities were well supervised by the Judiciary:

> So the first thing I want you to think about is, when you hear Patriot Act, is that we changed the law and the bureaucratic mind-set to allow for the sharing of information. It's vital. And others will describe what that means.
>
> Secondly, there are such things as roving wiretaps. **When we're talking about chasing down terrorists, we're talking about getting a court order before we do so.** It's important for our fellow citizens to understand, when you think Patriot Act, constitutional guarantees are in place when it comes to doing what is necessary to protect our homeland, because we value the Constitution.

"President Bush: Information Sharing, Patriot Act Vital to Homeland Security," Remarks by the President in a Conversation on the USA Patriot Act, Kleinshans Music Hall Buffalo, New York (Apr. 20, 2004), *available at* http://www.whitehouse.gov.news/releases/2004/04/print/20040420-2.html (emphasis added).

674. President George W. Bush, Remarks at Ohio State Highway Patrol Academy, June 9, 2005, *available at* http://www.whitehouse.gov/news/releases/2005/06/20050609.2.html.

675. "President Bush Encourages Renewal of Patriot Act Provisions," July 20, 2005, *available at* http://www.whitehouse.gov/news/releases/2005/07/20040720-4.html.

676. Risen & Lichtblau, "Bush Lets U.S. Spy on Callers Without Courts," *N.Y.Times*, Dec. 16, 2005 at A1.

677. Alberto Gonzales, Att'y Gen. of the United States, and Michael Hayden, Principal Deputy Director for National Intelligence, White House press briefing (Dec. 19, 2005), *available at* http://www.whitehouse.gov/news/releases/2005/12/20051219-1.html.

678. Foreign Intelligence Surveillance Act of 1978, Pub. L. 95-511, Title I, 92 Stat. 1796 (Oct. 25,1978) codified as amended.

679. Vice President's Remarks on Iraq and the War on Terror at the Manhattan Institute for Policy Research, New York, Jan. 19, 2006, *available at*

http://www.whitehouse.gov/news/releases/2006/01/20060119-5.html.

680. House Judiciary Committee Democratic Staff, *The Constitution in Crisis; The Downing Street Minutes and Deception, Manipulation, Torture, Retribution, and Coverups in the Iraq War, and Illegal Domestic Surveillance*, 135-36 (August 2006).

681.Wartime Executive Power and the NSA's Surveillance Authority: Hearing before the S. Comm. on the Judiciary, 109th Cong. (2006) (statement of Sen. Arlen Specter).

682.Risen & Lichtblau, "Bush Lets U.S. Spy on Callers Without Courts", *N.Y. Times*, Dec. 16, 2005, at A1.

683.Bamford, "Where Spying Starts and Stops: Tracking an Embattled CIA and a President at War", *N.Y. Times*, Jan. 9, 2006, at E6; Risen and Lichtblau, "Bush Lets U.S. Spy on Callers Without Courts", *N.Y. Times*, Dec. 16, 2005, at A1.

684.Eggen & Pincus, "Ex-Justice Lawyer Rips Case for Spying," *Wash. Post*, Mar. 9, 2006, at A03.

685. Lichtblau & Shane, "Basis for Spying in the U.S. is Doubted", *N.Y. Times*, Jan. 7, 2006, at A1.

686.Risen & Lichtblau, "Bush Lets U.S. Spy on Callers Without Courts", *N.Y. Times*, Dec. 16, 2005, at A1.

687.Lacayo, "The Spying Controversy: Has Bush Gone Too Far?", *Time*, Jan. 9, 2006, at 25.

688.Letter from William E. Moschella, Assistant Attorney General, to the Sen. Pat Roberts, Chairman, S. Select Comm. on Intelligence, Sen. John D. Rockefeller, IV, Vice Chairman, S. Select Comm. on Intelligence, the Rep. Peter Hoekstra, Chairman, H. Permanent Select Comm. on Intelligence, and Rep. Jane Harman, Ranking Member, H. Permanent Select Comm. on Intelligence (December 22, 2005) (hereinafter "Moschella letter").

689.U.S. Department of Justice White Paper, "Legal Authorities Supporting the Activities of the National Security Agency Described by the President" (Jan. 19, 2006), *available at* http://www.usdoj.gov/opa/whitepaperonnsalegalauthorities.pdf.

690.Authorization for the Use of Military Force, Pub. L. No. 107-40, 115 Stat. 224 (2001).

691.Alberto Gonzales, Att'y Gen. of the United States, and Michael Hayden, Principal Deputy for National Intelligence, White House press briefing, Dec. 19, 2005, *available at* http://www.whitehouse.gov/news/releases/2005/12/20051219-1.html.

692.*See* Grimmett, "Authorization for Use of Military Force in response to the 9/11 Attack (P.L. 107-40): Legislative History," *CRS Report for Congress RS 22357*, *available at* http://www.congress.gov/erp/rs/pdf/RS22357.pdf (emphasis added).

693.Democratic Briefing on the "Constitution in Crisis: Domestic Surveillance and Executive Power," Before the H. Comm. on the Judiciary, 109th Cong. (2006) (statement of Prof. Jonathan Turley).

694.*See* Grimmett, "Authorization for Use of Military Force in response to the 9/11 Attack (P.L. 107-40): Legislative History," *CRS Report for Congress RS 22357*, at 43, *available at* http://www.congress.gov/erp/rs/pdf/RS22357.pdf.

695.Hersh, "Listening In," *The New Yorker*, May 29, 2006, at 24.

696.Gellman, Linzer, & Leonnig, "Surveillance Net Yields Few Suspects," *Wash. Post,* Feb. 5, 2006, at A1

697."Wiretaps Fail to Make Dent in Terror War; al Qaeda Used Messengers", *Insight Magazine*, Dec. 26, 2005 - Jan. 1, 2006.

698.Lichtblau and Risen, "Spy Agency Mined Vast Data Trove, Officials Report," *N..Y. Times*, Dec. 24, 2005, at A1.

699.Meek, "Taps Found Clues, Not al Qaeda, FBI Chief Says," *N.Y. Daily News*, Feb. 3, 2006, at 17.

700.Gellman, Linzer & Leonnig, "Surveillance Net Yields Few Suspects," *Wash. Post*, Feb. 5, 2006, at A1.

701.Hosenball & Thomas, "Hold The Phone," *Newsweek*, May 22, 2006 at 22.

702.Gellman, Linzer & Leonnig, "Surveillance Net Yields Few Suspects," *Wash. Post*, Feb. 5, 2006, at A1.

703.Bergman, Shane, Van Natta, Jr. & Lichtblau, "Spy Agency Data After Sept. 11 Led F.B.I. to Dead Ends," *N.Y. Times*, Jan. 17, 2006, at A1.

704.*Worldwide Threats to the United States: Hearing Before the S. Select Intelligence Comm.*, 109th Cong. (2006) (Testimony of FBI Director Robert Mueller, III).

705."Interview with Bill Frist by Wolf Blitzer,"(CNN May 14, 2006), *available at* http://transcripts.cnn.com/TRANSCRIPTS/0605/14/le.01.html.

706.Roberts, "Debate on the Foreign Intelligence Surveillance Act," *El Paso Times* (August 22, 2007).

707.*See* Leonnig and Nakashima, "Ruling Limited Spying Efforts: Move to Amend FISA Sparked by Judge's Decision," *Wash. Post*, Aug. 3, 2007 at A1 ("[T]wo government officials privy to the details confirmed that [Boehner's] remarks concerned classified information.").

708.*See Hearing on Warrantless Surveillance and the Foreign Intelligence Surveillance Act: The Role of Checks and Balances in Protecting Americans' (Part II): Hearing Before the H. Comm. on the Judiciary*, 110th Cong. (2007) (Statement by Michael, McConnell, Director of National Intelligence on FISA/Protect America Act withdrawing DNI's claims concerning German terror bombing plot), and Eggen, "Iraq Wiretap Delay Not Quite as Presented: Lag Is Attributed to Internal Disputes and Time to Reach Gonzales, Not FISA Constraints," *Wash. Post*, Sept. 29, 2007 at A8 (debunking claims concerning 10th Mountain Division case).

709.In March 2007, the Department represented that: "[The Office of Professional Responsibility] sought assistance in obtaining security clearances tot he Terrorist Surveillance Program to conduct its investigation. This request reached the Attorney General. ... The Attorney General recommend to the President that OPR be granted security clearances to the Terrorist Surveillance Program. The President made the decision not to grant the requested security clearances." Letter from Richard A. Hertling, Acting Assistant Attorney General, to Rep. John Conyers, Jr., Chairman, H. Comm. on the Judiciary (March 22, 2007).

710.Shane, "Bush Gives Clearances for N.S.A. Inquiry," *N.Y. Times*, Nov. 14, 2007. *See also* Letter from H. Marshall Jarrett, Office of Professional Responsibility, to Rep. Maurice Hinchey (November 13, 2007) (informing Congressman Hinchey that clearances had been granted and the investigation re-opened).

711.*In re National Security Agency Telecommunications Records Litigation*, U.S. District Court for the Northern District of California, Case No. 06-cv-01791-VRW

712.Markoff, "Judge Declines to Dismiss Privacy Suit Against AT&T," *N.Y. Times*, July 21, 2006. The Administration's conscious choice to undertake a surveillance program that was not authorized by FISA placed the telecommunications carriers who cooperated with government requests for assistance at legal risk as they faced lawsuits from a number of parties. Under FISA, a carrier – or any other person or entity – is shielded from liability for complying with a request for cooperation when provided with a document that sets forth the legal basis for the request (most often 18 U.S.C. § 2511. It has been publicly confirmed that, under the President's surveillance program, the carriers were provided certain documents which represented that the activities requested had been authorized by the President, and had been determined to be lawful by either the Attorney General or the Counsel to the President; but th documents did not state that the request complied with Section 2511 or any other specific law. *See* S.Rep. No. 110-209 (2007). The carriers have publicly argued that they had sufficient legal justification for complying with requests for surveillance assistance even when such requests were not based on FISA but instead were based on other legal theories, such as the president's inherent authority or common law. *See, e.g.*, Letter from Wayne Watts, Senior Executive Vice President of AT&T to Rep. John Dingell, Chairman, H. Comm. on Energy and Commerce, Rep. Edward Markey, and Rep. Bart Stupak (October 12, 2007), *available at* http://markey.house.gov/docs/telecomm/ATT%20wiretapping%20response_101207.pdf

713.Order, *In re National Security Agency Telecommunications Records Litigation*, U.S. District Court for the Northern District of California, Case No. 06-cv-01791-VRW (Jan. 5, 2009), *available at* http://blog.wired.com/27bstroke6/files/walkercharityruling.pdf.

714.*American Civil Liberties Union et al v. National Security Agency*, U.S. District Court for the Eastern District of Michigan, Case No. 2:06-cv-10204 ("*ACLU v. NSA*"), *available at* http://www.aclu.org/pdfs/safefree/nsacomplaint.011706.pdf

715.Memorandum Opinion, *ACLU v. NSA*, (EDMI, August 17, 2006), *available at* http://www.aclu.org/pdfs/safefree/nsamemo.opinion.judge.taylor.081706.pdf

716.*Id.*

717.*Id.*

718.*American Civil Liberties Union v. National Security Agency*, 493 F.3d 644 (6th Cir. 2007).

719.Eggen, "Court Will Oversee Wiretap Program," *Wash. Post* , Jan. 17, 2007.

720.Letter from Alberto Gonzales, Attorney General, to Sen. Patrick Leahy, Chairman, S. Comm. on the Judiciary, and Sen. Arlen Specter, Ranking Member, S. Comm. on the Judiciary, (January 19, 2007), *available at* http://graphics8.nytimes.com/packages/pdf/politics/20060117gonzales_Letter.pdf

721.*See* Leonnig and Nakashima, "Ruling Limited Spying Efforts: Move to Amend FISA Sparked by Judge's Decision," *Wash. Post*, Aug. 3, 2007 at A1 (concerning revelations of court action by Minority Leader John Boehner).

722.Roberts, "Debate on the Foreign Intelligence Surveillance Act," *El Paso Times* (August 22, 2007).

723.*Constitutional Limitations on Domestic Surveillance: Hearing before the H. Subcomm on the Constitution, Civil Rights, and Civil Liberties of the H. Comm. on the Judiciary*, 110th Cong. 8 (2007) (statement of Steven Bradbury, Principal Deputy Assistant Attorney General, Office of Legal Counsel, U.S. Department of Justice).

724.*Constitutional Limitations on Domestic Surveillance: Hearing before the H. Subcomm on the Constitution, Civil Rights, and Civil Liberties of the H. Comm. on the Judiciary*, 110th Cong. 8 (2007) (statement of Steven Bradbury, Principal Deputy Assistant Attorney General, Office of Legal Counsel, U.S. Department of Justice).

725.Roberts, "Debate on the Foreign Intelligence Surveillance Act," *El Paso Times* (August 22, 2007), *available at* http://www.elpasotimes.com/news/ci_6685679. *See also* Leonnig and Nakashima, "Ruling Limited Spying Efforts: Move to Amend FISA Sparked by Judge's Decision," *Wash. Post*, Aug. 3, 2007 at A1 (concerning apparent revelations of Court action by

Minority Leader John Boehner).

726. Pub.L. No. 110-55.

727. Roberts, "Debate on the Foreign Intelligence Surveillance Act," *El Paso Times* (August 22, 2007), *available at* http://www.elpasotimes.com/news/ci_6685679 (emphasis added).

728. *Warrantless Surveillance and the Foreign Intelligence Surveillance Act: the Role Of Checks and Balances in Protecting Americans' Privacy Rights (Part I), Hearing before the H. Comm. on the Judiciary*, 110th Cong. 17 (2007) (statement of Suzanne Spaulding).

729. *Id*. at 23 (statement of Prof. Robert Turner).

730. *See FISA for the Future: Balancing Security and Liberty, Hearing before the H. Permanent Select Comm. on Intelligence*, 110th Cong. (2007); *Administration Views of FISA Authorities: Hearing before the H. Permanent Select Comm. on Intelligence*, 110th Cong. (2007).

731. *See, e.g.,* Letter from Rep. John Conyers, Jr., Chairman, H. Comm. on the Judiciary, Rep. Jerrold Nadler, and Rep. Bobby Scott to Fred Fielding, White House Counsel (September 11, 2007), *available at* http://old.judiciary.house.gov/Media/PDFS/Conyers-Nadler-Scott070911.pdf.

732. *See* Press Release, H. Comm. on Judiciary, Conyers Responds to WH Granting Committee Access to Wiretapping Documents (Jan. 24, 2008), *available at* http://judiciary.house.gov/news/012408.html

733. Hess, "Bush Opens Wiretap Documents to House," *Associated Press* (Jan. 24, 2008). In pursuit of both its oversight and its legislative responsibilities, the Judiciary Committee had sought access to the information as to the conduct of the carriers and whether they were entitled to the sort of immunity urged by the White House. For years, the Bush Administration had refused to permit House or Senate Judiciary Committee access to the FISA court orders or other details about how the program was conducted. Even while the Administration withheld information Congress believed necessary for legislating responsibly, DNI McConnell selectively revealed information about the program in the media in an attempt to justify his negotiating tactics around the PAA – information that the Administration had argued for years was too sensitive for even Members of Congress to review. *See* Letter from Rep. John Conyers, Jr., Chairman, H. Comm. on the Judiciary, Rep. Jerrold Nadler, and Rep. Bobby Scott to Michael McConnell, Director of National Intelligence (September 11, 2007), *available at* http://old.judiciary.house.gov/Media/PDFS/Conyers-Scott-Nadler070911.pdf.

734. *See* "Statement of Undersigned Members of the House Judiciary Committee Concerning the Administration's Terrorist Surveillance Program and the Issue of Retroactive Immunity," March 12, 2008, *available at* http://judiciary.house.gov/news/pdfs/Immunity080312.pdf.

735. "Statement of Undersigned Members of the House Judiciary Committee Concerning the Administration's Terrorist Surveillance Program and the Issue of Retroactive Immunity," March

12, 2008, at 5, *available at* http://judiciary.house.gov/news/pdfs/Immunity080312.pdf.

736. As discussed above, a critical aspect of the TSP was the claim of the Administration and its allies that there were legal bases for wiretapping other than in FISA, the exclusivity provision of the statute notwithstanding. *E.g.*, U.S. Department of Justice White Paper, "Legal Authorities Supporting the Activities of the National Security Agency Described by the President" (Jan. 19, 2006) *available at* http://www.usdoj.gov/opa/whitepaperonnsalegalauthorities.pdf, *and* Letter from Wayne Watts, Senior Executive Vice President of AT&T to Rep. John Dingell, Chairman, H. Comm. on Energy and Comerce, Rep. Edward, Markey, and Rep. Bart Stupak (Oct. 12, 2007) *available at* http://markey.house.gov/docs/telecomm/ATT%20wiretapping%20response_101207.pdf. While this claim was rejected by the district court in *ACLU v. NSA*, state secrets and standing issues have prevented any appellate court from resolving the issue.

737. Dept. of Justice, Office of Inspector General, "A Review of the Federal Bureau of Investigation's Use of National Security Letters," at 1, *available at* http://www.npr.org/documents/2007/mar/doj/doj_oig_nsl.pdf. (Hereinafter referred to as *DOJ OIG NSL Report*).

738. These statutes include: 1) The Right to Financial Privacy Act (RFPA), 12 U.S.C. § 3414(a)(5)(A), to obtain financial institution customer records; 2) The Electronic Communications Privacy Act (ECPA), 18 U.S.C. § 2709(a), to obtain certain communication service provider records; 3) The Fair Credit Reporting Act (FCRA), 15 U.S.C. §§ 1681u, 1681v, to obtain certain financial information and consumer reports, and credit agency consumer records for counterterrorism investigations; and 4) The National Security Act (NSA), 50 U.S.C. § 436, to obtain financial information, records, and consumer reports. Prior to September 11, 2001, and the enactment of the PATRIOT Act, the authorizing statutes which governed NSLs required the satisfaction of a more demanding standard, including certification by a senior FBI Headquarters official that the FBI had "specific and articulable facts giving reason to believe that the customer or entity whose records are sought is a foreign power or agent of a foreign power" as defined in FISA.

739. Gellman, "The FBI's Secret Scrutiny: In Hunt for Terrorists, Bureau Examines Records of Ordinary Americans," *Wash. Post*, Nov. 6, 2005, at A1.

740. *Anti-Terrorism Intelligence Tools Improvement Act of 2003: Hearing before the Subcomm. on Crime, Terrorism, and Homeland Security of the H. Comm. on the Judiciary*, 108th Cong. (November 24, 2004) (responses from Justice Department and FBI to post-hearing questions for the record).

741. Letter from the Office of Assistant Attorney General to the Honorable F. James Sensenbrenner, Chairman, H. Comm. on the Judiciary (Nov. 23, 2005).

742. Pub. L. No. 109-177, § 119. Congress directed the OIG's review to include:

1) an examination of the use of NSLs by the Justice Department during calendar years 2003 through 2006;

2) a description of any noteworthy facts or circumstances relating to such use, including any improper or illegal use of such authority;

3) an examination of the effectiveness of NSLs as an investigative tool, including-

    A) the importance of the information acquired by the Justice Department to the Intelligence activities of the Justice Department or to any other department or agency of the federal government;

    B) the manner in which such information is collected, retained, analyzed, and disseminated by the Justice Department, including any direct access to such information (such as to "raw data") provided to any other department, agency, or instrumentality of Federal, State, local, or tribal governments or any private sector entity;

    C) whether, and how often, the Justice Department utilized such information to produce an analytical intelligence product for distribution within the Justice Department, to the intelligence community... or to Federal, State, local, or tribal government departments, agencies or instrumentalities;

    D) whether, and how often, the Justice Department provided such information to law enforcement authorities for use in criminal proceedings;... *Id.*

The pre-PATRIOT Act statutes required the FBI to provide classified semi-annual reports to Congress disclosing summary information about national security letter usage. *See* I.G. Report at 9. The PATRIOT Act itself continued to require classified reports to Congress on the FBI's use of its NSL authorities. *Id.*

743. *DOJ OIG NSL Report*, at viii, 3

744. P. L. No. 109-177.

745. President's Statement on H.R. 3199, the USA PATRIOT Improvement and Reauthorization Act of 2005, http://www.whitehouse.gov/news/releases/2006/03/20060309-4.html (March 9, 2006).

746. *DOJ OIG NSL Report.*

747.*Id*. The FBI used exigent letters as a broad law enforcement tool that was not conditioned on meeting even the requirements for NSLs.

According to the Inspector Generals' report, the FBI General Counsel claimed that, *if challenged*, the FBI could rely on 18 U.S.C. § 2702(c)(4), as authority for obtaining information through exigent letters. *See DOJ OIG NSL Report* at 95 (emphasis added). During the period reviewed in the Inspector General's report, the statute permitted telecommunications providers to divulge records to "a governmental entity, if the provider *reasonably believes* that an emergency involving immediate danger of death or serious physical injury to any person justifies disclosure of the information." Note that the statute permits, but does not strictly require, the telecommunications provider to divulge the information. However, as further discussed in this section, the exigent letters were not always issued in emergency situations.

In the USA PATRIOT Improvement and Reauthorization Act of 2005, Pub. L. 109-177, signed into law in March 2006 – in section 107(b)(1)(B), a provision titled "Enhanced Oversight of Good-faith Emergency Disclosures under Section 212 of the USA Patriot Act" – Congress *relaxed* the standards in 18 U.S.C.§ 2702(c)(4). Now the telecommunications provider need only believe "*in good faith*"– a more forgiving standard – and the emergency no longer must be "immediate."

The Electronic Communications Privacy Act (ECPA) allows the FBI to compel the production of telephone toll billing records or subscriber information pursuant to an NSL. 18 U.S.C. § 2709. Thus, while 18 U.S.C. § 2702(c)(4) is a request for voluntary emergency disclosure, 18 U.S.C. § 2709 is compulsory. To date, though, the FBI has not specifically stated under which of these two statutes it was operating to justify its use of exigent letters.

748.*Id*. at 86. Specifically, the FBI provided copies of 739 exigent letters addressed to the three telephone carriers dated between March 11, 2003, and December 16, 2005, all but four of which had been signed. Together, the 739 exigent letters requested information on approximately 3,000 different telephone numbers. *Id*. at 89-90.

749.*Id*. at 86.

750.The practice of issuing exigent letters originally began in the FBI's New York office after the September 11, 2001 attacks. When agents from that office transferred to FBI Headquarters, they brought this practice with them. *DOJ OIG NSL Report* at 87, 89.

751.*DOJ OIG NSL Report* at 88. Although National Security Law Branch (NSLB) FBI attorneys told the OIG that they were not consulted about the three contracts, FBI Office of General Counsel procurement lawyers did in fact participate in reviewing the contracts. *Id*. at 89, n.126.

752.*Id*. at 89.

753.*Id.* at 123.

754.*Id.* at 86 .

755.*Id.*

756.*Id.*

757.*Id.* at 92-93.

758.*Id.* at 93.

759.*Id.* at 93-94

760.*DOJ OIG NSL Report* at 94; Appendix, FBI Director Robert Mueller's Letter to Inspector General Glenn Fine, at 6 (hereinafter, Mueller Letter).

761.*DOJ OIG NSL Report* at 97.

762.*Id.* at 123 .

763.*Id.* at 115-16.

764.*Id.* at 116.

765.*Id.* at 116-17. According to FBI Personnel who issued the certificate letters, the letters requested that the Bank determine whether it had information, as opposed to requesting the records themselves. *Id.* at 116.

766.*Id.* at 68.

767.*Id.*

768.The Inspector General concluded that some of these infractions occurred because agents do not always verify whether the received records match the original requests prior to their input into databases. *Id.* at 85.

769.*Id.* at 72.

770.*Id.* at 123.

771.*Id.* at 121.

772.*Id.*

773.*Id.* at 31.

774.*Id.*.

775.*Id.* at 36.   The OIG determined that the spike in calendar year 2004 was due in large part to the issuance of 9 NSLs in one investigation that contained requests for subscriber information on a total of 11,100 separate telephone numbers.

776.*Id.* at 33.

777.*Id.* at 34.

778.*Id.* at 98

779.*Id.*

780.*Id.* at 110.

781.*Id.*   In response to the problems identified in the report, OIG offered ten recommendations:

1. Require all Headquarters and field personnel who are authorized to issue national security letter to create a control file for the purpose of retaining signed copies of all national security letters they issue.

2. Improve the FBI-OGC NSL tracking database to ensure that I captures timely, complete, and accurate data on NSLs and NSL requests.

3. Improve the FBI-OGC NSL database to include data reflecting NSL requests for information about individuals who are not the investigative subjects but are the targets of NSL requests.

4. Consider issuing additional guidance to field offices that will assist in identifying possible IOB violations arising from use of national security letter authorities.

5. Consider seeking legislative amendment to the Electronic Communications Privacy Act to define the phrase "telephone toll billing records information."

6. Consider measures that would enable FBI agents and analysts to (a) label or tag their use of information derived from national security letters in analytical intelligence products and (b) identify when and how often information derived from NSLs is provided to law enforcement authorities for use in criminal proceedings.

7. Take steps to ensure that the FBI does not improperly issue exigent letters.

8. Take steps to ensure that, where appropriate, the FBI makes requests for

information in accordance with the requirements of national security letter authorities.

9. Implement measures to ensure that FBI-OGC is consulted about activities undertaken by FBI Headquarters National Security Branch, including its operational support activities, that could generate requests for records from third parties that the FBI is authorized to obtain exclusively though the use of its national security letter authorities.

10. Ensure that Chief Division Counsel and Assistant Division Counsel provide close and independent review of requests to issue national security letters.

DOJ OIG NSL Report at 125.

782. *Hearing on "The Inspector General's Independent Report on the FBI's Use of National Security Letters," Before the H. Comm. on the Judiciary*, (hereinafter *DOJ OIG NSL Report Hearing*), 110th Cong. at 1 (2007) (statement of Chairman John Conyers, Jr.).

783. *Id.* at 228 (statement of Justice Department Inspector General Glenn Fine).

784. *Id.*

785. *Id.* at 236. In light of these and other abuses that the Inspector General's office identified in its report, the OIG made a variety of recommendations to the FBI concerning the improved use of NSLs as investigative tools. *See DOJ OIG NSL Report.*

786. *DOJ OIG NSL Report Hearing* at 229 (testimony of FBI General Counsel Valerie Caproni).

787. *Id* at. 241.

788. *Id.* at 216.

789. *Id.* at 249.

790. *Id.* at 232 (statement of Rep. Sensenbrenner).

791. Dept. of Justice, Office of the Inspector General, "A Review of the FBI's Use of National Security Letters: Assessment of Corrective Actions and Examination of NSL Usage in 2006," (hereinafter *"DOJ OIG NSL Corrective Action Report"*) (2008).

792. *Id.* at 7-8.

793. *Id.* at 12.

794. *Id.* at 8.

795.*Id.*

796.*Id.*

797.*Id.*

798.*Id.* at 128-129.

799.*Id.* at 9.

800.*DOJ OIG NSL Report* at 35; *DOJ OIG NSL Corrective Action Report* at 9-10.

801.*DOJ OIG NSL Corrective Action Report* at 8.

802.*Id.* at 10-11.

803.*Id.* at 11. In addition, on the same day he issued the "Corrective Action Report," Inspector General Fine issued a report concerning his review of the FBI's use of Section 215 Orders. One aspect of that report implicated the FBI's use of NSLs. It noted that, after the FISC had denied a 2006 FBI request for a Section 215 business record order seeking "tangible things" as part of a counterterrorism case – citing First Amendment concerns – the FBI then circumvented the court's oversight and pursued the investigation using three NSLs that were predicated on the same information contained in the Section 215 application, despite the fact that NSLs contain the same First Amendment constraints. Dept. of Justice, Office of Inspector General, "A Review of the FBI's Use of Section 215 Orders for Business Records in 2006," at 68, 72 (2008).

804.*Id.*

805.*Id.*

806.*Id.* at 12. The recommendations included:

1.   Create blank mandatory fields in the database supporting the NSL data system for entering the U.S. person/non-U.S. person status of the target of NSLs and for entering the number of NSL requests in order to prevent inaccuracies that may otherwise result from the current default settings

2.   Implement measures to verify the accuracy of data entry into the new NSL data system.

3.   Implement measures to verify that data requested in NSLs is checked against serialized source documents to verify that the data extracted from the source document and used in the NSL is accurately recorded on the NSL and the approval EC.

4. Regularly monitor the preparation of NSL-related documents and the handling of NSL-derived information with periodic reviews and inspections.

5. Assign NSLB attorneys to participate in pertinent meetings of operational and operational support units in the Counterterrorism and Counterintelligence Divisions.

6. Consider increasing the staffing level of the OIC so that it can develop the sufficient skills, knowledge, and independence to lead or directly carry out critical elements of the OIC's work.

7. Reinforce the distinction between the FBI's two NSL authorities pursuant to the Fair Credit Reporting Act throughout all levels of the FBI's National Security Branch at FBI Headquarters.

8. Add procedures to include reviews of FCRA NSLs in counterintelligence investigations in the FBI Inspection Division's periodic reviews and in the NSD's national security reviews.

9. Reiterate in its continuing discussions with major credit reporting agencies that the agencies should not provide consumer full credit reports in response to FCRA NSLs and should ensure that they provide only requested information in response to FCRA NSLs.

10. Ensure that guidance and training continue to identify the circumstances under which FCRA NSL matters must be reported to the FBI OGC as possible intelligence violations.

11. Issue additional guidance addressing the filing and retention of NSL-derived information that will improve the ability to locate NSL-derived information.

12. Include in its routine case file reviews and the NSD's national security reviews an analysis of the FBI's compliance with requirements governing the filing and retention of NSL-derived information.

13. Periodically reissue guidance and training materials reminding case agents and supervisors assigned to national security investigations that they must carefully examine the circumstances surrounding the issuance of each NSL to determine whether there is adequate justification for imposing non-disclosure and confidentiality requirements on the NSL recipient.

14. Periodically reinforce in training and guidance provided to case agents and supervisors assigned to national security investigations the FBI OGC directive to

timely report to the FBI OGC possible intelligence violations arising from the use of NSL authorities.

15.   Require case agents and supervisors assigned to national security investigations to specify in any reports to the FBI OGC the precise remedial measures employed to handle any unauthorized information they obtain in response to NSLs and to address whether the inappropriately provided information was used or uploaded into FBI databases.

16.   Periodically provide case agents and supervisors assigned to national security investigations with examples of common errors in the use of NSLs, such as the examples used in the November 20, 2006, FBI OGC guidance memorandum regarding possible NSL-related intelligence violations.

17.   The Department of Justice should direct that the NSL Working Group, with the FBI's and the NSD's participation, re-examine measures for (a) addressing the privacy interests associated with NSL-derived information, including the benefits and feasibility of labeling or tagging NSL-derived information, and (b) minimizing the retention and dissemination of such information.

DOJ OIG NSL Corrective Action Report at 162-63.

807.*Hearing on H.R. 3189, the "National Security Letters Reform Act [NSLRA] of 2007," Before the Subcomm. on the Constitution, Civil Rights, and Civil Liberties of the H. Comm. On the Judiciary*, 110th Cong. (Apr. 15, 2008) (hereinafter "*NSLRA Hearing*") .

808.Inspector General Fine acknowledged that since only a year had passed since the 2007 report, it may have been too early to assess whether the FBI will implement all of the 2007 report's recommendations. *See NSLRA Hearing*. at 20.

809.*Id*. at 17.

810.*Id*. at 18.

811.*Id*. at 19.

812.*Id*. at 22 (testimony of FBI General Counsel Valerie Caproni).

813.*Id*. at 23

814.*Id* at 24 (testimony of FBI General Counsel Valerie Caproni).

815.*Id*. at 46 (testimony of Jameel Jaffer).

816.*Id*.

817.*Id.*

818.*Id.* at 52 (testimony of Bruce Fein).

819.*Id.*

820. *Id.* at 58 (testimony of Michael Woods).

821.*Id.*

822.*Id.* at 60 (testimony of David Kris).

823.*Id.*

824.Memorandum for William J. Haynes, General Counsel, Department of Defense, *Possible Habeas Jurisdiction Over Aliens Held in Guantanamo Bay*, from John Yoo, Deputy Assistant Attorney General, and Patrick F. Philbin, Deputy Assistant Attorney General (Dec.28, 2001).

825.*Boumediene v. Bush*, __ U.S. __ , 128 S.Ct. 2229 (2008)

826.*See* discussion Section II, Part I. On November 6, 2001, the Justice Department's OLC set forth the legal basis for the commissions. Memorandum for Alberto R. Gonzales, *Counsel to the President, Legality of the Use of Military Commissions to Try Terrorists*, from Patrick F. Philbin, Deputy Assistant Attorney General (Nov. 6, 2001). President Bush signed the order establishing a military commission system on November 13, 2001. "Military Order – Detention, Treatment and Trial of Certain Non-Citizens in the War Against Terrorism," Executive Order dated November 13, 2001, 66 Fed. Reg. 57833 (Nov. 16, 2001). A copy of this order may also be found at http://www.whitehouse.gov/news/releases/2001/11/20011113-27.html. The Supreme Court found the commissions in violation of the separation of powers principles of the Constitution, s*ee Hamdan v. Rumsfeld*, 548 U.S.557, 591-92 (2006) (footnote omitted) (citing *Ex Parte Milligan*, 4 Wall. 2, 139-40 (1866)) (emphasis added), and also in violation of both the Uniform Code of Military Justice and the Geneva Conventions. *Id.* at 613-625 (violates Uniform Code of Military Justice), 625-635 (violates the Geneva Conventions).

827.*See* discussion Section II (Assault on Individual Liberties), Part I (Detention) .

828.*See* discussion Section II (Assault on Individual Liberties), Part II (Interrogation) .

829.*See* discussion Section II (Assault on Individual Liberties), Part II (Interrogation).

830.*Hamdan v. Rumsfeld*, 548 U.S. 557 (2006).

831.*See* discussion Section II (Assault on Individual Liberties), Part II (Interrogation).

832.The use of these techniques, which went beyond the treatment allowed under the Army Field Manual, has been confirmed by, among other things, "interrogation logs" that have been disclosed, and the report of Department of Justice Inspector General Glenn Fine, which discussed the interrogation tactics used by the Department of Defense against Muhammad al-Khatani at Guantanamo. *Statement of Glenn A. Fine Inspector General, U.S. Department of Justice before the House Committee on Foreign Affairs Subcommittee on International Organizations, Human Rights, and Oversight concerning The Role of the FBI at Guantanamo Bay*, at 5-9 (June 4, 2008) *available at* http://www.usdoj.gov/oig/testimony/t0806/final.pdf. *See also* "Interrogation Log, Detainee 063," *reprinted in Time, available at* http://www.time.com/time/2006/log/log.pdf.

833.*See* discussion Section II (Assault on Individual Liberties), Part II (Interrogation).

834.As but one example, *The Washington Post* reported: "[S]taff sergeant, James Vincent Lucas, told Army investigators that he traveled from Cuba to Iraq from October to December 2003 as part of a six-person team to bring his 'lessons learned' and to 'provide guidelines' to interrogators at Abu Ghraib who were setting up their operation," according to investigative documents obtained by The Washington Post." White, "Abu Ghraib Dog Tactics Came From Guantanamo," *Wash. Post*, July 27, 1005, at A14, *available at* http://www.washingtonpost.com/wp-dyn/content/article/2005/07/26/AR2005072601792.html. Similarly, an internal Department of Defense report stated:

> In August 2003, [Major General] Geoffrey Miller [who was then the Commander of Guantanamo] arrived [in Iraq] to conduct an assessment of DoD counterterrorism interrogation and detention operations in Iraq. ... He brought to Iraq the Secretary of Defense's April 16, 2003 policy guidelines for Guantanamo – which he reportedly gave to CJTF-7 [the Combined Joint Task Force 7 – the U.S. Army in Iraq] as a potential model – recommending a command-wide policy be established. He noted, however, the Geneva Conventions did apply to Iraq. ... [T]here was also a store of common lore and practice within the interrogator community circulating through Guantanamo, Afghanistan and elsewhere.

"Final Report of the Independent Panel to Review DoD Interrogation Operations," (Hon. J. Schlesinger, Chairman), Aug. 2004 at 37, *available at* http://www.defenselink.mil/news/Aug2004/d20040824finalreport.pdf.

835.*See* discussion Section II (Assault on Individual Liberties), Part II (Interrogation).

836.*Id.*

837.*See, e.g.*, Mayer, "Outsourcing Torture, the Secret History of America's "Extraordinary Rendition" program," *The New Yorker*, Feb. 14, 2005, *available at* http://www.newyorker.com/archive/2005/02/14/050214fa_fact6; Campbell, "September 11: Six Months on: U.S. Sends Suspects to Face Torture," *The Guardian*, Mar. 12, 2002, at 4 (quoting an unnamed U.S. diplomat as acknowledging "[a]fter September 11, [renditions] have been occurring all the time....It allows us to get information from terrorists in a way we can't do on U.S. soil."); Jehl and Johnston, "Rule Change Lets C.I.A Freely Send Suspects Abroad to Jails," *N.Y. Times*, Mar. 6, 2005, at A1 ("former government officials say that since the Sept. 11 attacks, the CIA has flown 100 to 150 suspected terrorists from one foreign country to another, including to Egypt, Syria, Saudi Arabia, Jordan and Pakistan"); Satterthwaite & Fisher, *Beyond Guantanamo: Transfers to Torture One Year After Rasul v. Bush (2005)*, Ctr. For Human Rights & Global Justice, N.Y. Univ. Sch. of Law, *available at* http://www.chrgj.org/docs/Beyond%20Guantanamo%20Report%20FINAL.pdf .

838.*See, e.g,.* President George W. Bush, President Discusses Creation of Military Commissions to Try Suspected Terrorists, Sept. 6, 2006, *available at* www.whitehouse.gov/news/releases/2006/09/20060906-3.html.

839.*See* generally discussion, Section 2 (Extraordinary Rendition, Ghosting and Black Sites), Part III.

840.*See* generally discussion, Section 2 (Extraordinary Rendition, Ghosting and Black Sites), Part III.

841.*See* generally discussion, Section 2 (Extraordinary Rendition, Ghosting and Black Sites), Part III.

842.*See* generally discussion, Section 2 (Extraordinary Rendition, Ghosting and Black Sites), Part III.

843.Department of Homeland Security, Office of Inspector General, OIG-08-18, *The Removal of a Canadian Citizen to Syria*, at 22 (March 2008).

844.Letter from Clark Kent Ervin, Inspector General, Dept. Of Homeland Security, to Rep. John Conyers, Jr., Ranking Member, H. Comm. on the Judiciary, (July 14, 2004) (apologizing that "our work has been delayed and may not be completed in a timely matter" because access to information had been blocked based on claims of classification and legal privilege). Several other members of Congress, including Constitution Subcommittee Chairman Nadler, have also pressed the Administration for information regarding rendition of terror suspects. Many of those requests remain unanswered. *See, e.g.*, Letters from Hon. Jerrold Nadler and William D. Delahunt to Hon. Michael Mukasey, General Michael Hayden, Hon. Condoleezza Rice, and Hon. Michael Chertoff (July 10, 2008).

845.*See, e.g., El-Masri v. U.S.*, 479 F.3rd 296 (4th Cir.) (dismissing lawsuit based on state secret privilege), *cert. denied*, 128 S.Ct. 373 (2007).

846.*See, e.g.*, Mayer, "Outsourcing Torture, the Secret History of America's "Extraordinary Rendition" program," *The New Yorker*, Feb. 14, 2005, *available at* http://www.newyorker.com/archive/2005/02/14/050214fa_fact6 ; Johnson, "At a Secret Interrogation, Dispute Flared Over Tactics," *N.Y. Times*, Sept. 10, 2006, *available at* http://www.nytimes.com/2006/09/10/washington/10detain.html?pagewanted=all .

847.*See*, *e.g.*, Office of the Inspector General, Department of Justice, "A Review of the FBI's Involvement in and Observations of Detainee Interrogations in Guantanamo Bay, Afghanistan, and Iraq," 257 (2008) (referencing Vice Adm. Church's investigation into the abuse at Abu Ghraib prison and discovery that, through unwritten agreement, the Coalition Joint Task Force in Iraq provided a number of cells at Abu Ghraib for the CIA's exclusive use in holding ghost detainees); "AR 15-6 Investigation of the Abu Ghraib Prison and 205th Military Intelligence Brigade," by LTG Anthony R. Jones, at 23, *available at* http://fl1.findlaw.com/news.findlaw.com/hdocs/docs/dod/fay82504rpt.pdf. *See also* Press Release, Human Rights First, Latest Army Report: More Involved in Abuse Than Previously Reported (August 25, 2004), *available at* http://www.humanrightsfirst.org/media/2004_alerts/0825_b.htm ; Amnesty International et al., "Off the Record: U.S. Responsibility for Enforced Disappearances in the 'War on Terror,'" 4 (June 2007), *available at* http://www.hrw.org/backgrounder/usa/ct0607/ct0607web.pdf.

848.*See* generally discussion, Section 2 (Extraordinary Rendition, Ghosting and Black Sites), Part III.

849.50 U.S.C. §1809.

850.U.S. Department of Justice White Paper, "Legal Authorities Supporting the Activities of the National Security Agency Described by the President" (Jan. 19, 2006), *available at* http://www.usdoj.gov/opa/whitepaperonnsalegalauthorities.pdf.

851.The House version of [FISA] would have authorized the president to engage in warrantless electronic surveillance for the first year of a war, but the Conference Committee rejected so long a period of judicially unchecked eavesdropping as unnecessary inasmuch as the 15-day period would "allow time for consideration of any amendment to this act that may be appropriate during a wartime emergency." Letter from Professor Laurence H. Tribe, Harvard Law School , to Rep. John Conyers, Jr, Ranking Member, H. Comm. on the Judiciary (January 10, 2006).

852.U.S. Department of Justice White Paper, "Legal Authorities Supporting the Activities of the National Security Agency Described by the President" (Jan. 19, 2006), *available at* http://www.usdoj.gov/opa/whitepaperonnsalegalauthorities.pdf.

853.H.R. Conf. Rep. No. 95-1720, at 34 (1978).

854.Memorandum Opinion, *ACLU v. NSA*, (EDMI, August 17, 2006), *available at* http://www.aclu.org/pdfs/safefree/nsamemo.opinion.judge.taylor.081706.pdf. The Sixth Circuit Court of Appeals overturned the decision not on the merits, but on the grounds that the plaintiffs lacked standing because they had not "— and because of the State Secrets Doctrine [could] not" – produce any evidence that any of their own communications have ever been intercepted [without a warrant]." *American Civil Liberties Union v. National Sec. Agency*, 493 F.3d 644, 653 (6th Cir. 2007).

855. Press Briefing by Attorney General Alberto Gonzales and General Michael Hayden, Principal Deputy Director for National Intelligence, *available at* http://www.whitehouse.gov/news/releases/2005/12/20051219-1.html (December 19, 2005).

856. Klaidman, "Now We Know What the Battle Was About," *Newsweek*, December 13, 2008.

857. Lichtblau, "Debate and Protest at Spy Program's Inception," *N.Y. Times*, Mar. 30, 2008, *available at* http://www.nytimes.com/2008/03/30/washington/30nsa.html?_r=3&ref=us&oref=slogin&oref=slogin&oref=slogin .

858. Gellman, "Cheney Shielded Bush From Crisis," *Wash. Post*, September 15, 2008 ("'I decide what the law is for the executive branch,' [Bush] said").

859. Statement of Undersigned Members of the House Judiciary Committee Concerning the Administration's Terrorist Surveillance Program and the Issue of Retroactive Immunity," March 12, 2008, *available at* http://judiciary.house.gov/Media/PDFS/Immunity080312.pdf.

860. *Hamdan v. Rumsfeld*, 548 U.S. 557 (2006).

861. "President Bush Calls for Renewing the USA PATRIOT Act," Remarks by the President on the USA PATRIOT Act, Hershey Lodge and Convention Center, Hershey, Pennsylvania (Apr. 19, 2004), *available at* http://www.whitehouse.gov.news/releases/2004/04/print/20040419-4.htm (emphasis added).

862. *DOJ OIG NSL Report* at 97.

863. *DOJ OIG NSL Report* at 110.

864. *DOJ OIG NSL Report Hearing* at 228 (testimony of Inspector General Glenn Fine); *DOJ OIG NSL Report* at 82.

865. *DOJ OIG NSL Report Hearing* at 228 (testimony of Inspector General Glenn Fine).

866. Dept. of Justice, Office of Inspector General, "A Review of the FBI's Use of Section 215 Orders for Business Records in 2006," at 68, 72 (2008).

867. *DOJ OIG NSL Report* at 115-16.

868. *Id.* at 116.

869. *Id.* at 121; Gellman, "The FBI's Secret Scrutiny: In Hunt for Terrorists, Bureau Examines Records of Ordinary Americans," *Wash. Post*, Nov. 6, 2005, at A1.

870. *NSLRA Report Hearing* at 19 (testimony of Inspector General Glenn Fine).

871.*Id*. at 9.

872.*Id*.

873.The OIG determined that the spike in calendar year 2004 was due in large part to the issuance of 9 NSLs in one investigation that contained requests for subscriber information on a total of 11,100 separate telephone numbers. *Id*. at 36.

874.*DOJ OIG NSL Report* at 33.

875.*Id*. at 34.

876.*DOJ OIG NSL Report Hearing* at 216 (testimony of FBI General Counsel Valerie Caproni).

877. *Id*. at 9 (testimony of Inspector General Glenn Fine).

878.*Id*.

879.*Id*.

880.*NSLRA Hearing* at 9 (testimony of Inspector General Glenn Fine).

881.*DOJ OIG NSL Report*, at 86.

882.*Id*. at 93

883.*Id*.

884.*DOJ OIG NSL Corrective Action Report,* at 127.

885.*Amending Executive Order 12866: Good Governance or Regulatory Usurpation: Hearing Before the Subcommittee on Commercial and Administrative Law of the H. Comm. on the Judiciary,* 110th Cong. (2007) (prepared statement of Professor Peter L. Strauss, Columbia Law School).

886.Public Citizen, "New Executive Order is Latest White House Power Grab," Jan. 18, 2007, *available at* http://www.citizen.org/pressroom/release.cfm?ID=2361. *See also* Kriz, "Thumbing His Nose," *Nat'l J.*, July 28, 2007, at 32-34.

887.*Presidential Signing Statements under the Bush Administration: A Threat to Checks and Balances and the Rule of Law?: Hearing Before the H. Comm. on the Judiciary,* 110th Cong. (2007).

888.*Presidential Signing Statements: Hearing Before the S. Comm. on the Judiciary*, 109th Cong. (2006).

889. American Bar Association, Report of Task Force on Presidential Signing Statements and the Separation of Powers Doctrine (July 24, 2006).

890. Halstead, "Presidential Signing Statements: Constitutional and Institutional Implications," *CRS Report for Congress, RL33667*, at 2 (2006).

891. *Id.* at 2 (2006). A House report criticized Jackson's signing statement, declaring that a congressionally authorized road should not extend beyond Michigan, as tantamount to a line-item veto. Another House report called Tyler's signing statement regarding the constitutionality of an apportionment bill to be "a defacement of the public records and archives." *Id.*

892. *Id.* at 2.

893. *Id.* at 2.

894. *Id.* at 2.

895. Memorandum of Samuel A. Alito, Jr., U.S. Department of Justice, Office of Legal Counsel, Using Presidential Signing Statements to Make Fuller Use of the President's Constitutionally Assigned Role in the Process of Enacting Law (Feb. 5, 1986), *available at* http://www.archives.gov/news/samuel-alito/accession-060-89-269/Acc060-89-269-box6-SG-LSWG-AlitotoLSWG-Feb1986.pdf.

896. Halstead, "Presidential Signing Statements: Constitutional and Institutional Implications," *CRS Report for Congress, RL33667*, at 3-4 (2006); *See, e.g., Bowsher v. Synar*, 478 U.S. 714 (1986); *INS v. Chadha*, 462 U.S. 919 (1983).

897. Halstead, "Presidential Signing Statements: Constitutional and Institutional Implications," *CRS Report for Congress, RL33667*, at 4 (2006).

898. *Id.*

899. *Id.* at 5-6.

900. Department of Justice, Office of Legal Counsel, The Legal Significance of Presidential Signing Statements, 17 U.S. Op. Off. Legal Counsel 131 (1993).

901. Department of Justice, Office of Legal Counsel, Presidential Authority to Decline to Execute Unconstitutional Statutes, 18 U.S. Op. Office of Legal Counsel 199 (1994).

902. Special White House Briefing on Provision in the FY1996 Defense Authorization Bill Relating to HIV positive Armed Services Members, Feb. 9, 1996, Federal News Service, available on Lexis Nexis; *see also* Alison Mitchell, "President Finds a Way to Fight Mandate to Oust H.I.V. Troops," *N. Y. Times*, Feb. 10, 1996 (Clinton, "once signing the overall legislation, would have no choice but to enforce the law, in the absence of a court ruling against it").

903. *Presidential Signing Statements under the Bush Administration: A Threat to Checks and Balances and the Rule of Law?: Hearing Before the H. Comm. on the Judiciary,* 110th Cong. (2007).

904. Halstead, "Presidential Signing Statements: Constitutional and Institutional Implications," *CRS Report for Congress, RL33667,* at 9 (2006).

905. American Bar Association, "Task Force on Presidential Signing Statements and the Separation of Powers Doctrine," (July 24, 2006) *available at* http://www.abanet.org/op/signingstatements , which concluded that signing statements undermine separation of powers.

906. Christopher S. Kelley, Home Page, *available at* http://www.users.muohio.edu/kelleycs/.

907. Halstead, "Presidential Signing Statements: Constitutional and Institutional Implications," *CRS Report for Congress, RL33667,* at 9 (2006).

908. *Id.* at 9-11.

909. *Id.* at 11.

910. S. Admt. 1977, 109th Cong. (2006).

911. Savage, "Bush Could Bypass New Torture Ban," *Boston Globe,* Jan. 4, 2006, at A1.

912. The White House, President's Statement on Signing of H.R. 2863, the "Department of Defense, Emergency Supplemental Appropriations to Address Hurricanes in the Gulf of Mexico, and Pandemic Influenza Act, 2006," Dec. 30, 2005, *available at* http://www.whitehouse.gov/news/releases/2005/12/20051230-8.html.

913. Savage, "Bush Could Bypass New Torture Ban," *Boston Globe,* Jan. 4, 2006, at A1.

914. The White House, President's Statement on H.R. 199, the "USA PATRIOT Improvement and Reauthorization Act of 2005," Mar. 9, 2006, *available at* http://www.whitehouse.gov/news/releases/2006/03/20060309-8.html; Drew, "Power Grab," *N. Y. Review of Books,* June 22, 2006; Savage, "Bush Could Bypass New Torture Ban," *Boston Globe,* Jan. 4, 2006, at A1.

915. Drew, "Power Grab," *N. Y. Review of Books,* June 22, 2006.

916. The White House, President's Statement on H.R. 5441, Oct. 4, 2006; *see* Savage, "Bush Challenges Hundreds of Laws," *Boston Globe,* Apr. 30, 2006.

917. The White House, President's Statement on H.R. 5441, Oct. 4, 2006; *see* Savage, "Bush Challenges Hundreds of Laws," *Boston Globe,* Apr. 30, 2006.

918. *See* Pub. L. No. 108-458, Sec. 1011(a), Sec. 102A(f)(1)(B)(3)(A)(iv), at 118 Stat. 3649 (2004).

919. 539 U.S. 306 (2003).

920. *Presidential Signing Statements: Hearing Before the S. Comm. on the Judiciary,* 109th Cong. (2006) (statement of Sen. Patrick Leahy), *available at* http://leahy.senate.gov/press/200606/062706.html.

921. *Id.*

922. Savage, "Bush Challenges Hundreds of Laws," *Boston Globe*, Apr. 30, 2006.

923. GAO Informal Opinion B-308603, at 3, 11-12 (June 18, 2007).

924. *See* GAO Informal Opinion B-308603 (June 18, 2007); GAO Informal Opinion B-309928 (Dec. 20, 2007).

925. GAO Informal Opinion B-308603 (June 18, 2007); GAO Informal Opinion B-309928 (Dec. 20, 2007). With respect to whistleblower protections, the GAO found that, contrary to law, the Department of Energy had not notified its employees that they are covered by specified whistleblower protections and "did not state when it plans to" do so, and that the Nuclear Regulatory Commission had so notified its employees, but had done so some two years late. GAO Informal Opinion B-309928, at 12 (Dec. 20, 2007).

926. *See* Press Release, H. Comm. on the Judiciary, Conyers-Byrd GAO Report Shows Presidential Power Grab in Use of Signing Statements (Dec. 21, 2007).

927. *See Impact of Presidential Signing Statements on Implementation of the National Defense Authorization Act for FY 2008: Hearing Before the Subcomm. On Oversight and Investigations of the H. Comm. On Armed Services*, 110th Cong. (2008) (Statement of Subcommittee Chairman Vic Snyder).

928. Savage, "Bush Declares Exceptions to Sections of Two Bills He Signed into Law," *N. Y. Times,* Oct. 15, 2008, (quoting Rep. Jim Cooper).

929. *See* Risen, "The Executive Power Awaiting the Next President," *N. Y. Times*, June 22, 2008.

930. *See* Savage, "Barack Obama's Q&A," *Boston Globe*, Dec. 20, 2007.

931. Copeland, "The Federal Rulemaking Process: An Overview," *CRS Report for Congress, RL 32240*, at 1 (Feb. 7, 2005).

932. The terms "regulation" and "rule" are generally used "interchangeably in discussions of the federal regulatory process." Copeland, "The Federal Rulemaking Process: An Overview," *CRS Report for Congress, RL 32240*, at 1 (2005). In turn, "rulemaking" refers to "[t]he process by

which federal agencies develop, amend, or repeal rules." *Id.*

933.*Regulatory Reform: Are Regulations Hindering Our Competitiveness?: Hearing Before the Subcomm. on Regulatory Affairs of the H. Comm. on Government Reform,* 109th Cong. 56 (2005) (testimony of J. Christopher Mihm, Managing Director – Strategic Issues, U.S. Government Accountability Office).

934.5 U.S.C. §§ 551-59, 701-06, 1305, 3105, 3344, 5372, 7521 (2008).

935.Edles, "Lessons from the Administrative Conference of the United States," *2 Eur. Pub. L.* 571, 572 (1996).

936.Copeland, "The Federal Rulemaking Process: An Overview," *CRS Report for Congress, RL 32240,* at 1 (2005)

937.Exec. Order No. 10,934, 26 Fed. Reg. 3,233 (Apr. 13, 1961).

938.*OMB Management Watch List: $65 Billion Reasons to Ensure The Federal Government is Effectively Managing Information Technology Investments: Hearing Before the H. Comm. On Government Reform,* 109th Cong. (2005) (Testimony of David A. Powner, Director, Information Technology Management Issues, U.S. Government Accountability Office).

939.Committee Print: "Office of Management and Budget: Evolving Roles and Future Issues," *CRS Report,* S. Comm. on Governmental Affairs, 99th Cong. 185 (1986).

940.OIRA was established in 1980. Paperwork Reduction Act of 1980 § 3503, 44 U.S.C. ch. 35 (2008).

941.Interim Report on the Administrative Law, Process and Procedure Project for the 21st Century, Subcomm. on Commercial and Administrative Law of the H. Comm. on the Judiciary, 109th Cong. 39 (2006) available at http://judiciary.house.gov/Media/PDFS/Printers/109th/31505.pdf.

942.The Project was approved on January 26, 2005 by the House Judiciary Committee as part of its Oversight Plan for the 109th Congress and its continuation was approved as part of the Committee's Oversight Plan for the 110th Congress. The objective of the Project was to conduct a nonpartisan, academically credible analysis with the assistance of CRS. The Project culminated with the preparation of a detailed report with recommendations for immediate legislative reforms as well as suggested areas for further research and analysis to be conducted by the Administrative Conference of the United States, which was most recently reauthorized in the 110th Congress.

943.Interim Report on the Administrative Law, Process and Procedure Project for the 21st Century, Subcomm. on Commercial and Administrative Law of the H. Comm. on the Judiciary, 109th Cong. 39 (2006) *available at* http://judiciary.house.gov/Media/PDFS/Printers/109th/31505.pdf.

944. Vladeck, "Unreasonable Intervention: The Battle to Force Regulation of Ethylene Oxide," *Administrative Law Stories* 192, at 222 (2006).

945. Vladeck, "Unreasonable Intervention: The Battle to Force Regulation of Ethylene Oxide," *Administrative Law Stories* 192, at 222 (2006). Others defend OBM's role as an enforcer of the Administration's priorities and forum for centralized review. They cite, for example, how OMB can be a "brake on overly zealous, pro-regulatory bureaucrats and as a way for an Administration to manager and rationalize its regulatory policy." *Id.* at 225. Centralized review, they argue, allows a president to consolidate power.

The ramifications of this debate are significant as explained in the following:

> [T]he stakes are enormous, implicating the most basic principles of separation of powers. At bottom, the real question is whether the White House or agencies will make the policy decisions that Congress entrusted to the agencies, not to the President. These decisions may seem mundane in the abstract, but in fact they are breathtaking in their scope and importance: affecting, among other things, the purity of the air we breathe, the food we eat, and the water we drink, the safety of our drugs, medical devices, cars, airplanes, trains, and ships, and the security of our nation's airports, refineries, nuclear power plants, chemical plants, and even our nation's border.

Id. at 226.

946. Lisa Heinzerling, Deregulatory Review, Georgetown Law Faculty Blog, *available at* http://gulcfac.typepad.com/georgetown_university_law/2007/01/deregulatory_re.html (visited Jan. 24, 2007). A commentator similarly noted, "On Jan. 18, while the headlines in the U.S. focused on the war in Iraq, the new Democratic Congress, and actress Lindsay Lohan's alcohol problem, the Bush Administration rewrote the book on federal regulation." Skrzycki, "Bush Gains Power on Rules After Losing Congress," Bloomberg.com, *available at* http://bloomberg.com/apps/news?pid=206700001&refer=columnist.

947. Exec. Ord. No. 13,422, 72 Fed. Reg. 2,763 (Jan. 23, 2007).

948. Exec. Ord. No. 12,866, 58 Fed. Reg. 51,735 (Oct. 4, 1993).

949. Pear, "Bush Directive Increases Sway on Regulation," *N. Y. Times*, Jan. 30, 2007, at A1.

950. *See, e.g.,* Press Release, Public Citizen, New Executive Order Is Latest White House Power Grab (Jan. 18, 2007), *available at* http://www.citizen.org/pressroom/release.cfm?ID=2361; Epps, "The Power of King George," Salon.com, (Feb. 1, 2007) (describing Executive Order 13422 as a "power grab" by the Bush Administration), *available at*

http://www.salon.com/opinion/feature/2007/02/01/presidential_power/.

951. Krugman, Op-Ed., "The Green-Zoning of America," *N. Y. Times*, Feb. 5, 2007, at A25.

The Administration, on the other hand, claimed the Order was simply an exercise of "good government." For example, OMB General Counsel Jeffrey Rosen explained, "Simply put: what we are doing here is 'good government.' We are building upon a process that has been used by presidents of both parties to try to institutionalize best practices." Skrzycki, "Bush Gains Power on Rules After Losing Congress," Bloomberg.com (Jan. 30, 2007), at http://bloomberg.com/apps/news?pid=206700001&refer=columnist. In another statement to the press, Mr. Rosen noted, "'This is a class good-government measure that will make federal agencies more open and accountable." Pear, "Bush Directive Increases Sway on Regulation," *N. Y. Times*, Jan. 30, 2007, at A1. Paul Noe, a former OIRA advisor, similarly noted, "The executive order promotes better-informed and more accountable regulatory decisions." Skrzycki, "Bush Gains Power on Rules After Losing Congress," Bloomberg.com (Jan. 30, 2007), at http://bloomberg.com/apps/news?pid=206700001&refer=columnist. Other proponents of Executive Order 13422 argued that it represents "long overdue action to constrain the growing burden of federal regulation on the economy." Bartlett, "Regulatory Respite," *The Washington Times*, Feb. 7, 2007.

952. *Executive Order 13422: Good Governance or Regulatory Usurpation?: Hearing Before the Subcomm. on Commercial and Administrative Law of the H. Comm. on the Judiciary,* 110th Cong. (2007).

953. Exec. Ord. No. 13,422, 72 Fed. Reg. 2,763 (Jan. 23, 2007), at § 1(a).

954. Copeland, "Changes to the OMB Regulatory Review Process by Executive Order 13422," *CRS Report for Congress, RL 33862*, at 4 (2007).

955. Skrzycki, "Bush Gains Power on Rules After Losing Congress," Bloomberg.com (Jan. 30, 2007), at http://bloomberg.com/apps/news?pid+206700001&refer=columnist (quoting Professor Sally Katzen as stating, "'It's another thumb on the scale....There will be more boxes to check, more I's to dot, more T's to cross, and more analysis.'").

956. Copeland, "Changes to the OMB Regulatory Review Process by Executive Order 13422," *CRS Report for Congress, RL 33862*, at 5 (2007) (summarizing observations by certain outside groups).

957. *Hearing on the Rulemaking Process and the Unitary Executive Theory Before the Subcomm. on Commercial and Administrative Law of the H. Comm. on the Judiciary*, 110th Cong. (2008) (prepared statement of John Conyers, Jr., Chairman, H. Comm. on the Judiciary).

958. Skrzycki, "Bush Gains Power on Rules After Losing Congress," Bloomberg.com, (Jan. 30, 2007) *available at* http://bloomberg.com/apps/news?pid=206700001&refer=columnist

959.On the same day that Executive Order 13422 was issued, OMB issued a bulletin establishing "policies and procedures for the development, issuance, and use of significant guidance documents by Executive Branch departments and agencies." Office of Management and Budget, Final Bulletin for Agency Good Guidance Practices, 72 Fed. Reg. 3,432 (Jan. 18, 2007).

960.Exec. Ord. No. 13,422, 72 Fed. Reg. 2,763 (Jan. 23, 2007), at § 3(g). According to the OMB Bulletin interpreting this provision, the definition "is not limited only to written guidance materials and should not be so construed." Office of Management and Budget, Final Bulletin for Agency Good Guidance Practices, 72 Fed. Reg. 3,432, 3,434 (Jan. 18, 2007). The Bulletin explains that the term "encompasses all guidance materials, regardless of format," including "video or audio tapes, or interactive web-based software. *Id.*

961.Exec. Ord. No. 13,422, 72 Fed. Reg. 2,763 (Jan. 23, 2007), at § 3(h). In pertinent part, the definition provides that a "significant guidance document":

> (1) Means a guidance document disseminated to regulated entities or the general public that, for purposes of this order, may reasonably be anticipated to:
>
> > (A) Lead to an annual effect of $100 million or more or adversely affect in a material way the economy, a sector of the economy, productivity, competition, jobs, the environment, public health or safety, or State, local, or tribal governments or communities;
> >
> > (B) Create a serious inconsistency or otherwise interfere with an action taken or planned by another agency;
> >
> > (C) Materially alter the budgetary impact of entitlements, grants, user fees, or loan programs or the rights or obligations of recipients thereof; or
> >
> > (D) Raise novel legal or policy issues arising out of legal mandates, the President's priorities, or the principles set forth in this Executive Order[.]

Id.

962.Pursuant to these requirements, the agency must:

1. base its decision regarding the need for and consequences of each new guidance document on the best reasonably obtainable scientific, technical, economic or other information;

2. avoid issuing guidance documents that are inconsistent, incompatible or duplicative with other regulations or guidance documents;

3. tailor the guidance to impose the least burden on society, consistent with the regulatory objective, taking into account, *inter alia*, the costs of cumulative regulations, to the extent practicable;

4. draft the guidance document so that it is simple and easy to understand; and

5. ensure that the guidance document is consistent with applicable law, the President's priorities, and EO 12866, as amended.

Exec. Ord. No. 13,422, 72 Fed. Reg. 2,763 (Jan. 23, 2007), at §§ 1-2.

Executive Order 13422 also requires OMB to ensure that the guidance document is consistent with applicable law, the President's priorities, and Executive Order 12866, as amended. *Id.* at § 2(b). A further new requirement for significant guidance documents specifies that each agency must give OIRA advance notice of any such documents and, upon request of the OIRA Administrator, provide OIRA with the content of the draft guidance document together with a brief explanation of its need and how it will meet that need. The OIRA Administrator must notify the agency if additional consultation is required before the document may be issued. *Id.* at § 7.

963. Press Release, Public Citizen, New Executive Order Is Latest White House Power Grab (Jan. 18, 2007), *available at* http://www.citizen.org/pressroom/release.cfm?ID=2361. A representative of Public Citizen made the following additional observation, "'By requiring White House approval of important guidance, the White House will insert its political agenda and pro-business bias into every level of agency policy, so that our federal government will handcuff itself instead of the companies that violate the law and put the public in danger.'" *Id.* (quoting Robert Shull, Deputy Director for Auto Safety and Regulatory Policy, Public Citizen).

964. Copeland, "Changes to the OMB Regulatory Review Process by Executive Order 13422," *CRS Report for Congress, RL 33862*, at 10 (2007).

965. *Id.* at 10-11.

966. Exec. Ord. No. 13,422, 72 Fed. Reg. 2,763 (Jan. 23, 2007), at § 4(c).

967. *Amending Executive Order 12866: Good Governance or Regulatory Usurpation?: Hearing Before the Subcomm. on Commercial and Administrative Law of the H. Comm. on the Judiciary*, 110th Cong. 55 (2007).

968. Copeland, "Changes to the OMB Regulatory Review Process by Executive Order 13422," *CRS Report for Congress, RL 33862*, at 9 (2007).

969. Exec. Ord. No. 13,422, 72 Fed. Reg. 2,763 (Jan. 23, 2007), at § 5(b).

970. *Id.* at § 4(b).

971. Pear, "Bush Directive Increases Sway on Regulation", *N. Y. Times*, Jan. 30, 2007, at A1.

972. *Hearing on the Rulemaking Process and the Unitary Executive Theory Before the Subcomm. on Commercial and Administrative Law of the H. Comm. on the Judiciary*, 110th Cong. (2008) (prepared statement of Curtis W. Copeland, Specialist in American National Government, Congressional Research Service).

973. Copeland, "Changes to the OMB Regulatory Review Process by Executive Order 13422," *CRS Report for Congress, RL 33862*, at 6 (2007).

974. *Id.* at 7.

975. *Id.* at 6.

976. *Hearing on the Rulemaking Process and the Unitary Executive Theory Before the Subcomm. on Commercial and Administrative Law of the H. Comm. on the Judiciary*, 110th Cong. (2008) (prepared statement of John Conyers, Jr., Chairman, House Committee on the Judiciary).

977. Copeland, "Changes to the OMB Regulatory Review Process by Executive Order 13422," *CRS Report for Congress, RL 33862*, at 56 (2007) (quoting Office of Management and Budget, *Stimulating Smarter Regulation: 2002 Report to Congress on the Costs and Benefits of Federal Regulations and Unfunded Mandates on State, Local, and Tribal Entities*, Dec. 2002).

978. John Graham, Administrator, OIRA, Remarks to the Board of Trustees, The Keystone Center, at Washington, DC (June 18, 2002), *available at* http://www.whitehouse.gov/omb/inforeg/keystone_speech061802.html.

979. Administrative Law, Process, and Procedure Project for the 21st Century: Interim Report, *Subcomm. on Commercial and Administrative Law of the H. Comm. on the Judiciary, Comm. Print No. 10*, 109th Cong. 56 (2006).

980. Heinzerling, "Statutory Interpretation in the Era of OIRA," 33 Ford. Urb. L. Rev. 1097, 1117 (2006).

981. U.S. General Accounting Office, *Rulemaking: OMB's Role in Reviews of Agencies' Draft Rules and the Transparency of Those Reviews*, GAO-03-929, Sept. 22, 2003.

982. *The Rulemaking Process and the Unitary Executive Theory: Hearing Before the Subcomm. on Commercial and Administrative Law of the H. Comm. on the Judiciary*, 110th Cong. (2008) (prepared statement of Curtis W. Copeland, Specialist in American National Government, Congressional Research Service) (footnotes omitted). Additional instances of this heightened role include the following:

- the increased use of "informal" OIRA reviews in which agencies share preliminary drafts of rules and analyses before final decisionmaking at the agencies — a period when OIRA says it can have its greatest impact on the rules, but when OIRA says that some of the transparency requirements in Executive Order 12866 do not apply;

- extensions of OIRA review for certain rules for months or years beyond the 90-day time limit delineated in the executive order;

- using a general statutory requirement that OIRA provide Congress with "recommendations for reform" to request the public to identify rules that it believes should be eliminated or reformed;

- a leadership role for OIRA in the development of electronic rulemaking, which has led to the development of a centralized rulemaking docket, but which some observers believe can lead to increased presidential influence over the agencies;

- the development of an OMB bulletin on peer review that, in its original form, some believed could have led to a centralized system within OMB that could be vulnerable to political manipulation or control;

- the development of a proposed bulletin standardizing agency risk assessment procedures that the National Academy of Sciences concluded was "fundamentally flawed," and that OIRA later withdrew; and

- the development of a "good guidance practices" bulletin that standardizes certain agency guidance practices.

Id.

983. However, OIRA returned only two rules in 2003, one rule in 2004, one rule in 2005, no rules in 2006, and one rule in 2007. OIRA officials indicated that the pace of return letters declined after 2002 because agencies had gotten the message about the seriousness of OIRA reviews.

984. *The Rulemaking Process and the Unitary Executive Theory: Hearing Before the Subcomm. on Commercial and Administrative Law of the H. Comm. on the Judiciary*, 110th Cong. (2008) (prepared statement of Curtis W. Copeland, Specialist in American National Government, Congressional Research Service).

985. Eilperin, "Ozone Rules Weakened at Bush's Behest," *Wash. Post*, Mar. 14, 2008, at A1.

986. *Id.* (quoting OIRA Administrator Susan Dudley).

987.Skrzycki, "It's Not a Backroom Deal If the Call Is Made in the Oval Office," *Wash. Post*, Apr. 8, 2008, at D2.

988.*Hearing on the Rulemaking Process and the Unitary Executive Theory Before the Subcomm. on Commercial and Administrative Law of the H. Comm. on the Judiciary*, 110th Cong. (2008) (prepared statement of John Conyers, Jr., Chairman, H. Comm. on the Judiciary).

989.Exec. Ord. No. 12,866, 58 Fed. Reg. 51,735 (Oct. 4, 1993).

990.*See, e.g.,* Final Rule: Amendment of the Standards for Radioactive Waste Disposal in Yucca Mountain, Nevada (under review since Dec. 15, 2006); Final Rule: Concentrated Animal Feeding Operation Rule (under review since Aug. 13, 2007); Proposed Rule: Air Quality Index Reporting and Significant Harm Level for PM2.5 (under review since Sept. 19, 2007); Proposed Rule: Protection of Stratospheric Ozone: Ban on the Sale or Distribution of Pre-Charged Products (under review since Nov. 9, 2007). General Services Administration, RegInfo.gov, *available at* http://www.reginfo.gov/public/do/eAgendaViewRule?ruleID=273113

One of these long-delayed rules concerned North American right whales, which are among the most critically endangered species in the world. Endangered and Threatened Species; Petition to Initiate Emergency Rulemaking to Prevent the Extinction of the North American Right Whale; Final Determination, 70 Fed. Reg. 56,884 (Sept. 29, 2005). More than four years ago, the National Oceanic and Atmospheric Administration initiated a rulemaking to protect the North American right whale from ship collisions. Advanced Notice of Proposed Rulemaking for Right Whale Ship Strike Reduction, 69 Fed. Reg. 30,857 (June 1, 2004). After an exhaustive rulemaking process, a final rule was submitted to OMB on February 20, 2007 for review. More than 18 months later, the rule was still under review. General Services Administration, RegInfo.gov, *available at* http://www.reginfo.gov/public/do/eAgendaViewRule?ruleID=273113 (last visited Aug. 12, 2008). This delay is due to objections raised by White House officials, including officials in the Office of the Vice President. *See* Letter from Henry Waxman, Chairman, H. Comm. on Oversight and Gov't Reform, to Susan Dudley, Administrator, Office of Regulatory and Information Administration (Apr. 30, 2008); Hebert, "Delay in Ruling on Endangered Right Whales Criticized," *Wash. Post*, Apr. 30, 2008; Nat'l Oceanic and Atmospheric Admin. Fisheries Serv., Ship Strike Rulemaking (Oct. 2007). Critics of this delay, such as Rep. Henry Waxman, claim that the Administration is raising "'baseless objections' to findings by government scientists who for years had been studying the dangers posed to the whale by commercial shipping." Hebert, "Delay in Ruling on Endangered Right Whales Criticized," *Wash. Post*, Apr. 30, 2008.

991.Pub. L. No. 104-121, § 251, 110 Stat. 847, 868-74 (1996) (codified at 5 U.S.C. §§ 801-08).

992.Letter from Gary Kepplinger, General Counsel, U.S. Gov't Accountability Office, to Sen. John D. Rockefeller, IV (D-WV) (Apr. 17, 2008).

993.5 U.S.C. § 801(a) (2008).

994.5 U.S.C. § 801(a)(3)(A) (2008).

995.Letter from Dennis G. Smith, Director, Center for Medicaid and State Operations, Dept. of Health & Human Servs. Centers for Medicare & Medicaid Servs. (Aug. 17, 2007), *available at* http://www.cms.hhs.gov/smdl/downloads/SHO081707.pdf

996.Letter from Dennis G. Smith, Director, Center for Medicaid and State Operations, Dept. of Health & Human Servs. Centers for Medicare & Medicaid Servs. (Aug. 17, 2007), *available at* http://www.cms.hhs.gov/smdl/downloads/SHO081707.pdf. This directive has been widely criticized. For example, Senator John Rockefeller (D-WV) said, "The directive is a bold-faced attempt to subvert the law and prevent states from implementing their plans to provide health insurance coverage to millions of uninsured children nationwide." Teske, "Health Care: Lawmakers Cite GAO, CRS Findings in Faulting CMS's 2007 Enrollment Directive," *BNA, Inc. Daily Rep. for Executives*, at A-17 (Apr. 21, 2008) (quoting Sen. John D. Rockefeller (D-WV)). Similarly, Senator Olympia Snowe (R-ME) complained, "Rather than working with Congress and the Governors in an open, cooperative and transparent manner, CMS chose to circumvent the rules and go their own way." *Id.* (quoting Sen. Olympia Snowe (R-ME)).

997.Memorandum from Morton Rosenberg, Specialist in American Public Law, American Law Division, CRS, to Sen. John D. Rockefeller, IV (D-WV) (Jan. 10, 2008); Letter from Gary Kepplinger, General Counsel, U.S. Gov't Accountability Office, to Sen. John D. Rockefeller, IV (D-WV) (Apr. 17, 2008).

998.Teske, "Health Care: Lawmakers Cite GAO, CRS Findings in Faulting CMS's 2007 Enrollment Directive," *BNA, Inc. Daily Report for Executives*, at A-17 (Apr. 21, 2008) (quoting CMS spokesman Jeff Nelligan).

999.*See, e.g.*, Brito & de Rugy, *Midnight Regulations and Regulatory Review* (Mercatus Center Working Paper No. 08-34, 2008), at 1.

      Rulemaking can take any number of forms. *See generally* Stephen G. Breyer *et al.*, Administrative Law and Regulatory Policy 479-692 (6th ed. 2006). Most of the regulatory activity likely will fall into the category of notice-and-comment rulemaking. This form of rulemaking is usually "informal," which means that the agency need not conduct a trial-like evidentiary hearing. Formal rulemaking is seldom used, and only a few federal statutes require it. Notice-and-comment rulemaking, which is governed by section 553(b)-(d) of the Administrative Procedure Act, 5 U.S.C. § 553(b)-(d), begins with the publication of a proposed rule in the *Federal Register*. The agency must give interested persons sufficient time to provide written comments on the rule. The agency must consider any comments it receives and then decide whether to withdraw the rule or promulgate a final rule. Any final rule must be published at least 30 days before its effective date. *See id.* Some rules are exempted from these notice-and-comment procedures.

1000.*See, e.g.*, Brito & de Rugy, *Midnight Regulations and Regulatory Review* (Mercatus Center Working Paper No. 08-34, 2008), at 3-6.

1001.*See, e.g.*, Brito & de Rugy, *Midnight Regulations and Regulatory Review* (Mercatus Center Working Paper No. 08-34, 2008), at 4.

1002.*See, e.g.*, Brito & de Rugy, *Midnight Regulations and Regulatory Review* (Mercatus Center Working Paper No. 08-34, 2008), at 7; Morris *et al.*, "Between a Rock and a Hard Place: Politics, Midnight Regulations and Mining," *55 Admin. L. Rev.* 557 (2003).

1003.*See* Beermann, "Presidential Power in Transition," 83 *B.U. L. Rev.* 947, 957-58 (2002).

1004.*See, e.g.*, Pear, "Protests Over a Rule to Protect Health Providers," *N. Y. Times*, Nov. 18, 2008 ("A last-minute Bush Administration plan to grant sweeping new protections to health care providers who oppose abortion and other procedures on religious or moral grounds has provoked a torrent of objections, including a strenuous protest from the government agency that enforces job discrimination laws."); Cook *et al.*, "Dozens of Environmental Rules in Pipeline as Bush Administration Enters Final Weeks," *BNA Daily Rep. for Executives* (Nov. 14, 2008) (noting that the "Bush Administration is working to complete dozens of final environmental rules as it prepares to leave office").

1005.Smith, "A Last Push to Deregulate; White House to Ease Many Rules," *Wash. Post*, Oct. 31, 2008, at A1

1006.Copeland, "Midnight Rulemaking: Considerations for Congress and a New Administration" *CRS Report for Congress, RL34747*, at 2 (2008).

1007.*Id.* at 2.

1008.*See, e.g.*, Kolbert, "Comment Midnight Hour," *The New Yorker*, Nov. 24, 2008 (observing that the Bush Administration has proposed rules "that would: make it harder for the government to limit workers' exposure to toxins, eliminate environmental review from decisions affecting fisheries, and ease restrictions on companies that blow up montains to get at the coal underneath them"); Steven D. Cook *et al.*, "Dozens of Environmental Rules in Pipeline as Bush Administration Enters Final Weeks," *BNA Daily Rep. for Executives* (Nov. 14, 2008) (noting that among these last-minute rules "are measures that include several air pollution regulations, a rule to ease reporting requirements for certain farm emissions, and provisions to allow for 'mountaintop mining' by coal companies"); Skrzycki, "Democrats Eye Bush Midnight Regulations," *The Washington Post*, Nov. 11, 2008, at D3; Editorial, "So Little Time, So Much Damage," *N. Y. Times*, Nov. 4, 2008 (observing that "President Bush's aides have been scrambling to change rules and regulations on the environment, civil liberties and abortion rights, among others – few for the good"); Beamish, "Congress Has Fast-Track Power to Kill Bush Rules," *Associated Press*, Nov. 14, 2008 (noting that various environmental activists are compiling lists of problematic midnight regulations); Palmer, "As Bush Lines Up Late Regulations, Congress Has Choice About Intervening," Congressional Quarterly Today Online

News – Regulatory Policy, Nov. 6, 2008 *available at*
http://news.yahoo.com/s/cq/20081106/pl_cq_politics/politics2983778.

1009.Skrzycki, "Democrats Eye Bush Midnight Regulations", *Wash. Post*, Nov. 11, 2008, at D3 (quoting a letter from the Institute for the Study of Regulation at New York University School of Law sent to the White House).

1010.Copeland, "Midnight Rulemaking: Considerations for Congress and a New Administration," *CRS Report for Congress RL34747*, at 4-7 (footnotes omitted) (Nov. 18, 2008),. Additional examples identified by CRS include:

- a Justice Department proposed rule that would "clarify and update" the policies governing criminal intelligence systems that receive federal funding, but that some contend would make it easier for state and local police to collect, share, and retain sensitive information about Americans, even when no underlying crime is suspected.

- a Justice Department proposed rule that would "adopt enforceable accessibility standards under the Americans with Disabilities Act of 1990 (ADA)," but that critics contend would weaken those standards and reduce enforcement efforts.

- an EPA revision of the definition of "solid waste" that would exclude certain types of sludge and byproducts (referred to in the proposed rule as "hazardous secondary waste") from regulation under the Resource Conservation and Recovery Act.

- an EPA rule that is expected to change how pollution levels are measured under certain parts of the Clean Air Act, and that some contend will change emissions standards for industrial facilities operating near national parks.

- a National Park Service rule that, if consistent with the April 2008 proposal, would change the agency's current policy and permit state laws to determine whether concealed firearms could be carried in national parks.

- a proposed amendment to the Federal Acquisition Regulation to require certain contractors and subcontractors to use the E-Verify system to confirm that certain of their employees are eligible to work in the United States, but which the U.S. Chamber of Commerce and others said contravenes the intent of Congress and raises numerous practical difficulties.

- a Department of Labor proposed rule that would change the way that occupational health risk assessments are conducted within the department. Legislation has been introduced in the 110th Congress (H.R. 6660 and S. 3566) that would prohibit the issuance or enforcement of this rule.

Id.

1011.Copeland, "Midnight Rulemaking: Considerations for Congress and a New Administration," *CRS Report for Congress RL34747*, at 7 (2008),.

1012.*Id.* at 7-8.

1013.*Id.* at 8.

1014.*See* Memorandum from Andrew Card, White House Chief of Staff, to Heads and Acting Heads of Executive Departments and Agencies (Jan. 20, 2001), *available at* http://www.whitehouse.gov/omb/inforeg/regreview_plan.pdf.

1015.*See, e.g.*, Natural Res. Defense Council, Inc. v. EPA, 683 F.2d 752, 761 (3d Cir. 1982); Council on S. Mountains v. Donovan, 653 F.2d 573 (D.C. Cir. 1981).

1016.*See* Natural Res. Defense Council v. Abraham, 355 F.3d 179, 204-05 (2d Cir. 2004), in which the court rejected the Department of Energy's attempt to use procedural rule and good cause exceptions to suspend the effective date of energy conservation standards for air conditioners and heat pumps.

1017.Henry, *Patrick Henry: Life, Correspondence and Speeches*, at 496 (1891).

1018.*The Rulemaking Process and the Unitary Executive Theory: Hearing Before the Subcomm. on Commercial and Administrative Law of the H. Comm. on the Judiciary*, 110th Cong. (2008) (prepared statement of Curtis W. Copeland, Specialist in American National Government, Congressional Research Service) (footnotes omitted).

1019.*The Rulemaking Process and the Unitary Executive Theory: Hearing Before the Subcomm. on Commercial and Administrative Law of the H. Comm. on the Judiciary*, 110th Cong. (2008). Other witnesses at the hearing included: Susan E. Dudley, Administrator, Office of Information and Regulatory Affairs, Office of Management and Budget; James L. Gattuso, Senior Fellow in Regulatory Policy Roe Institute for Economic Policy Studies at The Heritage Foundation; Professor Peter L. Strauss, Columbia University School of Law; and Dr. Rick Melberth, Director of Regulatory Policy, OMB Watch.

1020.*The Rulemaking Process and the Unitary Executive Theory: Hearing Before the Subcomm. on Commercial and Administrative Law of the H. Comm. on the Judiciary*, 110th Cong. (2008) (testimony of Curtis W. Copeland, Specialist in American National Government, Congressional Research Service).

1021.*Id.*

1022.*Id.*

1023.U.S. General Accounting Office, *Rulemaking: OMB's Role in Review of Agencies' Draft Rules and the Transparency of Those Reviews*, GAO-03-929, Sept. 22, 2003.

1024.American Bar Association, Achieving the Potential – The Future of Federal E-Rulemaking, A Report to Congress and the President from the Committee on the Status and Future of Federal E-Rulemaking, at 3 (2008).

1025.*Id.* at 3.

1026.*Id.* at 4.

1027.Oversight Plan for the 109th Congress, Committee on the Judiciary, at 5 (Jan. 26, 2005) *available at*
http://judiciary.house.gov/media/pdfs/printers/109th/109th%20Oversight%20Plan.pdf.

1028.House Judiciary Committee Oversight Plan 110th Congress, *available at*
http://www.judiciary.house.gov/media/pdfs/110-Oversight.pdf

1029.*Administrative Law, Process, and Procedure Project for the 21st Century: Interim Report, Subcomm. on Commercial and Administrative Law of the H. Comm. on the Judiciary, Comm. Print No. 10*, 109th Cong. (2006). The report made recommendations for legislative proposals and suggested areas for further research and analysis to be considered by ACUS was issued in December 2006. The report addressed the: (1) agency adjudicatory process; (2) public participation in the rulemaking process; (3) the role of science in the regulatory process; (4) the utility of regulatory analysis and accountability requirements; and (5) congressional, presidential and judicial review of agency rulemaking.

1030.With respect to symposia, the Committee's Subcommittee on Commercial and Administrative sponsored three. On December 5, 2005, the Subcommittee convened a symposium on e-rulemaking. Representatives from the Legislative and Executive Branches as well as from academia and the private sector discussed whether e-rulemaking improves the regulatory process and encourages public participation. It also examined how advances in information technology may impact administrative rulemaking. On May 9, 2006, the Subcommittee sponsored a symposium that focused on the role that science plays in the rulemaking process. This program, which was held at American University, involved representatives from the public and private sectors who debated what the appropriate role of science should be. The third symposium, held on September 11, 2006, considered congressional, presidential and judiciary review of agency rulemaking. This program, hosted by CRS, also examined conflicting claims of legal authority over rulemaking by the Legislative and Executive Branches.

1031.The studies addressed the development of proposed rules before they are published, judicial review of rulemaking, and the role of advisory committees.

1032.*Reauthorization of the Administrative Conference of the United States: Hearing Before the Subcomm. on Commercial and Administrative Law of the H. Comm. on the Judiciary,* 110th Cong. (2007) (testimony of Morton Rosenberg, Specialist in American Public Law, Congressional Research Service).

1033.*Reauthorization of the Administrative Conference of the United States: Hearing Before the Subcomm. on Commercial and Administrative Law of the H. Comm. on the Judiciary,* 110th Cong. (2007) (testimony of Morton Rosenberg, Specialist in American Public Law, Congressional Research Service).

1034.Administrative Conference Act of 1964, Pub. L. No. 88-499, 5 U.S.C.A. §§ 591-96 (2002). Temporary conferences were established in 1953 by President Eisenhower, *Memorandum Convening the President's Commission on Administrative Procedure,* Pub. Papers 219-22 (Apr. 28, 1953), and in 1961 by President Kennedy. Exec. Order No. 10,934, 26 Fed. Reg. 3233 (Apr. 13, 1961).

The Conference's jurisdiction over administrative procedure was intentionally broad. It was authorized to study "the efficiency, adequacy, and fairness of the administrative procedure used by administrative agencies in carrying out administrative programs, and make recommendations to administrative agencies, collectively or individually, and to the president, Congress, or the Judicial Conference of the United States[.]" In addition, it facilitated the interchange among administrative agencies of information potentially useful in improving administrative procedure. The Conference also collected information and statistics from administrative agencies and published reports evaluating and improving administrative procedure. 5 U.S.C. § 594 (2008).

1035.Section 592 of title 5, for example, provided that the term "administrative procedure," was "to be broadly construed to include any aspect of agency organization, procedure, or management which may affect the equitable consideration of public and private interests, the fairness of agency decisions, the speed of agency action, and the relationship of operating methods to later judicial review . . . ." 5 U.S.C. § 592(3) (2008).

1036.*Reauthorization of the Administrative Conference of the United States Before the Subcomm. on Commercial and Administrative Law of the House Comm. on the Judiciary,* 104th Cong. 31 (1996) (statement of C. Boyden Gray).

1037.Over time, Congress assigned ACUS various responsibilities. For example, agencies seeking to implement the Government in the Sunshine Act, 5 U.S.C. § 552b(g) (2008), and the Equal Access to Justice Act, 5 U.S.C. § 504(c)(1) (2008), were required to consult with ACUS before promulgating rules to ensure uniformity. ACUS served as the key implementing agency for the Administrative Dispute Resolution Act, 5 U.S.C. §§ 571-583 (2008), the Negotiated Rulemaking Act, 5 U.S.C. §§ 561-570 (2008), the Equal Access to Justice Act, 5 U.S.C. § 504(c)(1), (e) (2008), the Congressional Accountability Act, Pub. L. No. 104-1, § 230, 109 Stat. 3 (1995), and the Magnusson-Moss Warranty-Federal Trade Commission Improvement Act, Pub.

L. No. 93-637, § 202(d), 88 Stat. 2183, 2198 (1974). ACUS also played a key role in the Clinton Administration's National Performance Review with respect to improving regulatory systems. *See, e.g.,* Letter from Elaine Kamarck, Senior Policy Advisor to the Vice President, to Rep. Steny H. Hoyer, Chair, Subcomm. on Treasury, Post Service, and General Government of the House Appropriations Comm. (Mar. 7, 1994) (citing the Conference's "valuable assistance" to the National Performance Review). Further, ACUS served as a resource for Members of Congress, Congressional Committees, the Internal Revenue Service, Department of Transportation, and the Federal Trade Commission, *See* Breger, "The Administrative Conference of the United States: A Quarter Century Perspective," *53 U. Pitt. L. Rev*. 835-37, 847 (1992); Toni Fine, "A Legislative Analysis of the Demise of the Administrative Conference of the United States," *30 Arizona St. L. J.* 19, at 46 (1998). Even after its demise in 1995, Congress continued to assign ACUS various responsibilities apparently unaware of the Conference's termination. *See, e.g.,* S. 1370, 107th Cong., § 12(b) (2001) (requiring the Attorney General and the Secretary of Health and Human Services to consult with the Conference with respect to developing guidelines for alternative dispute resolution mechanisms); S. 1613, 105th Cong., § 1(g) (1998) (requiring the Conference to report to Congress on the frequency of fee awards paid by certain federal agencies); S. 886, 105th Cong., § 111 (1997) (requiring the Attorney General and the Secretary of Health and Human Services to consult with the Conference with respect to developing guidelines for alternative dispute resolution mechanisms).

1038.H.R. Rep. No. 104-291, at 6 (1995).

1039.Pub. L. No. 110-290 (2008).

1040.*See* Pub. L. No. 109-148, Title X, Sec. 1003 (2005).

1041.*See* President's Statement on Signing of H.R. 2863, 41 WCPD 1918 (Jan. 2, 2006).

1042.*See* Savage, "Bush Challenges Hundreds of Laws," *Boston Globe*, Apr. 30, 2006, at A1; *Presidential Signing Statements under the Bush Administration: A Threat to Checks and Balances and the Rule of Law?: Hearing Before the H. Comm. on the Judiciary,* 110th Cong. (2007) (Testimony of Prof. Charles J. Ogletree, Jr.).

1043.*See* Savage, "Bush Challenges Hundreds of Laws," *Boston Globe*, Apr. 30, 2006, at A1.

1044.*See* Energy Policy Act of 2005, Pub. L. No. 109-58 (2005).

1045.*See* President's Statement on Energy Policy Act of 2005, 41 WCPD 1267 (Aug. 15, 2005); Savage, "Bush Challenges Hundreds of Laws", *Boston Globe*, Apr. 30, 2006, at A1.

1046.*See* Pub. L. No. 108-458, Sec. 1011(a), Sec. 102A(f)(1)(B)(3)(A)(iv), at 118 Stat. 3649 (2004).

1047.*See* Statement on Signing the Intelligence Reform and Terrorism Prevention Act of 2004, 40 WCPD 2993 (Dec. 27, 2004); Savage, "Bush Challenges Hundreds of Laws," *Boston Globe*,

Apr. 30, 2006, at A1.

1048.*See* GAO Informal Opinion B-308603, at 24 (June 18, 2007). The GAO noted that the Defense Department **did** submit the required data for operations in the Balkans and Guantanamo Bay but failed to do so with respect to operations in Iraq.

1049.*See* GAO Informal Opinion B-309928, at 12-13 (Dec. 20, 2007). The GAO concluded that the NRC implemented its obligations under the law approximately two years late.

1050.*See* Halstead, "Presidential Signing Statements: Constitutional and Institutional Implications," *CRS Report for Congress, RL33667*, at 9-11 (2006).

1051.*See Clinton v. New York*, 524 U.S. 417 (1998) (invalidating line-tem veto under Article I, section 7); Philip J. Cooper, *George W. Bush, Edgar Allen Poe, and the Use and Abuse of Presidential Signing Statements*, 35 *Presidential Studies Quarterly* 515, 518 (2005).

1052.*The Rulemaking Process and the Unitary Executive Theory: Hearing Before the Subcomm. on Commercial and Administrative Law of the H. Comm. on the Judiciary*, 110th Cong. (2008) (prepared statement of Curtis W. Copeland, Specialist in American National Government, Congressional Research Service) (footnotes omitted).

1053.Specific concerns about the Order are its requirements that agencies:

1. identify a specific "market failure" before initiating a rule. Doing so bypasses Congress by establishing standards for regulatory initiation that are not consistent with statutory requirements, and deters congressionally intended regulatory actions;

2. provide OIRA with advance notification of significant guidance documents. Doing so represents a major expansion of the office's (and therefore the president's) influence, particularly when coupled with the ability of OIRA to determine which guidance documents are "significant" and the ability of OIRA to conclude that "additional consultation will be required" before a document is issue; and

3. designate a presidential appointee to be a regulatory policy officer who must approve every proposed regulation before an agency may commence the rulemaking process and before such regulation may be included in the agency's regulatory plan. Representative Henry A. Waxman (D-CA), Chair of the Committee on Oversight and Government Reform, observed, "'The executive order allows the political staff at the White House to dictate decisions on health and safety issues, even if the government's own impartial experts disagree. This is a terrible way to govern, but great news for special interests." Pear, "Bush Directive Increases Sway on Regulation," *N.Y. Times*, Jan. 30, 2007, at A1. These appointees are problematic because they are accountable only to the Administration, yet they can effectively substitute their political judgment for agency decisionmaking. Also, very little is known about how these appointees

operate, how often they override proposed rules, and the extent to which they substitute their political judgment for the substantive expertise of the agencies.

1054. Examples include the following:

- the development of a detailed economic analysis circular and what agency officials described as a perceptible "stepping up the bar" in the amount of support required from agencies for their rules, with OIRA reportedly more often looking for regulatory benefits to be quantified and a cost-benefit analysis for every regulatory option that the agency considered, not just the option selected;

- the issuance of 21 letters returning rules to the agencies between July 2001 and March 2002 — three times the number of return letters issued during the last six years of the Clinton Administration. However, OIRA returned only two rules in 2003, one rule in 2004, one rule in 2005, no rules in 2006, and one rule in 2007. OIRA officials indicated that the pace of return letters declined after 2002 because agencies had gotten the message about the seriousness of OIRA reviews;

- the issuance of 13 "prompt letters" between September 2001 and December 2003 suggesting that agencies develop regulations in a particular area or encouraging ongoing efforts. However, OIRA issued two prompt letters in 2004, none in 2005, one in 2006, and none in 2007.;

- the increased use of "informal" OIRA reviews in which agencies share preliminary drafts of rules and analyses before final decisionmaking at the agencies — a period when OIRA says it can have its greatest impact on the rules, but when OIRA says that some of the transparency requirements in Executive Order 12866 do not apply;

- extensions of OIRA review for certain rules for months or years beyond the 90-day time limit delineated in the executive order;

- using a general statutory requirement that OIRA provide Congress with "recommendations for reform" to request the public to identify rules that it believes should be eliminated or reformed;

- a leadership role for OIRA in the development of electronic rulemaking, which has led to the development of a centralized rulemaking docket, but which some observers believe can lead to increased presidential influence over the agencies;

- the development of an OMB bulletin on peer review that, in its original form, some believed could have led to a centralized system within OMB that could be vulnerable to political manipulation or control;

- the development of a proposed bulletin standardizing agency risk assessment procedures that the National Academy of Sciences concluded was "fundamentally flawed," and that OIRA later withdrew; and

- the development of a "good guidance practices" bulletin that standardizes certain agency guidance practices.

The Rulemaking Process and the Unitary Executive Theory: Hearing Before the Subcomm. on Commercial and Administrative Law of the H. Comm. on the Judiciary, 110th Cong. (2008) (prepared statement of Curtis W. Copeland, Specialist in American National Government, Congressional Research Service) (footnotes omitted).

1055. Skrzycki, "It's Not a Backroom Deal If the Call Is Made in the Oval Office," *Wash. Post*, Apr. 8, 2008, at D2; Eilperin, "Ozone Rules Weakened at Bush's Behest," *Wash. Post*, Mar. 14, 2008, at A1.

1056. More than four years ago, the National Oceanic and Atmospheric Administration initiated a rulemaking to protect the North American right whale from ship collisions. Advanced Notice of Proposed Rulemaking for Right Whale Ship Strike Reduction, 69 Fed. Reg. 30,857 (June 1, 2004). After an exhaustive rulemaking process, a final rule was submitted to OMB on February 20, 2007 for review. More than 18 months later, the rule was still under review. General Serv. Admin., RegInfo.gov, at http://www.reginfo.gov/public/do/eAgendaViewRule?ruleID=273113 (last visited Aug. 12, 2008). This delay is due to objections raised by White House officials, including officials in the Office of the Vice President. *See* Letter from Henry Waxman, Chairman, H. Comm. on Oversight and Gov't Reform, to Susan Dudley, Administrator, Office of Regulatory and Information Admin. (Apr. 30, 2008); Hebert, "Delay in Ruling on Endangered Right Whales Criticized," *Wash. Post*, Apr. 30, 2008; Nat'l Oceanic and Atmospheric Admin. Fisheries Serv., Ship Strike Rulemaking (Oct. 2007). Critics of this delay, such as Rep. Henry Waxman, claim that the Administration is raising "'baseless objections' to findings by government scientists who for years had been studying the dangers posed to the whale by commercial shipping." Hebert, "Delay in Ruling on Endangered Right Whales Criticized," *Wash. Post*, Apr. 30, 2008.

1057. Press Release, U.S. Senator Jay Rockefeller (D-WV) & U.S. Senator Olympia Snowe (R-ME), With Law on Their Side, Senators Call on Bush Administration To Voluntarily Rescind August 17 Chip Directive (Apr. 18, 2008), at http://rockefeller.senate.gov/press/record.cfm?id=296411.

1058. Smith, "A Last Push to Deregulate; White House to Ease Many Rules," *Wash Post*, Oct. 31, 2008, at A1

1059. *See, e.g.*, Froomkin, "Approaching the Midnight Hour," *Wash. Post*, Nov. 20, 2008; OMB Watch, "Midnight at the White House: Bush Using Rules to Cement Legacy" (Nov. 4, 2008), http://www.ombwatch.org/article/articleview/4400/1; Letter from Richard L. Revesz, Dean,

New York University School of Law, & Michael A. Livermore, Executive Director, Institute for the Study of Regulation, to Jim Nussle, Director, Office of Management and Budget (Sept. 5, 2008).

1060.*See* Froomkin, "Approaching the Midnight Hour," *Wash. Post*, Nov. 20, 2008.

1061.OMB Watch, "Midnight at the White House: Bush Using Rules to Cement Legacy" (Nov. 4, 2008), http://www.ombwatch.org/article/articleview/4400/1.

1062.For example:

> 1. OIRA increasingly requires agencies to submit rules for "1" review before the agency heads have formally approved the rules, and OIRA has said it has its greatest influence on the rules during this period. However, OIRA has also said that the requirement in Executive Order 12866 that agencies disclose the changes made at the suggestion or recommendation of OIRA does not include informal reviews;

> 2. OIRA discloses its meetings with outside parties, but those disclosures often do not clearly indicate what rules were discussed or who those parties represent;

> 3. OIRA does not disclose how many "significant" guidance documents it has reviewed since the issuance of Executive Order 13422, or what changes were made to those documents as a result of those reviews; and

> 4. agency regulatory policy officers do not disclose how many rules they changed or completely prevented from being published in the *Federal Register*.

The Rulemaking Process and the Unitary Executive Theory: Hearing Before the Subcomm. on Commercial and Administrative Law of the H. Comm. on the Judiciary, 110th Cong. (2008) (prepared statement of Curtis W. Copeland, Specialist in American National Government, Congressional Research Service) (footnotes omitted).

1063.*See, e.g., The Rulemaking Process and the Unitary Executive Theory: Hearing Before the Subcomm. on Commercial and Administrative Law of the H. Comm. on the Judiciary*, 110th Cong. (2008) (prepared statement of Curtis W. Copeland, Specialist in American National Government, Congressional Research Service) (noting the it is currently unclear whether agency regulatory policy officers "have stopped any agency regulatory initiatives before they became draft rules, or, if so, whether there has there [sic] been an increase in such stoppages" since their authority was enhanced under Executive Order 13422).

1064.*Reauthorization of the Administrative Conference of the United States: Hearing Before the Subcomm. on Commercial and Administrative Law of the H. Comm. on the Judiciary,* 110th Cong. (testimony of Morton Rosenberg, Specialist in American Public Law, Congressional Research Service).

1065.Transcript of Record (Feb. 20, 2007), *United States v. Libby*, C.R. No. 05-394 (D.D.C.) (hereinafter *Libby*).

1066.Kristoff, "Missing in Action: Truth," *N.Y. Times*, May 6, 2003; *see also* Pincus, "CIA Did Not Share Doubt on Iraq Date; Bush Used Report of Uranium Bid," *Wash. Post*, June 12, 2003, at A-1.

1067.*Id.*

1068.Pincus, "CIA Did Not Share Doubt on Iraq Date; Bush Used Report of Uranium Bid," *Wash. Post*, June 12, 2003, at A-1.

1069.Ackerman & Judis, "The First Casualty: The Selling of the Iraq War," *New Republic*, June 19, 2003.

1070.*Id.*

1071.Wilson, "What I Didn't Find in Africa," *N.Y. Times*, July 6, 2003. The op-ed attracted considerable media attention. *See, e.g.*, Leiby & Pincus, "Retired Envoy: Nuclear Reports Ignored; Bush Cited Alleged Iraq Purchases," *Wash. Post*, July 6, 2003.

1072.*See* Transcript, *NBC Nightly News*, July 8, 2003, *appears as* Gov't Ex. 1A, *Libby*.

1073.*See* Wilson, "What I Didn't Find in Africa," *N.Y. Times*, July 6, 2003.

1074.*See, e.g.*, Leiby and Pincus, "Retired Envoy: Nuclear Report Ignored; Bush Cited Alleged Iraqi Purchases," *Wash. Post*, July 6, 2003.

1075.*See* Novak,"Mission to Niger," *Chicago Sun-Times*, July 14, 2003, at 3. *See generally* Phelps & Royce, "Columnist Blows CIA Agent's Cover," *Newsday*, July 22, 2003.

1076.*See, e.g.*, Cooper, Calabresi, & Dickerson, "A War on Wilson?," *Time*, July 17, 2003.

1077.*See, e.g.*, Transcript, CNN, *Wolf Blitzer Reports*, July 14, 2005, http://www.transcripts.cnn.com/transcripts/0507/14/wbr.01.html.

1078.Exec. Order No. 12,958, 68 Fed. Reg. 19,829 (Apr. 17, 1995).

1079.*See, e.g.*, *Disclosure of CIA Agent Valerie Plame Wilson's Identity and White House Procedures for Safeguarding Classified Information*, *Hearing Before the H. Comm. On Oversight and Gov't Reform*, 110th Cong. (2007) (hereinafter *Disclosure Hearing, Before H. Comm. On Oversight and Gov't Reform*), Preliminary Transcript at 4-5, *available at* http://oversight.house.gov/documents/20071114150609.pdf (statement of Henry A. Waxman, Chairman, H. Comm. on Oversight and Gov't Reform); *see also id.* at 15 (statement of Valerie Plame Wilson) ("In the run-up to the war with Iraq, I worked in the Counterproliferation Division of the CIA, still as a covert officer whose affiliation with the CIA was classified . . . . While I helped to manage and run secret worldwide operation against this WMD target from CIA headquarters in Washington, I also traveled to foreign countries on secret missions to find vital intelligence."); *id.* at 20 (statement of Valerie Plame Wilson) (testifying that on the day Mr. Novak's column appeared, she was a "covert officer"); *id.* at 34-35, 38 (statement of Valerie Plame Wilson) (testifying as to covert and classified status). The above-cited statement of Chairman Waxman was reviewed and approved by CIA Director Michael V. Hayden. *See Disclosure Hearing, Before H. Comm. On Oversight and Gov't Reform* at 4. Special counsel Patrick Fitzgerald, appointed by the Justice Department to investigate the leak of Ms. Wilson's identity, has confirmed that Ms. Wilson was a covert agent whose status was classified. *See, e.g.,* Indictment at 3, *Libby*; Press Conference, Patrick Fitzgerald, Special Counsel, U.S. Dept. of Justice (Oct. 28, 2005),http://washingtonpost.com/wp-dyn/content/article/2005/10/28/AR2005102801340; Statement, Patrick Fitzgerald, Special Counsel, U.S. Dept. of Justice, White House Official I. Lewis Libby Indicated on Obstruction of Justice False Statement and Perjury Charges Related to Leak of Classified Information Revealing CIA Officer's Identity ((Oct. 28, 2005), http://www.usdoj/usao/iln/os; Gov't Sentencing Mem. at 12, *Libby*. Journalistic accounts establish, based on interviews with confidential CIA sources, that Ms. Wilson was what is known as a "'non-official cover officer (NOC).' NOC's are the most clandestine of the CIA's frontline officers." Corn, "What Valerie Plame Really Did at the CIA," *The Nation*, Sept. 6, 2006; *see also* Corn and Isikoff, *Hubris: The Inside Story of Spin, Scandal, and the Selling of the Iraq War* (2006); Pincus & Allen, "Leak of Agent's Name Causes Exposure of CIA Front Firm," *Wash. Post*, Oct. 4, 2003, at A-3. This distinguishes them from "official cover" operatives who pretend to work for another government agency. *See, e.g.,* Corn, "What Valerie Plame Really Did at the CIA," *Nation*, Sept. 6, 2006. In Ms. Wilson's case, she pretended to work for an energy consulting firm (Brewster Jennings & Associates). Her actual job was overseeing the operations of the CIA's Joint Task Force an Iraq – part of the Counterproliferation Division of the CIA's Directorate of Operations. The Joint Task Force's mission was to find evidence to back the Bush Administration's claim that Iraq had or sought to acquire weapons of mass destruction. *See, e.g., id.* Her "main mission" with the Joint Task Force was to "gather agents for the CIA." *Id.*

1080.*See Disclosure Hearing, Before H. Comm. On Oversight and Gov't Reform* at 17 (statement of Valerie Plame Wilson); *id.* at 4-5 (statement of Henry A. Waxamn).

1081.*See, e.g., id.* at 6-7; Transcript of Record (Jan. 24, 2007), *Libby* (statement of Craig Schmall, Mr. Libby's regular daily intelligence briefer); Indictment at 2, *Libby*.

1082.*See Disclosure Hearing, Before H. Comm. On Oversight and Gov't Reform* at 22 (statement of Valerie Plame Wilson).

1083.Letter from Stanley M. Moskowitz, Director, Congressional Affairs, CIA, to John Conyers, Jr., Ranking Member, H. Comm. on the Judiciary (Jan. 30, 2004).

1084.On the background of the investigation, see, *e.g., United States v. Libby*, 429 F. Supp.2d 27, 28 (D.D.C.).

1085.Editorial, "Investigating Leaks," *N.Y. Times*, Oct. 2, 2003, at A30.

1086.*See, e.g.*, White House Press Secretary Scott McClellan, Press Briefing (Oct. 7, 2003), *available at available at* http://www.whitehouse.gov/news/releases/2003/10/20031007-4.html#2; Stevenson & Eric Lichtblau, "Leaker May Remain Elusive, Bush Suggests," *N.Y. Times*, Oct. 8, 2003, at A28.

1087. On October 21, 2003, the Assistant Attorney General for the Criminal Division, Christopher Wray, informed the Senate Committee on the Judiciary that he was keeping Attorney General Ashcroft up-to-date on the investigation. *See, e.g.*, Waas, "What Now, Karl? Rove and Ashcroft Face new Allegations in the Valerie Plame Affair," *Village Voice*, Aug. 13, 2005; Waas, "Ashcroft's Interest," *American Prospect*, July 8, 2004, *available at* http://www.prospect.org/cs/articles?article=ashcrofts_interest.

1088.Michael Duffy, "Leaking With a Vengeance," *Time*, Oct. 13, 2003, at 28.

1089.Press Statement, U.S. Dept. of Justice, Deputy Att'y Gen. James Comey, Appointment of Special Prosecutor to Oversee Investigation Into Alleged Leak of CIA Agent Identity and Recusal of Attorney General Ashchroft from the Investigation (Dec. 30, 2003); *see also, e.g.*, *United States v. Libby*, 498 F. Supp.2d 1, 6-8 (D.D.C. 2007); *United States v. Libby*, 429 F.Supp.2d 27, 28 (D.D.C. 2006) (same). The manner in which the Department appointed Fitrzgerald, however, led Fitzgerald to believe he was not granted the authority to issue a report at the conclusion of his investigation. *See* Letter from Patrick Fitzgerald, Special Counsel, U.S. Dept. of Justice, to John Conyers, Jr., Chairman, H. Comm. on the Judiciary, *et al.* (Oct. 28, 2005). If the Department instead had used their express regulatory authority to appoint Mr. Fitzgerald as special prosecutor, such a report would have been required. *See* .28 C.F.R. § 600.8-.9.

1090.*See, e.g.*, Leonnig & VandeHei, "Libby May Have Tried to Mask Cheney's Role," *Wash. Post*, Nov. 13, 2005, at A6.

1091.Much of the focus centered on Scooter Libby's refusal to sign a waiver. *See In re: Special Counsel Investigation*, 374 F. Supp.2d 238 (D.D.C. 2005). In an effort to prompt Mr. Libby to cooperate, Chairman Conyers and other Members of Congress wrote to Mr. Libby seeking his personal waiver for Ms. Miller. *See* Letter from John Conyers, Jr., Ranking Member, H. Comm. on the Judiciary, *et al.*, to I. Lewis Libby, Chief of Staff, Office of the Vice President (Aug. 8, 2005) ("Your failure to grant such a waiver to Ms. Miller has apparently lead her to refuse to testify about her conversation(s) with you and, in turn, led to her recent incarceration for civil contempt for days."). While Mr. Libby claimed to have provided Ms. Miller with a personal waiver, Ms. Miller denied that he had done so. *See* Letter from I. Lewis Libby, Chief of Staff, Office of the Vice President, to Judith Miller, *The New York Times* (Sept. 15, 2005); *see also* Miller, "Judith Miller's Farewell," *The New York Times*, Nov. 10, 2005 (letter to the editor) ("After 85 days, more than twice as long as any other American journalist has ever spent in jail for this cause, I agreed to testify before the special prosecutor Patrick J. Fitzgerald's grand jury about my conversations with my source, I. Lewis Libby Jr. I did so only after my two conditions were met: first, that Mr. Libby voluntarily relieve me in writing and by phone of my promise to protect our conversations; and second, that the special prosecutor limit his questions only to those germane to the Valerie Plame Wilson case. Contrary to inaccurate reports, these two agreements could not have been reached before I went to jail."). On September 12, 2005, Mr. Fitzgerald stated that he would welcome such a communication reaffirming Mr. Libby's waiver. *See* Letter from Patrick Fitzgerald, Special Counsel, Dept. of Justice, to Joseph A. Tate, Dechert LLP (Sept. 12, 2005).

1092.Press Conference, Patrick Fitzgerald, Special Counsel, U.S. Dept. of Justice (Oct. 28, 2005), *available at* http://washingtonpost.com/wp-dyn/content/article/2005/10/28/AR2005102801340. It has not gone unnoticed that the administration effectively delayed any indictment until after President Bush was reelected. *See, e.g.*,Dionne, "What the 'Shield' Covered Up," *Wash. Post*, Nov. 1, 2005, at A25 ("Has anyone noticed that the coverup worked? ... Note the significance of the two dates: October 2004, before President Bush was reelected, and October 2005, after the president was reelected. Those dates make clear why Libby threw sand in the eyes of prosecutors, in the special counsel's apt metaphor, and helped drag out the investigation. ... As long as he was claiming that journalists were responsible for spreading around the name and past CIA employment of Wilson's wife, Valerie Plame, Libby knew that at least some news organizations would resist having reporters testify. The journalistic 'shield' was converted into a shield for the Bush administration's coverup.").

1093.*See* Press Briefing, White House Press Secretary Scott McClellan (Sept. 29, 2003), *available at* http://www.whitehouse.gov/news/releases/2003/09/print/20030929-7.html.

1094.*Revelations by Former White House Press Secretary Scott McClellan: Hearings Before the H. Comm. on the Judiciary*, 110th Cong. (2007) (statement of Scott McClellan).

1095. Press Briefing, White House Press Secretary Scott McClellan (Oct. 7, 2003), *available at* http://www.whitehouse.gov/news/releases/2003/10/20031007-4.html#2.

1096.NBC, *The Today Show* (May 28, 2008).

1097.*Revelations by Former White House Press Secretary Scott McClellan: Hearing Before the H. Comm. on the Judiciary*, 110th Cong. (June 20, 2008) (statement of Scott McClellan).

1098.Press Briefing, White House Press Secretary Scott McClellan (Oct. 7, 2003), *available at* http://www.whitehouse.gov/news/releases/2003/10/20031007-4.html#2; *see also* Press Briefing,White House Press Secretary Scott McClellan (Sept. 29, 2003), *available at* http://www.whitehouse.gov/news/releases/2003/09/print/20030929-7.html.("If anyone in this administrationwas involved . . . [in the leak], they would no longer be in this administration.") (stating that anyone within the White House found to have leaked classified information would, "[a]t a minimum...lose their job").

1099. Press Briefing, White House Press Secretary Scott McClellan (Oct. 10, 2003), *available at* http://www.whitehouse.gov/news/releases/2003/102003/1010-6.html.

1100. ABC News, *The Note* (Sept. 29, 2003), *available at* http://www.abcnews.go.com/sections/politics/TheNote/TheNote_Sep29.html.

1101. Press Conference, George W. Bush (Oct. 28, 2003), *available at* http://www.whitehouse.gov/news/releases/2003/10/20031028-2.html.

1102. Compare President Bush's statement, just before the 2000 presidential election, about the need for integrity in the White House: "Americans are tired of investigations and scandal, and the best way to get rid of them is to elect a new president who will bring a new administration, who will restore honor and dignity to the White House." *CNN Today*, Sept. 14, 2000.

1103. Press Conference, President George W. Bush (July 18, 2005), *available at* http://www.whitehouse.gov/news/releases/2005/7/20050718-1.html.

1104. *Revelations by Former White House Press Secretary Scott McClellan: Hearing Before the H. Comm. on the Judiciary*, 110th Cong. (June 20, 2008) (statement of Scott McClellan).

1105. *See* Press Conference, Patrick Fitzgerald, Special Counsel, U.S. Dept. of Justice (Oct. 28, 2005), *available at* http://washingtonpost.com/wp-dyn/content/article/2005/10/28/AR2005102801340; *see also* Statement, Patrick Fitzgerald, Special Counsel, U.S. Dept. of Justice, White House Official I. Lewis Libby Indicted on Obstruction of Justice, False Statement, and Perjury Charges Relating to Leak of Classified Information Revealing CIA Officer's Identity (Oct. 28, 2005), *available at* http://www.usdoj.gov/usao/iln/osc.

1106. *See, e.g.*, *United States v. Libby*, 429 F. Supp.2d 1, 4 (D.D.C. 2006). The indictment included five felony counts. The "over-arching obstruction of justice" count was the principle one. Statement, Patrick Fitzgerald, Special Counsel, U.S. Dept. of Justice, White House Official I. Lewis Libby Indicated on Obstruction of Justice, False Statement, and Perjury Charges Relating to Leak of Classified Information Revealing CIA Officer's Identity, *available at* http://www.usdoj.gov/usao/iln/osc.

1107. *See, e.g.*, Lewis, "Libby Guilty of Lying in C.I.A. Leak Case," *N.Y. Times*, Mar. 6, 2007.

1108. For a reliable summary of many of the key facts narrated below, see Transcript of Record (Feb. 20, 2007), *Libby* (government's closing argument). For a reliable journalist account of the facts, see, *e.g.*, Corn & Isikoff, *Hubris: The Inside Store of Spin, Scandal, and the Selling of the Iraq War* (2006).

1109. The key facts cited below are summarized in the closing statement of the prosecutor in the Libby trial, Transcript of Record (Feb. 27, 2003), *Libby,*, and on a chart prepared by the House Committee on Gov't Oversight and Reform, *Disclosure of Valerie Plame Wilson's Classified*

CIA Employment (Mar. 16, 2007), *available at*
http://oversight.house.gov/documents/20070316173308-19288.pdf.

1110.Transcript of Record (Jan. 23, 2007), *Libby* (testimony of Marc Grossman).

1111.*See, e.g.*, Gov't Ex. 1 (Libby grand jury testimony, Mar. 5, 2004, at 29-34, 57-58, 67-68), *Libby*; Gov't Ex. 2 (Libby grand jury testimony, Mar. 24, 2004, at 27-28), *Libby*; Gov't Ex.104, *Libby*.

1112.*Disclosure Hearing, Before H. Comm. On Oversight and Gov't Reform* at 25 (statement of Rep. Hodes).

1113.*See, e.g.*, Waas, "Exclusive: Cheney's Admissions to the CIA Leak Prosecutor and FBI," *Crooks and Liars*, Dec. 23, 2008, *available at* http://www/murraywass.crooksandliars.com/2008/12/23/exclusive-cheneys-admissions-to-the-cia-leak-prosecutors-and-fbi; Transcript of Record (Feb. 20, 2007), *Libby* (government's closing argument) Hamburger & Wallsten, "Cheney Said to Have Told Aide of Plame," *L.A. Times*, Oct. 25, 2003, at A13; *see also* Transcript of Record (Jan. 24, 2007), *Libby* (testimony of Robert Grenier) (suggestion by defense counsel that Mr. Grenier or another CIA employee was asked to look into circumstances of Ambassador Wilson's trip, perhaps by Vice President Cheney, before Mr. Libby and Mr. Grenier discussed the matter).

1114.*See, e.g.*, Gov't Ex. 1 (Libby grand jury testimony, Mar. 5, 2004, at 61-63, 156), *Libby;* Gov't Ex. 2 (Libby grand jury testimony, Mar. 24, 2004, at 172), *Libby*.

1115.Transcript of Record (Feb. 20, 2007), *Libby* (government's closing argument).

1116.Transcript of Record (Jan. 24, 2003), *Libby* (testimony of Robert Grenier).

1117. Transcript of Record (Jan. 25, 2007), *Libby* (testimony of Robert Grenier); Transcript of Record (Jan. 25, 2007), *Libby* (testimony of Cathie Martin); Defendant's Ex. 104, *Libby*.

1118. Transcript of Record (Jan. 23, 2007), *Libby,* (testimony of Marc Grossman). It has been widely reported that on June 12, 2003, the State Department sent Secretary Powell a classified memorandum written a month earlier identifying Wilson's wife as a CIA employee and saying it was believed she recommended Wilson for the Niger mission. Secretary Powell was traveling with Bush to Africa, and sources said the memorandum was widely circulated among officials with appropriate clearances aboard Air Force One. *See* Gellman, "A Leak, Then a Deluge," *Wash. Post*, Oct. 30, 2005, at A-1.

1119.*See* Transcript of Record (Jan. 24, 2007) (testimony of Craig Schmall).

1120.*See, e.g.*, Gov't Ex. 205, *Libby*.

1121.Transcript of Record (Jan. 30, 2003), *Libby* (testimony of Judith Miller).

1122. Transcript of Record (Feb. 20, 2003), *Libby* (government's closing argument)*; see also, e.g.*, Gov't Ex. 2 (Libby grand jury testimony, Mar. 5, 2004, at 76, 78-80), *Libby;* Transcript of Record (Jan. 25, 2007), *Libby* (testimony of Cathie Martin). *See generally* Wallsten & Hamburger, "Bush Critic Became Target of Libby, Former Aides Say," *L.A. Times*, Oct. 21, 2005.

1123. Gov't Ex. 1 (Libby grand jury testimony, Mar. 5, 2004, at 79-80, 82), *Libby*; *see also* Gov't Sentencing Mem. at 10, *Libby* ("The evidence showed that Mr. Libby was aggravated about Ambassador Wilson and paid exceptionally close attention in June and July 2003 to media stories about Mr. Wilson. . . . Following Ambassador Wilson's Op Ed in the *New York Times* . . . , Mr. Libby inserted himself even more in the press response to Mr. Wilson.").

1124. Gov't Ex. 402, *Libby*; *see also* Gov't Ex. 2 (Libby grand jury testimony, Mar. 24, 2004, at 87-91), *Libby*.

1125. Gov't Ex. 403, *Libby*.

1126. Transcript of Record (Jan. 29, 2007), *Libby* (testimony of Ari Fleischer); Transcript of Record (Feb. 20, 2007), *Libby* (government's closing argument).

1127. Press Conference, Ari Flesicher, White House Press Secretary (July 7, 2003), http://www.whitehouse.gov/news/releases/2003/07/20030707-5.html; Gov't Ex. 540, *Libby;* Transcript of Record (Jan. 25, 2007), *Libby* (testimony of Cathie Martin).

1128. Transcript of Record (Jan. 25, 2007), *Libby* (testimony of Cathie Martin).

1129. Gov't Ex. 524, *Libby*.

1130. Waas, "Exclusive: Cheney's Admissions to the CIA Leak Prosecutor and FBI," *Crooks and Liars*, Dec. 23, 2008, *available at* http://www.murraywass.crooksandliars.com/2008/12/23/exclusive-cheneys-admissions-to-the-cia-leak-prosecutors-and-fbi

1131. *Id.*

1132. *See* Transcript of Record (Jan. 29, 2007) (testimony of Ari Fleischer), *Libby*.

1133. *Id.*

1134. Transcript of Record (Feb. 12, 2007), *Libby* (testimony of Walter Pincus); *see also* Pincus, "Anonymous Sources: Their Use in a Time of Prosecutorial Interest," *Neiman Reports*, Summer 2007, at 25.

1135. Transcript of Record (Feb. 12, 2007), *Libby* (testimony of Walter Pincus); *see also* Pincus & Allen, "Probe Focuses on Month Before Leak to Reporters," *Wash. Post*, Oct. 12, 2003, at A-

1.

1136.*See, e.g.*, Transcript of Record (Jan. 25, 2007), *Libby* (testimony of Cathie Martin).

1137.A day or so before this meeting, Mr. Libby had conferred with the Vice President's counsel (and later Chief of Staff) about the President's authority to declassify information. During this conversation, Mr. Libby brought up the subject of Ambassador Wilson and his wife's role in arranging his trip to Niger. He asked, in particular, what paperwork would exist if a CIA employee arranged to send her spouse on an oversees trip. *See, e.g.*, Transcript of Record (Jan. 29, 2007), *Libby* (testimony of David Addington).

1138.*See* Gov't Ex. 1 (Libby grand jury testimony, Mar. 5, 2004, at 114-20, 124-25, 140-42, 156; Mar. 23, 2004, at 29-37, 40-56, 61-65), *Libby*; Gov't Ex. 528B, *Libby;* Gov't Ex. 207, *Libby*.

1139.Transcript of Record (Jan. 30, 2007), *Libby* (testimony of Judith Miller).

1140.Gov't Ex. 352, *Libby*.

1141.Gov't Ex. 1 (Libby grand jury testimony, Mar. 5, 2004, at 173-84), *Libby*; Gov't Ex. 528B, *Libby*; Transcript of Record (Jan. 25, 2007), *Libby* (testimony of Cathie Martin).

1142.*See* Gov't Ex. 2 (Libby grand jury testimony, Mar. 24, 2004, at 70), *Libby;* Gov't Sentencing Mem. at 12, *Libby*; *see also* Govt' Ex. 2 (Libby grand jury testimony, Mar. 24, 2004, at 85, 169),
Libby. *See generally* Waas, "Exclusive: Cheney's Admissions to the CIA Leak Prosecutor and FBI," *Crooks and Liars*, Dec. 23, 2008, *available at* http://www/murraywass.crooksandliars.com/2008/12/23/exclusive-cheneys-admissions-to-the-cia-leak-prosecutors-and-fbi

1143. Transcript of Record (Jan. 31, 2007), *Libby* (testimony of Matt Cooper).

1144.Gov't Ex. 1 (Libby grand jury testimony, Mar. 5, 2004, at 187), *Libby*.

1145.*See, e.g.*, *Disclosure Hearing, Before H. Comm. On Oversight and Gov't Reform* at 25 (statement of Rep. Hodes).

1146. Transcript of Record (Jan. 31, 2007) (testimony of Matt Cooper), *Libby*); *see also* Johnston & Stevenson, *"Prosecutor Narrows Focus in Leak Case,"* *N.Y. Times*, Nov. 4, 2005, at A-1.

1147.According to the Libby indictment, "On or about July 10 or July 11, 2003, Libby spoke to a senior official in the White House ('Official A') who advised Libby of a conversation Official A had earlier that week with columnist Robert Novak in which Wilson's wife was discussed as a CIA employee involved in Wilson's trip. Libby was advised by Official A that Novak would be writing a story about Wilson's wife." Indictment at 8, *Libby*. "Official A" is Karl Rove. *See*

Yost, "Mysterious 'Official A' is Karl Rove," *Editor & Publisher*, Oct. 28, 2005. Mr. Libby told FBI investigators and later testified before the grand jury that, in a private meeting in Mr. Rove's office, Mr. Rove told him that Mr. Novak had informed Mr. Rove of Ms. Wilson's identity. Gov't Ex. 1 (Libby grant jury testimony, Mar. 5, 2003, at 163-65, 169-70), *Libby*; Gov't Exhibit 2 (Libby grand jury testimony, Mar. 24, 2004, at 113-15), *Libby*; Transcript of Record (Feb. 1, 2007) (testimony of Deborah Bond). As explained below, Mr. Novak disputes that account. *See* Transcript of Record (Feb. 12, 2007), *Libby* (testimony of Robert Novak).

1148. Transcript of Record (Feb. 12, 2003), *Libby* (testimony of Robert Novak); *see also* Gov't Sentencing Mem. at 11, *Libby*. Secretary Armitage also passed the information along to *Washington Post* reporter Bob Woodward during an interview that Woodward was writing about the Bush Presidency. *See* Transcript of Record (Feb. 12, 2007), *Libby* (testimony of Bob Woodward);VandeHei & Leonning, "Woodward Was Told of Plame More Than Two Years Ago," *Wash. Post*, Nov. 16, 2005, at A-1. According to Mr. Woodward, Secretary Armitage believed that Ms. Wilson was a non-covert analyst whose status was not classified. Transcript of Record (Feb. 12, 2007) (testimony of Bob Woodward), *Libby*. Secretary Armitage would later tell a State Department colleague that revealing Ms. Wilson's CIA employment was the "dumbest thing" he had done in his life." Transcript of Record (Jan. 23, 2007), *Libby* (testimony of Marc Grossman) (recounting conversation with Secretary Armitage just prior to Mr. Grossman's interview by FBI during fall of 2003). He is apparently the only leaker to have expressed any regret over his role in the leak.

1149.Phelps & Royce, "Columnist Blows CIA Agent's Cover," *Newsday*, July 22, 2003.

1150.Gov't Sentencing Memorandum at 5, *Libby*.

1151.For a summaries of the key facts, see, *e.g.*, *id.* at 9-12, *Libby*; Transcript of Record (Feb. 20, 2007) (government's closing argument), *Libby*; Indictment, *Libby*.

1152.*See* Transcript of Record (Feb. 1, 2007), *Libby* (testimony of Deborah Bond, an FBI agent present at Mr. Libby's two interviews with the FBI); *see also* Indictment at 8-9. *See generally* Phelps & Royce, "Columnist Blows CIA Agent's Cover," *Newsday*, July 22, 2003 at 9.

1153.*See* Gov't Ex. 1 (Libby grand jury testimony of Mar. 5, 2004), *Libby*; Gov't Ex. 2 (Libby grand jury testimony of Mar. 24, 2004), *Libby*; *see also* Indictment at 9-14, *Libby*.

1154.*See* discussion Section 4(I)(B).

1155.Transcript of Record (Feb. 7, 2007), *Libby* (testimony of Tim Russert).

1156.18 U.S.C. § 3143(b)(1).

1157.*See United States v. Libby*, 498 F. Supp.2d 1 (D.D.C. 2007).

1158.Press Conference, George W. Bush, Executive Clemency for Lewis Libby (July 2, 2007), *available at* http://whitehouse.gov/news/releases/2007/07/20070702-3.html.

1159.Snow, Op Ed, *USA Today*, July 5, 2007.

1160.Press Conference, Tony Snow, White House Press Secretary (July 3, 2007), *available at* http://www.white.house.gov/news/releases/2007/07/20070703-6.html. Mr. Snow also noted during the press conference that the district court had rejected a report by the "Parole Commission" calling for a sentence less than 30 months. *See id.* That mistaken reference to the Probation Department was based on a misunderstanding of the nature of the recommendation. The Probation Department made a recommendation as to the *legal* interpretation of the Federal Sentencing Guidelines – which the judge rejected – not a recommendation as to the appropriateness of a given punishment in the absence of the Guidelines (as Mr. Snow's comment implied).

1161.*See* Press Conference, Tony Snow, White House Press Secretary (July 3, 2007), *available at* http://www.white.house.gov/news/releases/2007/07/20070703-6.html.

1162.*See Use and Misuse of Presidential Clemency Power for Executive Branch Officials*: *Hearing Before the H. Comm. On the Judiciary*, 110th Cong. 33 (2007) (hereinafter *Misuse of Clemency Power Hearing*) (statement of Roger C. Adams); *see* U.S. Dept. of Justice, *Office of the Pardon Attorney*, *available at* http://www.usdoj.gov/pardon.

1163.Press Conference, Patrick Fitzgerald, Special Counsel, U.S. Dept. of Justice (Oct. 28, 2005), *available at* http://washingtonpost.com/wp-dyn/content/article/2005/10/28/AR2005102801340.

1164.*See* Letter from Henry A. Waxman, Chairman, H. Comm. on Oversight and Gov't Reform, to Patrick J. Fitzgerald, Special Counsel (Mar. 8, 2007), *available at* http://oversight.house.gov/documents/20070308134201-02108.pdf; Letter from Patrick J. Fitzgerald, Special Counsel (Mar. 14, 2008), *available at* http://oversight.house.gov/documents/20070314180406-55978.pdf; Transcript of Record (Feb. 20, 2007), *Libby* (government's closing argument).

1165.The Republican-controlled Congress had ignored repeated calls to investigate the leak. *See, e.g.*, Letter from Henry A. Waxman, Ranking Member, H. Comm. on Gov't Reform, to Tom Davis, Chairman, H. Comm. on Gov't Reform (June 13, 2006).

1166.*See* H. Comm. on Gov't Oversight and Reform, *Report on Recommendation that House of Representatives Find Michael B. Mukasey in Contempt of Congress* (July 16, 2008), *available at* http://oversight.house.gov/documents/20080716162943.pdf (hereinafter *H. Gov't Oversight Comm. Report on Resolution*); Letter from John Conyers, Jr., Chairman, H. Comm. on Judiciary, to Michael Mukasey, Attorney General (June 5, 2008).

1167.*Revelations by Former White House Press Secretary Scott McClellan: Hearing Before the H. Comm. on the Judiciary*, 110th Cong. (June 20, 2008) (statement of John Conyers).

1168.*See attached to Appendix to H. Gov't Oversight Comm. Report on Resolution*, *available at* http://oversight.house.gov/documents/20080716163617.pdf.; Subpoena of H. Judiciary Comm. to Michael Mukasey, Attorney General (June 27, 2008), *attached to Appendix to H. Gov't Oversight Comm. Report on Resolution*, *available at* http://oversight.house.gov/documents/20080716163617.pdf.

1169.*See* Letter from Henry A. Waxman, Chairman, H. Comm. on Oversight and Gov't Reform, to Michasel Mukasey, Attorney General (July 8, 2008), *attached to Appendix to H. Gov't Oversight Comm. Report on Resolution*, *available at* http://oversight.house.gov/documents/20080716163617.pdf.

1170.*See* Letter from Keith B. Nelson, Principal Deputy Assistant Attorney General, Dept. of Justice, to Henry A. Waxman, Chairman, H. Comm. on Oversight and Gov't Reform (July 16, 2008), *attached to Appendix to H. Gov't Oversight Comm. Report on Resolution*, *available at* http://oversight.house.gov/documents/20080716163617.pdf.

1171.For the specific argument raised by the President and an assessment of their validity, see the discussion in Section 5 of this Report.

1172.*H. Gov't Oversight Comm. Report on Resolution* Subpoena of H. Judiciary Comm. to Michael Mukasey, Attorney General (June 27, 2008).

1173.Letter from Henry A. Waxman, Chairman, H. Comm. on Gov't Oversight and Reform, to Michasel A. Mukasey, Attorney General of the U.S. (June 3, 2008), *attached to Appendix to H. Gov't Oversight Comm. Report on Resolution*; *see also H. Gov't Oversight Comm. Report on Resolution*; Subpoena of H. Judiciary Comm. to Michael Mukasey, Attorney General (June 27, 2008) (summarizing publicly available information that raises questions about Vice President Cheney's role), *attached to Appendix to H. Gov't Oversight Comm. Report on Resolution*; *see also H. Gov't Oversight Comm. Report on Resolution*.

1174.*Disclosure Hearing, Before H. Comm. On Oversight and Gov't Reform* at 3 (statement of Hon. Henry A. Waxman, Chairman, H. Comm. on Oversight and Gov't Reform).

1175.Exec. Order No. 12,958, 68 Fed. Reg. 19,829 (Apr. 17, 1995).

1176.*Id.* § 5.5(e)(1) (Apr. 17, 1995) (preamble); *see also Disclosure Hearing, Before H. Comm. On Oversight and Gov't Reform* (statement of James Knodell).

1177.Standard Form 312, Classified Information Nondisclosure Agreement (hereinafter "Form 312"), *available at* http://contacts.gsa.gov/webforms.nsf/0/03A78F16A522716785256A69004E23F6/$file/SF312.pdf.

1178.*See, e.g.*, Gov't Ex. 5A, *Libby* (Libby agreement).

1179.*Disclosure Hearing, Before H. Comm. On Oversight and Gov't Reform* (testimony of James Knodell and William Leonard); Exec. Order No. 12,958, 68 Fed. Reg. 19,829 § 5.5(e)(1) (Apr. 17, 1995).

1180.Exec. Order No. 12,958, 68 Fed. Reg. 19,829 § 5.7 (Apr. 17, 1995).

1181.Form 312. For a summary of the agreement's terms, see Information Security Office, National Archives and Records Administration, *Briefing Booklet: Classified Information Non-Disclosure Agreement (Standard Form 312)* 73, *available at* http://www.fas.org/sgp/isoo/sf312.html (hereinafter *Form 312 Booklet*).

1182.Form 312; *Form 312 Booklet*.

1183.*Disclosure Hearing ,Before H. Comm. on Oversight and Gov't Reform* at 96 (testimony of James Knodell).

1184.*Id.*

1185.*Form 312 Booklet*.

1186.*Id.*

1187.*Disclosure Hearing, Before H. Comm. On Oversight and Gov't Reform* at 88-93, 101-02, 104-05, 107, 109, 116, 122-23 (testimony of James Knodell). On the absence of any White House investigation into the leak, see *Revelations by Former White House Press Secretary Scott McClellan: Hearing Before the H. Comm. on the Judiciary*, 110th Cong. (2007) (testimony of Scott McClellan).

1188.Gov't Ex. 2 (Libby grand jury testimony, Mar. 24, 2004, at 140-68), *Libby*.

1189.Gov't Ex. 2 (Libby grand jury testimony, Mar. 24, 2004, at 149, 155-56), *Libby*.

1190.*Revelations by Former White House Press Secretary Scott McClellan: Hearing Before the H. Comm. on the Judiciary*, 110th Cong. (June 20, 2008) (statement of Scott McClellan).

1191.Gov't Ex. 532, *Libby*.

1192.*Revelations by Former White House Press Secretary Scott McClellan: Hearing Before the H. Comm. on the Judiciary*, 110th Cong. (June 20, 2008) (testimony of Scott McClellan).

1193.*Id.* at 1 (statement of John Conyers).

1194.Michael Isikoff, "2007 Pardon," *Newsweek*, July 16, 2007; *see also* Lewis, *Libby Guilty of Lying in C.I.A. Leak Case*, N.Y. Times, Mar. 6, 2007.

1195.*See* Letter from John Conyers, Jr., Chairman, H. Comm. on the Judiciary, to George W. Bush, President of the U.S. (July 6, 2007), *reprinted in Misuse of Clemency Power Hearing* at 190; Letter from John Conyers, Jr., Chairman, H. Comm. on the Judiciary, to George W. Bush, President of the U.S. (July 10, 2007), *reprinted in Misuse of Clemency Power Hearing* at 192.

1196.*See* Letter from Fried F. Fielding, Counsel to the President, to John Conyers, Jr., Chairman, H. Comm. on the Judiciary (July 11, 2007), *reprinted in Misuse of Clemency Power Hearing* at 193-94. On the legal issues surrounding Mr. Fielding's response, see the discussion in Section 5 of this Report.

1197.*See Misuse of Clemency Power Hearing* at 2 (statement of John Conyers, Jr.).

1198.*Id.* at 12 (statement of Douglas A. Berman).

1199.*Id.* at 15. It also established that the sentence was the result of careful consideration. The court imposed the sentence after "reviewing a detailed pre-sentencing report, lengthy sentencing memoranda from the parties, and hundreds of letters from interested persons. Judge Walton also held a sentencing hearing in which he heard arguments from the parties and provided Mr. Libby an opportunity to address the court directly." *Id.* at 13.

1200.18 U.S.C. § 3553(a).

1201.*See Misuse of Clemency Power Hearing* at 12-13 (statement of Douglas A. Berman).

1202.*Id.* at 12 (emphasis in original); *see also United States v. Libby*, 495 F. Supp.2d 49, 52 n.1 (D.D.C. 2007) (noting that sentence was "consistent with the bottom end of the applicable sentencing range as properly calculated under the United States Sentencing Guidelines"). According to one witness, the judge's decision to sentence Mr. Libby at the bottom of the sentencing guidelines "suggests that he was attentive to the collateral personal consequences that Mr. Libby's prosecution and convictions necessarily produce. *Id.* at 14 (statement of Douglas A. Berman).

1203.127 S. Ct. 2456 (2007).

1204.*See Presidential Clemency Decision*, 110th Cong. at 19-20 (statement of Douglas A. Berman).

1205.*Presidential Clemency Power* at 15 (statement of Douglas A. Berman) (emphasis in original); *see also* Statement of Special Counsel Patrick Judge Fitzgerald, *United States v. Libby*, Crim. No. 05-394 (RBW) (D.D.C.), *quoted* in *id.* at 14 n.2 (rejecting President's statement that sentence was excessive).

1206.*Misuse of Clemency Power Hearing* at 20 (statement of Douglas A. Berman); *id.* at 4-55 (statement of Thomas Cochran); *see also* Gov't Sentencing Mem. at 8-9, *Libby* (noting that Mr.

439

Libby was not entitled to leniency because of his public service). One witness testified that the defendant in *Rita*, whose underlying crimes were remarkably similar to Mr. Libby's, was required to report for a 33-month prison sentence on the same day that President Bush commuted Mr. Libby's sentence. *See Misuse of Clemency Power Hearing* at 47 (statement of Thomas Cochran). In a separate concurrence, Justices Scalia and Thomas called the defendant's sentence in *Rita* "relatively low" given his perjury conviction. 127 S. Ct. at 2474 (Scalia, J., joined by Thomas, J., concurring).

1207. Brief for U.S, *Rita v. United States*, 127 S. Ct. 2456 (2007), *available at* http://www.usdoj.gov/osg/briefs/2006/3mer/2mer/2006-5754.mer.aa.html.

1208. *See Misuse of Clemency Power Hearing* at 9 (testimony of Douglas A. Berman).

1209. *See id.* at 33, 39 (statement of Roger C. Adams); *id.* at 1-2 (statement of John Conyers, Jr.). The regulations appear at 28 C.F.R. §§ 1.1-1.11.

1210. *See Misuse of Clemency Power Hearing* at 40 (statement of Thomas Cochran).

1211. *See id.* at 34 (statement of Roger C. Adams).

1212. *See* Press Conference, George W. Bush, Executive Clemency for Lewis Libby (July 2, 2007), *available at* http://whitehouse.gov/news/releases/2007/07/20070702-3.html. ("[O]ur entire system of justice relies on people telling the truth. And if a person does not tell the truth, particularly if he serves in government and holds public trust, he must be held accountable.").

1213. *See Misuse of Clemency Power Hearing* at 116-65 (lists of pardons and commutations during Clinton and Bush administrations prepared by Office of Pardon Attorney).

1214. Isikoff & Hosenball, "Requests Come in for Last-minute Pardons from President Bush," *Newsweek*, Nov. 24, 2008.

1215. *See Misuse of Clemency Power Hearing 127* (list of commutations by President Bush prepared by Office of Pardon Attorney). The administration had by then received over 4,000 commutation petitions. *See id.* at 88 (testimony of Roger C. Adams). As governor of Texas, President Bush commuted only one death sentence. *See* Berlow, "The Texas Clemency Memos," *Atlantic Monthly*, July/Aug. 2003.

1216. *See Misuse of Clemency Power Hearing* at 16-21 (statement of Douglas A. Berman).

1217. Transcript of Record (Feb. 20, 2007), *Libby* (government's closing argument noting promise of testimony by Mr. Libby to this end).

1218. *Misuse of Clemency Power Hearing* at 77 (testimony of Joseph F. Wilson, IV).

1219.*See id.* at 6 (testimony of Joseph F. Wilson, IV); *see also id.* at 2 (statement of John Conyers) (raising issue).

1220.*See id.* at 89, 106 (testimony of Douglas A. Berman). Some conservative commentators have since called on President Bush to pardon Mr. Libby. *See, e.g.*, Editorial, "Bush and Scooter Libby," *Wall Street J.*, Dec. 22, 2008.

1221.Other examples have drawn recent media attention. *See, e.g.*, Isikoff, "The Fed Who Blew the Whistle," *Newsweek*, Dec. 22, 2008, at 40 (featuring ordeal of Thomas M. Tamm, a Justice Department whistleblower who exposed the Department's warantless wiretapping program).

1222. *DoD Budget: Hearing on FY2004 Defense Authorization Before the Senate Armed Services Comm.*, 108th Cong. (2003) (statement of Eric K. Shinseki).

1223.*Id.*

1224.Schmitt, *"Pentagon Contradicts on Iraq Occupation Force's Size,"* N.Y. Times, Feb. 8, 2003, at A1.

1225.Engel, "Scorned General's Tactics Proved Right," *Guardian*, Mar. 29, 2003, *available at* http://www.guardian.co.uk/international/story/0,3604,925140,00.html.

1226.Schmitt, *"Pentagon Contradicts on Iraq Occupation Force's Size,"* N.Y. Times, Feb. 8, 2003, at A1.

1227.Engel, "Scorned General's Tactics Proved Right," *Guardian*, Mar. 29, 2003, *available at* http://www.guardian.co.uk/international/story/0,3604,925140,00.html.

1228.Kessler & Connolly, "Plenty of Flaws Among the Facts: Candidates Made Questionable Claims," *Wash. Post*, Oct. 9, 2004, at A20.

1229.Fallows, "Bush's Lost Year," *Atlantic Monthly*, Oct. 1, 2004, at 68.

1230.Herbert, "No End in Sight," *N.Y. Times*, Apr. 2, 2004, at A19.

1231. *See* Interview with Secretary Paul O'Neill, *60 Minutes* (CBS television broadcast, Jan. 11, 2004), *available at* http://www.cbsnews.com/stories/2004/01/09/60minutes/main592330.shtml ("[N]ine days after that meeting in which O'Neill made it clear he could not publicly support another tax cut, the Vice President called and asked him to resign").

1232.*Id.*

1233.*Id.*

1234.*Id.*

1235.Shanker, "Rumsfeld Says He Contacted Ex-Official on Bush Book," *N.Y. Times*, Jan. 14, 2004, at A13.

1236.*See* Malveaux, *"O'Neill Cleared In Use of Classified Documents,"* CNN, Feb. 6, 2004, *availalbe at* http://www.cnn.com/2004/ALLPOLITICS/02/06/oneill.cleared/.

1237.Krugman, *"The Awful Truth,"* N.Y. Times, Jan. 13, 2004, at A25.

1238.Malveaux, "O'Neill Cleared In Use of Classified Documents," CNN, Feb. 6, 2004, *available at* http://www.cnn.com/2004/ALLPOLITICS/02/06/oneill.cleared/.

1239. *Id.*

1240. Blumenthal, "He Cannot Tell a Lie, Salon," Jan. 15, 2004, *available at* http://archive.salon.com/opinion/blumenthal/2004/01/15/o_neill/index_np.html?x.

1241.Andrews, *Bush,* "In Shake-Up of Cabinet, Ousts Treasury Leader," *N.Y. Times*, Dec. 7, 2002, at A1.

1242.Rich, "Bring Back Warren Harding," N.Y. Times, Sep. 25, 2005.

1243.*See* Corbett B. Daly, "Ex-Bush Aide: Iraq War Planning Began After 9/11," CNN, May 6, 2004, *available at* http://www.cnn.com/2004/US/03/20/clarke.cbs/.

1244.Interview with Richard Clarke, *60 Minutes* (CBS television broadcast, Mar. 21, 2004), http://www.cbsnews.com/stories/2004/03/19/60minutes/main607356.shtml.

1245.*Id.*

1246.*Id.*

1247. *See* Miller, "Former Terrorism Official Faults White House on 9/11," *N.Y. Times*, Mar. 22, 2004, at A18.

1248.Press Secretary Scott McClellan, White House Press Briefing (Mar. 22, 2004), *available at* http://www.whitehouse.gov/news/releases/2004/03/20040322 4.html.

1249.150 CONG. REC. S3209 (daily ed. Mar. 26, 2004) (statement of Sen. Frist).

1250. Lizza, "Logic Jam," *New Republic*, Mar. 24, 2004.

1251.Eckholm, "A Top U.S. Contracting Official for the Army Calls for an Inquiry in the Halliburton Case," *N.Y. Times*, Oct. 25, 2004, at A13.

1252.*Id.*

1253. *Oversight H. on Waste, Fraud, and Abuse in U.S. Gov't Contracting in Iraq Before the Senate Democratic Policy Comm.*, 109th Cong. (2005) (statement of Bunnatine Greenhouse).

1254. *Id.*

1255. *Id.*

1256. Miller, *Democrats Demand Probe of Demotion*, L.A. Times, Aug. 30, 2005, at A8.

1257. *See, e.g., Disclosure Hearing ,Before H. Comm. on Oversight and Gov't Reform* at 4-5 (statement of Henry A. Waxman approved by Michael Hayden, Director, CIA); Press Conference, Patrick Fitzgerald, Special Counsel, U.S. Dept. of Justice (Oct. 28, 2005), *available at* http://washingtonpost.com/wp-dyn/content/article/2005/10/28/AR2005102801340.

1258. 50 U.S.C. § 421. Special Counsel Patrick Fitzgerald so found. *See, e.g.*, Gov't Sentencing Mem. at 12, *Libby* ("[I]t was clear from very early in the investigation that Ms. Wilson qualified under the relevant statute Title 50, United States Code, Section 421, as a covert agent").

1259. *See, e.g.,* H. Comm.on Gov't Oversight and Reform, *Disclosure of Valerie Plame Wilson's Classified CIA Employment* (Mar. 16, 2007), *available at* http://oversight.house.gov/documents/20070316173308-19288.pdf.; *see also* Gov't Sentencing Memorandum at 2, *Libby*.

1260. H. Comm. on Gov't Oversight and Reform, *Disclosure of Valerie Plame Wilson's Classified CIA Employment* (Mar. 16, 2007), *available at* http://oversight.house.gov/documents/20070316173308-19288.pdf.

1261. *See* discussion Section 4(I)(C); Gov't Sentencing Mem. at 14, *Libby*.

1262. *Disclosure Hearing, Before H. Comm. On Oversight and Gov't Reform* (testimony of Valerie Plame Wilson).

1263. *See* discussion Section 4(I)(C).

1264. *Id.*

1265. *Id.*

1266. See *H. Gov't Oversight Comm. Report on Resolution* at 9 (July 16, 2008); *see also* Gov't Sentencing Mem. at 14, *Libby* (noting that "there was an indication from Mr. Libby himself that his disclosures to the press may have been personally sanctioned by the Vice President"); discussion Section 4(I)(C).

1267. *See, e.g..*, Waas, "Exclusive: Cheney's Admissions to the CIA Leak Prosecutor and FBI," *Crooks and Liars*, Dec. 23, 2008, *available at* http://www/murraywass.crooksandliars.com/2008/12/23/exclusive-cheneys-admissions-to-the-cia-leak-prosecutors-and-fbi; Transcript of Record (Feb. 20, 2007); discussion Section 4(I)(C).

1268.Gov't Ex. 532, *Libby*.

1269.*See* discussion Section 4(I)(A)-(B).

1270.*See Disclosure Hearing Before H. Comm. On Oversight and Gov't Reform* at 82, *available at* http://oversight.house.gov/documents/20071114150609.pdf (testimony of James Knodell).

1271.Exec. Or. No. 12958 § 5.1, 68 Fed. Reg. 15,315 (Mar. 28, 2003).

1272.*See, e.g.*, Transcript of Record (Jan. 31, 2007),*Libby* (testimony of *Time Magazine* reporter Matt Cooper that, after disclosing Ms. Wilson's identity, Mr. Rove said that he had "already said too much"); Transcript of Record (Jan. 24, 2007) (testimony of Robert Grenier, Associate Deputy Director for Operations, CIA, that he briefed Mr. Libby about Ms. Wilson).

1273.Form 312; *Form 312 Briefing Booklet; Disclosure Hearing Before H. Comm. On Oversight and Gov't Reform* (statement of James Knodell).

1274.50 U.S.C. § 421 (2006). While no defenders of the administration have contended that Ms. Wilson's cover status was not protected from disclosure under Executive Order 12958, at least one defender of the Administration, former Republican congressional staffer Victoria Toensing, has contended Ms. Wilson was not a "covert agent" under the Intelligence Identifies Protection Act. *See, e.g., Disclosure Hearing, Before H. Comm. On Oversight and Gov't Reform* (testimony of Victoria Toensing); *see also* Toensing and Sanford, Editorial, "The Plame Game: Was This a Crime?" *Wash. Post*, Jan. 12, 2005, at A21. The Act defines a covert agent, in relevant part, as a " a present or retired officer or employee of an intelligence agency who is serving outside the United States or has within the last five years served outside the United States." Ms. Toensing has contends that Ms. Wilson did not qualify as a covert agent because, at the time of the disclosure, she "resided" in Washington. *See id.* The statute, however, does not require that the agent resided outside the United States during the five-year period preceding the disclosure – only that he or she *served* outside the United States. It is undisputed that Ms. Plame performed covert missions outside the United States during the five years preceding the disclosure. *See, e.g., id.* at 164, 173 (testimony of Valerie Plame Wilson). Serious questions have been raised as to whether Ms. Toensing testified accurately and truthfully before the House Government Oversight and Reform Committee when she testified that Ms. Wilson was not a "covert agent" under the Act. *See Disclosure Hearing Before H. Comm. On Oversight and Gov't Reform* (statement of Henry A. Waxman, Chairman, H. Comm. on Gov't Reform); Corn, "Did GOP Lawyer Mislead Congress About Plame Case?" *Nation*, Mar. 19, 2007, *available at* http://www.thenation.com/blogs/capitalgames/177049.

1275.*See, e.g.*, Gov't Sentencing Mem. at 12, *Libby*.

1276.Press Conference, Patrick Fitzgerald, Special Counsel, U.S. Dept. of Justice (Oct. 28, 2005), *available at* http://washingtonpost.com/wp-dyn/content/article/2005/10/28/AR2005102801340

1277.*Disclosure Hearing Before H. Comm. on Oversight and Gov't Reform* at 88-93, 101-02, 104-05, 107, 109, 116, 122-23 (statement of James Knodell).

1278.*See, e.g.*, *H. Gov't Oversight Comm. Report on Resolution;* Letter from Keith B. Nelson, Principal Deputy Assistant Attorney General, Dept. of Justice, to John Conyers, Jr., Chairman, H. Comm. on Judiciary (June 13, 2008).

1279.*See, e.g.*, "Juror: Libby is guilty, but he was the fall guy," *CNN.com*, Mar. 6, 2007, *available at* http://www.cnn.com/2007/POLITICS/03/06/libby.juror/index.html; Collins, "Inside the Jury Room: Huffington Post Exclusive: What the Jury Thought, Day by Day, Witness by Witness, at the Scooter Libby Trial, *Huffington Post*, Mar. 7, 2007; Waas, "Exclusive: Cheney's Admissions to the CIA Leak Prosecutor and FBI," *Crooks and Liars*, Dec. 23, 2008, http://www/murraywass.crooksandliars.com/2008/12/23/exclusive-cheneys-admissions-to-the-cia-leak-prosecutors-and-fbi.

1280.Gov't Sentencing Mem. at 15, *Libby*.

1281.Transcript of Record (Feb. 20, 2007), *Libby* (government's closing argument); Gov't Sentencing Mem. at 5, *Libby*; *see also* Gov't Sentencing Mem. at 16, *Libby*.

1282.Press Conference, Patrick Fitzgerald, Special Counsel, U.S. Dept. of Justice (Oct. 28, 2005), *available at* http://washingtonpost.com/wp-dyn/content/article/2005/10/28/AR2005102801340.

1283.*See, e.g.,* H. Comm. on Gov't Oversight and Reform, *Disclosure of Valerie Plame Wilson's Classified CIA Employment* (Mar. 16, 2007), *available at* http://oversight.house.gov/documents/20070316173308-19288.pdf.

1284.*Revelations by Former White House Press Secretary Scott McClellan: Hearing Before the H. Comm. on the Judiciary*, 110th Cong. (June 20, 2008) (statement of Scott McClellan).

1285.*See id.* (statement of John Conyers, Jr.). Mr. Conyers read a statement the Committee from a former federal prosecutor (Barry Coburn) that read, in relevant part: "A substantial predicate exists for investigation of whether this conduct may constitute the criminal offense of obstruction of justice." *Id.*

1286.*See, e.g.*, Letter from John Conyers, Jr., Chairman, H. Comm. on Judiciary, to George W. Bush, President of the United States (July 6, 2007), *reprinted in Misuse of Clemency Power Hearing*.

1287.Press Conference, President George W. Bush (Oct. 28, 2003), *available at* http://www.whitehouse.gov/news/releases/2003/10/20031028-2.html.

1288. *Disclosure Hearing Before H. Comm. On Oversight and Gov't Reform* at 4-5 (statement of Hon. Henry A. Waxman, Chairman, H. Comm. on Gov't Oversight and Reform).

1289. *See, e.g., Revelations by Former White House Press Secretary Scott McClellan: Hearing Before the H. Comm. on the Judiciary*, 110th Cong. (2007) (testimony of Scott McLellan); Op-Ed, *"The Libby Affair," Wash. Times*, July 4, 2007; *see also* Government's Sentencing Mem. at 16-17., *Libby* (emphasizing that Mr. Libby's crimes were an affront to the rule of law).

1290. *See Misuse of Clemency Power Hearing* at 33 (2007) (testimony of Douglas Berman).

1291. *See* Letter from Fred W. Fielding, White House Counsel, to John Conyers, Jr., Chairman, H.Comm. on Judiciary (July 11, 2007), *reprinted in Misuse of Clemency Power Hearing* at 33 (2007); Letter from John Conyers, Jr., Chairman, H. Comm. on Judiciary, to George W. Bush, President of the United States (July 6, 2007), *reprinted in Misuse of Clemency Power Hearing* at 33.

1292. Taylor, An Inquiry Into the Principles and Policy of the Government of the United States 194, (The Lawbook Exchange, Ltd. 1998) (1814).

1293. Kornblut, "Bush's Stance on Secrecy Draws Criticism," *The Boston Globe*, Feb. 11, 2002.

1294. *Id.*

1295. Williamson, "White House Secrecy Starts To Give," *Washington Post*, Jan. 13, 2008, at A5.

1296. Examples include, but are not limited to, the Administration's selective declassification of the October 2002 National Intelligence Estimate on Iraq and its delayed release of a heavily-redacted version of the report of the Joint Inquiry into Intelligence Community Activities before and after the Terrorist Attacks of September 11, 2001 by the House and Senate Intelligence Committees.

1297. Graham, "Securing a Safe America Requires Accountability For 9/11 Mistakes," *The Forward*, Aug. 1, 2003, at 1.

1298. The "presidential communications privilege" and "deliberative process privilege" are facets of executive privilege. The presidential communications privilege protects from disclosure communications by the president directly or by his immediate advisers. The deliberative process privilege protects the confidentiality of internal government deliberations (including discussions, opinions, and recommendations) during the process of formulating policy. However, even when properly invoked, assertions of executive privilege can be overcome by showing a sufficient need for the requested information. *See* Huq, "Background on Executive Privilege," *The Brennan Center for Justice*, Mar. 23, 2007, *available at* http://www.brennancenter.org/content/resource/background_on_executive_privilege/.

1299.365 F.3d 1108.

1300.H. Rep. No. 108-414, at 129 (2004).

1301.*Id.* at 130.

1302.For a full accounting of the scandal, see Section 4 of this report. The Judiciary Committee's own investigation into the commutation of "Scooter" Libby's sentence is addressed later in this Section.

1303.*Report of the Comm. on Oversight and Gov't Reform, U.S. House of Representatives, Regarding President Bush's Assertion of Executive Privilege in Response to the Committee Subpoena to Attorney General Michael B. Mukasey* 2-3 (2008) (hereinafter 2008 Report on Mukasey Executive Privilege).

1304.Letter from Henry A. Waxman, Chairman, H. Comm. on Oversight and Gov't Reform, to Patrick J. Fitzgerald, Special Counsel, U.S. Dept. Of Justice (July 16, 2007).

1305.2008 Report on Mukasey Executive Privilege at 3.

1306.2008 Report on Mukasey Executive Privilege at 4-5.

1307.H. Comm. on Oversight and Gov't Reform, Subpoena to Attorney General Michael B. Mukasey (June 16, 2008).

1308.Letter from Keith B. Nelson, Principal Deputy Assistant Att'y Gen., U.S. Dept. Of Justice, to Henry A. Waxman, Chairman, H. Comm. On Oversight and Gov't Reform (June 24, 2008).

1309.Letter from Henry A. Waxman, Chairman, H. Comm. On Oversight and Gov't Reform to Keith B. Nelson, Principal Deputy Assistant Att'y Gen., U.S. Dept. Of Justice (July 8, 2008).

1310.Letter from Keith B. Nelson, Principal Deputy Assistant Att'y Gen., U.S. Dept. Of Justice, to Henry A. Waxman, Chairman, H. Comm. On Oversight and Gov't Reform (July 16, 2008).

1311.Letter from Michael B. Mukasey, Att'y Gen., to President George W. Bush (July 15, 2008).

1312.2008 Report on Mukasey Executive Privilege at 6.

1313.2008 Report on Mukasey Executive Privilege at 7.

1314.*Id.*, citing Letter from Patrick J. Fitzgerald, Special Counsel, U.S. Dept. of Justice, to Henry A. Waxman, Chairman, H. Comm. On Oversight and Gov't Reform (July 3, 2008).

1315.2008 Report on Mukasey Executive Privilege at 7, citing *In Re Sealed Case* and *Judicial Watch*.

1316. 2008 Report on Mukasey Executive Privilege at 7.

1317. *From the Department of Justice to Guantanamo Bay: Administration Lawyers and Administration Interrogation Rules, Part III Before the Subcomm. On the Constitution, Civil Rights and Civil Liberties of the H. Comm. on the Judiciary*, 110th Cong. (2008) (statement of David Addington, Chief of Staff, Vice President of the United States).

1318. Isikoff and Hosenball, "Closing the Door," *Newsweek*, July 16, 2008, *available at* http://www.newsweek.com/id/146651.

1319. *Id.*

1320. 2008 Report on Mukasey Executive Privilege at 8.

1321. Draft Report of the H. Comm. on Oversight and Gov't Reform Regarding The Bush Administration's Abuse of Power in Asserting Executive Privilege in Response to Committee Subpoenas to Stephen Johnson, Administrator, Environmental Protection Agency, and Susan Dudley, Administrator, White House Office of Management and Budget, 2-3 (2008) *available at* http://oversight.house.gov/documents/20081014104748.pdf.

1322. *Id.* at 2.

1323. *Id.* at 5.

1324. *Id.* at 5.

1325. *Id.* at 7.

1326. *Id.* at 8

1327. Letter from Susan Dudley, Administrator, Office of Information and Regulatory Affairs, Office of Management and Budget, to Stephen Johnson, Administrator, Environmental Protection Agency (Mar. 12, 2008) *available at* http://oversight.house.gov/documents/20080520092019.pdf. The letter is misdated as Mar. 13, but was actually transmitted Mar. 12.

1328. Draft Report of the H. Comm. on Oversight and Gov't Reform Regarding The Bush Administration's Abuse of Power in Asserting Executive Privilege in Response to Committee Subpoenas to Stephen Johnson, Administrator, Environmental Protection Agency, and Susan Dudley, Administrator, White House Office of Management and Budget, 12, 14 (2008) *available at* http://oversight.house.gov/documents/20081014104748.pdf.

1329. *Id.* at 10, 13.

1330. *Id.* at 15.

1331.*Id.* at 16, 17.

1332.Letter from Michael B. Mukasey, Att'y Gen., U.S. Dept. of Justice, to President George W. Bush (June 19, 2008).

1333.Draft Report of the H. Comm. on Oversight and Gov't Reform Regarding The Bush Administration's Abuse of Power in Asserting Executive Privilege in Response to Committee Subpoenas to Stephen Johnson, Administrator, Environmental Protection Agency, and Susan Dudley, Administrator, White House Office of Management and Budget, 1 (2008) *available at* http://oversight.house.gov/documents/20081014104748.pdf.

1334.The discussion that follows focuses on the related executive privilege and immunity claims made by the Bush Administration during the course of the Committee's investigation. For a further discussion of the factual details of this investigation, please refer to Section 1 of this Report.

1335.Letter from Fred Fielding, Counsel to the President, to Reps. John Conyers, Lamar Smith and Linda Sánchez and Sens. Patrick Leahy and Arlen Specter, (Mar. 20, 2007).

1336.*Ensuring Executive Branch Accountability: Hearing Before the Subcomm. on Comm. and Admin. Law of the H. Comm. On the Judiciary*, 110th Cong. 67-68 (2007).

1337.*Id.* at 73.

1338.*Id.* at 74.

1339.Letter from Fred Fielding, Counsel to the President, to Patrick Leahy, Chairman, S. Comm. on the Judiciary, John Conyers, Jr., Chairman, H. Comm. on the Judiciary (June 28, 2007).

1340.H.R. Rep. No. 110-423, (2007). *See* Proceedings against John M. Quinn, David Watkins, and Matthew Moore (Pursuant to 2 U.S.C. § 192 and 194), H.R. Rep. No. 104-598, (1996).

1341.*See, e.g.*, *Smith v. FTC*, 403 F. Supp. 1000, 1018 (D. Del. 1975); *Black v. Sheraton Corp.*, 371 F.Supp. 97, 101 (D.D.C. 1974; *Landry v. FDIC*, 204 F.3d 1125, 1135 (D.C. Cir. 2000); *In re Sealed Case*, 121 F.3d 729, 735 (D.C. Cir. 1997).

1342.*In re Sealed Case*, 121 F.3d 729, 752 (D.C. Cir. 1997).

1343.*See* Press Briefing, White House Press Secretary Dana Perino, Mar. 27, 2007, *available at* http://www.whitehouse.gov/news/releases/2007/03/20070327-4.html.

1344.Fein, "Executive Nonsense," *Slate*, July 11, 2007, *available at* http://www.slate.com/id/2170247/.

1345.Letter from Prof. Erwin Chemerinsky, Duke University School of Law, to John Conyers, Chairman, H. Comm. on the Judiciary (Sept. 20, 2007).

1346.Editorial, "In Contempt," *N.Y. Times*, Nov. 16, 2007, *available at* http://www.nytimes.com/2007/11/16/opinion/16fri1.html?scp=1&sq=in%20contempt&st=cse.

1347.2 U.S.C. § 194.

1348.Letter from Michael B. Mukasey, Att'y Gen., U.S. Dept. Of Justice, to Nancy Pelosi, Speaker of the House, (Feb. 29, 2008).

1349.Memorandum Opinion and Order, *Committee on the Judiciary v. Miers*, Civil Action No. 08-0409 (JDB) (United States District Court for the District of Columbia, July 31, 2008).

1350.*Id.*

1351.October 6, 2008, Opinion and Order Granting Motion for Stay Pending Appeal, *Committee on the Judiciary v. Miers*, Appeal No. 08-5357, United States Court of Appeals for the District of Columbia Circuit.

1352.For a full discussion of the Committee's investigation into selective prosecution, see Section 1 of this report.

1353.Letter from Robert D. Luskin, Att'y for Karl Rove, to Rep. John Conyers, Chairman, H. Comm. On the Judiciary, (July 9, 2008).

1354.Letter from Fred Fielding, Counsel to the President, to Robert D. Luskin, Att'y for Karl Rove, (July 9, 2008).

1355.Steven G. Bradbury, Principal Deputy Assistant Attorney General, U.S. Dept. Of Justice, Memorandum for the Counsel to the President, *Re: Immunity of Former Counsel to the President from Compelled Congressional Testimony*, July 10, 2007.

1356.Ruling of Chairwoman Linda T. Sánchez, Subcomm. on Commercial and Administrative Law of the H. Comm. On the Judiciary, July 10, 2008.

1357.Halstead, *Walker v. Cheney: District Court Decision and Related Statutory and Constitutional Issues*, CRS Report for Congress, RL31713, Mar. 8, 2004, at 2.

1358.*See, eg.* Alvarez and Schmitt, "Cheney Ever More Powerful As Crucial Link to Congress," *N.Y. Times*, May 13, 2001, at A1; Shenon, "Sensing a Bush Liability, Democrats Push an Energy Plan," *N.Y. Times*, May 16, 2001, at A1; Labaton, "Business Leaders Visit Bush at White House," *N.Y. Times*, Jun. 21, 2001, at A18.

1359.*Chronology of GAO's Efforts to Obtain NEPDG Documents from the Office of the Vice President*, Apr. 19, 2001 to Aug. 25, 2003, *available at* http://www.gao.gov/nepdgchron.pdf.

1360. *See id.*

1361. GAO Statement Concerning Litigation, Feb. 22, 2002, *available at* http://www.gao.gov/press/gaostatement0222.pdf.

1362. *Walker v. Cheney*, 230 F.Supp.2d 51 (D.D.C., 2002).

1363. Lukey, "At The Court, Inflating The White House's Power," *Washington Post*, Jul. 4, 2004, at B2.

1364. *Cheney v. U.S. Dist. Court for Dist. of Columbia*, 542 U.S. 367, 371 (2004).

1365. *In re Cheney*, 406 F.3d 723, 728, 365 U.S.App.D.C. 387, 392 (D.C. Cir. May 10, 2005).

1366. Shenon, "Bush to Limit Testimony Before 9/11 Panel", *N.Y. Times*, Feb. 26, 2004, at A23.

1367. *See, e.g.* Miller, "Panel Presses Rice to Testify," *L.A. Times*, Mar 29, 2004, at A1; Washington, "Democrats Push for Rice to Testify," *Boston Globe*, Mar. 24, 2004, at A12; Lewis, "Behind the Privilege That in the End Bowed to Politics," *N.Y. Times*, Mar. 31, 2004, at A21.

1368. Rauber, "A Privileged Conversation," *Richmond Times*, Apr. 3, 2004, at A2.

1369. Letter from Alberto Gonzales, Counsel to the President, to Hon. Thomas Kean and Hon. Lee Hamilton, Co-Chairs, National Commission on Terrorist Attacks Upon the United States, Mar. 31, 2004, *available at* http://edition.cnn.com/2004/ALLPOLITICS/03/30/gonzales.letter/index.html. It should be noted, however, that neither Dr. Rice's testimony nor the 9/11 Commission report included information about a July 10, 2001, meeting between Rice and CIA Director George Tenet at which he claims to have warned her of an "imminent" al Qaeda attack. (Eggen and Wright, "Tenet Recalled Warning Rice," *Washington Post*, Oct. 3, 2006, at A3.)

1370. Stolberg, "Two Decline to Testify on Drug Cost," *N.Y. Times*, Apr. 2, 2004, at A17.

1371. Letter from Alberto Gonzales, Counsel to the President, to Rep. Bill Thomas, Chairman, H. Comm. On Ways and Means, (Mar. 31, 2004).

1372. Press Release, Rep. Charles Rangel, Ranking Member, H. Comm. On Ways and Means, Apr. 1, 2004, *available at* http://www.house.gov/apps/list/press/wm31_democrats/040401_whitehouse_avoid_medicare_coverup.html.

1373. *Id.*

1374. Stolberg, "Two Decline to Testify on Drug Cost," *N.Y. Times*, Apr. 2, 2004, at A17.

1375.Letter from Rep. John Conyers, Chairman, H. Comm. On the Judiciary, to President George W. Bush, July 6, 2007; Letter from Rep. John Conyers, Chairman, H. Comm. On the Judiciary, to President George W. Bush, (July 10, 2007).

1376.Letter from Fred Fielding, Counsel to the President, to Rep. John Conyers, Chairman, H. Comm. On the Judiciary, (July 11, 2007).

1377.*Id.*

1378.345 U.S.C. § 1 (1953).

1379.Frost and Florence, "Reforming the State Secrets Privilege," *American Constitution Society for Law And Policy*, 4 (Oct. 2008), *available at* http://www.acslaw.org/files/Frost%20Florence%20Issue%20Brief.pdf.

1380.Hibbits, "Judge dismisses el-Masri CIA rendition suit on state secrets grounds," *Jurist*, *available at* http://jurist.law.pitt.edu/paperchase/2006/05/judge-dismisses-el-masri-cia-rendition.php.

1381.Lanman, "Secret Guarding," *Slate*, May 22, 2006, *available at* http://www.slate.com/id/2142155/.

1382.Frost and Florence, "Reforming the State Secrets Privilege," *American Constitution Society for Law And Policy*, 4 (Oct. 2008), *available at* http://www.acslaw.org/files/Frost%20Florence%20Issue%20Brief.pdf.

1383.Priest, "Secrecy Privilege Invoked in Fighting Ex-Detainee's Lawsuit," *Wash. Post*, May 13, 2006, at A3.

1384.*El-Masri v. Tenet*, 437 F.Supp.2d 530 (E.D.Va. May 12, 2006), *aff'd sub nom. El-Masri v. U.S.*, 479 F.3d 296 (4th Cir. 2007), *cert. denied* 128 S.Ct. 373 (2007).

1385.El-Masri, "I Am Not A State Secret," *L.A. Times*, Mar. 3, 2007.

1386. For a further discussion of the facts of the El-Masri and Arar renditions, please see Section 3.

1387.*Arar v. Ashcroft*, 414 F.Supp.2d 250 (E.D.N.Y. Feb. 16, 2006), *cert. denied* 2006 WL 1875375 (E.D.N.Y. Jul. 05, 2006), *judgment aff'd* 532 F.3d 157 (2nd Cir 2008), *rehearing en banc granted* (August 12, 2008).

1388.Tim Harper, "U.S. Ruling Dismisses Arar Lawsuit," *Toronto Star*, Feb. 17, 2006, *available at* http://www.commondreams.org/headlines06/0217-01.htm.

1389.For a further discussion of the Bush administration's warrantless wiretapping program, see Section 3.

1390.*Al-Haramain Islamic Foundation, Inc. v. Bush*, 451 F.Supp.2d 1215 (D.Or. Sep. 7, 2006), *reversed and remanded* 507 F.3d 1190 (9th Cir. 2007), *on remand sub nom. to In re National Security Agency Telecommunications Records Litigation*, 564 F.Supp.2d 1109 (N.D.Cal. Jul. 08, 2008).

1391.According to public sources, the document summarized phone conversations monitored by the government between foundation lawyers and directors. Associated Press, "Court: Charity Can't Use Call Log in Wiretap Case," *USA Today*, Dec. 16, 2007, *available at* http://www.usatoday.com/news/washington/2007-11-16-domestic-eavesdropping_N.htm.

1392. During arguments before the Ninth Circuit, Justice Harry Pregerson asked whether the government was arguing that the courts could only "rubber stamp" the decisions of the Executive once state secrets privilege had been invoked. Siegel, "State-secret Overreach," *L.A. Times*, Sept. 16, 2007, *available at* http://www.latimes.com/news/opinion/sunday/commentary/la-op-siegel16sep16,0,4333818.story.

1393.However, the Court of Appeals directed the lower courts (after a change of venue, the district court for the Northern District of California) to decide whether the 1978 Foreign Intelligence Surveillance Act trumps presidential claims of secrecy. *See* Associated Press, "Court: Charity Can't Use Call Log in Wiretap Case," *USA Today*, Dec. 16, 2007, *available at* http://www.usatoday.com/news/washington/2007-11-16-domestic-eavesdropping_N.htm. Upon remand to the district court of northern California, renamed *In re National Security Agency Telecommunications Records Litigation*, Judge Walker ruled that FISA did preempt state secrets privilege, but plaintiffs couldn't use the document in question to establish themselves as "aggrieved persons" under FISA, and since the caselaw for the remedial measures in FISA was so poorly developed (and since there had been little factual development for purposes of litigation in the instant litigation), plaintiffs were given leave to file an amended complaint, which they did. The government responded with a third motion for summary judgment or to dismiss (Sep 30, 2008), and the plaintiffs opposed (October 17, 2008). The Court also held that "[The] legislative history [of FISA] is evidence of Congressional intent that FISA should displace federal common law rules such as the state secrets privilege with regards to matters within FISA's purview."). *See* 564 F.Supp. 2d 1109, 1120 (N.D.Cal. Jul. 2, 2008).

1394."State secrets privilege upheld in whistleblower case," *available at* http://www.rcfp.org/news/2005/0509-foi-states.html.

1395.Giraldi, "What FBI Whistle-blower Sibel Edmonds Found in Translation," *Dallas Morning News*, Feb. 17, 2008, *available at* http://www.dallasnews.com/sharedcontent/dws/dn/opinion/points/stories/DN-sibeledmonds_17e di.ART.State.Edition1.45b446a.html.

1396.Holland, "Supreme Court Rejects CIA Officer's Appeal," *Associated Press*, Jan. 9, 2006.

1397.*Oversight Hearing on Reform of the State Secrets Privilege, Before the Subcomm. on the Constitution, Civil Rights, and Civil Liberties of the H. Comm. on the Judiciary*, 110th Cong. (2008) (statement of Judith Loether).

1398.*Oversight Hearing on Reform of the State Secrets Privilege, Before the Subcomm. on the Constitution, Civil Rights, and Civil Liberties of the H. Comm. on the Judiciary*, 110th Cong. (2008).

1399.*Oversight Hearing on Reform of the State Secrets Privilege, Before the Subcomm. on the Constitution, Civil Rights, and Civil Liberties of the H. Comm. on the Judiciary*, 110th Cong. (2008) (statement submitted for the record by Louis Fisher, Specialist in Constitutional Law, Law Library of the Library of Congress).

1400.Barone, *Secrecy in the Bush Administration* 39 (2006).

1401.*Id.*, at 39.

1402.The increase in decisions to classify information resulting from the Administration's actions is diametrically opposed to the September 11 Commission's recommendations, which seek to bolster oversight of intelligence agencies.

1403.Barone, *Secrecy in the Bush Administration* 40-41 (2006).

1404.*Id.*

1405.Silverglate and Takei, "Covering a Multitude of Sins," *The Boston Phoenix*, Apr. 30, 2004, *available at* http://www.bostonphoenix.com/boston/news_features/top/features/documents/03789077.asp.

1406.*Id.*

1407.Jacoby, "Sen Graham: Bush covered up Saudi involvement in 9/11," Salon.com, Sept. 8, 2004, *available at* http://dir.salon.com/story/news/feature/2004/09/08/graham/print.html.

1408.Memorandum for The Secretary of State, The Secretary of the Treasury, The Secretary of Defense, The Attorney General, The Director of Central Intelligence, and the Director of the Federal Bureau of Investigation, *Subject: Disclosures to the Congress*, From President George W. Bush (Oct. 5, 2001) *available at* http://www.fas.org/sgp/news/2001/10/gwb100501.pdf.

1409.Pierce, Mark and Sorrells, "Lawmakers Unahppy About Bush's Curb on Classified Briefings," *Congressional Quarterly Daily Monitor*, Oct. 9, 2001.

1410."Bush Easing Stand on Sharing of Secret Data," *The New York Times*, Oct. 13, 2001, *available at* http://query.nytimes.com/gst/fullpage.html?res=9501E4DC133FF930A25753C1A9679C8B63.

1411.Chairman Conyers and other Members of the House Judiciary Committee repeatedly requested, and were denied, access for all Committee Members to classified documents related to the program in advance of congressional reauthorization of the Foreign Intelligence Surveillance Act. *See, e.g.*, Letter from Rep. John Conyers, Jr., Chairman, H. Comm. on the Judiciary, and 20 other Democratic Members of the H. Comm. on the Judiciary, to Alberto Gonzales, Att'y Gen., U.S. Dept. of Justice, (Jan. 19, 2007); and Letter from Rep. John Conyers, Jr., Chairman, H. Comm. on the Judiciary, to Fred Fielding, Counsel to the President, (Feb. 12, 2008). For further discussion of the Judiciary Committee's efforts to obtain this information, see Section 2 of this Report.

1412.Hess, "Bush opens wiretapping documents to House members," *The Associated Press*, Jan. 24, 2008.

1413.*See, e.g.*, Letter from Rep. John Conyers, Jr., Chairman, H. Comm. on the Judiciary, to Michael B. Mukasey, Att'y Gen., U.S. Dept. of Justice, (Sept. 10, 2008); Letter from Keith B. Nelson, Principal Deputy Assistant Att'y Gen., U.S. Dept. of Justice, to Sen. Patrick Leahy, Chairman, S. Comm. on the Judiciary, (Nov. 14, 2008).

1414.*Moving Toward a 21st Century Right-to-Know Agenda: Recommendations to President-elect Obama and Congress* 36, OMB Watch (November 2008), *available at* http://www.ombwatch.org/21strtkrecs.pdf.

1415.Leonnig and Rich, "U.S. Seeks Silence on CIA Prisons; Court Is Asked to Bar Detainees From Talking About Interrogations," *Wash. Post*, Nov. 4, 2008 at A1.

1416.Lea, "Inside the Wire," *The Guardian*, Feb. 26, 2007, *available at* http://www.guardian.co.uk/books/2007/feb/26/poetry.guantanamo.

1417."Secrecy Hinders Progress of Terrorism Cases," *OMB Watch*, Vol. 8 No. 24, Dec. 4, 2007, *available at* http://www.ombwatch.org/article/articleview/4107/1/1?TopicID=1.

1418.*Id.*

1419.Finn, "Judge's Order Could Keep Public From Hearing Details of 9/11 Trials," *Wash. Post*, Jan. 7, 2009, at A2 (emphasis added).

1420.*Id.*

1421.*Id.*

1422.5 U.S.C. § 552.

1423.Memorandum from Attorney General John Ashcroft, For Heads of all Federal Departments and Agencies, *The Freedom of Information Act*, Oct. 12, 2001, *available at* http://www.usdoj.gov/oip/foiapost/2001foiapost19.htm.

1424.Memorandum from Andrew H. Card, Jr., Assistant to the President and Chief of Staff, For Heads of Executive Departments and Agencies, March 19, 2002, *available at* http://www.usdoj.gov/oip/foiapost/2002foiapost10.htm.

1425.*See* Part II (B) of Section 5 for a further discussion of the Office of the Vice President's confrontation with National Archives.

1426.44 U.S.C. §§ 2201-2207.

1427.Exec. Order No. 13233, Further Implementation of the Presidential Records Act, Nov. 1, 2001, *available at* http://www.whitehouse.gov/news/releases/2001/11/20011101-12.html.

1428.Professor Laurent Sacharoff has argued that former Presidents may not have the Constitutional authority to assert executive privilege after leaving office:

> The Constitution does not mention executive privilege, but the Court in *United States v. Nixon* (citations omitted) found that executive privilege derives from Article II of the Constitution. But the Term Clause of Article II, Section 1 limits a President's term to four years, and the Twenty-Second Amendment states that a person can be elected President only twice. Since these constitutional provisions end a particular President's Article II powers, and **since executive privilege is incident to Article II power, it follows that the President loses the right personally to assert executive privilege after he leaves office.** The privilege itself of course survives the tenure of any particular President, but the holder of the privilege shifts entirely from the former to the new President. Article II, Section 1 vests the executive power in the President, not the former President

Sacharoff, "Former Presidents and Executive Privilege," (December 2008) (unpublished) at 5.

1429.The position, that the Office of the Vice President exists in some sort of netherworld between the legislative and executive branches, was articulated by Vice President Cheney as early as 2004. In the 2004 directory of senior government officials known as The Plum Book, Vice President Cheney's position was articulated as follows: "The vice presidency is a unique office that is neither a part of the executive branch nor a part of the legislative branch, but is attached by the Constitution to the latter."

It is correct that the vice president is mentioned in Article II of the Constitution as part of the executive branch, but is given legislative powers in Art. 1, Sec. 3, which establishes the Senate. Historically, however, the office of the vice president has always been treated as part of the Executive Branch, and subject to the Executive Branch's rules and regulations. Vice President Cheney has taken a position that his office enjoys the benefits of both branches, while being subject to the requirements of neither.

1430.The order requires any "entity within the executive branch" that comes into the possession of classified information to report annually how much it is keeping secret.

1431.Baker, "Cheney Defiant on Classified Material, *Wash. Post* , June 22, 2007, at A1. The expected required transfer of the Bush White House's electronic messages and documents to the National Archives at the end of his Administration has been imperiled by lawsuits, some of which contest the Administration's assertion in federal court in December 2008 that Vice President Cheney alone may determine what constitutes vice presidential records or personal records and how his records will be created, maintained, managed, and disposed, without outside challenge or judicial review. *See* Smith, "Bush E-mails May Be Secret a Bit Longer: Legal Battles, Technical Difficulties Delay Required Transfer to Archives," *Wash. Post*, Dec. 21, 2008, A1.

1432.Silva, "Cheney Keeps Classification Activity Secret," *The Chicago Tribune*, May 27, 2006, at C4; Letter from Henry A. Waxman, Chairman, H. Comm. On Oversight and Gov't Reform, to Richard B. Cheney, Vice President of the United States, (June 21, 2007).

1433.Letter from Shannen W. Coffin, Counsel to the Vice President, to Sen. Patrick Leahy, Chairman, S. Comm. on the Judiciary, (Aug. 20, 2007).

1434.Associated Press, "Cheney Claims Power to Decide His Public Records," *N.Y. Times*, Dec. 18, 2008.

1435.Texas Governor George W. Bush's campaign focused on issues of "compassionate conservatism," his stated view that conservative policies could be brought to bear to address social ills. Another focus of his campaign was the perceived ethical transgressions of the Clinton Administration, and the Starr Investigation in particular. Governor Bush promised to restore "honor and dignity to the White House." *Capital Gang: Lieberman Takes the Heat; Bush, McCain Meet in Arizona; Are the Democrats Getting Tough on Hollywood?*, (CNN television broadcast Aug. 13, 2000), *available at* http://transcripts.cnn.com/TRANSCRIPTS/0008/13/cg.00.html.

1436.*See* Commission on Presidential Debates, Unofficial Debate Transcript, Oct. 3, 2000, *available at* http://www.debates.org/pages/trans2000a.html. Vice President Cheney also stated in an interview, in the midst the 2000 presidential campaign, that the U.S. should not act as though "we were an imperialist power, willy-nilly moving into capitals in that part of the world, taking down governments." *Meet the Press: Interview with Dick Cheney*, (NBC television broadcast Aug. 27, 2000).

1437.Burrough, Peretz, Rose & Wise, "The Path to War," *Vanity Fair*, May 1, 2004.

1438.Clarke, *Against All Enemies: Inside America's War on Terror* 32 (2004).

1439.*Meet the Press: Interview with General Wesley Clark*, (NBC television broadcast Jun. 15, 2003), *available at* http://securingamerica.com/ccn/node/1147.

1440. *The 9-11 Commission Report: Final Report of the National Commission on Terrorist Attacks Upon the United States* 559-560 (2004), *available at* http://www.9-11commission.gov/report/911Report.pdf.

1441. *Meet the Press*, (NBC television broadcast Dec. 9, 2001). Even after the invasion, on October 10, 2003, the Vice President stated that Saddam Hussein "had an established relationship with al Qaeda." *Fox News: Interview with Vice President Dick Cheney*, (Fox News television broadcast Jun. 28, 2004), *available at* http://www.foxnews.com/story/0,2933,123794,00.html).

1442. President George W. Bush, State of the Union Address, Jan. 29, 2002, *available at* http://www.whitehouse.gov/news/releases/2002/01/20020129-11.html.

1443. *Id.*

1444. President George W. Bush, Graduation Speech at West Point, Jun. 1, 2002, *available at* http://www.whitehouse.gov/news/releases/2002/06/20020601-3.html. He further noted that "[t]he war on terror will not be won on the defensive. We must take the battle to the enemy... And this nation will act." *Id.*

1445. On multiple occasions, Vice President Cheney and Mr. Libby questioned analysts studying alleged Iraq's weapons programs and links to al-Qaeda. Pincus, "Some Iraq Analysts Felt Pressure From Cheney," *Wash. Post*, Jun. 5, 2003, at A1.

1446. Strobel, "Some in Bush administration have misgivings about Iraq policy," *Knight Ridder Newspapers*, Oct. 7, 2002, *available at* http://www.mcclatchydc.com/128/story/8592.html. *See also*, Suskind, "Without a Doubt," *N.Y. Times Magazine*, Oct. 17, 2004, at 44; Treasury Secretary Paul O'Neill recounted, "If you operate in a certain way - by saying this is how I want to justify what I've already decided to do, and I don't care how you pull it off - you guarantee that you'll get faulty, one-sided information... [y]ou don't have to issue an edict, or twist arms, or be overt."; Kessler, "CIA Leak Linked to Dispute over Iraq Policy," *Wash. Post*, Oct. 25, 2005, at A3, Lawrence Wilkerson, former Chief of Staff to Secretary of State Colin Powell stated:

> The case that I saw for four-plus years was a case I have never seen in my studies of aberrations, bastardizations, perturbations, changes to the national security decision-making process,... What I saw was a cabal between the vice president of the United States, Richard Cheney, and the Secretary of Defense, Donald Rumsfeld, on critical issues that made decisions that the bureaucracy did not know were being made... [when a decision was presented to the bureaucracy], it was presented in such a disjointed, incredible way that the bureaucracy often didn't know what it was doing as it moved to carry them out. *Id.*

1447. For example, on August 22, 2002, the President stated that he was willing to "look at all options." Nagourney & Shanker, "A Patient Bush Says He'll Weigh All Iraq Options," *N.Y.*

Times, Aug. 22, 2002, at A1. Later that year, he stated, "Of course, I haven't made up my mind we're going to war with Iraq." President George W. Bush, Remarks on Terrorism Insurance, Oct. 1, 2002, *available at* http://www.whitehouse.gov/news/releases/2002/10/20021001-1.html.

1448.Rich, "It's Bush-Cheney, Not Rove-Libby," *N.Y. Times*, Oct. 16, 2005, *available at* http://select.nytimes.com/2005/10/16/opinion/16rich.html.

1449.S. Rep. 110-345, at 4 (2008).

1450.Vice President Cheney stated that "it is now public that, in fact, [Saddam Hussein] has been seeking to acquire, and we have been able to intercept and prevent him from acquiring through this particular channel, the kinds of [aluminum] tubes that are necessary to build a centrifuge... We do know, with absolute certainty, that [Saddam] is using his procurement system to acquire the equipment he needs in order to enrich uranium to build a nuclear weapon." *Meet the Press: Interview with Vice President Dick Cheney*, (NBC television broadcast Sept. 8, 2002).

National Security Advisor Condoleezza Rice told CNN, "We do know that there have been shipments going into...Iraq, for instance, of aluminum tubes that really are only suited to - high quality aluminum tools that are only really suited for nuclear weapons programs, centrifuge programs." *CNN Late Edition: Interview with Condoleezza Rice*, (CNN television broadcast Sept. 8, 2002).

President Bush would later state in his 2003 State of the Union Address that Saddam Hussein was trying to buy tubes "suitable for nuclear weapons production. President George W. Bush, State of the Union Address, Jan. 28, 2003, *available at* http://www.whitehouse.gov/news/releases/2003/01/20030128-19.html.

1451.Barstow, Broad, & Gerth, "How the White House Embraced Disputed Iraqi Arms Intelligence," *N.Y. Times*, Oct. 3, 2004, at A1. "The tubes, the report asserted, 'have little use other than for a uranium enrichment program.'"

1452.President George W. Bush, Remarks at the U.N. General Assembly, Sept. 12, 2002, *available at* http://www.whitehouse.gov/news/releases/2002/09/20020912-1.html. He also said that the U.S. would not allow any terrorist or tyrant to threaten civilization with weapons of mass murder. President George W. Bush, Remarks to the Nation on the Anniversary of Terrorist Attacks, Sept. 11, 2002, *available at* http://www.whitehouse.gov/news/releases/2002/09/20020911-3.html.

1453.S. Rep. 110-345, at 75 (2008).

1454.*Id*. at 29.

1455.Letter from Dr. Naji Sabri, Minister of Foreign Affairs, Iraq, to Kofi Annan, U.N. Secretary-General, Sept. 16, 2002, *available at* http://www.sfgate.com/cgi-bin/article.cgi?f=/news/archive/2002/09/16/international1954EDT0706.DTL.

1456.President George W. Bush, President Discusses Iraq, Domestic Agenda with Congressional Leaders, Sept. 18, 2002, *available at* http://www.whitehouse.gov/news/releases/2002/09/20020918-1.html. The next day, the President stated how important it was that Congress pass a resolution authorizing the use of force in Iraq. President George W. Bush, President Bush to Send Iraq Resolution to Congress Today, Sept. 19, 2002, http://www.whitehouse.gov/news/releases/2002/09/20020919-1.html.

1457.President George W. Bush, President Bush, Colombia President Uribe Discuss Terrorism, Sept. 25, 2002, *available at* http://www.whitehouse.gov/news/releases/2002/09/20020925-1.html.

1458.Schmitt, "Rumsfeld Says U.S. Has 'Bulletproof' Evidence of Iraq's Links to Al Qaeda," *N.Y. Times*, Sept. 28, 2002, at A9; In September 19, 2002, testimony before the Senate Armed Services Committee, the Defense Secretary claimed "We know that al Qaeda is operating in Iraq today, and that little happens in Iraq without the knowledge of the Saddam Hussein regime." *Hearing on U.S. Policy on Iraq: Before the U.S. Senate Comm. on Armed Services*, 107th Cong. (2002) (statement of Donald Rumsfeld, Secretary of Defense). Secretary Powell also described a "potentially...sinister nexus between Iraq and the al Qaeda terrorist network, a nexus that combines classic terrorist organizations and modern methods of murder." Judis and Ackerman, "The First Casualty," *The New Republic*, June 30, 2003. And on September 25, 2002, Rice insisted, "There clearly are contacts between al Qaeda and Iraq . . . There clearly is testimony that some of the contacts have been important contacts and that there's a relationship there." *Rice: Iraq trained al Qaeda in chemical weapons*, CNN.com, Sept. 26, 2002, *available at* http://archives.cnn.com/2002/US/09/25/us.iraq.alqaeda/.

1459.Stevenson, "After The War: C.I.A. Uproar; White House Tells How Bush Came to Talk of Iraq Uranium," *N.Y.Times*, July 19, 2003, at A6. *See also* Senior Administration Official Holds Background Briefing on Weapons of Mass Destruction in Iraq, As Released By the White House, July 18, 2003, *available at* http://www.fas.org/irp/news/2003/07/wh071803.html.

1460.Stroble, "Some in Bush administration Have Misgivings about Iraq Policy," *Knight Rider Newspapers*, Oct. 7, 2002, *available at* http://www.mcclatchydc.com/128/story/8592.html.

1461.President George W. Bush, Remarks by the President on Iraq, Cincinnati, Ohio, Oc. 7, 2002, *available at* http://www.whitehouse.gov/news/releases/2002/10/20021007-8.html.

1462.H.J. Res. 114, 107th Cong. 2d Sess. (2002) (enacted as Authorization for Use of Military Force Against Iraq Resolution of 2002, Pub. L. No. 107-243, 116 Stat. 1498 (2002)). Several Members of Congress, including Ranking Member Conyers, filed suit in Federal court arguing the resolution was Constitutionally deficient. Among other things, the suit alleged that the text of the resolution did not explicitly invoke the War Powers Act and unconstitutionally delegated the congressional power to declare war to the Executive Branch. The suit was ultimately unsuccessful. *Doe v. Bush*, 323 F.3d 133 (1st Cir. 2003). While substantial questions remain about whether this resolution appropriately authorized the use of force in Iraq, it has come to be known as a joint resolution for the use of force and will be referred to as such in this report.

1463.*See id.*

1464.President George W. Bush, Remarks at the Signing of the Iraq Resolution, Oct.16, 2002, *available at* http://www.whitehouse.gov/news/releases/2002/10/20021016-1.html.

1465.S.C. Res 1441, U.N. SCOR, 4644th mtg., S/2002/1198 (2002), http://www.un.int/usa/sres-iraq.htm. The resolution made clear that only the United Nations Security Council had the right to take punitive action against Iraq in the event of noncompliance.

1466.Mohamed ElBaradei, Report to the U.N. Security Council, Jan. 27, 2003, *available at* http://www.un.org/News/dh/iraq/elbaradei27jan03.htm. According to the IAEA, the tubes were not suitable for manufacturing centrifuges as the Administration had claimed.

1467.President George W. Bush, State of the Union Address, Jan. 28, 2003, *available at* www.whitehouse.gov/news/releases/2003/01/20030128-19.html.

1468.Secretary of State Colin Powell, Remarks to the U.N. Security Council, Feb. 5, 2003, *available at* http://www.whitehouse.gov/news/releases/2003/02/20030205-1.html. During his speech, Secretary Powell assured the world that, "every statement I make today is backed up by sources, solid sources. These are not assertions. What we're giving you are facts and conclusions based on solid intelligence."

1469.*Id.*

1470.*Id.*

1471.*Meet the Press: Interview with Vice President Cheney,* (NBC television broadcast Mar. 16, 2003), *available at* http://msnbc.msn.com/id/3080244/s.

1472.Letter from President George W. Bush to Congress, Mar. 18, 2003, *available at* http://www.whitehouse.gov/news/releases/2003/03/20030319-1.html. The letter stated, "Reliance by the United States on further diplomatic and other peaceful means alone will neither (A) adequately protect the national security of the United States against the continuing threat posed by Iraq nor (B) likely lead to enforcement of all relevant United Nations Security Council resolutions regarding Iraq."

1473.*Hearing to Receive Testimony on Efforts to Determine the Status of Iraqi Weapons of Mass Destruction and Related Programs Before the S. Comm. On Armed Services*, 108th Cong. 57 (2004) (statement of David Kay) (transcript *available at* http://www.cnn.com/2004/US/01/28/kay.transcript/).

1474.*Id.*

1475. Letter from Laurence Silberman and Charles Robb, Co-Chairs, The Commission on the Intelligence Capabilities of the United States Regarding Weapons of Mass Destruction, to George W. Bush, President of the United States (Mar. 31, 2005), *available at* http://www.wmd.gov/report/wmd_report.pdf.

1476. *The Situation Room: Debate Continues Over Iraq Withdrawal; Holiday Crunch Hits Home; Hillary vs. Condoleeza in 2008?*, (CNN television broadcast Nov. 23, 2005), *available at* http://transcripts.cnn.com/TRANSCRIPTS/0511/23/sitroom.01.html.

1477. Minority Staff of H. Comm. On Gov't Reform, 109th Cong., *Iraq on the Record*: *The Bush Administration's Public Statements on Iraq*, H. Comm. (2004), *available at* http://oversight.house.gov/IraqOnTheRecord/pdf_admin_iraq_on_the_record_rep.pdf.

1478. Burrough, Peretz, Rose & Wise, "The Path to War," *Vanity Fair*, May 1, 2004; Pincus & Priest, "Some Iraq Analysts Felt Pressure From Cheney Visits," *Wash. Post*, June 5, 2003, at A1. *The Washington Post* described the pressure on intelligence officials from a barrage of high-ranking Bush Administration officials:

> Former and current intelligence officials said they felt a continual drumbeat, not only from Cheney and Libby, but also from Deputy Defense Secretary Paul D. Wolfowitz, Feith and less so from CIA Director George J. Tenet, to find information or write reports in a way that would help the administration make the case that going into Iraq was urgent. "They were the browbeaters," said a former defense intelligence official who attended some of the meetings in which Wolfowitz and others pressed for a different approach to the assessments they were receiving. "In interagency meetings," he said, "Wolfowitz treated the analysts' work with contempt."

1479. Burrough, Peretz, Rose & Wise, "The Path to War," *Vanity Fair*, May 1, 2004.

1480. Chairman Rockefeller additional views, S. Rep. No. 110-345, at 455-456 (2008). Chairman Rockefeller's Additional Views also reported that, in his interview with SSCI, CIA Director Tenet confirmed that some officials at the CIA had complained to him about the repetitive tasking. *Id.*

1481. *Hearing on "The 9/11 Plot" Before the National Commission on Terrorist Attacks Upon the United States*, June 16, 2004, 70 (statement of Dietrich Snell) *available at* http://govinfo.library.unt.edu/911/archive/hearing12/9-11Commission_Hearing_2004-06-16.pdf.

1482. *Id.*

1483. *Hearing on "The 9/11 Plot" Before the National Commission on Terrorist Attacks Upon the United States*, June 16, 2004, 7 (statement of Douglas MacEachin) *available at* http://govinfo.library.unt.edu/911/archive/hearing12/9-11Commission_Hearing_2004-06-16.pdf.

1484. *The 9-11 Commission Report: Final Report of the National Commission on Terrorist Attacks Upon the United States* 66 (2004), *available at* http://www.9-11commission.gov/report/911Report.pdf.

In a footnote to its conclusions regarding the lack of a "collaborative operational relationship" (*Id.*) between Iraq and al Qaeda, the 9-11 Commission also noted that the "most detailed information alleging such ties came from an al Qaeda operative who recanted much of his original information." *Id.* at 470 (Footnote no. 76).

1485. S. Rep. No. 108-301, at 3 (2004).

1486. *Id.* at 347.

1487. *Id.* at 88.

1488. *Id.*, at 91-92. The Department concluded that because of the tubes' dimensions and mass, the tubes were consistent for use with standard rockets but that it would be too arduous, time-consuming, and expensive to use them as nuclear centrifuges. *See also* Barstow, Broad, & Gerth, "How the White House Embraced Disputed Iraqi Arms Intelligence," *N.Y. Times*, Oct. 3, 2004 *available at* http://www.nytimes.com/2004/10/03/international/middleeast/03tube.html.

1489. *Id.* at 91-92. Furthermore, in the October 2002 NIE, the State Department unequivocally concluded, "the tubes are not intended for use in Iraq's nuclear weapons program" and that it was "far more likely that the tubes are intended for another purpose, most likely the production of artillery rockets." National Intelligence Council, Iraq's Continuing Program for Weapons of Mass Destruction: Key Judgements, (From NIE 2002-16HC, declassified July 18, 2003). Even internal CIA memoranda from as early as June 2001 contained caveats, "divergent views," and discussions of disagreements about the tubes' intended use. Commission on the Intelligence of the U.S. Regarding Weapons of Mass Destruction, Report to the President of the United States (2005). In the end, according to the 2008 Senate Intelligence Committee's review of prewar intelligence, the IC never assessed whether Iraq possessed nuclear weapons. S. Rep. No. 110-345, at 40-41 (2008).

1490. Rose, "Bush and Blair Made Secret Pact for Iraq War," *The Observer*, Apr. 4, 2004, at 1.

1491. Memorandum from David Manning, U.K. Foreign Policy Advisor, to the Prime Minister, Mar. 14, 2002, *available at* http://downingstreetmemo.com/docs/manning.pdf. "Condi" refers to Secretary of State Condoleezza Rice.

1492. Memorandum from Jack Straw, U.K. Foreign Secretary, to the Prime Minister, Mar. 25, 2002, *available at* http://downingstreetmemo.com/docs/straw.pdf.

1493. Memorandum from Cabinet Office, *Iraq: Conditions for Military Action*, July 21, 2002, *available at* http://www.timesonline.co.uk/tol/news/world/article531957.ece.

1494. Testimony of Ambassador Joseph C. Wilson at June 16, 2005, Proceeding Regarding the Downing Street Memos at 15.

1495. O'Rourke, "Downing Street Memo a Growing Problem for Bush," *McClatchy Newspapers*, June 17, 2005.

1496. Press Release of S. Select Comm. On Intelligence, June 5, 2008, *available at* http://intelligence.senate.gov/press/record.cfm?id=298775. The same day, the Committee also released another report of the "Phase II" of the investigation into prewar intelligence, titled "Intelligence Activities Relating to Iraq Conducted By The Policy Counterterrorism Evaluation Group and the Office of Special Plans Within the Office of the Under Secretary of Defense for Policy." That report detailed "inappropriate, sensitive intelligence activities conducted by the DoD's Office of the Undersecretary of Defense for Policy, without the knowledge of the Intelligence Community or the State Department." *Id.*

1497. S. Rep. No. 110-345, at 1 (2008).

1498. These speeches include:
- Vice President Richard Cheney, Speech in Tennessee to the Veterans of Foreign Wars National Convention, August 26, 2006.
- President George W. Bush, Statement before the United Nations General Assembly, September 12, 2002.
- President George W. Bush, State of the Union address, January 28, 2003.

1499. S. Rep. No. 110-345, at 2 (2008).

1500. S. Rep. No. 110-345, at 2-3 (2008).

1501. Press Release of S. Select Comm. On Intelligence, June 5, 2008, *available at* http://intelligence.senate.gov/press/record.cfm?id=298775.

1502. S. Rep. No. 110-345, at 63 (2008), quoting Feb. 6, 2002, and Feb. 7, 2002 DIA Defense Intelligence Summaries (DITSUM) (No. 031-02 and No. 32-012).

1503. In February of 2002, intelligence sources began to question al-Libi's credibility. A DIA defense intelligence report noted that al-Libi:

> lacks specific details on the Iraqi involvement, the CBRN materials associated with the assistance, and the location where the training occurred. It is possible he does not know any further details; it is more likely this individual is intentionally misleading debriefers... Saddam's regime is intensely secular and is wary of Islamic revolutionary movements. Moreover, Baghdad is unlikely to provide assistance to a group it cannot control.

S. Rep. No. 110-345, at 65 (2008), quoting Feb. 22, 2002 DITSUM (No. 044-02).

1504.Press Release of S. Select Comm. On Intelligence, June 5, 2008, *available at* http://intelligence.senate.gov/press/record.cfm?id=298775 (emphasis added).

1505.S. Rep. No. 110-345, at 76 (2008), quoting National Intelligence Estimates, *Iraqi Military Capabilities through 2003*, (1999). In addition, the intelligence community thought that Saddam Hussein would decide to use WMDs only when he felt his personal survival was at risk and after having exhausted political, military, and diplomatic options. S. Rep. No. 110-345, at 76 (2008), quoting National Intelligence Estimates, *Iraq's Continuing Programs for Weapons of Mass Destruction October 2002.*

1506.Press Release of S. Select Comm. On Intelligence, June 5, 2008, *available at* http://intelligence.senate.gov/press/record.cfm?id=298775.

1507.*Id.*

1508.S. Rep. No. 110-345, at 57 (2008).

1509.*Id.* at 31-32, 35.

1510.*Id.* at 38.

1511.*Id.* at 50.

1512.Press Release of S. Select Comm. On Intelligence, June 5, 2008, *available at* http://intelligence.senate.gov/press/record.cfm?id=298775.

1513.S. Rep. No. 110-345, at 70-71 (2008), quoting CIA SPWR dated May 14, 2002 titled, *Iraq: Strenthening Its Terrorist Capabilities*. The CIA also concluded that ""the [f]ragmentary intelligence reporting points to indirect ties between Baghdad and the 11 September hijackers but offers no conclusive indication of Iraqi complicity or foreknowledge. Foreign government service sensitive reporting in September indicated that Muhammad Atta met with an IIS officer in Prague in April of 2001."

1514.S. Rep. No. 110-345, at 71 (2008), quoting DIA, July 31, 2002, Special Analysis, *Iraq's Inconclusive Ties to al-Qaida.*

1515.Pincus and Allen, "C.I.A. Got Uranium Reference Cut in October; Why Bush Cited It In January Is Unclear," *N.Y. Times*, July 13, 2008.

1516.S. Rep. No. 110-345, at 11 (2008).

1517.*Id.* at 12. Even after the IAEA Chair formally announced that the documents underlying the assertion were forgeries, the Vice President and the President continued to cite the supposed burchase as evidence of Iraq's unclear weapons program. Dozens of interviews with intelligence officials and policymakers have proved that the documents, and their claims, had been irrefutably forged. (Eisner, "How a Bogus Letter Became a Case for War," *Washington Post*, Apr. 3, 2007, at A1. Eisner describes that the documents' authenticity had been dismissed by as early as February 2002 within the intelligence community.) Although the distributor of the documents, identified by the Italian government in November 2005 as Italian spy Rocco Martino has been unclovered, the source and rationale for the documents remains unknown. (Sciolino & Povoledo, "Source of Forged Niger-Iraq Uranium Documents Identified," *N.Y. Times*, Nov. 4, 2005, *available at* http://www.nytimes.com/2005/11/04/international/europe/04italy.html?scp=1&sq=niger%20forgery&st=cse).

1518.*Executive Power and its Constitutional Limitations: Hearing before the H. Comm on the Judiciary*, 110th Cong. (2008) (statement of Rep. Dennis Kucinich).

1519.*Executive Power and its Constitutional Limitations: Hearing before the H. Comm. on the Judiciary*, 110th Cong (2008) (statement of Vincent Bugliosi).

1520.*Executive Power and its Constitutional Limitations: Hearing before the H. Comm. on the Judiciary*, 110th Cong (2008) (statement of Rep. Elizabeth Holtzman).

1521.Suskind, *The Way of the World: A Story of Truth and Hope in an Age of Extremism* (2008).

1522.*See* Letters from Rep. John Conyers, Jr., Chairman, H. Comm. on the Judiciary, to George Tenet, Rob Richer, John Maguire, A. B. "Buzzy" Krongard, John Hanna and I. Lewis Libby, Aug. 20, 2008.

1523.*See, e.g.,* Letter from Rob Richer to Rep. John Conyers, Jr., Chairman, H. Comm. on the Judiciary, Sept. 1, 2008.

1524.*Memorandum regarding the President's Claim that Iraq Sought Uranium from Niger*, Henry A. Waxman, Chairman, H. Comm. on Oversight and Gov't Reform, Dec. 18, 2008.

1525.*Id*. at 2.

1526.*Id*. at 7-8.

1527.Karl, "Exclusive: Cheney Holds Hardline Stance," *ABC News*, Dec. 15, 2008, *available at* http://abcnews.go.com/WN/story?id=6464919&page=1.

1528.Raddatz, "Bush 'Not Insulted' By Thrown Shoes," *ABC News*, Dec. 14, 2008, *available at* http://abcnews.go.com/print?id=6460837.

1529.*Id*.

1530.H. Comm. on Oversight and Gov't Reform, Subpoena to Condoleezza Rice, Secretary of State, (April 25, 2007).

1531.H. Comm. on the Judiciary, Subpoena to Harriet Miers, former Counsel to the President (June 13, 2007).

1532.H. Comm. on the Judiciary, Subpoena to Joshua Bolten, White House Chief of Staff, or appropriate custodian of records (June 13, 2007).

1533.S. Comm. on the Judiciary Subpoena to Karl Rove, White House Deputy Chief of Staff (June 26, 2007).

1534.H. Comm. on Oversight and Gov't Reform Subpoena to Stephen L. Johnson, Administrator, U.S. Environmental Protection Agency (Mar. 13, 2008).

1535.H. Comm. on Oversight and Gov't Reform Subpoena to Susan Dudley, Administrator, Office of Information and Regulatory Affairs, White House Office of Management and Budget (Apr. 16, 2008).

1536.H. Comm. on Oversight and Gov't Reform Subpoena to Stephen Johnson, Administrator, Environmental Protection Agency (Apr. 9, 2008); H. Comm. on Oversight and Gov't Reform Subpoena to Stephen Johnson, Administrator, Environmental Protection Agency (May 5, 2008).

1537.H. Comm. on the Judiciary Subpoena to Karl Rove, White House Deputy Chief of Staff (May 22, 2008).

1538.H. Comm. on Oversight and Gov't Reform Subpoena to Michael B. Mukasey, Att'y Gen. of the United States (June 16, 2008).

1539.H. Comm. on the Judiciary Subpoena to Michael B. Mukasey, Att'y Gen. of the United States (June 27, 2008).

1540.S. Comm. on the Judiciary Subpoena to Michael B. Mukasey, Att'y Gen. of the United States (Oct. 21, 2008).

1541.Huq, *Twelve Steps to Restore Checks and Balances*, Report by the Brennan Center for Justice at New York University School of Law 15 (2008).

1542.Giraldi, "What FBI Whistle-blower Sibel Edmonds Found in Translation," *Dallas Morning News* , Feb. 17, 2008, *available at* http://www.dallasnews.com/sharedcontent/dws/dn/opinion/points/stories/DN-sibeledmonds_17e di.ART.State.Edition1.45b446a.html.

1543.*See El-Masri v. Tenet*, 437 F.Supp.2d 530 (E.D.Va. May 12, 2006), *aff'd sub nom. El-Masri v. U.S.*, 479 F.3d 296 (4th Cir. 2002), *cert. denied* 128 S.Ct. 373 (2007).

1544.*See Arar v. Ashcroft*, 414 F.Supp.2d 250 (E.D.N.Y. Feb. 16, 2006), *cert. denied* 2006 WL 1875375 (E.D.N.Y. Jul. 05, 2006), *judgment aff'd* 532 F.3d 157 (2nd Cir 2008), *rehearing en banc granted* (August 12, 2008).

1545.*See Al-Haramain Islamic Foundation, Inc. v. Bush*, 451 F.Supp.2d 1215 (D.Or. Sep. 7, 2006), *reversed and remanded* 507 F.3d 1190 (9ᵗʰ Cir. 2007), *on remand sub nom. to In re National Security Agency Telecommunications Records Litigation*, 564 F.Supp.2d 1109 (N.D.Cal. Jul. 08, 2008).

1546.*See* Part II (B) of Section 5 for a further discussion of Executive Order 13292.

1547.*See* Part II (B) of Section 5 for a further discussion of the weakening of FOIA under the Bush Administration.

1548.*See* Part II (B) of Section 5 for a further discussion of Executive Order 13233.

1549.*See* Part II (B) of Section 5 for a further discussion of the Office of the Vice President's refusal to comply with disclosure obligations and its fights with the National Archives.

1550.*Meet the Press: Interview with the Vice President*, (NBC television broadcast Sept. 8, 2002).

1551.President George W. Bush, President George Bush Discusses Iraq in National Press Conference, Mar. 6, 2003, *available at* http://www.whitehouse.gov/news/releases/2003/03/20030306-8.html.

1552.Rose, "Bush and Blair Made Secret Pact for Iraq War," *The Observer*, Apr. 4, 2004, at 1.

1553.Memorandum from David Manning, U.K. Foreign Policy Advisor, to the Prime Minister, Mar. 14, 2002, *available at* http://downingstreetmemo.com/docs/manning.pdf.

1554.Memorandum from Jack Straw, U.K. Foreign Secretary, to the Prime Minister, Mar. 25, 2002, *available at* http://downingstreetmemo.com/docs/straw.pdf.

1555.Memorandum from Cabinet Office, July 21, 2002, *available at* http://www.timesonline.co.uk/tol/news/world/article531957.ece.

1556.Remarks Prior to Discussions With President Alvaro Uribe of Colombia and an Exchange With Reporters, 2002 PUB. PAPERS, at 1657 (September 25, 2002).

1557.Schmitt, "Rumsfeld Says U.S. Has 'Bulletproof' Evidence of Iraq's Links to Al Qaeda," *N.Y. Times*, Sept. 28, 2002, at A9.

1558.S. Rep. No. 110-345, at 63 (2004), quoting February 6, 2002, and February 7, 2002, DIA Defense Intelligence Summaries (DITSUM) (No. 031-02 and No. 32-012).

1559.*The 9-11 Commission Report: Final Report of the National Commission on Terrorist Attacks Upon the United States* 576 (2004), *available at* http://www.9-11commission.gov/report/911Report.pdf.

1560.*Meet the Press*, (NBC television broadcast Dec. 9, 2001).

1561.*The 9-11 Commission Report: Final Report of the National Commission on Terrorist Attacks Upon the United States* 579 (2004), *available at* http://www.9-11commission.gov/report/911Report.pdf.

1562.President George W. Bush, Remarks by the President on Iraq, Cincinnati, Ohio, Oc. 7, 2002, *available at* http://www.whitehouse.gov/news/releases/2002/10/20021007-8.html.

1563.Secretary of State Colin Powell, Remarks to the U.N. Security Council, Feb. 5, 2003, *available at* http://www.whitehouse.gov/news/releases/2003/02/20030205-1.html.

1564.S. Rep. No. 110-345, at 65 (2008), quoting DITSUM (No. 044-02 of February 22, 2002.

1565.S. Rep. No. 110-345, at 75 (2008), quoting President's Remarks at the United Nations General Assembly, Sept. 12, 2002.

1566.S. Rep. No. 110-345, at 76 (2008), quoting National Intelligence Estimates, *Iraqi Military Capabilities through 2003*, 1999.

1567.Vice President Cheney and Condoleezza Rice also referred several times to Iraq's alleged effort to purchase uranium from Niger in order to convince the American public that Iraq's nuclear weapons program was active. (Cheney, Jan. 29, 2003, "Saddam Hussein recently found to have sought uranium from Africa.")

1568.Pincus and Allen, "C.I.A. Got Uranium Reference Cut in October; Why Bush Cited It In January Is Unclear," *N.Y. Times,* July 13, 2008.

1569.Memorandum from Carl W. Ford, Jr., Assistant Secretary of State, Bureau of Intelligence and Research, to Marc Grossman, Under Secretary of State, *Niger/Iraq Uranium Story and Joe Wilson*, June 10, 2003.

1570.*Memorandum regarding the President's Claim that Iraq Sought Uranium from Niger*, Henry A. Waxman, Chairman, H. Comm. on Oversight and Gov't Reform, Dec. 18, 2008.

1571.Vice President Cheney stated that "it is now public that, in fact, he [Saddam] has been seeking to acquire, and we have been able to intercept and prevent him from acquiring through this particular channel, the kinds of [aluminum] tubes that are necessary to build a centrifuge... We do know, with absolute certainty, that [Saddam Hussein] is using his procurement system to acquire the equipment he needs in order to enrich uranium to build a nuclear weapon." *Meet the Press: Interview with Vice President Dick Cheney* (NBC television broadcast Sept. 8, 2002).

National Security Advisor Condoleezza Rice told CNN that "We do know that there have

469

been shipments going into... Iraq, for instance, of aluminum tubes that really are only suited to - high quality aluminum tools that are only really suited for nuclear weapons programs, centrifuge programs." *CNN Late Edition: Interview with Condoleezza Rice*, (CNN television broadcast Sept. 8, 2002).

1572. President George W. Bush, State of the Union Address, Jan. 28, 2003, *available at* http://www.whitehouse.gov/news/releases/2003/01/20030128-19.html.

1573. S. Rep. No. 108-301, at 88 (2004).

1574. Strobel, "Some in Bush administration have misgivings about Iraq policy," *Knight Ridder Newspapers*, Oct. 7, 2002, *available at* http://www.mcclatchydc.com/128/story/8592.html.

1575. Burrough, Peretz, Rose & Wise, "The Path to War," *Vanity Fair*, May 1, 2004.

1576. These materials and testimony were requested most recently in subpoenas dated June 13, 2007, July 13, 2007, May 22, 2008, June 27, 2008 and in letters dated July 26, 2007, June 6, 2008, and November 24, 2008, all of which are available in Judiciary Committee files. These requests overlap with requests made by the Senate Judiciary Committee and the House Committee on Oversight and Government Reform. The subpoenas to Joshua Bolten and Harriet Miers were reissued during the 111th Congress on January 7 and 9, 2009, respectively.

1577. With respect to secret OLC opinions that purport to set forth presidential powers, three appear particularly significant:

- Memorandum for Alberto R. Gonzales, Counsel to the President, and William J. Haynes II, General Counsel, Department of Defense ("DOD"), from John C. Yoo, Deputy Assistant Attorney General, OLC, Re: Authority for Use of Military Force to Combat Terrorist Activities Within the United States (Oct. 23,2001). – Committee staff have reviewed this unclassified memorandum, which contains extraordinary assertions of executive power and appears deeply flawed in its legal analysis. The memo relies on odd precedents, such as a 1933 decision of the New Mexico supreme court, while unhelpful precedents of seemingly greater weight – such as those discussing legal principles developed during the Civil War era involving non-battlefield actions – are dismissed in footnotes. The memo focuses on a startling hypothetical example involving a U.S. military commander seizing an apartment building in a major American city and detaining and interrogating every person found inside. The Department has claimed that this memo does not reflect current OLC thinking, but it is not clear if it has been formally withdrawn or revised. There is no excuse, moreover, for the Administration's refusal to make this memorandum public.

- Memorandum for Daniel Bryant, Assistant Attorney General, Office of Legislative Affairs, from John Yoo, Deputy Assistant Attorney General,

OLC, Re: Applicability of 18 U.S.C § 4001(a) to Military Detention of United States Citizens (June 27, 2002). — This Memorandum, based on its title and when it was prepared, appears to have been written to justify the military custody of Jose Padilla, a United States citizen.

- Memorandum for William J. Haynes II, General Counsel, DOD, from Jay S. Bybee, Assistant Attorney General, OLC, Re: The President's Power as Commander in Chief to Transfer Captured Terrorists to the Control and Custody of Foreign Nations (March 13, 2002). This Memorandum appears to address rendition practices.

In addition to these memoranda, there are a number of more recent and classified memoranda containing the legal justification for the Administration's current CIA detention and interrogation program.

1578. In testimony before the Senate Judiciary Committee, Frederick A.O. Schwartz, Senior Counsel to the Brennan Center for Justice, urged that "a bipartisan independent investigatory Commission should be established by the next Congress and President, first to determine what has gone wrong (and right) with our policies and practices in confronting terrorists since September 11, 2001, and then to recommend lasting solutions to address past mistakes...." *Restoring the Rule of Law, Hearing Before the Senate Judiciary Committee,* 110th Cong. (2008) (testimony of Frederick A. O. Schwartz). Schwartz also stressed that the Commission should be independent, have subpoena power, and access to secret information. The Brennan Center for Justice has called for a Church Committee-like approach. *See* Huq, *Twelve Steps to Restore Checks and Balances,* (Brennan Center for Justice, 2008) at 21, *available at* http://brennan.3cdn.net/543341179e6a856b9b_9um6batcl.pdf. ("The Church Committee is a model for how comprehensive oversight can clarify what has gone wrong and provide forward-looking guidance.")

1579. *See, e.g.,* "The Torture Report," *N.Y. Times,* Dec. 17, 2008, *available at* http://www.nytimes.com/2008/12/18/opinion/18thu1.html.

1580. *See, e.g.,* Mazzetti & Johnston, "Justice Dept. Sets Criminal Inquiry on C.I.A. Tapes," *N.Y. Times,* Jan. 3, 2008, *available at* http://www.nytimes.com/2008/01/03/washington/03intel.html?_r=1&ref=todayspaper.

1581. *See, e.g.,* Letter from Rep. Jan Schakowsky, John Conyers, Jr., and other Members of Congress to Michael B. Mukasey, Att'y Gen. U.S. Dep't of Justice (June 8, 2008) *available at* http://www.house.gov/schakowsky/Letter%20to%20Mukasey%20Special%20Counsel.pdf. That letter explicitly stated: "We are writing to request you appoint a special counsel to investigate whether the Bush Administration's policies regarding the interrogation of detainees have violated federal criminal laws. There is mounting evidence that the Bush Administration has sanctioned enhanced interrogation techniques against detainees under the control of the United Stats that warrant an investigation."

1582. A federal court in Michigan held that the program was unlawful before the case was thrown out on appeal due to lack of standing. The Michigan case, *American Civil Liberties Union v. National Security Agency*, is discussed specifically in Section 2.3.B.2.

1583. Memorandum from Attorney General Michael Mukasey to Heads of Department Components and United States Attorneys (Dec. 19, 2007).

1584. *See, e.g.*, Letter from Janet Reno, Att'y Gen. of the United States, to Lloyd Cutler, White House Counsel (Sept. 19, 1994); Letter from Jamie Gorelick, Deputy Att'y Gen., to Chairman Orrin Hatch, S. Comm. on the Judiciary (Mar. 16, 1995).

1585. Memorandum from Chief of Staff Josh Bolten to Cabinet and Executive Agency Heads (Dec. 1, 2008).

1586. H.Amdt. 831 - On agreeing to the Conyers amendment (A001) Agreed to by recorded vote: 217 - 192 (Roll no. 935), 110th Cong.

1587. Board of Immigration Appeals, *Procedural Reforms To Improve Case Management*, Final Rule, 8 C.F.R. § 3 (2002).

1588. Joint Report of the U.S. Dep. of Justice Office of Professional Responsibility and Office of the Inspector General, "An Investigation of Allegations of Politicized Hiring by Monica Goodling and Other Staff in the Office of the Attorney General" (July 2008) *available at* http://www.usdoj.gov/oig/special/s0807/final.pdf.

1589. An oversight hearing held on September 23, 2008, by the House Judiciary Subcommittee on Immigration, Citizenship, Refugees, Border Security, and International Law revealed some changes made by the Department and EOIR to improve the immigration courts but also showed a number of reform promises that were not fulfilled. *The Executive Office for Immigration Review: Hearing Before the Subcomm. on Immigration, Citizenship, Refugees, Border Security, and Int. Law of the H. Comm. on the Judiciary*, 110th Cong. (2008).

1590. *See* Eggen, "Staff Opinions Banned in Voting Rights Cases," *Wash. Post*, Dec. 10, 2005 at A3.

1591. In the 110th Congress, H.R. 1281, the" Deceptive Practices and Voter Intimidation Prevention Act of 2007," was reported out of the Committee on Judiciary on April 18, 2007.(H.R. Rep. 110-101, 110th Cong. [2007]); and passed the House on June 25, 2007, by voice vote. (Senator Barack Obama introduced a companion bill in the Senate, S.453).

1592. This remedy was proposed in H.R. 5038, the "Caging Prohibition Act of 2008."

1593. Many of these provisions were contained in the "Voting Opportunity and Technology Enhancement Rights (VOTER) Act", H.R. 533, introduced by Chairman Conyers in the 109th Congress.

1594.*See, e.g., Van Hollen v. Government Accountability Bd.*, No. O8CV4085, Hearing Tr. 7-16 (Wisc. Dane County Cir. Ct, Ovt. 23, 2008).

1595.*See, e.g.*, House Judiciary Comm. Democratic Staff, *Preserving Democracy: What Went Wrong in Ohio* (Status Report, Jan. 5, 2005); Perez, *Voter Purges* (Brennan Center for Justice, 2008); Lawyers' Comm. For Civil Rights, *Election Protection 2008 Primary Report: Looking Ahead to November* (July, 2008); Weiser and Goldman, *An Agenda for Reform* (Brennan Center for Justice, 2007).

1596.Dellinger and other former OLC Attorneys, *Principles to Guide the Office of Legal Counsel*, (Dec. 21, 2004), *available at* http://www.acslaw.org/files/2004%20programs_OLC%20principles_white%20paper.pdf.

1597.The country of Portugal has recently agreed to accept some Guantanamo detainees and has urged other European countries to do the same. *See* Glaberson, "Move May Help Shut Guantanamo Camp," *N.Y. Times*, Dec. 11, 2008.

1598.*See, e.g., In re Guantanamo Bay Detainee Litigation*, F.Supp.2d, 2008 WL 4539019 (D.D.C., Oct. 9, 2008), *app. pending* (ordering 17 Chinese Uighurs who were held at Guantanamo but who were not "enemy combatants" to be freed into the United States). *See also* Taylor, "Judge Orders 17 Guantanamo Detainees Released to U.S.," *McClatchy Newsapers*, Oct. 7, 2008, *available at* http://www.mcclatchydc.com/homepage/story/53595.html.

1599.The closing of Guantanamo can and should be accomplished by executive action by the incoming Obama Administration; in addition, at the beginning of the 111th Congress, Chairman Conyers, Rep. Jane Harman, Rep. Jerrold Nadler, and Rep. Anna Eshoo introduced H.R. 374, the Lawful Interrogation and Detention Act, which would mandate the closing of Guantanamo. H.R. 374 also concerns torture, abuse, and ghosting, which are discussed in recommendations 14 and 15 below.

1600.*See generally*, Wilner, "We Don't Need Guantanamo Bay," *Wall St. Jour.*, Dec. 22, 2008, *available at* http://online.wsj.com/article/SB122990491721225253.html .

1601.*See generally* the discussion in Section 2 of this Report.

1602.The decision to move al-Marri must be understood as reflecting the Administration's determination that the law does not support his continued military detention, not as an attempt by the Administration to avoid Supreme Court review of that legal contention. Thus, if, for unforeseen reasons, the Supreme Court or the Fourth Circuit are unwilling to permit al-Marri to be transferred from military custody, in effect forcing the incoming Administration to argue the al-Marri case before the Supreme Court, the Government, through the incoming Justice Department, should reverse the position of the Bush Administration and argue that the military detention of al-Marri was not authorized either under the Constitution or under the AUMF, and, accordingly, request that the Court order the Government to release al-Marri from military custody and be turned over to civilian custody to be charged with and held to answer federal terrorism charges. To the same end, if the Fourth Circuit refuses to vacate its opinion, the Administration should issue a clear statement that it is moving al-Marri because the Administration has concluded that it is not legally appropriate to keep him in military custody.

1603."This intolerable reading of the law would leave a president free to suspend the rights of anyone, including American citizens." "Tortured Justice," *N. Y. Times*, Dec. 8, 2008, *available at* http://www.nytimes.com/2008/12/08/opinion/08mon1.html?_r=1.

1604.*See, e.g.*, "The Torture Report," *N.Y.Times*, Dec. 18, 2008, *available at* http://www.nytimes.com/2008/12/18/opinion/18thu1.html?pagewanted=2&_r=1&sq=President%20Bush%20February%207%202002%20memo%20torture%20&st=cse&scp=1

1605.This provision is also contained in H.R. 374, 111th Cong. (2009). The Bush Administration has ignored previous attempts by Congress to end torture, and has stubbornly insisted that the ability to order torture was a presidential prerogative as Commander in Chief. In 2005, Congress passed the Detainee Treatment Act of 2005 (DTA) which required the Department of Defense (but not the CIA) to abide by the Army Field Manual, and prohibited allagencies (including the CIA), from using "cruel, inhuman, or degrading treatment or punishment" of persons in U.S. custody or control. Detainee Treatment Act of 2005 (DTA), Pub. L. No. 109-148, §§ 1001–1006 (2005). In signing the DTA into law, President Bush issued a signing statement: "The Executive Branch shall construe Title X in Division A of the Act, relating to detainees, in a manner consistent with the constitutional authority of the President to supervise the unitary Executive Branch and as Commander in Chief and consistent with the constitutional limitations on the judicial power, which will assist in achieving the shared objective of the Congress and the President, evidenced in Title X, of protecting the American people from further terrorist attacks." "President's Statement on Signing of H.R. 2863, the 'Department of Defense, Emergency Supplemental Appropriations to Address Hurricanes in the Gulf of Mexico, and Pandemic Influenza Act, 2006,'" *available at* http://www.whitehouse.gov/news/releases/2005/12/20051230-8.html. It has been reported that the Justice Department's OLC issued a memorandum that interpreted the DTA prohibition on cruel treatment to allow (not prohibit) the CIA to use extreme techniques like waterboarding. The *New York Times* reported in 2007: "Later that year [2005], as Congress moved toward outlawing 'cruel, inhuman and degrading' treatment, the Justice Department issued another secret opinion, one most lawmakers did not know existed, current and former officials said. The Justice Department document declared that none of the C.I.A. interrogation methods violated that standard." Shane, "Secret U.S. Endorsement of Severe Interrogations," *N.Y. Times*, Oct. 4, 2007, *available at* http://www.nytimes.com/2007/10/04/washington/04interrogate.html?_r=2&oref=slogin&oref=slogin.

Thereafter, provisions akin to those set forth in Rep. Nadler's bill (H.R. 2082) were made part of the Intelligence Authorization Act of 2008, section 327(a) of which specifically provided: "No individual in the custody or under the effective control of an element of the intelligence community or instrumentality thereof, regardless of nationality or physical location, shall be subject to any treatment or technique of interrogation not authorized by the United States Army Field Manual on Human Intelligence Collector Operations." "Intelligence Authorization Act for Fiscal Year 2008," H.R. 2082, 110th Cong., sec. 327(a). President Bush vetoed this legislation, and the House of Representatives failed to override the veto.

1606. Sept. 13, 2006 Letter from General Colin Powell (Ret.), to Sen. John McCain, *available at* http://msnbcmedia.msn.com/i/msnbc/sections/news/060914_Powell.pdf.

1607. This provision is also contained in H.R. 374, 111th Cong. (2009).

1608. *See* discussion in Section 2.

1609. For example, the U.N. Convention Against Torture and Cruel, Inhuman and Degrading Treatment prohibits torture and the transfer of individuals to countries where it is likely that they will be tortured. U.N. Convention Against Torture and Other Cruel, Inhuman or Degrading Treatment or Punishment, opened for signature December 10, 1984, G.A. Res. 39/46, 39 UN GAOR Supp. No. 51, at 197, UN Doc. A/RES/39/708 (1984), entered into force June 26, 1987, 1465 U.N.T.S. 85, 23 I.L.M. 1027 (1984), as modified, 24 I.L.M. 535. The Federal Torture Statute, 18 U.S.C. §§ 2340A-B, criminalizes torture committed outside the U.S. and the conspiracy to commit an act of torture outside the U.S. For an analysis of the full range of U.S. and international legal constraints on extraordinary rendition, *see* Comm. On Int'l Human Rights of the NY Bar Ass'n and Ctr. For Human Rights and global Justice, NYU School of Law, *Torture by Proxy: International and Domestic Law Applicable to "Extraordinary Renditions,"* at 55-83 (as modified June 2006), *available at* http://www.chrgj.org/docs/TortureByProxy.pdf; Satterthwaite, "Rendered Meaningless: Extraordinary Rendition and the Rule of Law," 75 *Geo. Wash. L.Rev.* 1333 (2007); *Rendition to Torture: the Case of Maher Arar: Joint Hearing before the Subcomm. on Int'l Orgs., Human Rights, and Oversight of the H. Comm. on Foreign Affairs and Subcomm on Constitution, Civil Rights, and Civil Liberties of the H. Comm. on the Judiciary*, Serial No. 110-52, at 93-102, 110th Cong., 1ˢᵗ Sess. (2007) (testimony of Professor David Cole); Garcia, "Renditions: Constraints Imposed by Laws on Torture," *CRS Report for Congress*, RL 32890, Jan. 25, 2008 at 3.

1610. U.S. officials, usually speaking off the record, have provided troubling indications that the practice has been used frequently following the 9/11 terrorist attacks. Campbell, "September 11: Six Months on: U.S. Sends Suspects to Face Torture," *Guardian (London)*, Mar. 12, 2002, at 4. (quoting an unnamed U.S. diplomat as acknowledging "[a]fter September 11, [renditions] have been occurring all the time....It allows us to get information from terrorists in a way we can't do on U.S. soil.") Estimates range anywhere from 100-150 to several thousand renditions of terror suspects to countries including Egypt, Syria, Saudi Arabia, Jordan and Pakistan. Jehl & Johnston, "Rule Change Lets C.I.A Freely Send Suspects Abroad to Jails," *N.Y. Times,* March 6, 2005 at A1 ("former government officials say that since the Sept. 11 attacks, the C.I.A. has flown 100 to 150 suspected terrorists from one foreign country to another, including to Egypt, Syria, Saudi Arabia, Jordan and Pakistan"); Satterthwaite & Fisher, *Beyond Guantanamo: Transfers to Torture One Year After Rasul v. Bush (2005), available at* http://www.chrgj.org/docs/Beyond%20Guantanamo%20Report%20FINAL.pdf) (quoting Jane Mayer: "one source knowledgeable about the rendition program suggested that the number of renditions since September may have reached as high as several thousand").

1611.*See, e.g., Rendition to Torture: the Case of Maher Arar: Joint Hearing before the Subcomm. on Int'l Orgs., Human Rights, and Oversight of the H. Comm. on Foreign Affairs and Subcomm on Constitution, Civil Rights, and Civil Liberties of the H. Comm. on the Judiciary,* Serial No. 110-52, at 80, 110th Cong. (2007) (testimony of Frederick P. Hitz) (after the September 11th attacks, renditions "resulted in the use of interrogation methods beyond what would have been permitted to U.S. authorities," which "is doing indirectly what U.S. officials would be prohibited from doing directly and is unwise, if not illegal."); Mayer, "Outsourcing Torture, the Secret History of America's 'Extraordinary Rendition' Program," *New Yorker,* Feb. 14, 2005, *available at* http://www.newyorker.com/archive/2005/02/14/050214fa_fact6; Comm. On Int'l Human Rights of the NY Bar Ass'n and Ctr. For Human Rights and Global Justice, NYU School of Law, *Torture by Proxy: International and Domestic Law Applicable to "Extraordinary Renditions"* (June 2006), http://www.chrgj.org/docs/TortureByProxy.pdf.

1612.*See, e.g.,* Burns, "CIA confirms British territory used in rendition flights," *Int'l Herald Tribune,* Feb. 22, 2008; Brinkley, "Rice is Challenged in Europe Over Secret Prisons," *N. Y. Times,* Dec. 7, 2005.; Garcia, "Renditions: Constraints Imposed by Laws on Torture," *CRS Report to Congress,* RL32890, at 2-3 & nn.6-7. The United Kingdom currently is investigating whether to bring criminal charges against the American CIA agents allegedly responsible for the rendition and torture of Binyam Mohamed. Verhaik, "CIA officers Could Face Trial in Britain over Torture Allegations," *The Independent,* Oct. 31, 2008.

1613.*See* Feb. 26, 2007 Letter from Richard A. Hertling, Acting Assistant Attorney General, U.S. Dept. Of Justice, at 4; *see also* Mayer, "Outsourcing Torture, the Secret History of America's "Extraordinary Rendition" Program," *New Yorker.* Feb. 14, 2005, *available at* http://www.newyorker.com/archive/2005/02/14/050214fa_fact6.

1614.*See, e.g.,* Priest, "CIA's Assurances on Transferred Suspects Doubted," *Washington Post,* March 17, 2005, at A1 (quoting one unnamed CIA officer involved in renditions as describing assurances from other countries as "a farce," while another U.S. government official took the position that "it's beyond that. It's widely understood that interrogation practices that would be illegal in the U.S. are being used."); *Rendition to Torture: the Case of Maher Arar, Joint Hearing before the Subcomm. on Int'l Orgs., Human Rights, and Oversight of the H. Comm. on Foreign Affairs and Subcomm on Constitution, Civil Rights, and Civil Liberties of the H. Comm. on the Judiciary,* Serial No. 110-52, 110th Cong, 1st Sess. at 80 (2007) (testimony of Frederick P. Hitz) (describing assurances as "meaningless as a restraint on the practices of nations with poor human rights records"); *id.* at 95, 101 (testimony of David Cole) (explaining that assurances are inherently unreliable because (1) countries that torture generally deny that they do so; and (2) there is no effective means to monitor such assurances once a suspect has been transferred and is out of the control of the sending state); Department of Homeland Security, Office of Inspector General, *OIG-08-18, The Removal of a Canadian Citizen to Syria,* at 5, 22 (March 2008) (INS officials concluded that it was "more likely than not" that Mr. Arar would be tortured if sent to Syria, but still sent him there even though the "assurances upon which INS based Arar's removal were ambiguous regarding the source or authority purporting to bind the Syrian government to protect Arar," and their "validity" "appears not to have been examined." *U.S. Department of Homeland Security Inspector General Report OIG-08-018, The Removal of a Canadian Citizen to Syria: Joint Hearing before the Subcomm. on the Constituion, Civil Rights, and Civil Liberties of the H.Comm. on the Judiciary and Subcomm. on Int'l Orgs., Human Rights, and Oversight of the H.Comm. on Foreign Affairs*, Serial No. 110-101, at 74, 110th Cong. (2008) (testimony of Clark Ervin and Richard Skinner) (further investigation into possible criminal misconduct in Mr. Arar's case is warranted).

1615.Pub. L. No. 105-277, section 2242 (a) and (b) (1998).

1616.*Warrantless Surveillance and the Foreign Intelligence Surveillance Act: The Role of Checks and Balances in Protecting Americans' Privacy Rights (Part II) : Hearing before the H. Comm. on the Judiciary,* 110th Cong., 1st Sess. (2007) at 46-47 (Statement of J.M. McConnell, Director of National Intelligence.

1617.Cauley, "NSA Has Massive Database of Americans' Phone Calls," *USA Today,* May 11, 2006, at A1.

1618.*Does the Protect America Act Protect Americans' Civil Liberties and Enhance Security?: Hearing before the S. Comm. on the Judiciary,* 110th Cong. (2007)at 82.

1619.*See, e.g.,* Dept. of Justice Ofc. of the Inspector General, *"A Review of the FBI's Use of National Security Letters: Assessment of Corrective Actions and Examination of NSL Usage in 2006"* (2008), at 48.

1620.Office of Inspector General, Dept. of Justice, *A Review of the Federal Bureau of Investigation's Use of National Security Letters* (2007), at 86, *available at* http://www.npr.org/documents/2007/mar/doj/doj_oig_nsl.pdf.

1621.Office of Inspector General, Dept. of Justice, *A Review of the Federal Bureau of Investigation's Use of National Security Letters* (2007), at 33-34, *available at* http://www.npr.org/documents/2007/mar/doj/doj_oig_nsl.pdf.

1622.Office of Inspector General, Dept. of Justice, *A Review of the Federal Bureau of Investigation's Use of National Security Letters* (2007), at 68, *available at* http://www.npr.org/documents/2007/mar/doj/doj_oig_nsl.pdf.

1623.*See, e.g.,* Office of Inspector General, Dept. of Justice, *A Review of the FBI's Use of National Security Letters: Assessment of Corrective Actions and Examination of NSL Usage in 2006* (2008), at 128-29; Office of Inspector General, Dept. of Justice, *A Review of the FBI's Use of Section 215 Orders for Business Records in 2006* (2008) at 68, 72.

1624. Office of Inspector General, Dept. of Justice, *A Review of the Federal Bureau of Investigation's Use of National Security Letters* (2007), at 110, *available at* http://www.npr.org/documents/2007/mar/doj/doj_oig_nsl.pdf.

1625. *See, e.g.*, Office of Inspector General, Dept. of Justice, *A Review of the FBI's Use of National Security Letters: Assessment of Corrective Actions and Examination of NSL Usage in 2006* (2008) at 48.

1626. Even though the FBI had attempted to comply with all of the Inspector General's 2007 recommendations, the Inspector General noted in his 2008 report that some of the recommendations need fuller implementation. Thus, despite the fact that the FBI may believe it has implemented the recommendations, the Inspector General is in a better position to assess whether the FBI has fully addressed his recommendations from both the 2007 and 2008 reports.

1627. A recent federal appellate court decision has invalidated parts of the statute that wrongly put the burden on NSL recipients to initiate court review of gag orders, ruling that the government must go to court and justify silencing NSL recipients. The ruling also invalidated parts of the statute that narrowly limited judicial review of the gag orders by requiring the courts to treat the government's claims about the need for secrecy as conclusive and to defer entirely to the Executive Branch. *See Doe v. Mukasey*, No. 07-4943-cv (2nd Cir. Dec. 15, 2008).

1628. *See* 73 Fed. Reg. 44673 (July 31, 2008) (Dept. of Justice; Office of Justice Programs).

1629. *See* C. Johnson, "Rule Changes Would Give FBI Agents Extensive New Powers," *Wash. Post*, Sept. 12, 2008.

1630. Pub. L. No. 108-408 (2004).

1631. Pub. L. No. 110-53, Title VIII, § 801 (2007)

1632. The United States ratified the International Convention on Civil and Political Rights (ICCPR) in 1992, the Convention Against Torture in 1994, and the Convention on the Elimination of All Forms of Racial Discrimination in 1994. The U.S. additionally ratified two international human rights protocols in 2003: the Optional Protocol to the Convention on the Rights of the Child on the involvement of children in armed conflict; and the Optional Protocol to the Convention on the Rights of the Child on the sale of children, child prostitution, and child pornography.

1633. National Security; Prevention of Acts of Violence and Terrorism, 28 C.F.R. §§ 500-501.

1634. *See* Savage, "Barack Obama Q&A," *Boston Globe* , Dec. 20, 2007.

1635. Mikva & Lane, *Legislative Process* 130 (2d ed. 2002).

1636. *See, e.g.* Huq, *Twelve Steps to Restore Checks and Balances*, at 7-8 (Brennan Center for Justice, 2008).

1637. Several House bills seeking to address presidential abuse of signing statements have been introduced in the 110th Congress by both Republicans and Democrats. H.R. 5993 by Rep. Jones provides that the president must promptly transmit to Congress and publish in the Federal Register any signing statement that "declares or insinuates" an intention to disregard parts of a signed law and, at the request of any member of the House or Senate Judiciary Committee, must make available the Attorney General, Deputy Attorney General, or White House Counsel to testify to "explain the meaning and justification" for any such signing statement. *See* H.R. 5993 (introduced May 8, 2008), sections 4 and 5. H.R. 3045, by Rep. Shea-Porter, states that no court can rely on or defer to any signing statement, and that in any lawsuit concerning the interpretation of a law as to which a signing statement has been issued, the House or Senate can participate as *amicus curiae* and Congress can pass a concurrent resolution concerning the law's meaning that will be included in the court record, with the court case to be expedited. *See* H.R. 3045 (introduced July 16, 2007), sections 4 and 5. H.R. 264, by Rep. Jackson-Lee, provides that government agencies cannot take signing statements into account in construing or applying laws and that no government funds can be used to produce or disseminate signing statements that are inconsistent with the intent of Congress. *See* H.R.264 (introduced January 5, 2007), sections 3 and 4. And H.R. 3835, introduced by Rep. Paul, seeks to provide standing to both the House and the Senate to bring a declaratory judgment action in federal court challenging the constitutionality of any signing statement declaring an intent to disregard a law's provisions. *See* H.R. 3835 (introduced October 15, 2007), section 6.

1638. Copeland, "Changes to the OMB Regulatory Review Process by Executive Order 13422," *CRS Report for Congress*, RL 33862, Feb. 5, 2007, at 56 (quoting Office of Management and Budget, *Stimulating Smarter Regulation: 2002 Report to Congress on the Costs and Benefits of Federal Regulations and Unfunded Mandates on State, Local, and Tribal Entities*, Dec. 2002).

1639. Other requirements of the Order likewise undermine congressional intent. These include the requirement that OIRA receive advance notification of significant guidance documents and specifying the appointment of a regulatory policy officer who must approve every proposed regulation before an agency may commence the rulemaking process and before such regulation may be included in the agency's regulatory plan. This mandate allows the White House to unduly influence regulatory matters – including health and safety issues – even if the agencies disagree with the outcome.

1640. Bass., *Advancing the Public Interest Through Regulatory Reform - Recommendations for President-Elect Obama and the 111th Congress*, Nov. 2008 ("*Regulatory Reform Recommendations*"), at 3, 17.

1641. U.S. Government Accountability Office, *Rulemaking – OMB's Role in Reviews of Agencies' Draft Rules and the Transparency of Those Reviews*, GAO-03-929 (Sept. 2003).

These recommendations included the following:

- Define the transparency requirements applicable to the agencies and OIRA in section 6 of Executive Order 12866 in such a way that they include not only the formal review period, but also the informal review period when OIRA says it can have its most important impact on agencies rules...

- Establish procedures whereby either OIRA or the agencies disclose the reasons why rules are withdrawn from OIRA review...

- Instruct agencies to put information about changes made in a rule after submission for OIRA's review and those made at OIRA's suggestion or recommendation in the agencies' public rulemaking dockets, and to do so within a reasonable period after the rules have been published[.] *Id.* at 14-16.

1642.E-rulemaking "has transformative potential to increase the comprehensibility, transparency and accountability of the regulatory process." American Bar Association, *Achieving the Potential – The Future of Federal E-Rulemaking, A Report to Congress and the President from the Committee on the Status and Future of Federal E-Rulemaking , 2008 ("ABA E-Rulemaking")* at 3.

1643.For example, while OIRA discloses its meetings with outside parties, those disclosures often do not clearly indicate what rules were discussed or who those individuals represented.

1644.*The Rulemaking Process and the Unitary Executive Theory: Hearing Before the Subcomm. on Commercial and Administrative Law of the H. Comm. on the Judiciary*, 110th Cong, 2d Sess.. (2008) (prepared statement of Curtis W. Copeland, Specialist in American National Government, Congressional Research Service) (footnotes omitted).

In developing facilities for electronic rulemaking and the associated dockets, agencies should be required to place all matters related to a rulemaking (other than those that are privileged under FOIA) on their electronic docket, beginning with the entry that commences the regulatory plan or places the item on the regulatory agenda, including all relevant studies, comments, and related materials, whether received electronically or in paper form, as recommended by the Committee on the Status and Future of e-Rulemaking under the auspices of the American Bar Association. *Regulatory Reform Recommendations* at 44-53.

1645.*Regulatory Reform Recommendations* at 44-53.

1646.Although "[f]ederal regulations are among the most important and widely used tools for implementing the laws of the land – affecting the food we eat, the air we breathe, the safety of consumer products, the quality of the workplace, the soundness of our financial institutions, the smooth operation of our businesses," it is extremely difficult to follow the regulatory process, as observed by the American Bar Association's Section of Administrative Law and Regulatory

Practice. *ABA E-Rulemaking* at 3.

1647.*See, e.g., ABA E-Rulemaking; Regulatory Reform Recommendations* at 45-50..

1648.ACUS was created by Congress to develop recommendations for improving procedures by which federal agencies administer regulatory, benefit, and other government programs. It served as a "private-public think tank" that conducted "basic research on how to improve the regulatory and legal process," and many of its recommendations resulted in saving millions in taxpayer dollars. *See Reauthorization of the Administrative Conference of the United States: Hearings Before the Subcomm. on Commercial and Administrative Law of the House Comm. on the Judiciary,* 104th Cong. 31(2005) (statement of C. Boyden Gray).

1649.For example, the Department of Health & Human Services issued a "directive," which the GAO and CRS determined was a "rule" within the meaning of the Act. The Centers for Medicare & Medicaid Services (CMS), in an apparent effort to avoid the Act's requirements, issued a letter on August 17, 2007 to state health officials concerning the State Children's Health Insurance Program for the purpose of "clarifying" how CMS intended to apply existing statutory and regulatory requirements in its review of requests by states to extend eligibility under the Program to children from lower-income families. Aug. 17, 2007 Letter from Dennis G. Smith, Director, Center for Medicaid and State Operations, Dept. of Health & Human Servs. Centers for Medicare & Medicaid Servs, *available at* http://www.cms.hhs.gov/smdl/downloads/SHO081707.pdf. Although both CRS and GAO concluded that this letter directive was a "rule" within the meaning of the Act and must therefore be submitted to Congress before it could take effect, Memorandum from Morton Rosenberg, Specialist in American Public Law - American Law Division, Congressional Research Service, to Sen. John D. Rockefeller, IV (D-WV) (Jan. 10, 2008); Apr. 17, 2008 Letter from Gary Kepplinger, General Counsel, U.S. Gov't Accountability Office, to Sen. John D. Rockefeller, IV (D-WV) , CMS stated that "'GAO's opinion does not change the department's conclusion that the Aug. 17 letter is still in effect.'" Teske, "Health Care: Lawmakers Cite GAO, CRS Findings in Faulting CMS's 2007 Enrollment Directive," *BNA, Daily Rep. for Executives,* Apr. 21, 2008, at A-17 (quoting CMS spokesman Jeff Nelligan). The agency refused to rescind its "directive" until just days before states would have lost funding for their failure to comply.

1650.Many of the Administration's most controversial midnight regulations appear to have been issued without allowing sufficient time for public comment and for the issuing agencies to consider public comments and (in appropriate cases) hold public hearings. There are also concerns that the Office of Management and Budget may not have adequate time to perform the substantive regulatory review mandated by executive order. These and other departures from well-accepted rulemaking procedures can threaten the integrity of the rulemaking process and, of still greater concern, may result in regulations detrimental to the public interest that the incoming administration will often find difficult to amend or repeal.

1651.*See, e.g., Regulatory Reform Recommendations* at 3, 13.

1652.A starting point for Congressional consideration may be the Midnight Rule Act, introduced by Representative Jerrold Nadler (D-NY). H.R. 7296, 110th Cong. (2008). The bill would amend the Administrative Procedure Act by delaying the effective date of a midnight regulation (subject to exceptions) until 90 days after the appointment of the responsible agency head by the incoming President. It would also authorize the incoming agency head to disapprove a midnight regulation.

1653.*See* Department of Justice, *Principles of Federal Prosecution of Business Organizations* (Aug. 28, 2008), available at http://www.usdoj.gov/opa/documents/corp-charging-guidelines.pdf

1654. "Journalists Need Protection at the Federal Level," *Wash. Post*, Aug. 1, 2007.

1655.Unlike previous legislative proposals to compensate these victims, this bill would allow them to recover only a portion of the judgments rendered or claims made – the POWs would agree to forego punitive damages and two-thirds of the compensatory damages awarded, and the human shields to forego all punitive damages. Iraq would be required to pay approximately $415 million.

1656. Pub. .L. No. 104-208, Title I, §101(c) (1996), 110 Stat. 3009-172; codified at 28 U.S.C. § 1605 note.

1657.On March 20, 2003, as the war began, President Bush issued an executive order placing those assets – then totaling approximately $1.73 billion – which had previously been frozen, into a dedicated Development Fund for Iraq, to be used in the post-war reconstruction of Iraq. E.O. 13290, 68 Fed. Reg. 14,305-08 (March 24, 2003). Assets that had previously been ordered attached in satisfaction of judgments against Iraq were excluded from the Executive Order, as was Iraq's diplomatic and consular property. Six weeks later, on May 7, he declared, based on general authority Congress had recently granted him to exempt Iraq from laws governing terrorist-supporting states, that the terrorism exception to FSIA would not apply to Iraq. *See* Emergency Wartime Supplemental Appropriations Act for FY2003, P.L. 108-11, §1503 (April 16, 2003). Memorandum for the Secretary of State (Presidential Determination No. 2003-23) (May 7, 2003), *available at* http://whitehouse.gov/news/releases/2003/05/20030507-13.html. Two weeks later, on May 22, he issued another executive order, prohibiting attachment of any assets in the Development Fund for Iraq. E.O. 13303, 68 Fed. Reg. 31, 931 (May 28, 2003).

1658.Pub. L. No. 110-181, §1083 (2008).

1659.Asserting that the section as originally drafted would jeopardize Iraq's economic development and security, he insisted that it be rewritten to give him authority to waive it with respect to Iraq, retroactively as to all pending cases, if he determined that a waiver would serve the United States' national security interest, promote U.S.- Iraq relations, and facilitate reconstruction and political development in Iraq, and that Iraq continued to be a reliable ally and partner in combating terrorism. Congress passed the revised version of the FY08 NDAA, and the President signed it into law January 28, 2008, exercising his waiver authority that very day. See

Pub.L.No. 110-181, §1083(d). White House Memorandum of Justification for Waiver of Section 1083 of the National Defense Authorization Act (January 28, 2008), *available at* http://www.whitehouse.gov/ news/releases/2008/01/20080128-12.html. The waiver effectively bars any type of recovery for terrorism victims. Anticipating the detrimental impact a waiver would have on pending suits, Congress inserted a provision in Section 1083 urging the President to work with the Iraqi government to help the American victims of Iraqi terrorism during the Gulf War obtain relief for the emotional and physical injuries they sustained. To date, the President has not indicated to Congress that any efforts have been made to do so.

1660.18 U.S.C. § 3261 (2006).

1661.H.R. 2740 also requires the Inspector General of the Justice Department to submit a report to Congress regarding the identification and prosecution of alleged contractor abuses overseas. This requirement is intended to address the Justice Department's apparent failure to aggressively investigate and prosecute crimes committed by contractors over which it currently has jurisdiction. Finally, H.R. 2740 requires the Federal Bureau of Investigation to establish a Theater Investigative Unit to investigate reports of criminal misconduct in regions where contractors are working. This is intended to underscore the importance of providing resources to enforce the law.

1662. Miller, "Private Contractors Outnumber U.S. Troops in Iraq", *Los Angeles Times*, July 4, 2007.

1663.The Military Extraterritorial Jurisdiction Act is limited jurisdictionally and only covers those contractors abroad who are employed by a federal agency supporting the mission of the Department of Defense overseas. As originally enacted in 2000, the Act authorized Federal courts to have jurisdiction over only civilian employees, contractors, and subcontractors affiliated with the Defense Department who commit crimes overseas. In 2005, the Act was amended to expand the court's jurisdiction to include employees of any other Federal agency "supporting the mission of the Department of Defense overseas." 18 U.S.C. § 3267 (2006).

1664.*See* Meyer, "U.S. Details Case Against Blackwater Guards," *L.A. Times,* Dec. 9, 2008. In addition, there are 17 pending cases of detainee abuse, including abuses that occurred at the Abu Ghraib prison in Iraq, with the U.S. Attorney's Office in the Eastern District of Virginia. *See War Profiteering and Other Contractor Crimes Committed Overseas: Hearing Before the Subcomm. on Crime, Terrorism, and Homeland Security of the H. Comm. on the Judiciary,* 110th Cong. (2007) (testimony of Erica Razook). In some of these cases, the Army has found "probable cause" that a crime has been committed, and referred the case to the Justice Department for prosecution.

1665.*See* Ross, "Victim: Gang-Rape Cover-up by U.S., Halliburton/KBR," *ABC News,* Dec. 10, 2007; *Enforcement of Federal Criminal Law to Protect Americans Working for U.S. Contractors in Iraq: Hearing Before the Subcomm. on Crime, Terrorism, and Homeland Security of the H. Comm. on the Judiciary,* 110th Cong. (2007). In addition to the Jones case, there are troubling reports of other similar sexual assault cases, with no apparent prosecutions. For example, letters to the Pentagon and the Justice Department from Sen. Bill Nelson, D-Fla., underscore congressional concern about an alleged sexual assault, this time of a woman from Florida who reportedly worked for a KBR subsidiary in Ramadi, Iraq in 2005. *See* Rood, "Another KBR Rape Claim Brings Scrutiny," *ABC News*, Dec. 13, 2007.

1666.H.R. 6492 was introduced by Rep. Bill Pascrell (D-NJ), Rep. Frank Pallone (D-NJ), and Commercial and Administrative Law Subcommittee Chairwoman Linda Sánchez (D-CA) in the 110th Congress.

1667.In DPAs and NPAs, a corporation against which the government has sufficient evidence to file criminal charges enters into an agreement with the government to a period of probation, subject to specific conditions. A DPA differs from a NPA in that a DPA typically includes a formal charging document – an indictment or a complaint – and the agreement is normally filed with the court, while in the NPA context, there is typically no charging document and the agreement is normally maintained by the parties rather than filed with a court.

1668.The guidance that has been issued by the Justice Department did not come until the eve of hearings on the subject by the Judiciary Committee's Subcommittee on Commercial and Administrative Law in March, 2008.

1669.For example, New Jersey U.S. Attorney Christopher Christie appointed John Ashcroft, under whom Mr. Christie served when he was Attorney General, to be an independent corporate monitor with neither public notice nor competitive bidding. As a result of that appointment, former Attorney General Ashcroft stood to collect fees of up to $52 million. Shenon, "Ashcroft Deal Brings Scrutiny in Justice Dept.," *N.Y. Times*, Jan. 10, 2008. *See Deferred Prosecutions: Should Corporate Settlement Agreements Be Without Guidelines?: Hearing Before the Subcomm. On Commercial and Admin. Law of the H. Comm. On the Judiciary,* 110th Cong. (2008).

An upcoming Government Accountability Office (GAO) study, requested on January 16, 2008 by the Chairmen of the House and Senate Judiciary Committees, will shed additional light on the Justice Department's use of DPAs, NPAs, and independent corporate monitors.

1670.*See, e.g.*, S. 645, 107th Cong. (2001).

1671.*See, e.g.* "Mr. Bush and the Pardon Power," *N.Y. Times*, Nov. 29, 2008.

1672.*See generally* Lardner, "A Pardon to Remember," *N.Y. Times,* Nov. 22, 2008.

1673.*See, e.g.*, Peterson, "Congressional Power Over Pardon and Amnesty: Legislative Authority in the Shadow of Presidential Prerogative", 38 *Wake Forest L. Rev.* 1225, 1258-59 (2003).

1674.*See, e.g.* Lardner, "A Pardon to Remember," *N.Y. Times,* Nov. 22, 2008.

1675. Documents were withheld on the basis of executive privilege in congressional investigations into interference with the EPA's regulatory process; the Valerie Plame leak; and the U.S. Attorneys firings. Executive privilege was also asserted with respect to documents in the possession of National Security Advisor Rice when requested by the bipartisan 9/11 Commission established by Congress.

1676. H. Rep. 110-423, 110th Cong. (2007). *See* H. Rep. 104-598, 104th Cong. 38 (1996). ("Under [procedures established by President Reagan on November 22, 1982, and adopted by President Clinton]....[i]f the President decides to invoke [executive] privilege, the decision is to be communicated to the congressional committee requesting the information that the claim is made with the specific approval of the President. In the past, Presidents in fact have executed and signed claims of privilege which have accompanied a detailed justification prepared by the subpoenaed official.")

1677. *Committee on the Judiciary v. Miers*, Civil No. 08-0409 (JDB), slip op. at 92 (D.D.C. July 31, 2008), *app. pending.*.

1678. "Report of the Commission on Protecting and Reducing Government Secrecy," *S. Doc. No. 105-2* (1997).

1679. "Iraq's Weapons of Mass Destruction Programs," *National Intelligence Estimate*, prepared by National Intelligence Counsel (October 2002).

1680. *See* "Memorandum for Heads of All Federal Departments and Agencies," from John Ashcroft, Attorney General (October 12, 2001), *available at* http://www.usdoj.gov/04foia/011012.htm.

1681. Right to Know Community, *Moving Toward a 21st Century Right-to-Know Agenda* 14 (Nov. 2008).

1682. *Id.* at 3.

1683. OPEN Government Act of 2007, Pub. L. No. 110-175, 121 Stat. 2524 (2007).

1684. On January 7, 2009, the House passed H.R. 35, the Presidential Records Act Amendments of 2009 (111th Cong., Roll Call Vote No. 5, *available at* http://clerk.house.gov/evs/2009/roll005.xml), which, among other things, would repeal Executive Order 13233 by statute.

1685. *See* House Comm. on Oversight and Government Reform, *Interim Report, Investigation of Possible Presidential Records Act Violations*, June 2007.

1686. *See* Baker, "Cheney Defiant on Classified Material." Wash. Post, June 22, 2007, at A1; Associated Press, "Cheney Claims Power to Decide his Public Records," *N. Y. Times*, Dec. 18, 2008.

1687.50 U.S.C. §413(a)(1)

1688.50 U.S.C. §413b(c)(2).

1689.Cumming, "Statutory Procedures under which Congress is to be Informed of U.S. Intelligence Activities, including Covert Actions," *CRS Memorandum for Congress,* Jan. 18, 2006 at 7.